THE CATHOLIC ORIGINS OF QUEBEC'S
QUIET REVOLUTION, 1931–1970

MCGILL-QUEEN'S STUDIES IN THE HISTORY OF RELIGION

Volumes in this series have been supported by the Jackman Foundation of Toronto.

SERIES TWO   In memory of George Rawlyk
Donald Harman Akenson, Editor

The Catholic Origins of Quebec's Quiet Revolution, 1931–1970

MICHAEL GAUVREAU

McGill-Queen's University Press
Montreal & Kingston · London · Ithaca

© McGill-Queen's University Press 2005
ISBN 0-7735-2874-1

Legal deposit fourth quarter 2005
Bibliothèque nationale du Québec

Printed in Canada on acid-free paper that is 100% ancient forest free
(100% post-consumer recycled), processed chlorine free.

This book has been published with the help of a grant from the Canadian
Federation for the Humanities and Social Sciences, through the Aid to
Scholarly Publications Programme, using funds provided by the Social Sci-
ences and Humanities Research Council of Canada.

McGill-Queen's University Press acknowledges the support of the Canada
Council for the Arts for our publishing program. We also acknowledge the
financial support of the Government of Canada through the Book Publishing Industry Development Program (BPIDP) for our publishing activities.

Library and Archives Canada Cataloguing in Publication

Gauvreau, Michael, 1956–
   The Catholic origins of Quebec's Quiet Revolution, 1931–1970 /
Michael Gauvreau.

(McGill-Queen's studies in the history of religion; 41)
Includes bibliographical references and index.
ISBN 0-7735-2874-1

   1. Catholic youth – Québec (Province) – History – 20th century.
2. Catholic action – Québec (Province) – History – 20th century.
3. Catholic Church – Québec (Province) – History – 20th century.
4. Youth movement – Québec (Province) – History – 20th century.
5. Social change – Québec (Province).   6. Québec (Province) – History –
1960–1976.   I. Title.   II. Series.

BX1422.Q8G38 2005   267'.622714   C2005–901847–X

Typeset in 10/12 Baskerville by True to Type

For my parents

Contents

Acknowledgments

While the writing of a scholarly monograph frequently abstracts the author from the daily round of human relationships because it necessarily involves many solitary hours spent in archives and the quiet of a study, this particular project has been for me a particularly satisfying one, as it has both deepened old friendships and forged new ones. Many individuals and institutions have given generously of their time and expertise to offer me the benefits of their support, insight, and advice. My most profound intellectual and personal debt, as always, is to Nancy Christie, who several years ago urged me to set aside a more amorphous research project on nineteenth-century Protestantism, and explore the twentieth-century relationship between religion and modernity. She also generously provided me with an opportunity to publish my early findings on the new relationship between Quebec Catholicism and ideas of gender and marriage, which form a critical pillar of this study. As the research progressed, I was fortunate to encounter many historians of Quebec who are fascinated with the role of religious identities and institutions. At an early stage of defining the topic more clearly, I benefited from the advice of Pierre Trépanier and Jacques Rouillard. Roberto Perin, from the perspective of his own researches into twentieth-century Catholicism, offered a piece of advice that I have endeavoured to apply – to avoid being caught up in the continued mythmaking surrounding the Quiet Revolution. Audiences at the Canadian Historical Association, the Université du Québec à Montréal, the Catholic University of America, McMaster University, and Université Laval heard various versions of the interpretation, and were open and fulsome with their criticism and advice. More importantly, long conversations over many coffee breaks and evening dinners in Toronto and Montreal with Ollivier Hubert sharpened my thinking about the nature of cultural history and the place of Catholicism in Quebec historiography.

I am also particularly indebted, in carrying out the research, to the generosity and assistance of archivists at the Archives Nationales du Québec, the Archives de l'Université du Québec à Montréal, and the Centre Lionel-Groulx. Among this fraternity, however, I would like to single out for special thanks Denis Plante of the Service des Archives de l'Université de Montréal, who went far beyond the call of duty, drawing my attention to collections of papers that had escaped my attention, and facilitating my research by making microfilm available when research funding did not enable me to travel to Montreal. The Arts Research Board of McMaster University and the Social Sciences and Humanities Research Council of Canada provided financial assistance towards the cost of carrying out research for this project.

Don Akenson, senior editor at McGill-Queen's University Press, expressed interest and encouragement from an early stage. He and his attentive team at the Queen's end, Roger Martin and Kyla Madden, have been a delight for any author to work with. During the lengthy process of publishing a scholarly book, I have benefited at critical junctures from their advice to keep things in perspective. Roger Martin, editor at McGill-Queen's University Press, has spent far too many telephone hours calming me down and explaining the intricacies of publishing in an underfunded system. At the McGill end, Joan McGilvray oversaw the production and design of the volume with the attentiveness, professionalism, and high sense of commitment to the aesthetics of book publishing that makes McGill-Queen's such a hospitable environment for scholars. I owe a very special debt of gratitude to David Schwinghamer, who copy-edited the book. David's meticulous and driving concern to make the prose accessible, and his flair for expression, have made this book immeasurably better. At the final stage, Tegan Hall turned a sharp, critical eye to proofreading a very lengthy manuscript, a task undertaken with rigorous devotion to accuracy. It goes without saying, however, that any remaining errors, infelicities, and egregious sins of omission or commission are entirely my responsibility.

THE CATHOLIC ORIGINS OF QUEBEC'S
QUIET REVOLUTION, 1931–1970

Introduction

Recasting Catholicism's Place in Modern Quebec

"The men and women of my generation," stated Jean-Paul Gignac in 1970, "were very traumatized by the Catholic Church."[1] His expression of the anxieties caused by the rapid erosion of the social and cultural authority of Quebec's Catholic Church in the late 1960s was delivered to the Commission d'étude sur les laïcs et l'Église (colloquially known as the Commission Dumont), a group of experts appointed to consider the reasons for the sudden decline in the social presence of Catholicism. At one level, because his comment was delivered at the end of a decade of extremely rapid social and cultural change, his perplexity can be read as an obvious response of conservative Catholics to a phenomenon historians have termed the "Quiet Revolution." Since the 1970s, the historical consensus – as expressed in the influential synthesis authored by Paul-André Linteau, René Durocher, Jean-Claude Robert, and François Ricard – is that the Quiet Revolution, in its most precise sense, described a series of political reforms undertaken by the Liberal government of Premier Jean Lesage between 1960 and 1966. In a larger sense, these historians apply the term to the period extending from 1960 to 1980, an era which they maintain was characterized by "the triumph of neo-liberalism and neo-nationalism."[2] Thus, the Quiet Revolution has been irrevocably associated with politics, either through a far-reaching campaign of accelerated state intervention during the 1960s in the areas of education, economic management, health and social services, through its frequent application to the acrimonious attempts of successive Quebec governments to assert greater constitutional authority vis-à-vis the federal government, or through the project to promote a vision of Quebec as a sovereign nation.

This historical consensus also has a religious dimension. Scholars have long been fascinated by the extremely rapid disintegration of Catholicism as an institutional presence and as a system of public and personal values during the 1960s. Indeed, the period of the Quiet Revolution has been

viewed as an era of intense secularization, if not outright de-Christianization, of a society that even in the late 1950s vaunted its Catholic identity.
The political reforms of the 1960s, it is generally accepted, compelled a
rapid deconfessionalization of Quebec society, with the church withdraw-
ing from the key sectors of education and social welfare in the face of a
political state that had acquired the expertise and will to exert an increasing primacy over the social and economic development of Quebec in the
name of rationality, competence, and efficiency. Of equal significance, the
identification of the Quiet Revolution with politics has rendered it synonymous with the rise of a secular "neo-nationalism" whose bonds consisted of economics, language, and the power of the state, instead of a
common religious faith. In a few short years, the expansion of the state
decisively marginalized the social and cultural role of Catholicism within
Quebec society.[3]

However, what is striking about Gignac's intervention before the Commission Dumont was that he was not a reactionary Catholic simply
lamenting the loss of a social and cultural cohesion that religion had
once provided. Indeed, as one of the principal assistants to René
Lévesque during the nationalization of Hydro-Québec in 1962, and later
as head of the state-operated steel corporation Sidbec, Gignac seemed to
epitomize the rational, technocratic, and anti-religious ethos of the
Quiet Revolution.[4] Significantly, he located the source of the disorienta-
tions and discontinuities experienced by members of his generation in
Catholicism itself, rather than in the expansion of the modern, secular
state. Here was no simple juxtaposition of Catholicism and the state as
opposed categories. Rather, it amounted to a far more ambiguous realization that within Catholicism itself there existed a profound and
ongoing tension over the nature and meaning of modernity. He did not
view Catholicism as the ubiquitous source of stasis, security, and unbending tradition. Thus, Gignac implicitly posed a set of questions that the
dominant currents of Quebec historical writing, themselves strongly
influenced by the secularizing, statist ethos of the Quiet Revolution,[5]
have either sought to negate or evade. It is these questions which form
the central concerns of this study: To begin, did certain tendencies
within Catholicism act as a significant force in the articulation, promotion, and permeation of modern cultural values into Quebec society after
1930? And if Catholicism did indeed maintain a positive, dynamic presence in the very definition and diffusion of certain modern values in the
Quebec context, this raises an even more problematic set of issues. Could
it be that the Quiet Revolution itself can be understood, not as a project
by which political elites sought a mutually-exclusive juxtaposition of
secular and religious identities, thus marginalizing Catholicism, but as a
more far-reaching cultural transformation enlisting the energies and

activities of a far broader range of less prominent men and women in Quebec, a transformation, therefore, whose central categories were in reality shaped to a considerable degree by religious ideologies and institutions? And if this was the case, did not the Quiet Revolution then mark a sustained attempt to enhance and strengthen, rather than weaken and ultimately sever, the relationship between Catholicism and Quebec society?

Perhaps the major difficulty facing anyone who undertakes a reassessment of the origins and nature of the Quiet Revolution lies in the assumption that it was a chain of primarily political events. Two major historiographical currents have dominated discussions of the genesis of the Quiet Revolution, but both privilege either the activity of the state or the changing political ideologies of groups of intellectuals who were disaffected with a prevailing political climate of conservatism. One current, which I term the "orthodox liberal" version of the Quiet Revolution, is closely linked to a number of key participants in Quebec political debates in the 1960s. It maintains that after 1945 Quebecers were confronted by a conflict between, on one side, the increasingly rapid modernization of the province under the impact of industrial expansion and the rise of mass culture, and on the other, institutions such as the Roman Catholic Church, which these historians identified as the guardians of values deemed traditional or anti-modern. According to this interpretation, Catholic values constituted one of the central pillars of the conservative political regime of Maurice Duplessis. Assailed by newer liberal and nationalist ideologies propagated by a small reformist coterie which included progressives within the trade unions, intellectual magazines such as *Cité libre*, and the Faculty of Social Sciences at Université Laval, Catholicism had entered into irreversible decline by the 1950s. By 1960, because of its very traditional character, and its clericalism and alliance with political conservatives, Catholicism had become increasingly unpopular with a rising middle class of professionals, academics, and administrators devoted to secular and technocratic ideals of economic progress and political modernization.[6]

Since 1970, a second interpretation, which can loosely be termed "revisionist," has been oriented to the study of economic structures and processes, and has sought to place Quebec society within the framework of modern liberal capitalism. Emphasizing the "normal," pluralist character of Quebec society, it locates the roots of Quebec's modern values in the nineteenth century, rather than in a sudden discovery by intellectuals of post-war social realities. By thus denying any particular significance to the period after World War II, it renders as increasingly problematic the "orthodox liberal" historiographic canon of a Quiet Revolution which separated church and state and in which Catholicism found its social role usurped by new secular elites. Proponents of this view have downplayed the existence of conservative ideologies and traditional social arrangements, and asserted that Quebec was dominated, not by an alliance of Roman Catholicism and political conservatism, but by a liberal capitalist outlook typical of English-speaking North American societies. Modernity did not work a revolutionary transformation of Quebec's values after 1945; rather, many historians writing in this vein have argued that Quebec's state and social structure had been fully "modern" as early as the 1840s.[7]

However, in both these accounts of the modernization of Quebec, Roman Catholicism and Catholic values loom as shadowy, elusive presences, and are rarely themselves considered as analytic subjects. For all their interpretive differences, when it comes to fitting religion into the Quebec past, "orthodox liberal" and "revisionist" accounts rest upon a series of hypotheses supplied by classic secularization theory. This theory asserts that modernization – generally defined as industrialization, urbanization, and the expansion of the capitalist market economy – necessarily diminishes the social significance of religion.[8] "Liberals" and "revisionists" alike have largely accepted that Catholicism was, in an age of rapid economic transformation, the repository of an unchanging "tradition"; it was an institution which prior to 1940 conserved considerable social power, but was mired in a rural, utopian past and thus inevitably destined to melt away in the march of industrialization and urbanization, a march which necessarily generated new secular ideologies and cultural practices that combined to marginalize religion. In both accounts, therefore, Catholicism was viewed as an object acted upon, rather than as a dynamic presence in the history of modern Quebec.[9] However, if we are to accept the argument proffered by the revisionists, namely, that "modernization" was a much longer process, how then to account for the impressive institutional expansion of Catholicism, not only in terms of parishes and number of clergy, but in greater Church activity in the areas of education and social welfare during the nineteenth century, the great age of liberal capitalism and the beginnings of industrialization? Can this be simply written off as a historical aberration, one in which Quebec stood outside the "normal" development of the Western world – thus invalidating a central tenet of the "revisionist" historiography? Or was there a set of deeper social and cultural connections between Catholicism and liberal capitalism that gave religion greater authority in a society characterized by voluntarism and political democracy?[10] More tellingly, a growing body of historical evidence, both from other industrial societies such as Britain, and from Quebec itself, suggests that there was no necessary equation between the rise of an urban, industrial society and religious decline. Indeed, the classic age of industrial capitalism was one of considerable religious vitality and expansion. It was an age in which churches, both Protestant and Catholic, assumed the challenges posed by social pluralism, and evolved creative, new strategies, making changes to their institutions and practices that in fact made religion more inclusive and accessible to new social groups in the urban community.[11]

When applied to the question of the origins of the Quiet Revolution, the achievements and difficulties of the "revisionist" historiographic trajectory are exemplified in the work of Gilles Bourque, Jules Duchastel, and Jacques Beauchemin, *La société libérale duplessiste*. In one sense, the authors of this seminal work sought to break with the prevailing view that Catholicism was merely the repository of tradition. They argued instead that it operated within a more complex context of liberal, "modern" social values and state formation. Defining "modernity" as a commitment to economic progress under a regime of liberal capitalism, the separation of public and private spheres, an explicit distinction between church and state, and a lack of reference to religious arguments in formulating public policy,[12] this work exonerated both Duplessis and the Church of the charge of reactionary traditionalism, and placed them firmly within a historical schema of continuity leading up to the Quiet Revolution itself. Such a procedure undercut the central assumptions that lay at the root of the "liberal" interpretation of the Quiet Revolution,[13] and indeed seemed to question the very chronological periodization that identified the post-1945 era as constituting a "revolution in mentalities" that produced the political changes of the 1960s. In one crucial respect, however, the authors of *La société libérale duplessiste* still adhered to one of the central conventions of both "orthodox liberal" and "revisionist" historiography: they equated Catholicism with the ideologies and actions of the upper clergy, and continued to view Catholicism as marginal to the elaboration of social ideologies in the period after 1945.[14] In this respect, their work simply echoed the view that the meaning of Catholicism was entirely encompassed by the perspective of the ordained clergy, and it subtly reinforced the older "orthodox liberal" view that, prior to 1960, Quebec was a society characterized by social and ideological conformity.

This raises a more fundamental difficulty for both historiographical trajectories. Where religion does enter their analytic framework, Catholicism is always ubiquitously identified with the activities and ideologies of the clergy. Further, it is assumed that Roman Catholicism was largely a conservative political force, of interest only when explaining the interaction of clerical and political elites. Thus, the relatively even-handed treatment of twentieth-century Quebec Catholicism authored by Jean Hamelin and Nicole Gagnon presents a picture of growing institutional ossification and internal confusion in which church and clergy are synonymous, and in which Catholicism is a complex of structures and values acted upon by secular forces from the outside.[15] However, since the mid-1980s, a new current of religious history in Quebec that has thoroughly reassessed the

rise of ultramontanism between 1840 and 1890 has presented a far more
nuanced portrait. In effect, these historians have argued that far from
being a fundamental, unchanging characteristic of Quebec society, clericalism was in effect a contingent and time-specific social and cultural construction. To be sure, the Quebec clergy during this period were by and
large successful in making Catholicism correspond to a series of beliefs,
values, and practices largely defined by them. However, this dominance of
the clergy – and the concomitant ultramontane social vision and set of religious practices that they espoused – did not characterize earlier periods of
Quebec history and, more significantly, it was a religious and social project
that was frequently resisted and contested, by groups both of Catholic laity
and clergy acting upon rival definitions of Catholic belief and practice.[16]

This study is an explicit attempt, both interpretively and methodologi-
cally, to decentre the "orthodox liberal" and "revisionist" master-narratives
of Quebec's Quiet Revolution. It is also a study which stands outside the
current vogue of "post-revisionism" because it is emphatically not an
attempt to refurbish Duplessis's "liberal" credentials, nor does it assert, as
does one recent treatment of the economic achievements of this period,
that the Quiet Revolution was a mistake. Further, it does not, as does
Ronald Rudin's critique of the "revisionist" school, assert that historians
need to devote greater attention to the "unique" elements in Quebec
society, such as "considerable clerical influence,"[17] an assertion that ultimately doubles back to a central tenet of Quiet Revolution ideology. And,
more significantly, this book is not a contribution to the current polemic
about history and memory in post–Quiet Revolution Quebec that is driven
by a discontent with modernity itself. "Revisionist" historians, according to
one such recent treatise, have, like other intellectuals since the 1960s,
drawn Quebec too closely into a scheme of modernity that is governed by
American identities and value-systems, and have essentially promoted a
"history without memory," one that ultimately denies any historical rele-
vance to attempts to promote a specific national destiny for Quebec
society.[18]

Indeed, if anything, this study simply argues for the extension of historical revisionism to the relationship of Catholicism and twentieth-century
Quebec society. Like the historians of Quebec's nineteenth-century ultramontane devotional revolution, whose work has largely exploded the myth
of a monolithic, unchanging Church, this work contends that we should
resist any a priori attempt to equate the categories "Catholicism" and "tradition." It is the central argument of the present study that particularly
after 1930, although powerful currents of conservatism certainly remained
within Catholicism, there was a growing ideological diversity in the
Church, one marked by powerful lay social and cultural initiatives. These
initiatives were generated by people belonging to Catholic Action, a group

of organizations that attracted groups that had hitherto been quite marginal to the intersection of church and society: youth, working-class people, and women.[19] The perspective of this study is that, from the beginning, these movements articulated a powerful critique of the Church hierarchy – a critique frequently verging on anticlericalism – as, by insisting that Church structures be responsive to the needs of laypeople, they emphasized the more democratic aspects of religion. Indeed, the very existence of these Catholic Action movements indicates the need for a reassessment of the way in which Quebec Catholicism intersected with the formation of the cultural values of a modern, liberal society during the middle decades of the twentieth century.

In contrast to the "orthodox liberal" and "revisionist" interpretations of the Quiet Revolution, both of which privilege the play of economic forces and political actors, this book approaches the problem by drawing upon two insights. The first, offered by Léon Dion in his celebrated work on Quebec intellectuals of the post-1945 generation, is that the religious beliefs of figures like Pierre Trudeau, Gérard Pelletier, André Laurendeau, and Gérard Filion were rather superficial and shallow.[20] The second was suggested more recently by the historian Jocelyn Létourneau, who observed that the Quiet Revolution might best be understood as a "category of identity" in modern Quebec.[21] While Dion's characterization cannot be taken at face value – because he was a direct participant in the critiques levelled at the Duplessis régime and in many of the subsequent events of the Quiet Revolution – it provides a point of entry into the mindset of a generation whose common experience was participation in Catholic social and youth movements of the 1930s and 1940s. In the case of Létourneau, the use of the term "identity" suggests the need for a cultural approach, rather than a political or economic one, to the origins and nature of the Quiet Revolution – although in his framework, "identity" is used purely in a geographic and economic sense. Taken together, the views of Dion and Létourneau lead to the formulation of the central questions that animate this study: Was the type of Catholicism promoted within the Catholic Action movements a bulwark of tradition, or was it a significant factor in the dynamic entry of modern cultural values into Quebec society? Was Catholicism, as both "liberal" and "revisionist" historiographies suggest, simply marginal to the formation of a modern urban society in Quebec and to the building of modern ideas of the state, or did it offer access to a range of more dynamic, democratic social identities? And, if "modernity" as a cultural phenomenon is to be understood as a search for authenticity and intensity of experience, and as a sense of profound rupture with the past,[22] given the pervasive nature of Catholicism in Quebec's public life and social values before 1960, should not historians look to religion, and in particular to transformations within Roman

Catholicism itself,[23] in order to examine the changes that helped define a series of "modern" values in the public ideologies and personal identities of youth, masculinity, femininity, and family?

To answer these questions, a methodological approach that relies on a different set of evidence is needed. The principal source for this study is the records generated from the 1930s to the 1960s by a number of Catholic Action lay organizations. The main collection, the Fonds Action Catholique Canadienne, is held at the Archives de l'Université de Montréal. Although "youth" was a major focus of specialized efforts by Catholic Action throughout this period, it would be a mistake to see the implications of this study as limited to this cultural category. Indeed, the leaders of Catholic Action collected material from a wide range of organizations and people who either were involved with an array of Catholic social, educational, and cultural initiatives, or expressed ideas about the role Catholicism should play in Quebec society. As well, although this study is not centred on the Catholic clergy, a wide range of clerical interest and opinion is represented in the archives of Catholic Action, ranging from episcopal attempts to regulate and discipline the orientations of the movement's leaders, to chaplains and parish priests involved with promoting specific aspects of Catholic endeavour. Because this book claims to be a study of Catholicism as public ideology, it has also explicitly drawn upon a particularly rich periodical literature and, more selectively, on daily newspapers such as *Le Devoir*. Some of this material was generated by laypeople, some, in the case of *Revue Dominicaine, Maintenant*, and *Relations*, by powerful religious orders such as the Dominicans and Jesuits who were active in various social initiatives throughout this period. Finally, because it aims to demonstrate certain connections between the cultural categories of youth, family, and female identity and some of the significant political reforms of the Quiet Revolution, particularly in the field of education, it gives serious consideration to collections such as the Fonds Paul-Larocque, which preserved the records of Quebec's Royal Commission on Education.

Particularly in the field of twentieth-century Quebec Catholicism, some scholars still privilege clerical prescriptions and leadership as defining the nature of "Catholicism," a story in which the bishops and upper clergy speak, and the faithful follow, either in a conservative or more liberal direction.[24] In one sense, this is understandable. Until very recently, the terrain of Canadian religious history, both Catholic and Protestant, was largely taken up with intellectual histories of clerical discourse, which was frequently taken to be coterminous with "religion" itself.[25] Increasingly, however, such approaches have been displaced by those offered by scholars interested in the ways in which lay men and women of a variety of classes and social groups experienced and appropriated the discourses and practices officially promulgated by the clergy, and then articulated definitions of religious belonging and authority that were, in many historical instances, at odds with the clerical version. This body of scholarship, crossing the traditional doctrinal barriers between Catholicism and Protestantism, has coalesced around the concept of religion as a body of mutable social and cultural practices, a view that gives considerable analytical weight to lay initiative.[26] This more recent type of social and cultural history of religion finds itself somewhat at odds with the discourse as constructed by international Catholicism, which at least since the Reformation, has presented the Church as offering a body of doctrine and ritual that is basically unchanged since the age of the primitive Church. Notably, such doctrine has also been articulated and preserved by a visible clerical hierarchy in which laypeople have very little scope or initiative.

While there have been historical periods within Catholicism in which there were closer approximations between lay and clerical definitions of what Catholic teaching really was, the twentieth century, with its conflicted history of ideologically-driven social strife and rapid evolution of gender identities, notions of family, social order, and visions of the self, was not one of them.[27] It was, in fact, an age of constantly renegotiated cultural boundaries between lay and clerical authority within Catholicism. Particularly in a society like Quebec, which had experienced an accentuated clerical presence during the mid-nineteenth century, the attempt by laypeople to assert greater authority over their religious beliefs and practices must stand as one of the great and exciting themes of that society's history. And the primary source for this study – the public discourses generated by the Catholic Action movements, which at times expressed a strong lay dissent from clerical teaching – offers historians privileged access through records of the Catholic institution itself into the complex ways in which religious and social change were articulated in Quebec society.

However, it should be emphasized at the outset that this study in no way aspires to offer a comprehensive treatment of mid-twentieth century Catholicism in Quebec. Histories centred on the clergy, such as the otherwise excellent study by Jean Hamelin and Nicole Gagnon, need not be once again recapitulated. Any attempt to revise such histories by going over the same terrain would be premature for two major reasons. First, the details of parish administration and of relations between the bishops, parish priests, and faithful, as well as the parish records themselves, are subject to a seventy-year rule of closure practiced by Quebec's episcopal archives. This restriction limits the ability of historians, until at least the middle of the twenty-first century, to contemplate accumulating the research base for such a history. Second, the fact that census records are currently unavailable after 1901 severely hobbles historians interested in determining the class bases of religious participation. The body of archival material left by Catholic Action thus offers the best record currently available – albeit from a perspective weighted towards the laity – of the encounter between the social and cultural authority of Catholicism and movements of social and cultural change in Quebec.

Finally, this book offers a cultural reassessment of the Quiet Revolution that diverges from both "revisionist" and "orthodox liberal" historiographic trajectories that privilege it as a mainly political event centred on either an abbreviated or longer teleology leading to the interventionist welfare state and a secular neo-nationalism. Thus, it seeks to apply to the mid-twentieth century a current of historical analysis recently outlined by younger cultural historians of the period of the French Revolution. Taking what is usually seen as a dramatic political event, these scholars have suggested that the impact of this period might best be understood, not according to conventional political categories of "liberal," "conservative," and "radical," but in terms of more profound shifts and discontinuities that people experienced as new ways of thinking about self-identity and the relationship of the self to the wider society. Thus, like both the "orthodox liberals" and the cultural historians of the French Revolution, my approach retains "a heavier investment in notions of radical rupture and discontinuity."[28] However, in contrast to the "orthodox liberals," who interpret the Quiet Revolution as a post-1945 "revolution in mentalities," accept the primacy of political categories and teleologies, and place inordinate weight on the role of intellectual minorities opposed to the conservative regime of Maurice Duplessis, this study situates the point of rupture and discontinuity further back in time, locating the cultural origins of the Quiet Revolution in the experiences young men and women acquired in the Catholic Action youth movements of the 1930s.[29] Centred particularly on the elaboration of a type of spirituality that emphasized both the human person and the formation of community, this type of Catholicism intersected with modernity in two key respects: it emphasized the importance of more democratic, egalitarian social relationships, and a generation's rejection of continuity with the past.

Unlike the studies of "revisionists," the present study is more attentive to the nuances of religion and culture, rather than to the impact of structural and macroeconomic changes. Further, it seeks to broaden the understanding of twentieth-century Catholicism to the social plane – by focusing on the initiatives of the laity in appropriating and deploying strands of Catholic thinking – and to the terrain of public ideologies, rather than narrowing it to the interests of a certain clerical elite. Read in a cultural sense, and through a range of social experience outside the immediate purview of political elites, the Quiet Revolution was not, as both "orthodox liberals" and "revisionists" have cast it, about the evisceration of Catholicism from Quebec society and state. Rather, it was an attempt through a variety of institutional strategies to make Catholicism coterminous with aspects of modernity, and in so doing, to anchor it more firmly in Quebec's public culture.

Last, and most importantly, I argue that two central tensions emerged from the 1930s Catholic youth movements that were to give a decisive cast to the Quiet Revolution. First, Catholic Action fostered a more "democratic" religious style, and in particular, spawned movements that were activist, inclusive, and oriented to the demands of working-class people and women, seeking in particular to reform what were seen as deficiencies in family relationships by emphasizing a more egalitarian status for youth and women. During the late 1940s and early 1950s, however, this activist current was challenged and eventually marginalized by a second emphasis that also derived from the experience of the 1930s. This was a consequence of Catholic Action's generational thinking – an elitist cult of spiritual authoritarianism rooted in theological, rather than social, priorities – articulated by a small, but influential circle of Catholic intellectuals that viewed working-class religious identities and practices with disdain and abhorrence for fear these were promoting both religious conformity and a cultural levelling that was rapidly Americanizing Quebec. From this religious critique flowed a political critique that assimilated the Catholic clergy and the conservatism of Maurice Duplessis. And because it was from this latter current that both "liberal" and "revisionist" historians drew their assumptions regarding the place of religion within the historical evolution of post-Conquest Quebec, their unquestioning appropriation of the categories of this Catholic intellectualism inadvertently obscured, in the name of politics, the social and cultural legacy of the Quiet Revolution.

1

"The Presence of Heroism in Our Lives"[1]
Youth, Catholicism, and the Cultural Origins of the Quiet Revolution, 1931–1945

We are not destined to live in a world that is comfortable for faith. One day, the least amongst us will have to bear witness in the wilderness of atheism. As a human community, we must testify to a reality that is supernatural. Under pain of death, our faith must express itself socially. And, as laymen, we must live our faith personally in a hostile environment, in the midst of incredible obstacles, in a solitude that is dizzying and disorienting.[2]

At first glance, Depression-era Catholicism in Quebec would seem an unlikely cultural crucible for the Quiet Revolution. The Church's response to the social crisis emphasized both caution and conservatism. Its economic panacea of social corporatism, which evoked a hierarchical, authoritarian order modelled on the patriarchal family, sought to restore an idealized social harmony among competing classes. When it launched the specialized Catholic Action movements in the early 1930s, the Church hierarchy also intended – through the education and disciplining of youth – to arrest what it considered the de-Christianizing tendencies of modern industrial workplaces and commercialized amusements and especially to forestall the enlistment of Quebec's Catholic youth under the banners of anti-Christian ideologies. However, although conservative in intent, the Catholic Action movements incarnated a vision of Quebec society that was profoundly unsettling and subversive of traditional social relations. This was the idea that youth constituted a separate "class" – an idea imported from a number of European youth associations that flourished during the 1920s and 1930s. Young people, promoters of youth associations claimed, differed radically from the previous generation because they were less docile and less inclined to be regulated by tradition. They were characterized by a desire for free expression without reference to their elders and by a fierce longing for adventure.[3] Here was a clear notion of generational separation which, when imported to Quebec under Catholic auspices, constituted from the first a serious challenge to the corporatist model of patriarchy and hierarchy that the same Church laboured so assiduously to promote. This new youth identity as expressed through Catholic Action profoundly transformed definitions of sexuality, marriage, family relationships, and gender identity between the mid-1930s and the mid-1950s.

However, one must be wary of accepting at face value the claims that Catholic Action created an overarching identity for youth. The numbers of young people enrolled in the various movements at any one time was never large, particularly among working-class youth, and the popularity of the various movements among young women far surpassed their appeal to men.[4] Only in the largely middle-class *collèges classiques* did Catholic Action succeed in enrolling a significant proportion of the total youth cohort. But to posit a direct relationship between numbers and social influence would fail to do justice to the inner logic of Catholic Action itself, whose members always claimed that their work was "one of influence and diffusion," and did not depend upon the actual number of people enrolled in a structured organization.[5] Any evaluation of the cultural impact of Catholic Action must therefore take as its starting point the meaning of words such as "solitude," "community," "anxiousness," and "authentic," which recurred over and over again in Quebec between 1931 and the mid-1950s. What was significant was that these words represented religious values that were always attributed positively to young people, and always in reference to the negative qualities of conformity, complacency, individualism, hypocrisy, a sterile obsession with moralizing, and bad faith, all of which marked the religious experience of the previous generation. Indeed, the attempt made during the Depression by Catholic lay activists and clergy to fuse the ideals of youthful endeavour and higher spiritual quality into a set of conflictual generational identities – in which certain Catholic leaders and educators encouraged young people to exalt their own psychological and spiritual qualities, and denigrate those of their parents – further distinguished Quebec Catholicism from its Protestant counterpart in English Canada. Like mainstream Protestantism, Catholicism was challenged by the emergence of totalitarian ideologies and public pressure for greater state intervention in the field of social welfare, and indeed, adopted a view similar to that of Protestantism, namely that the Depression was primarily a moral and spiritual crisis. But there the similarity between Catholics and Protestants ended. Unlike the United Church, whose leaders retreated from earlier efforts to promote a cultural climate of social reform and a series of alliances with the state in favour of an older emphasis upon evangelical conversion and revivalism, Quebec Catholics continued to view the task of social and spiritual reconstruction as seamlessly interwoven.[6] More significantly, Catholicism's emphasis on recasting youth identity, through the creation of specific organizations, as the central social and cultural axis of reconstruction had no institutional counterpart in Depression-era Protestantism.

It was the definitions of youth forged within Quebec's Catholic Action organizations – rather than any objective measurements of youth sociability – that captured what was in fact central to the mindset of the Quiet Revolution, and, indeed, to modernity itself: the overwhelming conviction, among many young men and women who grew up between the early 1930s and the late 1950s that their society's religious past incarnated only negative values. Catholicism, they believed, must be entirely made over with reference to a heroic present and future in which humans engaged in an unremitting struggle *against tradition* to forge new forms of community solidarity. As expressed in the Catholic Action movements of the 1930s, youth alone possessed the spiritual force, vigour, and purity necessary to reconstruct Quebec society along Christian lines.

After World War II, as the youthful Catholic militants of the 1930s moved into careers in media, law, and trade union activism, they did not shed this sense of generational divide upon entry into adulthood. Rather than helping youths re-cement their ties with their elders, the youth values of the 1930s, which were reinforced by a transatlantic current of French personalism, remained at the core of an uncompromising critique of mass culture and obsessive anxieties about "conformity" and the "proletarianization" of the middle classes. Indeed, by the mid-1950s, these cultural activists worried increasingly that contemporary adolescents had, through their encounter with prosperity and consumerism, lost any sense of spiritual purpose, and were slipping back into the practices of a decadent, "bourgeois" traditional Catholicism. Driven by the burning conviction that only through the wholesale adoption of their brand of elitist spirituality could Quebec's distinct identity as a Catholic and French society be preserved, these former Catholic Action leaders identified as their principal enemy an administratively powerful, omnicompetent Church. Catholicism, which had in the 1930s nurtured a "heroic humanism," by the 1950s offered only an emasculated version appropriate for spiritually-quiescent "organization men" devoid of any explicit Catholic or French character who were suited to staff corporate offices in a standardized, universal, North American society.

"YOUTH'S TASK IS THAT OF SPIRITUAL RECONSTRUCTION"[7]

The method of specialized Catholic Action was imported to Quebec in the early 1930s,[8] and adopted a Belgian model developed by Father Joseph Cardijn, a zealous advocate of Catholic activism among working-class youth. Cardijn's approach emphasized, not the winning of individuals to

Christian beliefs and practices, but an ideal of Catholicism whose concern was to transform the milieu, that is, the family, workplace, and leisure social settings and atmosphere in which modern workers lived their lives.[9] In rapid order between 1932 and 1937, the Quebec church hierarchy authorized the establishment of specialized Catholic youth organizations: for working-class youth, the Jeunesse Ouvrière Catholique (JOC); for college students, the Jeunesse Étudiante Catholique (JEC); for middle-class youth, the Jeunesse Indépendante Catholique (JIC); and for rural young people, the Jeunesse Agricole Catholique (JAC).[10] Catholic Action proffered, on the one hand, a conservative imperative that promised to restore traditional religious values among urban social groups which the clergy feared were becoming de-Christianized under the impact of modern class relations, ideologies, and commercialized amusements. On the other hand, the idea of grouping young people in associations established according to social function, rather than geographic residence, constituted a decisive break with older Catholic patterns of religious endeavour that had historically been based upon the local parish. Bishop Georges Gauthier, the archbishop-coadjutor of Montreal, initiated contacts with Belgian and French Catholic Action leaders in the late 1920s, in the hope that this new approach could win Quebec workers back to Christian practices and values. More tellingly, Gauthier hoped that the new style of Catholic Action would effectively promote the ideal of a Christian social order, based upon hierarchy, discipline, and class harmony between employers and workers, and would thus serve as a front-line defence against the spread of Communism.[11]

When imported to Quebec, Catholic Action entered a cultural and ideological environment that dramatically altered the direction of the international movement. In a European context of dynamic and strongly institutionalized Marxist and fascist ideologies, which in a number of countries aggressively enrolled young people into anti-Christian groups and associations, this brand of social Catholicism possessed a strongly conservative tinge and vociferously eschewed any relationship with politics.[12] The Quebec context, however, was one in which not only a relatively harmonious climate of relations prevailed between Catholicism and a "liberal" state,[13] but one in which the Church enjoyed a near-monopoly over the education and training of Catholic youth. Even more importantly, although working-class religious identity and participation, relative to rural Quebec, was somewhat weaker, it was still significantly stronger than that of the industrial working classes of large European cities.[14] Despite a good deal of clerical scare-mongering about "de-Christianization," it would be incorrect to posit this as occurring on a massive scale in Quebec during the 1920s and 1930s.[15]

During the Depression decade, Quebec's Catholic Action movements certainly followed the lead of the senior clergy in firmly supporting the social corporatist programme outlined in the 1931 encyclical *Quadragesimo Anno*. However, by the mid-1930s, Quebec's bishops became strongly influenced by an international climate of Catholicism that sought to distinguish Christian corporatism from the extreme nationalist applications of the ideology that had appeared in Italy, Portugal, and Spain. They therefore moved to draw a crucial distinction between the "spiritual" and social imperatives of the new Catholic Action movements, on the one hand, and the "national" action advocated by older youth groups such as the Association de la Jeunesse Canadienne-Française (ACJC) – associated with the Montreal priest-historian Abbé Lionel Groulx – and vocal nationalist organizations such as the Jeune-Canada dominated by younger spirits like André Laurendeau and his circle, on the other hand.[16] The episcopacy commissioned the Dominican Father Georges-Henri Lévesque to draw up a statement subordinating nationalism to Catholicism and, in so doing, bring the nationalist youth societies under firmer guidance and regulation by the Church hierarchy. Lévesque's own nationalist credentials were impeccable, as he was a firm promoter of the belief that religion and nationalism would remain symbiotically linked so much so that he proclaimed that the spiritual renaissance promised by Catholic Action would supply "a mysterious energy that promises to revive the French-Canadian social body."[17] Historians have focused on the resulting controversy between Lévesque and Abbé Groulx, the intellectual mentor of the earlier nationalist groups, and have read into the struggle over uncoupling "Catholic" action and "national" action as marking the first overt fissure that would later divide anti-nationalist, pro-federalist "liberals" and "neo-nationalist" partisans of greater Quebec independence.[18]

However, while this debate may have been of considerable moment to the evolution of twentieth-century political nationalism in Quebec, this relatively short-lived debate about the relationship of religion to political nationalism should not be allowed to marginalize other elements of great significance in Quebec Catholicism's encounter with the forces of modernity. First, it is necessary to remember that the dissension over the rival merits of "national" and "Catholic" action occurred between committed Catholic activists and was really a quarrel over organizational means and ambitions, rather than ends.[19] Second, it occurred in a society where Catholicism was not confronted by totalitarianisms or extreme nationalisms that occupied the political mainstream.[20] The fact that the Church occupied a dominant position in the field of education and in adolescent leisure activity and associational life meant that a large number of clerics and lay activists were quite comfortable in articulating a new intersection between Catholicism and youth that fostered and legitimized the spread of models of society that rested less upon hierarchy and social solidarity, than upon notions of tension and conflict. However, in the case of the Catholic Action movements, the partially successful attempt by Church authorities to excise nationalism from the Catholic youth movements accelerated a process in which oppositional identities were transposed from the terrain of class and economic relations, or from constitutional quarrels between the rival claims of French and English Canadians, to the realm of inter-generational ties. Catholic Action emphatically formulated a challenge to the bonds that had once linked parents and adolescents. In particular, this challenge helped foster a series of dichotomous pairings that firmly equated "youth" with a more "pure" and exalted type of Catholic spiritual-ity, and at the same time, linked the elder generation to religious formal-ism and routine. These, and not nationalism, were issues around which Quebec Catholicism dramatically reoriented itself, thus moving away from its historic role as a repository of tradition and a bridge between genera-tions, and serving instead as a means for elements within the Church to self-consciously promote an idea of Catholicism as the vanguard of mod-ernist notions of personal identity and visions of community.

Catholic Action's enunciation of the idea that the nature of the rela-tionship between adolescents and their parents was one that was adversar-ial in character was evident from the first implantation of the Jeunesse Ouvrière Catholique (JOC) in Montreal in the early 1930s. Writing in 1934 after several years of work among young people in the city's working-class parishes, Father Henri Roy, the Canadian founder of the JOC, bluntly stated that among youth, religious practice could be summed up by "atten-dance at Sunday mass." The decline of devotional practices in the home, he argued, was symptomatic of a wider breakdown in family relations, and he placed the blame squarely upon the shoulders of the elder generation. In his estimation, parents had neglected their traditional responsibility for the religious and moral education of their adolescents, and had come to regard the latter's relationship with the family as purely economic, with adolescents contributing wages in exchange for room and board. "Rare are the homes," Roy observed, "where evening prayers are held in common ... No one even takes the time to organize morning prayers any more, and in the evening, most are content with a mere *scrap* of prayer."[21] Archbishop Gauthier, Roy's superior, reflected upon the gravity of what confronted young people in industrial society. Forced to leave school at an early age to supplement the family budget, "our working-class children," Gauthier complained, "are simply left to themselves" by parents who were either unable or unwilling to further their religious and moral education. The potential for de-Christianization would emerge less from anti-Christ-ian ideologies than from the fact that young people "carry with them, on their life's journey, a very slim store of religious doctrine, and a few pious practices"[22] taught in elementary school and the parish church.

What the comments of these promoters of Catholic Action reveal is an acute awareness that the accelerated industrialization of large cities like Montreal in the 1920s and the impact of the Depression upon working-class families had irrevocably altered the context and nature of the relationship between parents and adolescents. Both Gauthier and Roy operated within a traditional ideological framework which exalted the interdependent character of the family, not only as an economic unit, but as an affectional one. In this framework, the bonds between parents and their children were vertical, supplying stability and continuity to society itself, because they were anchored upon the moral and religious education that the elder generation, in close association with the local parish clergy, provided.[23] However, in the eyes of many Catholic clergy, the pace of social change was seriously eroding the moral and affectional aspect of the interdependent family, to the point where, rather than serving as the foundation of social solidarity, the family had degenerated into a heterogeneous collection of individuals seeking personal economic gratification. The formation of specialized Catholic Action youth groups constituted an explicit statement by the Catholic Church that the older generation – and the traditional parish networks that had, since the early days of rural settlement, bound together local clergy and parents[24] – could no longer be trusted with the all-important task of socializing adolescents in their religious and family responsibilities.

The formation of movements like the JOC and the burgeoning of other Catholic youth associations were thus a deliberate acknowledgment by an important segment of the urban clergy that the old hierarchical links that ensured intergenerational solidarity and the very structure of the Church that had provided religious sanction for these bonds had broken down. In this situation, clergymen like the Dominican Father M.-Ceslas Forest acknowledged that the danger for Quebec Catholicism lay in a type of faith oriented towards "a former age of quiescence and repose," and which failed to demonstrate awareness that there now existed "a type of youth that was seething, one that found no solution to its problems in the paltry stock of convictions left to it by past generations, and which searches with a freedom that is as dangerous as it is new." For Forest, the central problem for the modern Church was the inchoate character of these new youth aspirations, which required organized and disciplined expression if they were not to manifest themselves as destructive urges. "Never before," he concluded, "have we so thoroughly felt the need of an intellectual and religious renewal."[25] How, then, to ensure that young people would effectively imbibe the traditions and imperatives of Catholicism? For clerical activists like Henri Roy, the eminently traditional goal of restoring the power of religion in Montreal's working-class neighbourhoods could only be accomplished through a method that was radically modernist. The new specialized youth movements simply short-circuited and bypassed the vertical solidarity of the parish that had bound generations of Catholics together, and did so through a virulent critique of the elder generation as spiritually and morally derelict. Instead of the old language of parish identity and respect for one's elders, Church leaders offered Depression-era youth an identity that exalted the language of vitalism and energy, always equated with youthfulness itself, and grounded in the categories of modern sociology, in which the keywords were "*life, milieu, and mass.*"[26]

What undoubtedly excited many young Quebecers about Catholic Action was that, at least in theory, young people themselves were responsible for leading and directing the new youth associations. In a society that had historically had a numerous and institutionally dynamic clergy, religious endeavours had followed the conventional lines of social and age hierarchy; specifically, they had relied upon the leadership supplied by parish priests, seconded by local notables who worked according to the time-honoured tradition that young unmarried men and women were at best unreliable from a religious and moral perspective, and at worst troublesome and disturbing elements in the community.[27] The priority placed upon lay initiative interposed a reordering of the lines of social authority in Catholicism. It was a direction which established from the outset a fundamental tension between the imperatives of the Church hierarchy, which saw Catholic Action as "a powerful, disciplined, conquering army" obedient to its spiritual leaders,[28] and young lay activists like Simonne Monet-Chartrand, who in 1939 emphatically declared that her commitment to the women's section of the Jeunesse Étudiante Catholique was "personal and free," and that she and her colleagues would not be regarded as the "mouthpieces" of the bishop. Catholic Action's religious message, she stated, "must be conceived and expressed by us, in our own style and manner, flowing in a collegial manner from our own study groups."[29] "It would be contrary to the character of Catholic Action," stated an internal memorandum prepared for the Jeunesse Catholique des Classes Moyennes in 1950, "for the movement to be directed by the clergy."[30]

The extent of youth control of these organizations should not, however, be overemphasized. In many respects, Quebec's Catholic Action paralleled similar initiatives in other societies that sought to reconstruct the idea of adolescence around the categories of instability and vulnerability. Ironically, these actually curbed the independence of youth by interposing the effective control of adult leadership.[31] However, it must be remembered that Quebec participated in French and Catholic youth initiatives, which differed sharply from parallel Anglo-American and German associations. Where the latter tended to emphasize the superior physical attributes of youth, thus divorcing it from older ties to morality and spiritual strength,[32] Catholicism actually enhanced the idea that the spiritual values of young people were superior to those of their parents. Thus, the novelty of specialized Catholic Action in the context of Quebec did not lie in the actual extent to which adolescent laity actually controlled the organizations themselves, but in a spiritual and moral reversal of the age hierarchy, in the legitimation by the Church of the assumption that young, unmarried men and women were qualified to lead because their spiritual potential transcended that of their parents and socially-established Catholic laity. Commenting on the accomplishments of the women's section of the Jeunesse Étudiante Catholique in the late 1930s, one observer grasped the cultural significance of a movement which, in a conservative society ruled by hierarchy, "was run by chaplains and young women students. The nuns only play an auxiliary role as technical assistants."[33] Indeed, adolescents who chafed under the rather austere morality and restrictive discipline of the male and female colleges run by Quebec's religious orders welcomed Catholic Action's programme as it emphasized "reflection and action, a right of discussion and organization."[34] And the watchwords of Catholic Action, to "See – Judge – Act," repeated over and over again in study sessions and devotional meetings, explicitly told young men and women that Catholicism was not simply another name for the time-tested wisdom of their parents, but was in fact the core of a self-education whose pace and content they themselves would control.

While it must be recognized that the promoters of Catholic Action were socially conservative in their desire to elevate the authority of the Church among adolescents, the whole tenor of this new religious approach introduced a jarring note as the point of reference in reconstructing and reinforcing the position of the Church was neither the past nor the attitudes and practices of the previous generation. By deploying the argument of parental incompetence, Depression-era Catholic activists formulated a direct relationship between Catholicism and youth that had the effect of identifying the Church *exclusively* with the qualities that the activists assigned to modern youth. As Father Guay declared in a series of lectures on youth held under the auspices of the Semaines Sociales du Canada in 1945, Christianity must be interpreted as "the doctrine of progress, and of the future, and not as that of a bygone era."[35] This had the effect of radically displacing the prevailing image of society, which had operated according to a hierarchy of age and social status. What Catholicism now offered adolescents was a vision of modern society defined along a more "democratic," horizontal axis premised upon two elements: the notion of equality among young laypeople and a functional notion of hierarchy derived not from ascribed social status but based on the engagement, service, and commitment that young people displayed to the movements themselves. For its promoters and lay activists, Catholic Action was simply the recognition that under the social conditions of a modern society young people lived their lives in workplaces and social situations in which they were largely autonomous from their parents. The priority, as Father Guay emphatically proclaimed in terms that brusquely dispensed with any notion of intergenerational solidarity, was to encourage adolescents to be "responsible for their own up-bringing,"[36] an injunction echoed by Gérard Pelletier, the national president of the Jeunesse Étudiante Catholique, who forcefully articulated the need for "a generation of Christians who are emancipated, autonomous, and able to stand on their own two feet," and not inclined to always look to parental or clerical authority figures for directions that would guide their thoughts and actions.[37]

The key element in the mindset of the clergy and lay militants who sought to implant Catholic Action in Quebec was the conviction that youth, as a social and cultural entity, constituted the vanguard of a revolution sweeping Western society during the 1930s. Such ideas were not unique to Quebec as they in fact imported wholesale elements of "nonconformist" intellectual and philosophical discussion then current in Depression-era France. These intellectual nonconformists clustered around a series of ethical concerns that operated under the rubric of "personalism." Personalism held particular appeal for Catholics during the 1930s, because it drew its inspiration in part from the "New Theology" of French Dominicans and Jesuits, and in part from the specialized Catholic Action movements, and thus stood very close to Catholic spiritual and social doctrines enunciated by the official Church. It emphasized a cult of personal engagement, insisted upon realism, rejected philosophical, scientific, and social determinisms, and sought to define what many labelled a new socialism, founded upon the sanctity of the human person, rather than upon strictly materialist imperatives.[38] Personalists also proclaimed that theirs was a revolutionary creed that could compete with Fascism and Marxism in enlisting the allegiance of modern youth. However, the personalist revolution, its exponents claimed, was "spiritual" in character, and did not look to Fascism or Marxism for its ideological sustenance, and as such would not be accomplished through the violent overthrow of the existing order. "Bourgeois" civilization, which they castigated as an unstable compound of individualism, excessive democracy, materialism, and rationalism, was already rotten to the core and would crumble from within, unable to sustain the violent assaults of economic failure and the competition of totalitarian ideologies. From the wreckage would emerge a new civilization, described by some as a "New Middle Ages," built around the "absolute value of the human person." Among these advocates of a new order, the "person" was not simply the equivalent of liberal society's "individual," for their underlying assumption was that the primary quality which defined the "person" was the cultural and spiritual bonds that linked humans to the community.[39] Here, then, was a brusque rejection of the old liberal order's view of society built around competing individuals.

The "spiritual revolutionaries" of the 1930s postulated a vision of community that would create an enduring order by harmonizing the flowering of the full potential of humans with the principle of authority and stability.[40] As explained by "Gilmard" in the pages of JEC – the publication of the Catholic student youth movement – individualism was an atheistic doctrine which failed to recognize the reality that human life was lived through "a network of determined solidarities that are both spiritual and material." However, while one aspect of this French "personalism" was founded upon a spiritual quest to revive heroic myths of community as a counterweight to modern individualism, it always insisted that "society was not an end in itself; its end resides in the completion of the human person,"[41] a view which established a firm barrier between "personalism" and various totalitarian doctrines.[42] Although "persons" stood in indissoluble relationship with their societies, community as an end served only to expand and fulfill the freedom and potentialities of each person. In this sense, "community," because it was primarily a spiritual and cultural bond, firmly reprobated Marxian visions of competing classes and the subordination of human individuals to the collective destiny. Moreover, because personalism drew upon Catholic social theory, its notion of community drew upon a heritage of corporatist thinking that linked the person to the intermediate collectivities of family, church, and nation. In this way, the individual would be protected from the depredations of the modern state. Significantly, in contrast to Fascism, which also deployed a communitarian, corporatist language, it refused to countenance the swallowing of these "natural" communities by the political state. However, the relationship between the community and individual was always an ambiguous one, and the exponents of personalism were always wary about assigning one priority over the other. Thus, depending on the historical context, personalism could be given a more individualistic or collectivist cast. During the 1930s, the personalism expressed in Quebec's Catholic Action movements had a distinctly communitarian, corporatist cast, while in the post-war period, the impact of a more democratic culture accentuated the individualistic elements within personalism.[43]

In contrast to France, however, Quebec lacked the variety of political tendencies, independent artistic movements, and intellectual journalism that articulated the canons of this "spiritual revolution." Its imperatives were thus not manifested openly in the political sphere, but in a violent rejection not of religion itself, but of a number of religious attitudes and practices associated with undesirable characteristics imputed to previous generations. It would be easy to dismiss this as evidence of an "apolitical" temper[44] that reinforced already-dominant tendencies of conservatism and traditionalism in Quebec society. However, what was of crucial cultural significance in this appropriation of the language of "spiritual revolution" was that it served, among an influential minority of young people, as the vehicle for the expression of an independent, adversarial youth culture shaped under the auspices of Catholicism itself. "Today's generation," trumpeted one young Catholic student, "is a new generation because it not only differs from the older generation, but more importantly, it is *opposed* to it."[45] In this respect, Quebec differed significantly from the English-speaking societies of North America because Catholicism, unlike Protestantism,[46] provided a favourable environment before the great "youth revolution" of the 1960s for the promotion of a collective youth identity based on a frank sense of spiritual and moral superiority over the older generation.

"Revolution," proclaimed JEC, "revolution that is not mere 'bluff' but authentic Christianity. Revolution that does not mean destruction, but the upbuilding of ... a *new world*."[47] Calls for the inauguration of an idealistic, new Christian order that would put an end to the "nearly complete economic, political, and moral failure"[48] then afflicting Western Europe and North America regularly appeared in Catholic Action youth publications. In the years after 1934, young Quebec Catholics were effectively introduced to the full spectrum of French "personalist" ideologies which "incarnated the thought and effort of that young France that is Christian and enthusiastic."[49] These ranged from the "integral humanism" of the neo-Thomist of Jacques Maritain, who visited Montreal in 1934, and whose views found a ready audience in a university climate tightly controlled by the Church and firmly wedded to scholastic philosophy, to more radical philosophical variants associated with the Nietzschean existentialism of *Ordre Nouveau* and the attempts of the *Esprit* group, under the intellectual leadership of Emmanuel Mounier, to forge an ideology of "permanent revolution" by engaging in a critical dialogue with Marxist intellectual tendencies.[50]

What young Quebec Catholics took from all this discussion, however, was not any specific allegiance to particular philosophical tendencies, but the abiding conviction that "spiritual revolution," and modernity itself, was nothing more than a distillation of the qualities, faith, and values of young people themselves, the confirmation that youth was "inalienably possessed of the truth."[51] As conveyed by the opening number of the official organ of the Jeunesse Étudiante Catholique, the "most modern characteristic of the most integral modernism" was nothing other than "the absolute, fierce will to follow a system to its final end." For these pioneers of Quebec Catholic Action, the essence of being a "young *modern* Catholic" involved "bringing to this condition an absolute, definitive quality that would be the enemy of any compromising or half-measures." For these young Catholics, the exigencies of modern life, as opposed to past centuries, offered little in the way of security or quiescence, but because it "encompasses impetuousness, ardour, violence, then let us be impetuous, ardent, and violent."[52] According to Father Maurice Lafond, a chaplain who worked closely with Catholic student youth, "today's generation is drawn to extremism and totalitarianism." In his estimation, Catholicism needed to provide a type of Christianity that enlisted the complete loyalty of young people who were "desirous of the total gift of themselves, who aspire to a doctrine of life that invades all their thoughts and desires, and monopolizes all their activities."[53] The dominant characteristics of modern youth were always expressed by words rife with violent analogies associated with revolution and the battering down of obstacles: "energy," "force," "virility," "power," and a willingness to risk all for an integral Christian faith. The principal quality that distinguished young people from their parents, declared Maurice Tremblay in 1936, was the "free response to each instant of life, which builds character," a mentality which gave adolescents a superior and privileged access to "a more intimate life with Christ."[54]

It was precisely this spontaneity that conferred upon youth a religious superiority. Father Adrien Malo evoked this element in 1941 when he wrote that the only true Christianity was neither acquired through Christ's merits nor through simple human conduct that modelled itself upon Christ's example. Such notions of spirituality all rested upon the past and relied for their effectiveness on tradition and precedent. Modern humans, in Malo's estimation, led Christian lives because they themselves "in their thoughts, affections, actions" directly and instantaneously reproduced Christ's divinity in themselves,[55] an action that relied upon the qualities which only youth possessed in abundance: vitality, energy, and spontaneity. The overt link drawn between the readiness and enthusiasm of youth and a superior form of religion offers the point of entry into what was central to the Catholic youth movements of the 1930s: this was nothing less than a spiritual Prometheanism that proclaimed a rupture with the past as it was seen as possessing nothing in the way of values that could guide modern youth. The notion of rupture, strongly developed among the leaders of Catholic Action, emerges in particularly acute form in the definition of the new Catholic spirituality offered in a 1940 lecture by Simonne Monet:

When parents speak of "their experience," they usually allude to their past, lived in the sense of tradition. ... for young people, experience possesses the meaning of invention, of experimentation, of assuming new roles, duties and responsibilities in their social environment. ...

We want to take risks ... the only valuable experience consists in experiment, in taking charge with the assistance of other people, young and adults, who believe in the same ideals and have the same objectives. ... Our daily life, lived under the sign of risk and enthusiasm, will be more Christian because it is at the same time more human.[56]

Monet's statement effectively encapsulates the views current in Quebec's Catholic Action circles. It should be noted that not all adults were suspect: sympathetic chaplains, and adult youth leaders were not lumped in with "parents" because their authority did not flow from "tradition," or "law," but from a more democratic, communitarian sociability of "shared" goals and values. Parents, because they lacked the qualities of "risk" and "enthusiasm" – both synonyms of the most desirable quality of all, spontaneity – were consequently placed on an inferior religious footing, and were even implicitly accused of being anti-human.

A matter of further significance stems from the line that young people like Monet drew between the new religious values and traditional, parental authority. The polarization between generations that many Quebec Catholics sought to promote was always articulated, not around issues of politics or ideology, but in terms of divergent meanings of Catholicism. And here precisely is another characteristic that distinguished Quebec from its Anglo-Saxon counterparts: conflicts over cultural values, the relative balance of tradition and modernity, the underpinnings of the social order, and the distinctive identity of French Canada within the larger Canadian society, prior to the mid-1960s, always centred on the problem of religion and the role of the Church. In Quebec, this debate was only partly related to the institutional power that the Church wielded over education and social welfare. What gave these debates their acute edge was something that lay far deeper for it resided in the transformation worked by Catholic Action in the realm of culture and personal identity among an important segment of young Catholics in the 1930s. Participants in the youth movements acquired the notion that Catholicism, which had hitherto been synonymous with the power of tradition and adult authority, was *itself* the incarnation of an irrefutable modernism indistinguishable from youth itself. The new current within Catholicism, one student leader explained, "is a *new movement* ... like youth full of promise for the future, extending a horizon that has many centuries before it."[57] Declared Guy Cormier, one of the leading spirits of the Jeunesse Étudiante Catholique, the Church "responded to all the exigencies of our youth, to all our problems and anguish. ... We sought to make our wildest dreams reality and the Church offered us the task of rebuilding the world. ... We demanded a strong, revolutionary doctrine, and the Church offered the unvarnished Gospel."[58]

The tight fusion that occurred in Depression-era Quebec between Catholicism and the qualities of youthfulness forged a mentality that was thoroughly "modernist" in its profound hostility to the past as a source of authority. This sensibility, as captured by Jean-Robert Bonnier, took as its starting-point the declaration that "history takes no account of individuals and peoples who are fixated upon a glorious but obsolete past."[59] The way young people expressed this futurist sensibility was not through abstract discussions of personalist doctrines, but through brusque declarations that conveyed a deep and abiding scorn for a world ruled, in the eyes of Guy Frégault – a Catholic student youth leader, future historian, and first deputy-minister of Cultural Affairs after 1960 – by "a heap of overstuffed, stupid, and selfish old people."[60] In religious terms, this attitude was summed up by one young woman, "Dorothée," who in 1935, wrote that "virtue is always young and beautiful, and vice is old and ugly."[61]

However, it is important to understand what the precise criteria were of this rejection of the past that prevailed within the framework of the Catholic Action movements. On the one hand, the leaders of Catholic Action were acutely aware that a distancing of young people and their values from parents was essential in firmly establishing a new Christian identity for youth. However, the need to maintain the authority of Catholic doctrine over this generation of "spiritual revolutionaries" implied that Catholic Action could not simply write off the totality of the past; rather, it had to find a method that would establish a creative bond between "tradition" and "modernity" that eviscerated the preceding generation from the equation. As one commentator warned, "youth possesses too much power, too much life, and proclaims too much hope to trust itself to its own lights. It needs the discipline of order, the power of work, the courage, and conviction, that is provided by an abiding Catholicism that is taught by the past, our history."[62]

Thus, what emerged out of the youth experience in Quebec between 1935 and 1945 was a highly ambiguous articulation of the links between past and present. Catholic Action evoked a past that was of value because it was a resource of communitarian values that surged from a long-distant history, from the quasi-mythical heroic communities of the Middle Ages or the early days of the origins of Christianity. The immediate past, that of the parents, should be expunged from collective experience because it was a record of failure and spiritual capitulation to the values of an alien and alienating "bourgeois" civilization.[63] As the apprentice historian Guy Frégault pessimistically observed in 1937, the "upward course of our history" had, for the past seventy years, experienced a reversal. French Canada's "national sense," he concluded, was not a quality that was transmitted continuously from generation to generation, but rather, was "truly hereditary" because it "leaped generations in whom it was nearly completely or totally absent."[64] The ideologists of Catholic Action firmly believed that present-day humans could immediately recover, and insert into modern society, the meaning and purpose of this primitive Christian past without recapitulating the experience of intervening generations. It was for this reason that many young Catholics were so enraptured with the communitarian doctrine of the Church as Christ's Mystical Body; this doctrine encouraged and legitimated the idea that the experience of fellowship and community that they themselves experienced was itself a "spontaneous" and instantaneous re-creation of the actual presence and divinity of Christ.[65]

At its most basic level, Catholic Action postulated a break in the continuity of history and identified the youth movements themselves as incarnating a kind of Catholicism that constituted a fundamental rupture with the religious values of the past. The fundamental achievement of modern youth, in the words of Father Lafond, was to "break with a host of bourgeois customs."[66] Indeed, it would be no exaggeration to state that a large part of the identity of Catholic youth of this era could be summed up in the vocal contrast drawn between the spiritual values of the "bourgeois" – always identified with the undesirable values and practices of the preceding generation – and those of Catholic Action, which embodied the original vitality and energy of a "real" Christianity.

Perhaps the most acute and compelling description of the "rupture" that Catholic Action hoped to accomplish within Quebec Catholicism, and what specifically so repelled these Catholic militants about the religious culture of former generations, was provided by the novelist-poet François Hertel. Hertel was none other than the Jesuit Father Rodolphe Dubé, professor of *Belles-Lettres* at Montreal's Collège St.-Jean-de-Brébeuf in the late 1930s, a vocal promoter of all the enthusiasms of Depression-era youth, who introduced young men like Gérard Pelletier, Pierre Trudeau and, indirectly, René Lévesque, to the luminaries of modernist literature, Ibsen, Dostoyevsky, Hardy, Léon Bloy, and Charles Péguy,[67] authors whose works were still viewed with suspicion in Jesuit colleges where scholasticism was the reigning intellectual fashion. Hertel's dissection of the cultural mentality of modern youth, *Leur inquiétude*, published under the imprint of Catholic Action, drew heavily upon the various French "nonconformist" intellectual currents of the 1930s, boldly proclaiming the "primacy of the spiritual," and sought to define a purpose for modern youth around the psycho-literary category of "anxiety." Because young people possessed this quality – one of the basic constituents of modernity itself – in greater measure than adults, Hertel argued, they had already achieved a higher level of humanity. Evoking the adversarial Catholicism that had made its way in Quebec since the early 1930s, Hertel praised the fact that over the past decade, "there has been a world upheaval that has altered the balance between an anxious and inquiring youth and those of mature age, who are satisfied and *embourgeoisés*."[68] However, "anxiety" was an exceedingly volatile condition which, unless properly directed and energized by some higher spiritual purpose, could mire the individual in a sterile psychological state which sought an "evasion of the real," expressive of "a fear of living."[69] Hertel celebrated the specialized Catholic Action movements for giving young people an ideal which enabled them to excoriate the "religious defections of their elders." "Young people," he concluded, "have surpassed us, the over-thirty generation, with our proper, placid, timid Catholicism."[70]

In Hertel's work, "bourgeois" was not an economic category, but a cultural and spiritual term of opprobrium. In *Leur Inquiétude*, this educator drew a forceful contrast between Anglo-Saxon liberal societies, whose spiritual potential was exhausted because liberal individualism was not conducive to creative surges of "anxiety,"[71] and France and Quebec, where Catholicism seemed to give shape and voice to this superior quality of modern youth. However, it was Hertel's 1939 novel *Le beau risque* that fully expressed the cultural distance which separated a younger generation devoted to the "primacy of the spiritual" and the "bourgeois" Christianity that was lived by their parents. As explained by Suzanne Manny, who headed the women's section of the Jeunesse Étudiante Catholique, *Le beau risque* was "a book that forms a part of our youth, it belongs to those of us who have been called the 'New Youth'... it expresses our entire aspiration towards INTEGRAL LIFE."[72] Set in a *collège classique*, Hertel's novel analysed the relationship that developed between the adolescent student Pierre Martel, a composite portrait of the young men taught by Hertel at Collège Brébeuf, and one of his college professors, who assumed the role of mentor. In this case, Pierre's coming of age was accompanied by the religious "anxiety" so well outlined in *Leur inquiétude*, an earnest, at times psychologically debilitating search for a Catholicism that would express vitality, meaning, and a desire for service in a world that seemed sunk in materialism, greed, and unthinking routine. The great difference between the generation of modern young people and all past generations, explained Hertel, lay in a realization that "our life is a continual tension." In religious terms, to achieve holiness, contemporary humans were called to "sacrifice a certain feeling of security that usually characterizes the conventional 'good Christian soul.'"[73] The element of generational conflict in *Le beau risque* was provided by the introduction of Pierre's father, a successful French-Canadian businessman who incarnated the "bourgeois" spirit that so repelled Hertel and his youthful acolytes. The father, a doctor who typified the culture of the French-Canadian petty bourgeoisie, was a conventionally moral and practicing Catholic in terms of punctiliously fulfilling his religious duties. However, he was described as "worldly and blasé," and "incurably decrepit,"[74] spiritually dead because his religion remained a surface affair, a quest for a limited individual satisfaction and salvation which did not penetrate and transform a social existence that remained, at the core, pagan, hedonistic, and materialistic and most certainly did not offer the life of heroic service dreamed of by the son and his sympathetic college instructor. Indeed, Hertel's message to the younger generation was that the old rituals and collective religious exercises that had once provided a sense of community and identity in Quebec's Catholic parishes were inappropriate for a generation forced to come to grips with modern values. Engagement, not renunciation or mortification, was for Hertel the key to elaborating a new intersection between Catholicism and twentieth-century human culture. Christ, he concluded, "had nothing about him of the Jansenist-tinged austerity of those saints of the sad epochs that preceded ours. ... The recipe for a contemporary holiness takes as its original element the substitution of the emulation of the living and concrete example of Christ for the cult of abstract observance."[75] As the novel closed, Pierre's awakening to manhood was consummated, not by assuming the values of his father, but through contact with his grandfather, the custodian of the heroic national values of the more distant past, in this case, the world of the rebels of 1837, while the teacher, a thinly-veiled portrait of Hertel himself, enlisted as a Catholic missionary in China.[76] Here was testimony to the notion that only the new youth Catholicism of energy, vitality, and the injunction to lead an integral life possessed the power to redeem adults as well. Salvation, the reconstruction of community in the Depression, and the future of Catholicism as the dominant element of French Canada's national identity were achieved not by the continuous handing of tradition and precedent from elder to younger generations, but rather through an abrupt backwash of values. Such a shock precipitated an adversarial action in which young people themselves, as part of their quest for self-identity, determined the content of the past.

Discussions of the spiritual method of Catholic Action that took place in Quebec during the 1930s and 1940s always proceeded from a negative reference-point: the values of previous generations could offer no guidance or salvation for young Catholics confronted with the pressures and challenges of modern society. The chaplains and lay activists who headed Quebec's Catholic Action movements were always most emphatic about the character of their organizations as marking a rupture with traditional Catholic piety. Specifically, they reproached old-style Catholicism with postulating a negative, overly-moralistic ideal of holiness, what Father Roy in his colourful language described as producing "nice little goody-two-shoes Christians removed from all occasions of sin" and who took no responsibility for transforming their social environment. The future of the Church required a training that stressed "activity, combat and conquest" as this would ensure that modern-day Christians would have the character of "fighters well-suited to live as workers and as Christians."[77] The overarching aim was thus, not the abstraction of the individual from

his surroundings and his enlistment in temperance leagues, pious confraternities, or philanthropic societies, which lacked a universal, collective
character, but to "leave the workers in their social settings so that, through
their lives, these can be transformed."[78] "The besetting sin of 19th century
apostolic efforts," explained Father Chenu, "was that it sanctified the individual without seeking to reach his natural *milieu* ... of sanctifying him *by
removing him from his milieu.*"[79] Here was an indictment that expressed the
fundamentally adversarial quality of the new Catholicism. Old-style parish
piety and social endeavours were associated with adults, the social and
economic failure of the Depression, quiescence, and false and unnatural
hierarchies compounded by a selfish egoism. The religious values of
parents incarnated a "spiritual protectionism" completely at odds with
"the spirit of conquest which is the decisive resource of modern youth."[80]

In defining itself as a "rupture" with the prevailing models and practices
of Quebec Catholicism, Catholic Action offered a religion in which spiritual priorities were radically shifted from the individual to an imperative to
transform the collective mentality of whole communities. The most
common indictment of old-style Catholicism was that its spiritual character
was flawed because it equated salvation with the mere performance of the
duties of individual piety and observance of a restrictive moral code, and
thus presented the Church as accessible only to certain elect individuals
who were able to conform to these moral imperatives, a view that hobbled
its ability to function in a modern world where collective effort and
purpose alone would assure the intersection of Catholicism with all facets
of human existence. Writing in 1943, Alexandrine and Gérard Pelletier,
two of the leading figures of the Jeunesse Étudiante Catholique, argued
that traditional ideals of holiness "have presented themselves too frequently as an individual adventure, as a *solitary voyage on a path bordered with
thorns* that featured in Jansenist hymns. ... if we read the Gospel ... we see
that, on the contrary, all of humanity is like a river, marching towards the
Kingdom of God. We are a small drop of water in that river. We are
members of Christ's Mystical Body, members of an immense multitude of
saints and sinners, and we are in solidarity with all of them."[81] The use of
the epithet "Jansenism" to describe older models of Catholic piety is, in
this context, a particularly revealing one. As used by the Pelletiers,
Jansenism was synonymous with a preoccupation with individual salvation
and a rather hypocritical moralizing, and it was always applied to the
"timid ... routine, crouching" [82] type of Catholicism practiced by the older
generation, what they castigated as the concomitant to the "bourgeois"
Catholicism so roundly denounced by Hertel. The model of "Jansenism,"
or "tradition," was always used for contrast in the context of promoting an
ideal of Catholicism as a dynamic religious community in which "democracy" was a spiritual fellowship forged between an elite and masses. This

new emphasis on religious community was outlined by Father André Picard, who stated in 1945 that "the spiritual level of the entire mass must be raised to the level of the Christian vocation of those who compose it ... We must live the life of the first centuries of the Church."[83] The religious ideal, to many lay activists and clergy who participated in Catholic Action, expressed the commitment and service of emancipated persons whose "violent" Christianity was thoroughly modern, potent enough to permeate and transform all social and cultural institutions.[84] The conviction that dominated the specialized Catholic Action movements, that this communitarian, "revolutionary" Christianity not only appealed more to youth, but had a precise and complete identity with the distinctive qualities of youth, convinced many of this generation that theirs was the only "authentic" Christianity present in their society. By conferring upon an active minority of the young an overweening sense of religious and moral superiority over their elders, it thrust generations of Catholics even further apart and, most importantly, made Catholicism itself a contested terrain in Quebec's struggle to articulate the values of modernity.

"*Spiritual Athletes*"[1]
Elites, Masses, and the Betrayal of Catholicism, 1945–1958

An anxiousness, a searching, a fidelity: this is the triple banner under which the authentic youth of French Canada must enlist.[2]

At a session of the Semaines Sociales du Canada in 1946, which assembled Catholic social thinkers and activists to launch a post-war wave of Catholic Action, Father Robert Fortin recapitulated what had emerged from the past decade of Quebec youth activism as the central theme of the new modernist Catholicism. Referring to the literary tradition launched earlier in the century by the French writer Charles Péguy, and to the communitarian spirituality of the leading personalist thinker Emmanuel Mounier, Fortin began his lecture with the assertion that youth constituted "a new social class."[3] At one level, this statement, and the fact that the entire Semaine Sociale was devoted to the characteristics of modern youth and their place in society, could be read as the acceptance by the mainstream of Catholic clergy and academic opinion of the cultural modernism so eloquently expressed in the idea of generational rupture, rampant in Quebec during the late 1930s. However, Fortin's attempt to define the younger generation as a new social class, redolent with its sociological implications of a separate milieu and distinctive mentality that established a clear line of demarcation between young people and other social groups,[4] was carefully balanced by the comments of a young social worker, Claude Ryan, who had recently been appointed national secretary of the new Action Catholique Canadienne, an umbrella organization designed to coordinate the welter of specialized movements that had sprung up during the Depression. Ryan's concern was less the restatement of adversarial notions of generational conflict, than an injunction to youth to re-cement their links and re-connect themselves to other groups in Quebec society. "Just as youth found its place in the totalitarian social order," Ryan observed, "it must find it in a Christian society."[5]

Ryan's contrast between "totalitarianism" and "Christianity" was a juxtaposition that was most revealing of a palpable shift that had occurred in conceptualizations of youth between the publication of Hertel's *Le beau risque* and the end of World War II. In the estimation of Ryan, and at least a segment of Catholic opinion, the modernistic view that young people and their elders were irrevocably opposed had been cynically employed by totalitarian regimes to cement their hold on power. These regimes, it was argued, rode to power by exploiting generational divisions, and then held onto power by incorporating and regimenting youth into state-controlled youth organizations. For these social activists, the future of democratic community depended, not on a prolongation of youth and the infusion of youth spontaneity into adult culture, but upon the rapid progress of the individual through the stage of adolescence, which was to be achieved through the creation of mechanisms that would *integrate* youth into adult responsibilities, duties, and lifestyles – a process which implied a reconnection of young people and their parents, and a forceful reassertion of adult leadership in youth movements. Henceforth, adult values and priorities must shape the values of post-war young people. More significantly, Ryan's reassertion of intergenerational solidarity marked the recession of the powerful wave of European modernism that had marked the pioneer generation of Catholic Action, faced by an encounter with Anglo-Canadian, Protestant definitions of the nature and role of modern youth.

The adversarial definitions of youth that had predominated in the Depression-era Catholic Action movements were modified by the participation of a number of Quebec youth leaders in the Canadian Youth Commission, which met between 1943 and 1946. From the outset, the Youth Commission – initially created under the auspices of the YMCA – was Anglo-Protestant in inspiration, and the inclusion of Quebec academics, youth leaders, and social activists was largely an afterthought. Indeed, as one of the commissioners, Father Georges-Henri Lévesque, critically observed, the publications of the Youth Commission were never translated into French.[6] However, as Claude Ryan indicated, the immediate post-war years had witnessed a proliferation of youth movements of all types, which necessitated the establishment of some permanent institutional machinery of coordination for identifying common issues and problems.[7] Operating from a more economic definition of society and a model of citizenship that had become widely accepted among Anglo-Canadian federal policymakers in the late 1930s,[8] the Youth Commission defined as its mandate not the exaltation of a "youth culture" or the superior spiritual qualities of adolescents, but the smooth integration of post-war young people into the world of family formation, steady employment, and the assumption of adult responsibilities.

Although Quebec Catholicism had been profoundly marked during the

1930s by a modernist current focused around an intergenerational rupture of religious values, a different priority began to assert itself in the Catholic youth groups during wartime. Writing in 1942, the official organ of the Jeunesse Ouvrière Catholique, while insisting that youth as a group was the only force that could save society from "anarchy and dictatorship," struck a far less confident note by abandoning the 1930s language of the self-confidence and vitality of youth, clamouring instead for adult assistance in "inculcating an ideal of life, work, love, family, and society."[9] Thus, the infusion of a collaborationist, rather than an adversarial, ideology of youth, affected far more than the sections of the Youth Commission that were devoted to employment, education, and training. For example, at the meeting of the Committee on Religion, held at the Université de Montréal in January 1945, what appeared on the surface to be an evocation of the modernist climate of "anxiety" and a denunciation of old-style religious sentimentalism in the name of youthful risk and spontaneity in fact sounded a far less confrontational note. "Anxiety" was now interpreted not as a positive quality that mercilessly exposed adult hypocrisy, but a rather pathetic state occasioned by adult refusals to listen and to provide "a definite orientation." Far from dwelling upon the superiority of the religious values of the young and the "bourgeois" derelictions of adult Christianity, the session called for a better, more positive presentation of religion in the schools, and a "collaboration in the study of religious problems" among young people and knowledgeable adults.[10]

Beneath the fulsome rhetoric that looked back to the Catholic modernist climate of the 1930s, that celebrated a "dynamic" youth that "lifted the surrounding world above the level of mediocrity," some Catholic youth leaders began to introduce a more conciliatory language that expressed a need for social integration with the adult generation. "Young people," stated Marcel Côté, president of the Jeunesse Indépendante Catholique in 1946, "do not constitute a world apart. They are in solidarity with the rest of the great social whole."[11] According to this analysis, the problems which modern youth confronted conferred no quality of distinctiveness: they were simply one part of the "social question," and were similar to the maladjustments that impeded the welfare of adults.[12] The reassertion of this more traditional view of youth explains in part why the Quebec church hierarchy established an effective national secretariat and bureaucracy to impose some order upon the welter of specialized Catholic Action movements that had sprung up during the 1930s. As explained by Claude Ryan, who carried out this task of coordination, it was important to avoid any suggestion that the Church was giving countenance to the notion that youth constituted a distinct social group, or that its organizations formed "a State within a State."[13] The post-war, central Action Catholique Canadienne thus grouped both organizations devoted to the needs of young people and those catering to adults, and while each specialized movement retained its distinctiveness and autonomy, it was compelled to participate in annual common programmes sanctioned by the bishops and *adult* lay leaders.

This attempt to reduce the gulf between generations, a social metaphor that had so characterized the new Catholic spirituality of the late 1930s, revealed a small, but nonetheless palpable fault line. On one side there was the outlook of men like Claude Ryan, whose commitment to social democracy stood closer to traditions of Anglo-American liberalism, and who emphatically refused to countenance "utopian" methods that would "push young people to attempt to create a separate youth polity, based upon distinct organizations, structures, and institutions."[14] And on the other side there was the emphatically modernist engagement of men like Gérard Pelletier, whose notion of fellowship and community was explicitly premised upon the superiority of youth values. Commenting on the Canadian Youth Commission in early 1945, Pelletier placed the Commission in an oppositional dialectic which allowed him to once again underscore the differences between an elder generation that had hypocritically and corruptly "accepted disorder," and a younger generation whose pristine spiritual convictions allowed its members to stand in judgment on their parents. Unlike adults, who expected such organizations to offer panaceas to solve all the world's problems, youth remained devoted to an uncorrupted spiritual fellowship anchored on "an internal reformation," and were justifiably sceptical of such "structures, impersonal revolutions, or promises of immediate rectification of social ills" that all too easily fell prey to economic need, or the compromises necessitated by political imperatives.[15] Pierre Juneau, another former president of the Jeunesse Étudiante Catholique, observed with alarm the technique of groups like the Canadian Youth Commission, which he believed sought to reinforce "the overly-tight grip that existing social structures have on young people." The latter's identity was affirmed, not through collaboration and acceptance of adult leadership, but through a heroic revolt against the "static character, authoritarianism, and individualism of family and school."[16]

Pelletier's hostility to the Youth Commission must be interpreted both in light of his growing disenchantment with the more conservative, hierarchical direction taken by Quebec Catholic Action during World War II, and from his position as a leading spokesman for a group of Catholic student leaders who in the late 1940s committed themselves to a series of international engagements with youth from other countries. Through these encounters and youth congresses, such as the 1947 Fédération mondiale de la jeunesse, activists like Pelletier, Guy Cormier, Réginald Boisvert, Pierre Juneau, and Jeanne Sauvé built upon earlier notions of youth's spiritual superiority and began to articulate a notion that "youth" now constituted an independent and universal class, culturally and socially distinct from adults.[17] In a series of articles written between 1944 and 1946, Pelletier, who was the president of the Jeunesse Étudiante Catholique, editor of JEC, and perhaps the leading lay intellectual figure in the youth movements, bemoaned the sterile climate of theoretical discussion, which he believed emanated from the lack of contact with French and European sources. This, he maintained, had led directly to the adoption of American-style bureaucratic, organizational methods by the Church hierarchy in order to put a damper on giving young laypeople effective responsibility and control.

For those who had grown up in the modernist climate of Depression-era Catholic Action, this change in direction, from heroism and spontaneity to a bureaucratic ethos and administrative rigidity, signalled a sabotage of the ideal communities of spiritual fellowship that they believed would rejuvenate modern Catholicism. In a thinly-veiled critique of the bishops' four-square support of the Allied war effort, Pelletier charged that Catholic Action, far from incarnating young people's aspirations for a pure, communitarian fellowship, had degenerated into "campaigns to enforce the curfew" or sterile denunciations of Marxism.[18] Young Catholics who shared Pelletier's vision of spirituality could not but view post-war Quebec as a spiritual nightmare. Adopting a reading of events that linked together the bureaucratization of the youth movements, what they saw as the growing rigidity of the Church hierarchy on cultural and social questions, and the political victory of Maurice Duplessis's brand of conservative liberalism in 1944, Pelletier and like-minded spirits discerned the reimposition of the religious values of the elder generation, assisted by a clergy that had only a few years before been the sympathetic allies of the young. Rather than following to the limits the modernist logic of progress through the adoption of youth values, Quebec Catholicism seemed to be lapsing into the cloying religious sentimentalism of old-style Catholicism, the victory of age, hypocrisy, and "routine" over "the cult of spiritual *realism*."[19] Catholic Action, Pelletier believed, had reached a crossroads, and was now confronted with "a certain climate of suspicion" on the part of clerical authorities who feared the "'exaggerated' autonomy" of lay activists, and sought to confine spontaneity and commitment in visible, "impersonal" institutional hierarchies.[20]

A significant and vocal group of young Catholics, all influenced by the Depression climate of Catholic Action, believed that the end of the war marked a particularly critical period during which they moved from adolescence to adulthood. Significantly, this transition was defined not only in terms of personal emotional development and the individual experience of international travel and encounter, but was transposed to the level of society, so that the drama that was played out within the maturing adolescent generation was equated with that occurring within the French-

Canadian "nation" as a collective entity. Thus, the new definition of "youth" as universal and independent was easily transferred to Quebec itself, and read as the need for the entire society to mature culturally by broadening its horizons, and in particular, to challenge the authority of those who were cast as its "traditional" leaders. "Our society," stated Gérard Pelletier in 1946, "was too small to fracture itself without serious apprehensions, and therefore crammed all its members together higgledy-piggledy, in a sort of large family where the children all sat up together of an evening, endlessly recycling the same topics of conversation, careful not to call attention to themselves." French Canada, Pelletier declared, was finally ceasing to become a family to become "a nation ... a complete society able to tolerate differences of opinion and resolve its internal conflicts without fratricidal outcries."[21]

What so distinguished this young Catholic elite was a particular view of history, one that rejected the Conquest and the long, unedifying series of constitutional squabbles as being central to national self-definition. Rather, they posited the industrial revolution as the real rupture, an event which to them had occurred in the relatively recent past, and which constituted both "a nightmare" and "the drama of an adolescent conscience" because it revealed the possibility of divergent ideologies as arising from the interests of different social classes.[22] Conflating the economic process of industrial modernization with the emotional and psychological stresses attendant upon entry into adolescence, their historical schema was one in which the category of "youth" remained the central hinge that bound Quebec's past to its future. The "crisis of authority" that they viewed as central to French Canada's post-war experience was thus interpreted as being a function of "a crisis of growth" that had long been stunted by generations of pre-war adults, leaders of church and state, who insisted on a monolithic ideological unity as the precondition for national survival.[23]

The linguistic benchmarks of this coming of age were words like "realism" and "lucidity," banners under which the spiritual values that the Catholicism of the 1930s had sanctioned – heroism, integrity, scathing exposés of "bourgeois" piety, and an adamantine unwillingness to compromise with the established order – could remain potent despite the leaving behind of one's physical youth. Catholic idealism and a commitment to "spiritual values," with the two viewed as forging a dynamic equilibrium between tradition and progress, and supplying also the distinctive elements of the French-Canadian national character, remained the dominant theme among this group of post-war intellectuals and activists.[24] According to Maurice Lamontagne, an economist at Université Laval, the "traditional Christian heritage" of Quebec had not simply withered away in a period of massive social change. In his estimation, the challenge facing post-war Catholics was to "remodel and uplift the essential elements of this heritage by a spirituality that was better adapted to our times."[25] It was this at times unbearable sense of superiority, conferred by international experience that reinforced the possession of a pure Catholicism incarnated in an enduring, eternal youth, that turned many of these Catholics to the task of expunging the nightmare of "bourgeois" Christianity, and in the process, legitimized in the wider Quebec society the notion that "contest" and "confrontation" were religious values superior to those of obedience and authority. And it was this sensibility that not only made competing visions of Catholicism a battleground in the 1950s, but also supplied the essential cultural dynamic of the Quiet Revolution by fostering a polarization around the following question: what relationship should prevail between Catholicism and the enhancement of both personal freedom and communitarian values in a modern society increasingly characterized by mass organizations and modes of communication?

Under the rubric of the "problem of freedom," Claude Ryan in 1950 summarized the discussion held at the Jeunesse Indépendante Catholique's annual École Civique d'Été. The summary was essentially a synthesis of the insights offered by the participants and guest lecturers, whose names constituted what was in effect a roll call of most of the major Quebec federalist and sovereigntist champions of the next three decades: the list included Gérard Pelletier, at that time a labour journalist and master-spirit of the recently founded critical journal *Cité libre*; Maurice Sauvé, president of the World Assembly of Youth; Dr Claude Mailhiot, a Montreal psychiatrist; Dr Camille Laurin, a young psychiatrist who earlier that year had written a perceptive internal assessment of the nature of Catholicism in Canada; Pierre Juneau, a former leader of the Jeunesse Étudiante Catholique, now active in the *Cité libre* group; André Laurendeau, former leader of the Bloc Populaire, now editor of *Le Devoir*; Guy Cormier, whose career had begun as a leader in the JEC, now editor of *Le Front Ouvrier*, the weekly newspaper of the Jeunesse Ouvrière Catholique, and a contributor to *Cité libre*; and Pierre Trudeau, a young federal civil servant fresh from graduate studies at Harvard and in Paris and London.

From Ryan's summary, it was evident that the tenor of discussion had centred on the more universal and compelling problem of the future of religion in the modern world, and not on rival definitions of Confederation. Most of the contributors had addressed themselves to the task of formulating an agenda for post-war Christians in a world divided into two rival power blocs. As might be expected in a venue under the sponsorship of Catholic Action, Ryan performed the ritual exorcism of the "Marxist current," which he categorized as unacceptable because it abstracted humanity from God. But significantly, while acknowledging that the "Christian current" was superior because it rested upon respect for the human person, he also stated that civilizations founded upon this principle of respect constituted a source of "personal frustration and a violation of ... freedom" for millions who lived in the "lower strata." Christianity, in his estimation, had much to learn from the Marxist imperative to deliver mankind from frustration, opposition, and alienation, and he urged modern Christians to bear witness to two kinds of freedom, defined as internal and external in nature. However, Ryan cautioned that while moving about in a world in which freedom was the watchword modern Christians must navigate carefully. In promoting human liberty and in building a civilization that was more just than the revolutionary order offered by Marxists, they must resist the temptation to confine the Christian message in rigid structures, and seek an intersection between Catholicism and modern society that offered humans security through a network of Christian political structures and social institutions.[26]

The hunger of the young "spiritual revolutionaries" of the 1930s for an order based on spontaneous fellowship and community had endured and gained wider credibility within Quebec culture in the 1950s. What animated them was the conviction that paralleling the universal struggle between Christianity and Marxism for adherents was the ongoing dialectical struggle within Christianity itself between a liberating "Christianity of freedom," which opened Catholics to a progressive future, and a constricting "Christianity of structures," always identified with the values of the past. During the five years immediately following World War II, many of these young Catholics rounded out their education at European universities, or participated in ongoing contacts with international student movements.[27] At one level, they accepted conservative definitions that the problem of civilization involved a spiritual struggle between Christianity and Marxism, and publicly proclaimed their hope for the victory of Christian civilization. However, their definition of Marxism as a form of "religion" allowed them to use the juxtaposition of Christian and Communist ideals as a critical vantage point from which to assess and critique the religious failings of Catholicism. Most would have accepted the view proffered by Jacques Dubuc, that "communism ... is above all a poetic form, a vision of the world voluntarily projected into the future and able to provide nourishment for the masses." In meeting the Communist challenge, Christians must at all costs avoid sterile opposition or a simple repetition of orthodox formulae that "passed over life's problems by shifting them to the level of moralism and offering hasty solutions."[28] "The greatest scandal of our century," lamented the young sociologist Guy Rocher in 1946, "lies in the fact that pagans were the first to dream of effectively relieving the misery of the proletariat. This situation must be laid at the door of the cowardice of Christians and the deficiency of the Church."[29] Even Claude Ryan, whose position as national secretary of Catholic Action placed him closer to the views of the Church hierarchy, urged young Catholics to obtain a deeper knowledge of Communism as "a social system ... a metaphysic," but above all to realize that it was "an assembly of human beings." Because the struggle was ideological, warnings and condemnations would not be sufficient to counter the Communist threat.[30]

The significance of these pronouncements on the relationship between Communism and Christianity did not lie in the fact that they constituted a mainstream. Quebec, like Canadian society as a whole, remained intensely anti-Communist, and Catholicism acted as a powerful contributory factor in the elaboration of an official culture that developed measures to eradicate any hint of Marxism from universities, labour unions, and government bureaucracies.[31] What is important about the views of these young Catholic activists was their contention that there was a *relationship* of affinity between Christianity and Marxism that existed at the level of engagement in the quest for social justice. More tellingly, they employed this notion of an ideological relationship with Marxism to reinvigorate the convictions they had learned from the 1930s – that the new youth Catholicism constituted a "revolution" in values. Thus, the encounter with Marxism simply reinforced the notion of a constant generational, dialectic tension within Catholicism between a religion of "tradition" and one incarnating "progress." Energy, commitment, and dynamism, qualities always associated with Communists, were contrasted to the "more or less conscious conformity to a moral system" displayed by Christians.[32] Read in this light, Gérard Pelletier's assertion that, "in spite of their irreducible objections to Marxist doctrine, sincere Christians are much closer to *Marxist men* dedicated to their cause than to selfish men who have sold themselves to the defence of capitalist abuses" should in no way be taken as an endorsement of Marxism.[33] Rather, what Pelletier intended was the infusion of a "revolutionary" vigour and activism into Christianity, one that would enable it to meet the enormous challenge of a "thirst for totality" and "a search for faith" that he discerned among post-war young people.[34] The notion of a "dialogue" between Christians and Marxists was, first and foremost, an exhortation to young Christian activists to assume their social responsibilities, and to offer a Christian ideology in which the youthful ideals of "risk" and spontaneity displaced what they roundly deprecated as a search for "security"[35] – a Catholicism typical of older generations that sought easy, "unrealistic" solutions in rigid structures of dogma and piety, and failed to speak to the post-war human desire for liberation.

This deployment of the oppositional formulation of spirit and structure indicated the high-water mark of the influence of a particularly radical strand of French personalism, that represented by Emmanuel Mounier and his periodical *Esprit.* Although Mounier's thought was familiar to a small coterie of Quebec Catholics in the 1930s, his personalism was then considered as simply one among many of the varieties of "nonconformity" that so excited Catholic youth during this period. It was in the decade after World War II that Mounier acquired his stature as the primary intellectual mentor and leading French exponent of "left Catholicism" and he became the object of admiring attempts to replicate in Quebec his notions of democratic community,[36] attempts based upon his willingness to synthesize Christian belief with currents of existentialism and Marxist social analysis. Writing on the subject of progressive Christian intellectuals like Mounier, Claude Ryan wrote in 1953 that "all that we can call a real intellectual and spiritual elite in French Canada can frequently trace a direct kinship" to them.[37]

That Mounier's personalism gave a definite shape and direction to the critical Catholicism of a vocal section of young Quebecers was, however, not simply a matter of intellectual affinity or reading. During the five years after World War II, a small but significant group whose ideas would indelibly mark religious, political, and social scientific discussion in Quebec during the 1950s and 1960s journeyed to Paris and personally experienced the cultural atmosphere in which Mounier formulated his brand of "left Catholicism." Young Canadians who visited France after 1945 entered an environment in which the left had acquired an overwhelming intellectual prestige as a result of its apparent leadership in the struggle against Fascism. Marxism, in fact, was the issue that dominated political and philosophical conversation in France because it symbolized the "masculine" values of engagement, commitment, and contempt for all moderation and compromise. Liberalism, the workings of parliamentary politics, and what was deemed "bourgeois" materialism – typified by the image of the United States – were enemies that both French Catholics and Marxists condemned and ridiculed.[38] Young Canadian Catholics thus imbibed this heady French intellectual climate which worked from the Marxist postulate that all society was divided into two irreconcilable parts. They were naturally drawn to post-war developments within French Catholicism which sought to bridge the contradictions between Christianity and Marxism by entering into a dialogue with the left. Tendencies such as the emerging worker-priest movement and the *Économie et humanisme* circle, which grouped together Christian economists and social scientists, provided a compelling vision of reconstruction in which human communities, based upon a fellowship that emerged from work, rested upon both spiritual and material elements.[39] In a world where the framework of social analysis was provided by Marxist categories, such movements inspired young Canadian visitors with the belief that a communitarian reconstruction of Christianity could transcend the atomization and alienation that modern industrial civilization had forced upon a suffering humanity.[40]

However, as stated earlier, it was the personalism of Emmanuel Mounier that provided the principal intellectual underpinnings to the culture of a

"Christian Left." What was fundamental to Mounier's appeal, and what conveyed such an excitement to Quebec's young Christian activists, was his definition of personalism not as a doctrine, but as a "postulate of research,"[41] a point of departure which, while insisting upon the spiritual dimensions of human existence, allowed Christians to easily incorporate elements of the post-war fashions in Marxist social analysis and existentialist psychology. Although he had flirted briefly with Vichy's "National Revolution" between 1940 and 1942, Mounier had overtly espoused an overture to the French Left in the post-war years. It was then that he insisted upon the affinities between Christianity and Marxism by mercilessly flaying "traditional" Christianity for its neglect of human biological and material necessities, and by locating the primary human imperative not in individual self-affirmation, but in the need to communicate with others, to create collectivities anchored upon fellowship and spiritual affinity.[42] More importantly, however, Mounier's personalist Christianity reassured young Quebec Catholics who discovered that their religion was not a reactionary force linked with discredited conservative regimes, but that they stood on the cutting edge of history; that in responding to the French thinker's call for a "revolution," they could answer their vocation of commitment not by removing themselves from the world, but by hurling themselves into the human struggle, by standing in effective spiritual solidarity with all progressive political, social, and cultural forces that sought "a profound revision of values";[43] and that they could thus secure the flowering of their personalities through allegiance to a communitarian ethos that exalted the common man over and against privileged classes.[44]

"I always feel a sort of envy," wrote Gilles Marcotte in 1957, "when I see the normal, natural way in which Mounier accomplished the renovation of his faith, and at the same time pursued an authentically human revolt."[45] In the symbiotic link he established between the renewal and affirmation of Christian faith and the overthrow of oppressive social structures, Marcotte perfectly captured the appeal to the post-war generation of this radical current of personalist Christianity. Indeed, the question of the place of the Christian committed to social justice in a Church that had all too frequently stood against the working classes was an issue that was particularly troubling for young Quebec Catholics who frequented Paris in the years after World War II. Commenting on his years spent in Europe just after the war, Gérard Pelletier remembered that the political divisions between left and right possessed universal significance, and described widely differing visions of society. His generation, he believed, was called to choose between "two conceptions of life, two explanations of the world, two modes of thinking that engaged the entire person and the totality of human activity." For him, the "communitarian personalism" of Mounier and the "left Christians" allowed him to maintain his Catholic allegiance by resolving the conflict with Marxism.[46] Personalism encouraged a similar intellectual choice in Pelletier's colleague Pierre Elliott Trudeau, who praised Mounier's insights for turning him away from the "doctrine of absolute liberalism."[47] Although young men of this stamp roundly rejected a Marxist political allegiance, the military success of the Soviet Union, the fall of China to the Communists in the late 1940s, and the electoral strength of Marxists in Western Europe persuaded them that human history was governed by a process of liberation easily recognizable as a throwing off of economic and class oppression. "Man," Trudeau declared in 1949, "seeks to free himself from all that oppresses him ... he rejects theocracy in favour of an anthropocentric view with the result that instead of considering authority as emanating from God and his ministers, he considers himself the sole authority. Thus, man himself becomes aware of his human consciousness, and we witness over the course of history, slaves gaining freedom from their masters, the middle classes from the aristocracy, and now, the proletariat from the bourgeoisie, each group seeking to free itself from the superior group."[48]

Trudeau was adamant that neither the Western liberal democracies, nor the Marxist regimes that described themselves as economic democracies, were in fact truly democratic societies. The problem lay in searching for "values where man will gain a consciousness of his freedom." In Trudeau's view, "only Christianity offers true freedom to the spirit of man, for himself and for the world. Lived Christianity is a social religion, the only one that gives an answer to all human problems."[49] In this case, it seems evident that personalism convinced Trudeau of the superiority of the Christian message as a force for human progress because it understood human needs in terms of "the individual enriched with a social conscience, integrated into the life of the communities around him and the economic context of his time, both of which must in turn give persons the means to exercise their freedom of choice." This analysis does not place Trudeau's democratic commitment in doubt; rather, it argues that Mounier's personalism supplied a democratic vision very different from the Anglo-American civil libertarian and welfare-state liberal alternatives which he also encountered in the years after World War II. The synthesis of personalism and democracy both dictated Trudeau's choice of thesis research at Harvard – he sought to examine the "interplay between two doctrines, Christianity and Marxism, which were competing for the loyalty of people in Asia"[50] – and his post-1950 engagement as a social activist and critic.

By carrying on a dialogue with modern ideologies that claimed to synthesize Christian faith and Marxist social analysis and political commitment, post-war personalism continued and reinvigorated the imperative of "spiritual revolution" among an influential section of Quebec Catholic youth. According to Maurice Blain, the attraction to Mounier's exaltation of spiritual freedom was the direct corollary of the "religious anxiety" and the desire for a religion of risk, heroism, and spontaneity which had characterized Quebec youth for the past two decades.[51] However, the fact that post-war personalism was permeated with quasi-Marxist categories of social analysis meant that "anxiety" for one's inner life was now balanced by the imperative for humans to "become communitarian." If the Church preached respect for the "interiority of man," it was not to enclose human beings in "a solitude or in a collective egoism," but rather, promoters of personalism expected that this would generate a communitarian imperative.[52] Given that personalists radically eschewed liberal individualism and placed such great emphasis on communication as the basis of human solidarity, it is not surprising that "community" occupied a central place in their attempt to infuse religious values into modern society. However, "community" was understood in a very specific way. "Life," stated the Laval University sociologist Jean-Charles Falardeau in 1961, "is inseparable from work." Appealing to the glorified, mythical images of "worker-monk" communities of the Middle Ages, which he believed provided the prototype of modern factories, Falardeau's conclusion that "work is also communion" glorified the spiritual possibilities of modern organized, automated, industrial work because membership in an organization increased the potential for friendship and fellowship.[53] By weaving together the insights of French nonconformist thinkers like Charles Péguy, who was most insistent upon the "spiritual" and "redemptive" qualities of work, and the Marxist emphasis on the superiority of the producing classes, post-war personalists argued that the community flowed from work, with work understood not as a means of individual salvation or of discipline, but as the precondition to "spiritual freedom" realized through collective effort and purpose.[54]

Indeed, because of the centrality of work, action, and effort to the personalist vision of community and spiritual fellowship, it is difficult to escape the conclusion that this "revolutionary" style of Christianity was an emphatically male-centred religion. Its presentation of a religion shorn of the trappings of conventional "bourgeois" morality was, in the words of Trudeau, analogous to the supreme effort and teamwork that young men expended during the course of an arduous wilderness canoe trip, where through vigorous physical energy men experienced a "more ardent faith that drew man back to an age where religion, like everything else, was simplified," and prayer, "a man-to-man chewing of the fat with the divinity," stripped away "the useless material baggage of the human heritage."[55] In the estimation of Gérard Pelletier, the ideal modern Christian must be "strong, muscled, lean, and virtuous. Certain sentimental tolerances, acceptable in other times, are in today's world not acceptable." To live the Christian life fully, the believer must have the character of a front-line soldier, who "performed a harsh duty," and not display what Pelletier excoriated as the cowardly, overdressed, sentimental religion of the French-Canadian parish *zouave*, a deliberately critical reference to the uniformed male laity whose religious zeal was limited to participating in the highly ritualized devotional processions characteristic of local Catholic religious life.[56]

Here then was a notion of religion in which discipline readied the believer not for a life of individual contemplation, but of activism. Mounier was always adamant that the commitment and engagement required by his modernist Christianity offered an ideal of "virile labour and communal discipline" that would be a tonic against the ultimate vices of "dissipation," with the latter being a demasculinizing form of alienation that resulted from modern capitalism's propensity to create an industrial class that was "uprooted and unoccupied."[57] Here was a Christianity whose message was consciously restricted to the few: spiritual reward was the fruit of superhuman effort, and more significantly, integral Christianity could only be found among an elite who, in their daily lives, could exemplify and sustain this level of commitment and engagement in the progressive march of history and were thus the only genuine Christian community. In this respect, such a spiritual elite limited the definition of "Christian" to a concept of religion that did not accept the orthodox message that humans were weak and in need of salvation, and consequently required the assistance of authority and tradition. Rather, the starting point of this Christian modernism was the radical, quasi-Nietzschean assertion of human self-sufficiency and divinity derived from St Paul's "you are gods."[58]

Personalism aimed its appeal at a group of Catholics whose self-image as a cultural elite did not rest upon inherited privilege; rather, they believed that their "violent and dominating" religious message conferred upon them a quasi-prophetic character. Possessing an "independence and power of thought, self-respect and arrogance," they were entitled to self-consciously proclaim their "Jupiterian superiority over the collective soul" and thus summon to a higher form of Christianity, by "surpassing, denouncing, and humiliating," a common mass of humanity whose faults could be summed up by "lack of historical importance, cultural impoverishment, naivete, preoccupied with the mundane, lacking glory."[59] For this group of post-war Christians, human divinity was achieved through a prophetic style that emphasized aggressive commitment and public action in the service of socially progressive causes, which in post-war Quebec were considered emphatically male domains. Such views thus served as the Catholic expression, and the religious exaltation of, a wider cultural imperative that emerged from the Depression in which only active male workers possessed the full rights of citizenship.[60] As such, it appealed strongly to the anxieties of young middle-class men exhilarated yet frightened by the revolutionary potential of a relapse into economic anarchy, and troubled by the questions raised by existentialist and Marxist critics about the "alienating" quality of modern mass civilization upon the culture both of workers and the middle classes.

As Henri-Irénée Marrou, the celebrated French historian and close associate of Emmanuel Mounier, observed in 1952, "*Cité libre*, a courageous little magazine, constitutes a veritable Canadian version of the *Esprit* team." Marrou's prose was redolent with admiration for a youthful group of Christian journalists and lawyers, fully engaged on the progressive side of history as sympathizers, ideologues, and activists in trade union movements, yet who found the time to test their still-youthful physiques in summer-long canoe journeys into the wilderness.[61] Transatlantic male back-slapping aside, the comments of this French intellectual, which centred upon the role of this "youthful" elite in a young and energetic society, provide a novel point of entry into the experience and significance of the *Cité libre* group.

Historians have so frequently attested to the centrality of *Cité libre* to the origins of the Quiet Revolution that the issue requires little further discussion. However, because the "Quiet Revolution" has been interpreted through the lens of a transformation of political ideologies, rather than through the perspective of culture, most historians have slotted the magazine into a liberal political teleology that reads back into the concerns of *Cité libre* the federalist, anti-separatist political choices made by Pierre Elliott Trudeau and Gérard Pelletier in the mid-1960s.[62] Scholars have, of course, been well aware that prior to 1960, much of the journal's commentary centred not on political questions, but on religion, and specifically, the nature of the relationship between Catholicism and Quebec society. Again, however, this religious engagement has been understood either and only in terms of the objection of "liberal" sympathizers to "clericalism" – the overweening power of the clergy in the province's political life and their occasionally distasteful compromises with the government of Maurice Duplessis[63] – or as a largely negative, and ultimately sterile critique of the still-vibrant "traditional" Catholicism of Quebec's small towns and rural parishes, with post-1960 Quebec Catholics left in a "spiritual vacuum in both interpretations."[64] However, to properly contextualize *Cité libre* and the values it promoted requires a reassessment of its relationship to post-1945 directions in Catholic Action, and more specifically, to the continuing fascination that the notion of a distinct youth culture exerted over a section of the Quebec Catholic intelligentsia.

One of the central difficulties faced by post-war Catholic Action in Quebec was the question of how to harness the Christian commitment of those activists whose age and marital status meant that they could no longer belong to the youth movements. This problem was particularly acute for young middle-class people in the years after 1945, for while

Catholic Action instituted the Ligue Ouvrière Catholique to enlist the energies of working-class married couples, no comparable organization or experience of community officially existed for middle-class Catholics. Once these individuals married, they were forced to relinquish their membership in the *Jeunesse Étudiante Catholique* or the Jeunesse Indépendante Catholique.[65] This organizational lacuna was one that particularly affected the young men whose earlier experience with Catholic Action had left them with a taste for greater responsibility in the form of some meaningful action,[66] and who chafed at belonging to older parish-based Catholic associations where they believed they would be under clerical tutelage. In the late 1940s, organizers like Claude Ryan undertook to fill this gap by sponsoring under the auspices of the Montreal Jeunesse Indépendante Catholique a series of experiments designed to foster the idea of fellowship and community among young professionals and intellectuals.

The first of these was "Présence," a group which existed between 1945 and 1950, in which fifty young men, journalists, labour leaders, social workers, lawyers, and students – all former members of Catholic Action youth groups – met on a regular basis at the Corso Pizzina, a Montreal restaurant. At their meetings, they discussed such issues as the future of the Canadian Confederation, the idea of federalism, the development of methods of popular culture, "co-management" of enterprises as a solution to industrial strife, social security, "the problem of relations between East and West,"[67] and the shocking revelations by Gérard Pelletier concerning "religious communities and handicapped children in Quebec."[68] Jacques Dubuc, who acted as secretary for Présence, frankly avowed the personalist and communitarian impulse that animated these young men. The group, in his words, "was the beginning of a vast movement which will awaken ... the need for spiritual reflection and solidarity in action among young Canadians."[69] Présence was reinforced by a monthly magazine, *Jeunesse Canadienne*, which was published between 1946 and 1949. Claude Ryan's circular that launched this journal frankly envisioned it as serving the needs of former Catholic Action militants, who still craved the need for "the sense of team-work and solidarity" that had characterized their lives in the youth movements, and who now felt isolated in their married and professional lives.[70] Through Jeunesse Canadienne and the annual Écoles Civiques d'Été, Catholic Action leaders like Ryan hoped not only to continue and enhance, among adults, the dynamism and energy that the 1930s youth movements had displayed. They believed that the challenge for the post-war generation, in a world that seemed descending into increasingly rancorous class conflict, was to evolve forms of civic action and popular education that would draw together middle-class professional and working-class elites in a creative synthesis of Catholicism and nationalism.[71]

Viewed from this perspective, *Cité libre* was hardly a novel experiment. Rather, it stood well within current attempts to give some definite organizational shape and identity to middle-class Catholic male cravings to re-experience youthful action and solidarity. Indeed, with the exception of Pierre Elliott Trudeau, the magazine's entire editorial team had once occupied prominent roles within the Jeunesse Étudiante Catholique. That the magazine represented an avowedly masculine imperative of public commitment is shown by the fact that although in his memoirs Gérard Pelletier named four women as having been involved in initially planning the journal, none of the four ever wrote articles for *Cité libre* and indeed, until 1960, the journal had run only *one* article by a woman.[72] From the outset, Pelletier and his associates were explicit about the aims of *Cité libre*: to rekindle the sense of spiritual and cultural distinctiveness and superiority among an elite of "college students who are today over thirty,"[73] and to speak to their need for association and common purpose in overcoming what many felt was "a certain silence."[74] "Silence," in this context, meant the loss of religious identity that many of these activists felt had marked their lives during the transition from youth to adulthood. *Cité libre* stood directly within the youth ideology formulated within the Catholic Action groups of the 1930s. "Our generation," loftily proclaimed the opening editorial, "did not receive the same upbringing, did not live the same experiences of the preceding ones. Thus, the questions that it poses and the answers that it brings possess a new, original, and distinct quality."[75]

The intra-generational solidarity that so fascinated the *Cité libre* team was not provided by a common political outlook, in spite of the virulently anti-Duplessis stand taken by the journal during the 1950s. The connection was provided by a cultural commitment, and more specifically, by the fact that so many had become adherents of a particular religious mentality they encountered through their careers in Catholic Action and later through their contacts with post-war French personalism and international encounters with student leaders from other countries. In what served as the journal's intellectual manifesto, Pelletier stated that all members of the team had "experienced profound transformations, of which the most important, without doubt, were within the realm of religious thought. Their Christianity, which had begun as traditional and implicit, had been violently decanted. From a somnolent, quiet conscience, one solely preoccupied with personal sins, they abruptly moved into a state of watchfulness ... and sometimes of revolt. They suddenly understood that their little bucolic world was cracking at all its seams under the formidable pressure of changing times and hostile ideologies."[76] Pelletier, as did François Hertel's *Leur inquiétude* before him, played upon the theme of "anxiety" to evoke what he considered the common qualities and experience of this generation that as young men had experienced the Depression and the earth-shattering conflict of ideologies – their "torment, instability, extreme self-consciousness" – but also to evoke this generation's "impatience, fiery and violent character, its need to go beyond itself."[77] However, what was fundamental to the identity that Pelletier wanted to recover, and what provided the constant pole of opposition to the positive values that he wished to awaken, was the metaphor of adult betrayal.

The reason his generation had failed to incarnate its ideals of heroism and action, and why its members currently felt so isolated and useless, "wasting their time,"[78] stemmed not from their own failings or lack of organizational ability, but directly from the inability of their college instructors – significantly all of them Catholic clergy – to present them with an ideal of holiness based on the activism they so craved and to which they could aspire. Even Catholic Action, which during the 1930s had awakened a sense of boundless purpose and dynamism, appeared to be "afflicted with psychological fatigue," "to be going in circles," to have limited its goals to fostering a "student vocation" rather than pressing for "vast modern transformations of mentality."[79] As a personalist, whose primary human and religious values rested upon "intimacy" and "communication," Pelletier was critical of a clergy that had so failed young men, by presenting a "sweetened Gospel" stripped of its "rough language, clear expression, of its demands, of the revolutionary violence that underlies it."[80] A distinctive, culturally fertile, dynamic youth culture had been quite simply emasculated and constrained, Pelletier concluded, by a religion reduced to a series of negative moral precepts that simply reproduced a "feminized" style of passive obedience to male clerical authority figures and a pervasive sense of mediocrity and failure among those forced to live under its discipline: "Instead of a cause to promote, barriers to respect. Instead of remedies to our anxieties, a diagnostic method that carefully weighed our symptoms. In sum, a law without spirit."[81]

Pelletier and *Cité libre* then moved one step beyond Hertel's characterization of the 1930s youth generation. Taking the general portrait of youth fostered by the 1930s sense of "spiritual revolution," and reinforced by their own sense of superfluity in a structure of Catholic Action that had found little place for male, adult militants, Pelletier and his team applied the by now conventional juxtaposition of youth's dynamic and energetic Christian humanism constrained and stifled by adult hypocrisy and conventionality as a description for the *entire* Quebec Catholic Church and culture. "Blockage" and "unblockage," the dialectic that was to provide the cultural and ideological code words for the Quiet Revolution itself, originated in the violent denunciation voiced by young men who felt cheated in their quest for "meaning" and "action" by a clerically-dominated educational system that had signally failed to cultivate holiness among laypeople. Pelletier argued that, for his generation, the entire problem of culture could be summed up by a paradox centering in religion: while he and his colleagues identified themselves with a Catholicism that was a force for social and cultural ferment, reactionary elements within the Church sought desperately to "shore up half-rotted support beams." "What we dreamed of as a postwar cultural revolution," lamented Pelletier, "has fallen short in the face of an all-powerful current of reaction. ... We are always menaced by a dogmatism that is difficult to overcome, one that evinces nothing in the way of life or Christian character."[82] First and foremost, *Cité libre*'s intent was to demonstrate that laypeople could, through their own efforts, incarnate the values of heroism and solidarity so admired by personalist Christians. By constituting "in all aspects a community,"[83] the journal sought to apply a spiritual remedy to the sense of isolation and powerlessness felt by a number of vocal young Catholics in a society that in their estimation was being increasingly vitiated by the anti-religion of North American individualism, which was breeding conformity, materialism, hypocrisy, and cultural mediocrity.

Indeed, the special meaning that Pelletier and the *Cité libre* circle attached to the notion of "community" provided the hinge for their entire interpretation of the relationship that they believed ought to prevail between Catholicism and Quebec society. Standard historical interpretations of post-war Quebec have identified *Cité libre* as one of the key cultural precursors of a modern, secular society because it spoke out vociferously, in the name of individual rights, against the tacit alliance between church and state, and because it mercilessly exposed the contradictions and spiritual folly of Catholicism's pursuit of temporal authority through its assumption of institutional responsibilities in the areas of education and social welfare.[84] However, it should be remembered that the personalist dynamic of history was a quasi-Marxist one in which movement, change, and direction were supplied by the opposition of increasingly well-organized human *collectivities*, an opposition that was consummated in the modern era by the acute stage of warfare in Western societies between organized labour and bureaucratized industrial enterprises. Mounier and his disciples diverged from older currents of Catholic corporatism by maintaining that such conflictual economic interests could never be fully harmonized or reconciled, and that attempts to create institutions based on corporatist principles would inevitably fail and breed further oppression of workers and an intolerable suppression of personal freedoms.[85] In the interests of social justice, modern society thus must recognize and give voice to this pluralism through laws and institutions that legitimated opposition and fundamentally divergent views on the nature of society.

However, the paradox of personalism lay in its continuous drive to reconcile a quasi-Marxist, conflictual model of society with the belief that "a new civilization" would only be realized to the extent that "Christians would uplift entire collectivities to a Christian and peaceful vision of the world."[86] For personalists, the counterpoint to a secular, conflictual model of society was the belief that in the modern world, with all its competing interests, Catholicism must play an even more fundamental role than it enjoyed in pre-modern societies structured around a series of organic, hierarchical relationships. In the pluralistic society exalted by personalists, religion was *the* ultimate source of the values of fellowship because it transcended and bridged the rival economic interests of competing classes. Because personalists viewed these interests as being in constant tension, religion's role was to overcome them by establishing a higher spiritual community, one that would be more valuable and enduring precisely because religion eschewed negative, institutional methods of control or restraint. The very power and appeal of Christianity lay in its "great emphasis upon personal responsibility and freedom ... the fact that it rests on free adhesion ... its resistance to propaganda and pressure."[87] In the personalist world, "society" or "state" were powerless in defining or promulgating these values of human freedom, because their only purpose was the purely functional one of institutionalizing, monitoring, and regulating conflict while warding off threats to the personal freedoms of its citizens. "Secular" institutions were thus powerless to erect and sustain a moral community. In the words of Charles Lussier, Christianity's value in modern society lay in the fact that it alone recognized that "man as person is above society" and spoke to "his perpetual drive for freedom" amidst social structures and institutions that were "purely conventional and amoral entities."[88] While such a spiritual fellowship was built upon the free adherence of individuals, personalists adamantly rejected the idea that religion was a source of individualism or that it simply began and ended with the notion of individual freedom. Rather, the type of Catholicism they envisioned was the crucible in which the individual not only learned, but actually *became* a communitarian being, a *person* in the true sense of the word.

In post-war Quebec, what gave the *Cité libre* group its novelty, hard edge, and what later commentators have dismissed as mere negativity was its importation and adaptation of the final, radical phase of Mounier's personalism. Taken in their French context, Mounier's writings between 1945 and 1950 were dominated by the conviction that the prevailing forms of Christianity had failed to effect a creative synthesis with other "massive" ideological realities that demonstrated their power to arouse "moral forces, heroism and even kinds of saintliness."[89] In order for Christians to constitute an "avant-garde," to establish a creative dialogue with modernity – read Marxism – it was Mounier's belief that Christianity had to divest itself of its tendency to incarnate itself in explicitly "Christian" ideologies, political parties, and institutions. Specifically, Mounier's call to Christians to separate themselves from "'established disorders'" was a scathing denunciation of the new post-war French Christian Democratic Party (Mouvement Républicain Populaire) which appropriated much of the personalist agenda into an explicitly anti-Marxist political platform.[90] However, Mounier's vision of crisis remained optimistic; he foresaw the end, not of Christianity itself, but "only of a kind of Christianity,"[91] one that he castigated as "bourgeois," one which expressed itself in organized institutions derived from nineteenth-century middle-class social endeavour and irremediably wedded to a cult of purely individual piety, rather than a collectivist preoccupation with social justice.

When imported to Quebec, this radical personalism took on a rather different tinge. Mounier's chief bugaboo was the existence of Christian political parties and political ideologies that acted as barriers to his creative dialogue with Marxism. In Quebec, despite considerable awareness of Mounier's direction in Catholic Action university circles,[92] politics remained tied to British parliamentary categories where explicitly "Christian" parties and ideological movements had no resonance. The process of transferring Mounier's radical personalism to Quebec entailed a shift from debating the place of Christian political ideologies to the social role of Christian institutional structures. In this respect, the product was far more conservative: Mounier's *citélibriste* disciples were less interested in promoting a "Christian agnosticism" that reached out at a cultural level to Marxism,[93] than in reasserting what they upheld as a purified Christianity, one that sought to enhance the place and authority of Catholicism in Quebec by persuading the Church to radically curtail its organizational, managerial role in Quebec society.

As Fernand Dumont, a young student of sociology and admirer of Mounier explained, the engagement of modern Christians with issues of social justice must be characterized by "an energetic refusal of a Christian politics and of a new Christendom." Because it was a "spiritual ferment," Christianity was most effective when believers participated actively in the ordinary structures of society, when their faith remained at the level of "mystique" rather than became incarnated in "politics." The strategy of permeation and engagement was preferable to attempting to create a system of parallel institutions, which tended, in the long run, to become spiritually "empty."[94] It was precisely this equation between institutional Catholicism, bureaucratization, compromises between the spiritual and temporal realms, and spiritual vacuity that animated the religious sensibility of *Cité libre*. Underneath this critique lurked the fear of de-Christianization, the withering away of Quebec's Catholic identity that supplied a source of cultural distinctiveness in North America. For Maurice Blain, later one of the leading figures in the Mouvement Laïque de Langue Française, the main impulse driving his criticisms of the Church was his fear that reforms would be undertaken by secularist intellectuals not working from the perspective of Christian dogma. Catholics themselves, he proclaimed, must demonstrate the force of their religion by offering "the scandal of a Catholicism that links itself with the tradition of an open humanism and an autonomous culture; the scandal of a Church reestablished in the real distinction between spiritual and temporal; the scandal of a spiritual freedom with no other condition than respect of conscience."[95]

However, unlike France, Quebec possessed a socially-prestigious Catholic Church, and more tellingly, an enormous network of clerically-controlled colleges, educational institutions, hospitals, and social agencies that were ripe targets for personalist notions of "revolution," which rested upon a virulently anti-institutional Christianity. Thus, conscious of their position as a moral and spiritual "avant-garde" and as promoters of a new spiritual fellowship between Christians and all "progressive" elements in society[96] that sought to "liquidate certain noxious traditions of spiritual separatism and ideas of a Christian ghetto,"[97] men like Pelletier and Trudeau singled out and lambasted "clericalism," the propensity of priests to blur the boundaries between spiritual and temporal by engaging in activities where the clergy had no technical or professional competence. "We are anxious," stated Pelletier in 1952, "because in French Canada the Church has strayed very far into the dangerous borderland between spiritual and temporal realms."[98]

What worried these Quebec personalists was that the encroachments of some of the clergy were beginning to constitute a spiritual danger to the faith on two levels. First, the large number of priests involved in administering schools and welfare bureaucracies meant that there was a shortage of parish clergy for the Church's primary mission of evangelization. Second, Pelletier estimated that the compromises and rather cynical horse-trading that went on between senior clergy and politicians in the interests of securing funding for these institutions actually impaired the spiritual hold of the Church over the faithful.[99] Significantly, Pelletier's anxious reflections appeared in the same year that Quebec's bishops had moved to further curtail the independent scope of lay militants in Catholic Action. Clearly worried in the wake of the Asbestos Strike that many participants in the Catholic Action organizations had been tempted to stray too far into the prohibited realm of political action, the Church hierarchy sought to inject a dose of conservatism and apoliticism into Catholic Action by establishing diocesan committees of Catholic Action. Through them it hoped to constrain more radical laity by associating such members with the more traditional structures of parish life, which were predominantly pious associations.[100]

What is significant in this context is not the historical accuracy of *Cité libre*'s portrayal of contemporary Quebec Catholicism, but what it reveals about the personalist religious mentality. Indeed, although during the 1950s more conservative Catholics frequently alleged that *Cité libre* stood at the centre of a web of crypto-Communist influence,[101] what is most striking is the relatively temperate critique that Pelletier and his associates engaged in when they addressed themselves to the social and cultural role of the Church. The dominant element that emerged from their discussions of Catholicism was not a desire to marginalize the Church or to secularize society, but rather the opposite: how to enhance the authority of Catholicism as the fabric of a vision of communitarian solidarity that was appropriate for a democratic society. Pelletier himself rigorously eschewed any hint that the *Cité libre* team were demanding the equivalent of the Protestant right of "free examination" of biblical and spiritual realities without reference to the magisterium of the Church.[102] Pierre Trudeau, who vaunted his credentials as an "anticlericalist," in fact was a conservative Catholic in terms of belief and commitment. He was always careful to qualify what he meant by "anticlerical," using this designation as synonymous with "integral Christian" as opposed to "clericalists," whom he derogatorily referred to as "veritable pagans." Interestingly, for all the shrill polemic about careful distinctions between spiritual and temporal realms, Trudeau admitted that in Quebec, such neat divisions of responsibility were not easy. Trudeau, as a firm Christian, maintained that the *Church* should be involved in all social and human questions, but contended that the *clergy* as a social group should refrain from such involvement if they possessed no special competence, leaving such concerns to activist Catholic laypeople instead.[103] Trudeau aimed not at a secular society which radically separated the Church and the public realm; rather, his urgent admonitions that the clergy act with restraint in the area of political and social issues was solely directed at fostering a "more serene collaboration" between clergy and laity in the interests of the "building of the Church and a civic realm that was truly Christian."[104]

A fundamental ambiguity thus lay at the core of *Cité libre*'s modernist interpretation of Catholicism. On the one hand, the magazine's merciless critique of the "unrealism," rigidity, and anti-intellectualism of traditionalist Catholics,[105] and its advocacy of "openness" and "dialogue" with current intellectual fashions in existentialism and Marxism – in the manner of Mounier's *Esprit* – greatly appealed to a coterie of highly educated university and college students and young faculty who had encountered these strands of thought first through Catholic Action and then through foreign study.[106] However, for all the evocation of "freedom," the primary mission of the editorial team of *Cité libre*, on the other hand, was to solidify the prestige of Catholicism as a doctrinal and spiritual force among the rising generation of young intellectuals, union leaders, and social activists by pruning those "medieval" and "Jansenist" excrescences – in particular, "clericalism" – that diminished its cultural authority and appeal. In 1952, writing in a piece intended for a French audience, Gérard Pelletier gave voice to what ultimately animated *Cité libre* by asking plaintively: "How long will the initiative for renewal remain in the hands of Christian believers"?[107] The post-war generation, he contended, was obsessed with social justice and activism, and threw themselves into unstinting lives of service. However, in so doing, they ran the risk of simply losing interest in dogma, the central elements of the Christian faith which were the ultimate source of spiritual commitment. "It is to be feared," he stated, "that the contents of their [modern intellectuals'] beliefs will interest them less than what contains them. One day, they will find themselves confronted with a situation in which they have regained their freedom and resolved a host of problems, but with a concern for their spiritual life that has been weakened to the point of death."[108] In the estimation of Jean-Guy Blain, a student leader at the Université de Montréal, the vast majority of the younger generation did not turn away from Christianity because they had become materialistic, or because they found Marxism more attractive, but "more as a protest against an unthinking Catholicism in which they have been raised." What they required was a spirituality anchored upon the "naked evangelical message," and the active assistance of the Church in attaining a personal Christian commitment.[109] What aroused the fears of both these Catholic intellectuals was the paradox that a society that was officially Christian and served by cultural and social institutions directly controlled by the Church – and which even proclaimed that Catholicism was its defining badge of identity – was also undergoing an insidious process of de-Christianization not through ideological challenge or social revolution, but through the erosion of the spirituality of its cultural elites.

In this key respect, *Cité libre*'s concern was not the production of political criticism or jibes at the moral failings and cynicism of senior clerics. Rather, like its Catholic Action predecessor, the group Présence, it sought to act as a cultural fulcrum, an antidote to what Maurice Blain termed "the religious malaise" of the post-war generation of young people.[110] It was, first and foremost, as Pelletier had intended it, a "community," the point of equilibrium for a particular group of middle-class professionals who sought to find a spiritual identity *as Catholics* through social engagement. Indeed, Pelletier's statement that "the Church needs saints, rather than reformers,"[111] was eloquent testimony to the primacy of religious concerns in *Cité libre*. In more than one respect, the opposition of this group of lay Catholics to the government of Maurice Duplessis flowed not from political issues themselves, but from the fact that Duplessis was the archetype of the Christian lay elites they so roundly despised: men who made a great public display of obeisance to the clergy, but, like Pierre Martel's father, whose lack of inner spirituality was ultimately responsible "for the poverty of our Catholicism, for its aridity, for its devitalization."[112] The magazine's firm insistence that the clergy should attend to spiritual matters of evangelization and sound doctrine, and less to institutional management and political leadership, was a banner that rallied an elite that worked from the premise of a distinctive religious sensibility they had acquired as adolescents. This religious identity had always exalted Catholicism as a spiritual dynamic that privileged the action of laypeople rather than institutional hierarchies, structures, and organizations that in Quebec were usually dominated by the clergy and religious orders. In the final analysis, *Cité libre* spoke to the need of a generation of former Catholic Action militants who now toiled in Catholic labour unions and welfare organizations, and whose spiritual yearnings demanded nothing less than a purified, vigorous Catholicism as the vehicle for the promotion of a new professional, elite leadership. Only in this way could the religious essence of French-Canadian national identity be preserved in a North American society of fundamental and troubling post-war cultural change.

"QUEBEC HAVING FABRICATED ITS *MIDDLETOWNS*, IS NOW PRODUCING ITS OWN *BABBITS*"[113]

In the years after 1945, what had begun during the Depression as the assertion that Catholicism set Quebec youth apart from the values of earlier generations was amplified and redirected into a particularly aggressive brand of cultural modernism. As the pioneer Catholic youth activists entered maturity, they sought ways to freeze their youthful years in time, to live in a realm of "eternal youth"[114] by preserving a type of religion that they believed had conferred upon them a moral and religious superiority anchored in a distinctive energy, commitment, and dynamism that they volubly contrasted with adult religious failings. However, in attempting to eradicate the religious experience of the previous generation in the name of a restored sense of spiritual fellowship, they imported into Catholicism itself the dialectical categories of distinction between "tradition" and "modernity," which they contended were in permanent opposition. By the late 1950s, there existed in Quebec intellectual circles a wide-ranging critique of various deficiencies of "traditional" Catholicism that was religious rather than secularist in its inspiration and goals. Like the exponents of "tradition," modernist Catholics fervently believed that religion was the foundation of civilization and, further, forcefully subscribed to the belief that what gave French Canada its cultural distinctiveness in North America was its Catholicism. However, their polemic against tradition was animated by a profound cultural anxiety and lack of confidence. They feared that old-style Catholicism, and in particular, its propensity towards clerical authority and institutional top-heaviness, had left modern Quebec spiritually bereft.

Although they were profoundly derogatory towards this form of religion, and regarded modernity, and especially urban, industrial civilization as its demise, what gave this religious debate in Quebec a distinctive twist was that by the early 1950s personalist Catholics had come to believe that this form of old-guard Catholicism was not simply dying a natural death. Rather, through a cruel and unexpected convergence between industrial capitalism and the impact of mass culture, and what they portrayed as the "invasion" of American civilization, old-style Catholicism had been rejuvenated. For those Catholic activists whose experience had been shaped by the equation of Catholicism and the dynamism of youth, it seemed that in post-war Quebec, Catholicism was endangering the soul of French Canada: this was because its organization had become the expression of and the conduit for the values of a "false" humanism – the North American invasion of individualism, mass culture, conformity, and impersonality – the very antithesis of the personalist quest for intimacy, communication, and spiritual fellowship. By the late 1950s, the crucible for this conflict of "religions" was the culture of the middle classes, and the stage was the Church-controlled educational system, and especially the elite *collèges classiques*.

The central contribution of Catholic Action to Quebec's religious culture was a definition of spiritual life as "conquest" and the absolute identity it posited between youthful energy, dynamism, and creativity, and a spiritually "pure" and energetic Catholicism powerful enough to compete with modern totalitarian ideologies. Because this type of Catholicism was bound up with a modernist notion of a generation of youth that was distinct from all previous generations, Catholic Action was implicitly premised upon two types of religious identity that were diametrically opposed and in fundamental conflict. Cultural and social change thus involved a "rupture" with the past, a rupture that was most palpably expressed around two forms of religious devotion. In his youth classic *Leur inquiétude*, François Hertel gave voice to this religious dichotomy in a devastating portrait of a rural religion that had become a "code of observances" rather than a "Christian life." "For three centuries," he declared, "we have been living off the old, rough and solid deposit of faith brought from France by our forefathers ... But any legacy, rich though it may be, is always used up in the long run. Ours is very close to being depleted. Among us, religion is still a habit to which the mass of people ... conform. Is it enough of a life, a dynamism, a religion? In many cases, it has simply degenerated into a ritualism."[115] Hertel's pejorative designations of "conformity," "ritualism," and "mass" that described old-style Catholicism were naturally contrasted with the soul-searching spiritual "anxiety" of the young intellectual elite whose values he aspired to shape. However, what added a hard, confrontational edge to this promulgation of a modern, authoritarian, elitist Catholic spirituality was

Hertel's belief that "traditional" Catholic religious practices were driving men away from the faith. Quebec society, he maintained, had entered a vicious circle in which the persistence of old-style ritualism had persuaded many middle-class and professional men that "religion was only good for women."[116] Although Hertel acknowledged that large numbers of men still frequented the sacraments, the long-term prospect was bleak, because such an inward-looking, feminized style of piety simply did not resonate with the needs of modern men for spiritual fellowship based on activity and engagement. The end result was that the emasculating of Catholicism would simply expose male, public elites to the inroads of more aggressive, secularist ideologies, and would inevitably, despite Quebec Catholicism's impressive institutional armature, privatize religion.

So central was this gendering of tradition and modernity to the enterprise of Catholic Action that modern spirituality was always assimilated to "male" qualities of activity and dynamism, while "traditional" Catholicism was described in terms of "female" characteristics of passivity, a search for personal comfort, a desire to conform, and an unthinking obeisance to the leadership of male clergy. Thus, in a 1939 article, Vianney Décarie sarcastically contrasted the "parlour Christianity" of the mass of Quebec Catholics and the urgent zeal of a youth elite, observing that "we have transformed the Cross into a comfortable chesterfield. The evangelical ideal has been reduced to attendance at Sunday Mass."[117] Writing in 1941, François Hertel pursued the metaphor by violently execrating a Catholicism that wallowed in "a sort of sickly-sweet romanticism and surface religious commitment," one that gloried in "meretricious pseudo-supernatural states, or one that simply sought to unburden itself of responsibility through an exaggerated 'churchiness.'"[118] The message that was widespread within Catholic Action was that "traditional" Catholicism was simply the equivalent of a kind of female religious hysteria, or the hypocritical conduct of middle-class women who sought social preferment through a constant display of pious practices.

"Bondieuserie" – a kind of knee-jerk Catholic attendance at regular devotions that was not animated by genuine intellectual understanding or commitment – was the particular hobby horse of Hertel's disciple Gérard Pelletier, who reckoned it a more dangerous enemy than Naziism. This type of Christianity, he maintained, was preoccupied merely with external matters, and had become simple social convention, a kind of no-man's land between "true Christianity and militant unbelief," the latter to be preferred because at least it carried the courage of conviction. In Quebec, Pelletier lamented, God was no longer addressed in sacred language, but in an artificial "vocabulary of pious women, as the 'Divine Lover', the 'Lover of Hearts', the 'Divine Consoler.'" "Masculine" religious simplicity and honest faith here confronted a "feminine" world of religious convention and artifice. Wartime hyperbole aside, Pelletier's fear was that what he thought was an artificial religion would ultimately poison and corrupt the "authenticity" that he exalted as the moral criterion of superiority that youth possessed over the older generation. Ultimately, because "traditional" Catholicism appeared to stress outward conformity and church attendance at all costs, it bred a species of social hypocrisy, Pelletier reckoned, as young people "would BELIEVE that they were obliged to appear Christian and to pretend to be someone that they are not."[119]

By the 1940s, it was apparent that the young elite of Christians who had imbibed the spirituality of Catholic Action accepted not only the notion of "rupture" between two kinds of religion, but had, even more crucially, discounted "traditional" religious practice as a valid form of Christianity. "A hollow, aching dichotomy" stated the young sociologist Jean-Charles Falardeau in 1941, "is tearing apart our Catholic souls and intellects." Rather than manifesting itself as a "conquest," the fruit of illumination and struggle, Falardeau worried that collective religious life in Quebec remained stunted, the product of endless "inoffensive repetitions of acts of piety."[120] According to Father André Guay, the formalistic, routine piety evinced by most Christians allowed them to "live lives that were practically pagan although coated with a Christian veneer."[121] Such negative assessments of "tradition" were reinforced among this modernist elite by the social scientific investigations of sociologists like Horace Miner and Everett C. Hughes, who in the late 1930s examined the impact of new urban mentalities on older rural folkways. Miner's account of Saint-Denis, a "traditional" rural parish, presented a picture of collective parish religious life that bore little relationship to personal religious commitment or Catholic doctrine, and resembled nothing more than anthropological social conventions. Individuals, Miner concluded, practiced religion for purely social reasons, and not because of any personal understanding of or commitment to Catholic doctrine.[122] Such views resonated with a coterie of young Catholic Action militants whose commitment to a youth religious identity predisposed them to view their own religious values, flowing from "anxiety," as "a return to the most naked simplicity, to the most exact truth,"[123] in profound contrast with the "lie of official Christianity"[124] mouthed by the well-established elder generation.

By the mid-1950s, a vocal section of Catholic opinion in Quebec had adopted the notion of an unbridgeable chasm between two diametrically opposed religious mentalities as the key to the historical development of French-Canadian society. In a speech to the members of Quebec's university and college student press in 1955, Claude Ryan outlined a balance sheet of French Canada's history, organized, of course, around the relationship of Catholicism to the social evolution of Quebec. Ryan argued that Quebec was currently traversing a religious crisis, characterized by the sudden appearance of negative critiques of religion and a "crumbling of structures" as institutional Catholicism experienced difficulties in coping with the spiritual needs of a mushrooming urban population. However, what most troubled him about this "spiritual drama" was the evidence of "a pronounced divorce that separates the older generation from the younger one."[125] While Ryan conceded that both groups displayed positive qualities, the danger was that each group was the prisoner of certain "myths" they sustained about one another: that the older generation's immutable doctrines were equated with outmoded nationalist creeds and a clericalist type of religion; that the younger generation, in advocating progress at all costs, would eradicate the religious basis of human society.

However, despite his avowed purpose of locating some common spiritual basis for generational cooperation, Ryan's assessment of "tradition" and the older generation was far harsher than that which he meted out to the progressive yearnings of the rising generation. The solution, he maintained, was the cultivation of a climate of spiritual "adulthood" founded upon "*an aptitude for communion*." The clear message was that only the spiritual experience promoted by Catholic Action, available most particularly to young people, had the potential to enable people to attain the status of spiritual adulthood, and that the elder generation's propensity was to remain mired in a kind of religious infantilism. The only way to restore a sense of common spiritual fellowship and purpose to Quebec society was for the older generation to relinquish its old-style nationalism, and for French Canada to "dissociate itself definitively from the equation of religion and nation." Rather than being a barrier that fostered a spiritual protectionism, modern Catholicism must be the conduit for universal values that opened Quebec society to broader social and ideological realities.[126]

Basing his insights on a reading of the University of Chicago sociologist Everett C. Hughes, whose *French Canada in Transition* inspired much sociological inquiry and debate during the 1940s and 1950s, Ryan argued that Quebec Catholicism had developed in a rural setting and thus preserved "something of a medieval flavour." Strongly characterized by "a climate of orthodoxy and submission to authority," Quebec Catholicism displayed a close rapprochement between clergy and people, which in his estimation contributed greatly to the progress of religion, while on the negative side, it imposed a powerful barrier to the "effective achievement of freedom."[127] French Canada's Catholicism, despite its many positive qualities, including the still-vibrant devotional life of many ordinary people and the overwhelming allegiance that it maintained among all social groups, both rural and urban in the 1950s, was on balance a negative force. Its Catholicism was, for the most part, purely "sociological,"[128] an adjective that was always contrasted with the "personalist" religion that post-war religious reformers laboured to promote. "Sociological" religion was an amalgam of long-standing popular folk practices that had been translated into an unthinking reflex of conformity to a series of devotional acts not anchored in any intellectual commitment or understanding of Catholic doctrine. For this reason, Ryan assessed that "the religious life of the average French-Canadian is totally devoid of cultural roots."[129] Of crucial concern to the cultural historian is not the accuracy of the portrayal;[130] rather, the definition of two competing religious mentalities, one with the negative reference of "traditional," the other identified with the superior spiritual values of modernity, was nothing less than the starting-point for the notion of a cultural "Quiet Revolution" among an increasingly influential elite minority of reformist clergy and lay academics and professionals.

Ryan was not alone in describing the post-war social transformation of Quebec as a cultural and spiritual crisis. Indeed, during the latter half of the 1950s, a host of Catholic commentators eagerly seized upon the notion of a sundering of religious mentalities as the key to social transformation, a compelling indication that Catholic Action's notion of generational rupture, developed during the 1930s, had entered the cultural mainstream. At a symposium held in 1956 at the Université de Montréal, "traditionalist" and "modernist" Catholic spokesmen discussed the nature and contours of Quebec society's religious crisis. Conservative Catholics, including law professor Maximilien Caron, repudiated the notion of a generalized religious crisis, pointing to the virtual non-existence of anticlericalist ideologies in Quebec, although he did discern signs of trouble in the fact that the younger generation possessed a higher level of religious knowledge and consequently demanded a more intelligent presentation of the faith. For Gérard Pelletier, the prime evidence for a spiritual crisis lay in the bloated growth of a clericalized, bureaucratized Church, and the fact that Catholics increasingly moved in a spiritual ghetto while the great social and political issues confronting the world were settled elsewhere. "We do not," argued Pelletier, "even agree on the existence of a religious crisis or the problems with which it confronts us."[131] Claude Ryan, however, contended that the spiritual malaise went far deeper than a clash of ideologies, but was most evident at a cultural level, in the most mundane activities and choices made by ordinary Christians on a daily basis. While the essential elements of the Church were not in danger, the positive content of the faith was "so thin that it collapses rapidly when brought into contact with a civilization that is more seductive and dynamic." Though omnipresent in a number of areas, religion was totally absent from the daily lives of ordinary Christians, which were increasingly governed by "a practical agnosticism."[132]

For men like Ryan and Pelletier, the impact of a more accessible North American consumer culture during the late 1950s laid bare the failure of old-style Catholicism in providing a framework of personal and social identity that could offer a spiritual counterweight to this wave of materialism, with its homogenizing pressures to conformity. "We are moving," warned Gérard Pelletier in 1946, "towards a spiritual vacuum and the anemic religiosity ... typical of North America."[133] What these Catholic activists feared was developing was an actual convergence between the formalist, sociological traditional Christianity and the conformist pressures of standardized North American society. In 1953, Jean-Charles Falardeau outlined what in effect was the fundamental ambiguity that confronted contemporary Quebec Catholics. "An industrial invasion," he wrote concerning the massive infusion of American capital investment, "is always accompanied by a cultural invasion, and any process of industrialization implies, in addition to technological transformation and alterations to the external social structure, far-reaching moral and spiritual perturbations."[134] For Falardeau, the primary issue at stake was the "historical indissolubility of French Canadian culture and Catholic religion," which he adamantly believed must be maintained as the foundation of collective identity. But how to reconcile the desire for material gratification felt by ordinary French Canadians, the need to achieve a higher standard of living by integrating themselves into North American society, with their "psychology," which remained "theological" in articulating its "supreme values?"[135] If, as a result of industrial change, many French Canadians began to "think like Americans,"[136] how could society cope with the massive experience of "uprooting" that such a process would naturally entail?[137] And, as François Hertel asked in more troubled tones, how could this shedding of French Catholic values in favour of North American ones contribute to preserving "our originality as a people?"[138]

In their anxieties over the conformist nature of post-war culture, the concerns of these Catholic activists closely paralleled those of other prominent North American social thinkers, who worried about the depersonalizing consequences of the routinized, mass-production labour in large-scale corporate bureaucracies experienced by North American males. Firmly committed to a democratic ideal of citizen activism and participation, these critics ultimately feared that the conditions of such work bred not only loss of personal creativity and spontaneity and its attendant psychological frustrations, but also political passivity and apathy. Modern individuals faced an ultimately bleak prospect of seeking relief through soporific, commercialized mass entertainment which did not engage the critical or creative faculties, or expressing their alienation through withdrawal from society.[139] However, the focus chosen by French-Canadian Catholic reformers differed from that of American social scientists. For the reformers, the discussion centred less around criticisms of modern work and the nature of the political process, than on the character of religion itself. Because this post-war group of young Catholics all displayed a common allegiance to personalism, they accepted that religion was the source of the values of spontaneity and creativity that made sense of individual lives and provided the sense of higher purpose that lifted modern humans out of a merely standardized existence. More significantly, Catholicism remained for them the spiritual undergirding of any viable political order, for they maintained that the sense of community provided by religion reconciled class polarizations in an industrial society.

For Quebec's Catholic activists, only the urgent and imperative transfusion of a new kind of spirituality would eradicate "conformity," "routine," and "individualism," the failings of Quebec's traditional form of religious expression. What this language indicated was the prevalent fear among Catholic militants that religion was becoming simply another expression of the vapid North American mass culture of self-gratification, in which all cultural values tended to coalesce around the lowest common denominator.[140] In its sentimentalism, its preoccupation with "secondary and artificial emotions," Quebec's Catholic liturgy exhibited all the human appeal of "a funeral parlour." "People here," wrote Claude Ryan in 1955, "are Catholic to avoid eternal damnation; they go to confession to free their consciences from guilt. They pray solely to obtain personal favours. They practice their religion because, in a society that is sociologically Catholic, it avoids a lot of problems and even helps them succeed in a number of areas of professional life."[141] Prominent Catholic leaders like Ryan eagerly ascribed gendered qualities to what they defined as two divergent religious mentalities. The worst danger facing modern democracy, Ryan claimed, was that in most Western societies, religion interested women more than it did men. Particular devotions, external conventions, and habitual practices were not in themselves evils, but when placed at the centre of religion, as they were in traditional Quebec Catholicism, "they had the unfortunate propensity to age and degenerate," by which Ryan meant that religion would simply be banished from public life as something that energetic, educated, and active – read male – elites would regard as simply obsolete and unnecessary.[142]

Such derogatory views of Quebec's popular Catholicism, which during the 1950s still commanded widespread adherence, did not go unchallenged. Both lay and clerical commentators argued that mass popular devotions such as those offered at St Joseph's Oratory were not simply an "infantile regression." The Catholicism of the French-Canadian masses, argued Father Louis-M. Régis in 1955, was in fact the "normal existential condition of the doctrine of Christ: that it must be lived not simply by individuals as such, but by peoples taken in their collective sense." In offering such an assessment, Régis hit upon what he considered the principal flaw in the personalist religious dynamic: that it certainly offered solace to a spiritual elite who were able to follow its exhortations to live in a world of anxiety, risk, and effort, but it failed to meet the needs of the "poor, the little people, the ignorant and the beggars" who had as much right to salvation as the "spiritual athletes" of Catholic Action.[143]

The personalist critics of old-style Catholicism condescendingly conceded that conformity could have "a positive value in terms of preserving collective religious values," but argued that in the case of French Canada the real Christian value of this collective behaviour had become anemic and empty of significance. French Canada's Catholic religious sensibility, in the words of Father Louis O'Neill, was "impoverished and deficient," and resembled that found in the poorest societies in Europe, Eamon de Valera's Ireland, and Francisco Franco's Spain. In both cases, the Catholic Church enjoyed a privileged relationship with an authoritarian state.[144] O'Neill's comparison appealed greatly to this vocal group of Catholic reformers because it implicitly linked the venial sins of artistic bad taste and habitual mass religious practices to more serious evidences of corruption – the economic backwardness, political reaction, and above all, the failure of Quebec's Catholic society to "grant a place to active and creative Christian intellectuals."[145] Rather than affording a critical and responsible perspective on modern social and cultural developments, and stimulate a collective sense of engagement in the compelling issues of the day, this type of religion tended to underscore political passivity and an unthinking conservatism by offering a false sense of security through mass conformity, as the faithful were encouraged simply to work for individual salvation through endless repetition of pious acts. Ultimately, religious traditionalism tended to lapse into "pious mythology," which was vilified as "a falsification of the Christian hope,"[146] because it removed the imperative for humans to engage in collective action on the side of social progress.

The analysis of Quebec's post-war cultural situation offered by Catholic Action and *Cité libre* might at first sight appear to present an intellectually confused, scatter-gun polemic against the inroads of American-style mass culture and routinized religion. Indeed, their explanation of Quebec's contemporary history presented these modernist Catholics with a conundrum. On the one hand, "traditional" expressions of Catholicism, and the conservative mentality they engendered, were supposed to be withering away under the inevitable cultural solvent of urban and industrial realities. But if this was true, how to explain the continued ability of the institutional Church to adapt itself to urban and industrial social situations, and to define and take possession of new social roles, a point conceded even by so stern and unbending a critic of overweening clerical pretension as Pierre Trudeau?[147] In so desiring to demonstrate the failure and futility of "tradition," and to resolve the dichotomy between what they saw as the inevitable historical displacement of tradition and its evident appeal to masses of ordinary people, these Catholic reformers were forced even further towards the modernist notion of spiritual rupture. The 1950s saw the elaboration of a bleak, pessimistic interpretation of Quebec's religious past, one in which even the instititutional enterprise and dynamism displayed by the Catholic Church was *itself* the source of spiritual defection and vacuity. As expressed by the sociologist Hubert Guindon in 1960, "having achieved complete control over the social organization, the clergy may discover, perhaps too late, that its population no longer knows what religion and its cherished symbols mean. ... And not because of alien and foreign culture, but as a direct result of the clergy's own successful control of the whole society."[148]

In constructing such a vision of Quebec history, it must be remembered that this group of Catholic activists was strongly marked by the virulently anti-institutional personalism of Emmanuel Mounier, and a quasi-Marxist vision of economic relations. Institutional power thus stood in inverse proportion to spiritual vitality. Worse, as Gérard Pelletier had observed in 1952, the increasing bureaucratization of the Church, necessitated by its taking on increased social responsibilities in an urban setting, had reduced ordinary French Canadians to the status of "spiritual proletarians."[149] Although urban churches might be full every Sunday, they had ceased to be real communities. They were simply administrative mechanisms where "the worker is faced with 'office hours' tacked on the presbytery door, and the impersonal contact with one of the five or six assistant priests who is 'on call' on that particular evening. The sermon, carried on loudspeakers to the furthest recesses of the church, has become the exposition of a cold doctrine, or simply the endless enumeration of promises of marriage or intentions. The parish no longer exists as a centre of life, it structures a religious practice that is less and less vibrant; it has become a place, a territory, and gradually ceases to be a community."[150] Here, the personalist exaltation of spiritual fellowship was the key consideration in evaluating the ability of Quebec Catholicism to respond to the spiritual needs of modern urban workers.

In the estimation of men like Pelletier, the principal dereliction of the Catholic clergy lay in the fact that they had contributed to breaking down traditional bonds of rural community solidarity without offering any modern vision in its place. Rather than holding out a way of transcending class and wealth divisions, or of working for the displacement of traditional lines of authority, the Church's "administrative revolution" had simply reinforced the position of traditional elites in Quebec society, and worse, had done so by importing the impersonal mentality of the modern capitalist business enterprise into what should have been a place of spiritual solace. Already heavily indebted to Mounier's Christian incorporation of Marxist notions of conflict and progress, these Catholic activists saw in the modern urban parish the ultimate sign of a thoroughly perverted society, a world in which the clergy had become "bureaucratic overlords,"[151] a "bourgeoisie"[152] totally abstracted from working-class people. The failure of Quebec's historic Catholic tradition lay in the fact that working-class French-Canadians were increasingly drawn to the alternatives of "the most disorderly Protestant sects," and in "the imperceptible flight" of many from religious observances "that indicates the slow ebbing away of the very substance of our Christian life."[153]

In one respect, Pelletier's depressing vision of working-class religious apostasy and his vehement denunciation of the modern Catholic clergy as mere "organization men" drew heavily upon his post-war experience in France, where a generation of French Catholics were obsessed with the de-Christianization of large sections of the French working class.[154] The term "proletarianization," however, had a different resonance in Quebec where, by any standard, the commitment of working-class people to Catholicism remained exceedingly high. In Quebec, "proletarianization" was synonymous with "conformity," a reference to those aspects of mass culture and North American values that Catholic activists found most troubling. Pelletier's Cité libre associate Maurice Blain, for example, removed the class descriptor from "proletarian" by arguing that the entire Catholic laity in fact constituted a spiritual proletariat.[155] It was this characterization that most accurately translated the vision of post-war Catholic activists on the conflict of religious mentalities that was rupturing their society. On the one hand, the assigning of "proletarian" qualities to all lay Catholics and the depiction of the clergy as greedy administrative professional bureaucrats – a "bourgeoisie" – afforded these middle-class intellectuals the luxury of viewing themselves as a historically underprivileged, oppressed group, rendered superfluous and prevented from occupying its true role as a social elite because its leadership functions in modern educational and social welfare organizations had been usurped by the institutional Church in a process that had begun during the 1840s. However, more significantly, it identified the Quebec middle class, rather than the working class, as the critical hinge of modernity, as where the battle between "traditional" and "personalist" religious mentalities would be most decisively waged.

In the years between 1945 and 1960, Quebec's Catholic reformers embraced a variety of strategies to incorporate Quebec workers into the civic polity, including popular education and an espousal of certain aspects of labour ideology. While historians have concentrated on key turning points – such as the 1949 Asbestos Strike and the subsequent 1950 Pastoral Letter of the Quebec Bishops that advocated the Christianization of industrial relations – as indicative of the attitudes and obstacles faced by progressive Catholic elites,[156] another key element has been relegated to the background. Spurring the efforts of these reformist Catholics was an underlying belief that what was essential to the articulation of this new social partnership – the vision of a true Christian fellowship that straddled class boundaries – was a transformation of middle-class values. Specifically, Quebec's educated professional elites had to be won from an individualistic concern for material well-being and self-gratification, to a consciousness of social responsibility for the welfare of less advantaged social groups. In this respect, post-war Catholic activists stood within a rather traditional current – its advocates during the 1930s included older Catholic nationalist intellectuals such as Esdras Minville, director of the École des Hautes Études Commerciales at the Université de Montréal, and Abbé Lionel Groulx – that viewed the leadership of educated and socially conscious middle-class elites as essential to balancing social stability and progress.[157]

However, in the immediate post-war years, this older strand of reflection had been given new currency and enhanced anxiety through an encounter with a new consciousness. Specifically, encounters with European youth leaders more narrowly defined the category "youth" to mean "student," which, as opposed to Depression-era definitions, automatically possessed a more middle-class inflection.[158] However, this more limited definition of youth identity automatically exposed post-war youth to greater social and cultural temptation, in particular, the footloose, American-style, socially-disconnected individualism and access to consumer gratification offered by a more leisured lifestyle in which paid work was pushed back into a more distant future. These Catholic activists could only view the emergence of this cultural type as the antithesis of their ideals of elite leadership and socially-engaged spiritual fellowship. In order to counter this, reformist Catholics adopted two cultural strategies: one was to define student youth as "intellectual workers,"[159] thus attempting to establish a refurbished notion of engagement and solidarity with the working-class; the second, was to carry on a close scrutiny of Quebec's Catholic college and university institutions so that these might properly harmonize elitism, democracy, religious conviction, and social commitment.

Writing in 1951, Claude Ryan restated this emphasis on elite leadership, but superimposed a notion of the centrality of the middle classes to the definition and survival of democracy. "The middle classes," he observed, "are a sort of crossroads where the transition from one class to another occurs. The more a society is open and anchored on the principles and traditions of democracy, the more easily and frequently the movement from one class to another occurs."[160] However, the principal obstacle to the realization of this democratic society founded upon education, merit, and social mobility lay in the character of many middle-class people: an unthinking conservatism, pessimism, and timidity that translated itself into a blind traditionalism that, in Ryan's estimation, stifled the development of individual personalities and induced middle-class professionals to a culture that slavishly imitated that of financiers and the haute bourgeoisie, rather than encouraged them to seek an open culture based on social partnership with responsible working-class elites. The presence of such a mentality inhibited middle-class professionals from performing their true social function, that of being spiritual guardians of Quebec's distinctive national and religious culture.[161]

Perhaps no polemicist more effectively joined together the generational thinking of 1930s Catholic Action with a virulent cultural critique of the failure of Quebec's middle classes than Pierre Elliott Trudeau. Although widely viewed as a social-democratic sympathizer of Quebec's beleaguered post-war labour movement because of his celebrated intervention in the 1949 Asbestos Strike, he also epitomized a strain of cultural conservatism during the early 1950s as he at times appeared to be far more concerned about exposing what he considered to be the spiritual and cultural deficiencies of the Catholic middle classes. This was a group he dismissively referred to as "petty financiers, petty civil servants, and failed academics." What most troubled Trudeau was that the "traditional" bourgeois professions of medicine, law, and the Church languished at the level of "prescribers of pills, pawns in the courtroom, and commentators on the *petit catéchisme* [abridged catechism]," utterly lacking in the "fearless qualities of the evangelists, the explorers and the *coureurs-de-bois* who were willing to risk everything."[162]

Spurring Trudeau's negative characterization of middle-class leadership was a fear that his society stood on the brink of class warfare, and that under conditions of modern industrial conflict, nationalism, in which Catholicism played such a prominent place, might itself fail to reconcile religious belief and human freedom and thus preserve a solidarity among classes that alone could stem the tide of Marxism.[163] Writing in 1947, he pessimistically observed, "I do not believe that many avenues of salvation are still open to us." Citing the failure of "the three courageous efforts of Bourassa, Paul Gouin, and the Bloc," he blamed middle-class leadership for erecting both nationalism and Catholicism into an unreasoning, dogmatic orthodoxy. "Our Catholicism," he concluded, is not a faith, but a system of assurances where entry into paradise is guaranteed by the performance of a prescribed number of laudable and ostentatious practices. … Our pharisaic religion is a doctrine of comfort, and is, in truth, the opium of the people."[164] For this young Catholic purist, the only hope for Quebec lay in the social promotion of new middle-class elites, whose religion was more socially conscious. Trudeau described this group as "some Catholic Action militants, certain artists, writers, and union leaders who have placed themselves on the side of freedom."[165]

The arresting feature of this discussion was the explicit articulation of two types of middle-class mentality, one that was properly modern and democratic, based on an ideal of responsible civic leadership, and the other, contemptuously described as "bourgeois," spiritually-barren, and devoted to conformity, imitation, and the cult of making money. Not coincidentally, this description exactly paralleled both the notion of irrepressible conflict between two diametrically opposed types of Catholicism, and the notion of "rupture" between a spiritually vital youth generation and an adult generation whose spirituality was obsolete. Viewed through the categories offered by Catholic Action, "bourgeois" was less an economic indicator than a testimony to one's lack of proper cultural and spiritual values,[166] and in this respect, such denunciations simply recapitulated tropes articulated since the turn of the twentieth century by French literary intellectuals for whom modern society was divided between the official culture of the bourgeoisie and a spiritually and morally superior culture of an elite avant-garde.[167]

However, after the late 1940s, the fundamental dichotomy between conformist "bourgeois" and a spiritual vanguard of youth was increasingly expressed in the concerns felt by post-war Catholics about the "conformist" implications of modern mass media and Quebec's exposure to North American prosperity, which amplified their fears surrounding their society's middle class. Catholic social commentators reckoned that, because of its status and stable employment, the middle class had the opportunity to participate more fully in a culture of material prosperity. This, participation, however, would automatically expose their Catholic heritage to more spiritual risks, and worse, because they constituted an elite class whose values influenced others, the choices made by Quebec's middle class would ultimately determine the values of the entire society. Would they opt for a comfortable life as "organization men," passive consumers living the lives of "erratic nouveaux-riches" in comfortable suburbias utterly divorced from French Canada's working classes,[168] or would they accept the engagement of personalist Catholicism and opt for forms of social leadership that would challenge the hold of materialist values?[169]

By the late 1950s, a profound mood of cultural pessimism enveloped the post-war generation of reformist Catholics. For those who had imbibed the energetic Catholic Action spirituality of the 1930s, it was apparent that the French-Canadian middle classes, and by extension the entire nation, had largely surrendered their souls to the North American values of mass conformity. Because their dynamic of culture and social change centred around the spiritual qualities of youth, what so perplexed them about post-war society was that the cohort who entered adolescence during the 1950s seemed eager to embrace, not an ideal of spiritual activism, but a culture of consumerism, imitation of movie-star idols, and the quest for personal wealth, the very negative qualities ascribed to "bourgeois" adults. Indeed, in what constitutes one of the fundamental ironies of Quebec's cultural history, at the very moment that North American youth appeared to acquire an autonomy, a cohesiveness, and an awareness that they constituted a distinct community, Catholic youth activists abandoned an older European vision of youth's cultural superiority in favour of a bleaker Anglo-American post-war vision that equated adolescent assertiveness with egotism and potential delinquency.[170] However, in contrast to the United States, where the public debate on the danger of the new adolescent was dominated by a critique of a mass culture of films, comics, and advertising,[171] the concerns of Quebec elites remained closely tied to religion. During the course of this polemic, three elements that originated with Catholic Action were inextricably welded together: the older modernist notion of a fundamental dichotomy between an official middle class and a spiritual avant-garde, a growing conviction that Quebec youth were simply being swamped by a spiritually vapid North American middle-class culture, and a belief that this moral vacuity was being actively assisted and promoted by institutional Catholicism through its educational institutions.

Speaking to the faculty of arts at Université Laval in 1958, professor of literature Jeanne Lapointe characterized students in the *collèges classiques* as "pervaded by a materialism that is more crude and brutal than that with which we reproach the Americans." Humanism in Quebec, she contended, rather than offering a vision of the world founded upon the dignity of man, was straitjacketed by a religious mentality and a scholastic philosophy. These, rather than opening the student to a positive vision of the world, were dominated by a "degraded form of dualism" that led to "a species of moral nihilism ... to an anarchy of practical conduct which flows from a Christianity that has become pure formalism." In a merciless indictment, Lapointe castigated the religious engagement of Quebec Catholics as resembling that of Dostoyevsky's Grand Inquisitor, who demanded obedience and the surrender of critical faculties, and exposed as hollow Catholicism's oft-vaunted claim to have preserved, in the face of Anglo-American materialism, the higher spiritual qualities of French culture and language.[172] Two key considerations emerge from Lapointe's discussion. First, the fact that these views were being enunciated within the precincts of French Canada's major university indicated that the personalist critique of institutional Catholicism had gained adherents beyond the specific purview of Catholic Action and its exponents in *Cité libre*. It now included a vocal group of reformist clergy, educators, and university academics.

Second, Lapointe and a number of other participants conflated a defective, authoritarian religious education, which they believed produced an amoral conformity; a compartmentalization between secular and religious life, which they characterized as a "practical atheism"; a lack of social responsibility and a culture of individualism, which they discerned among middle-class youth; and the poverty of written and spoken French, which was dragging Quebec even further within the anglophone ambit of North America.[173] Adopting the personalist definition that "[a] language is a communication that presupposes interior courage and true freedom,"[174] this group of educators, all committed to the notion of preserving a symbiotic link between Catholicism and French culture, argued that an authoritarian, formalist religious training fostered cultural impoverishment and exposed Quebec youth to the inroads of North American mass culture. Most alarmingly, they concluded that the "spiritual revolt" that they discerned among Quebec youth during the late 1950s, one that expressed itself through a reaction against all forms of regimentation, could be directly attributed to the way Catholicism was presented in the schools by the clergy and members of religious orders.[175]

The stated concern of this group centred on clerical control of the educational system, and in particular, the perceived inability of the clergy to provide a *religious* education that would inspire middle-class youth to counter materialist values. As emphatically stated by Pierre Dansereau in 1956, the rising cultural level among the masses in Western society "poses serious problems for religious education: training in doctrine and catechesis can no longer rest upon the rudimentary traditions that we have inherited from the past." To neglect this problem, argued Dansereau, would place Quebec on the same trajectory as Europe, where the masses of people had become completely de-Christianized. What particularly worried him as the main contributing factor to this evisceration of religion from society was that "the level of non-religious instruction among all classes is considerably more advanced than is religious instruction."[176] However, the confrontation that they believed existed between their personalist Catholic ideals and North American civilization drew reformers like Dansereau towards a far more aggressive assault on institutional Catholicism. The Church-controlled educational system did not simply need reforming because it had failed to inspire youth with Christian values. Rather, institutional Catholicism, despite its claim to preserve the "higher" spiritual values of French and Catholic civilization, was actively *promoting* an accommodation between French Canada and the "bourgeois" culture of North American consumerism. By 1958, many of those most influenced by Catholic Action had come to a radically revisionist sense of the clergy's historic role in their society, one that dictated the urgent removal of priests and members of religious orders from their spiritual guardianship of culture.

The cause of the spiritual dereliction of post-war middle-class adolescents was laid squarely at the door of the *collèges classiques*, an educational network completely controlled by diocesan authorities and religious orders, where the vast majority of middle-class French-Canadian Catholic youth received their secondary education. Prior to 1945, these colleges were comfortable teaching a curriculum dominated by classical humanism, in which the study of the sciences played little part, and which claimed to preserve French culture and civilization by identifying it with Catholicism.[177] Although many of the Depression-era Catholic Action movements began in these colleges, the movements as a whole, even before 1945, had adopted a critical attitude towards the type of religious instruction available to adolescents. Writing in 1941, Jean LeMoyne castigated what he saw as a complete absence of the "Christian reflex" among young people trained in these institutions, as they displayed an almost complete ignorance of the Bible, Catholic dogma, or the history of the Church. The colleges, he maintained, were mired in the "formalist," bourgeois piety that created a generation of lukewarm, indifferent Catholics for whom religion was separated from life.[178] Frequent surveys of adolescent religious attitudes done in the *collèges classiques* during the 1950s revealed a similar pattern. Religious educators, strongly marked by the communalist ethic of Catholic Action, were persistently confronted with the "individualist" practices of most students, for whom attendance at mass was simply an occasion for a rather routine, conformist piety. According to Father Guy Bélanger, "their Christianity is situated first and foremost at the level of doctrine, and then ready-made responses, abstract and intemporal solutions."[179]

In the eyes of Catholic reformers concerned for the spiritual dynamism of their society, such a routinized expression of Catholic religious practice made a mockery of the lofty humanist ideals of the *collèges classiques*, which were supposed to stand as a bulwark against the inroads of American materialist values. Indeed, during the 1950s, a growing number of Catholic educators began to question the very "humanistic" quality of this education in light of the kind of Christian that these institutions appeared to produce. In an influential report written for Catholic Action in 1950, Camille Laurin, evidently relying on information obtained from Esdras Minville, proffered a few tepid criticisms of the colleges and their need to offer more scientific subjects, but concluded that this should not be done at the expense of the teaching of Thomist philosophy. Reforms, he suggested, could be accomplished by integrating more lay teachers into the college and more state assistance for cash-strapped institutions.[180] Two years later, however, Fernand Cadieux, president of the Jeunesse Étudiante Catholique, raised a question that was fundamental to the intersection of Catholicism and the preservation of humanistic values. Most middle-class students, he argued, were destined to occupy jobs as minor functionaries in the North American service economy, yet as no less a figure than the archbishop of Montreal, Cardinal Léger, had forcefully intimated, the colleges did not teach students to become socially-conscious Christians.[181]

The message was clear: at best, Quebec's system of clerically-dominated

secondary schooling was teaching a kind of Christianity that was appropriate for middle-class "organization men." In a cruel irony, the very system
that was designed to protect French Canada from the inroads of North
American civilization was, through clerical authoritarianism and insistence
upon a conformist piety and a Jansenist religion of prohibitions that "sun-
dered soul and body,"[182] actually producing an entire generation of
passive, bureaucratic, ultimately "feminized" individuals oriented to a neurotic pursuit of wealth and self-gratification. The Church, in the estimation
of Maurice Blain, offered modern French Canadians a debased humanism
which was leading the vast majority to simply think like Americans even
after attending colleges ostensibly devoted to the loftiest ideals of French
classical humanism.[183] In the final analysis, what angered these personalist
Catholics about Quebec's institutional Catholicism was less its financial
servitude towards powerful politicians like Maurice Duplessis, than its cultural and spiritual failings. In the hands of the clergy, concluded this
growing chorus of reformist voices, the *collège classique*'s expression of
French cultural values had become truncated, "unreal," and utterly perverse, incarnating not youth's need for anxiety, engagement, and dialogue,
but "the necessity to get to the top, make money, and procure for oneself
the greatest possible material comfort."[184]

By the late 1950s, a growing chorus of critical voices had begun to question institutional Catholicism's custodianship of French humanistic values
in the face of a new youth culture that exhibited the alarming symptoms
of integration into a North American mass culture of consumerism and
spiritual vacuity. In what must stand as one of the great discontinuities of
modern Quebec's cultural history, the institutional Church, which had so
assiduously promoted a vision of Catholicism as a cultural renewal
premised upon the moral and spiritual qualities of an activist youth,
became increasingly suspect during the years after 1945. A generation of
youth leaders, mostly trained within the environment of the *collèges classiques* in the 1930s and early 1940s, now sought through a variety of
methods to graft the religious ideals of their youth onto an entire society.
In so doing, they sought to maintain the centrality of Catholicism by
forging a modernist vision which married French personalism to a vision
of "eternal youth" in such a way as to continually reinforce their consciousness of their generation's spiritual superiority as the key to the articulation of modern values in Quebec. However, in the years after 1950,
they found their vision increasingly challenged, not by a cultural and
political conservatism that worked within the framework of religious "tradition," but by a rival version of modernity. This modernity, which they
saw at work within institutional Catholicism itself, was imbuing youth with
an antimorality of passivity, a feminized subservience to authority, and a

hedonistic desire to participate in a North American, standardized, consumerist society. It was the enunciation, after the mid-1950s, that this new
youth culture constituted the direct antithesis of the personalist values of
those Catholics who had since the 1930s affirmed that youth was the
fulcrum for spiritual renewal, which ushered in a climate of cultural pessimism in Quebec Catholicism. And it was precisely this pessimism that
profoundly dictated the shape and pace of the Quiet Revolution of the
1960s.

3

"A New World Is Born, and with It a New Family"[1]

Marriage, Sexuality, Nuclearity, and the Reconstruction of the French-Canadian Family, 1931–1955

Many political and religious revolts are but delayed reactions against the family past.[2]

In standard historical treatments of the post-war years in North America, the family has emerged as synonymous with a broader cultural yearning for quiescent domesticity and security in response to the upheavals of World War II and the subsequent climate of fear engendered by the Cold War.[3] Quebec, a society in which many aspects of institutional life and public ideologies were shaped by Roman Catholicism, would seem at first glance to encapsulate an accentuated version of the "traditional" patterns of family relations that held sway in English Canada and the United States. However, instead of helping maintain an immobile, timeless family or a static pattern of gender and age relations, Roman Catholicism was a dynamic element which overtly recast a number of key definitions of family life in the Great Depression and the immediate post-war era that ended in the mid-1950s.

During the late 1930s, a new ideal of marriage and an emphatically nuclear concept of family structure and relationships emerged within the framework of the Catholic Action movements. Such ideas formed a key component of the reformist Catholic response to definitions of family and male authority that were oriented solely around wages and work and which came from social science experts and policy-makers in Ottawa, as well as a number of Canadian provinces.[4] Although it was on one level an attempt to reassert older ideals of family cohesion, this Depression-era Catholic thinking centred the idea of family almost exclusively upon the affectional nature of the marriage partnership, and more precisely upon the emotional fulfillment and satisfactions that it provided for husbands and wives. By elevating marriage as a sacramental, sexual relationship predicated entirely upon the quest for intimacy, it excluded, almost entirely, ideas of family that had held sway until the 1930s which had stressed multi-generational kinship ties or economic productive functions.

What was central to this new Catholic vision was the conviction that the family formed the essential core of the personalist ideal of individual self-affirmation through a quest for the values of community. In an industrial society whose work processes, ideologies, and leisure entertainments were characterized by impersonality, anonymity, and alienation, the family, especially for men, was the repository of those human relations, primarily sexual ones, that were deemed most creative and the source of ultimate values. For this reason, Catholic reformers invested a great deal of energy in refurbishing the family as a visible, public, institutional entity in which the domestic authority of the affectionate father – a kind of "spiritual" paternity – ultimately underpinned the authority of Catholicism over educational and social institutions in the wider Quebec society. The Catholic family ideology of the late Depression and the first decade of the post-war period thus attempted to straddle the social corporatist imperative, which located social reconstruction in the restoration of hierarchical, institutional relationships, and a personalist current, which placed a heightened value on individual fulfillment.

"INSTEAD OF LINKING MARRIAGE TO RELIGION, WE HAVE MADE A RELIGION OUT OF MARRIAGE"[5]

In its attempt to recast the place of youth in modern society, Catholic Action imparted an ambivalent message to Depression-era Quebec. During the early part of the decade, Catholicism in certain contexts appeared to veer in the direction of generational conflict, using the term "revolution" to enlist young people into the new working-class and student movements by promoting a more "democratic," communitarian type of sociability and a personalist spirituality superior to that of the "routine" and "conformity" that characterized the religious practice of earlier generations. However, by the late 1930s, Quebec Catholic clergy and elements of the lay leadership had begun to downplay ideas of generational rupture and the creation of youthful communities, and actually began to backpedal towards restoring the hierarchical generational continuities that socialized young people into the assumption of social and civic responsibilities centering on family formation. Two major concerns underlay this shift in emphasis, one drawn from Catholicism's cultural apprehension of the threat from European totalitarian ideologies, the other drawn directly from the Canadian social reality of high and persistent youth unemployment.

Although Catholic Action had, during the early part of the decade, invested considerable effort in building movements around the incarnation of a separate youth culture based upon a generational critique of adult, "bourgeois" values, the example of interwar German and Italian youth movements, which had become totally incorporated into the Nazi and Fascist social orders, served as a powerful negative influence. Indeed, it seemed that in these countries the ideology of youth separateness had actually hastened the complete subservience and dependency of youth to totalitarian dictators, and the submergence of spirituality in the all-powerful state apparatus.[6] Reinforcing this mood of ideological apprehension was a preoccupation with the spectre of high and persistent youth unemployment, a concern that Catholic social activists shared with their Anglo-Canadian counterparts. Despite indications that the Canadian economy as a whole seemed to be showing signs of recovery by the late 1930s, the problem of youth unemployment constituted an ongoing social crisis on two levels. First, the lack of steady work opportunities forced hundreds of thousands of young men into a period of prolonged childhood dependency or semi-permanent transiency, and, second, this in turn was translated into declining marriage and birth rates, which then raised fears of sexual delinquency and an inadequate preparation of young men for the responsibilities of family formation, with the end result being an erosion of the twinned civic values of work and family solidarity.[7]

Thus, by the waning years of the Depression, Quebec Catholicism's heroic language of youth's revolutionary possibilities was more and more nuanced by fear that modern youth's smooth progression into adulthood was barred by an incapacity to assume the tasks of family formation. The most serious consequence of the Depression, declared one member of the Jeunesse Ouvrière Catholique, was the alarming number of unemployed young men who "would normally be married ... if only they had had better opportunities."[8] The explicit linking of work and marriage under the rubric of "opportunity" pointed to an awareness among Catholic social commentators that the Depression had irrevocably weakened older patterns of connection between family and workplace. Writing in 1938, Father Léon Lebel argued that in modern industrial society prolonged periods of unemployment shortened the productive years of most workers, thus producing large-scale family poverty. However, the Depression had, in his estimation, exacerbated the precarious condition of Quebec families because they were unable to replicate the model of the interdependent family typical of an earlier phase of the society's industrialization. Because young people were unable to marry and form a family until they were much older, many working-class families faced the Depression encumbered with young school-age children who were unable to enter the workforce to supplement the family income. "Today's father," Lebel lugubriously concluded, "must by his own efforts, feed, clothe, and house ten or twelve children."[9]

What so troubled Catholic social commentators was the fact that these children, by the end of the 1930s, had grown into late adolescence without any work experience or skills, and thus lacked the essential attributes of responsibility that would enable them, in their turn, to embark on marriage and adulthood. "In practice," stated Father Guillaume Lavallée in 1937, "today's young people want to avoid, as long as possible, the duties and responsibilities of the married state. They may court their girlfriends for years without getting any closer to the goal. They do not live with the prospect of marriage in mind and thus neglect to prepare for it."[10] Adolescent insouciance regarding family formation was a telling indicator of a wider breakdown of family solidarity: by decisively weakening the economically interdependent family, the Depression had gone far to dissolve those intergenerational connections, the "*family spirit*"[11] by which parents had smoothly prepared adolescents for marriage. For it was through the function of the family as a unit of economic production that the values of "love of work, devotion, generosity, sincerity"[12] – which together were the foundations of successful marriage and family life – had been inculcated in the younger generation.

The growing propensity among Quebec working-class youth to defer marriage in fact constituted a double menace to the close connection that Catholicism wished to foster between family and religious values. First, as the lay Catholic militant Fernand Jolicoeur observed in 1946, paternal authority had "atrophied" in working-class homes, where younger men, inadequately prepared for the domestic responsibilities of fatherhood, tended to live separate lives, returning to their homes only to eat and sleep. The absence of male authority figures meant, according to Father Bernard Verville, that the spirit of adolescent subordination had percolated downward to include even younger children, who were displaying signs of insubordination, a situation which most parents seemed to tolerate with an indulgent resignation.[13] Second, the reluctance of adolescent males to contemplate marriage was further evidence of a "practical emancipation," by which Catholic promoters of the family meant sexual delinquency.[14] They discerned this delinquency in the rising number of divorces, illicit liaisons, or "concubinage," and the spread of "prevention of the family" through birth control, the ultimate challenge to Catholic moral teaching and family solidarity.[15]

How then to reconstruct vertical lines of socialization, by which youth were effectively initiated by the older generation into the values of steady work and family responsibility? Significantly, in attempting to reassert age hierarchies within the family, Depression-era Catholic activists eschewed a strategy that would have simply reinvested into the hands of parents the task of educating adolescents into the duties and responsibilities of marriage. While Father Verville admitted that, ideally, such education should be given by the adolescent's family – because such a setting best accorded with the papal directive of avoiding "exaggerated physiological education,"[16] – letters such as that of "Simone," a twenty-year-old woman who complained that her mother refused to inform her about the nature and purpose of the marital act, thus making her easy prey to "unhealthy curiosity and brutal indiscretions,"[17] compelled Catholic activists to somehow compensate for parental incompetence in educating adolescents for family roles. As Father Verville bluntly concluded: "today's child can no longer receive precise ideas about the nature and role of the family or ... be educated in the domestic virtues in the home." Thus, the need was not so much to reform relations within individual families, but to create "*modern institutions* capable of consolidating the home."[18]

It was precisely this concern to at once restore an imperilled family solidarity while compensating for the deficiencies of parents as authority figures in the modern family that drove a number of organizational initiatives in Quebec Catholicism. Beginning in the late 1930s and attaining greater institutional cohesion in the decade following World War II, groups such as the Service de Préparation au Mariage (SPM) and the École des Parents were created through the stimulus of Catholic Action. By the mid-1950s, these efforts encompassed a plethora of journals, family institutes, and movements of spirituality which sought to inform working-class and lower-middle-class Catholics about Catholic moral teaching on marriage, sexuality, and the proper relationships that ought to prevail in modern families. The goal was to both infuse these values into Catholics' daily lives and to provide expert psychological advice to parents regarding "modern" methods of educating children and adolescents.[19] The activities of these Catholic social movements married modern educational techniques to a traditional language which claimed to "restore" the family to a type of original, pristine solidarity of age and gender relations. However, these attempts to elevate the family as something immutable and eternal in an age of economic crisis and social turmoil in fact entailed a radical shift in Catholic thinking about the nature, purpose, and composition of the family. The effect of this revision was to abruptly shift the function of the family from older economic, political, or institutional considerations to the terrain of psychological satisfaction and emotional fulfillment.

Archbishop Gauthier's sermon, delivered at the JOC's mass-marriage ceremony in Montreal in July 1939, evoked the family as "holding pride of place among those things that do not die. Through all changes, there is something profound and durable that is revealed: love and the ties of blood. Whatever may be the times, customs, and social conventions, a father is still a father, a mother is still a mother."[20] The audience of young working-class Catholics who filled Montreal's Delorimier Stadium to witness the mass-marriage spectacle were undoubtedly reminded of the stability of the family and the enduring character of the Catholic Church's doctrines concerning marriage and family. However, both Gauthier's sermon and the weeks of intensive study that preceded the ceremony[21] presented a view that in important respects altered older understandings of the relationship between family and marriage. Prior to the Depression, a number of concepts of family prevailed within Quebec Catholicism, many of which conflated affectional links and functions with economic, productive criteria. Such family ideologies tended to stress that the relationship of spouses took place primarily on the level of reproduction, and they elevated multi-generational, kinship types of family in which all family members worked. They assigned relatively little attention to the cultivation of the emotional relationship between husband and wife. Elements of the Catholic clergy, intent on maintaining the church's institutional hold on orphanages and the social welfare system, at that time articulated notions of family that completely eviscerated husbands and wives, substituting the institution itself as central to the task of child-rearing.[22]

However, the combined upsurge of Catholic Action, with its new emphasis on the spiritual eminence of laypeople, and the perceived crisis in the commitment of Quebec youth to family formation pushed these economic, legalistic, and clerico-institutional concepts of family into the background. Central to the new lay spirituality was the elaboration of a mystique of marriage, which insisted upon the exclusive, sacramental nature of the bond between husband and wife. Those Catholics who sought to elevate the stature of the laity and to reassert a besieged family solidarity eagerly seized upon the 1930 papal encyclical on Christian marriage, *Casti Connubii*. At one level, in its prescriptions on the nature of the family, this document seemed simply to refurbish an unbending conservatism, evoking the traditional Catholic doctrine of the indissolubility and inviolability of marriage, rigidly reprobating divorce and forms of "companionate" marriage.[23] However, in so doing, Catholic doctrine also defined a new order of priority between marriage and family, one in which kin relations, economic functions, and even children either disappeared or moved to a lower scale of value. Religious value, in the terms outlined by the encyclical, was not attached to the family as an institution, and humans were not sanctified by participation in the legal, customary, economic, and political ties of the family. Rather, the family had no existence prior to the act of marriage itself, a "sacred partnership" between husband and wife, and at another level, between God and humans, which stood prior to any previous family bonds or commitments.[24] "Marriage," stated lay activist Adélard Provencher in 1940, "is not the family, but it is its governing principle."[25]

The desacralization of the family, and the new evocation of the absolute, sacred quality of the marriage partnership formed a central element of the Catholic thinking of this period. At the core of this strand of thought was the explicit link drawn between the sacramental character of marriage and the participation of both spouses in the divine act of creation. It was this spiritual quality of human creativity – flowing from a personal bond in which husband and wife gained access to God's grace – and not legal or social convention, which in turn dictated that marriage, once contracted, was indissoluble. The encyclical naturally restated, in the face of the growing inroads of neo-Malthusian attempts to popularize birth control, that the primary purpose of marriage was procreation and the education of children,[26] and that the first duty of spouses was "to transmit life."[27] However, its notion of "partnership" and "creation" was not restricted to bringing children into the world. Indeed, the insistence on procreation – the Church explicitly avoided the spiritually-neutral term "reproduction" in order to remind spouses that through sexual relations they were in fact exercising a divine imperative – had less to do with the cultivation of the ties between parent and child than with the spiritual benefits accruing personally to the husband and wife from marital intercourse. Procreation and child-rearing, declared Father M.-A. Lamarche in 1940, were naturally the central purposes of marriage, but he significantly added another element that overshadowed even these in importance: "the mutual sanctification of spouses." It was something which in his estimation drastically shifted the essence of marriage from "a legal institution to one that was simply a sharing of life by two people."[28] The implication of *Casti Connubii* was that marriage was not an economic relationship, social convention, or legal contract, but that its value from the religious perspective lay explicitly in the mutual spiritual satisfaction that husband and wife conferred upon each other. Thus, although the encyclical overtly insisted on procreation, it actually had the effect of subtly downplaying the purely reproductive, or social nature of the family, and of sanctioning a far more individualist current, privileging the psychological, and emotional realm of the affections, namely, the mutual enjoyment and physical and spiritual fulfillment of the married couple. This identified the married couple itself, and not children or extended kin relations, as the most important element in the family, because it alone was constituted by a sacrament. The fact that the marital relationship itself assumed an all-encompassing character required constant attention by both husband and wife to the process of mutual self-discovery and the cultivation of intimacy, what the encyclical termed a "deep attachment of the heart."[29]

Thus, from the late 1930s until well into the post-war decade, many Quebec Catholics imbibed the message that the primary spiritual value of marriage was the partnership between husband and wife primarily on an emotional, sexual, and psychological level. As a corollary, they maintained that the success of any marriage depended on the level of intimacy that the couple were able to achieve in their daily lives. While conservative clergy expatiated upon the new papal teaching on marriage as a political bulwark against Communism and the inroads of materialist ideologies,[30] lay promoters of the new specialized Catholic Action were more intent on using the new mystique of marriage, with its promise of happiness and mutual fulfillment, as a way of reintroducing young men and women to the responsibility of family formation by combining this imperative with a new scale of individual satisfactions. Personal choice and an ongoing commitment to mutual sharing and intimacy were notions that resonated strongly with those Depression-era adolescents who had been induced by the new youth movements to exalt spiritual authenticity and the quest for community as the touchstone of human society. Marriage, stated one contributor to *Jeunesse Ouvrière* in 1939, flowed from the free choice and consent of spouses, and conjugal love brought together "two souls, even more than two bodies, in intimate union." The degree to which spouses were able to attain a high level of spiritual satisfaction was wholly a function of "the generous gift that one human being gives to another of their whole being, extending over the course of their entire life."[31]

In identifying spiritual partnership and intimacy as the essential core of a new "*communitarian*" vision of marriage, Catholic Action's spirituality brusquely dismissed as obsolete all notions of institution or contract that still remained attached to the marital relationship. "It is not important," stated one commentator in 1947, "that young people who marry envision marriage as a function they perform together; the key is that they must together engage in a process of *becoming*."[32] The restriction of the family's primary spiritual community to the husband-wife couple implied, in turn, the popularization of a far more dynamic view of marriage. The core of this new conjugal vision stressed that it was the spouses' ongoing mutual emotional and psychological adjustment, rather than any adherence to precisely codified customary or legal duties, or conventional social expectations, that now comprised the essential criteria of a successful marriage.[33] According to one working-class Catholic commentator in 1935, true love was "a sentiment of affection that brings two souls together, that allows them to understand and derive mutual pleasure from one another."[34] The pairing of "understanding" and "mutual pleasure" revealed the direction of the inner logic of reformist Catholic thinking on marriage and family in post-Depression Quebec. By the end of the post-war decade, the reworking of marriage as a spiritual partnership between husband and wife entailed an explicit divinization of the sexual act itself within the bonds of marriage, thus assigning almost exclusive weight to the sexual act as the one element that provided an ongoing sanctification for marriage.[35] And because the quality of spiritual intimacy and thus stability depended on the degree to which husband and wife were capable of a satisfying sexual relationship, this strand of Catholicism maintained that young people had to be overtly prepared for the psychological and emotional demands of marriage. As stated by the columnist "José" in *Le Front ouvrier* in 1946, prospective husbands and wives had to begin from the perspective that men and women had different psychological natures and emotional needs that had to be understood and communicated. Being a good person, she stated, was in itself not sufficient to ensure marital happiness. "In addition," she admonished, "you must seek to understand your spouse, beginning from the fact that male and female natures, although destined to complete one another, are in fact quite different."[36]

Beginning in the waning years of World War II, Catholic Action's Service de Préparation au Mariage (SPM), formed in a number of working-class parishes under the auspices of the Jeunesse Ouvrière Catholique after 1942, sought to inextricably equate psychological compatibility of husband and wife and mutual sexual satisfaction, which in turn were defined as the distinguishing marks of a post-war lay spirituality. Catholic Action militants maintained that only through the conflation of spirituality and sexuality, which alone conferred personal satisfaction upon each partner to maintain the indissolubility of modern marriage, could young men and women be persuaded to form stable families and provide emotional security and a climate in which their own children could achieve psychological maturity. After 1944, the SPM, the most widely-diffused of all the forms of Catholic Action in Quebec, elaborated a comprehensive fourteen-week marriage preparation course designed to address the issues of psychological, sexual, and emotional adjustment between men and women; to inform them of the teachings of the Church on the nature of marriage; and to prepare the newlyweds to assume the financial responsibility of establishing a household and the complex task of parenting and raising a family.[37] By the mid-1950s, nearly fifty per cent of all engaged couples in the diocese of Montreal were attending the premarital study sessions.[38]

From the outset, the lay leaders of the SPM made it clear that, given the medical, psychological, and legal implications of marriage, the bulk of the instruction would fall to lay experts,[39] and after 1949 the key role in animating the program was played by experienced married couples themselves, whose personal testimony provided the centrepiece of the course. Until that year, instruction throughout the entire fourteen-week curriculum had been segregated along male-female lines, but the use of married couples as team leaders required the introduction of some coeducational sessions.[40] Indeed, the expectation of lay participants was that the clergy would be, by and large, an "invisible presence," confining themselves to the treatment of Christian morals, the rights and duties of spouses, and the laws of the Church regarding marriage and male and female psychology, and respecting the expertise of those who had either the knowledge or the experience to pronounce on marriage.[41] Those aspects of the course which treated the psychology of men and women were appreciated far more than doctrinal teaching because they dealt with the actual problem of how to create and maintain sexual intimacy on a daily basis, especially in the midst of ongoing family and financial stresses.[42]

Begun during the late Depression, the Catholic revaluation of marriage as an intimate partnership was inspired by socially conservative motives. Family stability would, its proponents believed, be affirmed through a reconnection of generations, which would occur by reawakening adolescents to a sense of responsibility in family formation. However, in the immediate post-war years, and particularly after the inception of the SPM in 1944 as a part of Catholic Action,[43] the conservative ideology of the marriage ideal was subtly altered by the injection of the notion of generational conflict which had been present in the Catholic youth movements of the 1930s, but shifted into the background during wartime. The ideal of marriage preparation, particularly during the late 1940s, was advanced in reference to a strident metaphor of sharply conflicting generational sexual awareness and values. "The mystique of marriage," observed Father Thomas Audet in 1945, "has remained for too long a prisoner of a certain strand of medieval theology, which, rather than elevating the sacrament of the marital act as a source of divine grace, considered it at best a remedy for sin and at worst, sexuality was imputed to sin itself."[44] Gérard Pelletier, the former national Catholic student leader and one of the principal advocates of clashing generational cultural sensibilities, declaimed sarcastically on the rigid social customs of the older generation, "where people still enter into marriage to serve the needs of family considerations or strategies. These are completely contrary to the will of the spouses. It is a scandal among us that there are parents who allow their children no freedom of choice, even that most basic one of choosing their life's companion." In defending the new personalist vision of marriage based on love, free choice, emotional compatibility and sexual intimacy, Pelletier openly mocked the values and experience of the pre-Depression generation, and he lambasted as hypocrisy the silence that surrounded the sexual facts of marriage. In the past, he declared, "we supposed that only haste was responsible for so many botched marriages. But we did not think of helping young people to prepare for married life. The entire discussion of marriage was taboo. We only sought to ensure that the trousseau of the bride was in order and that the groom was chaste. We never stopped to ask how young people, in a working world that is largely indifferent to their needs, and often morally suspect, could find the means to prepare themselves emotionally and spiritually for the greatest decision of their life. Abandoned and ignorant, many young people were literally forced to the altar."[45] To these Catholic activists, the focal point of generational difference, indeed, the key to explaining why the religious values of Depression-era and post-war youth were superior to those of the past, did not ultimately rest in conflicting values and practices in the political or economic realms. Rather, generational rupture involved nothing less than the core of personal identity, the worth that one attached to psychological and emotional fulfillment and satisfaction, which centred on the moral and spiritual value attached to the expression of sexuality within the marriage sacrament.

"A new consciousness of the sacramental character of marriage," proclaimed university student Charles Terreault in 1953, "is one of the most wonderful developments of the twentieth century."[46] For young men like Terreault who were about to embark on marriage, the radical novelty of post-war Catholicism's sacralization of marriage revolved entirely upon the revaluation of the place of sexual relations within marriage, and their equation with the highest form of spiritual perfection. "The absolute intimacy that occurs between two bodies," he reminded his listeners, "is the sign and instrument of the absolute intimacy of souls." In his estimation, the heightened intimacy that the promoters of the new Catholic vision of marriage believed occurred within the context of marriage could only be achieved through "the marital act," because it was completely free and justified by its ends: "propagation of the species, total fulfillment of husband and wife, and sense of peace and well-being in both body and soul."[47] Through sexual intercourse, argued the literary critic Jean LeMoyne, husband and wife attained a superior form of intimate communion, one that surpassed even language because it involved the essence of the individual being. Although many Catholic clergy would not have agreed with LeMoyne's inference from *Casti Connubii* that the personalist community which sex created between husband and wife in fact surpassed procreation as the primary purpose of marriage,[48] the spiritualization of sex as the key to an indissoluble marriage was eagerly promoted by a number of priests. Father Robert Llewellyn, closely involved in a number of Catholic Action movements, affirmed the religious nature of the sexual partnership in stating that "the normal human vocation is marriage, and conjugal love is humanity's most widespread method of sanctification."[49] While the need for sexual intimacy was biological, one writer explained, in the next breath he hastened to loosen that biology from its animal connotations. The biological order, he concluded, was "both carnal and spiritual," and the sexual act implied both the search for physical intimacy, as well as an intense communion of the soul.[50] The exaltation of sex was echoed by more conservative commentators such as the Jesuit Father Marie-Joseph d'Anjou who expatiated in 1952 upon the "sacred dignity of the sexual function," and warned that "any abuse of sex constitutes a veritable profanation."[51]

At one level, this sacralization of sex was simply a popularization of a marital spirituality that was already available in France through the works of promoters such as Father Jean Viollet, whose works, which envisioned a total sexualization of body, mind, and soul, were widely diffused in Quebec's marriage preparation movement.[52] However, in the religious atmosphere of post-war Quebec, which was strongly permeated by a tension between Catholic Action and the more institutional side of Catholicism, the positive revaluation of sex within marriage served, for many Catholic activists, to demarcate a cultural and moral fissure between clergy and laity, a division which had repercussions for the wider social authority of Catholicism in Quebec. As a way of overcoming their own sense of insecurity in the face of what they believed was their own relegation to adolescent status under clerical tutelage, lay Catholic militants drew upon new psychological theories which equated a healthy sexuality with emotional maturity, and thus human freedom.[53] By implication, those, like the clergy, who failed through lack of sex to move to a higher plateau of humanity remained repressed and thus stunted as persons, with a question mark over their fitness to wield social authority.

It was thus not surprising that Catholic lay activists were fond of drawing an absolute moral dualism between the new values of youth, directed to fulfillment, community, and spiritual authenticity – in which mutual sexual satisfaction sanctified marriage itself – and those of an older generation, whose puritanism – linked to immature, "medieval," and clerically-inspired definitions of the human personality – tolerated marital sex as a necessary evil to ensure reproduction, but certainly not as something to be openly discussed by engaged couples about to be married, much less to be enjoyed once married. Alexandrine and Gérard Pelletier, former leaders of the Jeunesse Étudiante Catholique who married during the 1940s, complained that earlier generations of Catholics had participated in a "conspiracy of silence" on the subject of the marriage vocation, a "conspiracy" which many laypeople in Catholic Action believed indicated a "return to old Origenist and Jansenist errors which presented human sexual and passionate tendencies as evil in themselves, whereas in fact they are beautiful and good."[54] In a letter written to his fiancée Simonne in 1941, Michel Chartrand commented on attending a Catholic Action study session that "priests and educators are still mired in Jansenism." What he found particularly stifling was the fact that they were still warning young men about "the dangers of sexuality, of seduction by women, of the loss of religious vocations ... by the evils of the flesh," and held "sexual life, even within the confines of marriage, as contemptible. They see in it only occasions of sin and not of spiritual growth."[55] In this context, the deployment of the term "Jansenism," far from evoking the old seventeenth-century French Catholic doctrinal controversies, was in fact a term of opprobrium used by youthful Catholic activists to distinguish their own superior spirituality – of which sexuality formed a central part – from older, more clerical traditions which identified puritanism and self-abnegation as testimony of a higher spiritual life.

Indeed, it is difficult to escape the conclusion that a number of articulate Catholics used promotion of the new sexualized marital spirituality to foster anticlerical attitudes, and in particular, to dispute the control that an unmarried clergy had always exercised over the realm of marriage and family. By sacralizing marriage and by identifying sexuality with spiritual satisfaction, a number of these Catholic militants came close to proclaiming a sacerdotal conception of marriage and sexuality that raised these above virginity and the religious vocation. In 1951, in a speech significantly entitled "Le laique marié, image de l'union du Christ et de son Église" ("The Married Layman, Image of the Union of Christ and His Church"), Gérard Pelletier argued that Quebec Catholicism, which overprivileged the authority of the clergy, had failed to provide married laity – especially men – with a status or spirituality that raised them above "realities that are too current, mundane, and without grandeur." Marriage, he claimed, had lost its original sense of "mystery" and "sacredness," and had been shackled by a defective clerical concept of spirituality to that ultimate lowest circle of spiritual hell, the sphere of "routine."[56] So seriously did elements of the clergy view this challenge, given the post-war decline in religious vocations, that the Jesuit Father Paul Vanier was called upon to refute the central tenets of this emerging lay spirituality of marriage. Vanier tartly reminded his opponent that Christ himself was a virgin who did not need human love or the personal experience of paternity to compensate for his solitude. Virginity thus stood above marriage because it was a "prophetic gift," representing the influx of the redemptive force of a supra-human world. Significantly, Vanier warned darkly that the day that Christians forgot the spiritual value of virginity – and by implication the high status attached to the clergy – they would "lose the sense of their vocation" and would fall prey to a "messianism of family" that would be as illusory and destructive as any social or political utopianism. Indeed, Vanier adamantly rejected Catholic Action's sacralization of sex, admonishing Christian couples that it was simply a form of self-fulfillment that, instead of celebrating human love and paternity as natural pleasures, arrogantly equated these with the act of adoring God.[57]

With its overtones of conflict between lay and clerical visions of Catholicism, Vanier's debate with Pelletier marked the rising cultural prestige of the new marital spirituality. During the late 1940s and early 1950s, Quebec Catholic commentators on marriage, like many of their European Catholic counterparts, overtly celebrated what they believed was the junction of family stability and personal happiness in the modern world. This, they believed, was achieved by the post-Depression generation of young adults who had effectively combined conjugal fidelity and a new eroticism in marital relations. Philippe Ariès, a conservative French Catholic and later a world-renowned historian of the family, discerned a cultural pre-eminence of youth in the post-war demographic tendency to younger marriages and the spacing of births within a few years, but a pre-eminence in which marriage, rather than marking the end of adolescence, was now the continuation of youthful "insouciance." However, Ariès did not deplore the existence of these attitudes; rather, he observed that conjugal love, which now included spiritual and erotic aspects, had made of marriage "no longer a customary necessity, but an existential situation."[58] Among Quebec Catholics, similar celebrations of the new spiritualized sexuality and its explicit links to the religious superiority of youth were frequently voiced. Marguerite Cardinal, for example, praised the efforts of the young generation to "reintegrate what is totally human in the divine" and argued that post-war youth's greatest field of endeavour would lie in anchoring conjugal fidelity on the pursuit of sexual intimacy.[59] The sociologist Gérald Fortin spoke of a "revolution of the sentiments" in Quebec that had paralleled that society's "economic revolution." Utilitarian marriages, he believed, had been replaced by those based on a notion of love that now sought a balance between "spirituality ... and animality in the marriage."[60]

However important the spiritualization of the sexual impulse was to post-war Catholic definitions of marriage and family in Quebec, it was still hedged about with a number of important limitations. Prior to the late 1950s, both conservative and reformist Catholic social activists were adamant that sex, in order to attain spiritual value, must be entirely confined to the marital relationship, and that there must be a psychological equilibrium between mutual pleasure and the desire of both spouses to collaborate in the work of divine creation – either from the perspective of a quest for spiritual perfection, or more usually, for the purposes of procreation. Social surveys such as those of the famous Kinsey Reports, the first of which on male sexual behaviour was published in 1948, posed a serious challenge to the Catholic spirituality of marriage. Although both Kinsey and Catholic family advocates accepted that the sexual impulse was the basis of human psychological and emotional identity, the implication of Kinsey's work was that sex was itself a form of mystical fulfillment and should be substituted for religion, which he believed merely imposed moral restrictions on natural imperatives. His work preached that any and all sexual activity could be considered spiritually fulfilling, and therefore sacred.[61] Interestingly, Catholic promoters of the new marriage doctrines rejected Kinsey's pansexualism for the same reasons that they criticized older Catholic mystical traditions of sexual abstinence:[62] it divorced the human sexual impulse from its creative imperative, and thus desacralized sexuality. In addition, for all the new openness of post-war Catholic attitudes, the spiritualization of sex was entirely restricted to intimacy between spouses. And because of the elevated spiritual value the new Catholicism attached to marriage, the attitudes of both clergy and lay experts towards premarital adolescent sexuality remained quite conventional until the late 1950s. For all the impact of new psychological knowledge regarding adolescent development, Catholic family reformers followed tradition in channelling and curbing adolescent expressions of sexuality until marriage, when it was allowed free rein.[63] Gérald Fortin stated the limits of Catholic thinking on sex when he drew a sharp distinction between current forms of romance-love, which he characterized as "materialist and childish," the Kinseyite celebration of sex as a tonic against "psychological and physical perils," and post-war concepts of Christian love, which he described as "more reasoned, stable, and complete." In his estimation, the two former types could lead only to free love, which amounted to the evisceration of the sexual impulse and the moral imperative. Sex, the sensual manifestation of love, must, in addition to providing individual satisfaction, have procreation and the acceptance of children as its primary purpose. "The sexual or conjugal act," Fortin maintained, had its place only within marriage, and "lost its human value if it is not the expression of a deeper and more spiritual love"[64] that was ultimately directed towards the cultivation and transmission of values.

"THE NEW FAMILY SEEKS ITS IDENTITY"[65]

At one level, the post-war Catholic assertion of marriage as the crucible of sexual fulfillment, emotional intimacy, and personal communion for both husband and wife was a conservative social imperative that sought to ease the path from youth to adulthood by removing a psychological barrier to family formation erected by the long Depression. However, the implication of the new primacy placed upon partnership and sexual adjustment as central to family stability formed the leading edge of a much larger effort to resituate the Quebec family in the context of what many believed was a period of bewildering social and cultural change. This not only entailed a restructuring and redefinition of who, in fact, comprised the family under the conditions of intense industrialization and urbanization, but, as a corollary, also subtly recast the lines of hierarchy and function within the family itself.

By shifting the essential function of the family away from economic production to the delicate calibration of the emotions and psychological
development of its members, family promoters, sociologists, psychologists,
and childhood educators who were overwhelmingly committed Catholics
continued to cast their thinking in what was at one level a conservative language aimed at restoring family solidarity. These efforts were especially
directed towards defining a type of family which would provide a field for
the exercise of male activity and leadership in the domestic realm.[66] By
contrast to family ideologies prevalent in English-speaking North
America,[67] in which the domestic sphere was viewed as the realm of
women's activity, and associated with the "female" qualities of privatization
and quiescence, the Quebec Catholic outlook preserved a strong public
emphasis for the family. This flowed from the personalist emphasis in
Catholic thinking on the family that advocated a continued connection
between the individual and his or her community. Thus, Catholic family
activists emphasized the family as a site in which the "male" qualities of
activity and public endeavour could be developed, and in so doing, elaborated a privileged role for the male head of the family as the personal link
between the domestic family and the wider world of public citizenship.
However, the effect of these attempts to readjust family structure and relations was to make the Quebec family the central nexus in which competing currents of democracy and authority were held in a creative equilibrium, with democracy represented by the tendency of youth to seek
horizontal, intra-generational forms of sociability, and authority seeking to
revalorize intergenerational hierarchies. In so doing, these Catholic
activists sought to heal the cultural fissure between generations that they
feared the Depression had opened in Quebec society. But ultimately, the
precarious balance they achieved in the years between the end of World
War II and the mid-1950s rested upon the continuing ability of the family
to fulfil a role that mediated between the private realm of individual emotional satisfaction and the public realm of social citizenship. Thus, by locating the family at the nexus of competing ideological currents, the Quebec
Catholic reconstruction of the family contained within it the potential to
make the family itself a contested political terrain if democratic cultural
aspirations, which post-war Catholics always interpreted in generational
terms, pierced the carapace of authority.

Writing in 1952, Father Gonzalve Poulin, director of the École de
Service Social at Université Laval, detailed the profound upheavals experienced by the French-Canadian working-class family during the process of
industrialization. The classic type of family, he stated, had either disappeared or was rapidly withering away. Traditional family solidarity, which
had been fostered by a joint productive effort of all family members,
taught the values of "acceptance of hard work, the praise of thrift and of

self-denial ... a type of asceticism in which the doctrine of the large family was considered one's Christian duty."[68] What was significant about this statement from one of Quebec's leading post-war social commentators was that it did not take the form of a jeremiad, or the nostalgic evocation of traditional family structures or practices. Casting the family's function as one of economic production had worked under the conditions of a largely rural economy, but under the conditions of urbanization and the industrial wage economy, Poulin believed, these economically-driven values had contributed to uprooting and proletarianizing the family. "The idea that family solidarity must be founded on a rigid structure of property," he intoned, "is definitely obsolete." Stability must be sought by reconceptualizing the family according to a different scale of values that would replace economic cohesion with something more profound. "We must," Poulin concluded, "accept the family as a spiritual and humanizing condition of our existence, and seek to deepen its essential functions," which he believed flowed outward from the new sacramental concept of marriage.[69] The totality of the emotional bond between husband and wife held within it enough creative potential to make of the entire family an intimate spiritual community that would "sanctify its members" by cultivating the "habits of intimacy" that would govern relations between spouses, parents, and children.[70]

This redefinition of the structure and functions of the family away from a productivist model towards a cultural typology which stressed the psychological qualities of intimacy and emotional fulfillment entailed, in turn, an explicit evocation of the closed, nuclear family as coterminous with the positive values of modernity. Indeed, a number of Catholic social commentators depicted the pre-Depression Quebec family as "autarchic": because it was a self-sufficient economic unit defined purely around the work of its members, it was incapable of eliciting in its members those human qualities that area essential to the complex social interactions of modern society. The post-war Quebec family, stated Catholic Action militant Camille Laurin in 1950, "has become a strictly functional entity, limited to its immediate members."[71] Catholic social commentators interpreted this development in largely positive terms, situating it within a long process of historical evolution in which the premodern "*grande famille*" (the extended kinship family) had been replaced by "family cells" limited to immediate kin. While some worried about the temporary social "disequilibrium" that would arise from the cultural clash between the two models of family, they maintained that only in the modern nuclear family could parents and children effectively cultivate "personal relationships," the type of spiritual, psychological, and emotional intimacy which alone could balance individual satisfaction and maturity with social responsibility. This combination of values was impossible to envision within the context of the older, economically-interdependent extended kin family, which fostered economic rather than cultural or spiritual values in its members.[72]

The attempt by a number of Catholic reformers to elevate the exclusive nuclear family as a new cultural ideal involved the explicit marginalization of other types of family entities that included wider kin networks or relied upon the interdependent economic contributions of all family members. Their concern was driven by the belief that the nuclear family, comprised solely of husband, wife, and children, *was* the essential touchstone of a type of modernity they earnestly endeavoured to promote, one conceived in terms of sharp, decisive contrasts in cultural mentalities between the values of the immediate past and those of the present. Social equilibrium, they maintained, was not the fruit of continuity and evolution, but of a rapid infusion of new spiritual values which would rapidly modify current practices. New patterns of social relations were seen as emerging not from the conflictual realm of politics or from models derived from the institutional Church, but from a personalist spirituality which in its conception of family privileged the emotional connections between parents and children and the psychological roles children learned by example and observation. In this respect, there was a nearly perfect fit between the ideal of the exclusive nuclear family and the type of spiritual culture characteristic of the Catholic Action movements.

Post-war social analysis of the Quebec family therefore took two forms. The first debated the extent to which "traditional" patterns of kin relations, characteristic of a recent rural past, persisted among urban dwellers and modified the ideal nuclear family type.[73] The second sought to use the cultural prestige of the nuclear family to reduce the Catholic Church's institutional control over child welfare, and to forge an alliance between lay expertise and the preservation of family relations. Journalists like Gérard Pelletier, who in 1947 published a celebrated inquiry into the management of Quebec's orphanages, explicitly assaulted the Church's official stance, which had elaborated the notion of the orphanage as a type of "extended" family in order to stave off pressure during the 1930s and wartime to establish a system of family placements. Pelletier was particularly concerned to apply Catholic Action's notion of rupture between "routine" and spiritual vitality to prove his thesis that for young children only the family could replace the family. Although he conceded that the young inmates of the Church-controlled orphanages were in good physical health, on the emotional level they "received about as much attention as an automobile chassis on the Ford assembly-line."[74]

Here, the debate over the extent to which Catholic Quebec had assimilated the nuclear family norm[75] stood as the shorthand for the adaptation of French-Canadian society to the social structure and cultural practices of the new urban society. More significantly, it attested to an agonized questioning among post-war social thinkers over whether Catholicism could incarnate and dictate the criteria of modernity, rather than simply undertake a passive defence of "tradition." Younger social scientists like Guy Rocher and Fernand Dumont who, as students, had taken a prominent role in Catholic Action,[76] were the most intent on identifying the connection between family nuclearity, the achievement of "modern" cultural values, and spiritual efficacy. They drew avidly upon recent studies undertaken by two Chicago sociologists: Horace Miner, who studied the transformations occurring in a rural parish at the end of the 1930s, and Everett C. Hughes, whose research, published in 1943, examined the adjustment of French-Canadian Catholics to urban life in the context of an industrial town. The ideas of these social investigators secured wide currency at Université Laval in the immediate post-war years, in large part because they provided scientific confirmation for Catholic Action's definition of the process of modernity as one of unbridgeable cultural rupture between two world views. Hughes, whose works enormously influenced a number of sociologists trained at Université Laval in the immediate post-war years,[77] described the institutional character of the "traditional" French-Canadian family, identifying as its primary function as economic, the "intimate union of the family and its farm plant"[78] in the rural districts of Quebec. Horace Miner applied the category of "folk society" – a concept which acquired axiomatic status in post-war Quebec social thinking[79] – to the rural parishes, painstakingly etching a family type that was "more primitive and outside of the European world," an economic unit in which all members of both ages and sexes shared in agricultural work. Such families, Miner stated, were extended rather than nuclear, including all relatives and direct descendants, and even collateral kin through the degree of third cousin. As outlined by the criteria of "folk society," the extended, economic family stood as the central pillar of "tradition." It was inseparable from the rythms of nature and incarnated the values of unchanging tradition and immobility[80] such that when confronted with rapid industrial transformation it could offer Quebec Catholics no spiritual sustenance or principle of social cohesion.

During the late 1930s and the immediate post-war years, Catholic family activists incorporated this American social analysis into their own ideas about the nature of the family, and drew a number of important corollaries. Miner's characterization of the extended, productive economic family as a "primitive," non-Western type challenged the way in which Quebec families, prior to the Depression, had lived both in rural areas and had adapted to the conditions of urban and industrial life. For many Quebec social commentators, especially those who had imbibed the personalist directives of Catholic Action, the "objective" sociological data of Miner and

Hughes proved that values associated with economic productivity and property – the values which had historically induced families to rely upon extended kin – would ultimately atomize and destabilize the family by bringing an individualistic ethos of competition and purely material pleasure into what should be a spiritual community. In 1939, Father Gonzalve Poulin reacted sharply against this type of economic family because it was a "modern ideal" that encouraged the "the slow slide of our family into materiality" by promoting values completely contrary to "our Christian family traditions."[81] Although Catholic reformers certainly evoked "tradition," their intention was not to shore up older notions of the extended family as a productive unit. It is significant that in the context of Quebec many Catholic commentators inveighed against federal welfare state interventions such as family allowances, juxtaposing the spiritual nature of the family against the "materialism" that these policies appeared to foster.[82] However, in articulating this opposition that insisted upon the primordial spiritual essence of the family, Quebec Catholicism, like the federal policies it critiqued, acted to subvert older family ideologies and practices.

As stated by Father Bernardin Verville in 1940, the "familial regime of the 'stem family'" had kept tradition intact, but French Canadians needed to evolve "in order to attain a higher life." He thus posited the family as "an institution of common life grouped around the parents" and as having an overtly psychological purpose: the fostering of "culture, relaxation, recreation, and conversation," an intimate refuge from the "promiscuity" of the outer world.[83] The portrayal of the extended family as incarnating a spiritually inferior scale of economic values in turn quickly eviscerated any lingering nostalgia in Catholic circles for the old-style rural family. The nuclear family, shorn of its extended kin, purged of its economic function, and directed towards the cultivation of the emotional and psychological maturity of its members, was the only entity capable of fostering the spiritual values that could orient Catholic society under modern conditions. Again, it must be reiterated that although Catholic activists claimed to be engaged in restoring the solidarity of "traditional" communities, their conscious purpose was to identify the family as the primary site where both the individual and the wider society would most intensely experience the cultural rupturing of mentalities between past and present.

"The biological and spiritual links that exist between parents and children," declared Father Gérard Dion, director of the School of Industrial Relations at Université Laval in 1959, "must be as strong as those that derive from economic dependency. A society where parental authority rested primarily upon the economic ties of children with their parents would already be a very sick one."[84] Dion's statement, which privileged the biological and spiritual nature of the family, implicitly evoked both the status that the closed nuclear family had achieved in post-war Catholicism and, in so doing, neatly articulated the far-ranging transformation in Catholic thinking that had occurred with the impact of Catholic Action on Quebec society after the mid-1930s.

The extent of this change is evident when Dion's lecture to the Semaines Sociales is contrasted with that of C.J. Magnan, delivered in the same venue in 1935. In praising the new spirituality of marriage, Magnan had defined the family's function as primarily educative, and had been especially concerned to demonstrate that husband and wife attained a higher degree of personal spiritual fulfillment by educating their children for family responsibilities. Thus far, his views testified to the inroads at that time of a newer sensibility in family relations, for he singled out the new "active" methods of childhood education for particular commendation, arguing for a "reasonable initiative" accorded to childhood "curiosity" as the stimulus to learning.[85] However much Magnan advocated newer concepts of marriage and family, however, his lecture also harkened back to an older vision of family in which the best educational environment was provided within the context of a multi-generational household. He thus evoked the presence of aged grandparents, who were honoured and supported as symbols of the continuity between present and past, and as living reminders to growing children of the need for family cohesion.[86] However, by the end of World War II, both working-class Catholic activists and middle-class social analysts concurred that the family could only fulfill its function of fostering personalist values if extended kin – by now a pejorative codeword for economic definitions of the family – were rigorously excluded in order better to allow for "*communication*"[87] – a term that expressed both the flowering of the sexual partnership and emotional intimacy between spouses, and the psychological connection between parents and children.

Indeed, this post-war conjunction between enhanced sexual intimacy, the restriction of the bounds of the family to parents and biological children, and the shifting definition of the family away from the economic towards emotional and psychological well-being was most apparent within the framework of the Catholic marriage preparation movement. As such, the nuclear family constituted the leading edge of the intergenerational contest of values which, for post-war Catholics, offered the ambivalent possibilities of either reconstructing solidarity between parents and youth, or of asserting a radical disjuncture between pre-war practices and the much-desired "modern" spiritual values. Thus, Fernand Jolicoeur, a leading activist within the Catholic labour movement, sounded the death knell of the economically-interdependent family in 1946, observing that such families were characterized by an "atrophy of paternal authority." Referring particularly to the wartime industrial environment, which had enlisted the labour of married women and adolescents in the name of increased production, Jolicoeur argued that such arrangements atomized the family by making wives and older children the economic competitors of the male breadwinner. Worse still, such families abjectly failed to assist young people in making the transition to adulthood, exposing them to a double proletarianization, the first, in which they had to work in appalling factory conditions, and the second, within the home itself, where in the interests of working to support the family, their psychological development was neglected and they were treated as inmates of a boarding-house.[88] What workers desired above all, declared the JOC in 1939, was "a home where it feels good to live and where one can be oneself," cultivating sincere and enduring bonds with family members.[89] In a brief presented to the Canadian Youth Congress in 1945, Catholic activists singled out the problem of working-class housing for special attention, arguing that the lack of separate lodging hampered the formation of stable nuclear families by "obliging young couples to live with their parents, with all the misunderstandings and quarrels" that would only lead to the disintegration of the marriage.[90] A home, in the view of marriage ideologists, "must shelter all the members of the *same* family; otherwise, its solidarity is in danger." Normal family development required a separate dwelling; only thus would the "emotional and moral life" of all its members find satisfaction.[91]

Specifically, elements of the marriage preparation course were designed to equip young couples to establish exclusive nuclear families. The course on budgeting the family finances aimed directly at enabling the newlyweds to secure their own separate dwelling. Indeed, many of these young people came to the courses expressing considerable frustration at the fact that they were unable to own their own homes and thus establish an independent identity as a married couple. One survey done in the mid-1950s revealed that only 5 per cent of newlyweds would be homeowners; another 10 per cent would live in a single room, 16 per cent with parents or in-laws, and 69 per cent in apartments.[92] As the Catholic labour journalist Renée Geoffroy hinted darkly in 1954, such intergenerational cohabitation caused by poor housing conditions would corrode the sexual bond between the married couple by creating a situation where "husband and wife would no longer recognize each other, and their relationship would be marked by indifference and routine. ... While love itself might not be dead, it is barely alive in such homes."[93] Consequently, young couples were repeatedly advised by the SPM that living with parents or in-laws was a prime cause of marital dispute and would stunt the emotional maturity of their own children. The sessions on intimacy and harmonization of personality had as their aim the resolution of the conflict by the couple themselves, and young women, in particular, were advised not to divulge anything about their intimate lives to their mothers. Family self-sufficiency meant independence from the interference of parents and in-laws as the bedrock of a solid marriage.[94] It was for this reason that, in addition to marriage preparation, one of the main thrusts of the Catholic Action movement was the advocacy of affordable housing for young, working-class families; having their own home would allow them the proper environmental setting to put into practice the new ideal of marital intimacy,[95] this being an ideal which could only be attained within the context of the closed nuclear family.

If post-war Catholic social commentators purveyed the notion that the transformation from the economic mentality of the kinship family to the emotional intimacy of the nuclear family epitomized the passage of their society from tradition to modernity, they were, however, aware of a profound dilemma. By eagerly accepting the loss of the family's productive functions, they also acquiesced in the fact that the family no longer played an exclusive role in educating children in those skills and values that would allow them to participate in the wider society. In other words, had the realization of modern values by their society made the family marginal given the role now played by public institutions?

Father Gonzalve Poulin observed in 1956 that the family was now dominated by the school and the mass media in the task of teaching values, and that the teacher had become "a competitor of the parents in the education of youth, in the transmission of the cultural heritage, values, ideals and modes of behaviour." To the older view that the school was simply the extension of the family, Poulin counterpoised the idea that the school was no longer simply a means or a mechanism that provided a continuum between the individual, the family, and the wider society, but now communicated the global values of the society directly to the individual child."[96] In order to find an exit from this conundrum, Quebec Catholic social thinkers drew upon strands of French personalism and American sociology. Both currents had, during the late 1930s, located the family as the key to recovering the meaning of community and, thus, as a counterweight to the impersonality and routinization of modern work, bureaucratic structures, and totalitarian ideologies which had completely submerged the individual personality. Although drawn from different sources, both strands of social thinking centred their attention on the role of the family in the emotional and psychological formation of its individual members. Both French and American currents insisted that the acquisition of a healthy, stable personality was the key to initiating and integrating the individual into the social relationships of larger modern communities. The Chicago sociologists and Talcott Parsons, both highly influential in post-war Quebec,[97] demonstrated that the loss of certain family functions, especially the productive and educative functions, was the inevitable concomitant of a process of industrialization that affected all Western societies.

Parsons, however, sought to counter this apparent marginalization of the family by asserting that the "private" nature of the family was in fact more important than its economic, customary, or institutional aspects. Through a creative use of Freudian psychology, Parsons underscored the family's critical role in the transmission of value-systems and learned patterns of behaviour. Among these, the most important were undoubtedly individual male and female sexual identities and roles, which he regarded as essential to the development of a psychological equilibrium. He thus inextricably linked the function of the modern family to the service it rendered to the development of the individual personality.[98]

While French personalists agreed with this interpretation of the family's changing roles, and privileged the cultivation of values through intimacy, they sought to avoid the privatizing implications of an over-emphasis on personal intimacy by revalorizing the family's role as a mediatory community that synthesized and transmitted private and public values. Emmanuel Mounier, for example, echoed an older-style Catholic social thought by characterizing the family as a "social cell," but he was emphatic that its purpose transcended biology or simple utility. Indeed, Mounier, the spiritual mentor of many post-war Catholic laity, was most concerned that the family should be completely detached from economic, institutional, or authoritarian ideologies that he excoriated as simply "reactionary," because they placed women and children under an unquestioning male authority.[99] Thus, personalists significantly altered the earlier corporatist tendencies of Catholicism, maintaining that, because the family was by its nature different from economic enterprises or the state, it could not serve as a model for hierarchical or authoritarian social ideologies. Its primary purpose lay rather in the terrain of psychology and the emotions, to promote the growth of the individual. However, personalists eschewed what they interpreted as the more extreme individualism of American sociology by retaining a notion of the family as a community with a definite institutional identity. Its central function derived from the fact that it was a community where children first learned values; that is, family taught them the nature of human relations. Stated at its simplest by the philosopher Jean Lacroix, "what the family transmits is its own self."[100] Thus, the family's essential function was to assist individuals in constructing a "personal universe" by combining social relations and "intimacy." The family's essence or "soul" was nothing less than the "free endeavour ... to develop its members mutually,"[101] or, as stated by Stanislas de Lestapis, to "*create personalism.*"[102] So all-encompassing was the cultivation of "intimacy" in the firmament of family functions that personalists warned against overly-confining expressions of this quality, because too much emphasis upon intimacy's purely interior aspect would stifle the development of the individual by severing the family from creative interactions with other forms of human community.[103]

In 1951, Claude Ryan, the national secretary of Catholic Action, exalted the family as the environment where "man is at his most natural, the most spontaneous, and the most free from conventions." The family was a privileged entity, one that allowed the individual to escape the constraints of routine by creating the conditions under which personality could express itself and flourish.[104] Ryan's view was thus part of a movement to reconstitute the family as a spiritual and emotional entity, a movement which drew further sustenance from another key element of the Catholic post-war sensibility: the fear that individual creativity and values – the "personal" universe – would vanish in the face of economic technique and bureaucratic institutions that reduced human qualities to the level of conformity. It was thus critical that Catholic reformers invest the family with those qualities of spontaneity and intimacy that would allow a privileged space for the individual to recuperate after working in industries and organizations that tended to eviscerate the personality.[105] In terms of the communitarian vision espoused by Catholic Action, family was, in contrast to the artificial organization of modern urban life, a "natural community" essential for the defence and nurture of a realm of "private sociability"[106] where instead of being simply "useful cogs," modern humans were endowed with "autonomy and dignity" and thus became "truly men."[107]

Encompassed under the rubric "intimacy," the attempt to recast family functions in terms of the individual personality expressed the hope of Catholic social scientists and family advocates that the immediate post-war era marked a series of fundamental cultural cleavages in which the family could be literally recreated and revitalized as both the dynamic and stabilizing factor in modern society. "The family as reconceived and lived anew as a community of destiny and love," proclaimed the French Jesuit Stanislas de Lestapis in 1957, "is a young idea, one that is courageous and all-conquering."[108] Undertaken during the late Depression and the immediate post-war years, Catholic attempts to restrict the nuclear family to immediate biological kin also signalled a transformation that social thinkers and activists wished to accomplish in the family's functions, from an orientation around reproduction in the interests of economic production to a more cultural emphasis that served exclusively the psychological and emotional needs of its members. "The mental health of our post-war society," warned the omnipresent Father Gonzalve Poulin in 1940, "is especially influenced by the emotional equilibrium and the totality of the affectionate life that is established within the family."[109]

Significantly, post-war Catholics maintained that the cultivation of intimacy encompassed the complete range of the modern family's functions. Speaking to the Semaines Sociales in 1940, Adélard Provencher stated that "humans live in families, and it is inside the family home where they experience the most sustained and intimate human ties."[110] His address made no reference to other family activities such as production or the technical training of children for specific economic roles which had hitherto been important family functions. So powerful was this leitmotif in Catholic discussion of the family that even conservatives who sought to revitalize rural life were constrained to admit that only by completely recasting the "traditional" family as a set of psychological and affectional ties[111] could it survive as a social entity. Thus, the colonization agent C.-E. Couture severely reprobated the relations that had developed between parents and youth on Quebec's family farms. Fathers increasingly treated their sons as "mere employees who are not even paid a fair wage." Young men and women, he warned, fled the countryside because "they did not receive any orientation from their parents. It has become more and more rare for families to discuss matters around the dinner table."[112] The juxtaposition of the materialistic values of the economically-interdependent family and the warm intimacy of the family table, which established enduring bonds between parents and children, precisely captured the way in which Catholic activists sought to transform the family. "Although the modern family has been shorn of its ancient economic and educative functions," declared Father Gonzalve Poulin, "this has freed it so that a greater expression of love can flourish. It is no longer interests but affections that enable members of the modern family to live together."[113]

The all-pervasive language of intimacy, however, possessed a very particular meaning in the context of post-Depression Quebec Catholicism, one that returned insistently to the problem of individual sexual identity as the nexus that harmonized the private and public functions of the family. If the new personalist ideals that so deeply marked a generation of Quebec Catholics dictated that the family could no longer be regarded as an economic or political entity, at the same time, they were emphatic that the family was not a mere collection of atomized individuals in pursuit of their own gratification. The building of a personal universe – the notion of community – was, above all, the way in which the individual psyche was shaped through encounter with wider social relations. In this respect, because personalism maintained that "sexual differences pervade each of the cells of the human organism,"[114] it in turn defined the family's absolutely essential function as the disciplining and education of the sexual impulse which formed the basis for all other systems of human law.[115] In asserting the "fidelity" of the French-Canadian family to its ancestral spiritual traditions, Father Gonzalve Poulin drew a portrait of family life in New France that was far less a historical account than a promotional tract for a post-war Catholic movement to reform the family by interweaving spirituality, emotional intimacy, and the need to define family stability through precise sexual identities:

The father, who presided over the life of the family group with a just and charitable authority, watched over the internal harmony of the home and the perpetuation of Christian traditions. As for the mother, she exercised that primacy of love that can only be founded upon a welcoming security, intimacy, and protection; by her self-effacement, devotion and understanding, she symbolized the soul of the family home. The oldest son was a living example for the younger children, a revelation of growing maturity. The sister, in her relations with other members of the family, incarnated womanhood, fostered the blossoming of mutual respect, and signified to her brothers that modesty that was the purification of sexual desire and thus constituted the first affirmation of the rights of the spirit over the body. ... Finally, the youngest maintained an atmosphere of grace and innocence within the home which was the centre around which all other family members converged.[116]

Although very much a conservative in his exaltation of the family as the fulcrum of post-war equilibrium, Poulin did not look back to the model of the multi-generational kinship family. Rather, his overriding concern for the moralization of the sex instinct dictated that his idealized *ancien régime* family was "of the 'nuclear' type," restricted to immediate biological kin, and actually quite limited in terms of numbers of children. It thus perfectly testified to the post-war conjunction between the new communitarian ideals of Catholicism and American social psychology, a fact that Poulin himself recognized in his conflation of "personalist spirit" with "individualism."[117]

In the post-war cultural climate shaped by Quebec Catholicism, such thinking had enormous resonance precisely because the discussion of family functions took as their point of departure the new Catholic doctrines that had recast the nature of marriage in terms of an emotional, intimate partnership in which the quality of the sexual relationship between husband and wife assumed overwhelming importance. Married love, the SPM courses in premarital counselling never tired of repeating, was "a gift of the self,"[118] and such a total communion at the sexual and emotional levels was only possible if husband and wife were psychologically secure in their identities of male and female. Catholic family activists in Quebec fully accepted the prevailing psychological wisdom that such identities were shaped very early in childhood, and that naturally, the most important element of family formation, after marriage itself, was to "apprentice children to conjugal life."[119] The guiding principle of the modern marriage ideal, aside from procreation and the cultivation of intimacy between husband and wife, was to enable children to in turn replicate this spiritual partnership in their own marriages by assuming the primary parental responsibility, "in a simple, truthful manner" to undertake by stages the sexual education of their children."[120]

However, it was at this point that the new Catholic family ideal exhibited a profound ambivalence. On the one hand, post-war Catholics of both conservative and reformist tendencies were agreed that education in sex roles and responsibilities was of primary importance and that it was best given by parents within the intimate setting of the family itself,[121] rather than in schools or in large group settings. However, contacts between Catholic activists and Quebec adolescents during the post-war period, particularly within the context of the SPM's premarital advice courses, seemed to reveal an appallingly low level of sexual knowledge and self-awareness exhibited by young men and women. The recurring phrase was that "sexual education and thus emotional maturity is clearly unsatisfactory,"[122] an impression borne out in surveys conducted at the end of the fourteen-week course. Even as late as 1962, 55 per cent of women and 57 per cent of men attending the courses stated that they had not been well informed by either parents or teachers about sexuality.[123] Of those who felt that their knowledge of these matters was adequate, what was more telling was that only 61 per cent of women and 34 per cent of men credited their parents with providing them with such information. A shockingly high percentage of young men and women had *never* been informed about marriage, sex, and reproduction before attending the SPM courses.[124]

The central purpose of these surveys was not to be an accurate measure of the state of sexual knowledge among post-war Quebec youth. Rather, they marked an ongoing attempt to define the family – and sexual identity itself – as the central terrain of cultural difference between the religious values of "youth" and those of the previous generation. Although on the one hand "intimacy," with all its connotations of sexual partnership, and the cultivation of the emotions represented aspirations for family solidarity and community in an ideologically troubled, impersonal world of mass institutions, its pervasive use by an influential group of Catholics also indicated that it was a slogan in an ongoing effort to elaborate a cultural polarization between present and past in Quebec society. Youth's lack of sexual awareness and therefore the firm psychological identity essential to form stable marriages and families was unanimously interpreted as the inadequacy and abdication of the previous generation of parents in fulfilling the primary function of the modern family: the psychological integration of all its members through education in sex roles.[125] Such failure would mean social disequilibrium because inability to impose the new model of family structure and function meant the persistence of older economic and extended-kin family ideals and practices. This, Catholic reformers believed, would prolong and intensify a state of cultural adolescence, a perpetual identity crisis that would affect not only the individual, but, because of the public character of the family, the wider Quebec society. It was to avert these consequences, therefore, that in the immediate post-war decade Catholic activists adamantly eschewed the privatization of the family, and continued to posit the necessity of institutional solutions such as the marriage preparation movement to foster the smooth integration of both the nuclear family ideal and the definition of the family as an emotional-psychological entity into the lives of ordinary Catholics.

"A DOMESTIC PONTIFICATE"[126]

In 1956, the Université Laval sociologist Fernand Dumont summarized the new post-war wisdom regarding the far-reaching structural and functional transformations that had affected the Quebec family. Following the trajectory of American sociology, he drew a striking portrait of the disintegration of the "traditional family" tied to a particular rural ecological setting, rooted in property, and forming a total institution which encompassed all educative and leisure activities. Such families, governed by a highly visible patriarchal authority, formed a "veritable clan in which the most distant kinship links are lived with intensity." By contrast, he observed, "the members of the modern family were bound by no ties other than those of the affections."[127] However, Dumont refused to contemplate that the displacement of the family from a number of these activities entailed either an atomization of the family unit into a congeries of individuals, or a radical disjuncture between a nuclear family restricted to a closed, private sphere and the "public" activities and values which occurred in the wider society. He employed the work of the French personalist thinker Jean Lacroix to argue that the loss of certain functions did not shatter or impair the meaning of the family. While the utility of the family would change according to alterations in social structure, it was more important, concluded Dumont, "to conserve ... its deeper *meaning*, its spiritual significance."[128] As just shown, in conceptualizing the family, post-war Catholic thinkers viewed it as the fundamental repository for the safeguard and creation of human values, the entity which fostered the assertion of the individual personality and the spiritual values of community in the face of "technique and automation."[129] However, if the family was the repository of those values of intimacy that underpinned human culture and individuality, it was not a refuge hived off from the outside world. Rather, it existed always in critical balance with other social institutions, participating in the process of clarifying their values. Dumont thus characterized the family as "the fundamental mechanism in which are elaborated the socio-cultural models of the social structure," and as such, it occupied a critical situation, the realm of "private sociability" or "social intimacy." It was within the nuclear family that the individual integrated the values of the culture by learning his or her "*role*" or achieving a firm sense of individual identity – a psychological process established through a critical dialectic between intra-family relations and the norms of the public realm – as defined by professional organizations, the civic culture, and the state.[130] And in a striking evocation of the language of Catholic Action diffused to thousands of young couples through the marriage preparation movement, Dumont explicitly declared that the creation of the new personalist family was the particular task of post-war youth, whose search for a new identity through rupture with the past would renew the institution of family by giving it "a new face."[131]

This optimistic interpretation of post-war family dynamics centred particularly around what Dumont maintained was a new equilibrium that he saw emerging between authority and self-expression. Personalists sought the antidote to modern bureaucracy and excessive individualism in the affectionate bonds that characterized family relationships. On a practical level, Catholic social commentators believed that this desired idea of community between parents and children was best expressed through common leisure and recreational activities, rather than the more formal relationships that supposedly characterized the older type of family oriented toward work and production. This transformation of the family allowed post-war Catholic family activists to assert that "a new type of family is in the process of formation," one that under the impact of "Freudian theories, the laws of modern psychology and the contact with American civilization," as Camille Laurin noted in 1950, had "altered the relationship between paternal authority and the children, encouraging a greater independence of the latter, and a greater indulgence and camaraderie on the part of the father."[132] They placed this new formula for family unity squarely within a more widely diffused "democratic" social and cultural imperative, which in the realm of family relationships "treated its members as equals, rather than relying upon the authority of the parents."[133]

At one level, this appropriation of the language of the "democratic family" by Quebec Catholics was not unusual in the immediate post-war years. Indeed, the same American social scientists and French personalists who informed the thinking of these Quebec Catholics had envisioned a "democratization" of family relations – the term was always used in connection with the rise of the nuclear, affectional family, which was regarded as the normal pattern of urban, industrial societies – to explain the cultural abyss that separated the structure and function of the modern family from older practices, which were increasingly dismissed as "authoritarian," "abnormal," and thus inimical to the development of both a balanced personality and social equilibrium. More recently, however, historians have subjected the post-war construction of the "normal democratic family" to increasingly savage criticism. Under their scrutiny, the promotion of the democratic family after 1945 was little more than empty rhetoric, an attempt by Anglo-Saxon social scientists to refurbish authoritarian ideologies that would ensure conformity to a middle-class, white, heterosexual, patriarchal family ideal. As a corollary, promulgation of the democratic family as "normal" effectively marginalized and in some cases criminalized such groups as homosexuals, sexually delinquent youth, and single mothers.[134] Although this analysis is undoubtedly attractive to historians that are strongly influenced by a postmodern revolt against what appear to be totalizing, monolithic formulations by a hegemonic elite of experts, its one-dimensional dichotomy of imposition and resistance fails to properly expose the nuances and ambivalences[135] which the "democratic family" ideal evoked among Catholic family promoters in Quebec.

Beginning in the late 1930s, a number of associations, such as the École des Parents, were formed in order to popularize the insights of psychological and educational experts so that parents could apply these insights in the task of child-rearing. Inspired by new methods of "active" education then current in a number of reform Catholic circles in France and Belgium, the central concern of promoters such as Mme Claudine Vallerand expressed what seemed at first sight a reversal of traditional lines of family authority: "the education of the parent through the child."[136] But Vallerand's vision was far from revolutionary, as it differed little from that of those Catholic commentators who had chosen as their primary concern maintaining family solidarity in the face of the corrosive effects of Depression and war. They frequently expatiated upon the need for a more "positive" concept of child-rearing, one that simply did not regard the child as the passive recipient of parental commands that must be punctiliously obeyed.[137] The communal imperative, stated one observer, could be so overweening that the family would fail "to respect the child's right to individuality." A sense of responsibility for the common good of the family could be best fostered in children by permitting them "a just autonomy."[138] Psychologists and childhood educators were quick to admonish parents that they must navigate carefully in attempting to nurture the child's need for individual self-expression and the necessity of authority, which alone could ensure the cohesion of the family community. "Parents," advised Marguerite St. Germain-Lefebvre, "must never exercise their authority in a dictatorial manner," but must do so "with respect, dignity, and love, remembering at all times that they represent divine authority."[139]

Because it sought to modulate individual satisfaction with the discipline of community, however, the personalism so influential among post-war Quebec Catholic activists was adamant on the continuing need for authority. Although they severely castigated "paternalism" as obsolete, family reformers were adamant that authority was essential to channel the potential clash of individual wills into a set of reciprocal, cooperative relationships. "We are witnessing," stated Catholic Action's brief to the Canadian Youth Commission, "the emergence of a democratic type of family where conjugal and familial activities are undertaken with the free consent of the father and the mother, and even of the children, although these remain under the direction of the head of the family."[140] However, it was believed that the most effective type of parental authority was one that was supple and less overt: its principal task was to enable the individual to internalize a sense of responsibility, or values, by establishing an atmosphere within the family that would "prepare the child to live without external constraint."[141] According to Father Stéphane Valiquette, parents, and especially fathers, needed to shed the old-fashioned role of "judge, executioner, and torturer" that obsolete concepts of family relations forced them to assume. Citing the damage to the fragile psyches of younger children, many of whom populated post-war psychological clinics complaining that their fathers reminded them of Hitler, Valiquette emphatically stated that the modern father must incarnate "gentleness and joy." However, he cautioned that a "paternal firmness" associated with a respect for authority was even more essential because, psychologically, children were a mass of undirected instincts and emotions.[142]

Thus, at the level of relationships between parents and children, the "democratic family" remained a rather limited concept, one associated not with a formal egalitarianism derived from political democracy with its insistence on universal suffrage, but one in which parents were consciously preoccupied with making their home a "proper setting for the physical, intellectual, and moral formation of their children."[143] For all of their child-centred language, groups such as the École des Parents sought to enlist the expertise of psychologists and child educators in reasserting the authority of parents to directly monitor the emotional maturity and sexual identity of children and youth. However, in a social context in which the education of children and adolescents, and the oversight of family organizations themselves, had long been the purview of the institutional Church, any attempt to endow parents with an independent expertise was tantamount to an assault on the traditional prerogatives of the clergy.[144] Indeed, although the 1944 debate between Claudine Vallerand and the Jesuit Jean Laramée focused on whether the new egalitarian language of child-centred pedagogy sufficiently emphasized the acquisition of self-discipline, the subtext was, in fact, whether the "modern" family, with its omnicompetent parents applying a new psychological expertise, or the Church-controlled school or college, was the proper educational environment. Vallerand fired a parting shot at the Catholic clergy, musing that while the school and college "regime of monolithic authority, of an ominipotent director who, in the image of God, lone creates, ordains, and permits" offered the advantage of simplicity, it actually required less thought, care, and "especially less competence" than the parent who began from the premise that "the child is the principal agent of his own formation."[145] In this critically important respect, the expression of the ideal of the "democratic family" formed part of the same impulse that sought to postulate an overt cultural and moral rupture between the values of "traditionalism" and those of "modernity." A major component of this disjuncture was provided by affirming an overt connection, in the post-war period, between psychological expertise and parenthood. For example, Gérard Lemieux, director of the Institut Familial of the Université de Montréal, employed a generational metaphor in asserting that for those men and women educated in the 1930s "*the family could not serve as our guide or stimulus*" for new ideas of parenting. He thus explicitly linked the "democratization of family relations," by which he meant "the abandonment of a certain type of paternalism in the name of the values of personal autonomy,"[146] to the new lay Catholicism that was coextensive with Quebec's post-Depression experience.

In tandem with the spiritualized sexuality of the marriage preparation movement, the promotion of "democratic" family relations by the Catholic Action movements was a key component of an attempt to re-establish intergenerational solidarities that many believed had been eroded by the cultural and social disruptions of Depression and wartime. In an article written in 1944, Jeanne Benoît, one of the national leaders of the Jeunesse Étudiante Catholique, and later to become a vocal advocate of women's rights, a federal minister, and governor-general, outlined the ideal of a power-sharing between parents and adolescents in the family as a post-war antidote to "materialist concepts of family output." Parents, as "heads of the family," must continue to direct and orient relationships and activities, but this authority, she maintained, "is often shared with the older children of the family. This type of arrangement, by which the adolescent acquires a voice in the 'family council' is entirely normal. ... While parents hold the authority, our role is that of collaboration ... a collaboration that must be as complete as possible although it must not supplant parental authority. ... Without the cooperation of youth in the running of the family, the home would have no attraction other than of a cheesy boarding house where one would enter or leave freely, unceremoniously and with scant politeness."[147] At one level, the insistence of Catholic youth leaders on the urgent need to develop relations of "friendship" and "camaraderie" between parents and adolescents sought to import into the family the horizontal, more egalitarian concepts of sociability that had evolved among middle-class and working-class Quebec youth during the 1930s. "Our young people," stated David Bosset of the Ligue Ouvrière Catholique, "no longer accept a system of prohibitions ... because our current way of life actually promotes greater freedom." However, the onus in fostering this new cultural mentality lay with the parents, who, above all, "must become real friends for their children, and enter into the spirit of the game where relationships have become more equal."[148] Parents were explicitly admonished that in addition to addressing their adolescents in a less authoritarian tone, "as companions, not as supervisors or masters who try to direct their activities or impose their own views,"[149] they were themselves to adopt a more youthful, approachable style. "José," the family advice columnist of the *Front Ouvrier*, exhorted parents to shed "their kill-joy image." "Don't stand in the way of them going out with friends," she urged; rather, let them invite their friends over and organize "small parties" for them; "that way, you will convince them that you are understanding friends and really young at heart."[150]

However, it must be recognized that these portraits of more "democratic" relations between parents and adolescents were not intended as descriptions of reality,[151] but rather sought to enlist Catholic youth behind a refurbished ideal of family relations. Two main concerns governed the deployment of egalitarian notions of "camaraderie" and more open notions of family decision-making. By downplaying older notions of hierarchy, Catholic activists hoped to re-initiate adolescents into a sense of responsibility for family formation that they feared had been seriously attenuated during the hiatus of Depression and war. It was with this goal in mind that Gérard Lemieux proclaimed in his presidential address to the Montreal diocese SPM that social reconstruction depended upon "the return of youth to the family home and the return of parents to the abundant and promising life of youth."[152] Second, the reconnection of older and younger generations had become even more imperative in light of the recent conflict with totalitarian ideologies. During the immediate post-war years, many leaders of the Catholic Action movements accepted that fascism and communism had succeeded in enrolling thousands of discontented young men by strategically making use of the notion that youth constituted a separate culture apart from the wider society. It was to refute this notion that Marcel Côté, president of the Jeunesse Indépendante Catholique declared in 1946 that "young people do not form a world apart. They are in solidarity with the whole society ... as they are the sensitive barometer which faithfully registers the health of the society made up by their families."[153] Thus, the elaboration of a common set of values – a partnership – that would reconnect the older and younger generation was deemed essential to the definition of a viable notion of democratic, participatory citizenship. Again, it should be reiterated that this did not rest upon the assertion of a formal political type of equality between youth and adults, or "self-determination" by adolescents. Like a number of their Anglo-Canadian counterparts, post-war Catholic reformers stressed the idea of the adolescent as a "citizen-in-training"[154] who was progressively initiated into civic life, first through the medium of family relations in the home and then in the school and recreational organizations through a flexible adult leadership provided by parents and sympathetic adult volunteers who had imbibed the new "pedagogy of *self-government* (restricted to certain zones)."[155] Young people should be allowed some free initiative in cultural, spiritual, and sporting activities, but democratic participation was limited to consultation rather than actual decision-making, with citizenship emphasized in its cultural and social, rather than overtly political aspects.

But how to discern, calibrate, and institutionalize the proper equilibrium between democracy and authority that ought to exist within the family, and by extension, in the wider post-war society? Did the nuclear family, oriented exclusively around a marital partnership that emphasized cultivation of sexuality and the affections, and the psychological maturity and satisfaction of its members, provide sufficient cohesion to operate as a personalist community that was competent to fulfill its institutional task, the transmission of spiritual and cultural values? The key barometer that indicated the thinking of Catholic family activists on these issues was the amount of attention they devoted to the status and role of the father within the family. Recent historical treatments of English Canada have emphasized both the extent to which post-war ideas of fatherhood became dissociated from notions of active partnership in child-rearing, and identified almost exclusively with the material aspects of being a breadwinner, and that notions of masculinity tended to fixate upon a flight from the family home into a type of escapism in which men asserted themselves by combining consumerism with a nostalgia for wilderness endeavour.[156] During the immediate post-war period, however, Quebec Catholic discussions of the meaning of modern fatherhood emphatically distanced themselves both from authoritarian concepts of patriarchy, usually identified with obsolete models of family, and from the economically-driven concepts current in English Canada. Instead, they articulated an overt association between fatherhood and the family home, insisting upon a male domesticity – which they termed a "spiritual paternity" – that retained the notion of male headship of the family, not as an ascribed status, but achieved as a function of the father's active involvement as a partner in child-rearing.

Post-war Catholics maintained that the anchoring of the father in the family home was imperative for two reasons. First, the personalism that influenced so many Catholic laypeople firmly projected the family as an entity that forged relationships that were in the first instance intimate and private, but more importantly served to orient the public conduct of the individual in the wider society. Thus, the family most definitely bridged the private and the public, and only the presence of the male head in the home, who brought the "rational" values of the profession and the political order to constrain the excessive and at times cloying emotional intimacy of the family ensured that the wife and children would experience the interaction of private and public values that alone would make them complete and mature persons. As such, male domesticity was regarded as a necessary corrective to a number of potential "deviations" inherent in the nuclear family. Second, it should be remembered that much post-war Catholic social thinking in Quebec remained tied to a corporatist sensibility, one that eschewed compulsion and excessive state planning and regimentation. This corporatist current identified the family and voluntary civic organizations as both the fundamental organizations of modern society and the primary agencies that socialized youth into the values of citizenship. In particular, this type of corporatism was especially concerned to elaborate a set of relationships within the family itself, and between the family and other civic organizations. The key dynamic to this "familist corporatism" was the continued valorization and exercise of male authority both within the family and the wider culture. In this way, post-war Catholicism in Quebec preserved an emphatically "public" definition of the family as an institutional channel between religious values and the socio-political order. The family, in addition to its "private" functions of providing individual emotional security and psychological adjustment, stood at the centre of a public culture of democratic voluntarism which was expected to act as a necessary restraint upon the aggrandizing tendencies of the modern state.

Writing in 1954, Jean-Marc Chicoine took aim at the "conspiracy of silence" with which modern life surrounded fatherhood. From his perspective, modern notions of masculinity accentuated either the movie star or the successful businessman whose status was acquired by attention to social position or dominance over others. The cultural power of these images fostered a view among young men that "being a father was not something that required much talent or special aptitudes." In the end, the father's status in the modern household derived purely from the fact that he was a "breadwinner."[157] The restriction of the male familial role to a purely economic one, a process that in the post-war years was encouraged by federal social policies that sought to reconstruct patriarchy by identifying the male head of family as the sole provider,[158] raised, however, a particular problem for Catholic family activists. Because they defined the nuclear-affective family as one of the key indicators of their society's allegiance to a more spiritually-authentic modern culture, the evidence that the modern father's contribution to the family seemed to be confined to the act of procreation and material provision appeared to them both as a sign of religious decline and as a symptom of a prolonged and debilitating identity crisis that could only paralyze their society. Indeed, the "bewildering materialism"[159] exemplified by defective and truncated notions surrounding the person of the male head of family seemed to indicate a childish hankering for the much-maligned economic extended-kinship family.

Worse still, for those young men inspired by the heroic ideals of Depression-era Catholic Action, the paucity of male roles attested to their own social superfluity as perpetual adolescent acolytes held in tutelage to a ruling elite of celibate clerical polymaths. As Gérard Pelletier explained in 1951, while the Church-dominated educational system successfully prepared young women for their maternal vocation, the clerical education offered in the *collèges classiques* taught young men that their choice lay between the priesthood, which was assigned the highest status as a spiritual vocation, and the world of professional work, which was placed on a lower scale of value as being concerned with material things. Clerical educators failed to teach young male Catholics that "their highest and most authentic vocation was marriage" and the concomitant spiritual responsibilities of fatherhood. The consequences, Pelletier maintained, were deleterious for religion and family life in Quebec. At the level of institutions and society, by inducing young males who did not opt for clerical vocations to conceive their work roles in purely material terms, this type of education distanced middle-class professional men from the Church and created a "disoriented laity" – a whole class of psychically-damaged men who oscillated between "passivity ... and internal rage," and were thus incapable of assuming the tasks of social leadership. But worse, within the family, the clergy's failure to educate men for fatherhood led to an abdication on the part of husbands and fathers: specifically, their consequent failure to recognize the primacy of their conjugal vocation rendered marriage a "deception" for wives, which in turn introduced a dangerous spirit of dissension and disintegration into the home.[160]

Although not all Catholic Action militants would have sanctioned Pelletier's vocal anticlericalism, many of those who were influenced by the Catholic youth and family movements regularly lampooned those pathetic fathers who were content with being a "banker provided by biology,"[161] whose interaction with the family consisted of being "squirreled away behind their newspaper and pipe, emerging in a rage only when bothered by their children, or when their wife needs a disciplinarian to make the older children obey."[162] Given the seamless connection drawn between the Catholic doctrine of the indissolubility of marriage and its new definition as an emotional, spiritual partnership in which both husband and wife could derive happiness and fulfillment, the purely economic definition of fatherhood constituted a sure recipe for disaster. "We need look no further for the reasons for the emancipation of modern wives, why they refuse to have children," declared "Miriam" in 1944, "than the fact that husbands come home only to enjoy good home-cooking, read the paper, put on their slippers and go to bed." Such male abdication from family roles was entirely subversive of the Catholic personalist definition of marriage as a spiritual community: it led only to compartmentalization, lack of communication, solitude, and ultimately marital breakdown[163] because its consequence would create such discontent as to force married women themselves out of the family and into the workforce in a quest for psychological satisfaction. For post-war Catholic family activists, the key to reconstructing family solidarity lay in elaborating an explicitly affectional, educative role for men within the family, one in which the head of family would delicately combine the obligations of fatherhood and professional work in "becoming the companion of his wife and the associate of his children."[164]

During the decade following World War II, Catholic commentators on the family defined the father's role within the family from the standpoint of the values of intimacy and partnership that governed the newer concepts of marriage that had emerged at the end of the 1930s. This does not mean that Catholic activists minimized the father's role as sole economic provider. Indeed, one of the explicit goals of the Catholic Action movements was to ensure, both through state initiative and through the marriage preparation courses, that wives not work outside the home after marriage and that male wages be sufficient to entirely cover the cost of raising a family.[165] However, because Catholic thinking on marriage and family drew so heavily upon the notion of different, but complementary male and female psychologies, social commentators were explicit that *both* mother and father were jointly responsible within the home for child-rearing,[166] a partnership whose balance and equilibrium urgently depended upon a strongly exercised and well-defined male paternal role. While most accepted that mothers were primarily responsible for nurturing the affections, this alone was not enough to create that familial climate of psychological equilibrium in which individuals could develop their full potential. The father's contribution must impart to the family a logical direction that brought to children and adolescents the rational values they would need to make the successful transition to adulthood.[167] Théo Chentrier, a Montreal child psychologist, reminded his readers that while children belonged to the mother through the biological order, the father represented the infusion of the higher spiritual values of the social and spiritual order. He affirmed that the modern father must incarnate the characteristics of youth that gave a creative direction to society. Within the family, the ideal father was a type of "coach," a constant presence whose "silent authority" enthusiastically inspired the creative initiative of his children, yet regulated and moderated their instincts.[168] "Whoever thinks that the maternal role is primordial," observed his colleague in 1951, the psychoanalyst André LaRivière, "is in error."[169]

The association of male headship with the value of rationality and the gradual process of educating instincts directed attention to the relative instability of the affectional nuclear family as a new cultural ideal in post-war Quebec. The continued evocation of the need for male authority – albeit an authority that did not flow from traditional allegiance to juridical patriarchy, but from a respect earned from the father's service and dedication to the well-being of wives and children[170] – expressed the fears of a number of post-war Catholic activists and social scientists that absent or ill-prepared fathers could pervert the internal psychodynamics of the nuclear family, and thus sever the bond between the family and the cultivation of civic values. Writing in 1954, Laval sociologist Guy Rocher noted that the isolation of the modern nuclear family caused a "hypertrophying of the maternal figure." By exclusively monopolizing the young child's affectional life, this excessive mothering provoked psychological imbalance as the developing emotional life fluctuated wildly between extremes of love and hate. Echoing Gérard Pelletier, Rocher lamented the fact that the idea of the father as a simple breadwinner did nothing to modulate this emotional chaos. Rather, because the father was associated in the child's subconscious with the competitive, materialistic values of the world outside the family, contact with the father only deepened and prolonged the adolescent identity crisis, and perpetuated a male domestic enfeeblement that would only further institutionalize a matriarchy.[171] Catholic Action militants like Rocher could only view this type of development with alarm, because they associated excessive feminization with an inferior type of spirituality that both mired the individual in a debilitating routine and dependence on the clergy and "traditional" religious devotions and promoted a cultural conformity that would weaken the personality in the face of modern mass institutions. The result of such a divorce between fatherhood and domesticity would be the complete privatization of the nuclear family, thus reducing the family to a unit of material and emotional consumption which fails to prepare its members for participation in the full life of the civic culture.

Indeed, it was the constant and effective presence of the father that brought the values of professional endeavour, work, and social and civic action into a creative synthesis with the intimate life of the family. This was a double necessity, both from the perspective of the family's responsibility to educate children and adolescents into maturity through the transmission of cultural values, and also from the standpoint of making the family a satisfying social and cultural environment for women. The personalist philosopher Jean Lacroix reminded his readers that one of the sources of the feminist movement lay in married women's rejection of the notion that they were simply biological and educative instruments for perpetuating the family. In order to overcome this source of family disintegration, he urged husbands to bring into the family circle and communicate to their wives those values of creativity and renewal that were present in public institutions and organizations, thus lifting women out of mundane, entirely emotional preoccupations. In turn, fathers themselves would experience greater communion by participating with their wives in the process of educating their children,[172] and the result would be a seamless relationship between the values of the public and private realm. In a similar vein, the Catholic labour journalist Renée Geoffroy urged in 1954 that "our education as union wives will not be accomplished by ourselves alone. It is the duty of our husbands to open up to us the full extent of their work, the necessity of trade unionism, so that as a consequence, union life will be fully integrated with our family life and shape the education of our children."[173]

It should be reiterated at this point that personalists, while endorsing the idea of the affectional, nuclear family, refused to view the family as a private entity. Jean Lacroix, for example, defended the concept of the "open family," and while he eschewed any facile elision between family and state, desiring at all costs to safeguard the crucible of human values and creativity from the inroads of totalitarianism, he argued that the values taught within the family in fact served as the foundation for the civic order, which he termed the "nation."[174] Catholic social commentators on both the "right" and "left" of the ideological spectrum emphatically endorsed the necessary link between family and nation. Esdras Minville, director of the École des Hautes Études Commerciales at the Université de Montréal and a leading social corporatist, declared in a post-war study of citizenship that the family was the basic cell and wellspring of the nation. "'We pass from the family to the nation without any break in continuity, because both are dedicated to the transmission of life.'" [175] And although younger social democrats like Fernand Dumont certainly sought to revise the more authoritarian, institutional concepts of fatherhood inherent in the corporatist vision, they still chose to express their ideal of the "democratic" family in a way that retained fatherhood as the key element that permitted "a profound opening of the family onto the central issues and values of civic life."[176]

The post-war Catholic insistence upon the father's strong spiritual and educative presence in the family was, therefore, indissolubly related to a personalist concept of public and spiritual order in which fatherhood was the operative principle. This can best be described as a male domestic pontificate – the term is Abbé Groulx's – if "pontificate" is kept close to its Latin root of "pontus," a bridge or connection. This bridge operated, first, with fathers creating and monitoring the biological relationships between family members, and then, through exercise of a spiritual mandate, his linking of wives and children to God. Finally, through the role of the father as a male citizen, the family as an institution was joined to the nation and the wider political culture. As elaborated by Father Gonzalve Poulin, "fatherhood imitates God more closely than any other creative activity. It imitates Him in its intimate life, for God is first and foremost a father. The Holy Trinity is constituted by personal relations that can only be understood through membership in a family, because it reproduces these in tangible form."[177] Poulin then went on to outline the essentially political concept of the domestic pontificate: "The father ... exercises here, depending upon God alone, his kingship of prime mover. His wife and children belong to no one other than him. If they belong to the Fatherland, the Nation, to Humanity, they do so only through him. ... And these bonds by which he has attached them to his person are bonds that no power – not his own, not even that of God – can ever break, because they are the ties of blood."[178] "Whoever becomes a father," declared the Jesuit Stéphane Valiquette in 1952, "becomes at that same moment the keystone of familial society, which is itself the cell of that larger society that we call the nation. If you remove the father, the whole edifice crumbles."[179]

The fact that fatherhood was viewed as being the central nexus between the nuclear family as a spiritual-psychological entity and the family as an entity occupying a place in the post-war political order testifies to the existence of a powerful strand of familist corporatism among Quebec Catholic reformers at that time. During the years between 1940 and 1955, this type of corporatism sought to maintain and further elaborate an explicit institutional identity for the family, and, in so doing, sought ways to limit and constrain modern democracy by attempting to harmonize it with models of patriarchy in which power flowed from God to male heads of families. Familist corporatism rested upon the central premise, frequently stated in Catholic social commentary, that the "family is the cell of society,"[180] and that any lasting reconstruction of the social order must begin by instituting measures that reaffirmed family cohesion and solidarity. During the 1930s, corporatism had become synonymous with a number of authoritarian European regimes, which is why, in the post-war period, Emmanuel Mounier and a number of his associates were either sceptical of, or hostile to, ideas that founded social authority upon a continuity between family structure and the organization of industry or the state.[181] However, during both the Depression and World War II, Quebec had remained comfortably within a framework of political liberalism, and, for Catholic activists of both "left" and "right," corporatism was thus not tainted with associations with fascism. This enabled an array of Catholic-inspired publications, business organizations, labour unions, and social thinkers to move seamlessly between definitions of democracy and notions of social reconstruction that were premised upon corporatist concepts which stressed family solidarity.[182]

How easily corporatism and democracy could be synthesized by Quebec Catholics is best exemplified in an article written by Gérard Pelletier and

Alexandrine Leduc, wartime student leaders of the Jeunesse Étudiante Catholique who later became principal advocates for left-leaning personalist currents within post-war Catholicism. While the two were vocal promoters of Catholic Action's horizontal youth sociability and its notion of a more "democratic" spirituality, they enthusiastically cited a publication by Marshal Pétain which declared that "'the right of the family is prior to and superior to that of the individual.'"[183] What concerned them was less the authoritarian character of the Vichy regime than the usefulness of Pétain's slogan in publicizing a concept of social and political organization that they believed was superior to the rather individualistic type of liberalism that had dominated the political scene in Quebec prior to the Depression. They would have emphatically agreed with the perspective of Esdras Minville, who in 1938 had called for a policy of "economic readaptation" that was conceived not "from the standpoint of the individual, that unstable and fragmentary social unit, but from the perspective of the family, the mother-cell and true foundation of society."[184] Again and again during the 1940s and early post-war years, Catholic reformers called for a "family policy" that would enshrine a new social order, anchored not on the individual, but on the family as the basic unit.[185]

What underlay this type of thinking was a desire to bring the family, with its attributes of internal hierarchy and solidarity, into a creative dialectic with notions of modern democracy. Post-war Quebec Catholic activists, although working within a framework of cultural and social democracy, followed the lead of a number of influential European personalists and refused to assign an absolute notion of good to political democracy, with its grounding in universal suffrage and majority rule.[186] Pre-war liberal democracy, many Catholics believed, had over-privileged the individual at the expense of natural communities such as the family, and had led to increasing anarchy in the economic and social realm, revealed most catastrophically in the Great Depression. Any lasting reconstruction would have to bring to bear the value of solidarity that was incarnated in the institutional family, with its ongoing reciprocal dynamic between "private" – the fostering of individual psychological well-being – and "public" – educating children and youth into the culture of modern citizenship. In both realms, the family's central foundation was the explicit connection betwen spiritual and political fatherhood. However, in post-war Catholic thinking on the family, there was an acute awareness that because of the cultural prestige of "democracy" – evident even in new ideals of family relationships – authoritarian models of fatherhood would fail at legitimizing the new corporatism. "Modern democracy," observed Father Poulin, "does not so much reject authority as it does one that is imposed." What he advocated was precisely the more open, accessible type of fatherhood elaborated in Catholic personalist concepts of the "democratic" family, one in which "authority was acquired or deserved."[187] Expressed in familial models in which individual realization was a function of the corporate good, the intention was to create an equilibrium that would balance the tendency of democracy towards excessive individualism. In transposing family authority to the public sphere, familist corporatism hoped to both maintain a framework of parliamentary institutions and universal suffrage and to institutionalize consultative mechanisms, such as a Superior Council of the Family, which would recognize the family as a constitutive unit of society, give family experts and organizations a voice in the shaping of state policy, and, most importantly, establish a chain of civic organisms that would stand between the individual citizen and the state[188] by organizing voluntary efforts in ways that would diffuse and deflect any encroachments of the state upon the rights of families. Post-war promoters of family stability sought to employ a refurbished political theory of the family – namely, familist corporatism – that enlisted voluntary civic organizations to assist the family in resisting the encroachments of the modern state. This, they believed, would enhance the authority of the male head of the household. In advancing this view of the family, they hoped to limit "democracy" by containing it within an institutional framework in which both the private and public identity of all family members was a function of the effective spiritual capacity of the father. Familist corporatism thus articulated a fragile equilibrium that held in balance the tensions its proponents discerned in society between egalitarianism – or individual self-realization – and the continuing need for authority – or paternalism. However, its politicization of the family was to leave it vulnerable to contestation that stemmed from the social aspirations of youth and women and ultimately compelled the family's privatization.

4

"The Defeat of the Father"[1]

The Disaggregation and Privatization of the French-Canadian Family, 1955–1970

Those young people who seek sympathetic understanding from adults frequently find that they are speaking to overgrown teenagers.[2]

Speaking to an audience of Catholic bishops in 1970, Philippe Garigue, the eminent Université de Montréal sociologist, forcefully underscored the transformations that had occurred in Quebec's Catholic families during the 1960s. He described an older Catholic ideal of the family unit: it was a family anchored on an affectional relationship between husbands, wives, and children and which required constant mutual self-sacrifice, charity in the exercise of authority, and the "communion" of spouses in the task of procreation and child-rearing, by which he meant a common participation of husband and wife in the process of divine creation. However, Garigue informed his listeners that this idea of the family unit, which a legion of Catholic commentators and social activists had laboured to uphold as the fundamental "social reality," was now "in crisis," "besieged" among a younger generation of Quebecers[3] whose conduct, ranging from juvenile delinquency to public flauntings of sexual openness to wholesale defections from Catholic teaching on birth control, had utterly desacralized and corroded the solidarity of the Catholic family, resolving it into a collection of disaggregated individuals in pursuit of individual self-fulfillment.

At one level, Garigue's speech can be read as a conservative fulmination against the forces of a rampant secularism, the final lament of old Catholic Quebec as it sought to reassert traditional family values in the face of a series of challenges posed by student revolt, the sexual revolution, women's liberation, and the loss of religious influence within the educational and social welfare system. However, Garigue's speech contained a number of puzzling assertions that compel a reassessment of the precise relationship between Catholicism, Quebec families, and the timing and nature of social and cultural change in post-war Quebec. Significantly, in accounting for the disconcerting magnitude of family disaggregation in the 1960s, the Montreal sociologist did not identify as primary forces those secular ideologies generally associated with this period of cultural revolution, namely, feminism and youth revolt. Rather, he blamed two currents within Catholic tradition for the crisis.

First, he stated that the Church had fundamentally erred in assigning sacramental status to marriage, but not to the family itself. By so exalting the marriage partnership and the need for emotional intimacy between husband and wife, Catholicism had lost sight of an essential element of balance: the need to infuse the same affectional values into parent-child relationships. The absence of such intimacy had allowed authoritarian, pre-Christian concepts of duty and private property to persist, which, Garigue argued, simply fuelled the anger of Quebec's young people against constricting family structures and morality. Second, Garigue complained that Catholic tradition had become thoroughly subservient to a "personalizing individualism," which had led Roman Catholics to privilege a cultural quest for individual values and satisfactions that ultimately isolated the individual household in modern society, and allowed media, schools, and government to usurp the authority of parents and carve out relationships with separate constituencies within the family unit itself. By failing to articulate ways in which the family as an institution could remain the foundation of society, and by so elevating the individual, Quebec Catholicism had, in Garigue's estimation, consciously devalued the family and had ultimately caused its invisibility and irrelevance as a mediator between the individual and the state.[4]

Several considerations emerge from this conservative sociologist's surprising arraignment in which Catholicism did not play its expected political role of conservator of the tradition of the institutional, hierarchical Quebec family. The deliberate weakening of this connection began in the mid-1950s when a vocal chorus of Catholic educators, youth workers, psychologists, and marriage counsellors, both lay and clerical, became acutely aware of what they interpreted as highly sexualized youth subcultures and patterns of behaviour which they feared functioned outside the hierarchical lines of family authority and adult role models. According to a strand of Catholic personalism that had become increasingly powerful in Quebec since the late Depression, marriage and family rested upon a sacramentalized sexuality. Thus, the primary private and public purpose of the family, both in terms of social citizenship and religious participation, was the initiation of adolescents into a consciousness of their sexual natures and responsibilities. If, as these Catholic activists believed, contemporary adolescent behaviour indicated that there was a massive failure by parents to educate and socialize their adolescents into a value system of spiritualized sexuality, then the family, and in the final analysis, Catholicism itself, was simply a conduit for the more hedonistic impulses of a consumerist, pleasure-seeking, conformist civilization.

This critique of the family reflected, in fact, an intensification of the cultural Quiet Revolution. What has largely escaped historical attention is that most Catholic Quebecers did not experience the Quiet Revolution in the realm of high politics, but through a fissure between Catholicism and the idea of the institutional family with its hierarchy of roles and responsibilities. The central element in this process was the definition of family problems in terms of conflicting generational mentalities, and the focus on adult values as the primary cause of family breakdown. The discovery of a seemingly independent youth sociability resulted, between 1955 and 1970, in a bifurcation of Quebec Catholicism. On one side was a conservative wing, led by social thinkers like Philippe Garigue, which sought to reinforce parental authority by giving the family a precise institutional definition within the machinery of the Quiet Revolution state. On the other side of the spectrum, more radical Catholic personalists, including some key members of the Church hierarchy, actually privileged elements of the new youth culture as more spiritually "authentic" than the economically-driven values of their Depression-era parents. Sections of Quebec Catholicism thus fostered a widening "generation gap" from the late 1950s to the mid-1960s by engaging in a harsh, frequently sarcastic send-up of parental authority in the sphere not only of personal and social values, but of religious beliefs and practices. This ultimately desacralized the older Catholic model of the public family, and in no small way contributed to the emergence of a new vision of political society in Quebec, one in which public authority simply bypassed the family as a collective entity to design particular social policies concerned with the needs of women, children, and young people *as individuals* consuming social services.

"WE SHOULD WORRY IF ANY ADOLESCENT DISPLAYS A LACK OF INTEREST IN THE OPPOSITE SEX"[5]

Two principal images of youth, the "teenager" and the "juvenile delinquent," are intimately associated with moments of cultural transformation within post-war society. The first, the figure of the "teenager," conjures up visions of social and cultural consensus created by a rather bland period of mass prosperity that North America universally experienced after 1945. In both the United States and Canada, historians frequently observe, a depoliticized generation of young men and women, in quest of security and conformity, shaped a largely homogeneous culture oriented to patterns of consumption shaped by mass-advertising. The distinctive features of this culture were dating, clothing styles, automobiles, and the music and dance rhythms of rock 'n roll.[6] The second image, that of the juvenile delinquent, also preoccupied post-war family experts and social commentators, and has in recent years drawn the attention of historians who, while accepting a dominant consensus and conformity that governed post-war culture, have viewed youth culture as a subversive element within post-war society. While accepting the general framework of a dominant consensus and conformity, recent historical writing has sought to treat facets of youth culture as a subversive element within post-war society. Here, scholars have identified a monolithic, conservative, and hegemonic discourse about youth, constructed largely around the assumed importance of the issue of "juvenile delinquency," with the latter representing a new and violent working-class "subculture" that would exist permanently on the margins of the adult world. As a result, the focus has been almost exclusively on interpreting the "moral panics" occasioned by the sexual delinquency of youth as symptomatic of massive breakdowns in the structures of institutional control and the weakening of parental authority, or as reflecting the fears of conservative elites about the overwhelming influences of the mass media.[7] This formulation of a dialectic of consensus/subversion as characteristic of the period 1945–60 serves to highlight what historians maintain is the central social and cultural transition of the post-war period, the contrast between the relatively placid behaviour of young people in the 1950s and the sudden emergence of "revolutionary youth" engaged in radical, counter-cultural activities that spurred a number of movements of social and cultural liberation that reshaped institutions and values in a number of Western societies in the years after 1963.[8]

"On nearing adolescence," observed the Canadian Youth Commission in 1948, "the child enters the distinctive world of teen-agers where 'having a good time' becomes an extremely important business. ... the bond between generations is often weakened more than it need be."[9] This commission, which originated during World War II as part of a national effort at social and cultural reconstruction, included a substantial number of Quebec Catholic activists and youth leaders. Their analysis appeared, at first glance, to concur with conventional historiography in finding that the post-war era marked the emergence in Canada of an American-style "teenager" culture of language, clothes, and social events separate from the family. However, a close reading of the Youth Commission's thinking about "teenagers" suggests that the values of youth were not conceived of as being separate, but rather as existing in a continuum with those of adults, and that intergenerational tensions were caused, not by a fundamental clash of values or mentalities, but by a failure of adults to "provide opportunities" for young people to "grow into those responsibilities they must shortly assume as adults."[10]

Indeed, studies of youth undertaken in the immediate post-war years by the Canadian Youth Commission offered a rather benign interpretation of youthful rebellion symbolized by the figures of the "teenager" and the "juvenile delinquent," generally concurring that these were but temporary phenomena related either to insecurities caused by wartime family upheavals or associated with the breakdown of the obsolete ideal of the authoritarian, economically-driven materialist family. It was expected that the emergence of the "democratic family," whose essence was the provision of psychological security and emotional satisfaction, would provide a set of values that was more attractive than any quest for an independent youth culture. In 1948, the Commission concluded that the "teenager" phenomenon was in fact restricted to certain urban high schools, and as such, evoked no fundamental opposition between a new consumerist leisure ethic and the productivist civic values that assumed that young people would be streamed into steady employment and family formation through education and training programs. The causes of any "teenage" rebellion could therefore be ascribed to a temporary inability of governments, community institutions, and families to find a formula that would smoothly integrate male adolescents into the family and civic responsibilities of adults.[11]

The implicit assumption of the Canadian Youth Commission was that post-war Canada differed from the United States because it lacked an independent youth culture, a conclusion reinforced by one crucial, raw, demographic consideration. Indeed, in contrast to one of the cherished assumptions of Canada's post-war historiography – that, for better or for worse, post-war prosperity carried Canada and Quebec along in the wake of American popular culture – recent American studies of "teenager" culture offer a significant *caveat*. The "teenager" was less the creation of prosperity itself than of the culturally homogenizing effects of the comprehensive, coeducational high school, where, as early as 1940, fully 80 per cent of young American men and women aged fourteen to seventeen were enrolled.[12] By contrast, in Canada as a whole, it was not until 1954 that even a bare majority of this age group attended high school,[13] and in Quebec, where the Church throughout the post-war period controlled secondary education for the middle classes, there were no coeducational comprehensive high schools until 1964. Although media and advertising depictions of a highly sexualized, affluent American youth culture certainly abounded in Canada and Quebec after 1945,[14] it would be incorrect to assume either that young people simply imbibed these patterns of behaviour, becoming passive participants in a one-way process of Americanization or, more tellingly, that young Canadians had as much consumer purchasing power as American teens.[15] Thus, it is not surprising that, between 1948 and 1954, most Canadian social commentators remained reasonably confident that the socialization of youth was occurring within the family and the framework provided by adult-led youth movements, churches, and organized leisure activities, and that the new "democratic family" had successfully forged a new intergenerational partnership. Sociological studies of wealthier Anglo-Canadian urban neighbourhoods, where income levels might have spawned elements of the American-style teenager culture, suggested important continuities between the behaviour patterns and values of adults and high school youth. Teenage rebellion, where it did occur, invariably happened "within the framework of the general patterns of the culture," and usually involved different career and work choices, not deviant sexual behaviour or divergent patterns of consumption.[16]

Like their Anglo-Canadian counterparts, Quebec's Catholic youth activists in the early 1950s were intent on demonstrating that adolescent freedom could only occur within a framework of socialization into adult roles and responsibilities that was best accomplished within the family, and that manifestations of a separate youth culture, based upon easy access to material pleasure, popularity, and superficial romances based solely on sexual attraction, should be kept at bay by watchful parents and teachers. In 1953, *Cahiers d'Action Catholique*, a review intended for educators and youth workers, reiterated that "left to themselves, today's students will elaborate a false doctrinal synthesis on sexuality, love, the roles of men and women, marriage and chastity, basing their ideas on modern propaganda and current slogans." Manifestations of a separate youth culture were simply denounced as evidence of materialism, individualism, and Americanization.[17]

However, Catholic family activists rarely ascribed this youthful independence to a "teenager" culture based on a high school peer group. For example, while a 1955 survey of young men and women aged seventeen to twenty-four undertaken by the JOC revealed lamentably low levels of interest in household skills or sense of family roles and obligations, it concluded optimistically that young people were massively committed to ideals of stable family formation. Indeed, fully 95 per cent of the youth questioned believed that it was necessary to know how to keep house, and 80 per cent rejected current images of love as pleasure, romance, and self-gratification, maintaining that lasting marriages were built upon "a great deal of self-sacrifice that often must last one's entire life."[18] The principal stimulus to adolescent rejection of the family was not participation in the various leisure activities of "teen" culture, but, as Father Léopold Godbout concluded as late as 1956, the entry of young men and women into the workforce. Possession of an income, he estimated, inexorably drew youth away from family sociability by conferring access to a whole array of dubious pleasures that aroused sexual appetites.[19] Because entry into the workforce still constituted the central life-transition, the problem of relations between adolescents and their families was thus cast in terms of older Catholic injunctions that enjoined parents to exercise proper leadership in preparing children for adult roles within the framework of the family itself. Thus, although highly charged with denunciations of adolescent defections, the Quebec Catholic discussion about youth was still framed within the categories set by the immediate post-war priority on preserving intergenerational solidarities and continuities.

Beginning in the middle years of the 1950s, a new strand of thinking began to permeate Quebec Catholicism, one that broke decisively with the trajectory of family ideology that had been elaborated in the latter stages of the Depression and was more fully articulated in the climate of post-war reconstruction. This new notion was that the values and behaviour of youth were shaped less by the family or adult-led institutions than by canons defined by their own peer group. Youth effectively formed a separate culture that paralleled the adult world but did not communicate with it. In an internal memorandum written for the Jeunesse Étudiante Catholique in 1955, youth leader André Juneau reported on the social and cultural values of male students aged twelve to fifteen, observing that until a few years ago the activities of this age group had centred largely on the institutions of family and school. However, he stated that they now found these institutions "too narrow" and in consequence "had been effectively drawn towards a world of values outside family and school." What perplexed Juneau was that the problem was not the expected one of youth claiming independence by following a prescribed life-course trajectory culminating in access to work after age seventeen. Young teenagers, he stated, had apparently created their own patterns of sociability, derived entirely from relations with their own age group, that telescoped the conventional age-progression, and had secured direct access, without the mediation of the family, to "the structures of the adult world and the cultural environment of the modern world."[20] Such an assessment of the new authority of the peer group was echoed by Brother Albini Girouard, whose analysis of the activities of working-class male adolescents concluded that "life in the gang," emphasizing "all that pleasure-seeking and commercial entertainments can offer," had shouldered aside "good old-fashioned family life."[21] So pronounced was this social and cultural separateness of youth, that Catholic activists raised the possibility of serious generational conflicts, particularly if family and school presented values and tried to prescribe patterns of behaviour that ran counter to the tenets of the teen peer group.[22]

But what precisely was it about the replication by young adolescents of the "structures of the adult world" that so preoccupied Catholic educators? Post-war Catholicism placed immense weight upon the concept of the nuclear, "democratic" family, especially the notion that the individual attained adulthood – defined as psychological maturity – largely through the assimilation, from parental example, of prescribed male and female sex roles. If Quebec adolescents, as early as ages twelve to fifteen had already evolved their own way of defining these roles, and thus their own norms of sexual conduct outside and without reference to the educative mechanisms of family and school, then it followed that a fully-fledged "teenager" culture, predicated on horizontal peer-group solidarities, and largely impervious to adult values and influence, was already in existence. In an article written for an audience of Catholic family experts in 1954, the French historian Philippe Ariès outlined the central aspect of this fundamental transformation in family structure and relations. He posited that the central gulf in generational sensibilities now revolved around "the role that is consciously reserved for sexuality in daily life, and a pervasive eroticism in literature and art."[23] If this was indeed the case, then these conflicting sexual standards were already eroding the laboriously-reconstructed intergenerational solidarity upon which both the structure and the public and private functions of the Quebec Catholic family rested. And, as a corollary, the question then arises of whether this highly-sexualized new youth culture would require Catholicism to reconceptualize its cherished notion that participation in the hierarchical sociabilities of the family was an instrument for the transmission of religious values.

The most overt intimation that a seismic shift was occurring in Catholic thinking about the family was the evidence provided in a series of discussions about the phenomenon of teen dating that took place between 1954 and the early 1960s. As late as 1953, the consensus among educators and youth workers was that dating, especially among younger teens, and indeed any kind of sexual initiation that adolescents engaged in without adult supervision, led only to unrealistic ideals about love and marriage that lacked reality. Dating was, in their estimation, a function of "social conditioning" and, because it dissociated the sexual instinct from sacrificial and communitarian concepts of love, making it entirely a function of physical attraction and a consumerist quest for personal popularity and self-satisfaction, it "*did not foreshadow adult love.*"[24] However, the following year, Agatha Sidlauskas stated that dating, especially for young women, served a highly positive function, both at individual and social levels, because it helped female teens mature by developing a "self-consciousness" based on sexual self-awareness. While she agreed with conservative Catholic critics that there were certainly selfish and materialistic elements associated with the dating culture, the fact that young women "were concerned for making themselves attractive" was something to be praised and encouraged rather than reprobated, because it "developed self-respect."[25]

However, it was Father Roch Duval's analysis of dating from the perspective of young males that was the most indicative of a palpable shift that was occurring in the relationship of Catholicism to the family. Duval opened by declaring that frontal attacks on dating would only be counterproductive, because they would run up against "the absolutist temper of the adolescent." Rather, educators should see dating as a positive opportunity to educate young people in the values of "freedom, sensitivity to others, and sexuality" that would serve as a prelude to the cultivation of intimacy that was so essential to the post-war Catholic marriage ideal. Far from being a symptom of a selfish consumerism, or a psychological immaturity, "the mutual discovery of intimacy that occurs between teenage boys and girls already presupposes that they have achieved a certain level of concern for the other. This discovery is a manifestation of the beginning of the adolescent's integration to society; by this type of dating that is exclusive to adolescents there thus appears a new type of community that is premised upon a degree of responsibility and possibilities of development hitherto unknown in the life of the child."[26] Duval's assessment constituted an overt challenge to the entire post-war intersection of Catholicism and the family, because it implied that it was the values and practices of the ostensibly self-absorbed independent teenage peer culture, and not the family itself, that nourished the affections and psychological mechanisms that were essential for the individual's acquisition of that emotional maturity and stability that would assure proper socialization into sex roles, and thus, family formation. Significantly, Duval's was not an isolated opinion. The editors of *Cahiers d'Action Catholique* generally endorsed his perspective, stating that "the adolescent has his own affectional life whose normal channels must be opened. An authentic experience of the affectional life, achieved at the moment of adolescence, will give him the equilibrium necessary to become an adult."[27]

Given the specific context of Catholic education in Quebec, which diverged significantly from the North American pattern through the dominant presence of same-sex educational institutions at the secondary level, conservatives were bound to lump together a more liberalized adolescent heterosexual sociability with advocacy of coeducation. Writing in 1959, Norbert Fournier argued that dating could serve a positive role in mutual self-discovery for adolescents, but only if it was undertaken with a view to preparing for marriage. Such relationships were unsuitable for those too immature to contemplate marriage, or for those intending to consecrate themselves to a religious vocation. Teachers and parents should certainly foster opportunities for camaraderie with the opposite sex, but should not place young people in situations "where they would have relations that were too frequent or where they would compete in same-sex athletic or cultural activities."[28] In the final analysis, what conservative critics found objectionable about dating was that such relations tended to evolve into "amours précoces"[29] – what the Anglo-American world would term "going steady." This type of relationship, which became the predominant form of adolescent heterosexual sociability in the 1950s, held forth the prospect of longer-term monogamous commitment and as such, offered to adolescents some of the emotional, and what many North American parents and educators feared, sexual comforts of marriage itself.[30] For this reason, conservatives like the Jesuit Father Jean-Paul Labelle contemptuously dismissed the whole culture of dating as largely female-inspired, elaborated to compensate for the emotional and psychological insecurities of young women who had just entered adolescence. Young men who were drawn into these "steady" relationships either by female seduction or emotional tyranny were inevitably "emasculated," lost "their spirit of initiative," and became "flabby and sentimental creatures; they lose their moral and psychological consistency and they have no more backbone."[31]

This debate over the emotional and psychological value of teenage dating indicated the emergence of a new synthesis, among an influential section of Quebec Catholicism, between the category of "adolescence" and concepts of cultural modernity. However, in contrast to the 1930s, when "youth" had expressed a series of cultural and spiritual qualities which, much as they had been equated with a particular generation, did not exclude the presence of adult sympathies or institutional leadership,[32] the tone of discussion in the mid-1950s revolved to a far greater extent around psychological theories that defined "adolescence" as an age-specific quest for identity that focused most intently on decisive, brutal moments of transition that were most marked in the teenage years. Adolescence, a number of theorists argued, centred on sexuality, and phenomena such as precocious dating and sexual initiation and juvenile delinquency – all attempts to exclude adult scrutiny – were thus interpreted as essential to the establishment of relations between self and others, and to the articulation of an emotionally-balanced personality.[33] From this standpoint, the experimental heterosexual sociability represented by teenage dating and "going steady" marked not a moral declension or a challenge to social order, but a necessary and highly formative stage in the quest for an adult personality.[34] At worst, such youth cultures demonstrated a confusion of identities that direct adult guidance could do little to alleviate. Indeed, because sexuality was the basis of identity itself, the message heard with ever-increasing volume and frequency in Quebec by the late 1950s was that independent teenager cultures and a "generation gap" were necessary because adults ignored literally everything concerning the "*human and divine nature of the sexual instinct*" and had communicated to adolescents only the barest, and most evasive, physiological facts. This was due, not simply to misunderstanding, but to a fundamental divergence in the appreciation of the role sexuality played in the formation of the human personality. Youth, it was frequently asserted, saw in sexual expression the pathway to personal growth, while adults regarded it as a source of shame.[35] Indeed, as the Catholic youth leaders Maurice Pinard and Albert Breton declared at the conclusion of a 1954 survey, teachers and parents were derelict, and had themselves broken the solidarity with their teenagers through their silence on questions pertaining to sexuality.[36]

In other cultural contexts, opinions advanced by Catholic reformers in the 1954 forum on dating might be dismissed as but heavy-handed conservative impositions of "compulsory heterosexuality," a monolithic discourse that subverted free sexual expression and repressed "deviant" forms of sexuality by encouraging and regulating teen dating as the prelude to the formation of monogamous and patriarchal family relationships.[37] However, in the context of Catholic Quebec, where male and female teens were educated in separate, homosocial institutions run by priests and nuns, and where these *collèges classiques* were widely viewed as recruiting bureaus for religious vocations, these articles served as signals of cultural liberalization. Indeed, Duval was reprimanded by his superiors for writing that parents and teachers should be wary of young men and women who evinced no interest in the opposite sex,[38] thus hinting that conservatives who sought to repress dating in their same-sex schools inadvertently created occasions for sin, the fostering of homosexual relationships. More outrageously, in the estimation of traditionalists, Duval apparently suggested that dating could be of positive benefit to those young men contemplating the priesthood, because it would give them access to normal patterns of emotional and psychological development which were, after all, anchored upon sexual maturity. Father Duval later recanted some of his ideas and gave a more precise definition to what he considered acceptable standards of dating and supervision of adolescents by educational authorities. However, his central point, that the family was in crisis because it had failed young people from the standpoint of their emotional and sexual development, and that young people needed a separate culture defined by their peer group because they found the family "*psychologically unacceptable*,"[39] indicated not a continuity with late-Depression and post-war notions of youth, but the dawn of a new sensibility.

From the mid-1930s throughout the immediate post-war period, the priority had been on forging intergenerational emotional connections as a way of specifically enlisting young men in the task of family formation. Manifestations of independence on the part of youth were then viewed as explicit challenges to a political and social order founded on the family. However, between 1955 and 1960, a far more psychological interpretation of adolescence carved out a larger sphere for the idea of a self-sufficient, independent youth culture predicated on the necessity of sexual self-

expression in the acquisition of maturity, a climate that was far more attentive to the activities and needs of young women.[40] Ultimately, this new
climate held significant implications for the future of the relationship
between Quebec Catholicism and the family. In accepting the existence of
two utterly incompatible psychological states, that of youth and that of
adulthood, elements of Catholicism lent credence to the idea that the
family was largely marginal, and perhaps even baneful, to the emotional
development of young people. Ultimately, this was to seriously erode
attempts to maintain an institutional or public identity for the family.

The revaluation by a substantial section of Catholic opinion of a less constrained, sexualized youth culture of dating was not an attempt by social
and cultural conservatives to reinvigorate pre-war ideals of family hierarchy. In many ways, its emphasis upon the teenage years as the most crucial
psychological stage in creating the human personality fostered an attitude
that subtly shifted the balance of power within the family away from
parents. Ultimately, allowing teenagers to determine their own identities
through the cultivation of forms of sociability that were independent from
adult control led rather easily to assertions that manifestations of an independent teen culture were not only a normal stage on the road to adulthood, but in fact represented a search for values that were spiritually and
morally superior to those of their parents. This marked a distinct shift in
cultural sensibilities, one that presaged the more radical climate of the
1960s,[41] with its association of the social and cultural power of youth with
the privileging of new forms of democratic egalitarianism that placed overweening value on unconstrained personal freedom and the satisfaction of
individual needs.

"TO GUARD OURSELVES AGAINST THE DANGERS OF STATE PATERNALISM"[42]

However, in the context of Quebec, this current, which was increasingly
critical of the family as an institution and sought a more explicit identification between religion and youth, was balanced, at least until the mid-
1960s, by a second strand of Catholic activism. This drew upon the continued prominence, among sections of the clergy, lay family organizations,
social science experts, and government officials, of models of familist corporatism that aimed at reinforcing family solidarity and the position of the
family as a public entity. This, its promoters imagined, would be achieved
through the creation of new government organs which, while not subordinating the family to the state, would accord it a consultative role in the
shaping of policy initiatives, thus explicitly recognizing the family as an
element of a new political corporatism. To a number of influential architects of provincial social policy in the early 1960s, the institutional family

was the principal guarantor of an equilibrium between a social service sector in which ongoing management and initiative would be left to private agencies, but in which the government would have a regulatory and financial control in the name of greater efficiency. It was the tension between these two divergent tendencies within Catholic opinion – the one accepting many of the tenets of the new psychological definitions of youth and more oriented to accenting egalitarianism, personal freedom, and the satisfaction of individual needs by society, and the other, that sought to reinforce the institutional solidarity of the family community and, by so doing, preserve a more decentralized concept of the state – that brought the family itself into a volatile climate of political contestation.

The family, stated the Université de Montréal sociologist Philippe Garigue in 1957, continued to be a "universal institution," because although its structure was modified by the same causes that were changing the wider society, it still fulfilled two fundamental functions: procreation and child-rearing.[43] Garigue's portrait of the institutional continuity and resilience of the family in a time of rapid social change reflected his position within the emerging discipline of sociology in Quebec. Unlike a number of his counterparts, he rejected the hypothesis of the "folk" society, which identified the patriarchal, extended kinship family with the immutable, natural traditions of rural society, and posited urbanization as a series of stresses which had acted upon the family from outside, profoundly destabilizing and narrowing the functions of the modern family. He questioned the whole concept that such a "crisis" existed in the family, asserting that "among French Canadians ... there is a link between the family of the eighteenth century and that of modern times because the extremes of change have been less abrupt."[44] Rather, Garigue's celebrated 1962 study of family relations and practices dwelt on the "cultural homogeneity" of rural and urban families, describing how even in the burgeoning suburbs around Montreal, French-Canadian families, though "modern" in their nuclear structure, continued to hold paternal authority in high regard, to place a high value upon intergenerational solidarity, and to be closely involved with their kin.[45] Garigue believed that the history of the French-Canadian family was characterized by a continuity governed by an internal cultural dynamic, rather than ruptures occasioned by the impact of Anglo-Saxon values or industrial capitalism. This outlook was particularly exemplified in his praise of the Catholic Church for its "innovative teachings on family relations," which, he maintained, had been of central importance in articulating a close connection between the family and the national particularism of French Canadians.[46]

Garigue's eulogy of Catholicism referred less to a set of particular doctrinal teachings than to a series of institutional initiatives that had been promoted at the end of the 1950s by a group of laypeople and clergy.

Inspired by corporatist doctrines which sought explicit representation of families and voluntary economic and social organizations within the political structure of the state,[47] a number of family movements led by the École des Parents sought to create an umbrella organization or association whose purpose, according to the Jesuit periodical *Relations*, was to "remedy the insufficiency of the family."[48] What was intended was not a campaign for greater state intervention into the sphere of family welfare. The intention, rather, was to counterbalance what many viewed as the fumbling and inefficiency of the conservative liberal government of Maurice Duplessis. In response to mushrooming social service expenditures and a recession after a long period of prosperity, the provincial government tended increasingly after 1957 to centralize the fiscal management of a number of social services, thus threatening to curtail the independence of private welfare bodies which in the Quebec context were frequently charities managed by the Catholic Church.[49] To resist what some Catholics feared was the beginning of significant government meddling into the family itself, a number of groups created a Fédération des Unions de Familles, which would function as something of a trade union for parents, engaging in a programme of popular education aimed at securing representation for families in public bodies so that the family would cease to be "an eternal minor child, waiting for a few meagre crumbs of assistance to be doled out by the welfare state."[50]

The 1959 meeting of the Semaines Sociales held in Quebec City was explicitly devoted to recommending measures that would confer upon the family a formal, public, institutional identity. The session's chief organizer, Father Richard Arès, opened by reminding his audience of one of the central canons of Catholic social theory, that "the family's rights were sacred, prior to, and superior to those of any other institution, including those of the State itself."[51] After enumerating a number of fundamental moral and economic "rights" possessed by families, Arès concluded that a purely private acknowledgment of these was insufficient, and indeed, out of step with the times, especially since the 1948 United Nations Declaration of Human Rights had urged governments to recognize that the family was a natural and fundamental element of society. In the case of Quebec, Arés was especially critical of the provincial government, whose policies were predicated upon "juxtaposed categories of individuals, from infancy to old age," and did not recognize the family as the vital cell and fundamental unit of human society.[52] Such an individualistic calculus was, in his estimation, a prime recipe for deviations like over-zealous state intervention and a planned economy, which might "even lead to totalitarianism."[53]

Father Arès's criticisms were directed most particularly against Catholic colleagues like Father Gérard Dion, director of the school of industrial relations at Université Laval, whose discussion of the modern family's need for social security started from the premise that rights pertained not to the family itself as a community, but to individuals within the family, such as wage-earning parents and children. Dion maintained that in terms of economic security, the family had no inherent rights as a social institution but, rather, was "a function of its members." This emphasis on individual rights, rather than family rights, led him to break with Catholic corporatism's insistence on the priority of the family over the state, and to countenance a far greater degree of direct state intervention into the hierarchy of the family itself in order to guarantee and enhance the individual's right to security.[54] In refuting Dion's arguments, Arès enjoined that the state should seek not to replace the family, but, instead, follow the prescriptions of Catholic social teaching which respected "the communitarian nature and personalist mission of the family, at once to facilitate the common life of its members and their personal fulfillment."[55] Arès elaborated a new partnership between the state and the public family, based upon the creation, in tandem, of a ministry of family and a powerful umbrella association launched by family movements themselves.[56] This would enable the family, through direct representation in the organs of the state, to express its needs and participate in the making of policy, while allowing the family to maintain a barrier against state encroachments into the internal structure of its relationships.

What was signficant about this debate was that it occurred just after the death of Maurice Duplessis, which provided an opportunity to correct what many experts believed was a haphazard welter of provincial welfare policies that had grown up during the post-war period. Father Arès's attempt to balance and coordinate state responsibility and private initiative around the corporatist priority of family rights might, at first sight, smack of a blinkered conservatism that failed to appreciate the need for massive state expenditures and institutional presence to cope with a modern industrial society. It would be premature to reach such a conclusion, however, without first considering the views of Claude Morin, a professor of social work in the faculty of social science at Université Laval, another of the participants in the 1959 Semaines Sociales, and a figure closely linked to the massive expansion of the Quebec state. Morin was soon to be recruited into the Liberal government of Jean Lesage, becoming one of the major architects of the political Quiet Revolution, first as one of its leading technocrats and a principal advisor in the constitutional negotiations between Quebec and Ottawa over the provision of universal social security, and later as a prominent member of the first Parti Québécois government, in which he was the minister of intergovernmental affairs responsible for the 1980 referendum strategy. Despite his association with the statist currents of the 1960s and 1970s, Morin's 1959 address closely mirrored the corporatism enunciated by Father Arès, with

its model of the limited state respecting the rights of families and intermediate bodies.

"The family," declared Morin, "has always had precise responsibilities,
chief among these being to support its members. This duty is the obverse
of an inalienable natural right of being the first line of support for its
members. The family itself, and not the State, must thus take the initiative
in proposing solutions designed to alleviate its own problems."[57] This
approach, he maintained, constituted a new departure for the formulation
of social policy in Quebec, which, hitherto, had been too strongly influenced by "an Anglo-Saxon and Protestant concept of life and society."[58] He
was thus in full agreement with corporatist ideals in which the communal
rights of institutions were superior to those of the individual. Morin consequently issued an explicit warning against social policies that sought to
marginalize the family by cultivating a direct relationship between the individual and the state, arguing that "the individual cannot be isolated from
his family."[59] However, as a welfare expert, he recognized that any reorganization of the provincial social services, even one that enhanced the
rights and public character of the family and preserved the principle of
private management of charitable agencies, would require greater state
involvement than had been the case under Maurice Duplessis. Private
charity, he reminded his audience, could not cover all social risks, and
greater state funding and planning was essential to ensure that the costs of
public welfare would be borne by society as a whole, and not by the most
needy families. "The ultimate effect of a reorganization of social security as
a function of the family," Morin concluded, "would be to give the role of
the State a heightened economic and social importance."[60] But despite its
new importance, the role of the state in social welfare was clearly circumscribed by the requirement that it respect the prior rights of families in
matters of assistance and education. In assisting families, rather than individuals, the state would also respect Quebec's long-standing tradition of
religious involvement in the day-to-day planning and provision of social
welfare.

It was this familist corporatism, which stressed the close public coordination and consultation between the institutional family, private social
service organizations, and the government, and not a desire to centralize
social security in the hands of the state, that dominated the early efforts
of the reformist Liberal government of Premier Jean Lesage. In their
efforts to rationalize Quebec's public welfare system, the provincial Liberals were guided by Lesage's own beliefs on the subject, which had been
outlined as early as 1951 when he was still a federal Liberal backbencher.
Speaking to a conference of welfare experts, Lesage categorically stated
that "we must never ... allow the unjustified intervention of the State
to destroy our Christian concept of the family." Lesage adhered closely to

the post-war personalist Catholic ideal which proclaimed a key public role and institutional identity for the affectional nuclear family as the creator of those "personal bonds" which created a "sense of security," enabling individuals to overcome the anonymity of mass urban civilization.[61] Lesage's evocation of the personal character of family relations led him to insist on the preservation and enhancement of private initiative in social welfare, rather than greater state intervention, as the best way to maintain the solidarities of the family.

Upon assuming office, Lesage moved to reform the provincial public welfare system by appointing a commission consisting of J.-Émile Boucher, Marcel Bélanger, and Claude Morin to study the various social assistance schemes, and the relationship between public authority and private agencies.[62] Although the 1963 Boucher Commission Report cited the UN's Universal Declaration of Human Rights, advocating the rights of persons and families to social assistance sufficient to ensure a healthy standard of living, the major organizations consulted by the commissioners were the seventeen diocesan Catholic welfare federations. Quebec's traditions of public assistance, stated the report, were entirely praiseworthy because, in making "individual and communal rights and responsibilities gravitate around the family," a culture of family self-sufficiency and solidarity had been preserved.[63] While the authors certainly wished to amplify the "rather ancillary role" that the State had occupied in social matters, they did not desire any "organic modifications to the private sector,"[64] fearing that this would legitimate what they observed was a "sponging attitude" among sectors of the Quebec populace, "which could easily be transformed into a mentality of dependency."[65]

The main failing of Quebec's system of public assistance, in the estimation of the Boucher Commission, was not the incompetence of the private sector, but the "partitions" that existed between government programs and agencies that had been created at different times, and between the state and private social welfare agencies.[66] Although the commission called upon the government to recognize that it had a more creative and dynamic role to play in social security, particularly in articulating a new definition of welfare that was not merely palliative, but was oriented to prevention and readaptation, it argued that, in terms of day-to-day administration, government's role was largely regulatory. The state should establish uniform regulations to which private bodies must adhere in order to qualify for stable financial assistance, but the commissioners unanimously concluded that private social services possessed greater administrative expertise. Consequently, the key to reform was not the incursion of the state through direct administration or creation of new services,[67] but a clearer definition of the roles and responsibilities of the state and private sector, and the creation of overtly corporatist machinery, such as a *Conseil*

Supérieur (Superior Council) within the ministry of public welfare, to provide a consultative representation of private welfare agencies and family organizations.[68]

The individual primarily responsible for erecting this new relationship between family, social security, and the state during the early years of the Lesage government was Émilien Lafrance, the minister of public welfare. Lafrance was a member of the conservative wing of the Liberal party and had close ties to the social corporatism of the École Sociale Populaire and the Jesuit periodical *Relations*. His implementation of the recommendations of the Boucher Commission began, significantly, with the more than symbolic change of name from Ministère du Bien-être public (Ministry of Public Welfare) to Ministère de la Famille et du Bien-être public (Ministry of Family and Public Welfare), which gave concrete recognition to the Catholic concept of familist corporatism. In his speech on Bill 25 creating the new ministry, Lafrance lambasted the social policy of the Duplessis years, charging that government action had hitherto been purely palliative, and had enacted no measures designed to "prevent the disaggregation of the home."[69] The fundamental aim of his new ministry, he stated, was to "recognize and respect the primacy of the family," and because the family, in his estimation, was the keystone of society, the function of the state in the field of public welfare was compensatory, to protect the family *"without absorbing it* or *substituting itself for it."* This imperative, the priority of the family to the state, he concluded, was fully safeguarded in the very structure of the ministry of family and public welfare, the key to which was the new Conseil Supérieur de la Famille, which would allow family organizations and heads of private welfare agencies a consultative voice over policy and a right to state their views on legislation. This, Lafrance maintained, would free the family even further from "government tutelage," which inevitably tended to substitute the state for "the authority of the father."[70]

The actions of Émilien Lafrance and recommendations of the 1963 Report on Public Assistance provided clear indication that the direction of Quebec Liberal social policy lay not in a unilateral centralization of social services[71] and the creation of a direct, unmediated relationship between the individual and the welfare state. Rather, far from being a break with the past, the views of Lesage, Lafrance, and Morin displayed important affinities with and drew upon the effort of Catholic activists to reconstruct the family in the wake of the Depression. By emphasizing that the achievement of social security by individuals was attained within the context of family relations, Liberal policy rested upon the premise that social order obeyed a communitarian ethos in which the state cultivated relationships with the family as an entity, rather than directly with the individual. However, unlike the liberalism of the Duplessis regime, which insisted upon an explicit separation between the political government and a civic order of autonomous social bodies, the reformism of the post-1960 Quebec Liberals sought to elaborate a new idea of citizenship and society[72] that rested upon the creation of structures of coordination and policy consultation *within the state* that would make natural communities like the family and intermediate bodies like the private welfare agencies part of a much expanded political sphere shared by government, the Church, private social services, and business and labour organizations.

Far from being incipient social democrats, key figures like Premier Lesage and Claude Morin thus articulated a neo-corporatist ideology which continued to respect families and private welfare agencies as visible communities that made political authority accessible to the individual. However, the attempt to anchor the authority of the state upon the hierarchical sociability of the family – in which adults, and particularly the male head of the household, exercised authority over their children, and in the case of husbands, over their wives as well – was to encounter heavy weather beginning in the mid-1960s. Both Catholic family activists and architects of the neo-corporatist state were challenged by a new public sensibility, fostered by elements of Catholicism itself, that accorded overwhelming cultural prestige to a new democratic ideal of personal self-expression and fulfillment, represented most visibly by a vocal, independent, and apparently anarchic youth culture.

"OUR YOUNG PEOPLE ARE REVOLTED BY THE FUNDAMENTAL IMMORALITY OF THEIR ELDERS"[73]

By the mid-1960s, Quebec, in common with a number of other Western societies, evinced an immense fascination with the spectacle of youth countercultures. These, many commentators and experts proclaimed, presented a libertarian challenge to political, racial, educational, and even religious "establishments" that at times verged upon a wholesale attack on institutions in the name of personal freedom. Here, apparently incarnated in the experience of an entire generation that transcended class, gender, and racial categories, was a new insistence upon individual freedom[74] founded on the egalitarian ideal of creative self-expression, which permitted unconstrained behaviour, most explicitly in the realm of sexuality and personal choice, without reference to older moral codes or cultural authorities. Stated most succinctly by the Montreal journalist Judith Jasmin, young people "thrust aside any form of authority, whether it be familial, clerical or social."[75] From an international perspective, what was ultimately compelling about the 1960s was the drama of contestation between this new cultural climate of freedom, represented by assertive youth, and the still-powerful forces of reaction, concentrated in police forces and religious bodies. Writing from a perspective that tends to universalize Anglo-Saxon traditions and cultural categories, the British historian Arthur Marwick grudgingly conceded that the Catholic Church contained more "enlightened" elements and was thus far from being a monolithic entity in the 1960s. Nonetheless, his overall assessment, couched in terms worthy of a long tradition of Protestant apologists, was that Catholicism tended to operate as "a centre of opposition to all the great movements aiming towards greater freedom for ordinary human beings."[76]

In the case of Quebec, however, the precise relationship between Catholicism and youth revolt in the mid-1960s provides a corrective to Marwick's conflation of Protestant cultural traditions and the types of personal freedom that came to the fore. Indeed, although conservative elements within Catholicism certainly existed, systematic opposition to the new libertarian attitudes was muted. Other strands of Catholicism, intent on renewing both the institution and belief, eagerly adopted some of the egalitarian attitudes associated with the youth "counterculture," and thus consciously acted as one of its principal conduits and promoters. First, building upon the more benign appreciation of youth subcultures evident after the mid-1950s among some Quebec psychologists and educators, many Catholics accepted, popularized, and legitimized the existence of a "generation gap" that privileged the moral and cultural attributes of young people. Second, in so doing, they increasingly validated the link between social freedom and sexual freedom, openly proclaiming that Quebec's institutions and structures of authority, many of which were controlled by the Church, must be revised in light of the new climate of sexual openness. Finally, between 1964 and 1970, Catholicism overtly withdrew its earlier post-war support for promotion of the institutional family and, in so doing, implicitly proclaimed the superiority of individual wants and satisfactions over the maintenance of family hierarchies and solidarities.

In this respect, Catholicism was thus a principal contributor to a key attribute of modernity. This revolved around the idea that the family itself was the scene of a fundamental social and cultural rupture because it tended to constrain and repress the individual's psychological need for free personal expression. The family, in the estimation of many Quebec Catholic observers, was incompetent to reconcile the tensions between the imperative needs of its members – mainly young people – for personal fulfillment and the maintenance of parental authority. This failing, they believed, meant that the family had irrevocably entered into a state of permanent "crisis," characterized by sharply increasing rates of individual psychopathologies and social contestation. "The family in crisis," one of the principal concepts to emerge from the encounter of Quebec Catholicism and the countercultural revolt of youth in the 1960s, was a cultural metaphor that increasingly dominated the thinking of both liberal and conservative Catholics in the 1960s and early 1970s. It dictated a radical recasting both of the notion that the family hierarchy transmitted religious knowledge to the individual, and that, in terms of public authority, the institutional family mediated between the individual and the state.

In early 1964, the Jesuit journal *Collège et Famille* attempted to discern the dominant values of contemporary youth by surveying 2,000 young men and women aged twenty and attending the *collèges classiques*. It should be remembered that during the late 1950s, this journal had been in the forefront of critiquing and ridiculing the teenager culture of dating and any manifestations of independent sexual expression among young people. The survey opened by remarking that this generation lacked the experience of World War II, and the editor described the dominant feature of those born in 1944 as one of "ideological pluralism," symbolized by the liberalism of such leaders as John F. Kennedy and Pope John XXIII. "The present age of prosperity," he stated, "has precociously taught them a very exaggerated use of their freedom among all the delicacies of the earth. They were not born under the sign of constraint and they wish to live only for today, finding their own way with no dependence upon the past. This leads to some curiosities, like finding the young *beatnik* who advocates poverty like Saint Francis of Assisi and free love like Simone de Beauvoir. ... What a blending of tradition and novelty, what an unstable and chaotic psychological cocktail!"[77] What was markedly different about this particular set of conclusions was that similar studies of youth attitudes undertaken in the first post-war decade had sought to demonstrate continuities in social and cultural values between young people and their parents, or had expressed concern about the existence of deviant "subcultures" that were outside the norms of work and family formation. By contrast, those of the 1960s sought, by applying overarching concepts such as "freedom" to encompass the mentality of an entire generation, to ascribe a totality and separateness to youth, one that obliterated older demarcations of wealth and education among this age group and distinguished it spiritually and culturally from the older generation.

In 1962, Catholic Action commissioned a sociological study significantly entitled "The World of Youth and the World of Adults," thus explicitly accepting the postulate of a cultural divide between generations. Such a rupture was, observed the inquiry, "a relatively new phenomenon in our country and in the world, and it is expressed by a tendency of young people to organize their life in institutions and structures parallel to those of the adult world."[78] Among Quebec Catholics, liberal and conservative educators and social commentators vociferously debated the supposed contradictions between youthful aspirations for "freedom" and the apparent "conformism" of musical tastes, clothing, and hair styles,[79] but they concurred on one fundamental issue – that for better or for worse, "youth" as an overarching cultural category now constituted the primary force of creative historical agency. "Youth," proclaimed the founding congress of the Mouvements de Jeunesse du Québec, "possesses its own distinct vision of society, and the resulting shock between youth's vision and the established order is an essential factor of social evolution."[80] An influential federal government study of youth attitudes concluded in 1971 that "youth dissatisfactions are not a function of age but are a forecast by the young of larger societal changes."[81]

For a number of influential social analysts, age, not class, now constituted the central dynamic of revolutionary change in Western societies. Interviewed by the Montreal daily *Le Devoir* in 1965, sociologist Marcel Rioux stated that in post-industrial societies, socio-political struggles would be intergenerational rather than economic in character, because, worldwide, young people had developed a "true *sub-culture*, markedly distinct from that of adults." In a hopeful reworking of Lenin's theorizing about the superior revolutionary potential of "backward" societies, Rioux argued that because Quebec youth were the most dynamic in North America, relations of historical agency within the society had in fact shifted. Familiar rites of passage such as work and marriage had, for the younger generation, lost their relative importance, and social authority had actually shifted to the young, who "were now actually making adults evolve." Thus, the entire society might, through the efforts of its young people, be lifted by its bootstraps to not only catch up to the rest of North America, but to surpass it in attaining an advanced stage of post-industrial social organization.[82] Rioux's liberal colleague, the Université Laval political scientist Léon Dion, was somewhat less optimistic, believing that few young people possessed the type of maturity necessary to lead such a social revolution, but he nonetheless acknowledged that the ideals of personal engagement and heightened communitarian sensibility constituted the "germs of a new humanism."[83] From a more conservative perspective, the Belgian educator Anselme d'Haese, whose views were disseminated in *Collège et Famille*, wrote in 1966 that what most profoundly marked the contemporary world was "the massive accession of youth onto the social scene. They form a class apart."[84]

In one respect, these views built upon the acceptance, by some Catholic educators in the mid-1950s, of elements of an independent teenager culture. However, it should be remembered that the dating culture and adolescent independence were condoned insofar as they were regarded as essential steps in the psychological and emotional development of adult, heterosexual relationships. Thus, while it was possible to countenance a certain amount of generational conflict as normal and desirable, this was still, as late as 1961, cast in terms of enabling young people to enter adulthood by forming families of their own.[85] The absolute sense of generational separateness – evoked most poignantly by Gilles Desmarais's statement at the 1964 Canadian Conference on the Family that "we are living in a world completely different, where the same facts don't mean the same thing to adults and youth"[86] – was regarded as something entirely unprecedented. It was this apartness, concluded Jean Brassard, a professor of education at Université Laval in 1967, that explained why generational tension, apparent in all societies and historical periods, had reached "such a paroxysm"[87] in modern Western cultures. This type of generational thinking penetrated even within the precincts of the *collèges classiques*, those bastions of Catholic conservatism. There, by the mid-1960s, many educators delineated and at times openly celebrated a profound sense of generational difference and rupture. Even in situations where youth expressed no sense of overt opposition or contestation, and where their opinions indicated a continuity between their values and those of the older generation, educators and social observers were quick to point out that "19 out of 20 recognize themselves as simply different" from their parents.[88]

This widespread apprehension of discontinuity between the social and cultural values of older and younger generations had immediate repercussions for Catholic notions of family structure and authority. Perhaps the most striking element of Quebec's generational debate in Catholic circles during the 1960s was the opprobrium attached to parents, and particularly to fathers, whose moral and psychological failings had primarily instigated the youth counterculture. "Youth," declared Léon Girard in 1964, "is being frustrated today by a false paternalism; the gradual disintegration of the family spirit arises from the fact that youth is seeking for something outside the home that should have been available in the home."[89] The articulation of an exclusive, egalitarian youth sociability was testimony to the failure of the family to fulfill and enrich the individual personality, a theme sounded by René and Claudine Vallerand in 1963. Reflecting on the urban terrorism of the Front de Libération du Québec and how it differed from the rather tame radicalism of the immediate post-war generation, they portentously exclaimed that "the generation that has now reached twenty has seen the masks of hypocrisy ripped away." Quebec's rising level of social tension reflected the fact that young people had been driven to the realization that admired adult figures were no more than "con-men and cheats." Despite the unprecedented freedom that Quebec's young people enjoyed, the Vallerands characterized the 1960s generation as tortured and profoundly alienated, a pathological state that they traced to "the absent father."[90]

What was most significant was not the somewhat hackneyed existential juxtaposition of the psychological categories of freedom and alienation, but the fact that Claudine Vallerand had, during the 1940s, been one of the central figures in the formulation of the Quebec Catholic version of the "democratic family" built upon a firm notion of parental authority acquired through access to psychological expertise. Faced with the spectacle of youth revolt and the actual prospect of social violence, the Vallerands now advocated, not a reassertion of familial authority, but parental "humility" and the need for adults to "gradually efface themselves ... when confronted with new manifestations of life that emerge, take shape, and affirm themselves." More tellingly, by employing the metaphor of a "telescoping of generations" – in which they designated the younger generation's quest for more fulfilling personal relationships and a more humanistic society as more emotionally and spiritually mature than the values held by their parents,[91] and they dismissed the latter as "adolescent" in their conformist enslavement to material goods and passion for acquisition – the Vallerands overtly dispensed with any physiological or psychological barrier between adolescence and adulthood, asserting that "one's chronological age has very little to do with human maturity."[92]

The views of Gérard Pelletier, once a prominent Catholic Action youth leader and a major advocate in the late 1940s of the marriage preparation movement, also served as a sensitive indicator of the cultural change the youth counterculture produced in Quebec Catholic circles during the 1960s. As federal secretary of state after 1968, Pelletier was the minister chiefly responsible for youth policy, and although he was less overtly critical of parents than the Vallerands, he similarly maintained that dialogue and continuity between generations, though socially desirable, no longer rested upon an age hierarchy. Sound family relationships, according to his definition, functioned according to the new egalitarian, presentist criteria of the youth counterculture, and depended exclusively upon "love" and the ability of parents to earn the respect of their children, not by invoking the past, "but by the value of what we accomplish today."[93] Pelletier's reflections, which had been articulated in a series of articles in *Châtelaine* in late 1965, became the template for a major federal statement of youth policy, published in 1971, which praised the "counterculture" for inspiring a "counter-ideology" that was founded on new values and committed to effecting cultural and political change. Parents and the entire older generation, the report's authors charged, had "abdicated responsibility" for social transformation, and, at best, had watched passively "as the institutions into which their children are expected to march have become overgrown and inhuman."[94] This reversal of the lines of authority between adolescence and adulthood, a technique also employed by no less an authority figure than Cardinal Léger,[95] at a stroke eviscerated any notion of family hierarchy, and assigned an unprecedented moral legitimacy to the egalitarian aspirations of young people and their demands for personal freedom. In this way, those quintessential bastions of adult authority – family, church, and state – were turned into symbols of an ossified social and cultural stasis, and made accountable to the plastic, energetic, and imaginative qualities that characterized adolescence.

Nowhere was this assumed gulf that divided the youth counterculture and the adult generation – the divide between what a growing chorus of Catholic educators termed the healthy exercise of personal freedom and a hypocritical system of compulsion and restraint – more pronounced than in the realm of sexuality. The spectacle of young men and women asserting their right to fulfilling sexual relationships *before* and *outside* of marriage came to be recognized as a "sexual revolution," the central hallmark of many of the wider social and cultural transformations of the 1960s.[96] Efforts to account for this liberated sexual climate spurred the most hard-edged Catholic critiques of contemporary family structures and relationships, and ultimately compelled, by the end of the 1960s, a drastic reinterpretation of the family's functions that placed almost total weight upon that entity's ability to satisfy individual needs.

Already, in the late 1950s, some Catholic educators and psychologists had begun to comment, with some urgency, on the highly sexualized dating culture of teenagers. What distinguished liberals and conservatives was that the former were prepared to concede considerable moral and spiritual validity to teenage practices and relationships. However, both groups agreed on one central issue: that the advent of the "dating culture" – and, in particular, "going steady" – was a symptom of the postwar family's signal failure to accomplish its most important task in modern society, the emotional and psychological preparation of adolescents to assume adult sexual roles which alone could produce stable marriages and families.

In the mid-1950s, the major preoccupation of Quebec Catholic educators when confronted by the teenager dating culture had been the socially baneful effects of the supposed "feminization" of adolescent males brought about by their participation in semi-permanent relationships that apparently duplicated some elements of marriage. However, between 1958 and 1963, the principal focus had shifted from young men to young women. The sudden explosion in Canada and a number of European societies of a mass teenager consumer market[97] induced a number of Catholics to consider the implications of what behavioural surveys and mass media indicated was the convergence of male and female musical and dance tastes (rock 'n roll), clothing styles (denim), and hair styles, with the popularity of longer hair as unisex fashion. What was most troubling was that all of these cultural activities seemed to revel in an uninhibited sexual openness, and seemed to indicate that a single standard of precocious sexual knowledge and experimentation was acceptable for *both* young men and young women and had supplanted the older social conventions of female virginity, hesitancy, and restraint.[98]

The first intimations that a sea-change in the sexual attitudes of female adolescents presaged a wider revolution in sexual values was apparent in the lengthy debates held at the faculty of arts at Université Laval over the modernization of the *collège classique* curriculum. Worried about falling attendance at mass and sacraments, and indications of declining membership in Catholic Action movements, Mgr Guillaume Miville-Dechêne noted the prevalence, among young women aged fifteen to eighteen, of the unconstrained pursuit of gratification. "Our young women," he lugubriously concluded, "feel a hysterical need to live a 'bachelor's' life."[99] Father Hozaël Aganier, national chaplain of the Jeunesse Étudiante Catholique, described a "disaffection from the supernatural" among most of the age cohort attending Quebec's *collèges classiques*. However, what in his estimation was the most striking factor was that, for two or three years, educators had observed a troubling pattern, whereby female students manifested "far more internal revolts" than their male counterparts, a rejection of Catholicism that rarely occurred on the level of doctrine, or religious practice, but at the level of the emotions.[100] Educators realized that these alterations in the climate of female spirituality were of immense significance. Young women identified religion with emotion, and when they were unable to engage religious devotion with the senses, they "experienced the real anguish of having 'lost their faith,'" leaving an empty shell of religious practice.[101]

For Catholics concerned with the continued infusion of spirituality into youth culture, the sudden prominence of young women in discussions about adolescence marked the end of the religious culture of the post-war era and the dawn of a new set of cultural concerns. The key element was the shift in attention from creating a spirituality of marriage and family to attract young males into the task of family formation, to agonizing over the extent to which an apparently independent youth culture legitimized new patterns of adolescent female sexuality. In reference to young women, the term "emotions" implied a whole gamut of psychological states and standards of sexual conduct, and the almost complete interchangeability of religion and sexuality. The rejection by young women of Catholic sexual morality – especially in the realm of premarital and extramarital sex – in the name of pleasure and greater freedom of choice while they continued to pay lip-service to the institutional church raised serious worries about the commitment of young women to the task of forming stable families. Second, women had, from the beginning of specialized Catholic Action in the 1930s, heavily outnumbered men in nearly all the lay movements.[102] Post-war Catholicism's intersection with Quebec society required committed female lay militants to infuse a public Catholic presence into the family and through this channel into other social movements. From this perspective, the question became what future lay ahead for Catholicism, given the distaste that young women displayed for movements such as the Jeunesse Étudiante Catholique, and their adoption of more fashionable role-models such as Simone de Beauvoir, Françoise Sagan, and Brigitte Bardot,[103] all of whom celebrated an open sexuality calibrated purely upon pleasure and individual satisfaction.

Most treatments of the cultural climate of the 1960s generally follow a model driven by social changes in the United States and date the shift in public attention to questioning the status of women to the later years of the decade, citing the rapidly rising numbers of married women in paid work and the foundations laid by the civil rights movement as factors that spurred the resurgence of a more assertive type of feminist political organization.[104] However, in the context of Quebec, it was not the creation of an organized secular feminist movement – which did not exist prior to 1966 – but changes that Catholic educators apprehended in the sexuality of female adolescents that presaged the seismic shift in women's status. In the late 1950s, it was sexuality, not debates over women's political or economic status, that had captured public attention, because of two central considerations that were specific to the way in which Catholicism had come to define its relationship to the family and the wider culture.

From the late 1930s onward, through the impetus of Catholic Action endeavours such as the marriage preparation movement, Catholic religious practice had subtly shifted away from clerical prescriptions and, in the minds of many laypeople, become inextricably intertwined with a type of affectional nuclear family which rested almost wholly upon a sacramentalized sexuality exclusive to marriage. In so doing, Catholic Action had created a situation whereby *any* alteration of sexual values that moved in the direction of sexuality outside of marriage entailed, almost by definition, a decline in religious standards. "Religion," declared one Catholic youth activist, "has in our country traditionally presented itself as the defender of the family. On its side, the family has contributed to religion for many years by transmitting and nourishing a robust faith. But it appears more and more that this liaison between the family and Christianity is becoming artificial, and in some cases is entirely ruptured. ... A certain conformity in attendance at sacraments still binds together the members of the family, but increasingly, religion does not seem to be an internal principal of spiritual animation."[105]

By the late 1950s, even conservative apologists for the Quebec family like Philippe Garigue wondered whether the acceptance of family life as a "'universe of rules'" had in fact created a close identification of religion and family that was unhealthy because it stressed only the more restrictive aspects of both: the imperatives to "sacrifice" and "duty" that the more pleasure-seeking adolescent culture openly flouted.[106] When, in the mid-1950s, some Catholic educators and family experts began advocating greater sexual freedom and experimentation for young people as the pre-condition of a healthy psychological transition to adulthood, they both implicitly and explicitly devalued the family as the foundation of both individual well-being and of the democratic order so painstakingly reconstructed after the depression and war. This in turn simply reinforced a polarized climate that was increasingly evident in Quebec Catholicism during the 1950s, as some articulate Catholics began to identify the positive values of "modernity" with the aspirations of youth to escape the hierarchical and psychological constraints of the family. They therefore identified the family – and by extension its defenders – with "tradition," and in so doing, explicitly articulated a critique of the family as the transmitter of a code of sexual morality and religious values, hitherto its primary function in a Catholic society. From this emerged the view that, at the level of the most basic functions of the family, there was an irreconcilable rupture between the values of tradition and modernity. To identify the family with "tradition" thus meant casting it as one of the principal culprits that was constraining social and cultural progress in both Catholicism and the wider culture because it incarnated the very counter-values of routine, stasis, and conformity that repressed, and thus deformed at both an individual and social level, the impulse towards a healthy identification with the modern era.

It might well be expected that the crisis occasioned by the discrepancy between the actual sexual behaviour of youth and the post-war equation of Catholicism with the idea that sex should be restricted to marriage would have provoked a conservative reaction among Quebec Catholics aimed at increasing the control of families and educational authorities over their teenagers. However, in a rather surprising reversal, a number of articulate Catholics during the early 1960s used adolescents' apparent rejection of the idea that sex should be restricted to marriage as the occasion for an assault on one of the most venerable Quebec social institutions: the tradition of education separated by sex that was enshrined in papal teaching[107] and represented most visibly by the Church-controlled *collèges classiques*. Supporters of the old system, like Father Jean Genest, charged that coeducation was false because it rested upon "a naturalism that negates original sin" and that it would make the school system the social architect of "*promiscuity and egalitarian levelling.*"[108] However, critics of the old system argued that the main reason that young people had increasingly turned to the seductions of the mass media and the structures of their own independent culture was that separate educational institutions had failed them. The colleges, they charged, had erected "a species of *apartheid*" between men and women, and they hinted, not so subtly, that in trying to repress the adolescent sexual instinct, colleges were only succeeding at driving it underground or deforming it into homosexuality.[109] "It is very dangerous," concluded one Catholic Action study, "that those who do not date develop certain complexes which might lead them to believe that they are different from others."[110]

To illustrate how the colleges had created an internal, and mutually-exclusive tension between teenagers' "religious aspirations and the need that they feel to meet young people of the opposite sex," opponents of the *collèges classiques* seized upon vivid examples of nuns admonishing young women that they had to "choose between God and boys" and young men likewise warned by male clergy that girls were "an obstacle to vocations."[111] Separate education, charged Professor J.E. Havel, was immoral, because it did not prevent "young people boiling with desire to engage in sexual experimentation. It is better that they do so with the opposite sex, rather than keeping them apart and thereby fostering homosexuality."[112] The Parent Commission, which between 1963 and 1965 recommended sweeping reforms to Quebec's educational system, drew heavily upon these discussions in recommending that coeducation be made a subject of serious consideration. The commissioners reasoned that ending separate male and female education would avoid duplication at the level of secondary schooling, and they essentially agreed with the position taken by many Catholic youth workers on the culture of teen dating, that bringing male and female adolescents into closer proximity would establish a "sounder basis for relationships" between young men and young women. In addressing the moral arguments that some Catholics had always used to defend sex-segregated education, the commission argued that papal teaching was not immutable, and it wondered whether opposition to coeducation, "the product of an age when the family and religious environment was restrictive," remained valid "under the conditions in which adolescents are brought up today."[113]

The debate on coeducation was significant because it brought church institutions, and the way in which the Catholic religion had structured and defined youth, under the sharp scrutiny of those who not only accepted but exalted the existence of a generation gap that was based on a healthy sexual freedom for adolescents, as opposed to the narrow puritanism of adults. However, the musings of the Parent Commission, which adopted the radical metaphors of cultural rupture by using words like "restrictive" to label the family and the Catholic educational environment, pointed to a far more profound anxiety. If some Catholics were willing to concede a degree of social legitimacy and independence to the new youth culture, did not this independence signal a profound crisis in the institutional family? And if this was the case, and young people had actually created a cultural world apart from their families, would Catholicism have to drastically uncouple its post-war triad of religious values, the affectional nuclear family, and the stability of public authority?

By the mid-1960s, advocates of Catholic marriage were acutely conscious of a crisis of authority that was eating away at the very structure of the family itself. "Today's married couple," declared Dr Camille Laurin, a prominent Montreal psychiatrist at the 1966 banquet of the Service de Préparation au Mariage, "is going through a very difficult phase because the foundations, ideals, norms and values upon which it was inspired are undergoing an unprecedented upheaval." As a psychiatrist, Laurin diagnosed the most common symptoms of this upheaval, which, he felt, were typified by a pathology of "incoherence" in the relations between husbands and wives, by which he meant a lack of correspondence between values and behaviour. Family breakdown, he maintained, was increasingly evident in a "conflict of generations" expressed in increasingly violent and abusive language. "It is our modern age that has coined," Laurin lamented, "those adjectives of sell-out, morally bankrupt" used by the young to describe the older generation.[114] What was most significant about Laurin's address was his equation of these symptoms of family breakdown with a wider cultural phenomenon – the "desacralization" of Quebec society, revealed in the growing propensity of many of the younger generation to dispense with all forms of authority[115] and to reject even marriage itself, because it restricted the free expression of the sexual self. "Chastity," Laurin ruefully observed, "is beginning to supplant masturbation as 'the principal cause of physical and mental maladjustment.'"[116]

As a prominent Catholic layman and a veteran of a number of Catholic Action movements, Laurin remained hopeful that the family would be able to renew itself by tapping into new reservoirs of psychological and social strength. In this way, he remained outwardly confident that Catholicism would be able to negotiate a new relationship with youth, and thus sustain the continuum between religious values and public authority that had "preserved and maintained the moral fibre of the family and our nation."[117]

However, by this point in time, Laurin's own career had reached something of a crossroads. In an interview with Alice Parizeau in early 1966, he reflected on the growing number of unsatisfied, resentful wives and psychologically-maladapted children that he had encountered in his clinic. He reckoned that these individuals experiencing intense personal unhappiness were the products of a pathology produced by an irrepressible conflict between the need for personal satisfaction and a repressive, authoritarian family structure that afflicted many Quebec families, one that rested upon "the infallibility of parents." Taking a none-too-subtle potshot at clericalism, Laurin charged that within the wider society, this pathology was most overtly illustrated in the tight control religious orders exercised over education, a situation that had arisen because of the need to break "strong-willed individuals."[118] The intensity of the individual psychological dissatisfaction he encountered led him to intimate that "those three great lodestars of authority, God, country, and family have lost their magic power." Current social science thinking, he admitted, "undermined the authority of the family by introducing the idea that it was no longer a supreme tribunal" and could actually be described as good or bad, depending on the extent to which it enhanced or impaired the personality development of individuals, the once-subordinate adolescents, wives, and children.[119] In the following year, Laurin began a personal quest for what he ardently believed was a new, more consensual mode of social authority, becoming one of the founding members of the Mouvement Souveraineté-Association (Sovereignty-Association Movement) and later a leading member of its successor political movement, the Parti Québécois.[120] Through his sponsorship of Bill 101, the controversial language legislation of 1977, Laurin was among those who were primarily responsible for articulating the vision of a unilingual, independent French society as a new form of social cohesion in Quebec.

Laurin's advocacy of independence as the path to resolving the crisis of authority occasioned by the breakdown of the symbiotic relationship of family and religion ultimately failed to enlist the overwhelming support of Quebec Catholics.[121] However, in the mid-1960s, both liberal and conservative tendencies within Catholicism increasingly agreed that there existed alarming symptoms of family "crisis," and that these had been provoked by a breakdown in the post-war equilibrium that once harmonized personal fulfillment and institutional cohesion. Commenting on the rising divorce rate among North American couples aged twenty-five to thirty-four, Quebec social worker René Raymond explained the situation by alluding to the "secularization of values" that had afflicted the modern family. This was a catch-all phrase meant to encompass religious decline, the growing role of material comfort, and the disproportionate attention given to children. Instead of making the family the centre of personal, intimate values in an increasingly bureaucratic, impersonal society, Raymond stated that "the increased freedom given to the sexual aspects of marriage" had merely accentuated the potential for discord. He estimated that the abrupt conjunction of material prosperity and a democratic cultural climate had undermined the status of the family as a social institution anchored on procreation, child-rearing, and "the gift of mutual affection," and had transformed it instead into a temporary collection of individuals seeking self-fulfillment. Secularization of the family – the "desacralization" identified by Camille Laurin – had brought in its train "certain forms of marginality" which had made the family the "black sheep of social life."[122]

Similarly, sociologist Philippe Garigue, who presided over the Conseil

Supérieur de la Famille and was a leading defender of the institutional family, drew attention to the disintegration of the French-Canadian family, sounding the alarm over the rising rate of juvenile delinquency and the flurry of legal separations that had occurred after the reforms to the Civil Code in 1964. What especially preoccupied Garigue, however, was the increasingly paradoxical behaviour of young people. While the rising rate of marriage and the declining age of newlyweds might otherwise have indicated that there was still adherence to post-war Catholic ideals of family, this was belied by the increasing tendency of couples to have fewer children. From Garigue's standpoint, what this meant was that young couples placed a premium on individual self-satisfaction, while at the same time rejecting the notions of parental duty and responsibility that sustained the institutional role of the family. For him, this tendency marked "the crumbling of the large and exuberant French-Canadian family."[123] Activists in the Jeunesse Étudiante Catholique agreed with Garigue that relations between adolescents and their families had reached a point of crisis, but they traced the confrontation to the failure of the family to engage in a profound revision of its structure and function in the light of new conditions. The family, they charged, had largely ceased to provide intimacy and spiritual sustenance, and was now a mechanism of consumption where contact between parents and children had been reduced to meals, watching television, and superficial conversations.[124]

It was precisely the mid-1960s discussion surrounding "deviancy" – the social pathology of separation, divorce, juvenile delinquency, rebellious youth – that revealed that the family had become a terrain of political and religious controversy between liberal and conservative Catholics. On the one hand, there were those like Governor-General Georges Vanier who both celebrated the family as being founded upon the "sacred bonds" of marriage and in the next breath inveighed against the modern tendency to insist so much upon personal liberty that "even motherhood may appear not as a glory but as a fetter to woman."[125] In contrast was a new current of public wisdom that was coming increasingly to the fore, and was evident even in the precincts of the prestigious Vanier Institute of the Family. This view, premised upon the individual's need for greater freedom and self-realization, explicitly sanctioned a new view of social deviance. Rather than interpret it as a personal moral failing or a symptom of a cultural conflict between the institutional family and the imperatives of mass civilization, this view increasingly regarded social deviance as the product of deficient family relationships. "When one considers the antecedents of the criminal, of the prostitute, of the delinquent adolescent," intoned one memorandum, "one always finds that there is some deep-seated flaw in his family life."[126] As the influential 1971 Report of the Secretary of State's Committee on Youth concluded, deviant forms of youth behaviour were but the reflection of the "very intensity of the family relationship," which tended to warp the human personality, either by making children conformist "duplicates of their parents," or inspiring in them a wholesale revulsion, turning them into "photographic negatives of everything for which their parents stand."[127]

In the years after 1964, the responses of young people to questions about marriage and sexuality revealed that Quebec Catholicism was faced with a massive rejection of the institutional concept of the family that it had formulated and aggressively articulated during the post-war era. A survey conducted among high school students in the St Jérôme diocese in 1970 revealed that on issues of Catholic moral teaching, 50 per cent agreed with the use of contraceptives, 60 per cent approved of divorce, and 57 per cent supported the idea of free love, although it must be emphasized that in the latter case the approval was in the abstract, and most respondents rejected it as a standard for their own relationships.[128] What was more perplexing was that even within the confines of the church-controlled *collèges classiques*, where conservative notions of family might have prevailed, the defection of young women from conventional notions of marriage was particularly compelling. For example, at Collège Ste-Anne-de-la-Pocatière, which had become coeducational in 1965, the Conseil Étudiant des Filles (Girls' Student Council) reported the result of a survey undertaken as part of its brief to the Royal Commission on the Status of Women. Fifty per cent of responses stated that marriage was less respected in contemporary society, and while the authors of the statement supported the idea of premarital chastity, they admitted that it was not a principle that their respondents expected to honour.[129] What was most significant, however, was the highly individualistic definition of marriage itself that seemed to prevail among these young women. "The meaning of the marriage partnership," declared the brief, "is founded upon the total self-realization of two individuals, rather than upon the idea that marriage exists for procreation."[130]

In light of the cultural shock waves of youth revolt and the prevalence, among social scientists, of the view that the family was responsible for a host of individual and social pathologies, many liberal Catholics concluded that the family's survival depended on the explicit promotion of more individualistic views of marriage which openly embraced personal fulfillments and satisfactions, rather than a set of institutional duties and responsibilities centred on procreation and child-rearing. Fernande Saint-Martin, editor of *Châtelaine*, castigated older religious and legal concepts of marriage, arguing that "the idea that spouses had to abstract their individual existences and the satisfaction of their emotional needs, and think only of the stability and permanence of the family" was obsolete and psychologically harmful, and would foster only "sick families that would impair the healthy personal development of their children."[131] The post-war model of the patriarchal family, charged Alice Parizeau, gave little scope to "the aspirations of wives and mothers for fulfillment. Why, they didn't even exist as individuals."[132] Though Catholic Action's highly popular marriage preparation movement – still rated in the early 1960s as a "national institution"[133] – continued to educate close to 50 per cent of engaged couples in the Montreal diocese and retained its appeal among the more prosperous elements of the working class and lower middle class,[134] leaders of the movement increasingly downplayed permanence and solidarity as the hallmarks of a successful marriage. Madeleine Trottier, the secretary of the Montreal SPM, declared that in the future those contemplating marriage would have to commit themselves to an ongoing effort to ensure mutual happiness, satisfactory sexual adjustment, integration and unity, and self-adjustment in the relationship.[135]

However, in the final analysis, one factor overrode all others as the key to explaining why the family had developed pathological tendencies in an era of rapid cultural change, and why the family institution needed to be downplayed in favour of individual identity and personal fulfillment. This revolved around perceived defects in what both liberal and conservative Catholics accepted as the primary function of the affectional nuclear family: the articulation and transmission of sexual knowledge and roles, which alone could prepare children and adolescents for emotionally secure adult lives. Both tendencies within Catholicism used the evidence of a transformation in youth sexual attitudes to launch an overt assault upon lines of authority and how knowledge was transmitted from parent to child within the family itself. In the words of the Dominican Father Hyacinthe-Marie Robillard, Quebec's families were not the "democratic" model of camaraderie and mutual trust, but rather, institutions ruled by authority and subordination. The test was how parents handled the healthy sexual curiosity of their adolescents. Instead of using it as an opportunity to educate the affections and emotions, they repressed all manifestations of adolescent sexual activity as leading to occasions of sin.[136] Robillard's conservative colleague, the Jesuit Father Joseph d'Anjou, similarly castigated modern parents for "failing to understand their educative responsibilities through their own lack of education, and failing to create in their homes the elevating and comfortable atmosphere that their daughters need to mature." The result was that young women increasingly sought sexual knowledge in "scabrous" workplace conversations or from the highly eroticized setting of mass-circulation magazines or films.[137] Even in smaller centres outside of Montreal, surveys undertaken by Catholic Action demonstrated a widespread breakdown in the family's most crucial function: the training of the young in adult sex roles. "Young people," lamented a study undertaken of Chicoutimi working-class youth in 1961, "are largely left to themselves for their sexual and sentimental education. They attribute little importance to their families in this area, and it is evident that the family is far from accomplishing its mission to educate adolescents in matters of love."[138]

In Catholic circles by the mid-1960s, the most popular interpretation of the family crisis was that the entire structure of pathology, and the consequent marginalization of the institutional family by the needs of the individuals comprising it, returned to the problem of deficient male sex roles and the interaction of fathers with their families. One 1964 Catholic Action study summed up the problem in the following terms: "Men have hitherto not been the centre of the French-Canadian family, but they are the final authority, giving approval to all family decisions. Women are more mothers than wives."[139] The description evoked a rather distant, authoritarian, and emotionally uninvolved male parent who left child-rearing to his wife in order to pursue his job or career. One consequence of such an attitude was that the values of intimacy and sexual partnership between husband and wife suffered, leading to a profound lack of individual fulfillment on the part of women. More tellingly, the distant, authoritarian figure of the father fostered a revulsion against the family on the part of the young. Even so eloquent a defender of the institutional family as Philippe Garigue, whose 1962 *Vie familiale des Canadiens-français* portrayed the survival of older concepts of male authority in the modern nuclear family, admitted at the Canadian Conference on the Family in 1964 that the solution to the various pathologies of the modern family did not lie in measures designed to reinforce parental authority and family solidarity. These might simply produce more revolts against the family, as "in some situations," he stated, "the existence of particular rules of conduct in the family can be enough in itself to drive members into asocial and even deviant modes of behaviour, despite the family's complete structural stability."[140]

However, conservative family experts like Garigue were quick to point out that the crisis of the modern Quebec family would not be solved by enhancing the individualist side of the post-war equation. Rather, the solution lay in a refurbishing of many of the post-war Catholic prescriptions which had asserted a close link between the presence of husbands and fathers in the family and male authority in the wider society. The key lay in rendering male role models more intimate as this would counteract what analysts like Garigue believed was one of the leading causes of pathological behaviour: the existence, through male distance or absence, of a cloying, emotionally voracious matriarchy. Indeed, a number of Quebec commentators in the early 1960s devoted considerable attention to diagnosing and decrying what they assumed was the causal relationship between first and foremost a lack of sexual intimacy between husbands and wives, the transformation of mothers into overprotective matriarchs, and the "Jansenist," repressive climate of family relations[141] that lay at the root of the yawning generation gap. The existence of this "Jansenism" was most evident in adult responses to adolescent sexuality. André Thibault's 1963 study revealed that adults had more concern for protecting youth against supposed outside threats to moral behaviour than they had real interest in the problems of adolescence. "Our society," he concluded, "offers little support to adolescents from the moment they become conscious of the awakening of their sexuality and the new exuberant state of their emotions." Teenagers experienced an intense solitude, an atmosphere in which they felt "ashamed and disapproved of in advance."[142]

What distinguished liberals from conservatives in this discussion was that the former believed that the root causes of this pathological climate of family life lay in the inner dynamics of the Quebec Catholic family itself, and in particular, in what they believed was Catholicism's promotion of a positively immoral concept of marriage. Reformers accused Catholicism of teaching that "the primary goal of marriage is to satisfy lusts of the flesh, and in the second instance, procreation,"[143] thus eviscerating any notion that women had a right to individual sexual satisfaction outside of child-bearing. This, explained the journalist Michelle Lasnier in 1962, forced wives to become emotional predators upon their children, enclosing the children in "a devouring and authoritarian tenderness." This also forced husbands to sunder their own selves by organizing their lives into public and private compartments in which work and career had no contact with family concerns and responsibilities. It was this sexual malaise, she concluded, that had forced the family to become a set of "rigid structures against which individuals have to run counter in order to express themselves. And from this encounter, they can only emerge as wounded and truncated beings."[144]

Conservatives, on the other hand, maintained that the breakdown in sex roles flowed from the recent introduction of American models of family practice into Quebec as a consequence of late post-war prosperity. Thus, in analysing the differences between American and French-Canadian families, Garigue drew attention to the fact that family life was "much idealized," but not considered an institution, because it gave priority to the individual rather than to the group. The result of this faulty scale of priorities was a frantic quest for material satisfaction to fill an emotional void, and, as a corollary, the reduction of the husband's role to "one of economic support and influence, rather than of final authority," as, because of his wife's intimate contact with and ability to satisfy the emotional needs of the children, he abdicated to her the most important role of "'operational' centre of family life."[145] In assessing these characteristics of a modern matriarchy, Garigue darkly stated the consequences of the male absence in families: "Is this the kind of family I want to live in? I think not."[146]

Garigue's dislike of matriarchy was shared by more liberal-minded Catholic social scientists, like his Laval colleague Guy Rocher. However, as early as 1954, Rocher was willing to admit that the causes of this social deviation might be inherent to Quebec's own model of post-war family relations. He observed that because the modern family centred almost completely on the emotional and affectional fulfillment of its members, there was always the potential for a "hypertrophy of the maternal figure." Although, as post-war Catholic Action had emphasized, he firmly believed that strict male and female role definitions were essential for the healthy emotional development of children, he also located within them the seeds of the child's resentment and hatred of parents. The father, in his estimation, represented the world outside the family, the modern, competitive ethic of success, while the woman-as-emotional-nurturer, identified completely with the inner, psychological realm of the affections, frequently became, through overprotection, an obstacle to the child's adaptation to the world,[147] and the source of a host of deviant behaviours: male alcoholism, sexual incompatibility, homosexuality, juvenile delinquency, and youth revolt.

A more overtly politicized current of discontent surrounded the Quebec Catholic family as issues related to the status of women grew in intensity after the mid-1960s. Wanting to ensure the continued achievement of legal and social measures for women's emancipation, advocates like Fernande Saint-Martin, the editor of *Châtelaine*, refuted the supposed existence of a Quebec matriarchy. She sarcastically turned Garigue's own sociological investigations against him by arguing that the persistence of strong lines of male authority in the family had scarcely allowed any female presence to register in family councils. Rather, Saint-Martin acidly observed that "it was impossible to dialogue" with husbands and fathers "precisely because of the distance" they maintained from the daily problems of their children "in the interests of preserving the prestige and inflexibility of the head of the family group."[148] Solange Chalvin, her colleague at *Le Devoir*, conceded that while there had been a very powerful maternal influence on the family, this could scarcely be described as a matriarchy, and indeed, because it had been exercised more subtly and surreptitiously, the overweening identification of women with the family had simply allowed husbands and fathers "to escape responsibility, which left him as a role model of no account in the eyes of his children."[149] For feminists, the path to resolving the crisis caused by rigid structures of family sex roles and authority, and thus the pathological aspects of the family itself, lay not in governmental or institutional measures designed to reinforce traditional role expectations. Such legislative solutions would only perpetuate inequities by restricting the access of women to the realm of individual satisfactions offered by careers and the possibility of making an economic contribution to family life. Rather, many feminists enjoined husbands and fathers to adopt more "feminized" roles that would enable them to interact more constructively with their children through the expression of understanding and intuition.[150] However much these feminists might have resembled immediate post-war Catholic family advocates in their appeals for male involvement with the family, the intention was not to shore up older models of family solidarity, but rather to enunciate the primacy of the fulfillment of women *as individuals* as the touchstone of modern family relations.

By 1964, the Catholic family was the scene of increasingly discordant polemics over one of its most essential functions as an institutional entity, namely, its continued ability to ensure, through the authoritative example of parents, the orderly transmission of adult male and female sex roles to the next generation. From the late 1950s onward, Catholic clergy and lay social scientists and educators had been increasingly divided over the question of the moral and cultural legitimacy of an independent adolescent form of sociability, and whether the convergent phenomena of youth revolt and sexual revolution indicated the existence of individual and social pathologies caused by the repressive character of the family itself. In particular, investigations of the defection of young women from the standard of premarital chastity seemed to provide overwhelming evidence that Catholic marriage itself was deeply flawed as a religious and cultural ideal. Many Catholics now accepted that the ultimate source of pathological behaviours was the deformation of sex roles caused by the family structure itself. Specifically, this structure was viewed as having produced overly-authoritarian and distant fathers, and sexually repressed, emotionally cloying wives and mothers.

The realization, during the early 1960s, of the potentially deviant nature of these very sex roles that were once taken as the basis of family solidarity and equilibrium led in turn to one of the most drastic reversals of cultural authority, one accepted by both liberal Catholics and by a number of influential conservative Catholics. From the 1930s and throughout most of the post-war period, Catholic opinion in Quebec had always resisted mass sex education,[151] believing that this was the one task that belonged solely to the modern family institution, which would fulfill this education on an individual basis. However, as Fernande Saint-Martin observed in 1961, this expectation depended entirely upon "the degree of maturity" exhibited by the parents.[152] The prominence, in social science discussion of the 1960s, of pathological family conditions, and of the highly visible manifestations of the sexual revolution, in which the sex act itself was desacralized, separated from love and marriage, and increasingly linked to personal physical and mental hygiene, convinced a wide swath of Catholic opinion that the family had abjectly failed its most essential social task. As the psychologist André Lussier asserted in 1966, Quebec had passed, in a few short years, from being "stifled by taboos, inhibitions, and repressions, to being drugged by an excess of sexuality, lacking all direction or rule."[153]

The advent of mass state-controlled secondary education after 1964, and the concomitant introduction of coeducational comprehensive high schools and public collegiate institutions, persuaded even the most ardent conservative apologists that massive institutional intervention was warranted to compensate for the family's deficiencies. It was in the school, and not in the family, that adolescents could ultimately find not only accurate instruction, but also sympathetic understanding from a new generation of teachers, counsellors, and chaplains, who could undertake the task of sex education more effectively than indifferent, distant, or rigidly repressive parents. Prominent Catholic social scientists, and even the authorities of the Archdiocese of Montreal, took a leading role in 1966 in establishing the Institut de Sexologie at the Université de Montréal,[154] anticipating the need for sex education teachers in the new public high school system. Even so rabid an opponent of coeducation as Father Jean Genest admitted in 1967 that young people "had the right to know" and needed to acquire ideals and the ability to measure the consequences of their acts – all of which would only occur through sex education. Because, in his estimation, parents had shirked their responsibilities in transmitting this type of culture, the school presented itself as "the best means for a corrective type of teaching."[155] Father Gaston Lapointe castigated the decision of the Montreal Catholic School Commission – a decision the commission based on its wish not to intrude on the prerogatives of parents – to dispense twenty-seven secondary schools from sex instruction. Few parents, he stated, even attempted to undertake this task with their adolescents. He was even more concerned about ensuring that high schools not present human sexuality "in the way that many of today's parents were educated. The horrible jansenism in which many of the older generation were raised prevents them from fulfilling their responsibility towards their children. Some ways of doing this have traumatized human beings for the rest of their lives."[156]

The initiative undertaken by more reformist Catholics to forge a new relationship with youth through mass sex education also amounted to an overt attack upon the nexus that post-war Catholic Action had forged between the affectional nuclear family and models of familist corporatism. The context for mass sex education was the new, state-controlled public secondary school system, one in which Catholicism had, in the wake of the wide-ranging educational reforms, a moral and cultural presence, but in which Catholic teachers and clergy were to undertake sex instruction on behalf of the public authorities. It was a situation that did not go uncriticized. In some schools, sex education was introduced under the rubric of catechism, a conflation that earned the opprobrium of many conservative parents and clergy, because, in their view, it tended to dissolve under the rather vague concept of "love" the crucial distinction between sin and redemption. One report described how modern catechism classes had degenerated from an authoritative presentation of doctrine to endless discussions "on themes like freedom, war, world poverty, love, dating ... and we come out of these rap-sessions as mixed-up and as ignorant as when we went in."[157] "Young people," declared one concerned group from the diocese of Nicolet, "interpret the word Love in the erotic sense and do not consider its implications of self-sacrifice."[158] A group of women in Roberval who wrote to the Royal Commission on the Status of Women in 1968 accused Catholicism of "taking the child out of the family" by "removing religious teaching from the schools and adding the teaching of sexuality. What kind of common sense is this, that collectivizes a type of instruction that must be individual and discreet, and undertaken without false modesty?"[159] Perhaps the most devastating comment on Catholicism's overt attempt to substitute its new institutional alliance with the state for the function of the family was offered in 1971 by Father J. Alphonse Beaulieu, parish priest of Mont-Joli. "I find it most curious," he remonstrated, "how in the last few years both State and Church have discovered a philanthropic mission in the field of sexology. Sex for being a better citizen, sex for encountering God. In school and elsewhere, young people are constantly bombarded with sex education. They are saturated. ... Besides, it is utterly laughable to believe that one can encounter God through sexual experience."[160]

"THE BRAYING OF TRANSISTORS HAS, IN MOST FAMILIES, INCREASINGLY REPLACED THE LITANY OF THE ROSARY"[161]

Hélène Pelletier-Baillargeon conveyed to the readers of *Maintenant*, Quebec's leading liberal Catholic review, a sense of the deep moral gulf between tradition and modernity in 1960s Quebec. She resorted to an arresting image, one that contrasted the transistor radio, international symbol and primary accoutrement of the contemporary youth culture's claim to a cultural space independent from their parents, with the ordered, calm, hierarchical world of family prayer.[162] In so doing, Pelletier-Baillargeon articulated what was in fact the most corrosive assault of an influential section of Quebec Catholicism on the structure and functions of the family. In its reaction to the youth revolt and the broader implications of the sexual revolution, Quebec resembled other Western societies in which sexuality and gender roles occupied a terrain of generational contestation. However, what accentuated the impact of the cultural revolution of the 1960s in Quebec was that the separation between youth and adults was interpreted as primarily revolving around radically divergent religious values.

Increasingly, mainstream opinion within Catholicism emphatically deployed "youth" as a separate and privileged religious category which was used to flay and excoriate what was brusquely dismissed as old-style, routine, and conformist religious beliefs and practices among the older generation. In delineating the religious sphere as the scene of a cultural fault line between parents and adolescents, reformist Catholics like Pelletier-Baillargeon and the *Maintenant* circle built upon the virulently anti-institutional polemics that a number of vocal personalists had voiced during the 1950s. By the late 1960s, their attempts to formulate a conflictual dialectic between tradition and modernity had resulted in the evisceration of what had been one of the post-war Catholic family's principal cultural functions: the transmission, from parent to child, of religious knowledge. In terms of the way Catholics envisioned internal family dynamics, this in turn eroded one of the most important bonds of family solidarity. This was the belief that parental authority was legitimate because parents had superior access to religion through age and experience. The overt identity that Catholicism established in the 1960s between adolescence and religious virtue sanctioned a more individualistic scheme of family relations, and implicitly gave credence to many of youth's other cultural demands.

The most telling effects of Catholicism's new approach became rapidly evident in the way in which the family now related to the public culture. In the name of aggressively accelerating Quebec's path to religious modernity, influential Catholics sought to carve out a separate relationship with youth, one that relied upon an educational alliance between religion and the state that allowed the Church to bypass Catholic parents in the name of providing better religious instruction. It thus tacitly abandoned its post-war synthesis of religion, the sacrament of marriage, and the institutional family. And in resolving the family into a number of competing age-specific categories of individuals, it overturned the concept of the family as the hinge between the public realm and the private sphere by advancing a view of Catholicism that turned its back on the familist corporatism that had enjoyed a revival under the Lesage Liberal reforms of social policy. By 1970, Catholic clergy and laity promoted a new vision of public authority, decreeing in the name of social development the demolition of all institutional barriers between the individual and the state.

One of the peculiar features of the discovery of "teenager" culture by Quebec Catholics at the end of the 1950s was that the surveys and debates that accompanied the discovery encouraged the widespread belief that generational differences were not simply a matter of sexual conduct, but were most visibly demarcated in the area of religion. For example, one 1955 survey of adolescent student attitudes to the Catholic mass revealed, despite the strong institutional presence of Catholic Action in the *collèges classiques*, the strong persistence of "traditional" attitudes. In this context, "tradition" was interpreted as a type of individualistic, anthropological piety that conformed to an unconscious, routine calculus of obligation and reward. Educators vociferously expressed their disgust with the fact that most adolescents attended mass "out of habit" and "only in the expectation that they will receive personal favours" from their prayers.[163] A self-conscious avant-garde of Quebec Catholic reformers eagerly applied the same virulently anti-institutional critique that had encapsulated apprehensions during the 1950s that "traditional" or conformist religion was simply accelerating the spiritual vacuity of their society's middle-class elites. The fear was that the pressures of life in standardized North American society would actually reinforce the formalist, sociological "traditional" Christianity based on individual piety and devotional rituals.

One of the most important considerations that emerged from these reflections was a notion of religious dichotomy or "spiritual schizophrenia" indicated by mass devotional participation that was ultimately empty of real commitment or meaning.[164] Thus, for Brother Albini Girouard, Quebec youth were simply swallowing wholesale the values and attitudes of American mass culture, which provided the lure of a "spiritual drug or barbiturate"[165] subversive of Catholicism's call to energy and action. At a conference on educational reform held at Université Laval in 1958, Father Hozaël Aganier, the national chaplain of the Jeunesse Étudiante Catholique, spoke with alarm about what he described as a "general inassimilation of Catholicism by the majority of students." The difficulty, he explained, lay not in an intellectual rejection of Catholicism in favour of secularist or materialist ideologies, but in the "wholesale rejection" of the Christian life, particularly at the level of "affectivity," a term which denoted the entire spectrum of sexual conduct, family relationships, and gender identities. Aganier drew a sombre picture of modern students who had no interest in even discussing the principles of Christianity, even though the vast majority continued to go through the motions of church attendance and participation at the sacraments. "Our young Christians," he lamented, are "*Christians without vocation*; this is the contemporary religious drama of our society."[166] As Father Marcel Marcotte outlined the problem, modern adolescents were aware of, and increasingly accepted a sharp break or "latent contradiction" between religious and secular life. The danger lay in the fact that young people felt powerless to resolve the contradiction, and thus opted increasingly either to detach themselves from all sources of religion or to preserve a shallow adherence to certain religious "traditions" and external devotional forms that they had personally selected out of a need for security.[167] This replacement of faith by what these critics haughtily dismissed as "religion" – understood to mean a shallow system of rituals and behaviour patterns – would surely lead to unbelief flowing from what they discerned as "strong impulses towards protest and anger" against the Church and the conventions of family life.[168]

Significantly, however, these radical Catholic personalists did not direct the blame at young people or at the new youth culture's emphasis on greater personal freedom and self-realization. Rather, they worried that modern youth's propensity to rebellion against adult values held the potential for a massive rejection of religious values, insofar as these were identified with adult authority.[169] As a response to this worry, those Catholics who accepted that youth culture contained legitimate spiritual and cultural values began an open campaign to align the values of Catholicism with those of youth, frequently evoking the language of renewal and greater openness to the secular world that inspired the reforms of Vatican II. However, it should be emphasized that the impulse behind this change was less the external pressure for reform emanating from Rome, and more the attempt of a number of vocal Quebec Catholic personalists to find an accommodation between Catholic doctrine and the libertarian currents of modern youth culture. Writing in 1961, Emmanuel Rioux stated that "a breeze of renovation is blowing over the world and the Church, and in this new climate, youth deserves a far greater hearing because it is the repository of specific values."[170] Some educators increasingly accepted that the best way to channel the new adolescent aggression towards authority and received wisdom was to "emphasize the revolutionary aspects of Christianity, and to insist upon the affinities between the spirit of revolt that resides within youth and the authentic Christian spirit."[171]

In Quebec, the religious socialization of children and youth had in the past been accomplished by a reciprocal modelling of hierarchical educational authority carried out by the family and parish. In a manner similar to the transmission of sex and gender roles, children and adolescents assimilated religious values almost unconsciously, by participating, under the authority of their parents, in Catholic devotions and sacraments which emphasized the seamless unity between family solidarity and the parish community.[172] This acquisition of religious knowledge was reinforced in the first instance by the compulsory religious devotions of the public school, which prior to the 1964 reforms were overtly confessional, and were defined, at least in terms of Catholic social theory, as an adjunct of family and parish. The collèges classiques, attended by the children of professional and middle-class elites, were for the most part directly controlled by diocesan bishops or religious orders, and because teachers and clergy in these schools acted in a parental capacity, students were also ostensibly required to participate in prayers and devotional culture. In this context, it is therefore to be expected that the attempt to incorporate some of the libertarian elements of the new youth sociability immediately disturbed the equation of the educational authority of Catholicism and that of the family. Specifically, some more radical clergy and lay educators began to draw the link between free choice in religious matters and a more authentic faith,[173] and the corresponding negative identification of compulsory religious attendance with conformity, sterility, and hypocrisy.

This conflict reached a crescendo by the mid-1960s, encouraged by evidence garnered from investigations of schools and colleges during the process of reforming the system of public education in Quebec. Modern students, observed a 1964 survey, interpreted religion in highly personal terms, and tended to reject any institutional framework that assimilated faith to morality, a legalistic code, or intellectual doctrines. "Our young people," the survey stated, "will no longer accept a religion of 'thou shalt not.' In the contemporary world, they can no longer rest content with a faith that they have received as a social heritage. They need to find the reason behind moral values with their prohibitions and the mediation of the sacraments; otherwise, they reject them. ... They will not have anything that smacks of an 'imposed religion.' Here, parents and teachers are at fault. To them, compulsory daily mass runs directly counter to personal religion."[174] The colleges, declared Guy Paiement in 1962, had ultimately failed as religious educators because, by adopting as a standard an "overly *quantitative* way" of attending mass, they had imposed a monastic pattern of religious observance upon students whose vocations did not lie in the clerical life. The result was "a spirituality ill-adapted to the student's concrete situation and the ultimate impoverishment of the Christian vitality of the wider society."[175]

Interpreted through the Catholic personalist categories of these educational reformers, although contemporary youth were increasingly permeated by mass values of consumption and pleasure, they remained open to spiritual appeals. A 1962 survey of 207 young Quebec women revealed a disappointingly low level of knowledge concerning Catholic social teachings and a lack of "personal effort" to cultivate a more authentic faith. However, Catholic critics could point to hopeful signs that the younger generation possessed a refreshing spiritual ethic more oriented to communitarian imperatives, and they estimated that in the sphere of religion "youth truly constitutes an avant-garde."[176] Reformist Catholics discerned an opportunity in the paradox of the continued high rate of church attendance of this group of Quebec youth and the group's sense of profound rupture with the values of the older generation. What has recently been termed the "*génération lyrique*" (lyrical generation), the first phase of the baby boom, born between 1942 and 1950, were exactly the cohort surveyed by anxious educators. In the eyes of sympathetic clergy and educators, because these youths had completed their education in settings where Catholicism remained institutionally strong, this group's sense of identification with Christianity remained firm, though it was often expressed in a manner critical of the Church.[177] However, the presentation of Catholicism in a manner appealing to youth – the underscoring of personal commitment by contrasting it with allegiance to institutions and rituals – inexorably entailed a recasting of the social role of Catholicism. By insisting on the radical disparity between the "authentic" faith of youth that flowed from free choice, and the "conformity" engendered by adult-controlled institutions of family and school, Catholicism turned its back upon its immediate post-war role of soldering together youth and adults through a common commitment to family solidarity. Catholicism had become, by the mid-1960s, the primary element in an increasingly strident cultural conflict between generations, one whose message as articulated by a growing group of personalist critics, fuelled the individualism of young people by ruthlessly exposing the deficiencies of parents in the transmission of religious knowledge.

"I wonder," mused college student André Beaudet in 1964, "whether our parents are truly Christian. I believe that we must not base our faith on that of our parents."[178] While his casting of conflicting generational identities in religious terms might have been expected from participants in a student symposium during the 1960s, it was a perspective shared by many influential Catholic activists. Father Henri Bradet, the editor of the liberal Catholic monthly *Maintenant*, advised his audience of religious educators that "we can no longer believe what our parents believed yesterday, and young people will not believe tomorrow what we believe today."[179] In 1964, the sociologist André Thibault described the spirituality of the older generation as being one that is primarily circumscribed by a legalistic observance of rituals, amounts to a devotional cult built around mortifications and sacrifices, and is dedicated to enforcing prohibitions against sexual sins. Young people, he concluded, were often alienated from religious practices and the authority of the clergy, but they had one important advantage over their elders: the conviction that religion ultimately rested upon a personal relationship with God.[180] Intent on elaborating an adamantly personalist religion freed from institutional forms, a growing number of reformist Catholics cast Quebec youth as the bearers of the desirable religious attitudes of free choice and commitment. They drew a stark contrast between the sense of social and humanitarian engagement of modern youth, their longing for a vital spirituality, and the "disappointment and dissatisfaction" they experienced when confronted with the religious conformity, rampant individualism and moralizing of the "sell-outs," the elder generation.[181] Montreal student leader Pierre Marois, later a prominent member of the first Parti Québécois government, dismissed the complaint that students as an entire group had lost their faith. Rather, he stated that they rejected a type of Catholicism "that has been systematized into questions and answers in the *petit catéchisme* (abridged catechism), in duties and obligations. They reject what appears to them a huge body without a soul, a whole mechanism of life that is collapsing under its own weight. Temporarily, faith is buried under a morass of garbage."[182]

Between 1960 and 1965, official Catholic opinion shifted markedly away from the notion that Quebec's identity as a Catholic society was a function of the Church's direct control of educational institutions. In a more pluralistic society, many Catholic leaders now maintained that the way to inculcate religious values lay in improved techniques of pastoral education, anchored upon the free adherence of the child or youth to religious doctrine. The proponents of this new catechesis assimilated the new currents of religious education to the Quiet Revolution itself,[183] and argued that it would ensure an influential Catholic presence among young people through the quality of the presentation of faith itself, and not through institutional management. However, the new program of pastoral education was itself governed by the assumption that religious values constituted a terrain of generational conflict.[184] Although many Catholics feared that much of contemporary youth culture displayed symptoms of anarchic rebellion against authority, an influential personalist minority subscribed to the notion that the greater freedom that young people craved was spiritually superior to the "sociological" observances of adults. Thus, they were prepared to actively promote a massive rethinking of the Church's relationship with the family, because their central premise was that Quebec's religious crisis had, in fact, been caused by the deficiency of parents as religious educators. To ensure the presence of Catholicism at the core of the values of the new generation, they urged that Catholicism must engage in a massive institutional intervention, bypassing family relationships to bring a new spiritually authentic pastoral technique directly to secondary school students, unmediated by the "traditional," and thus spiritually inferior, religious practices of either family or parish. In this way, they believed, the ideal of Quebec as a Catholic society could be preserved only through a dramatic reversal of the channel of cultural transmission, by using the school to enlist children and adolescents behind "modern" criteria of faith. In turn, adolescents, and not parents, would be the arbiters of religious authority, because they would bring this energetic new Catholicism from the school to home, galvanizing the older generation out of their routine of religious conformity.

Given the Parent Report's conscious separation of "sacred" and "profane" subject matter in education, much of official Catholic opinion accepted that catechism and liturgy now constituted the twin pillars upon which a Christian educational climate would be founded. As the Centre de Catéchèse de Montréal confidently observed in 1965, the old pedagogical style which depended upon an "infiltration" of religious messages into religious subjects like literature and mathematics was in contradiction with the new priority of pastoral education, which demanded a more precise and specific study of religious doctrine in order to awaken the experience of faith.[185] According to Father Jean-Paul Labelle, the old catechism had relied exclusively upon a scholastic method that stressed memorization. Religious teaching in the school did not always engage the child's whole being, because the Church had believed that it could always rely upon the community life of family and parish to compensate for any deficiencies. However, as Labelle concluded, such assumptions could no longer serve in a society where "our young people must confront a pronounced crisis of faith" in their daily lives.[186] At one level, proponents of the new religious education hoped that it would re-cement cultural bonds within the family by fostering in the home a new conception of prayer that would open lines of communication between parents and children.[187] However, the basis of the new catechism and its relationship to the new structure of education was, for a number of radical Catholic personalists, a complete breach with the traditions of the past. The spirit of the new catechism must, they believed, animate a modernized multi-confessional, pluralistic educational environment, one that was "individualistic and active, allergic to maintaining the past for its own sake, to all that reeks of the museum and older forms."[188] What was required, in the estimation of Marthe Henripin, a prominent activist in the reform of religious education, was less a definition by adults of new curricular structures and programmes than a new starting point for the entire enterprise, which lay in the nature of young people's mentalities and needs.[189]

Translated to the classroom, the new religious education hoped to overcome what personalists decried as a gulf between religious knowledge and lived experience[190] by explicitly downplaying the knowledge and superiority of authority figures like priests, teachers, and especially parents. In the modern school, urged Father Paul-Marcel Lemaire, Catholic educators must abandon the old idea of catechism as the transmission of a static body of categorical imperatives and incomprehensible and useless affirmations. Even in the context of a Catholic confessional structure, he enjoined instructors against "judging or categorizing students according to their devotional prowess,"[191] by which he meant attendance at mass, sacraments, and other liturgical exercises. In responding to the new challenges posed by Quebec youth, Catholic modernizers were adamant that the teaching of religion must frankly eschew notions of sin, suffering, and moral exhortation, to focus on Christianity as a "psychology"[192] linked to living human realities. Ginette Deschênes, a Montreal catechism teacher, stated that modern Catholicism's compelling need was to replace the crucifix in school classrooms, because it bore no relationship to modern values. The image of Christ's suffering and death only taught students a "morality of failure," a "cult of mortification," and a religion of "boredom."[193] Such a re-presentation of the faith in effect reversed the structure of authority by privileging the religious experiences of young people over the adult-defined teachings of doctrine and sacramental obligation.

Many articulate Catholic clergy and academics gave more than tacit approval and enlisted themselves as publicists in this radical reversal of cultural authority in the sphere of religious education because they envisioned youth as a cohort who "lived at the very heart of today's crisis," and whose values and activities would ultimately transform the nature of religion, politics, and society in Quebec. Young people, they believed, were more open to a religion of personal faith because they experienced God more directly than adults, who remained mired in empty words and stereotypic formulae.[194] Mother Ste.-Thérèse-de-Lisieux, a teacher at a women's *collège classique*, placed the blame for Quebec's religious crisis squarely upon the adult generation, and particularly parents, when she stated that even more than the teaching of doctrine and morality, "the spectacle of certain adults whose religion consists of devotional exercises,"[195] was alienating young people from Christianity.

The intent of this vocal group of Catholic reformers was apparent through the constant refrain that juxtaposed the authenticity, freedom, and experiential values of youth with the materialism, conformity, and formalistic religion of the older generation. It was nothing less than a radical recasting of the place of the family in relation to church, school, and the transmission of cultural values. Traditionally, Catholicism had assigned a large role to the clergy and the institutional church in the transmission of religious knowledge, but had always viewed the family hierarchy as the fundamental principle of social organization. In the immediate post-war period, as part of a massive effort to reconstruct family solidarity, Quebec Catholics had privileged the family as the principal repository of religious truth and cultural values, with the parish community and school functioning as the deputies of the parents, who held final and ultimate reponsibility. By now emphatically privileging as the locus of spiritual authority the religious consciousness of individuals, and more particularly of *young* individuals, influential sections of Catholicism exploded this earlier synthesis.

Opinion among many prominent Catholic clergy and laypeople had now swung towards the view that, if anything, children and adolescents must become the educators of their parents. In attempting to explain why social phenomena such as television addiction, drug-taking, and religious doubt and unbelief had become prevalent among both young people and adults in Quebec, the sociologist Guy Rocher pithily stated that "many children have undertaken the education of their parents," a process that had reversed lines of cultural authority.[196] Fernand Dumont, the Université Laval sociologist and perhaps one of the most influential Catholic voices during the 1960s, castigated Quebec's clerical heritage for erasing the family as a factor of religious formation. However, far from wishing to restore the family to its central position in the transmission of religious values, Dumont contended that the "stereotyped religious formulae" and "vague sentimentalism"[197] that summed up the religious consciousness of Quebec's parents offered no hope of enlisting them in a meaningful educational partnership with the Church. At times, Catholic reformers of the 1960s seemed particularly intent on demonstrating the positive deficiency and unreliability of parents as proper religious educators. In 1966, a committee studying the question of school catechism reported that 62 per cent of fathers attended no parent-teacher meetings on the new religious curriculum, and a further 17 per cent only participated in one meeting. Only 50 per cent of mothers attended all three meetings.[198] Pierre Ménard, in a study undertaken for the Commission Dumont, observed that while the new catechism required a sustained involvement on the part of parents in the task of religious formation, most of them displayed a positive "ineptness" when confronted with the "personalist humanism" of the new catechism. Disgusted by the endless hectoring about "new.values" and worried that the new catechism did not build its explanations on what the previous generation had learned, most parents took the line of least resistance and simply abandoned religious instruction to the school.[199]

"It has become very difficult," observed the Mouvements Familiaux of the St Jérôme diocese in 1970, "to express faith at the level of the family." Catholic religious practices, which until very recently had publicly testified to family solidarity, had become a source of intergenerational tension. "When the children are young," observed this organization, "parents can bring them to Mass; but once they reach adolescence, their desire for independence prevents parents from enforcing religious practice."[200] No better analysis of the breakdown of the family's religious role could be provided than the portrait drawn by one participant in the round-table interviews conducted under the auspices of the Commission Dumont in 1970. "I wonder," mused a devout postal worker, "how teachers, educators, and we the parents are going to convince children that the Catholic religion is good. In my time "we were forced to line up to go to Church on Sunday and then to Vespers. And, the good people of that era acquired, by force of habit, a faith which ... they professed. A few have wavered but let's say that the vast majority have remained Catholic. However ... the young people growing up under the new system, how are they going to acquire the belief that there is a God, a religion to respect, a belief?"[201]

The lament of Madame Paul David expressed a similar perplexity. Children, she declared, once absorbed faith by being integrated through the family into a well-organized society, and understood "the laws of good conduct which would secure entry into eternal life." Quebec's Catholic parents had preserved the memory of this world, but they felt increasingly insecure and powerless for as "the religious acts imprinted upon us disappear little by little ... we are ... deprived of all aids to faith, emptied of language and religious heritage."[202] That the reforms of religious education constituted an explicit assault on parental authority was acutely recognized by the Association des Parents of Sainte-Anne-de-la-Pocatière. "We have seen," they charged, "what disorder results ... from those who contest the authority of the Pope. By obscure connections ... it is the very authority of parents that is challenged. A faulty religious teaching in the schools sets young people in revolt against their parents at an earlier stage and more irrationally than in former times."[203]

The increasingly contested nature of the family's religious role simply amplified the propensity of reformers to rely upon a new context of large regional, coeducational, comprehensive high schools and state-controlled senior colleges (the CEGEPs) as the most effective framework for the pastoral teaching of Catholicism. However, the disconnection of family from the transmission of religion hastened the marginalization of the family as a distinct entity that was more than the sum of the needs of its individual members. Indeed, in characterizing the high school as more effective than the family in teaching religious values,[204] reformist clergy and educators simply underscored the notion that it was the new horizontal sociability of youth, and not the hierarchical solidarity of family, that was the ultimate repository of personal values. In so doing, they deprived the family of one of its final remaining public institutional attributes, its intimate association with teaching the moral and cultural values that enabled the private individual to act in a civic capacity. In turn, this short-circuiting of the family by Catholic educational reforms in the 1960s hastened the articulation of a new concept of state activity and public order, one that hinged upon the formulation of social policies that eschewed the inspiration of familist corporatism and instead created a direct connection between the individual citizen and the state.

Between 1964 and 1970, confronted with a new climate created by educational reform, the visibility of youth rebellion, and a more politicized feminism – the latter most poignantly evinced by a rapidly falling birth rate – many Quebec Catholics had come to believe that the family had become a contested generational terrain. It had thus lost its primary institutional functions of teaching stable gender roles and assuring the wider society's cultural cohesion through the transmission of religious values, and, to some critics, the family's inability to resolve the competing claims of authority and personal fulfillment made it the root cause of individual and social psychological malaise. In such a cultural climate, both liberal and conservative voices wondered what functions, if any, remained specific to the family, and whether it was worth articulating and preserving an identity for the family as an entity that mediated between the individual and the state.

After the mid-1960s, reformist Catholics increasingly accepted the proposition that the family, because of its potential to oppress the individual psyche through excessive authoritarianism, ought to be reinterpreted solely in reference to the priority of individual fulfillment. At the 1964 Canadian Conference on the Family, Abbé Gérard Dion explicitly rejected the central premise of much post-war Catholic social thinking, the idea that the family was the "mother-cell" of society, and thus the model for all other forms of social relations. Indeed, Dion went so far as to undercut any public role for the family by challenging the central premise of familist corporatism, that is, the analogy between the hierarchical authority within the family and that which ought to prevail in other social institutions in which parents were recognized as the sole spokespersons for the interests of the family. He expressed a radical individualism in his argument that the family was important only insofar as it provided "both the fulfilment of the child and the fulfilment of the married partners."[205] Other prominent Quebec voices at this gathering rallied to Dion's exaltation of the individual. In his concluding address, Gérard Pelletier urged the audience to evaluate family relations from a new perspective, that of the good of "children or ... individuals in the family."[206] From the perspective of psychology, Thérèse Gouin-Décarie argued that individuals who insisted upon their needs did not weaken the family. Rather, this type of individualism, although it might produce conflict between parents and children, was a positive good, because it was essential for personal emotional development and sound mental health.[207]

Within this liberal framework, the family's sole functions were exclusively of a private order. They revolved less around the premise of maintaining solidarity or of preparing children and adolescents for public or spiritual citizenship than they did around satisfying individual cravings for emotional and psychological security. Most of these social commentators had fully ingested the "folk society" paradigm which posited an irrecoverable rupture between the traditions of rural social organization and the modernity of life in the city. Thus, sociologists like Gérald Fortin were adamant that the "family can no longer be said to form a social entity; it has become a juxtaposition of individual consumers."[208] Where this observation would have once been cause for alarm and consternation in Quebec

Catholic circles, a number of family activists were now prepared to view the inroads of consumerism with equanimity. Indeed, even if the family was in the process of losing all functions – except for the purely biological one of procreation – to workplace, school, and state, liberal voices proclaimed that this new cultural environment offered unparalleled opportunities for the refurbishing of family relations. These, however, would no longer depend upon a model of authority derived from gradations of age or gender, but upon individual family members finding a common endeavour as consumers of leisure activities.[209] "Within families," stated one study, there has developed a "type of morality that rests on the right of the individual to happiness. We now judge family success according to its ability to procure the individual and collective satisfaction of its members."[210] Thus, the shrinking of the public functions of the family was not synonymous with disorganization, because the family's most important role lay entirely in another sphere, that of retreat from the outside world, a space divorced from the constraints and demands of a technological society, one where individuals could rest and recoup their emotional energies. In this way, the family would come to fulfill a privatized function as a set of relations that would fulfill the needs of its individual members for "calm and security at the physical and psychological levels."[211]

The views of sociologist Philippe Garigue were most illustrative of the ambiguous nature of conservative thinking on the family during the late 1960s. At one level, Garigue deplored the tendency of Catholic educational reformers to oppose school and family, which had, in his estimation, compromised social development by erecting a barrier between generations. In a number of public pronouncements, Garigue traced the cause of this social malaise to a conflict between the desire to promote individual aspirations and the claims of family responsibilities, a juxtaposition which, in his estimation, had introduced "a fragility into family relations."[212] However, Garigue and a number of his conservative associates accepted the substance of the reformist argument that the family no longer possessed the wherewithal to synthesize the imperatives of social cohesion and the new cultural climate of egalitarian individualism. Increasingly, the pronouncements of the Conseil Supérieur de la Famille, the linch-pin of the current of familist corporatism that had shaped the social policy reforms of the early Lesage administration, insisted on the necessity of a massive state intervention in the form of a general family policy. Jean-Paul Cloutier, the minister of family and public welfare in the Union Nationale administration that replaced the Lesage Liberals in 1966, flatly declared that "without the assistance of the State, the family is unable by itself to face the difficulties of the modern world."[213] Significantly, however, these proposals were couched less in terms of an authoritarian evocation of older gender roles, than in formulating policies that would offer financial inducements, in the form of provincial family allowances, that would allow women to make the individual choices necessary to resolve the conflict between child-rearing and career aspirations.[214]

Indeed, when queried about the type of relationships that ought to prevail within the modern family, Garigue and his supporters appeared to make a number of accommodations to the democratic cultural climate of the 1960s. Although he vociferously dissented from what he regarded as modern Catholicism's over-privileging of the individual, he deliberately rejected any authoritarian reimposition of older family patterns. Garigue maintained that in restoring the central link between the family and the transmission of human values, it was necessary to "go beyond the traditional institutions" and to judge the family not according to the standard of responsibility, duty, or control, but from a more egalitarian standard, namely, the affectional quality of family relations which alone could reconcile individuals to membership in the family institution.[215] More significantly, although Garigue's policy prescriptions sought to preserve the notion of the family as a public entity, he in fact adhered to the central postulate of his liberal critics: that in modern society, the family's key function was an emphatically private one, that of "being the place where personal happiness is realized, because it is the only place where one can be entirely one's self."[216]

Both liberal and conservative Catholics increasingly formulated family relationships, not in terms of a continuity of institutional connections between private and public spheres, but almost exclusively in terms of private happiness and individual fulfillment. The effacement of the family in the name of individualism was a key factor underlying a new series of social policy imperatives that were articulated by the Quebec government in the years between 1965 and 1971. At the end of 1965, the minister of family and social welfare, Émilien Lafrance, the chief political promoter of familist corporatism, resigned from the Liberal cabinet in disagreement over the government's refusal to enforce a ban against the public sale of liquor on Sunday. His replacement was none other than René Lévesque, architect of the nationalization of Hydro-Québec and a vigorous proponent of greater state intervention in affirming the priority of Quebec over Ottawa in the field of social security.[217] Lévesque immediately assailed the mixed public-private social welfare structure that Lafrance had created,[218] castigating it as "retrograde" in subjecting "deprived classes of our community" to a regime of "State charity." Rather, Lévesque believed that welfare, health, and social security allowances were a "strict individual right." His goal was the ultimate recovery of all social security powers from Ottawa, an action that would undergird what he understood was a new relationship between the state and the individual, one in which benefits would no longer be understood as merely residual, but as an actual insurance scheme.[219] At times, Lévesque's initiatives appeared to bypass the family as an entity by formulating policies for state intervention that would assert the rights of women as a special constituency of individuals within the family, a position which won him the plaudits of those who aspired to a "democratic socialism" in Quebec.[220] However, at other times he seemed to pursue a more conservative adherence to the familist corporatism of his predecessor, insisting even when defining the parameters of a sovereign Quebec that the point of departure for social policy was "the family as a base community," and that future social policy initiatives should be undertaken by the state after consultation with organizations representing families.[221]

Lévesque's attempt to navigate between social democracy and familist corporatism reflected, at the level of government, the unresolved debate on the family between Catholic reformers and conservatives. It was the return of the Liberals to power under Robert Bourassa in 1970, and not Lévesque's option for Quebec independence, which marked the final stage in the elaboration of a new relationship between the state and the individual, one that was adamant in excluding the family from any institutional recognition by the state. Claude Castonguay, the minister responsible for social welfare, moved to implement the reforms of a high-powered royal commission of inquiry on health and social security (which he himself had chaired before his entry into politics) that reported in 1971. Significantly, the change in nomenclature of the new ministry, from Famille et Bien-être social (Family and Social Welfare) to Santé et Affaires sociales (Health and Social Affairs), was indicative of the displacement of the family from its public role as mediator between the individual and the state.[222] The findings of the Royal Commission on Health and Social Welfare began from the premise that the family was in crisis, assailed by a bevy of socio-economic and psychological problems, and was increasingly unable to meet the needs of its individual members, let alone represent these needs to government bodies. Moreover, Castonguay and his associates recognized the youth revolt of the previous decade as a universal phenomenon, one that required responding to the critique that the failure of the family was part of the "establishment's" failure, and they accepted that youth now formed a social constituency of individuals independent of the family.[223]

Castonguay's most open break with previous traditions of social policy, however, lay in his assertion of the concept of "social rights," which pertained not to families, as in the older Catholic concept of order, but to the natural and inalienable rights of individuals. This in turn placed a new responsibility upon the state: the decree being that government intervention should flow from the principle of "social investment" or "social development," rather than from notions of remedialism or regulation. Such a new definition of the state consciously rested upon the sole criterion of individual well-being, and not the recognition of vested interests, such as private welfare agencies, the Church, or older lines of authority. The establishing of a permanent, unmediated relationship between the only two valid public actors, the individual and the state, would promote not only individual well-being, through the fulfillment of personal potential, but have overt collectivist implications for the advancement of the entire society.[224] What was missing from the equation was the notion that the family was the interlocutor of the state in the articulation of social policy by virtue of the fact that it mediated the ongoing dialectic between private values and the requirements of public citizenship. This lacuna was seized upon by conservatives like Garigue, who charged that Castonguay was engaged in a "'carving up' of family relations," one that sought to create services for particular groups of individuals in abstraction from their parents. Such a departure was flawed from the beginning because, in Garigue's estimation, it failed to consider the family as a "system of interpersonal relations," preferring to design policies for "a sum of individuals."[225]

The Castonguay reforms of 1970–71 marked the end of the ambiguous and complicated post-war relationship between Quebec Catholicism and the family. In this process, Catholicism itself, in its efforts to accommodate elements of the more democratic, horizontal sociability of youth, made the family the scene of contestation between liberal and conservative values, a struggle that destabilized and eroded older, more institutional concepts of the family. By focusing in particular upon the failure of adult authority to properly inculcate fulfilling sex and gender roles, influential currents within Catholicism paved the way for a wholesale reversal of lines of authority within the family, one that openly privileged the spiritual values of youth over those of parents. In resolving this crisis of religious values, mainstream Catholicism increasingly insisted upon a direct, unmediated relationship in religious education between the Church and young people, one that deliberately excluded the family, the latter having been deemed incompetent. It was this struggle over the transmission of sexual and religious knowledge that in no small way ultimately legitimized an egalitarian type of individualism that was a key component in casting a new structure of public authority. This closed off what had since the 1930s been the central current of the cultural Quiet Revolution: the revitalization of the institutional family as a mediator between the individual and the state. By proclaiming this as a barrier to the self-realization of individuals, the cultural transformations of the late 1960s decisively consigned religion and the family to the private sphere.

5

"The Epic of Contemporary Feminism Has Unfolded in the Church"[1]

Sexuality, Birth Control, and Personalist Feminism, 1931–1971

We have forced woman to enter a territory that she does not know, and thus, she still remains dependent upon what she has left behind without really occupying the terrain that we have assigned to her. She is divided within herself ... In one breath, she agrees with the feminists who demand new rights, but in the next, she will say with Betty Fredon[sic] that she is afflicted by a malaise that has no name, a sickness that is composed in equal parts of a fear of the future, of what is to become of her and at the same time, feelings of nostalgia for a situation which, despite its disadvantages ... conferred upon her a number of compensations.[2]

The assertion that there existed a close and mutually-sustaining relationship between modern feminism and Catholicism would strike most students of twentieth-century Quebec history as simply wrong-headed, if not downright perverse. After all, did not the Church authorities consistently seek to dictate a set of prescriptions regarding woman's nature and maternal role that, at least until the 1960s, drastically curtailed any attempt by women to obtain equal rights within the family, the workplace, and the political sphere? At best, it is argued, Catholicism tolerated a type of "maternalism," or "social feminism," which assigned a limited public role to women not by virtue of equal citizenship, but as a consequence of biological function. More darkly, those women's organizations that promoted this vision found themselves in the paradoxical position of promulgating a feminist message, all the while being enlisted as junior partners in propping up a deeply paternalist society. According to this interpretation, the egalitarian potential of these movements was constrained, recuperated, and deflected by the need to adhere to a dominant clerico-nationalist set of priorities that overtly privileged male power in church, state, and society.[3] Hélène Pelletier-Baillargeon's article "*Un Concile pour le deuxième sexe?*" ("A Vatican Council for the Second Sex?"), written in the midst of the reforms within the Catholic Church, the intense debates in the 1960s on free access to sexual pleasure and birth control, and a thoroughgoing reassessment of the relationship of married women to both family and paid work, was significant because it expressed the possibility of a compromise between the tenets of the Church and the revolutionary aspirations of "*le deuxième sexe*," a phrase that evoked the radical, politicized feminism of economic and sexual choice, advocated most prominently by Simone de Beauvoir.

If we are to situate women like Pelletier-Baillargeon as having been engaged in something more than just wishful thinking or the deliberate promotion of a false consciousness, the attempt to find common ground between Catholicism and feminism opens an intriguing interpretive pathway to the delineation of Quebec's cultural history between the Great Depression and the 1960s. First, one might ask whether the conventional teachings on women's maternal nature and role that were founded upon the assertion of the existence of separate male and female natures and which underpinned the Church's activism in reconstructing family and gender relations after 1931 offer, beneath their ostensible evocation of stasis and tradition, more egalitarian possibilities for women? More fundamentally, such a question challenges the usual, overly simplified chronology which takes the relationship between the Church hierarchy and the middle-class professional women of the Fédération Nationale de Saint-Jean-Baptiste as archetypal of the fate of feminism before the mid-1960s. Indeed, the creation of various Catholic Action movements in the mid-1930s which enlisted the energies of thousands of young women marked the beginning of a subtle, but nonetheless palpable, transformation of early twentieth-century maternalist tenets which held that women's public activism followed from a conception of a separate female biological role.[4] Although these movements appeared conservative because they imbibed the Catholic discourse of separate male and female natures and destinies, and thus emphatically warned women against the perils of the quest for equal political rights and participation in the workplace, the consequence was not a mechanical oscillation between the unfolding of initial "feminist" potential and subsequent recuperation by the forces of traditional order.[5] Rather, they marked the beginnings of a type of "personalist feminism" that on the one hand preserved some links to maternalist tenets, but also advanced increasingly egalitarian notions,[6] especially in the realm of sexuality and reproduction.

Increasingly during the years after World War II, the very period most closely associated by historians with the reinforcement of older gender hierarchies and, in the case of women, an extreme separation between workplace and home, personalist feminism popularized an increasingly culturalist or "spiritual" rather than strictly biological definition of maternity. It was a definition which advocated a more individualist ethos, especially in terms of relations between husbands and wives, as well as a number of new educational and professional directions for young women. Far from resolutely opposing women's freedom to assume economic roles outside the family, this strand of Catholicism presented a far more ambivalent message, one that increasingly postulated the satisfactions of paid work and career as psychological salves to an alienation stemming from routine and inactivity. More importantly, however, the energy that the Catholic Action movements invested in refurbishing gender relationships within marriage and the family rested upon the ideal of "intimacy," or emotional and sexual partnership between spouses. This, in turn, conferred religious legitimacy upon arguments that proclaimed women's right to equal sexual pleasure and satisfaction and, in the name of this freer sexuality and Catholic notions that maternity is primarily cultural and educative, actually affirmed a certain individual female control over reproductive choice. In the Quebec context, women's demands for sexual freedom and political equality were not coincident products of the cultural revolution of the 1960s after a long era of repression and silence. Rather, the Catholic personalist feminism that had taken form in the youth movements of the 1930s actually anticipated many of the demands of second-wave feminism, especially in its individualist assertion of control over reproduction, although these demands were, prior to the mid-1960s, articulated in a less politicized manner.

The presence of a feminist current within post-Depression Quebec Catholicism also goes far to explain the rapid de-Christianization of Quebec that occurred after 1965. Catholic Action's insistence upon radically separate gender roles and destinies was designed, on the one hand, to appeal to conservative desires for family stability, but in a religious sense, it in fact fostered, during the post-war years, a profound sense of cultural rupture and opposition between men and women. Personalist notions of "spiritual maternity," which at one level might be read as promoting female subordination within the family, served to fuel the increasingly shrill critique of fatherhood and male authority. More tellingly, lay male Catholic militants and clergy responded by likening female spirituality to the much-abhorred routine and conformity – viewed as "tradition" – that was the enemy of community and authenticity, the latter being the desired spiritual values of "modernity." Prior to the mid-1960s, Catholicism was seen as the cockpit of an increasingly polarized struggle between gendered notions of religious adherence and practice, a sensibility that awakened, among a religious elite, a sense of fragmentation within the very precincts of Catholicism. However, what was even more problematic was that by the 1960s the seamless link that Catholic Action had, in the context of female-friendly environments such as the marriage preparation movement, established between marriage, sexuality, and family had convinced many Quebec women that the Catholic religion itself was coextensive with a series of moral teachings on sexual practices and birth control. Moreover, many believed that the prohibitory restrictions surrounding the latter had become increasingly porous and negotiable, and subject to the dictates of individual conscience on a situational basis. The 1968 papal encyclical *Humanae vitae* was widely interpreted as reimposing constraints where, in the minds of many faithful, none had really existed for several decades, and worse, of refurbishing a resolutely antipersonalist credo that denied the equality of married women within the family. The massive and silent abandonment of Catholic identity was but the consequence of a logical connection that Catholicism had itself established among thousands of Quebec women, namely, that the practice of Catholicism and the morality of birth control were one and the same. However, although this conviction had constituted one of the cultural strengths of post-war Catholicism, if inability or conscientious refusal to adhere to the new restrictions on birth control were to become widespread among young women, the mass abandonment of the Catholic faith itself by its female constituency would ineluctably follow.

"IT SEEMS THAT OUR YOUNG WOMEN ARE IGNORANT OF THE MOST BASIC ANXIETIES"[7]

For François Hertel, that influential mentor and astute commentator on Quebec youth mentalities in the late 1930s, the much-desired attribute of "anxiety," by which he proclaimed the superiority of the heroic, modernist spirituality of Depression-era young people over the routine, compromises, and conformity of the older generation, was a peculiarly gendered quality. He explicitly identified the cult of spiritual anxiety with Quebec's young men and, in so doing, affirmed that the spirituality of their female counterparts remained mired in "tradition," unaffected by and potentially resistant to the revolutionary, modernist currents that stressed cultural rupture, the breach with individualism, and the re-creation, through Catholic Action and a host of similar youth movements, of enduring bonds of community. Hertel voiced what was, in fact, the paramount imperative of the Catholic Action movements that took hold in a number of Quebec circles after the mid-1930s; through the metaphor of youth, this was the attempt to articulate new social and cultural definitions of male leadership roles encompassing both family and public life. Of equal significance, his equation of masculinity with desirable, "modern," spiritual achievements bore witness to two currents that profoundly affected post-war Catholicism in Quebec. The first, the lack of "anxiety" among young women, was welcomed by some as an essential guarantee of stability: it rested upon notions that male and female roles were separate but complementary, and dictated largely by biology and the separation between the public sphere of work and the private sphere of family. This revolved around the expectation that female roles would remain fixed around older cultural priorities of maternity and family, thus ensuring both social and spiritual cohesion by respecting the conventional gender hierarchies. Secondly, a number of male educators and youth activists went further, employing the theory of male/female role division to assert, first, that two distinct religious styles existed, one heroic, "anxious," communitarian, and modern, the other, individualist, conformist, mired in routine and tradition, and, second, that these corresponded exactly to the largely immutable natures of men and women. Thus, to the cultural and spiritual dichotomy between youth and the older generation was added a further religious fissure which traversed post-war Quebec society along gender lines, and had, by the 1960s, further amplified what many Catholics experienced as the dissonance between tradition and modernity.

Upon closer scrutiny, however, Hertel was incorrect in his belief that young women were largely impervious to "anxiety," or that female roles and expectations were entirely dominated by conservatism and stasis. Indeed, strands of Catholicism which influenced Quebec during the Depression and the immediate post-war era brought considerable nuance and a more egalitarian cast to the conventional female destiny of maternity and family. The 1930 papal encyclical on marriage, *Casti connubii* – the starting point for Catholic thinking and activism about gender and family roles – was, underneath its reiteration of "the primacy of the husband with regard to the wife and children, the ready subjection of the wife and her willing obedience," considerably more open-ended. Indeed, such hierarchical language was balanced by more egalitarian considerations, particularly in its framing of the ideal of marriage as a "blending of life as a whole" which privileged relationships based upon mutual interchange and sharing, and not those of hierarchy and servitude.[8] In this respect, the pope wished to draw a critical and necessary distinction between Catholicism and forms of fascism and ultra-conservatism, movements which often used similar language, referring to the "eternal feminine" and woman's inescapable maternal destiny, to describe women's place.

One of the more popular expressions of this extreme biologism which was familiar to Quebec Catholics in the 1930s was Gina Lombroso's *The Soul of Woman*, published in 1923 as a refutation of feminist campaigns to secure political rights and women's access to higher education. Lombroso, the daughter of the celebrated Italian criminologist Cesare Lombroso, began emphatically from the premise that "woman is not man's equal." She defined contrasting male and female natures, summarized as "egotism" and "alterocentrism," which underscored her idea that women were beings characterized by intuition and passionality, and that these were immutable, being derived from woman's biological function of motherhood. According to her schema, "maternity gives to woman's mind an imprint of altruism that colors her whole life,"[9] and this extreme determinism led Lombroso to declare that, in terms of education, female activity was best directed away from abstract, theoretical studies, where women displayed little aptitude, to practical fields of life, especially those most closely associated with household tasks, where they could deploy their superior abilities of observation, imitation, and caring for others. Because maternity formed the core of women's essence, no amount of education, religion, or legislative "coercion" would ever change or improve woman's position, and Lombroso emphatically rejected male-female relationships based upon notions of reciprocal independence. Feminist campaigns to widen women's sphere outside the home, she concluded, would not provide security and peace of mind. This could only be found within the framework of "traditional marriage," where men would continue to exercise authority. For Lombroso, inequality between the sexes was not fundamentally unjust nor the product of male tyranny, because it was a consequence of biology. Her efforts were thus directed to fostering harmony between the sexes, not by opening male spheres to women, but through better reciprocal understanding of the immutable, separate male and female natures, and especially by men, who were exhorted to greater "chivalry." Indeed, improvement in the position of women would not come from feminist activism, but from cultivating greater understanding among men, who would retain the primacy of authority both in the family and the wider society.[10]

Although Catholic thinking on marriage and family was certainly infused with notions of maternalism and distinct male and female natures and roles, a number of developments in the 1930s dictated a distancing from biological determinism. By the early 1930s, several European fascist and ultra-conservative movements were using a version of Lombroso's biologism to further racialist campaigns for maternity and pronatalism, arguments which sought to completely identify women with reproduction and family. In his encyclical, the pope explicitly drew a distinction between Catholicism and these right-wing political movements, because in his estimation they had over-privileged male authority in both family and public life, and deployed an exclusively biologist maternalism to constrict women's roles. Indeed, Pope Pius XI was careful to caution that his primary concern in defining the reciprocal duties of husband and wife was less to uphold the power relationships within the family than to affirm "the liberty which fully belongs to the woman both in view of her dignity as a human person and in view of her most noble office as wife and mother and companion." Although he reminded women that the Church did not countenance "that exaggerated liberty" which defined the interests of women as being in opposition to those of the family, he nonetheless raised the possibility that women's rights as individual persons would not always coincide with the corporate interests of the family. Catholicism thus affirmed a more egalitarian and personalist dimension, because it did not require women to "obey her husband's every request not in harmony with right reason or with the dignity due to wife." In the final analysis, the Catholic Church rejected, because of its desire to uphold the alliance that it had struck in a number of European countries with moderate and conservative groups which demanded the extension of women's political rights and activism, the idea that in the social and political spheres, married women "should be put on a level with those persons who in law are called minors."[11]

Although the pope's intent was to strike a balance between gender hierarchy and egalitarianism in the modern family, influential minority currents within French Catholicism eagerly seized upon and sought a wider application for the personalist implications of the encyclical. While the radical views of Emmanuel Mounier limited the extent of his impact on Quebec Catholics in the mid-1930s, his influential essays "Woman also a Person" and "The Person of the Married Woman," an overt challenge to reigning biologist definitions of femininity, were read by young women college activists like Alexandrine Leduc soon after they were published. Women, contended Mounier, constituted a "spiritual proletariat," to whom bourgeois society had denied a spiritual life of conquest and freedom, imprisoning them in "a flowery but sealed prison – of a false femininity" defined by the biological imperative of maternity. Mounier mercilessly flayed conservative notions of the "eternal feminine," exposing them as constructions of male egoism designed simply to exclude women from public life and intellectual creation, and he insisted upon equality between the sexes that was based on a similar vocation entirely removed from biology: the call for both men and women to seek the highest spiritual perfection as persons. It was wrong, insisted Mounier, to assume that female spirituality was somehow different, that women developed their spiritual faculties by "an artificial accentuation of what is femininely picturesque in her." Woman's person, Mounier concluded, was not entirely separable from her maternal functions, but in the final analysis, he maintained that the foundation of personality transcended, and frequently struggled against, purely functional attributes.[12]

However, in advancing a cultural and religious argument for women's equality, this French personalist wished to distance his own thinking from the currents of secular feminism, especially when it came to discussing the rights of married women. While Mounier declared that women who had attained a consciousness of their mission as persons would naturally revolt against social expectations that they be merely passive reflections of their husbands, and he castigated conservatives for a "purely quantitative conception of maternity," he at the same time dissented from one of the central feminist canons that the precondition of the emancipation of women was their entry into the sphere of paid work outside the home. Although Mounier believed that personalists must assiduously resist arguments for the enforced idleness of women or reactionary legislation that sought to return women to the domestic sphere – he believed that married women must, in the name of equality, have full benefits of income from their work, equality of rights and duties with their husbands, and equal pay for equal work – Mounier refused to countenance the argument of what he termed "vengeful feminism," specifically that household work was of less value than that carried on in public workplaces. The context of married women's activity would still be a familial one because, for personalists like Mounier, the family remained a viable natural community, especially if permeated by the new Catholic ideals of mutual dependence, intimacy, and sharing between husband and wife.[13] It must be recognized, however, that in seeking to broaden the scope of the social and cultural role of married women, what personalists like Mounier were engaged in was less a rejection of the primacy of woman's maternal function than the offering of a more open-ended, cultural definition of this function that emphatically rejected closed, biologically-determined notions of woman's nature and destiny.

Thus from the mid-1930s onwards, Quebec Catholics who sought to define women's nature and social role encountered two currents that operated in increasing mutual tension. On the one hand, the concern to preserve the centrality of motherhood as a central quality of the female personality meant that within the context of Quebec's Catholic Action youth and family movements, there continued to be a great deal of maternalist language that viewed marriage and motherhood as the primary destiny of all women, a belief in the relative immutability of male and female natures and roles, and conservative-sounding rejections of feminism. "In my opinion," stated Mariana Jodoin in 1940, "all little girls are born mothers."[14] Father Ferdinand, a leading family promoter, contended that modern feminism – which he summed up as the emancipation of women from family duties, the notion that wives could manage their own economic interests independently from their husbands, and that, in order to devote themselves to public functions, women were entitled to be liberated from domestic tasks – was contrary to both nature and morality. Although men and women were equal on a spiritual plane, Ferdinand insisted upon the verity that "God built them differently so that they could mutually complete one another." Natural differences, he maintained, constituted different rights that both church and state must uphold. "It is not a real emancipation," he concluded, "for women to conflate these rights, to want to appropriate men's rights, to play at being a man when God has made you a woman."[15] However, within the framework of this insistence upon separate male and female natures and summonses to refurbish the conventions of gender hierarchy, there arose a second current. The more personalist, egalitarian, and cultural interpretations that posited the relationship between husband and wife as involving reciprocal understanding of each partner's imagination, will, and sensibility, rather than legalistic notions of hierarchy and subordination, began to appear in the waning years of the Depression. Such views placed a premium less upon women's capacity for biological generation, the reproductive act of motherhood itself, and more upon the status of wife as being that of spiritual partner within the family, as "collaborators" and "co-operators,"[16] concepts which seemed to accentuate the element of personal choice and expressed the ideal of a more egalitarian sharing of authority within the family.

What was most significant about Quebec's cultural dynamic in the late 1930s was that the personalist belief that women's essential nature was not completely encapsulated within the notion of motherhood did not emanate from the political sphere or from earlier strands of public maternalism like the Fédération Nationale de Saint-Jean-Baptiste. Even leaders of the successful campaign for women's voting rights like Thérèse Casgrain continued to operate within a maternalist ethos, justifying female suffrage on the grounds that "the primordial mission of woman is to be the guardian of the home" and that access to the ballot was a "defensive weapon" to defend the family cell, for which the woman-as-mother was primarily responsible.[17] In this respect, Casgrain would have agreed with conservative Catholic social thinkers like Esdras Minville, who relied upon highly differentiated male and female roles and woman's maternal vocation to promote an enhanced participation of women in popular institutions and social movements, which he believed would restore the primacy of home and family during post-war reconstruction.[18] Rather, it was within the supposedly non-political setting of the Catholic Action youth movements that there occurred a palpable shift away from deterministic notions of reproductive motherhood. In these organizations, based on the principle of parallelism between male and female wings, a common language of adventure, exalted spirituality as a particular trait of the younger generation, aspirations to self-education and autonomy, and a clear sense of difference with the elder generation resonated in particular among a cohort of younger women who contrasted this heroic imperative with the rather restricted social and cultural choices of marriage, singleness, and the religious life available to Quebec women before World War II.

Indeed, although women's movements that arose during the 1930s, such as the Jeunesse Étudiante Catholique Feminine (JECF) and the Jeunesse Ouvrière Catholique Feminine (JOCF), were to some extent constrained by the presence of male chaplains and spiritual directors, they were far from merely refurbishing traditional gender hierarchies or conventional notions of female identity. As Simonne Monet Chartrand later recalled, the novelty and "revolution of mentalities" represented by Catholic Action movements like the JECF was that they did not arbitrarily consign young women to the categories of potential wife or potential religious novice, but instead placed them on an equal level with young men by conferring upon them the status of student.[19] By adopting this more egalitarian framework, these movements became particularly appealing to young women, who, as Robert Charbonneau observed in 1935, were considerably more advanced than their male counterparts in their receptiveness to the new youth Catholicism. Female college students and young working-class women "were already prepared for Catholic Action because they experienced a tonic in the mutual assistance of their comrades and already had a more concrete setting for social action because their functions gave them more contact with others."[20] Thus, these movements were able to assert a new model of women's energy and engagement,[21] one that, like its male counterpart, distinguished itself from the formalism and routine of the older generation by defining as the desirable qualities of the human personality "youthful ardour, vibrant enthusiasm, profound conviction ... a living faith and ... a true piety."[22] Through a juxtaposition of these traits with the more static concept of maternity, there began to emerge intimations of a freer and more egalitarian identity for women, one based less upon an ineluctable biological destiny than upon women's choice above all to affirm and perfect their spiritual natures as persons.

"The right of every human person," proclaimed college student Lucette St. Cyr in 1936, "the only one that exerts an imperative call upon us, is the natural right to develop ourselves fully."[23] The presence of such language that invoked the rights of the human person and the need to attain the highest perfection bespoke a dynamic tension that young women experienced when they reflected upon their social roles. As much as these youthful Catholic activists of the 1930s imbibed the culturally pervasive notion of radically different, and biologically dictated male and female essences, which reinforced the message that they might one day be potential mothers and that maternity was "the wonderful future, common to all of us,"[24] this was filtered by a more personalist, non–gender-specific, quasi-military priority, one that was especially fostered within the Catholic Action movements. Reflecting upon Gina Lombroso's deterministic separation of male and female essential natures, which was used by conservatives in Quebec society to limit women's access to higher education and the professions, Claire Gélinas wrote in 1937 that because the author was "an ardent anti-feminist" it was impossible to accept wholesale her ideas concerning the biological and cultural differences between the sexes. Catholicism, Gélinas argued, "provides other answers to the same questions."[25]

The central contribution of 1930s Catholicism to the ongoing debate on separate male and female social and cultural destinies was the emphasis that youth of both sexes should place upon the cultivation of personal spirituality, the "forging of a soul of steel," whose characteristics were exemplified by physical hardiness, deep commitment to self-sacrifice, and a constant exertion of will.[26] So pervasive was the metaphor of conquest and heroism within Catholic Action that the whole notion of biological maternity seemed at times to recede and be overshadowed by the imperative demand that young women be first and foremost "modern" and "revolutionary." They were to engage in the task of spiritual reconstruction by incarnating in their own lives the values of life, movement, growth, and conquest, which translated into a refusal at all costs to be ground down by cultural and religious formalism, and they were to resist the social pressures to blindly assume the conventional female roles dictated by adult society.[27] Indeed, so compelling was this personalist impulse that, despite the opprobrium attached to the term "feminist" in a highly conservative society, elements within the middle-class student JECF actually used this term to describe their outlook and implicitly challenged the dichotomized biological thinking of Lombroso which assigned the realm of emotion and sensitivity to women, and the domain of intelligence and action to men. As one militant stated, "women, and especially those living in the 20th century, have always been carried away by sensibility. What will happen to us if we allow ourselves to be completely led by the senses and the emotions?"[28] However, they carefully qualified the term "feminist," and distanced themselves from the charge that they were trying to emancipate women from their duties, or "desiring to change women into men."[29]

Most modern feminist doctrines, maintained these Catholic activists, simply ignored the real nature of women in trying to make the sexes absolutely alike. These activists instead cast their definition of feminist doctrine not in terms of political demands, but as being a doctrine that "permits the full flowering of woman's nature, with all the qualities that are particular to them."[30] Promoters of Catholic Action women's organizations were always careful to proclaim that their efforts to make their members "true Christian women, who can bring real solutions to all questions,"[31] be understood not as an attempt to overturn prescribed gender roles, in the sense of imputing masculine tendencies to women.[32] Rather, Christianity taught that "woman is a person ... whose being was characterized by freedom, intelligence and will." From this, they interpreted the vocation of modern woman as being "identical to that of man, which is to realize fully the likeness of God (both natural and supernatural) that I carry within myself. This is actualized in a special vocation (as a woman) ... which is not identical to man's, but is complementary ... This places us completely outside those notions of woman-as-slave or adversarial relationships in which the woman seeks to become a man. Without losing a single element of my own Person, I become two within one flesh and by one love. Through me – which is now 'us' – life is transmitted. ... My Person finds its true fulfillment in this role and this vocation which is to transmit life – and as a consequence of it, to transmit Love."[33] Read at one level, this statement might appear to represent but a conservative celebration of woman's ineluctable maternal destiny. However, closer scrutiny reveals a radically different set of expectations, with the primacy placed upon a cultivation of spiritual elements of personality that placed women on an equal footing with men. However, what is most interesting is that even within the language of motherhood, the emphasis was not upon the familial or social connection between the mother and the child, but upon the bond between husband and wife established by emotional and sexual intimacy, and the sense of woman's individual fulfillment *as a person* conferred by the equal participation in creating and transmitting life. Thus, in an influential section of Quebec Catholicism from the late 1930s through the immediate post-war period, woman's maternal identity was severed from its original deterministic basis in reproduction, and was frequently sublimated, becoming but one element in a culture of personal spiritual perfection, translated in the youthful language of heroism as a "gift of the self." As stated by one student activist, young women should realize that "neither marriage, nor celibacy nor the religious life are choices to be imposed upon us, but are vocations prepared in the most intimate recesses of our conscience."[34]

"A NEW PROBLEM: THAT OF CATHOLICS PRACTICING A BAPTIZED NEOMALTHUSIANISM"[35]

The infusion of these Catholic, personalist, egalitarian spiritual tenets into earlier definitions of women's maternal destiny and duty during the late 1930s might at first sight be dismissed as a current of minor intellectual interest, restricted to a privileged, college-educated elite. However, between 1944 and the early 1960s, thousands of young working-class and lower-middle-class women encountered these ideas in a more popularized form through their participation in Catholic Action's Service de Préparation au Mariage (SPM), whose premarital counselling courses reached some 5,925 of the 11,000 couples married in the Montreal diocese in 1955.[36] Here, the message was not cast in such exalted spiritual terms, but rather in language that placed a premium on women's right to equal access to sexual satisfaction. A glance at the content of the marriage preparation courses might justify the view that this type of Catholic social endeavour did little to advance a more egalitarian notion of woman's nature and role, because the accent was upon limiting sexual expression to the context of marriage, an institution where, in the post-war period, traditions of female subordination would be expected to persist because husbands still retained the balance of legal and economic power. However, Quebec Catholic women did find a number of possibilities to elaborate more egalitarian female identities within personalist notions of a refurbished ideal of Christian marriage, an ideal that defined the relationship as one of partnership and community at the levels of emotional sharing, sexual intimacy, and enhanced mutual spirituality.

From the outset, the marriage preparation courses rested upon conventional Catholic notions of separate, but complementary male and female psychologies that were largely the function of distinct biological roles. By insisting upon "complementarity" rather than reciprocal independence, Catholic marriage promoters explicitly sought to distance themselves from the notion of the achievement of equality between the sexes through competition in the workplace. Such competition, they maintained, would "deprive woman of her soul, of her spirituality."[37] According to Simone Comeau, "men and women are destined to fulfill different roles, and thus they differ in nature and constitution." She estimated that the error from the outset in most male-female relationships lay in "the imputation by one sex to the other of its own way of thinking and reacting, and this is the main source of a great deal of mutual incomprehension."[38] However, these role definitions were not simply used to inculcate conservative social injunctions against the paid work of married women outside the home. Rather, the insistence upon the need for couples to understand the "complementarity" of fixed psychological natures and roles was given a decidedly feminist tincture by identifying male arrogance and ignorance as the major source of the dissatisfaction of wives and the consequent marital breakdown. "Young women," stated Jacques B. in 1944, "preserve a natural idea of the mission that they must accomplish. They know that they must give life, sustain the home, and raise their children." However, he was not at all certain that men were as equally well-prepared to respond to the stringent demands of the new personalist marriage ideal. "Will today's young woman find," he asked, "in the young men that they are courting all the understanding that she has the right to expect from him?"[39] What especially aroused the ire of these Catholic marriage promoters was the idea, which they maintained was prevalent among both middle-class professional and working-class men, that wives were simply housekeepers who maintained a comfortable retreat for their husbands to retire to in the evening, and had no right to expect anything more than an uninvolved, aloof husband who was simply an economic provider. Such male attitudes, stated Rémy Gagné in 1953, would simply lead to young wives resenting the fact that they were "reduced to a life of housework and just being a good mother, their lives summed up by the frying pan, the washing machine, and the dishrag."[40]

Implicitly, the SPM thus recognized that it was the emotional satisfaction of wives that provided the key to the stability of post-war Catholic marriages and, in a wider sense, because the family remained a public institution in the social Catholic lexicon, to Quebec society as a whole. Because the sexual impulse was the key to individual emotional adjustment and personality, it thus lay at the foundation of personalist notions of marriage and family as viable communities. Those who frequented the SPM courses in the post-war decades would have heard the message that in the modern era marital success should not be evaluated according to the standard of mere permanence. Over and over again, promoters and organizers insisted that factors such as the happiness of the couple, sexual satisfaction, unity, and self-adjustment had to be considered as crucial standards in evaluating marriage.[41] To begin the task of teaching husbands how to foster this climate of intimacy within marriage, the marriage preparation courses placed an emphasis on techniques of mutual psychological exploration. Group leaders and instructors were emphatically enjoined to "get at least one word out of each of them [the fiancés, to] make them advance their opinions" on matters ranging from budgeting to their emotional needs to their ideas about sex and their aspirations for married life.[42] Apparently, the prospective brides who attended these sessions regarded the frankness that the lectures and discussions encouraged, together with the emphasis on intimacy and partnership, as something both novel and refreshing. Writing in 1947, one young woman, "Marie-Ange," stated that "the study of the psychology of the male simply stunned me. What a revelation for me – and how useful – to learn that men think and act differently than we do." For her, this new psychological self-awareness encouraged a new intimacy with her fiancé: "we have often discussed together the subjects treated in the course. We are very happy to have settled before our marriage a host of problems: balancing a family budget, mutual trust, a proper sense of our sexual life and of its responsibilities, and child-rearing."[43] Throughout the history of the SPM, it was invariably the women who appreciated that the focus on the psychology of the sexes and the cultivation of intimacy was particularly tailored to their needs and desires.[44]

From a contemporary perspective, the psychological and physiological advice offered to these young women would appear both patronizing, and designed to keep them in a state of economic and sexual subordination to their husbands. Quebec Catholic reformers, in their desire to refurbish marriage as a source of sexual satisfaction to women, seemed at one level to participate in a North American stream of wartime and post-war conservatism in which sexuality was exalted as a way of satisfying women within the domestic sphere, thus obviating demands for greater access to paid work opportunities outside the home.[45] However conservative the equation between female sexual satisfaction and marital stability within this strand of Catholicism, it was apparent that the notions of intimacy and psychological "complementarity" taught by the SPM were not conservative in the sense of representing a simple continuity with pre-war definitions of marriage. Although the desire for family harmony and marital stability certainly remained constant, what was different about post-war Catholic activism was the emphasis placed upon the sexual satisfaction of the female partner, a female sexual expression that was not simply coextensive with motherhood and reproduction. In this key respect, this current of Catholic activism marked a substantial departure from pre-war sexual attitudes and practices, where both Church teachings and social values affirmed both the impurity and sinfulness of the sexual act, and explicitly identified it with the satisfaction of male needs and dominance within the conjugal relationship. Where female sexuality was acknowledged, it was limited to reproduction and motherhood with no consideration of a pleasurable component.[46]

Indeed, the message presented was that young women needed to think quite differently about their choice of husband than did their counterparts who married before the war. Prior to 1940, women's marriage ideals seemed to extend only to finding a husband who held a steady job, did not drink, and did not cheat, but who was not terribly intimate or communicative.[47] Access to the psychology and sexology presented by the SPM went far towards reassuring large numbers of young Catholic women that, in a conservative society in which marriage was still considered the full achievement of adulthood, the choice of a husband was not simply a "roll of the dice" that might confine them to a lifetime of emotional solitude and sexual unhappiness.

However, it was clear that what the prospective brides attending the sessions most appreciated and desired was the message that both women and men had entirely natural sexual urges which did not have to be repressed, but could be openly discussed and satisfied within the context of marriage.[48] Writing to her prospective fiancé Michel Chartrand in 1941, former JEC activist Simonne Monet intimated her apprehensions surrounding the "mysteries" of sexual intercourse, but insisted upon "*the right to love (which signifies pleasure) for the woman.*"[49] As part of their commitment to foster the closed affectional conjugal family, shorn of its intergenerational ties, Catholic marriage promoters and family activists were intent on demonstrating the novelty of their approach to female sexuality. They therefore drew a radical contrast between the type of up-to-date knowledge available to young women in the post-war period and that imparted by nuns and mothers just a few years before, with the latter amounting either to a "prudish" conspiracy of silence or a consigning of sex to the realm of animal impulses in the name of recruiting "well-bred" young girls for a life of religious celibacy.[50]

It was no coincidence that the most popular aspect of the SPM's marriage preparation course was the focus on male and female anatomies in sessions ten and eleven, and the expounding of the new Catholic moral teaching on sexuality in session thirteen. These lectures, delivered by medical professionals and clergy, invariably included instructions as to proper sexual techniques that would, it was believed, satisfy both husband and wife. It was small wonder, then, that SPM organizers frequently complained that young people were "flocking to the courses for sexual information and not to explore the spirituality of marriage."[51] One of the key features of post-war Catholic activism was the casting of generational difference in terms of young women's access to sexual knowledge, a sense of cultural discontinuity that was aptly, if somewhat rudely expressed by one anonymous critic in a perturbed letter to the Jeunesse Ouvrière Catholique's weekly newspaper, the *Front Ouvrier*. This critic charged that the SPM activists were telling young people to simply bypass the advice given by their parents, and were "making young girls wild to sleep with men and have children quickly ... You have no business in these matters ... and instead of bothering young women with this nonsense about marriage preparation, you should be teaching them how to earn an honest living. ... You are no better than Italian Fascists ... in allowing young men and women to associate in your Catholic youth groups; you are corrupting the young generation; you are simply making them horny."[52]

The element in the SPM's courses on marriage and sexuality that most clearly expressed the disjuncture that Catholicism hoped to effect within the culture surrounding women's identities and family roles was the notion that, because gender identities were psychological, they went beyond mere outward physical characteristics. Thus, according to this definition, women's sexual needs and response existed on an emotional and psychological level and were not determined solely by maternal function and reproduction. "Human sexuality," stated Father Bernard Mailhiot, a lecturer to the Montreal SPM, "is a psycho-sexuality that is bound up with the mystery of the human soul,"[53] an observation that precisely expressed the personalist conjunction that considered marriage as a sexual, psychological, and spiritual partnership which had less to do with the act of reproduction than with an ongoing cultivation of intimacy. While the marriage preparation courses generally assumed that women's sexual knowledge was not as well developed as that of their prospective husbands and that women should allow men to take the initiative in sexual matters, Catholic activists emphatically enjoined that the "gift of self," which was the watchword of the new ideal of Christian marriage, in fact conferred the right to sexual pleasure and satisfaction on both sexes. Catholic lay activists and clergy involved in the marriage preparation movement were acutely aware of the Kinsey Report and its implications regarding the promiscuous sexual behaviour of North American youth. The centering of marital stability on emotional and psychological fulfillment also meant that they located sexual incompatibility as the primary cause of marriage breakdown, a failure which they explained as arising primarily from the failure of husbands to properly understand female psychology and sexual needs.[54]

Post-war Catholic marriage activists were compelled to negotiate more egalitarian notions of female sexuality within the framework of a moral teaching whose traditional canons on sexual relations seemed to reflect a male-centred focus on the satisfaction of animal needs and women's passivity during the sexual act. Furthermore, traditional Catholic teaching viewed with suspicion any sexual contact that did not lead to reproduction. Within this rubric, however, post-war Catholic commentators on sexuality, although largely male clergy and activists, found considerable latitude for a more female-centred interpretation, one that reflected the need to appeal to a numerically-dominant female constituency within the Catholic Action movements.[55] Commentators like the Jesuit Father Marie-Joseph d'Anjou reminded prospective couples that conjugal love was not "a slavery to one's own instincts or the instincts of the other – but as a free gift of the self."[56] What is significant is that the personalist phraseology of reciprocal psychological satisfaction contained, in fact, an implicit critique and limitation of impulsive male sexual behaviour – always denounced under the rubric of "egoism" – that placed little emphasis on mutuality or even recognized that wives had sexual impulses that needed to be satisfied.[57] "The sexual gift," d'Anjou reminded couples, "must under no circumstances be a forced one." Indeed, he went even further, stating that during intercourse, because men were so rarely deprived of sexual satisfaction, the purpose of intercourse was, in fact, "the fulfillment of the wife," an obligation that must at all times take precedence in recognition of the fact that "sexuality has a hundred times the importance for a woman than it does for the man."[58] In this key respect – the notion that male activity must serve the achievement of a fulfilling female sexual experience – the sexology presented by the marriage preparation movement was not part of a post-war reassertion of conventional male-centred family hierarchies. Quebec Catholics drew upon a strand of thinking that made female orgasm central to "successful" intercourse, and aimed to correct faulty male technique because men were assumed to be the active agents in sexual initiation. By contrast, after World War II, most American treatments of sexuality, reflecting prevalent anxieties about masculinity, not only prioritized effective male sexual functioning, but placed the entire responsibility for satisfying husbands' needs upon wives.[59]

The ways in which a more woman-centred, personalist interpretation of sexuality could be formulated and accommodated within the traditions of Catholic moral teaching were aptly demonstrated during a question-and-answer session given by Father Jules Paquin in 1960 to SPM group leaders, and recorded in fairly graphic detail by a zealous lay note-taker anxious to communicate the knowledge to the participants in the marriage preparation courses. In the first place, many within this movement were aware of situations in which male and female sexual desires did not always coincide, and if the wife refused sexual relations, either through male clumsiness, drunkenness, or marital problems, did this contravene Catholic doctrine that it was the imperative duty of each spouse to satisfy the other's needs? Paquin responded that persistent refusal would certainly constitute a "serious sin," but what really counted between couples was that sexual need should never be framed in terms of a demand, which implied a relationship of subordination, but as an invitation between equals. Indeed, Paquin countenanced refusal if one spouse asked to have sexual relations "at the wrong time," or was drunk, or had committed adultery – moral shortcomings far more associated with men than with women. Implicitly, Paquin and his colleagues placed women's personal decision ahead of the Church's more legalistic prescription.[60] The real priority in sexual relations between married spouses was, however, female satisfaction, as Paquin was the promoter of a sexual technique called "reserved coupling" that taught married couples how to have satisfying intercourse without male ejaculation, which remained emphatically prohibited by the laws of the Church unless it occurred during vaginal sex and with the aim of procreation. While this imposed a decided boundary upon male sexual pleasure, by contrast, no such restrictions applied to the female orgasm, which could be achieved either vaginally or through caressing other organs, and was thus exempt from the natural law emphasis on procreation. Paquin informed his audience that during conjugal relations, "all the forms of caressing are permissible as preparation. Even without full intercourse, all these intimacies are permitted so long as they are not prolonged to the point where the husband ejaculates. Acts like a 69 are not contrary to chastity ... but there are certain forms of intimacy that are repugnant to women ... and they should thus be avoided."[61] Paquin's presentation, and the insistence throughout the SPM's courses on the husband's "duty of conscience to see to and further the complete orgasm, the physical and psychological satisfaction of your wives,"[62] provided a concise statement of two ideas that were central to post-war Quebec Catholicism: that although the main purpose of sexual relations might be procreative, there were many aspects of sexual relations between husband and wife that served a more

important function – that of building emotional and psychological intimacy between the couple as persons. And in so doing, male ejaculation –
the procreative act itself – came to be seen as actually quite secondary to
the achievement of mutual pleasure and emotional affinity.

In one sense, at the level of the sexual practices that occurred between
individual married couples, it is difficult to determine the extent to which
the prescriptions of this personalist sexology actually impinged upon the
lived experience of post-war Quebec Catholics. However, it is possible to
trace the enduring cultural influence of these more egalitarian values
through another avenue. A key element of this personalist reorientation of
Catholic teaching on marriage was a partial, if never complete, disentan-
gling of sexuality from strictly reproductive imperatives. The recognition
by a powerful current within the religiosity of lay Roman Catholics that the
psychological, sexual, and emotional components of marriage were at least
as important as the procreative aspects played a crucial role in articulating
and popularizing what was perhaps one of the most central attributes of
modernity in post-war Quebec culture: the growing assertion, between the
mid-1930s and the 1960s, of women's control over reproductive choice.
Again, the role of a Roman Catholic movement in such a liberalizing cultural process may seem paradoxical and counter to mainstream historical
wisdom, which takes as a given the oft-stated equation between French-
Canadian national identity and pronatalism, the latter constituting a directive to couples to raise large families. According to these scholars, this cultural imperative was reinforced by the clergy's unflinching opposition to
birth control, and they thus interpret the growing tendency of the faithful,
between 1930 and 1960, to limit and space births, as part of a master-narrative of secularization. Here, historians postulate an ongoing dialectic
tension between "normalization" – the conservative, pronatalist prescriptions of the male-dominated Church and medical establishment – and
"subversion" – the permeation of counter-religious, secular values into
Quebec society through the agency of women who manifested a silent
resistance to Catholicism's moral prescriptions, and quietly practiced birth
control in defiance of official teachings. Following historical convention,
this opposition emerged from underground and became the cultural
mainstream during the sexual revolution of the 1960s, when it became
especially associated with a rejection by young women of Catholic moral
codes regarding sexual conduct.[63] In this chronological schema, the widespread acceptance of contraception by Catholic women follows the advent
of the political phase of the Quiet Revolution after 1960.

There are two central difficulties with this line of interpretation as
applied to the cultural experience of Quebec Catholics in the post-war
period. First, although the Quebec clergy as a social group certainly paid
considerable ideological adherence to pronatalism, post-war Quebec

culture did not exhibit an extreme preoccupation with the problem of the birth rate. Indeed, a number of demographers and cultural historians have argued that in Quebec the celebrated "baby boom" did not constitute a reversal of an overall pattern of declining fertility that had been going on from at least the early twentieth century, and, because the pre-war birth rate among Catholic Quebecers had been higher than in other regions of the country, that the post-war increase had less demographic impact than the corresponding phenomenon in English Canada.[64] Despite the power of religion in Quebec, when compared to other societies where Catholicism was also strong, Quebec displayed a far weaker official commitment to pronatalism than did a number of European countries. In the wake of population losses suffered during World War II, governments in France and Germany evolved a panoply of state policies designed to foster a high birth rate. Lacking this social imperative, the commitment of Quebec Catholicism to a natalist direction remained at the level of culture and moral injunction. It did not extend to the more overt realm of social policy, where policies like family allowances, though ostensibly pronatalist in paying mothers benefits according to the number of children, were in fact intended to foster full employment and consumption, rather than raise the birth rate.[65]

More problematic still is the assumption that birth control – read modernity – and Catholicism – read tradition – were quite simply incompatible and destined to be always in opposition. This conclusion overlooks the considerable impact of personalism upon the post-Depression age cohorts through the mediating influence of Catholic Action. Although this type of Catholicism vigorously eschewed "artificial" forms of birth control and most certainly exalted the injunction that married couples should have children, it must be remembered that at its centre stood the immense priority it placed upon marriage as an emotional and sexual partnership that aimed at the spiritual perfection of husband and wife. In furthering this, it actively fostered the ideal of the closed, affectional, nuclear family in which the reproductive and economic function of parenting was highly modified by the emotional, psychological, and educative attention parents would bestow upon their children. Given this priority, Catholic personalism thus raised several questions: Could parents, and especially mothers, who were more directly implicated in education and child-rearing, best cultivate these roles by having large numbers of children or by exercising some prudent planning and foresight in order to adjust the parents' available physical and emotional resources to the numbers of children that they could effectively raise? And could husband and wife effectively cultivate their own intimate relationship under the pressures of raising large numbers of children, or have a satisfying sexual relationship under the psychological stress of the wife always becoming pregnant? Of equal significance, if women's sexuality – the foundation of post-war family stability itself – was not just synonymous with reproduction, could the sexual needs of wives be satisfied without some form of family limitation? In answering these questions, an important current of Quebec Catholicism did far more than simply oppose or haltingly accommodate itself to the supposedly "secular" practice of birth control. Through various forms of lay activism, Catholic Action promoted an ideal of family planning that emphasized women's control, because it was based upon using recent scientific knowledge of the female menstrual cycle, and relied upon the "mutuality" and intimacy which the marriage preparation movement sought to instill in the very relationship between husband and wife to allow couples to adjust the frequency, nature, and timing of their sexual expression. In so doing, the promoters of Catholic family planning deliberately attempted to balance self-sacrifice and sexual satisfaction, and thus navigated between what they considered two materialistic and irresponsible extremes: the extended, "economic" family model of having as many children as possible in order to supply the labour and income needs of the household, and a culture of hedonism which, they believed, sought to sever the connection between sexuality and procreation in the name of a mechanistic sexuality based entirely upon instinctive drives. In Quebec between the mid-1930s and the widespread use of the pill during the later 1960s, one type of birth control – the much-maligned Ogino-Knaus or rhythm method – was in fact central to the type of religiosity that Catholic Action aspired to promote, and it was this influential personalist current within Catholicism that became the principal vehicle through which values and practices of contraception infused the wider society.

A surface reading of the SPM's marriage preparation course would indicate that it was firmly anchored in the traditional Catholic notion that the purpose of marriage which legitimated the sexual relationship was childbearing and parenthood, exalted as the central ends of marriage for the modern husband and wife. In the eyes of the Church, the only acceptable method of birth control was abstinence, and even that was governed by the overriding insistence on the right of a spouse to demand sexual intercourse for the purposes of procreation. At the beginning of the 1930s, the papal encyclical *Casti connubii* had reiterated this doctrine, with the explicit proviso that *all* forms of birth control were "shameful and intrinsically vicious" because they perverted the conjugal act from its central purpose, "the begetting of children."[66] However, the pope's statement contained a number of ambiguous sentences that qualified to some extent this stern prohibition. *Casti connubii* absolved from blame "those … who in the married state use their right in the proper manner, although on account of natural reasons either of time or of certain defects, new life cannot be brought forth." The pope cited a number of secondary ends of marriage –

"mutual aid, the cultivation of mutual love, and the quieting of concupis-cence" – which were not forbidden to the married couple,[67] language which seemed to open the possibility that sexual intercourse within mar-riage had other uses not solely bound up with procreation. But what was the pope actually referring to when he spoke of instances when sexual intercourse did not result in procreation, and that on those occasions, the sexual act could serve other aspects of the marriage? The pope's teachings on marriage reflected, in fact, what many believed was the discovery during the 1920s of a reliable "natural" method of birth control based upon calculating the fertile and infertile days of the female cycle. Indeed, by acknowledging the possibility that on some occasions couples might engage in sexual intercourse that did not lead to procreation, the pope was in fact implicitly giving sanction to the Ogino-Knaus or rhythm method. During the 1930s, a number of Quebec clergy wrote treatises that popularized this form of contraception,[68] although until the efforts of the marriage preparation movement in the post-war period, the access to this knowledge by most ordinary Catholics would have remained quite limited.

However, the support of the institutional Church for the rhythm method should not be overstated. What emerged from most statements by the clergy both before and after World War II was that this practice was intended not so much as a form of birth control on an ongoing basis, but, as Father M.-C. Forest stated, as "a remedy for an exceptional and transi-tory situation" in the lives of married couples. It was not intended to replace the basic method, abstinence from intercourse, or to modify the primary doctrinal imperative, the subordination of sex to the purpose of procreation.[69] Progressive clergy like Forest recognized, however, that there were circumstances in the lives of many married couples, such as poverty and illness, that made constant pregnancies extremely difficult both for individual partners and for the stability of the marriage itself. In such cases, it was better to permit the limited use of the rhythm method for periods of time within the marriage – the lesser evil – rather than to have the faithful resort to prohibited birth control practices – the "pre-vention of the family" through "Malthusian doctrines propagated with con-siderable skill and refinement" through modern media outside the purview of the Church.[70] Indeed, by the early 1940s, Catholic clergy who were involved in a variety of family movements accepted that couples had the right to "deliberately plan a coincidence between the performance of conjugal duties and the return of the infertile period of the menstrual cycle" so long as couples did not explicitly desire to avoid procreation.[71] In other words, Catholic couples could use the rhythm method so long as they accepted all the pregnancies that might result from sexual inter-course. From the perspective of Catholic doctrine, the rhythm method had the advantage of being "natural" in the sense that it could be practiced without the use of artificial means, and it preserved the subordination of sexuality to the Christian imperatives of self-sacrifice and self-control, while its emphasis upon predictability and planning allowed women a greater amount of freedom to express their sexuality without the constant presence of undesired pregnancies. More significantly, however, its successful practice precisely mirrored the new Catholic emphasis upon mutuality and partnership in marriage, because it depended upon the joint decision of husband and wife to abstain from vaginal intercourse during the fertile days of the female cycle.

The real intent, however, was to have couples use the rhythm method in a limited fashion, not to allow couples to practice contraception, but to space births. As Father Hervé Blais advised the participants in the *École des parents* in 1942, "in the rhythm of a normal conjugal life, a moderate use of periodic abstinence can find its place in order to obtain a reasonable spacing of births."[72] However, most post-war Catholic commentators on contraception were quite adamant that the use of Ogino-Knaus was not to be regarded as a universal solution to the demands and dilemmas of Christian marriage, or as canceling the natural law responsibility of parents to procreate. To the fallacious claim by Dr Brock Chisholm, head of the World Health Organization, that the rhythm method was not contrary to Roman Catholic teaching, Camille L'Heureux retorted in 1952 that "the Church has never suggested to the individual family, and still less to an entire people, the use of the 'rhythm' method. It is only the conscience … individually guided by the moral law that can decide if, for serious reasons, in precisely determined circumstances, and in what ways, the use of the 'rhythm' method is compatible with the laws of God."[73] And among the "serious reasons" for practicing this method, the sole motive of family limitation would not have been deemed sufficient. Indeed, orthodox opinion was not even prepared to countenance family poverty as an excuse for derogations from natural law.[74] Nor was this hedging of the rhythm method with restrictions confined to Catholic conservatives or to the clergy. Writing to the *Front Ouvrier* in 1953 in reply to a question posed by "Jeune mari," who wondered what latitude he had within the religious injunction to "have as many children as circumstances permit," claiming that he was not rich and his wife not in sound health, Mme Berthe Lepage lauded the practice of large families, observing that these provided the atmosphere in which religious vocations could flourish. As for those who felt that they had borne enough children, and wanted the pleasures of sexual intercourse without the disadvantages of procreation, she tartly reminded them that "total abstinence" was something pleasing in the eyes of God, and that she personally had little time for those who "display such weakness as to slaver at the mere prospect of an ice-cream cone."[75]

From a somewhat different perspective, Catholic promoters of the new ideal of the affectional nuclear family, like Jeanne Grisé-Allard, were likewise opposed to the use of the rhythm method as a form of contraception because an overweening concern with limiting family size could cause problems with the proper psychological functioning of the family itself. Interestingly, although during the late 1930s and early 1940s the journal *La Famille,* one of the major mediators of the Catholic reformist family ideal in Quebec, always photographed families as comprising mother, father, and no more than three children, advocates of the modern nuclear family were concerned that families with only one child risked becoming the breeding ground of "superiority complexes that predispose to egoism."[76] Even radical personalists like Emmanuel Mounier, who otherwise opposed state-sponsored forms of pronatalism, condemned childless marriages, arguing that they tended towards "sexual isolation" because the union of husband and wife "only finds its fulfillment in the child."[77]

Within the SPM's marriage preparation courses, group leaders regularly extolled the primary procreative purpose of marriage, telling their audiences that the child was the confirmation of the marriage bond, and that from the perspective of marital harmony it was unwise to delay the birth of the first child unduly. However, given the prevailing emphasis upon the marriage bond as one of intimacy and emotional fulfillment of both husband and wife, these Catholic activists cast the injunction to have children in terms of the maturity of the spouses themselves, maintaining that the decision to postpone having children would merely prolong a species of "egotism" and prevent the psychological growth of husband and wife as a couple.[78] Indeed, most of the young men and women who attended the premarital counselling sessions appear to have been quite traditional in their attitudes regarding family size. As late as 1962, those questioned in a survey indicated that they desired a family of approximately four or five children.[79] However, from a very early stage in the history of the SPM, the presence of a large number of doctors and nurses as lecturers was intended not merely to inform prospective brides and grooms about human anatomy and the technical aspects of sexual intercourse, or to reassure young women about the naturalness and safety of childbirth, but to popularize the Ogino-Knaus method of birth control.[80]

During the so-called "sexual revolution" that followed when access to the birth control pill became widespread after the late 1960s, the rhythm method was much ridiculed as both ineffective and a symbol of women's subjection to patriarchal clerical dogma. While it was later seen this way, its promotion by Catholic Action must be placed in the context of the period before 1960. Given the lack of access in Quebec to reliable means of birth control, as evinced by the prevalence before the Depression of practices such as long-term abstinence, *coitus interruptus,* and more "folkloric" expedients to prevent conception,[81] knowledge of the rhythm method gave Catholic women, for the first time, a sense that they possessed the technical means, sanctioned by religion, to determine the timing of conception and thus, ultimately, the power to control the size of their families. Because Catholic laity, and especially women, dominated the post-war Catholic Action movements, within the SPM there began to emerge a palpable gap between the official doctrines that stressed the imperative of procreation, and the way the issue was dealt with and softened in practice by chaplains and spiritual directors who instructed young couples in the principles of Catholic morality. Clergy such as Father Jules Paquin explained that Catholic doctrine permitted the use of the rhythm method – what he termed "periodic continence" – to allow the spacing of children so as to ensure their proper care and education. Paquin nuanced official teachings by emphasizing that the key factor was not external authority, but the consent of both spouses, and their own personal identification of their needs and resources. "The church," he stated, "has never advocated giving birth to the most children in the quickest possible time."[82]

Father Paquin's statement precisely captured the conflicting imperatives in the dynamic of Catholicism and women's fertility that personalism had worked in Quebec society between 1930 and 1960. In response to the official subordination of marriage and family life to procreation, clergy and lay leaders in touch with Catholic Action advanced the idea that the decision to have children must be governed by a new, and even more overarching consideration: the ability of parents to raise and educate their children. It must be remembered that Catholic personalism in Quebec was closely bound up with a psychological-affectional concept of family, and that this reformist vision of family relations had implications not only for the private sphere, but for the synthesis of democracy and authority that Catholic Action desired to implant in Quebec culture. Catholic family advocates in the post-Depression era redefined child-rearing as a demanding parental task, and called upon husbands and wives to provide their children with far more than material need or preparation for work roles.

Given the rather total emotional involvement that the reconstruction of family life imposed upon parents, and especially upon mothers, could the all-encompassing older Catholic natural law emphasis upon parent-as-procreator really be reconciled to these newer conceptions of the family and cultural democracy that were coming to be regarded as integral to Catholicism? Did not the new personalist vision of marriage and parenting actually dictate the necessity of making a choice to limit family size? And what of *Casti connubii*'s own emphasis upon marriage as an intimate partnership between husband and wife? Did this itself not at least implicitly enjoin placing limits upon constant pregnancy, in order that the spouses could attend to the health and improvement of their own spiritual and physical relationship?

In an article written in 1943, Rodolphe and Germaine Laplante argued that, while it was certainly important to respect the principle of "natural fertility," it was important to place this doctrine in the context of fathers crushed by the "ungrateful role of provider," a role rendered difficult by the conditions of modern industry, and especially of those mothers who were called upon to be "educator ... and at the same time a housekeeper, cook, waitress, and nurse." Such mothers, the Laplantes claimed, were generally poor and had little time to keep abreast of all the latest developments in the science of child-rearing. Thus, such parents adopted the educational expedient of telling their numerous children simply to "keep quiet,"[83] a negation of Quebec's post-war ideal of the democratic family. Until the early 1960s, Catholic promoters of contraception never used the phrase "birth control" (*limitation des naissances*), preferring to couch their language in terms of the popular phraseology of "birth planning" (*régulation des naissances*). Such "planning," in which parents periodically resorted to the rhythm method to bring their fertility into line with the family's economic, psychological, emotional, and educative resources, was upheld in terms of the religious values of responsibility and prudence; it also enlisted a pervasive post-war sensibility devoted to planning and rationality that extended outside the conventional spheres of economic and social policy to encompass a variety of other cultural practices. [84] Through organizations like the SPM, reformist Catholics juxtaposed this new synthesis of personalist religiosity and commitment to rational management of resources with older practices of uncontrolled fertility. The latter were characterized in the language of personalism as "instinctual," and thus implicitly cast as being contrary to humanism. Thus, in the early 1940s social Catholic laity like Adélard Provencher reiterated the traditional ideal of the "natural and simple union of the spouses, with acceptance of all the potential children that might result," but he qualified this by declaring that "procreation must never be abandoned to an instinct that is not controlled by reason and virtuous effort." Citing the views of the German theologian Mgr Von Streng, Provencher advanced the argument that natural law injunctions must be modified by important considerations such as the health of the parents, the economic situation of the family relative to social rank, and especially by "the educative capacities, primarily of the mother, and by the facilities that the social environment offers for the education of the children."[85]

Significantly, although Catholic personalism certainly kept fertility to the fore as an important component of marriage, there began to emerge by the late 1940s among articulate Catholic laity, those most involved in the marriage preparation and family life movements, a reversal of the paired doctrinal priorities of procreation and mutual aid of spouses that papal teaching had enunciated at the beginning of the 1930s. "Marriage," in the view of family activists Jeanne d'Arc and Bernard Trottier, "has for its central goals the mutual aid of spouses and procreation." In their estimation, however, procreation had quite specific meanings that extended beyond the act of reproduction. It was "not limited to giving birth to children; it is bringing the personality of our children, day after day, into the world," a process that "involved the soul and intelligence as much as material comfort and food."[86] Other reformist Catholics turned the new psychological and affective ideal of modern marriage and parenting into what amounted to a full-scale assault on popular values of pre-Depression Quebec which had lauded a high rate of fertility. They severed these from any connection with Christianity, and assimilated the older cultural ideal of the unremitting cycles of birth with the instinctual, "irrational" social and cultural forms of a rural society that subordinated human values to the play of blind natural forces. "The procreation of children," stated the proceedings of one post-war conference on family spirituality, "is not necessarily the expression of chastity: it is perhaps more closely linked to a purely bestial sexual instinct, or to ignorance, what some would call 'bad luck.'" [87] Dr Albert Guilbeault, the director of *Nos Enfants*, the organ of the École des Parents, informed his readers that child-rearing was not simply a matter of making them gain weight like farm animals, or ensuring that they attended church and school. Parents must, he declared, "induce the child to surpass himself" through constant attention to the development of physical, intellectual, and moral faculties. This new and more responsible parental attitude to child-rearing constituted, in his words, "an educative procreation."[88]

Despite the claim of Catholic Action's marriage preparation movement that "our traditions regarding large families have been respected,"[89] the tenor of the movement after the mid-1950s emphasized a "prudent" attitude to family size and reproduction – stressing the planning and regulation of births made possible by the rhythm method – and downplayed the older doctrinal prescriptions of natural fertility. Personalism and demography came together in the thinking of Jacques Henripin, the Université de Montréal demographer who turned to the legacy of the old Catholic nationalist champion Henri Bourassa to critique the equation between nationalism and natalism. The premium that had once been placed upon quantity, observed Henripin, would actually work to the detriment of French Canada in an era when the society ought to be thinking in terms of qualitative progress through compulsory schooling and more sophisticated intellectual and technical training, which were the avenues to social promotion.[90] This reasoning also lay behind the statements of the SPM, whose group leaders were increasingly told to inform their audiences of working-class and lower-middle-class couples that "it is nearly impossible to determine today what is the ideal family size. All that we can say is that for a couple to voluntarily limit themselves to a single child might suggest a lack of generosity and that, on the other hand, consecutive maternities every ten months might not be a prudent use of human reproductive capacity."[91] The potential to plan and space births that the rhythm method held out was, for this post-war generation of Quebec Catholic women, a confirmation of the personalist emphasis upon human freedom, and in light of the priority that women within the movement placed upon sexuality and personal satisfaction within marriage, no longer would spouses have to rely upon the mere denial of sexual intimacy in order to limit family size: "The human heart, human reason, and human sense of responsibility can now intervene to assure a sensible regulation of births. This human progress in the mastery of fertility is possible thanks to recent scientific advances ... With the progress of science, the time is not far off when humanity will become more completely the master of fertility."[92] In a similar vein, the 1957 study session of the École des Parents evoked the "realism" of the modern family, the connection of rational practices of fertility to the quest for human values. These activists explicitly linked Catholicism to the progress of science and education – by which they implicitly meant the rhythm method, whose precise laws permitted the "spacing of maternities and the diminution in the number of children," thus assuring "the opening of possibilities for wives and children."[93]

But can it be said that the new Catholic culture of regulating births through the rhythm method had any long-term effects on demographic attitudes in Quebec and practices regarding fertility? In a little-known series of articles written in 1954, the French historian Philippe Ariès observed that despite a post-war rise in the birth rate in a number of Western societies, there had been no return to the "ancient" family where natural patterns of fertility had forced mothers to experience yearly births. Writing at the height of the post-war baby boom, Ariès characterized even the larger families of this era, those with four or five children, as "Malthusian" in their practices, because "young parents are deciding to have two or three children within the first five years of marriage, and after that, barring unfortunate accidents, the dimensions of the family do not increase further."[94] This pattern deduced from the French context also seems to have been evident in Quebec, where after 1945 such a "contraceptive revolution" occurred among the cohorts of women born between 1921 and 1935. It should be noted that this "revolution" in social practices was not at first manifest in an actual decline in the birth rate; indeed, the female age cohorts of 1921–35 appear to have had the same average number of children as women born between 1906 and 1910. However, within the later age cohorts, women increasingly chose to space and limit births over the course of their child-bearing years, and more particularly, made the decision to have all their children while younger, then employing a combination of contraceptive practices to ensure that the cycle of births was brought to an end. Of women born between 1921 and 1925, 47 per cent used some form of contraception; those born between 1926 and 1930, 59 per cent; and those born 1931 and 1936, 64 per cent.[95] Significantly, the latter two groups, whose fertility was the focal point of the revolution, were those women most likely to be influenced by the personalist teachings of Catholic Action and, in particular, to have had some contact with the marriage preparation movement. Women of these age groups relied upon the supposedly "traditional" combination of the rhythm method and periodic abstinence, the only forms sanctioned by Roman Catholicism, to introduce into Quebec the "modern" practice of limiting births. More tellingly, a culture of birth control occurred prior to and without the "sexual revolution" of the 1960s, and was largely elaborated by married women acting within the framework of religiously-sanctioned domestic roles. It was not the byproduct of widespread access to the pill or artificial means of birth control, and was not the result either of external pressure applied by non-Catholic advocates of "artificial" birth control or the rejection of Catholic morality by baby-boom youth.[96] Quebec's introduction to contraception between 1931 and the early 1960s signalled not the mass rejection of Catholic values, but the engrafting of a particular strand of Catholicism onto wider social practices.

The "modernity" of the Catholic personalist advocacy of the rhythm method was not lost upon contemporary social observers. Both the conservative Philippe Garigue and his more liberal colleague Jacques Henripin wrote articles on the subject in 1957, at the very height of the postwar upsurge in births, when women's commitment to domesticity might have been expected to be at its apogee. Both estimated that Catholic Action's emphasis on family planning, far from being a persistence of "tradition," constituted in fact something entirely new in the cultural experience of women and of the wider society: it was the harbinger of more individualist values and a new valorizing of women's social position that contained the possibility of a wider disruption in family relationships. For Garigue, on the one hand, Catholicism's promotion of the "natural regulation of births through a spiritual mastery of fertility" held forth the possibility of maintaining the historically close relationship between the family and the Catholic Church. On the other hand, he recognized that the new personalist marriage doctrines required "a control of human psycho-biological reactions that is foreign both to North American culture and, to a certain extent, to French-Canadian traditions. However, it is a solution that demands an acceptance of new values, which are not part of the cultural heritage of French Canadians."[97]

What troubled these two social scientists was that the efforts of Catholic organizations such as the SPM seemed to indicate the emergence of mass, rather than individual, birth control practices, which meant for Henripin and Garigue that the core values of stability, cohesion, and intimacy of the family had possibly been downgraded. "It is not impossible," mused Henripin, "that the anti-Malthusian doctrine carried some wisdom, some part of a social perspicacity, some warning that birth control might be used excessively if officially sponsored."[98] The new values of rational fertility increasingly identified with Catholic women "seemed to indicate the prevalence of the individual over his family rather than the subordination of the individual to the family."[99] What men like Garigue and Henripin most feared was that once the equation between Catholicism and the legitimacy of contraception was engrained in popular sensibilities and practices – largely through the choice of married women to assert control over reproduction – these same women would be able to use the personalist current within Catholicism to take the more equal status that the assertion of the right to sexual pleasure and greater freedom from constant maternity conferred to argue for greater equality and independence in the wider public sphere? This in turn raised the prospect of Catholicism actually weakening women's commitment to an ideal of domesticity founded upon maternity, and this, in a larger sense, would erode one of the central pillars of Quebec's laboriously constructed post-war synthesis of democracy and authority, that is, the close identification of married women with family roles.

"WE BELIEVE THAT SEXUAL EQUALITY IS FOUNDED ON DISSIMILARITY"[100]

It has been widely accepted that from the post-war years until the early 1960s, North America experienced the zenith of an extremely confining form of domesticity.[101] This was manifest in a desire for quiescence, a rapidly-rising birth rate, and the proliferation of passive, subordinate, and maternal female roles that reinforced older gender hierarchies in family and society, verities that were displaced only by the combined effect of the 1960s sexual revolution and the reemergence of a wave of egalitarian feminism. However, during the past decade, a number of scholars have challenged this historical truism, arguing that women in the post-war period experienced a tension between cultural messages that enjoined domesticity and more "feminist" currents that assigned a positive value to individual achievement and more diversified, egalitarian notions of women's roles.[102] What was striking about Quebec in the post-war era was that what might be termed "feminist" messages in the culture were given institutional expression and promoted in a most unexpected place, not in the sphere of the economic relations of the workplace or in the realm of politics, but within the context of what at first sight would be deemed the repository of an extreme form of "traditionalism," namely, the intersection between Catholicism and the definition of family roles. The spread of contraceptive practices like the rhythm method that was legitimized by a more egalitarian interpretation of personal relations among Quebec women during the post-war period reflected a larger set of tensions that Catholic Action fostered within public ideologies, one that articulated and defined the roles of married women both within the family and the wider society.

The fact that this process occurred in the years that lay between post-war reconstruction and the end of the 1950s is surprising. Indeed, until the late 1960s, Quebec, by comparison with other North American jurisdictions, had one of the lowest proportions of married women in the paid labour force.[103] During the immediate post-war years, the bifurcation of genders – that is, the identification of men with the public sphere of work, and women with the private sanctum of the family – seemed to be an unquestioned social and cultural verity, as both conservative and reformist Catholics, ranging from family activists to the leadership of the Catholic trade unions, participated fully in a culture and set of social policies that upheld paid work as a singularly masculine attribute. In relation to current concepts of woman's nature, Catholics assigned no positive cultural or spiritual value to paid work, regarding it at best as a necessary evil that could only be countenanced under the pressures of family economic exigency, and, at worst, as something "abnormal" that "crushed, deformed" and ultimately enslaved women by turning them away from their "sublime mission" of motherhood.[104] Even so staunch a political feminist as Thérèse Casgrain was constrained to admit that "the mother of a family who is truly conscious of her duties will not leave her children to go to the factory unless compelled to do so by absolute necessity."[105]

Catholicism's set of postulates surrounding gender and family that accepted masculinity and femininity as a system of fixed and immutable identities and roles appeared at first sight to be one of the main cultural vehicles of an extremely conservative form of domesticity, one that would only be dislodged by the combined effects of the "sexual revolution" of the 1960s and the measures of political and social liberalization accomplished in Quebec after the death of Maurice Duplessis. However, such a historical scheme fails to consider how the cultural currents that came to the fore within Catholic Action expressed and articulated domesticity in a way that envisioned a more egalitarian and flexible spectrum of possibilities, especially for married women. This brand of reformist Catholicism never openly dispensed with the conventional gender categories that assigned women a primarily maternal role; however, during the immediate post-war period, it continued to work out the implications of what had begun in embryonic form during the 1930s, namely, a distancing of women's nature and destiny from biological definitions of maternity. Even though female identities continued to be construed in relation to husbands and families, they were also susceptible to an increasingly individualist tincture. By posing the problem of women's nature and role in psychological and cultural terms, rather than biological ones, Catholic Action placed the accent upon a more egalitarian idea of the expression and self-fulfillment of women as persons within roles that from a contemporary perspective might be considered conventional and confining.

In a paean to motherhood written in 1948, Marguerite Perroy described the modern married woman as a "modern vestal" who must "maintain in an undiminished fashion the visible warmth of the home." [106] At one level, this might be regarded as an expression of post-war cultural conservatism, a celebration of a constraining cult of domesticity that urged women to sacrifice their aspirations in order to reaffirm older patterns of authority in the family that many felt had been disturbed by wartime exigencies. Conservatives, wishing to reinvigorate pre-war gender hierarchies and identities, frequently evoked the image of women attending to motherhood and household in the hope of creating a psychological placebo that would deflect married women away from seeking fulfillment through economic equality in work roles.

Such conservative concerns were not lacking among Catholic social activists in post-war Quebec. Father Gonzalve Poulin, one of the principal promoters of family life, discerned a "current that is rapidly pushing us towards the equality of the sexes." This, he believed, was opening a social and cultural fissure between women's own demands for more "comprehensive activities and a widening of their social role," and a reactionary tendency which sought to keep women in their traditional functions and family roles. It was not enough, he urged fellow conservatives, to remind women of their weaknesses and inability to work, because this would only engender "a real aversion to the home" among women. Rather, wartime had revealed not only "the flexibility, the spirit of adaptation, and the infinite resources that women possess," but also an "endurance, force, and courage" equivalent to that of men in most trades and professions. In Poulin's estimation, it was unrealistic to expect that the "woman problem" in modern society could be solved by legislation forcing women to return to the home, because wartime demographic changes had ineluctably created a need for female labour. He was, however, concerned to counter this tendency, and offered a double-edged strategy founded upon the notion of radically separate male and female natures and destinies. What was necessary was the elaboration of a "female humanism," one that entailed the reorganization of work around specifically feminine characteristics in such a way that work would "not destroy, but complete woman's personality" – in other words, not turn young women permanently away from maternal functions. In practice, however, Poulin resisted the idea of married women working outside the home, arguing instead that women could be persuaded that marriage and family life were superior to paid work by offering them better domestic preparation through specific instruction centering on household science and child psychology. Such a policy would maintain the old equation of nationalism and natalism. What women needed was a spiritual awakening that would encourage them to "bring large numbers of children into the world and to raise them in a healthy spiritual and patriotic atmosphere."[107]

While Poulin enlisted the notions of a separate female nature to articulate a comprehensive vision of female domesticity founded upon conservative, natalist priorities, his was not the only version of domesticity that Catholicism promoted in post-war Quebec. A closer reading of Marguerite Perroy's praise of motherhood would suggest that Catholicism in post-war Quebec incarnated a more personalist definition that in fact set in play a profound tension within the ideology of maternalism and domesticity. Perroy regarded purely biological interpretations of female destiny as "profanation," and vociferously condemned those "who wish to relegate the mother to a strictly *reproductive* role." She explicitly indicated that she considered motherhood as an ideal that was essentially "spiritual." Significantly, this contained a set of important implications for the lives of married women and the way in which their role was defined within the family. The tasks incumbent upon woman as household manager and mother, Perroy warned, "must not absorb her body and soul, because she must light, protect, and nourish another flame, the spiritual flame in the soul of her family and first and foremost ... in her own soul."[108] Here, buried within conservative sounding language, lay a rather compelling reversal of priorities, one that placed supreme emphasis, not upon the biological imperative to have children, but upon the need to cultivate women's individuality through cultural and psychological means that involved access to ideas and activities beyond the raising of children. Indeed, this quest for personal fulfillment was an imperative one because women's ability to effectively engage in other familial relationships with husbands and children worked outwards from her own cultural and spiritual achievements as a person. "Before even becoming a female being," stated "José," a columnist in the working-class *Front Ouvrier,* "woman is first a human being possessing a supreme dignity. This dignity must be appreciated and respected."[109]

It would be difficult to find any post-war Catholic discussion of women's roles that dissented from the central importance of motherhood in the making of women's identities, or any positive value attributed before the late 1950s to the work of married women outside the home. However, what is important to understand is the variety of meanings that different groups of Catholics attached to the concept of "motherhood." While Rita

Racette, a leader of the Jeunesse Étudiante Catholique, could write in 1949 that "maternity is what we all tend towards, because it is the full achievement of our personalities as women," in the next breath she could use the "eternal," maternal qualities of women's nature to advocate professional careers for single women that ostensibly had little to do with women's biological functions.[110] One set of reflections on woman's social role, outlined in 1945, noted that "maternity" did not simply confine women to reproduction or household tasks. Indeed, women's roles could assume the shape of wife, mother, widow, and single person, which offered the possibility of a variety of activities and careers, but, significantly, in each case and in different ways a combination of "physical" and "spiritual" maternity was considered present.[111] What some have read as a "sublimation" of maternity – that the subsuming of all female activities and functions under the rubric of motherhood marked the advent of a heightened cultural conservatism with a tighter sense of constraints upon women's roles and expectations after World War II – was in fact used by some Catholic women to affirm a greater degree of status and independence for single women by legitimizing more diverse careers and social endeavour for them outside the home. Thus, Madeleine Vaillancourt observed that, while earlier ideals of womanhood definitively identified all women with the private sphere of the home, modern life had enlarged and transformed single women's roles beyond "the restricted circle of the family." Such women, she averred, were "'true women' and ... not just attempting to copy or to imitate men. Their contribution to their respective fields has been a female contribution equal or superior to that of their male contemporaries and this should put an end to the controversy of which sex is superior."[112]

Far from simply representing a heightened form of conservatism, the sublimation of maternity and its close identification with the spiritual that characterized a number of influential Catholic Action circles after World War II was in fact an explicit movement away from the overriding biological imperatives which had always characterized twentieth-century conservative thinking about women's roles. Present as a minor current among some middle-class college women in the 1930s, the more forceful assertion of the concept of "spiritual maternity" was given added intellectual weight with the impact of Gertrud Von Le Fort's *The Eternal Woman* (*La Femme Eternelle*), translated from German in the late 1940s. From the perspective of present-day feminism, Von Le Fort's treatise seems archaic because, unlike thinkers like Simone de Beauvoir who form part of the canon of intellectual feminism, her views did not rest upon an a priori assertion of woman's autonomy. Von Le Fort identified woman with the "unpretentious" elements of culture and civilization, and promulgated the notion that "wherever woman is most profoundly herself, she is so not as herself but as surrendered; and wherever she is surrendered, she is both bride and mother." The use of such language seemed to place her in the tradition of those who accepted distinct "masculine" and "feminine" natures, which postulated a definition of woman's being as an "other" in relation to the social and cultural centrality of a masculine subject. Indeed, *The Eternal Woman* was replete with symbolic images, drawn from history and literature, of woman's sacrifice, self-effacement, and collaboration, as the "bearer of salvation," which to Von Le Fort, represented the epitome and essence of the feminine nature.[113] However, in the cultural context of Quebec in the late 1940s, it would be more accurate to juxtapose Von Le Fort's work with the biologism of Gina Lombroso. When viewed from this perspective, the former's appreciation of woman's nature and role appears far less constraining. Indeed, what was significant about *The Eternal Woman* was that its argument did not emanate from biology or psychology, but from religious symbolism, and thus did not consider masculine and feminine natures as biologically-determined, "essential," or immutable: through such symbols as the "Mystical Rose," "Mirror of Justice," and "Tower of David," men and women participated and collaborated in one another's natures and roles.[114]

More appealing to a generation of young women exposed to ideas of Catholic personalism was the fact that Von Le Fort's starting point for considering women's nature and social function was cultural, and not reproductive. Woman's value was not bound up with the activity of physical motherhood. Rather, as a person, her value was tied to "the eternal value," whose meaning, Von Le Fort asserted, "is the religious exaltation and affirmation of a person's value, as directly and intimately related to God alone."[115] Women appeared under three symbolic figures: the "bride," the "virgin," and the "mother" – all spiritual archetypes that in her estimation flowed from the realm of values rather than literally from biology or sexual activities, although these figures all revealed attributes of "spiritual motherhood."[116] Unlike Lombroso, whose appreciation of woman's social role was completely limited to the domestic setting, in *The Eternal Woman* Von Le Fort deployed woman's primary values of self-effacement and capacity for cooperation to assert a wider sphere of activity. Modern civilization, she argued, was no longer an environment dominated by great personalities: what ultimately mattered in the creative process was the anonymous work of cooperation that was epitomized by the feminine spirit, and here, women's actions assumed primary importance in humanizing modern life by "breaking up the cold pattern of mere organization."[117]

What was most significant, however, was that although Von Le Fort assiduously distanced herself from feminist movements that stressed economic and political equality, and she extolled the fostering of relationships and cooperation between men and women because these implied the creation of life, in both the physical and cultural sense,[118] her ideal types were severed from marital status itself or exclusively domestic or familial settings, and were applied to women, both single and married, engaged in the professions or even politics. While not rejecting the language of maternalism, *The Eternal Woman* was clearly transitional between the older social maternalism and the "modern" feminism typified by Simone de Beauvoir, precisely because by sublimating and spiritualizing maternity, and thus disconnecting it from biology, Von Le Fort's work assigned woman a largely autonomous value. Unlike an earlier generation of maternalists who argued for a literal extension of reproductive function to social endeavour, "motherliness" for Von Le Fort meant the activity of "protecting and fostering cultural values,"[119] not functions attendant on actual biological procreation. *The Eternal Woman* made clear that, of these archetypes, the ones most closely related to personalist priorities were that of the "bride" – a status which revealed woman not so much as a mother-in-waiting, but as "primarily a person in her own right," exercising a "co-operative" and "co-creative" impulse with her male counterparts[120] – and that of "virgin" – a value which she believed women should consider not as failure or a transitory state, but as conferring legitimacy upon a species of individualism, as being the choice of single women who, by avoiding marriage, attained a capacity and release for action.[121] Culture, values, the primacy of the female person, and diversity of roles – given its presentation of these elements and its firm rejection of biological determinism, it was not surprising that *The Eternal Woman* would resonate among Catholic Action militants in Quebec, and that women leaders like Rita Racette would see in the personalist injunction of "the gift of self" a privileged means by which women could accomplish their own "self-liberation."[122]

Von Le Fort's idea that woman's nature constituted an independent source of personal values found its most immediate expression in post-war Quebec in the way in which women understood and interpreted the post-war Catholic ideal of marriage. However much the Church authorities might have wanted to stress the continuity of natalist and procreative imperatives, it is clear that a number of Catholic woman preferred the more egalitarian notion that they were partners and collaborators with their husbands, and that conjugal love, with its strong overtones of sexual satisfaction, was of greater value than maternal love. Joined to this sensibility, and flowing from their personalist Catholicism, was the conviction that modern marriage was a partnership between two equal persons and did not entail a sacrifice or abridgment of personal autonomy. "True maternal love," stated Françoise Lavigne in a radio talk given in 1954, "can only take form after women have experienced conjugal love,"[123] a declaration that clearly encapsulated the more egalitarian post-Depression Catholic marriage ideal – extolled both by clergy and lay Catholics influenced by Catholic Action – of the primacy of emotional and psychological intimacy within the married couple,[124] a notion which implicitly and clearly viewed maternity as coming second to being a wife. More significant, however, was her explicitly personalist evocation of the type of relationship that ought to prevail between men and women. "Every woman," Lavigne reminded her listeners, "whether she is a wife or not, must feel that she is equal to men, that she herself is a person in her own right, able to give and to receive, capable of personal interests and exchanges, joined together with man in all things, a helpmeet who resembles him."[125]

To the modern eye, this Catholic personalist call to equality between the sexes might strike a jarringly archaic note because of the use of the term "helpmeet," which implied a relationship of subordination to men, and studiously avoided asserting arguments based upon equal access to paid work. However, what is significant is the elaboration of a type of domesticity around the autonomy and mutual collaboration of two persons, organized not around status or legal prescription, but around a relationship that both spouses were called upon to foster. "I insist," stated Fernande Juneau in 1950, "on the idea of sharing between husband and wife. ... in my opinion, maternity is not separated from paternity: the wife is first and foremost a companion to her husband and then an educator in mutual agreement with him. We no longer view mothers confined to manual household tasks. We ask her to truly share in all the concerns of her husband, whether they be intellectual or spiritual as well as material. Sharing means holding things in common. It is thus necessary that the wife also have concerns other than those of the household or the washing. ... Women must attend to this conjugal spirituality."[126]

During the early post-war period, a number of lay Catholic family activists were adamant that the precondition to a vital marital partnership was the conservation of personal autonomy. As stated by Simonne Monet Chartrand in a lecture given in 1945, the Church's teaching that absolute unity must prevail between the spouses was "unrealistic." "Two beings," she stated, "have to perform the conjugal act and share in the joys and trials of a life in common. While spouses should do their utmost to adjust to and please the other partner, it is even normal and good that each spouse retains their own personality, and seeks to nourish it individually, resisting the self-destruction that too often happens in and through marriage."[127] Although women like Monet Chartrand, strongly influenced by Catholic Action, subscribed to the prevailing notion of specific and highly gendered male and female natures, as personalists they emphatically distanced themselves from the view that biology dictated that woman's nature was more passive and confined her role to a domestic one. The fact that sex roles were highly differentiated was, in their opinion, far more a function of cultural "atavism" and defective education, complicated by the social and legal traditions of Quebec in which "the man – father and husband – has total authority over daughters and wives. He often gravely abuses it."[128]

Prior to the 1960s, the tension that the personalism exemplified by Catholic Action created within older conventions surrounding women's natures and domestic roles was most publicly evinced in two realms. The first was the abortive 1947 attempt to amend the Quebec Civil Code to give greater status and autonomy to married women within the family, and the particularly acrimonious debate over female education that was carried on between the end of World War II and the late 1950s between partisans of the humanistic *collèges classiques*, who favoured a common education for both men and women (albeit carried on in sex-segregated institutions), and proponents of a system of vocational household education, who maintained that highly differentiated male and female natures required a completely different type of education for women. The pressure to reform the Civil Code paralleled the marriage preparation movement, as both stemmed in part from a desire to counter the potential for family destabilization inherent in the wartime movement of large numbers of women into paid work, what Camille Laurin described in 1950 as the "*emancipation of women*," not so much through economic necessity, but by an "ideological campaign."[129] However, personalist Catholics sought to achieve this less through jeremiads that equated women's paid work outside the domestic sphere with family disintegration, or the conservative solution of legislative prohibitions against women working, than by taking concrete measures to adapt civil law to the new Catholic marriage ideal which, according to papal teaching, was founded upon the equality of rights between husband and wife in all matters pertaining to the family and the rearing of children.[130] This, its promoters believed, would enhance the status of married women vis-à-vis their husbands, thus making marriage more attractive, and making it easier to assert that it was in the context of the family that "women develop most normally, that they attain their full social potential."[131]

From the perspective of Catholic family reformers, one of the most troubling features of the Quebec Civil Code, promulgated in 1866, was the legal incapacity of married women and the almost absolute authority of the husband and father within the family. At the end of the 1920s, the Quebec government had instituted the Dorion Commission to investigate ways in which greater recognition could be given to married women, but apart from some relatively anodyne reforms that allowed married women to participate in family councils, the balance of power within the family and the subordinate status of married women remained unaffected.[132] One of the major objections to further reform centred on a problem stemming from the 1930 papal encyclical on marriage and family. Although the encyclical had apparently sought to modify absolute paternal power through the recognition of what some termed a "family directorate"[133] that accorded women an equal status in all decisions that affected the family, the pope had insisted that, because the family was a hierarchy, there needed to be a final authority, and that that authority was vested in the husband. Opponents of reform, like Professor Maximilien Caron of the Université de Montréal, argued that the incapacity of wives needed to be maintained without modification because it was Quebec's bulwark against individualism. In his estimation, husband and wife were not two separate entities: marriage was a "community of moral and material interests," where the husband must continue to oversee the wife's property, and in cases of conflict, the husband's authority, which he designated an "obligation" that did not tread upon woman's dignity as a person, must carry the final weight. Otherwise, "anarchy would result."[134]

Significantly, however, proponents of reform could point to the 1937 French legislation which had taken a compromise position, suppressing articles of the Napoleonic Code that decreed the civil incapacity of married women, while continuing to assert the husband's headship of the family.[135] Supporters of reform were thus hardly radical in their demands, arguing that the concomitant of greater capacity for married women was an explicit legal injunction stating that the first duty of the wife was the maintenance of the household and the care of children. From this standpoint, while married women should obtain unimpaired control of their own personal property, they would still require the husband's express authorization to engage in long-term economic activities outside the home. This reflected the commitment of Quebec's Catholic Action movements to a type of familist corporatism that sought to democratize relations within the family, while continuing to assert male headship as the vital link between the family sphere and public order.

However, reformist Catholics' main critique of the Civil Code lay in what they believed was its excessive concern to facilitate the husband's authority, deemed its pagan aspect,[136] as they believed this to be the antithesis of Christianity because it often led to real injustices that placed married women in an intolerable degree of personal and economic subordination. To this end, they believed that making separation of property the "default" legal regime, rather than the community, would more effectively protect the interests of married women. They adduced two major arguments. The first was an appeal to the personalist current within Catholicism, which asserted that, because women were human persons created by God to fulfill the same ends as men, this entailed a "recognition of the personal rights of women, of their equality and legal capacity." Men and women might have separate functions within the marriage, but, above all, they were "two collaborators, two partners, responsible for the well-being of their families, jointly and severally responsible for the work of the family."[137] The second argument was an appeal to Quebec's post-Depression economic and social realities. While full male authority and the community of property regime might have suited a rural society where immovable property was the predominant form, such a system did not accord well with an urban society where women had vastly increased family responsibilities as educators because the husband's workplace was completely separate from the home. Women's greater independence, in the weighty opinion of Me Antonio Perreault, president of the prestigious legal review *Revue du Barreau*, fully justified a greater capacity to own and administer property.[138] Although the Quebec government did not overhaul the Civil Code's limitations on the rights of married women until 1964, the assumptions of the reformers worked their way subtly into Catholic Action's marriage preparation movement. Not only was marriage presented to post-war couples under the more egalitarian rubric of partnership and the joint responsibility of spouses, the sponsors of the movement also recruited notaries to advise wives to insist in advance on retaining control over their own property through marriage contracts and the choice of the separation of property regime.[139]

It was in the debate over the content of female education during the post-war era, however, that a conflict between two rival Catholic concepts of maternity and domesticity was played out. This debate took the form of a contest for cultural power between two parallel, divergent, and expanding institutional forms, and it testified to the fundamental shift that Catholic Action had worked within Quebec society over the way in which women's roles were conceived and structured. One current, organized around the Instituts Familiaux – or schools of domestic education and household science which had been systematized under the leadership of Father Albert Tessier after 1937 and given increasing state support between 1948 and 1955[140] – was natalist and conservative and revolved around an older, explicit equation of femininity and biological function. The other current affirmed the necessity of what at first sight might appear a more "traditional" form of education, the highly structured curriculum of the *collèges classiques* which under the auspices of religious orders trained the male Catholic elites of Quebec and, after 1932, expanded to create a growing network of women's colleges which taught the same humanistic curriculum as in male institutions.[141] Significantly, while the proponents of classical education for women would have certainly agreed with the promoters of household education that marriage and domesticity certainly constituted the primary vocation of most women, their concept of womanhood was a far less constraining one. It rested upon a rejection of the ideology of fixed biological roles, favouring instead a more egalitarian and cultural definition of women's potential, both within the family and in the wider society.

Writing in 1950, Father Albert Léonard explained the rationale behind the Institut Familiaux's insistence on a separate educational curriculum for women at the secondary level. Women, he recognized, had an equal entitlement with men to develop their intellect and culture, but he cited the many psychological differences between young men and young women that necessitated, in his estimation, a different educational system and curriculum. "One wonders," he mused, "whether those young women who have applied themselves to a 'masculine' type of higher education have not starved themselves of their real potential and qualities by abdicating, under the pretext of acquiring a supposed culture, their status as queen of the household." In particular, Leonard took aim at the education provided in the *collèges classiques*, judging it as too cerebral because it was not organized from the standpoint of the family, and thus did not sufficiently prepare young women to be wives and mothers. A well-organized system of household education, he concluded, must foster in young women the desire to be "smart without affectation, happy and spontaneous without being silly," a female ideal especially cultivated through a curriculum that stressed psychology and activity rather than the acquisition of dead languages. Through "solid but not necessarily abundant reading," such wives and mothers would be able to expose their children to literature, history, art, and the sciences, and be attractive companions to their husbands through their ability to "carry on a conversation that is not merely a tour of her kitchen."[142]

Proponents of household education employed a liberal language that rested upon a critique of educational formalism and the need to cultivate diversity. Thus, Louise Mireault condemned the notion, which she associated with the *collèges classiques*, that all young women were destined for a religious vocation, an idea that led to a false representation of marriage and family as a "second-best," and worse still, systematically denied young women knowledge about their own bodies and its functions. Marriage and maternity, she advised her readers, "are not careers that can be improvised on the spur-of-the-moment." They had to be taught through a curriculum that would channel women towards "the family and social action rather than into speculative studies that will never satisfy them."[143] Publicly, the Instituts Familiaux claimed that they provided their students with a home-like atmosphere, in contrast to the "monasticism" that characterized the *collèges classiques*, and that they sought to provide their students with a "harmonious education" which would enable them to avoid, unlike the unfortunate inmates of girls' colleges, being constrained within a rigid curriculum and "obsessed with marriage and maternity, unable to acquire that personal flexibility that they will need in their real lives."[144]

However, this appeal to educational diversity indicated, not a greater openness in definitions of women's roles, but the need of the advocates of household education to make headway in the face of the cultural prestige and power of the Catholic religious orders in Quebec society. The public ideology that animated these schools, according to Fathers Albert Tessier and Paul Carignan, their chief organizers and propagandists, was not Catholic Action's personalist expression of a more democratic family, which stressed, in fact, some gender role flexibility by advocating a greater participation of husbands and fathers in the domestic sphere and argued against exclusively reproductive definitions of maternity. Despite Father Carignan's claim that insisting on the priority of women's family vocation did not entail their subjection to household routine, the "universal role of women"[145] that he envisioned rested on the assertion of a male-centred family based on an inflexible, biological, maternal destiny for women. It was not entirely coincidental that in 1950, Father Carignan cited both Dr Alexis Carrel, whose psychological views had animated a number of Vichy France's social policies, and Gina Lombroso in arguing for the priority of the maternal function among women. "Generation," he intoned, "is so intimately linked to woman's physiology that she can only find her complete fulfillment after the birth of many children."[146] Tessier believed that the main purpose of the household science schools was the inculcation of the central notion, in the minds of young women, of the "irreplaceable wealth of patriarchal families." By doing so, such schools would enable him to create among his students a "snobbery of the large, happy, generous, working, and Christian family."[147]

The "functional" or activist education that Tessier eagerly constrasted with the more formal classical curriculum rested upon Gina Lombroso's assumption that the intellects and psychologies of the sexes diverged fundamentally: women lacked the powers of synthesis and speculative reason that men possessed, although their more instinctual nature made them more effective in the practical, repetitive tasks required by child-rearing and household management.[148] Consequently, from a purely educational point of view, the humanities curriculum would simply be wasted upon them, and worse, the lack of vital experience fostered by these institutions was, in the estimation of one young woman, the source of "homophobia," which prevented women from realizing that God created woman for man, and not man for woman,[149] a relationship that automatically dictated subordination. As one male student, André Raynauld, put the matter in 1945, woman's role was purely familial and, as a wife, she was obligated to stay at home. Indeed, as a wife, a woman had the duty to "attract her husband to the home by her kindness, her good cheer, and her ardent love." Because the domain of the intellect was reserved to men, and women were destined by nature to remain in the domestic sphere and maternal roles, Raynauld objected to the "vain idea that in order to establish a happy home, women need to have finished a course of classical studies."[150]

At first sight, partisans of classical education appeared as conservative as their opponents because they relied upon the same concepts of divergent gender psychologies, and adopted the same language of domesticity to argue that the acquisition of an education equivalent to that received by men, far from masculinizing young women, would in fact make them more attractive companions and more competent mothers. Reporting the results of a 1951 survey undertaken by the Societé des Femmes of the Université de Montréal, Monique Dufresne rejected the notion that higher education would turn women away from their mission of being wives and mothers. Rather, she claimed, a young woman would still "obey the irresistible imperative" of her nature, but she would approach her tasks with a "mature spirit, a culture that is broad enough to give her the desire to continually increase her knowledge, and this would work to the greater benefit of her husband and children."[151] While Dufresne's formulation appeared to indicate that the advocates of a common college curriculum for men and women were forced to function within the parameters of a debate set by conservative, biologist views of women's role,[152] even their domestic, familial justification of why women needed this type of higher education displayed a far more personalist element.

In the first instance, such highly-educated women were better placed to achieve the post-war Catholic desideratum of marriage as a total partnership of emotional intimacy, because they would not "bore" their husbands with conversation that revolved around an endless litany of internal household tasks. In this respect, Françoise Lavigne considered most women to be "so intellectually apathetic" that one day their husbands and children would simply write them off as "superficial" beings.[153] Indeed, within the framework of a society that hardly favoured the work of married women outside the home, an intellectually substantive type of higher education would better place wives to understand and support their husbands' career aspirations, and they would themselves be able to derive a personal, ongoing cultural and spiritual fulfillment as individuals from these contacts with the world outside the bonds of family. However much these ideas expressed current notions of gender hierarchy, they also derived from a personalist outlook that did not define the family as an entirely closed, private entity, and vigorously eschewed reducing wives and mothers to the status of "machines in the service of the household."[154] As stated by Micheline Robitaille, a college student in 1953, "in our future homes, we have no intention of being 'maids' for our husbands and children. We also want dialogue on the intellectual and spiritual levels."[155] In particular, proponents of the women's colleges believed that the Quebec Catholic version of the democratic family, which accented the central role of parents in the total psychological and intellectual development of the individual child, required the presence of mothers who had mastered the classical curriculum's emphasis upon synthesis and organization as only such mothers would be able to properly cultivate the intellectual side of the child's development.[156]

What is significant in this debate, however, is that although at one level arguments favouring classical education for women remained tied to concepts of home and family, they also contained another element, one that was far more self-consciously feminist in that it interpreted access to education, in terms of women's individual intellectual potential, as being equal to that of men. Young women, stated Sister Saint-Madeleine-des-Anges in 1948, sought to "surpass themselves." She therefore advised educators that it would be useless to confine or repress this "frenzy to externalize themselves" through an education aimed narrowly at preparing them for maternity, and she cited no less an authority than Pope Pius XII in advocating a type of education that would cultivate a modern female heroism.[157] "There is no fundamentally different procedure," observed the Association des Collèges Féminins in 1958, "to educate the spirit of a man or a woman," and it would be a grave injustice to adopt the unitary model of female education proposed by the Instituts Familiaux because woman's role was "not completely bound up with the material tasks of housekeeping."[158]

In the context of post-war Quebec, such views established a cultural bridgehead and were accorded a relatively high level of authority because they were sponsored both by the religious orders, which had a vested interest in securing access to public funds for their network of women's colleges,[159] and by the francophone middle classes, which in the years following World War II were susceptible to appeals that equated a broader access to higher education with the cultivation of "individual values" through which Quebec society could achieve intellectual and spiritual maturity.[160] Here, during this tortuous educational polemic of the early 1950s, the more liberal implications of the Catholic personalist notion of "spiritual maternity" were brought sharply into focus, as this notion was used by a number of influential Catholic spokesmen to counteract and erode the conservative belief that separate male and female psychologies dictated an ineluctable maternal destiny and a perpetual subordinate status for women in the family and society.

In a series of articles written in the Jesuit-sponsored periodical *Collège et Famille* in the early 1950s, Monique Béchard, an educational psychologist, used the debate on female education to launch a full-scale assault on the sexually-determined, biologistic notions of gender that underpinned not only the arguments for universal household education, but the entire structure of role differentiation that restricted women's career choices. Indeed, though her argument was cast within the framework of current Catholic doctrines of spiritual maternity, Béchard advanced a series of questions that were, in fact, central to the elaboration of modern feminism: Did women have a value as individuals, independent of their sex? Were they worth something outside of maternity? Were women individuals, or were they a sexual function? Adopting language reminiscent of Simone de Beauvoir, Béchard informed her readers that the central flaw in conservative arguments lay in explaining woman always "as a function of *someone else*," and in conceiving her nature and role, not from the standpoint of her own being, but from functions that derived solely from maternity.[161] "What I find extremely dangerous," she declared, "is that educators see in man 'an individual' and in woman 'a family.'"[162]

In keeping with Catholic Action's personalism, Béchard was unwilling to abandon the doctrine that maternity constituted woman's "biological vocation" and that there existed psychological distinctions between the sexes. However, she relied upon reformist Catholicism's assertion of the primacy of conjugal love over maternal love to argue that woman's nature and vocation could be completely encompassed within notions of reproductive maternity.[163] Thus, for all their religious rhetoric, those who relied upon the formulations of conservatives like Gina Lombroso, whose views underpinned the philosophy of household education, were anti-Christian "fascists" because, rather than accepting the full implications of Catholic notions of the complementarity of men and women, their attempts to constrain women within ironclad maternal and household roles reflected an "infantile fear" that women were dangerous rivals to men.[164] Furthermore, such rigid role definitions, far from promoting family solidarity, were ultimately destructive. They created intolerable stresses both within the psychology of individual women and in the wider society, because the exigencies of modern life had widened the gap between women's personal aspirations and the traditional psychological norms that dictated the universal path to reproductive motherhood.[165] In this respect, Béchard anticipated elements of Betty Friedan's social criticism popularized in her 1963 classic, *The Feminine Mystique*. In Béchard's estimation, the values taught in Quebec's household science schools merely affirmed and institutionalized an oppressive "virility complex" in which women were taught to fear men and resent not being masculine. Béchard diagnosed the symptoms of this psychological malaise as "neurosis of housework," passive, dominant, and overprotective mothers, and an inward-looking female narcissism characterized by timidity, indecisiveness, extreme dependency, and frustration that submerged women's identities in an unthinking conformity produced by "our whole philosophy of womanhood, our narrow conception of female education, and the whole surrounding mentality of our culture."[166]

Béchard's standpoint was the Catholic personalist vision of "spiritual motherhood," whose fundamental conviction was the transcendence of the sexual by human values. In this respect, she explicitly rejected notions that psychological laws had the same inexorable application as those of the physical world: thus, the "maternal" characteristics of women were only aspects of humanity, and applied in the same limited way that men's paternal destiny did not encompass the whole of a man's human qualities. Assimilating personalism and the insights of social thinkers such as Margaret Mead and Simone de Beauvoir, Béchard concluded that the rigid biological division of intelligence into masculine logic and feminine intuition was a false one, and that, in fact, those explicitly "female" psychological traits which did exist were more the product of social customs and structures that had made women historically marginal.[167] From these considerations, personalist Catholicism, with its belief that women were in the first instance persons and only secondarily social beings, legitimized a bisexual gender role theory in which pure masculine and feminine types did not exist, which in turn implied that careers and activities deemed "male" could not be barred to women on the basis that their intellects were different. "We persist in believing," urged Béchard, "that professions have no sex."[168] This in turn underpinned a firm conviction that women, far from being imprisoned by a sexual determinism, accepted motherhood as a free individual choice. Thus, unlike among animals, motherhood was a role that must be accepted by the free choice of women as individuals; human maternity was first and foremost a cultural and spiritual process, not simply a reproductive act, one that should not constrict women's choices, but in fact open a whole array of careers and social roles for women outside the home. Indeed, queried Béchard, were "women who chose motherhood and the domestic sphere more *essentially feminine*" than professionals and intellectuals who chose to express their womanhood through careers? The answer to this question lay not with social traditions or customs, or through an imposed, monolithic educational direction, but "was up to each woman to determine ... according to her individual nature and particular vocation."[169]

While it might seem that this rather high-flown debate over the substance of women's higher education concerned only a professional middle-class elite of Catholics whose daughters might attend the *collège classiques*, the ideology of "spiritual maternity," with its more egalitarian evocation of personal choice and fulfillment expressed during this controversy, in fact sounded themes that resonated with a broader group of women, drawn from the middle and working classes, who participated in the Catholic Action movements. Throughout the late 1930s and the immediate post-war period, an influential facet of Catholic Action sought to use the new spirituality, with its confrontational vision of rupture between tradition and modernity, to assert the leadership of a male laity over realms of social endeavour that they viewed as dominated by the clergy. Despite the fact that resistance to clerical pretensions drew Catholic lay men and women together, the Catholic Action organizations themselves incarnated an implicit dynamic of opposition. All the movements operated on the principle of parallelism between male and female branches of the same organization, and the women's movements far outnumbered those of men. In this cultural climate, women activists, while subscribing to the concept of psychological differences between men and women, did not see their role as subordinate to male dictation. Women activists often chafed at the official injunction that women be "understanding," "disinterested," "self-sacrificing" workers behind the scenes. One 1947 position paper written by women directors criticized their male counterparts for dismissing their suggestions, although they ruefully observed that male organizers were quite prepared to appropriate ideas advanced by the women's sections. "We have the unfortunate propensity," concluded the leaders of the Jeunesse Étudiante Catholique Féminine, "to fall back too much on feminine diplomacy to secure the agreement of the men on a number of issues."[170] In a 1957 survey of twenty-two women activists, they cited their own superior organizational skills and a well-developed experiential grasp of the Catholic Action philosophy of spiritual community as reasons for their ability to accede to leadership roles. They viewed their participation in these movements as a self-enriching process, one that offered them a transformed spiritual life by enhancing their "feminine" qualities of capacity for adaptation and understanding people, and the opportunity to bring to the fore their personal discoveries, devotion, and spirit of service.[171] It was during the 1950s, precisely within this group of Catholic women activists, that these "female" attributes, coextensive with a conservative-sounding "spiritual maternity" were further elaborated into a "personalist feminism" in which equality between the sexes and a greatly expanded social sphere for women derived, not from workplace achievements or abstract political rights that tended to place men and women on the same level, but from the explicitly cultural and psychological attributes of the female person, qualities that differentiated men from women, while positing the need for modern society to elaborate new relationships of reciprocity between the sexes.

Writing in 1956, Denise Messier articulated the balance between equality and difference that existed in the Catholic Action movements, and delineated ways in which personalist feminism both resembled and diverged from individualist and collectivist forms of modern feminism. "Woman," she declared, "has a goal that is personal in nature. ... She is thus a free being vis-à-vis her husband, the civic order, and the family."[172] In her estimation, personalism and feminism were one and the same, provided that feminism was understood as "a liberation and an ascent towards the recognition of female values by having them brought to the fore." However, where Marxist and individualist forms of feminism had erred, explained Messier, was in identifying the equality and independence solely with access to paid work, which ignored the "healthy balance and the need of the human personality for total fulfillment."[173] True freedom, in the reasoning of Catholic activists like Messier, was conditioned by specific functions of the female nature which placed a priority on women's roles as wives and mothers, which meant, in her estimation, that the actualization of their freedom would come not from women assuming economic roles, but from a deepened cultural appreciation of woman's "family self," by which women could acquire a far more diverse range of functions and roles based upon their dual nature of wife and mother. By devoting so much attention to the workplace, Marxists and liberal feminists had deflected the movement towards secondary issues, and worse, according to Messier, they exalted gender conflict as the mechanism of social change. The home, and not the workplace, was the key to the achievement of women's equality in modern society, because "it was ... the centre of gravity for the equilibrium of the human person," which for personalists meant the nature and quality of human relationships. In addition, shifting the feminist axis from workplace to home would obviate the need for conflict. "To suppress the love of the home," stated Messier, "is to suppress the equilibrium of persons and merely introduces incomprehension, injustice, and inequality." In the personalist feminist equation, equality between men and women would be realized through "love as communion," the cultivation of greater interdependence, and reciprocity between husband and wife.[174]

Significantly, while Messier's elaboration of feminism might sound confused and contradictory because it derived from family categories, it must be reiterated that personalism did not see the family as a closed or merely private entity, but as a system of relationships in which individuals acquired the attributes of public, democratic citizenship. Her exposition thus warned explicitly against an exaggerated stress upon "the craft of housekeeping," because this would so interiorize women that all work and activities outside the home would be dismissed as harmful and vulgar. Women's self-fulfillment through the cultivation of family roles thus emphatically required a broadened access to culture and enhanced political awareness on the part of women. "In the full sense of the word," rang Messier's existential conclusion, "the independence of women is not an adolescent demand or a matter of stubbornness on the part of certain ambitious women ... but a fundamental question that involves the metaphysics of the female being *in the situation* of the home."[175]

The use of such words as "equality" and "independence" and the conviction that the source of female identity lay in the development of women's individual personalities, rather than in their reproductive, maternal functions, clearly positioned this type of Catholic thinking within a feminist, rather than an older maternalist, trajectory. However, it displayed close affinities to what Karen Offen has described as "relational feminism," particularly influential among French social Catholics, which stressed the rights of women *as women* within a framework of male-female complementarity based upon sexual differences.[176] Advocates of this type of feminism were always intent to draw a studious distinction between their views – what they termed a "reasonable feminism"[177] – and what they considered the "economic rationalism"[178] of feminists like Simone de Beauvoir, whose exaltation of paid work as the wellspring of female identity, they believed, ultimately placed women in an impasse because her philosophy ignored spiritual qualities that were essentially "feminine" and ultimately rested upon an adversarial model of gender relations.[179]

As stated by the student activist Rita Racette in 1950, the freedom of women to work outside the home was an important condition of economic and social evolution, but it was a limited ideal, benefitting only middle-class women, given the inhumane conditions of modern industry in which, for working-class women, freedom to work meant freedom to be exploited.[180] In an article written in 1950, Adèle Lauzon carefully elaborated the central dynamic of personalist feminism. Instead of linking it to the maternalist ideology of the past, she inserted it into contemporary history's revolutionary demands for equality. However, she distinguished it both from de Beauvoir's existential Marxism and from older Catholic views that subordinated men to women. Man's apparent superiority was only "accidental"; despite different functions, men and women were equal but different. However, Lauzon's retort to adversarial feminism was that in seeking equality women had to collaborate with men. "Men and women," she declared, "are made to love; this love is not only sexual – which is good but insufficient – but it is a profound friendship that allows their spirits and souls to complete one another as much as their bodies." Such friendship and collaboration, however, could only occur through accommodation of woman's desire for equality, which went beyond maternalism's recognition of woman's role in generation. Ultimately, woman must become "fully conscious of her right to participate in all manifestations of life and being."[181]

Though it was still premised on the idea that women had a special vocation for motherhood, Catholic personalist feminism maintained that "motherhood" was less a functional category than a set of spiritual and cultural qualities, and it thus subordinated the older notion of woman as "both mother and queen of the family circle" to woman's achievement of "a status worthy of her dignity as a human person."[182] As stated by Alex Pelletier in 1951, "we can no longer be inward-looking women. Our husbands and children ask far more than this."[183] Proponents of this strand of thinking within the various Catholic Action movements were adamant that it

marked an "innovation" on the past. For them it legitimized both professional endeavour and public activism that was based on distinctly female
spiritual qualities and in which women's presence was "a duty owed to both
persons and events."[184] That such participation flowed from the female
spirit meant that women "would not become men but remain women,
remain mothers, remain linked to a specifically female world of being and
action which is theirs, in both culture and history."[185] Indeed, during the
1950s, supposedly the zenith of domesticity, reformist Catholics devoted
far more attention, not to exhortations reminding women of their moth-
erly duties in the private sphere of the home, but to what historians would
now consider central issues to the elaboration of the next wave of feminism, namely, the "liberation of women from the servitude of certain
household tasks"[186] in order to rectify what women castigated as the deficiencies of their cultural life and their low level of social and civic participation. "Canadian women," lamented one report, "display a tendency to
neglect their social responsibilities, especially given the fact that the aces-
sion of women to public, social, political, and economic life is one of the
most important phenomena of our age."[187]

Perhaps the most important clue that post-war Catholic personalist feminism marked a cultural innovation, despite its overlay of maternalist language, lay in a palpable shift that in the late 1940s began to assign a positive value to paid work in the articulation of an autonomous female
personality. Initially, arguments justifying paid work and careers for
women deferred to powerful currents of an ideology of family stabilization
that was characteristic of the immediate post-war period, as such arguments enjoined married women to stay at home to see to the household
and attend to the tasks of child-rearing.[188] Young women were thus advised
to choose careers that would prepare them culturally for marriage and
motherhood. However, what was interesting about this advice was that,
increasingly, the Depression-era and wartime notion that work was incompatible with the female personality, or that some careers and jobs were, all
but disappeared. All careers were viewed as legitimate, because they all
taught young women to balance intelligence and will, and to cultivate the
explicitly feminine qualities of "gift of self and adaptation."[189] Speaking in
1952, Jean-Paul Gagnon, a Catholic labour activist, observed that women
were propelled into the sphere of paid work less from economic necessity
than by psychological factors. Adopting the trajectory of modernization
that had become standard in reformist Catholic circles, he argued that
women increasingly sought work outside the domestic sphere because the
"social community" had increasingly assumed the functions of the home,
and these conditions had fostered a psychological vacuum that had
created a consequent loss of autonomy on the part of married women who
felt alienated, useless, and inadequate.[190] Though firm proponents of

family stability, these Catholic personalists also cautioned married women against an excessive preoccupation with their children, which they believed when carried to extremes would act as a constraining force on women. "How many women," asked the journalist Germaine Bernier in 1954, in an article that presaged Betty Friedan's "disease that has no name," "gave themselves unstintingly for so many years, only to reach middle age where they found only an extremely cruel moral solitude, and not even the justice and appreciation they were entitled to from their husbands?"[191]

Catholic personalists, particularly those associated with the labour movement, began in the 1950s to interpret work for women not as a threat to the family, but as a pole of stability in a period of bewildering social and cultural change. The modern age, Gagnon declared, exalted work and productivity as the source of a balanced psychological identity. The appropriate response was not to bar married women from work either through legislation or ideology, but to ensure that women were not pushed into secondary occupations that prevented them from "conserving female dignity and virtue."[192] In particular, he believed that modern automated industries, or women's professions like nursing, teaching, and social work, because they did not entail brutalizing labour, could offer the conditions under which the instincts of spiritual maternity could be awakened. In Gagnon's estimation, work was not the antithesis of specifically feminine elements of identity, but a way to widen the horizons of the domestic sphere, a cultural process by which women could "conserve all their aptitudes for physical, spiritual, or social maternity."[193] In a similar vein, Adèle Lauzon upheld the notion that paid work for women, if properly regulated, could be one of the primary pillars of equilibrium for the individual psyche, the family, and the wider social order.[194] What was significant about these formulations was that they explicitly linked, in a positive sense, the notion of work and female identity. Woman's quest for public identity exemplified through entry into the workforce was henceforth, in Gagnon's estimation, as much a characteristic of female nature – hitherto deemed more "passive" than the more "activist" psychological temperament of men – and it was governed by the same humanizing imperative. Although he was careful to indicate to his audience of Catholic militants and labour activists that he was not advocating manual work for women, he distanced himself from older religious imperatives that took the notion of fixed gender essences too literally. "It belongs to each generation," he concluded, "to renew eternal principles by a fertile effort of thought and adaptation."[195]

Catholic personalist feminism, by attempting during the early 1950s to balance the claims of a relatively static, domestic female nature and individual achievement and satisfaction by articulating a positive dynamic between female identity and paid work outside the home, stretched the outermost boundaries of the fixed gender essences that had held sway during the Depression and the immediate post-war period. Intimations that personalist feminism held increasing authority within Quebec's Catholic culture was perhaps best indicated by one of its principal opponents, Father Paul Carignan, one of the leading ideologists of the maternalist Instituts Familiaux. In a 1958 brief presented to the commission to reform the Université Laval arts faculty, he claimed that the insistence on the family vocation of women, what he termed the "universal role of woman," precluded considering her a "servile manual worker or even as a compulsory mother."[196] That motherhood was seen by both reformists and conservatives as no longer "compulsory" raised a central question: if work was essential to the construction of balanced male and female individual and social identities, to what extent could these Catholic reformers argue that maternity retained its status as a primary spiritual signifier of identity for modern women? If Catholic activists sought to sustain within the wider culture the belief that the values of maternity and female difference, and their corollary, the structure of fixed gender roles, were not just contingent and accidental, but actually should retain their priority, were they not implicitly limiting the access of women to full human fulfillment, by consigning them to a second-rate status in a culture that increasingly accepted individual achievement in the public sphere as its yardstick of values? Were not the stable gender identities that underwrote the post-war family but straitjackets that constrained and subordinated women? And if so, did not Catholicism's attempt to adhere, at least in part, to this public ideology undercut the personalist claim that religion promoted the egalitarian aspirations of women? And if, as Catholic personalists seemed to be increasingly saying, work, the key to personal self-fulfillment – and not reproduction and child-rearing – constituted the ultimate cultural value for both men and women, how could Quebec Catholicism presume to offer a system of doctrinal and moral cautions against the mass appropriation of attitudes and techniques that equated an increasingly precise control of fertility and biological parenthood with those central personalist priorities of marital intimacy, sexual fulfillment as the source of individual psychological balance, and the promotion of the equality of the sexes in both private and public spheres?

"WOMAN MUST NOT BE OBEDIENT TO MAN, AS THE CHURCH IS TO GOD"[197]

At the conclusion of a Jeunesse Étudiante Catholique study session for university students held in 1952, Rita Racette aptly captured the expectations of those who sought to yoke Catholic personalism and feminist aspiration by declaring that "it does not belong to men alone to make history."[198] What was significant about the exhortation of this woman activist was that its central concept of woman as historical agent ran in many ways counter to the way in which Quebec Catholic Action had, since the Depression, defined the content of and the dynamic that prevailed between those central categories of tradition and modernity. Although during the immediate post-war period the Catholic Action movements had tried to accommodate women's aspirations by articulating more "democratic" and egalitarian notions of gender identity and family relations, these were circumscribed within a bipolar framework in which the essential natures, and therefore the social functions, of men and women remained relatively fixed and static – although it should be remembered that reformist Catholics viewed these differences as determined less by biology than by cultural and spiritual forces. The equilibrium of individuals, family, and the wider public society rested upon a reciprocal tension between male activity, reason, and creativity, and female passivity, intuition, and conservation.

However, the idea that men and women had distinct natures had particular implications in Catholic Action circles. When situated within the dominant post-war imperative to assert the claims of a male elite to social and cultural leadership, and the vision of cultural rupture that the movements sought to work within society, this gender dynamic could easily be interpreted as a conflictual dialectic. In Catholic Action circles, it was widely believed that male and female psychologies manifested strikingly different varieties of religiosity, with a "natural," instinctive, devotional type of Catholicism ascribed to women. Women's Catholicism was thus relegated to the pre-modern, ahistorical realm, usually dismissed with the epithet of "practices more or less devoid of substance." This "feminized" Catholicism was regarded by male activists as completely out of step with the modernist spirituality they sought so assiduously to foster among the new elites of post-war Quebec.[199]

Writing in 1953, Claude Ryan, the national secretary of Catholic Action, lamented the fact that over two-thirds of his movement's effectives were female, and he worried that this gender imbalance had long-term implications for the continued intersection of Catholicism and Quebec society. Ryan believed, in the first instance, that this female predominance in Catholic Action reflected a more general "devirilization" of Western societies, in which the daily practice of religion had become "an affair of women." An emasculated religion, he stated, was "an institution exhibiting signs of decadence" that were characterized by an attachment to external and superficial devotional forms and to a facile moralism. It was an institution that failed to incarnate values that would foster "adult and responsible" attitudes among Christians.[200] In a larger sense, what preoccupied Ryan was his belief that a feminized Christianity was the engine of secularization: educated, socially prominent, and active men evinced little interest in a Catholicism that seemed to epitomize female values. In the long run, he told fellow activist Madeleine Guay (who later became his wife), the preponderant influence of women in the daily practice of religion, which made it a realm of conservatism, passivity, emotionalism and superficiality, would lead to the loss of Christian identity in those facets of human endeavour – namely, the "activist" realms of politics, cultural institutions, and the trade unions – in which men needed a more "real" and "adult" religion to express their aspirations.[201]

However, Ryan's musings were less a social description of post-war Quebec than a profound reflection of North American cultural anxieties over the effects of "Momism" on the fragile male ego,[202] which in Ryan's case was accentuated by his leadership of a movement where women acted as both a strong numerical and intellectual presence. Indeed, Ryan's views neatly encapsulated the main line of argument of post-war secularization theory, in that they posited a growing dichotomy, worked by the corrosive acids of industrialization and urbanization, between a "real" world of large public institutions, characterized by rationality and purpose, and a "private" sphere of individual emotions where instinct and religious values still held sway, and he simply read this fissure into the language of post-war Catholic gender role theory. The danger for Quebec Catholicism that he discerned, in this period of acute modernization, lay in its association with a largely private, feminine, inward-looking type of spirituality that would simply make Catholicism irrelevant to whole sectors of public life in which men wanted to express their identities, which were oriented to ambition and self-realization. The male "public" sphere of work and civic activism was identified with the desirable characteristics of historical progress, and women were identified with the "private" sphere of instinct and emotion, which mired Quebec in a cultural stasis that was retarding the advent of modernizing currents, thus aggravating an adolescent "identity crisis" in the entire society.

Ryan's gender dichotomy underscored a shift that was occurring in Catholic Action in the early 1950s, where a style of family activism, oriented to women's concerns, was pushed aside by an emphasis on purifying Catholic theology, and affirming the connections of religion and the sphere of high politics. In hindsight, because Ryan's modernist spirituality seemed to take women's religiosity for granted, he grossly misread the direction of his culture's secularization. Indeed, the rapid de-Christianization that Quebec experienced during the 1960s, undoubtedly one of the most rapid in the Western world,[203] and in particular the massive loss of personal adherence to religious values, was less the result of Catholicism's loss of influence in the public, institutional, "masculine" realms of social endeavour, than of its inability to articulate an equilibrium between domesticity and work that would continue to inform female identities. In this key respect, Quebec women began to equate rejection of the conventional gender divisions and hierarchies with rejection of the Catholic religion itself. This was compounded by a failure on the part of Quebec Catholicism, during the late 1960s, to pursue the logic of personalism in the realm of sexuality and contraceptive practices, thus further sundering the links between Catholicism and women. And in this respect, Rita Racette's call for women's agency as integral to historical change offered a more prescient insight into the nature of her society's secularization than did Claude Ryan's equation of modernity with masculine assertion.

Despite a number of personalist feminist voices that attributed an increasing value to paid work as the wellspring of female identity, post-war Quebec Catholicism's reconstruction of the family rested on a set of prescribed gender roles and hierarchies in which the "vocation" of married women was interpreted as primarily bound up with the domestic sphere and child-rearing. In a process remarkably similar to the way in which discovery of an independent adolescent culture in the mid-1950s posed a challenge to paternal authority in the family, the growing realization, especially after 1955, that paid work, far from being exceptional, had emerged as a reality in the lives of married women, prompted a far-reaching questioning among Catholics. Between 1957 and 1964, a number of vocal Catholic critics mercilessly exposed the ideology of post-war psychological gender differences, because it had created an enormous reservoir of dissatisfaction and frustrated aspirations among Quebec women, and actually blocked them from the personalist self-fulfillment so important to Catholic reformers. At one level, the 1957 federal Department of Labour study *La Femme Canadienne au Travail (Canadian Women at Work)*, appeared to give comfort to the conventional Catholic equation of women and domesticity, because it revealed that 23.8 per cent of the workforce was female, and predicted that by 1980, this figure would stand at only 30 per cent – a figure lower than in the United States or Britain. However, it noted that there had been a rapid increase in the employment of married women outside of agriculture. Most of the growth in female employment during the 1950s had come in the 25–44 age group, the very age cohort in which there had been a significant decline in the birth rate.[204] Indeed, the statistics seemed to indicate that married women preferred paid work to motherhood or domestic roles. By 1962, Jeanne Duval, the vice-president of the Confédération des Syndicats Nationaux observed that female employment statistics already belied the Department of Labour's predictions, for in that year, in Canada as a whole, 47.3 per cent of all women workers were married, and in Quebec, this figure had quadrupled during the course of a single decade, from 7.6 per cent to 32.6 per cent, prompting her to declare that women were increasingly "torn between two conceptions: that of the woman at work and that of the wife at home." What was more significant, however, was the result of a 1959 survey by the Jeunesse Ouvrière Catholique Féminine, which discovered that 57 per cent of single women intended to work after marriage, and that 40 to 45 per cent of married working women were mothers with children at home.[205]

It was an indicator of Quebec's participation in a profound cultural shift in the late 1950s that this apparent breach in post-war domesticity did not arouse noisy conservative denunciations or jeremiads from Catholic activists,[206] but, rather, something completely new within Quebec Catholicism: an appreciation of the dilemma facing married women, who were asked not only to fulfill their domestic obligations prescribed by current post-war ideologies, but also to live up to the call of personalist feminists to participate fully in a culture of individual and social achievement through work. The Catholic labour journalist Renée Geoffroy, who a few years earlier had been a principal voice upholding the single-job male-breadwinner family, wondered in 1956 whether "the mother of a family could have both a career and a domestic life." She asked her readers to consider that "in spite of the already heavy burden of household tasks that is given to them automatically and without discussion, married women must take upon themselves an even more imperious responsibility: she must please her husband, please her children, please her neighbours, please her social environment, be beautiful and remain so, because she has to compete unjustly against the movie stars who invade her home through television and magazines. ... Can this woman, who already works a seven-day week, really take on a paying job or career, which demands as much energy and talent as those required by her work in the home?" What particularly worried Geoffroy was that given such a burden, could working wives even contemplate the additional burden of raising young children?[207] Because Geoffroy subscribed to an increasingly powerful current within Catholic feminism that viewed professional work that was "freely chosen by woman" as "allowing her to fulfill herself, to create, to render as service,"[208] as the mechanism through which the individual reached psychological maturity by achieving a synthesis of personal and social values, "a type of fulfillment that women no longer find by remaining at home," the solutions that she envisaged were the immediate institution of equal pay for equal work, and legislative measures such as daycare to ease the double burden of work and child-rearing.[209]

"Today's society," declared the Montreal Service de Préparation au Marriage (SPM), is "very hard on the married woman who works."[210] In a presentation given to an international conference of Catholic women's organizations in 1961, the Quebec delegation outlined the fact that a new model of womanhood, the epitome of a new consumerist ethos, had in a few short years replaced the traditional model of the French-Canadian mother, oriented to biological reproduction. Such images of maternity had been replaced by the figure of a young and elegant woman, able to organize everything for her husband, raise her children, "fulfill the demands of professional work outside the home and be involved in civic life." However, Catholic activists warned that this new role did not entail personal fulfillment for women. "Today's woman," they concluded, "does not feel that she is up to the demands of such roles, for which her overly-theoretical and idealistic education has not prepared her, except in what narrowly pertains to household tasks," and they noted with alarm the fact that many women displayed symptoms of "impatience, and mental exhaustion."[211]

Even the Montreal SPM, which, during the late 1940s and early 1950s, had subscribed to the view that the work of married women could be countenanced only in certain exceptional circumstances,[212] was aware by 1957 that among its audience of working-class and lower-middle-class women, nearly 80 per cent wanted to work after marriage. According to Solange Pitre, one of the SPM group leaders, it was important to still convey the message that work for women "harmed the adaptation of the couple at all levels: sexual, cultural, and social," but she insisted that the organization's lecturers approach the subject with "flexibility" and not engage in categorical denunciations.[213] For example, the SPM increasingly accepted a reformist logic, propagated by a number of influential Catholic social scientists like Guy Rocher, that upheld the work of married women as a key condition of Quebec's self-identity as a "modern" society, fully integrated in a general Western culture of social and cultural progress whose axis revolved around the social "dynamism" created by the cultivation of a female personality whose functions and activities were the product of individual choice.[214] In this reasoning, the work of married women was portrayed not as a detriment, but in increasingly positive terms as an "indicator of the evolution of our society" that would lead to a more far-reaching transformation of Quebec society.[215] In particular, the SPM was adamant that women's desire to work signalled their dissatisfaction with a culture where "the authority exercised by the husband is such that the wife is relegated to the role of a servant and the status of a minor," a form of male tyranny that stood as a barrier against the fulfillment of the female person. However, the SPM cautioned against the materialist-feminist error of denying all differences between men and women, an attitude that would merely subject women to "an unequal competition" with men and force women to perform functions for which they were not equipped psychologically.[216] In this way, the marriage preparation movement sought to preserve the post-war personalist equilibrium between familialism, in which maternal roles still held pride of place, and individualism, which stressed psychological fulfillment through public activity and recognition.

In the early 1960s, reformist Catholics found this synthesis increasingly difficult to sustain, as two sets of negative images of the complementary gender roles and family relationships came increasingly to public attention. "When I look around me," declared Alex Pelletier, a former national president of the Jeunesse Étudiante Catholique Féminine in a 1962 interview, "I see many women, the heads of large families, the children going off to school one by one, who find themselves without purpose, with nothing, they have nothing to say, and very little to do." Adopting an analogy from the world of industrial employment, Pelletier remarked that these women reminded her of "aging employees put out to retirement, except that these women are all under the age of forty. What would men say if we blocked their future prospects at age thirty-eight or forty? ... Are we then surprised that mothers are overprotective of their children, and that they exhibit symptoms of neuroticism?"[217]

Pelletier's critique, which from the perspective of Catholic personalist feminism approximated that of Betty Friedan, displayed a new sensibility, the idea that maternity and domestic roles, far from being the core of women's identities, were a source of deep resentment, psychological stress, and dissatisfaction that were constraining and perverting the female personality. However, what accelerated the rapid erosion of familialism as a public ideology among Quebec Catholics was that women's dissatisfaction revealed a whole range of inadequacies in the way in which men had fulfilled their own domestic roles within the post-war "democratic" family. This awareness reinforced the urgent need to elaborate a new basis of gender relations in which the older balance of hierarchy and democracy, and the functional separation of male and female roles, was replaced by the absolute equality of men and women in both private and public spheres.

Writing in 1962, the conservative sociologist Philippe Garigue portrayed the French-Canadian family as, in effect, a highly authoritarian structure centred upon the continued reality of male authority. While most of the men and women he surveyed indicated an acceptance of the Catholic definition of complementary roles, Garigue observed that gender complementarity did not mean equality. In language reminiscent of Simone de Beauvoir, he observed that "it is the woman who is 'complementary' to the man and not vice versa. Men possess, in their role of husbands and fathers, a legal priority, and in nearly all cases authority in the family is presented as a male, and not a female prerogative."[218] However, the increasing range of social problems within the family – psychologically stunted wives, increasingly independent youth – were in the early 1960s blamed less upon maternal deficiency, and more on absent or incompetent husbands and fathers, who had failed to live up to the canons of the Catholic marriage ideal as a partnership of sharing and intimacy, or upon the stresses and strains occasioned by the impossible demands of conventional male and female roles. This was a view shared even by those most devoted to older views of gender psychologies. For example, the Instituts Familiaux reiterated the conventional wisdom that "women were ordained for maternity," but in the same breath flayed what it maintained was "a lack of preparation on the part of men for their conjugal and familial responsibilities," a situation that rendered them insensitive towards "helping women find their balance between dependence and independence."[219] The culprit was with increasing frequency identified as the public/private role dichotomy, which in a post-war world of mass consumer prosperity had, in the harsh assessment of Camille Laurin, relegated women to a "golden cage" that was inconsistent with prevailing notions of democratic order, which in his estimation rested on the "authentic aspirations of the human person."[220]

Laurin's explicit link between women's personal aspirations and a new culture of democracy encompassing the entire spectrum of social relationships urges us to consider that the rapid erosion of older meanings of what it meant to be male and female was perhaps *the* central transformation of Quebec during the 1960s. Like other Western societies, Quebec did not experience a social revolution in the sense that the ruling economic or political elites were overthrown.[221] However, in the years after 1955, men and women in Quebec encountered through the critique of domesticity one of the central axioms of cultural modernity: that for the individual, gender did not entail fixed private or public sexual identities, and that individual happiness and self-fulfillment required the removal of the social and cultural constraints that rigid role definitions dictated. That women were now enjoined to seek "self-fulfilment as human beings rather than merely as females"[222] emerged, in a few short years, as part of the conventional wisdom of liberal states and societies testifies to the profound alteration in basic cultural values and assumptions. As stated by the French sociologist Violette Morin, who visited Montreal in 1967, because women now had acquired access to public identities based on work, the sexes increasingly resembled one another; thus, "the feminized male and the masculinized female are better placed to understand and to complete one another."[223] What was different about the 1960s version of modernity was that it was based on the notion that *both* male and female identities must move seamlessly from the family to the wider society, and recognized woman as the "*co-artisan* of a new humanity."[224] Quebec Catholicism, in particular, found the imperatives of this cultural modernity increasingly difficult to navigate because of the very ambiguities of the ways in which it had sought to balance the claims of authority and individualism. On the one hand, its assimilation of personalist values after the Depression had rested on a delicate balance between male authority and female aspiration contained within a system of psychologies and roles which, while often displaying a certain flexibility, emphasized the stability of woman's maternal role. On the other hand, Catholicism had, by postulating " spiritual" rather than physical definitions of maternity, and by actively promoting access to forms of contraception, encouraged the idea that maternity was an act of female choice.

The prevalence of these critiques of domesticity during the early 1960s prompted Raymond Doyle, the secretary of the Canadian Conference on the Family, to ask in 1964, "Is it still correct to say that we must render the tasks of mother and mistress of the household more attractive because women no longer (or never did) find these roles personally fulfilling?"[225] What Doyle's uncertainty reveals was that during the early 1960s an influential group of Catholic social scientists and reformers increasingly accepted that an exclusive focus on familial roles was stunting the female identity, and that work had opened the possibility of new public identities for married women, and that this in turn necessitated a wholesale change in the way Catholicism conceptualized the nature and role of women, and the relationship of the sexes both in the family and society. The SPM's resigned tolerance for the work of married women was in one sense an attempt to retain a balance between "family duties and professional obligations," by which some hoped to sustain the basic assumptions of the public ideology of Catholic domesticity.[226] However, where the direction of personalist feminism in the early 1950s had always worked within some overarching idea of separate male and female roles, with domesticity equated with women, the debates that occurred in Quebec over women's identity in the 1960s were significant, not just because they eroded the psychologies and family hierarchies, but because, increasingly, these older gender definitions – the epitome of static "tradition" – came to be equated with Catholicism itself. In Quebec, the process that marked the transformation of personalist feminism into individualist (or in American parlance "second-wave") feminism was marked by the formulation of the modern wisdom that Catholicism and women's aspirations were irreconcilably opposed.

Indicative of these currents at work was the 1962 symposium held under the auspices of the Canadian Broadcasting Corporation, *The Real World of Women*, that brought together a number of prominent social commentators from both English Canada and Quebec. The audience was treated to a lecture by Dr Mirra Komarovsky, professor of sociology at Columbia University, who reiterated what had become a standard observation during the late 1950s: that family roles and expectations had become highly problematic for the articulation of female identity because modern women were faced with nearly impossible psychological demands, as they were required to live up to higher standards of child care, which insisted upon parental responsibility for every facet of the child's personality. However, in what was to become the historical periodization of both second-wave feminism and much subsequent historical scholarship, Komarovsky characterized the whole culture of post-war domesticity as a "neo-anti-feminism," the belief that the solution to modern woman's dilemma lay in a reassertion of fixed and separate gender roles, and the exclusive identification of women with the domestic sphere. She juxtaposed against this a far more flexible definition of gender roles, arguing instead that "what is a masculine or feminine activity varies considerably with tradition and circumstances." Women, she believed, could "happily combine motherhood and employment," and, in light of demographic tendencies to have fewer children, this had become a psychological necessity.[227]

Komarovsky's portrait of the domestic sphere and conventional male and female roles as psychologically unfulfilling was forcefully echoed by the Montreal psychiatrist Camille Laurin, who argued that, far from being natural or biological, these roles had been defined, constructed, and imposed by male fears of women. In a critique that closely approximated that of Betty Friedan's *The Feminine Mystique*, published a year later, he declared that concepts of femininity based on beauty, intuition, cleverness, industriousness, and a self-sacrificing sense of duty had only succeeded in psychologically damaging women, making them victims of a "merciless repression and inhibition" which resulted in "the production of the inert, asexual type of woman, lacking in vitality and spontaneity, dragging her empty life throughout space and time, passing from one conformism to another, adept at daily chores but unable to give her husband or children any warmth or incentives."[228] While Christianity, in his estimation, had improved the lot of women by assigning them a spiritual equality with men, it had contributed to their subordination by curtailing a healthy expression of sexuality, and had created an idealized image of women that fed into the subordinating definitions of female passivity, which Laurin believed were fuelling a psychologically unhealthy climate of competition, resentment, and revenge between men and women, which brought to the surface alienations and aberrations such as the all-devouring matriarch, and an increasing refusal on the part of women to bear children.[229] For Laurin, the only road out of the dilemma lay in reconstructing gender relations by putting into practice Simone de Beauvoir's dictum that women's passivity was not biological, but socially-imposed, and that by taking responsibility for the full gratification of their sexual needs, they could actually attain a degree of heightened subjectivity in which sexuality, rather than being the sole determinant of female identity, assumed its proper role within a system of human values.[230]

The 1962 CBC symposium also stands as the beginning of a process by which personalist feminism became uncoupled from the post-war Catholic prescriptive identities for women, and by which Catholicism, by basing its

post-war public ideology of family so affirmedly on distinctive but complementary roles, became identified in the minds of a number of prominent
feminists as an obstacle to the equality and social progress of women.
Jeanne Sauvé, a prominent journalist and a former national president of
the Jeunesse Étudiante Catholique Féminine was a participant in the *Real
World of Women* discussions. Her own account of the intersection of Catholicism and female identity was far less harsh than that of her male counterpart, Camille Laurin. She informed the audience that her inherited definition of a woman was an asexual one, that of a well-balanced, reserved
person, lovingly devoted to her husband and bound by her faith and duty
to accept all chidren resulting from their life together and happy to be
indispensable to her family. Woman's reward for her self-sacrifice was
enhanced prestige in the home, with external recognition "only for her
qualities as a mother, very little as a wife." Sauvé praised the type of
Catholic Action she encountered in college as valuable for having
debunked "the mystery of sex relations," and while the notions of female
sexuality prevalent in Catholic Action may have been "a bit too sublime" –
an obvious reference to the personalist cult of "spiritual maternity" – she
maintained that "this spiritualization of sexual life helped to accept natural
instinctive desires which religion had taught to me."[231]

In her response to liberal feminists like Mirra Komarovsky and Thelma
McCormack, Sauvé sought to reaffirm some priority on motherhood,
stating that for woman "it is the only specifically feminine thing she can
do," but she also firmly indicated her adherence to the new currents within
Catholic personalism, declaring that women could never be fully satisfied
by "imprisoning" themselves in maternal roles, and in the interests of realizing the full attributes of their personality, had to project themselves into
the outside world and experience its challenges.[232] She reckoned that
much of the anxiety and psychic stress that post-war women were experiencing derived from a conflict between the competitive world of work and
their lack of preparation for it, a fissure that created among women "an
unbearable sense of defeat at work and at home," and a tremendous
resentment of men. In particular, Sauvé singled out for special blame the
Catholic classification of the sexes into feminine and masculine personalities, which extrapolated from anatomic differences roles that were specific
and clear-cut, if not opposed. "Opposed categories," she concluded, "are
bound to invite antagonism,"[233] a view that called into question, not only
the theory of gender roles that underpinned post-war domesticity, but the
very notion of a close fit between Catholic values and the aspirations of
women that activists of her generation had laboured so assiduously to
establish.

In Quebec, this growing tension between religion and feminism was
amplified by the activities of a number of "left" Catholics that were either

prominent in the mass media and academe, clustered around the journal *Maintenant,* or active in "secularist" organizations like the Mouvement Laïque de Langue Française (MLLF). Their ostensible aim was to reduce what they perceived as "clerical" control of education and social services, and in this campaign they came to believe that, despite the hopeful rhetoric of the political "quiet revolution," the rather tepid reforms such as the 1964 Civil Code amendments which improved the status of married women[234] signalled that church and state were engaged in a joint effort to refurbish older gender roles and patriarchy. In particular, they charged that Catholicism was notoriously lacking in ways to articulate female roles that corresponded to women's demands for new public identities. Writing in *Maintenant,* Father Bernard Mailhiot, evoking the philosophy of Simone de Beauvoir, stated that there was an imperative need to rethink sexual myths and stereotypes, and in particular, older Catholic notions regarding male and female psychology. "Our occidental patriarchies," he averred, assigned women only an "erotic" value, and failed to recognize women as "a subject, having the right to her own life, to her needs as a woman, to her specific functions in a human universe."[235]

Speaking in 1966, Fernande Saint-Martin, editor of *Châtelaine* and one of the most influential feminist voices, praised Catholicism as being linked to many profound human values and, indeed, she eschewed any desire to weaken the bonds between religious values and feminist aspirations. "If the female population of Quebec," she proclaimed, "appears to be a group of human beings far more evolved, sensible, and mature than its male counterparts, it is because of her attachment to religion that the French-Canadian woman owes these particular qualities ... It is within the framework of religion that women have been able to open themselves to a universe of spirituality which transcends the prosaic necessities of daily life, and which offered her a superior mode of human achievement, symbols and transcendence."[236] At one level, Saint-Martin was well aware of the extent to which her audience remained indebted to Catholic notions of female identity, to the older post-war premise of "equality, yes ... but not identity,"[237] for her address evoked a clear awareness of differences between men and women, and referred to women's fundamental aspiration to "realize a maternity that is even more vast" than the maternal function. However, she urged women to consider that, in Quebec, the personalist primacy of the spirit that characterized woman's nature had become perverted by the clericalism of the institutional Church and was actually contributing to the "alienation of women in our society," because Catholicism had consistently refused to accord them the status of autonomous persons. In addition, in an era when social and cultural values were rapidly changing, Catholicism's tendency was to prop up established authority, a choice which worked against women who, she maintained, massively rejected the idea that "the family was structured along the lines of autocratic societies, whether lay or clerical, and were seeking, in a sharing of power, the achievement of a real democracy."[238] Saint-Martin's message was that the personalism exemplified by those explicitly feminine qualities of "profound concern for life and for the well-being of humanity" could be preserved, but only by severing all ties to Catholicism's post-war familialism which had articulated these values within a culture that, she maintained, emphasized the constraints of duty and sacrifice. For Saint-Martin, personalist feminism must break from these artificially constructed gender roles by forging a dynamic relationship between female values and an individualist credo of limitless possibilities, one that recognized women's autonomy in the spheres of family, state, and society.[239]

The shift of personalist feminism from familialism to individualism – what Hélène Pelletier-Baillargeon termed "an optimistic feminism"[240] – after the mid-1960s was reflected in an uncoupling of mainstream organized feminism and Catholic institutions. In 1966, the same year that the Church authorities chose to close down the national offices of Catholic Action, a number of activists, including Jeanne Sauvé, made a crucial choice to inaugurate the Fédération des Femmes du Québec (FFQ), a body that grouped together a number of secular and religious women's organizations and had no official ties to Catholicism. Despite the continued presence of more conservative voices who condemned "an aggressive at-all-costs feminism which seeks equality with men by imitating their irresponsibilities and lack of moral fibre," and insisted upon the priority of a maternal role for women,[241] what was especially innovative about the FFQ was its complete lack of reference to the language of the complementary natures and roles of the sexes, and a firm articulation of the concept of women as autonomous individuals entitled to rights that would ensure their self-fulfillment *both* in the paid work force and in relation to family roles. Indeed, the promoters of this organization, and in particular Monique Bégin, who was to play a crucial role as executive director of the federal Royal Commission on the Status of Women later in the decade, sought to break "the more or less rigid cultural models that tied men and women to distinct and opposed gender roles" because they viewed this as a necessity "given the complexity of a highly industrialized society."[242]

At another level, the FFQ sought to put into practice Fernande Saint-Martin's exhortation to anchor personalist values in a culture of individualism. As the organization's brief on revising the Quebec Civil Code suggested, its intention was to advance a personalist conception of society that would "preserve the individuality and dignity of the human being." Its stated goal was to make the family "an authentic civil society" by predicating its relationships upon reciprocity between individual men and women, rather than upon prescribed notions of gender hierarchy,[243] and by forging a direct relationship between woman-as-individual and the state through individual access to rights-based government benefits and programs, an approach that in the words of the FFQ's principal government interlocutor, René Lévesque, minister of social affairs, would "offer women a free choice between a career and her vocation of 'housewife-educator-guardian of the home.'"[244] Indeed, by the late 1960s, even those who advocated the ostensibly "conservative" identity of stay-at-home mother justified it not in terms of an allegiance to familialism or to woman's duty, but in terms of personal choice. More tellingly, those who opted for this older expression of maternity claimed access, based upon the new idea of reciprocity, to benefits from the state.[245] Here, in the sphere of maternity itself, was the most important indicator of the way in which, during the course of a single decade, women's identities had become severed both from religious institutions and from the Catholic public ideology of family, and had been integrated and recast according to the new imperatives of individualism.

"SOMETIMES I REGRET HAVING BEEN BORN CATHOLIC, BUT ONLY FOR THIS REASON"[246]

The tensions between Quebec Catholicism and individualism that became particularly evident after the late 1950s affected not only the public ideological fit that feminist activists discerned between women's identities and religion. Indeed, the way in which most Quebec women had experienced personalism was through the post-war ideology of Catholic marriage and familialism. Through organizations such as the SPM, Catholic Action had, after the late 1930s, sought an equilibrium between Catholic doctrines and contraception and so established an accommodation between maternity and personal sexual satisfaction that assigned a high psychological and spiritual value to each element. "In all sections of society," concluded one 1961 Catholic Action assessment, "it is believed that the sexual compatibility of husband and wife can facilitate all marital conflicts, while the inverse will give rise to tensions within the marriage."[247] However, because this Catholic culture of "regulated births" eschewed artificial means of contraception, it had relied almost entirely for its effect upon an exalted sense of personal responsibility. This entailed a precise awareness, by individual women, of the fertile and infertile periods of their own menstrual cycle as a precondition to sexual intercourse, but even more significantly, upon a delicate, and frequently frustrating calibration of sexual pleasure and the self-sacrifice demanded by abstinence. However, by the early 1960s, two wider tendencies within Quebec culture, the psychological critique of female domesticity and an exaltation of personal sexual expression within the wider ambit of Western society began to unsettle this Catholic synthesis.

The same strand of social criticism that identified what it believed were overly-constrictive gender hierarchies and roles as the source of married women's feelings of psychological and social inadequacy also claimed to uncover a seething morass of female sexual frustration and frigidity within modern marriages that left most women in a perpetual state of "hysteria" that was damaging both to the individual psyche and to wider familial and social relationships.[248] And in a social environment increasingly influenced after the late 1960s by "permissiveness," a more uninhibited sexuality both within and outside of marriage came to be accepted by the cultural mainstream[249] – and not simply by baby-boomer youth – as the dominant criterion of both individual and social well-being. In the Quebec context, an increasingly vocal section of opinion came to identify Catholicism's morality of contraception, the delicate balance of pleasure and abstinence, as "a received cultural heritage of 'the evils of the flesh,'" as a particularly oppressive compound of interdictions, folklore, fears and taboos that acted as the primary obstacle to women's sexual fulfillment,[250] and by implication contributed to their alienation and inability to find personal fulfillment at all other levels of endeavour. As one young mother stated, "I deplore the fact that my sexual desires are being eaten away by being pregnant once again (although I do not deplore the pregnancy itself), because I am very much in love with my husband, and I would like to respond more frequently to his sexual advances."[251]

Catholic organizations such as the SPM recognized the need to adapt their message to this new, more open climate of sexual liberalization by articulating an increasingly individualist message that emphasized marriage as entailing the personal sexual satisfaction of each spouse. "Our society," declared Camille Laurin at the 1966 annual banquet of Montreal SPM activists, "has hitherto placed an unduly high value upon the maternal virtues. We must now valorize conjugal virtues, to articulate a new theology of marriage ... and at the same time, valorize them on the individual level. We must learn that woman has a responsibility to herself for her own pleasure, for the pleasure of her husband, and for the harmony of her home."[252] For Catholics like Laurin, it was possible, by following the logic of personalism, to construct a new theology of marriage that would reconcile both Catholicism and the new culture of individual sexual gratification.

Other Catholics, however, began to doubt whether the new culture of sexual openness – particularly as it touched upon the female identity – could in fact be harmonized with religious imperatives. Even Gérard Pelletier, one of the most articulate proponents of Catholic liberalism throughout the 1950s, worried about what he considered the new fashion of talking about the physical aspects of sexuality in what he castigated as "a tone of false detachment" that seemed to be reducing sex to a series of impersonal exchanges. This, he believed, testified to a "confusion between the whole and the part, between those aspects of sexuality that we want to bring out of the background and free them from their baggage of false shame, and the total love that must characterize the relationship between men and women."[253] However, what especially concerned Pelletier was an attitude prevalent among Quebec intellectuals and middle-class elites that sexual liberalization was the consequence of religious disaffection, and that freeing oneself from sexual inhibition involved the complete evisceration of personal religious beliefs and practices. Although he himself fully participated in denouncing religious education as being completely obsessed by a preoccupation with sexual sins, he concluded regretfully that "the spiritual anxiety of these social groups revolves entirely around sexual questions."[254]

The great irony here was that the link between sexuality and the abandonment of Catholicism was less a cultural phenomenon of rebellious youth than of stable, married couples of the previous generation. Post-war Catholic Action itself, of which Pelletier had been one of the most articulate leaders, had insisted upon an almost seamless connection between religious practice and sexuality in promoting its personalist vision of the conjugal, affectional family. However, the difficulty was that it was difficult for ordinary believers to draw the precise theological distinctions between what was Catholic moral teaching and what was the prescriptive ideology of the post-war family. If, for Catholics – as was happening increasingly during the late 1950s – having a family founded upon emotional satisfaction and affection depended on successfully balancing sexual pleasure and abstinence both for the spouses' emotional cohesion and for the determination of the family's size, would any difficulties that married women had in achieving this balance have repercussions for religious practice? And would Quebec Catholics opt for a vision of marriage in which contraception epitomized a more hedonistic quest for private satisfaction, or would contraception preserve its reference to a system of spiritual values, and thus to an ongoing Catholic ideology of marrige and family that continued to inform the public sphere?

By the early 1960s, evidence from a number of Quebec urban centres indicated a rather striking defection from the Church, most evident among Catholics who were trying to limit family size. A survey undertaken by the Ligue Ouvrière Catholique in 1963 found that 60 per cent of Catholic couples practiced birth control, but that of this number a shockingly high 65 per cent had entirely abandoned religious practice.[255] This prompted the Catholic activist Jean Francoeur to expatiate upon a troubling new phenomenon that seemed to characterize religious practice among married couples. Because many couples felt that it was necessary to practice contraception, and encountered difficulties with the approved combination of the rhythm method and abstinence, many "found themselves drawn towards practices reproved by Catholic morality as defined by the church. They then conclude that because they are already in a state of mortal sin, it avails them little to attend mass or to resort to the aid of sacraments like penance."[256] It was in order to avert this potential disjuncture between, on the one hand, the personalist definition of marriage and sexuality and, on the other hand, Catholic moral teaching – a development that would make sexual and reproductive choice a purely private act – that a growing chorus of reformist Catholics urged greater flexibility in Catholic moral teaching regarding birth control.

However, it must be emphasized that while these reformers sought to allow a greater scope for the choice of the individual couple according to their conscience, and they urged a drastic restructuring of what they believed was the rather negative official Catholic attitude to sexuality, they remained adamant that, in an age of permissiveness, contraceptive practices, and by extension sexuality itself, should remain "public," subject to the higher religious imperatives implicit in the Catholic vision of marriage as a spiritual partnership. Thus, they believed that what would evolve was a "positive chastity" in which sexuality, while not completely encompassed by the procreative act, would conserve connections to it in a way that would not simply legitimize individual or collective "selfishness."[257] Until the absolute papal prohibition against the birth control pill was announced in 1968, a number of Quebec Catholic organizations engaged in efforts which had as their effect the introduction of a wider range of contraceptive practices to ordinary Catholics. However, the partially unintended effect on a wide section of Catholic laity was to establish a firm identification between Catholicism and the notion that sexuality and contraception were purely private acts subject only to the dictates of individual conscience. When the pope reiterated Catholic moral teaching and the Church's opposition to what he termed "artificial" types of birth control, there followed a rapid, and massive erosion of adherence among Catholicism's traditional constituency: married couples with families.

Writing in 1961, Dr Jacques Baillargeon and Hélène Pelletier-Baillargeon reflected uneasily upon the "painful and silent antagonism that all too frequently opposes those husbands and wives obliged to literally flee one another to realize the total abstinence" necessary to the successful integration of contraception and Christian morality.[258] Like other reformist Catholics, the Baillargeons were well aware of the physical and psychological limitations of the rhythm method, the form of contraception employed most frequently by Quebec women, and the only method, other than total abstinence, that the Church deemed fully compatible with its doctrines. In the first place, the Ogino-Knaus method could only be successfully practiced by a minority of women who had completely regular menstrual cycles, and because it was not entirely reliable it was increasingly judged as a technique that favoured fertility and natality. Second, the rhythm method was identified as a principal culprit in the sexual and psychological dissatisfaction of women, especially in light of the accepted sexual wisdom (also propagated by the Church) that both husband and wife both needed a complete orgasm to achieve sexual fulfillment. "The long periods of abstinence required to assure the maximum effect of the rhythm method," stated Marie-Josée Beaudoin in 1964, "often led to serious difficulties in the home, the husband feeling frustrated, and the wife, fearing that she was already less sexually ardent, risked becoming completely frigid."[259] Judged in light of the personalist emphasis on the need for emotional intimacy and spontaneity in marriage, the rhythm method actually risked producing the opposite effect. In addition, although most surveys from the early 1960s revealed a strong commitment among Quebec Catholic couples to having four to five children during the course of their marriage, there was also compelling evidence of widespread acceptance, particularly among the expanding middle classes, of the logic of the affectional conjugal family which argued that child-rearing required the total psychological and emotional commitment of parents for each child, something that could only be effectively accomplished in situations where the parents had deliberately chosen to restrict family size.[260]

Within Catholic organizations like the SPM, which had, since the 1940s particularly, sought to address women's sexual and emotional needs within marriage, the existence of such a cultural climate fostered an accommodationist mentality among both clergy and lay activists towards new techniques of birth control. The birth control pill, especially, because it was based on "natural" substances, and did not create chemical or mechanical barriers to fertility, seemed to fall within the rubric of Church approval. Perhaps the most powerful testimony to the identification in the public mind of Catholicism and the fact that the choice of birth control techniques had become a matter of private choice, especially in the spacing of births, was a 1966 *Maclean's* survey in which 65 per cent of the women questioned claimed that priests advised them that the pill was acceptable, and the women believed that this technique seemed to resolve all problems of conscience occasioned by other methods. Indeed, 80 per cent of couples questioned in the Montreal diocese stated that they "found birth control such a normal practice that they did not even speak about it any more in the confessional because the Church had nothing to say in the matter."[261] Although a number of clergy were unhappy about the idea that the pill might free female sexuality from any restraint, they sought ways of integrating this new technique with Catholic teaching. Father Jules Paquin, for example, although he clearly preferred abstinence in conjunction with the rhythm method, sanctioned the use of the pill as a means of regularizing the female cycle in those cases where medical problems existed,[262] a view also adhered to by the women activists who lectured at the marriage preparation sessions. For them, the pill was an *aide à la nature* (a help to nature) because it assisted in breast-feeding and regularized the female cycle. However, in their estimation, the decision to use the pill was increasingly not a matter of doctrine or morality but a private decision to be determined by the woman herself in consultation with medical professionals.[263]

Indeed, by the mid-1960s, there appeared to be widespread popular acceptance of the notion that the Church's position on the issue of birth control had undergone considerable liberalization, and that the Catholic hierarchy had increasingly left the choice of method to "the conscience of couples enlightened by the values of their mutual love,"[264] so long as abortion was rigorously excluded. Thus, a number of Catholic clergy and social agencies eagerly participated in the experiment of the Montreal Centre du Planning Familial, inaugurated in 1966 by Dr Serge Mongeau. A committee of theologians, led by the liberal Dominican Father Vincent Harvey, underwrote the centre's view that Catholic welfare organizations had a positive duty to set up services that were designed to promote "responsible parenthood." Harvey, one of the editors of the "left" Catholic journal *Maintenant*, went even further, arguing that the existence of organizations such as the Centre du Planning Familial signified the passage from a "casuistic morality" to one based on "values considered in their whole context," a change that would contribute to a more fulfilling vision of family life, allowing Christian couples to navigate between an older "Jansenist" sexual morality of prohibitions, and the hedonism characteristic of modern life.[265] Harvey and his allies did not accept that the existence of family planning centres signified a privatization of sexuality and birth control, as they continued to believe that the Church, medical professionals, and social workers would encourage the exercise of birth control in a context shaped by the "social philosophy" of Quebec, which they maintained was committed to balancing the claims of individualism and familialism.[266]

However, the position of the theological committee masked a number of disagreements and confusions. As astutely noted by Father Ulysse Desrosiers, head of the Montreal Centre de Consultation Matrimonial and one of the leading participants in the family planning experiment, "the watchword seems to be family planning, but to those who are unable to make the distinction, family planning means family restriction." Many social workers employed by Catholic agencies were clearly uncomfortable with Dr Mongeau's emphasis on birth control, preferring to place the accent on the more acceptable terrain of the couple's sexual education and mutual adjustment.[267] From the perspective of personalism, the quasi-acceptance of the birth control pill was clearly unsatisfactory. It left contraception purely on the level of technique as it did not clearly define a Catholic position or exhort couples to link sexuality, fertility, and spiritual values. According to two perceptive "left" Catholics, the new Catholic attitude to sexuality and contraception was a "pastoral of exceptions," which prescribed "the pill for women with irregular cycles, the pill for menopausal women, the pill for neurotic women ... even some understanding moralists would prescribe the pill for wives of philandering husbands!" Worse, it simply encouraged what they lamented as a rather legalistic tendency for ordinary Catholics to seek easy, ready-made solutions to what were fundamental moral choices.[268] More conservative Catholics, however, warned that, in so exalting the scope of conscience, accommodationist clergy and laity had fundamentally erred because they were arousing expectations that they could not fulfill. According to Marthe Handfield, the term "conscience" had become fraught with serious difficulties. In former times, it had had a public reference because it was defined around particular applications of moral law; in recent years, it had come to mean something entirely privatized, nothing more than "the personal way in which we follow our passions." Morality, however, was eternal and transcendent, and she warned that the Church would never abandon its ultimate standard in face of the vagaries of the individual conscience.[269]

In the summer of 1968, Handfield's prophecy came to pass with the publication of Pope Paul VI's encyclical *Humanae Vitae*, which reiterated the conservative features of Catholic moral teaching and, by imposing a particular prohibition on the birth control pill, firmly tied sexuality and procreation. At one level, the encyclical had little effect on those Catholics who already considered contraception a private matter between husband and wife,[270] beyond confirming their view that the Church was associated with a negative set of prohibitions upon human freedom. This compelled a further alienation from religious practice for many married couples, who felt unable to live up to these doctrinal standards. However, the pope's legalism and his assumption that seemed to equate human and animal sexuality bitterly disappointed those personalists who had wanted, through the enunciation of a more flexible doctrinal position, to preserve a type of society in which Catholicism had continued to articulate a public ideology of marriage, sexuality, and family, and more especially, retained ties with the way in which women's identities were shaped.[271]

By restating what many castigated as a medieval theological position, the pope in two ways symbolically legitimized what in late 1960s Quebec was an emergent liberalism whose ultimate effect was to relegate Catholicism to the private sphere. In the first place, he gave credence to those who wanted to excise Catholicism out of a desire to foster an extreme individualism that was based on the exclusive right of the private conscience in all matters pertaining to personal values. Secondly, the implicit reaffirmation of older gender roles oriented around biological maternity confirmed the wisdom of Fernande Saint-Martin's dictum that the state was a more reliable ally for women's aspirations than was Catholicism. In this way, the final irony of the institutional Church's conservative turn on contraception was to further one of the central developments of a cultural revolution that rapidly displaced the public culture that both religious and political authorities had sought to build during the Quiet Revolution, one which assumed that Catholic religious values would provide the element of social consensus that would underwrite a broader climate of reform. In other words, the encyclical helped accelerate the privatization and individualization of all matters pertaining to family, and the failure of personalism to maintain a precarious balance between individual assertion and the public, institutional character of the family. Thus, a new form of social liberalism, premised on the sovereignty of the individual in the private sphere of sexuality and reproduction, emerged in Quebec as the dominant public ideology. It effectively relegated Catholicism to the background of public debate, and in so doing effectively closed off the cultural possibilities of the Quiet Revolution.

6

The Final Concordat
Catholicism and Education Reform in
Quebec, 1960–1964

God-damned old bishops! By offering these amendments to us like candy, they are trying to screw the province, like they have been screwing the altar boys for years. ... God-damned old bishops! What refinement, what vice! First, we'll dangle a noble declaration of freedom of conscience in front of you, and while the confused agnostics thank us, then we'll amend your little Bill in the ass ... until the whole nation, finally enslaved and trembling, falls at the feet of our spiritual lords, armed with croziers, while their robes undulate with unmitigated pleasure.[1]

Any reform of our school system can only impair the beneficial influence of religious institutions upon our society. Our educational system is impregnated with religion to the very marrow. Successive generations of priests and nuns have dedicated themselves to the awakening of your intelligences. Even our most anticlerical intellectuals have contracted an enormous debt with the Church.[2]

The Quiet Revolution – the very phrase conjures up visions of the collective liberation of Quebec from the constraints of a backward, best forgotten past. In a tale that still influences how the period is seen in both English Canada and Quebec, the then recently-elected Liberal provincial government, representing the will of the nation to launch itself on the path of reform, committed its resources to a massive effort of *déblocage* (unblocking), the removal of outmoded value-systems and institutions. In short order, so the story goes, the Quiet Revolutionaries replaced these with state structures that incarnated the canons of a secular modernity. Between 1960 and 1964, a rising elite of new professionals and technocrats, inspired by visions of economic progress, managerial competence, and a nationalism founded upon the power of the Quebec state, built a series of new educational structures that displaced Roman Catholicism from what had been a near-monopoly of clerical influence. More importantly, the creation of a new state educational system eviscerated

Catholicism from its traditional place as the focus of public life and social cohesion in Quebec, thus clearing the way for the free play of new secular ideologies like Marxism, social democracy, and the ideal of a sovereign Quebec.

The obscenities hurled at Quebec's Roman Catholic bishops at the conclusion of the public debate on education by Jacques Godbout, a young filmmaker passionately committed to the ideal of an independent, secular Quebec, indicate that those who most forcefully advocated the removal of Catholicism from the public realm believed that they had, in fact, lost a key battle to build a new, dynamic Quebec. Men like Godbout and Maurice Blain, the president of the Mouvement Laïque de Langue Française, an association founded in 1961, promoted both a radical separation of church and state and a new concept of social cohesion based on language and culture. Holding to the ideal of full civic equality for religious dissidents, including agnostics and unbelievers, this movement maintained that Quebec's Royal Commission on Education (Parent Commission), which sat between 1961 and 1963, and Bill 60, which enacted a new public system of education, simply perpetuated the "holy alliance of secular and sacred" spheres. What so angered them was that, in the framework of a modern democratic state, the Quebec government's decision to harness the ideal of a public system of state schools to the principle of confessional religious instruction appeared to consecrate what they denounced as the traditional confusion between French cultural values, Christian faith, and membership in the political community.[3]

The choice made by the government to overtly enshrine Catholic religion in public educational structures imperatively underscores the need to reconsider the causal sequence that underlies all historical treatments of the Quiet Revolution: the link between a rising tide of secular values and the expansion of the Quebec state in the early 1960s. The major signposts of the education debate – the creation of the Mouvement Laïque de Langue Française, the discussions surrounding the Parent Report, and the public debate on Bill 60 itself – point to the overwhelming desire, even among many elements committed to a diminution of clerical influence in Quebec society, to avoid choosing the polarized alternatives of either a theocracy or a state completely severed from all religious principles.[4] "I believe," stated Réginald Boisvert in 1961, "that the State can separate itself from the Church without divorcing itself from God. I believe in the possibility, for the salvation of all citizens, of a concordat between an adult State and an equally adult Church."[5] With its insistence that both state and church were jointly responsible for the task of "salvation," Boisvert's credo endowed the modern state with spiritual purpose and at the same time placed the values of Catholicism at the core of the new democratic order that many Quebec reformers desired to build. The new concordat which

Bill 60 ratified was not simply an agreement between a secular political elite and the Church hierarchy. Rather, it was an attempt to navigate between competing concepts of civic order, national identity, and social cohesion. Indeed, between 1960 and 1964, the fact that the Quebec government committed itself to something more than the bare recognition of the fact of confessionality, and openly directed its financial resources and teaching and administrative personnel to the task of *teaching* Roman Catholic religion at both the primary and secondary levels, firmly indicates that much of Quebec's new "secular" elite believed that Catholicism had a decisive role to play in the formation of a modern state.

In one sense, although the deal hammered out between the bishops and the Lesage government appeared to be an ultimately untenable alliance of clerical conservatism and aggressively secularizing liberal reformism, there were in fact parallels between the educational reforms of the 1960s and earlier state initiatives in the field of public schooling. For example, the compulsory school law enacted in 1943 by the Liberal government of Adélard Godbout brought together a similar series of odd political bedfellows: reformist Liberals committed to "managerial" reform, a coalition of anglophone and francophone businessmen anxious to secure a more stable and well-educated workforce, and senior clergy who, from motives of nationalism, wanted to keep rural children and adolescents in school longer in order to avert the spectre of rural depopulation, which they believed was sapping the French-Canadian Catholic social fabric.[6] However, by the 1960s, even if considerations of "managerial" liberalism and access to enhanced technical skill remained powerful arguments driving the creation of a completely state-controlled education system, three other important considerations were at work that dictated an even closer alliance between church and state.

First, as outlined in the opening chapter, the changing character of cultural notions of youth and adolescence that emerged by the mid-1950s, and in particular the linking of public youth identities to a rising tide of individualism and consumerist hedonism, led to a widespread cultural pessimism among both lay and clerical elements. Educational activists and reformist Catholics shared the belief that, especially in Church-run institutions, religious instruction and practice among middle-class youth had broken down, and Catholic values were being overcome and inverted by an overwhelming tide of North American materialist culture. To a considerable extent, these Catholic critics blamed a whole set of popular Catholic religious devotions and practices, and clerical institutions themselves for furthering Quebec's Americanization and consequent decline of humanistic values.

Second, as we have seen in the preceding chapters that have analysed Catholic discourse about the family, both reformist Catholic clergy and lay social scientists were being rapidly drawn towards the view that the nuclear family had failed as an educative entity both in instructing children and adolescents in the tenets of the Catholic faith, but also in teaching them proper sex roles and initiating them into family formation. This "crisis," it was widely maintained, could only be mastered by a systematic and massive campaign of institutional intervention by both church and state, one which must displace the family in order to rapidly re-educate a new generation of parents in vital Christianity. The school was thus elevated as the agency which could, in the final analysis, compensate for the social and cultural deficiencies of the Quebec family, and many Catholics came to enthusiastically accept that the state must assume an enhanced role not only in managing the school system, but in making the presentation of Catholic doctrine more effective.

Finally, the arrival in power of a reformist Liberal government in the early 1960s coincided with the inauguration of the Second Vatican Council. The fact that the new political elites of Quebec saw their identity as both Catholic and modern was given further cultural purchase by the highest authorities of the international Church, who endorsed the view that Catholicism, both as a system of private belief and public action, was fully compatible with the structure and dynamism of modern industrial nations characterized by social pluralism. Although historians have treated the reforms of the Second Vatican Council primarily from the standpoint of changes within the internal structures, attitudes, and practices of the Church,[7] it must be emphasized that because the Catholic Church in Quebec expressed the religion of the vast majority, and moreover, because the Church was a key public player in the areas of family, education, and social assistance, Vatican II cannot be understood purely as an internal process in which Catholicism can be treated apart from the wider public culture. Indeed, between 1960 and 1965, the combined effect of the Second Vatican Council and the institutional reforms undertaken by Quebec's Liberal government, particularly in the field of public education, marked not a retreat of religion, but a significant amplification of Catholicism's presence in Quebec society. Significantly, the elites who effected the educational reforms of the 1960s conceived of no necessary opposition between church and state, and no formal compartmentalization between religion and nationalism. Indeed, apart from a small minority – the secularists of the Mouvement Laïque de Langue Française – the majority of francophone Quebec Catholics until the mid-1960s continued to act as though the boundary between these categories was quite porous. This meant that throughout the 1960s, Quebec nationalism retained a strong Catholic reference. Consequently, it was with no sense of incongruity that the chief political architect of education reform, Paul Gérin-Lajoie, could insist that the new educational structures that he proposed were designed to break down the "watertight compartments" between church and state. "Whether we envisage the welfare and greatness of the nation; whether we think of the expansion and influence of the Church … on all levels, education is the foundation upon which we must in future rely."[8] The nature of the partnership hammered out between church and state between 1960 and 1964, which seemed to establish a closer relationship between the two entities, suggests the need to revise the political teleology of the Quiet Revolution that posits the existence of a powerful strain of secular neo-nationalism in the early 1960s that aggressively sought to eviscerate Catholicism from the public sphere. It may be suggestively argued that the emergence of such an ideology was contingent upon other social and cultural factors that came into play more powerfully in the late 1960s and weakened the commitment of Quebec's francophone elites to Catholicism as a source of social cohesion.

"THERE ARE PLENTY OF STRANGERS IN THE ROOM"[9]

The reform of Quebec's educational structures to meet both the demographic pressures of the baby-boom generation and the scientific and technological imperatives of post-war culture had been discussed at great length during the 1950s. Quebec's education system until 1964 can best be described as a "semi-public" entity designed to preserve both Protestant and Catholic confessional institutions from overt state interference. By 1960, the financing for most of the system came from the Quebec government, but the Department of Public Instruction lacked a responsible minister or upper administrative structures to assure accountability and coordination. Divided into Catholic and Protestant confessional committees, the department's mandate extended only to primary schools and to part of the secondary sector, which remained poorly-organized and chronically underfunded. A whole network of *collèges classiques*, originally designed to train the province's elite for careers in the priesthood, law, and medicine, had grown up in the twentieth century, the private preserve of diocesan bishops and religious orders. Technical education and other forms of specialized training were administered by the Ministry of Youth. The French-language universities were institutions of the Catholic Church, governed as independent corporations by pontifical charters.[10]

The Duplessis-appointed Royal Commission of Inquiry on Constitutional Problems (Tremblay Commission), which sat between 1953 and 1954, heard briefs from a wide variety of universities, classical colleges, business associations, trade unions, and educational organizations all stressing the need for enhanced financing, greater government initiative, and the modernization of the curriculum. However, what must be stressed about the submissions to the Tremblay Commission, and the subsequent critiques of the education system by pertinacious opponents of the Duplessis regime like André Laurendeau, Gérard Filion, and Pierre Trudeau, was that the debate was a discussion among Catholics. While subtle differences were present over whether education should promote "nationalism" or "democracy," none ever imagined the possibility of a system of education in which Roman Catholic religious values would not have a preponderant influence, or in which private religious initiative in education would ever be completely displaced by the state. Indeed, what united all these critics was a common training in the elitist *collèges classiques*, and, consequently, most of their attention was directed to an emotional debate over the place of the humanities, a shorthand for concern over the role of traditional elites in a society increasingly exhibiting the disconcerting attributes of mass culture.[11]

Premier Jean Lesage's new Liberal government, elected in 1960, moved to remedy certain deficiencies of the educational structure. A series of laws enacted in 1961 raised the school leaving age, combined a number of school commissions into larger regional bodies, extended free schooling to Grade 12, provided more public funding for *collèges classiques* and universities, and appointed a Royal Commission on Education to study the wider ramifications of school reform.[12] However, upon closer study, the Liberal reforms of 1961 were marked by a profound ambiguity. In many respects, the Liberal plan simply seemed designed to perpetuate aspects of the "semipublic" character of the education system, especially at the secondary and university levels, where religious bodies would now manage and direct their institutions with more secure government funding. More tellingly, three bills were introduced into the Legislative Assembly, proposing to charter three new private Jesuit universities, with two in Montreal and one in Trois-Rivières.[13] The attitude of the new premier was itself decidedly conservative, and from the outset Lesage pledged that he would never institute state control of education by establishing a ministry of education.[14] Even the Royal Commission, from which much was expected, seemed dominated by clerical and anti-statist elements. The commission's chairman, Mgr Alphonse-Marie Parent, was the vice-rector of Université Laval, while the vice-chair, Gérard Filion, was editor of the Catholic daily *Le Devoir*, and a prominent advocate of the autonomy of local school commissions. Although a prominent opponent of Maurice Duplessis during the 1950s, Filion had consistently stood for a decentralized state and for the rights of private educational institutions, steadfastly opposing the creation of a ministry of education. English-language interests, both Protestant and Catholic, who had much to fear from over-centralization, were well represented on the Parent Commission, as were Quebec's religious orders themselves, in the person of Marie-Laurent de Rome, a sister of the Holy Cross.[15]

However, in 1960 there occurred two sensational media events which, taken together, brought a good deal of public opprobrium upon the prominent role played by the clergy in Quebec's system of public education. The first of these was the bombshell of *Les Insolences du Frère Untel*, a critique of Quebec's public secondary education written by Frère Pierre-Jérôme (Jean-Paul Desbiens), a Marist teaching brother, and published as a series of letters in *Le Devoir* in 1960. At the heart of Frère Untel's arraignment of secondary education, and by implication the presence of clergy and religious orders in the system, was a thoroughgoing assault upon what he identified as the messianic confusion of religious and national values. This conflation had been the means by which the Catholic Church had justified its role in education in claiming to be acting as the guardian of the French language and culture. The result of this "concubinage of temporal and spiritual," according to Frère Untel, was that Catholic schools had failed the people of Quebec in teaching both language *and* religious values. Adolescents emerged from the system speaking "joual," a term coined by Untel to describe a bastardized, corrupted form of French that reflected "our inability to affirm ourselves, our refusal to accept the future, our obsession with the past."[16]

Despite the iconic status of *Les Insolences du Frère Untel*, the humorous jibes directed at clerical excesses and the incompetence of the Department of Public Instruction, and the heavy-handed attempts by Untel's ecclesiastical superiors to silence him, what resonated with a larger educated public was the author's rather snobbish cultural conservatism. Brother Pierre-Jérôme was, in fact, an ardent *believer* in the unity of Catholic piety and French-Canadian national sentiment. However, his exposé of pedagogical and administrative incompetence in secondary schools where the clergy's presence bulked large convinced many vocal members of Quebec's media and university elites that Catholicism's educational mission no longer served as a rampart against Americanization. Untel insisted that the "joual" taught in secondary schools was but the entering wedge of an empty, conformist, North American mass youth culture of fast foods, fast cars, and rock n'roll, which could only corrode Quebec's French identity.[17] Indeed, what was compelling about Untel's views was the explicit link that he drew between the corrupt, soulless, materialistic French typified by "joual," and the Catholicism of the younger generation. "Things are even worse than we thought," wrote this passionate young cleric. "Without openly declaring themselves atheists, the young people whom we teach are as far from Christianity as they can be in their values concerning money, women, success, and love. Here is a total failure of our religious teaching."[18]

Most of Untel's criticisms were hardly original. They simply introduced a larger public to ideas about the nature of Roman Catholicism in Quebec that had been in vogue in educated circles since 1945. Catholic Action movements had long complained about the lack of spirituality in the religious values and practices of Quebec's working-class and rural people. However, Untel's polemic quickly shed any acerbic humour. He castigated teaching brothers, priests, nuns, and educational bureaucrats with the same hectoring, condescending tones he had previously reserved for the working-class and rural adolescents who attended Quebec's secondary schools. The author blamed educators for failing to teach religion as a heroic, existential faith of anxiety, personal affirmation, mystery, and choice, and offering instead a religion of orthodoxy and routine, a Catholicism that was "withered, fearful, ignorant, reduced to a negative morality preoccupied with sexual transgressions." What he feared most about a deficient school system was that it would cause "a widespread disaffection of the French-Canadian people from the Catholic faith."[19]

The second event brought to public attention, not only clerical incompetence, but also the supposed existence of a dark religio-political conspiracy apparently designed to fetter the province to a perpetual second-rate intellectual status. The revival of the Jesuit proposal to create two new universities in Montreal occasioned an immediate firestorm of protest from faculty and university administrators, both clerical and lay, of the Université de Montréal, who saw in this a plan to make the universities permanent tributaries of powerful religious orders. The Jesuit arguments in favour of their universities turned upon raw demographic facts, that Montreal needed new facilities to accommodate the anticipated surge in enrolment resulting from baby boomers' demands for higher education. In addition, the Jesuits' legal counsel, a young lawyer named Marc Lalonde, destined for a brilliant career in the federal cabinet, reminded the Parent Commission that the Jesuits had a historic teaching mission in the province, one explicitly recognized by papal authority which, through the Apostolic Constitution "Jamdudum," had allowed the Jesuits to dispense instruction in theology and philosophy despite the pontifical charters given to Université Laval and the Université de Montréal. Why not adopt, argued Lalonde, a broad construction of the term "philosophy" to include all profane knowledge, and enable the Jesuits to open a full-service university which could only provide greater democracy and accessibility in Quebec's system of higher education?[20]

In order to refute the rather compelling demographic argument, the newly-constituted Association des Professeurs de l'Université de Montréal had, in effect, to defend the indefensible in a democratic age: the preservation of a de facto university monopoly by the Université de Montréal, itself a papally-chartered institution, which would deny access to higher education to large numbers of young French Canadians. In its argument, the university's faculty touched the same nerve of an endangered French culture that had already been rubbed raw by Frère Untel's revelations. The central point at issue, declared the faculty, was simply the question of whether Quebec wanted the French or the North American system. In the former, universities were a centralized arm of the state, the "heart of the nation," and their existence was thus a vital matter of public, rather than private, interest. A vigilant government should ensure that through proper management and public funding, the Université de Montréal would emerge as a world-class research and intellectual facility.[21] The Jesuit plan, the university's faculty charged, would create anarchy in the university system by saddling Quebec with the American system of small ill-funded liberal-arts colleges where specialized research and cultural excellence would be, quite simply, absent. Worse, such an initiative would emasculate any further government efforts to bring order and cohesion to the educational system, and would stifle all state efforts in the field of culture by solidifying an alliance between various religious orders which already controlled the *collèges classiques*.[22] Why would any modern democratic state, even one with a Catholic majority, allow itself to be boxed in by the arcane legalisms of the Apostolic Constitution "Jamdudum" – promulgated during the palmy days of ultramontanism in the 1880s – which apparently elevated the authority of powerful religious orders over that of an elected government? By implication, the Jesuit plan, by scattering energy and resources that should be concentrated, would open the door to the further anglicization and Americanization of French culture that Untel had already identified as a feature of secondary education.

Thus, by the spring of 1961, many articulate opinion makers in Quebec[23] viewed the prominence of the Roman Catholic Church in the field of education with considerable suspicion. In particular, the Church's claim to preserve the treasures of French language and culture through religious faith had been shaken by the Untel and Jesuit imbroglios. The founding of the *Mouvement Laïque de Langue Française* (MLLF) on 8 April 1961 decisively reoriented the whole tenor of the debate on education by bringing to public attention the existence of a French-speaking, non-Catholic minority that emphatically rejected confessional schools. This raised, for the first time in twentieth-century Quebec, the broader question of whether Christian religious belief itself was compatible with democratic public institutions, and whether faith had a continuing role to play as the central organizing principle of public education. The MLLF was an association of Montreal personalities who were prominent in the media, higher education, and the performing arts. Some of its members had, in fact, figured prominently in the Jesuit controversy of the previous year.[24] The consultative committee was composed of Rev. Jacques Beaudon, a pastor of the United Church of Canada; Jacques Bobet, a writer and movie producer; Solange Chaput-Rolland, a journalist; Théo Chentrier, a psychoanalyst and professor at the Université de Montréal; Pierre Cinq-Mars,

principal of the École Cinq-Mars; Pierre de Bellefeuille, editor-in-chief of
Magazine Maclean; Marcel Dubé, president of the Fédération des Auteurs
et Écrivains; Guy Dubreuil, head of the anthropology department, Université de Montréal; Robert Élie, a writer; Jacques Lussier, psychoanalyst, professor at the Université de Montréal; Jacques V. Morin, a union represen-
tative; Bertrand Rioux, professor of philosophy, Université de Montréal;
Marcel Rioux, professor of anthropology, Université de Montréal; Jean-
Louis Roux, actor, president of the Société des Dramatistes; and Jean
Simard, professor at the École des Beaux-Arts.[25]

Arguing from the premise that French-Canadian society had been
Catholic and confessional for much of its existence, a situation in which
French-speaking unbelievers and non-Catholics had found themselves
ostracized from the national community, the MLLF proclaimed as its objective the "restoration of the respect for individual freedom." It publicly
maintained that the close links that had developed historically between the
Catholic Church and educational and social institutions in Quebec were
undemocratic and therefore indefensible, because they abridged the
rights of individuals on the grounds of religious belief. From this, the MLLF
deduced the necessity of "the recognition and establishment of the secular,
non-confessional character of public institutions, while respecting the religious fact and the legitimate interests of all groups in our society."[26]
Central to this ideal of a secular society was the very character of the school
system. The new association proposed the creation by the state of a non-
confessional or religiously "neutral" school sector, equal in rights and parallel to the Protestant and Catholic systems. Here, maintained spokesmen
like Jacques Mackay, a psychiatrist at Montreal's Hôpital Ste-Justine, education would be founded upon the notion that religion was a private
matter, to be taught at home by parents, although optional courses in religion could become a feature of the curriculum if desired by parents.[27]

From the outset, the founding of the MLLF was regarded as an event that
was heavily-laden with symbolism. The association's insistence upon the
rights of unbelievers and non-Catholics to full civic and social equality in
Quebec apparently marked, in a public sense, the end of Quebec's identity as a religiously-homogeneous society. To André Langevin, the grouping of so many intellectuals in the MLLF constituted the final rupturing of
an ideology which confounded "faith, language, culture, State and Church
in the name of a suffocating, paralyzing messianic quest."[28] For the liberal
cleric Father Georges-Henri Lévesque, the mentor to so many reformers of
the Quiet Revolution, the proclamation of secularism as the foundation
stone of a new democratic order signalled the end of the infallible equation between Catholic faith and being a French Canadian which had
underpinned the old nationalist credo.[29] However, for public consumption, the MLLF's platform stopped well short of advocating complete secu-

larization of Quebec's public school system. There were nonetheless some radical elements in the audience at the founding convention – associated with the "young left" who linked the achievement of Quebec independence to the creation of a socialist, secular society – who did in fact press for a "fundamentally secular" school system in which the state would exercise complete authority.[30] Marcel Rioux, a professor of anthropology at the Université de Montréal, demanded a completely secularized educational system, with the establishment of a system of state-subsidized private schools to accommodate religion as a kind of "exception" from the national norm. These private schools would meet the needs of those who wanted confessional education.[31] Here, the implication was that in a modern society all religions were a matter of private, personal belief that should not impinge upon a public system in which the nation would coalesce, not around the homogenizing factor of Catholicism, but in reference to the canons of secular reason.[32]

Moderate leaders like Jacques Mackay, however, were quick to insist that, in order to maintain public sympathy for its campaign against theocracy, the MLLF had to back away from any suggestion that it might impose secularist ideology on Quebec's school system.[33] This public reticence indicated that, in spite of the lofty claims that the MLLF was the cutting-edge of a new religious and social pluralism in French-speaking Quebec, and that a growing minority of non-Catholic francophones needed full civic equality and appropriate non-confessional educational institutions, the association's leaders were aware that such pluralism was, in fact, more potential than actual. At its height, the membership in the MLLF stood at about 3,000,[34] and was largely concentrated in Montreal. Despite the organization's public claim that there existed a large and growing cohort of French-speaking unbelievers and Protestants demanding educational and civil rights, the fact remained that in the demographic context of the early 1960s any public success the MLLF might enjoy would depend, in large measure, not upon the recruitment of large numbers of agnostics to their cause, but upon convincing the Catholic majority of the need for justice for minorities. This situation was rather graphically revealed when the MLLF attempted to found a branch in Quebec City. As reported by Jean Lebas, the secretary of the Quebec City section, only eight people attended the founding meeting. Some, he stated, "are partisans of a more open Catholic schooling with a reduced religious curriculum; others, like Mr. Marcel Trudel [the Université Laval historian], regret the fact that they can't get the type of French schooling that their children experienced when they were in France. However, I sensed no intense enthusiasm for the cause."[35] Many prominent members of the MLLF would hardly have qualified as hardline agnostics. The historian Marcel Trudel, for example, hoped that by separating Catholic religion from political citizenship, the

Church would be freed from "a political context" in which priests had usurped state functions to the detriment of their spiritual role.[36]

The MLLF was correct in asserting that since World War II, Quebec society had, indeed, become more pluralist, with over 400,000 new immigrants entering the province between 1945 and 1961. However, as the conservative Jesuit commentator, Father Richard Arès perceptively noted in 1963, the recent census had revealed that the society was still, by and large, divided as it traditionally had been into Catholic and Protestant. Quebec, Arès pointed out, was 97 per cent Christian and 88 per cent Catholic; "others," including non-believers, numbered only 0.3 per cent of the population, and only 0.2 per cent of the Montreal metropolitan area. Catholicism, far from losing ground, as the MLLF and alarmist liberal Catholics like Gérard Pelletier were wont to claim, had more than kept pace with population growth in the post-war period.[37]

It was to avoid overtly antagonizing Catholic opinion that Thérèse Dumouchel of the faculty of philosophy at the Université de Montréal urged the movement's leadership to "avoid ill-considered pronouncements on secularism," which in her estimation would achieve nothing by tarring the MLLF with the brush of anticlericalism. It would be far better, she explained, to concentrate their energies on securing "respect for individual freedom."[38] Indeed, just before the founding convention, Gérard Filion, the powerful editor of Le Devoir, warned that the term laïque was a potential pitfall that might destroy the fledgling movement and set back the cause of minority rights for many years.[39] Gérard Pelletier, one of the darlings of Quebec's liberal intelligentsia of the 1950s, cautiously advised the gathering that the word laïque was best reserved to suggest a distinction within the Catholic Church itself between clergy and laity. Otherwise, he feared that the new movement was casting itself as a Quebec imitator of the early twentieth-century radical French anticlericals, who in their sectarian zeal attacked all religious faith. It would be far better, Pelletier maintained, if the new association adopted a designation that would appeal to "Christian sources of justice." Anticlericalism would simply provoke the formation of a conservative religio-political faction to defend an endangered Catholicism, which in turn would only ensure that the majority would turn its face against the minority's claims for educational and civic fair play.[40] Indeed, as part of a tactic to marginalize the new MLLF by undercutting its appeals to linguistic solidarity, commentators like the Jesuit Richard Arès obliquely asserted that many of its members were speakers of French from overseas. Their French, though "excellent," was clearly a foreign import from France, Morocco, and Romania.[41] The implications of Arès's characterization were not lost. The secular ideals of state, society, and education that the MLLF sought to graft onto Quebec were utterly foreign to French Canada's preponderantly Catholic culture. Worse still, from the perspective of conservative and moderate Catholics, the movement was simply a front for a discordant and disturbing element which sought to bring European religio-political quarrels to the harmonious social environment of Quebec.

Although the new association rejected Pelletier's advice and adopted the designation "laïque," it eagerly sought to garner the support of Catholics. From the outset, many in the association were aware that the real constituency for secular education was not the minuscule group of radical "unbelievers," but Catholic parents discontented with the confessional system who desired, not "atheist schools," but merely the possibility of a non-sectarian education in which all religions would be treated with respect.[42] The MLLF thus quickly backed away from demanding the complete secularization of the public school system.[43] Throughout the public debate on education, the association insisted that its aim was not an explosive confrontation between Catholicism and secularism, but coexistence between confessional and non-sectarian schools. The latter would, they maintained, serve as common ground where children of all religious groups could meet and forge a harmonious civic culture based on a creative tension between reason and faith.[44] The leadership studiously argued that "non-confessional" did not mean "non-religious," and stated to the Parent Commission that it envisioned optional, non-dogmatic religious instruction as a central feature of the minority schools it wished to create.[45] Consequently, its language was anchored less in anti-Catholic polemic than in appeals to social peace and justice, which borrowed concepts from "intellectual personalism" and "political socialism."[46] Such values, which underwrote freedom of conscience and minority rights, appealed to an audience which included a number of reformist clergy and Catholic laity who saw in the creation of non-confessional schools a fulcrum that would assist their own efforts to declericalize, reform, and open the Catholic Church.

Writing in April 1961, Gilbert Beloeil of Rimouski declared that, while he was not an atheist or unbeliever, he preferred to link himself with these elements because he was tired of the "intolerable dictatorship of the · Catholic religion."[47] To a number of Catholics influenced by personalist canons of faith and spirituality, which postulated that faith was a free choice of the individual in the face of God, the compelling element in the MLLF's programme was freedom of conscience and advocacy of natural rights for religious minorities. This concern even overrode worries about the negative, anti-religious tone of certain elements in the movement.[48] From the outset, Cardinal Léger, archbishop of Montreal, insisted that while Catholic parents had a strict duty to send their children to confessional schools, neither state nor church could violate the consciences of unbelievers. "French-Canadian Catholicism," the cardinal declared, "has always treated the non-Catholic minority with justice, and will surely adopt the same attitude in the face of 'new minorities.'"[49] Reform-minded clergy like Abbé Louis O'Neill urged Catholics to draw careful distinctions between "godless" schools and the "non-confessional" schools proposed by the MLLF, and reminded his audience that even unbelief was a legitimate option in modern society, because faith was not something that could be imposed upon the individual conscience.[50] According to Gérard Pelletier, civil justice for non-believing minorities was a positive injuction of Catholic social teaching, a conclusion supported even by the more conservative Université Laval philosopher Charles de Koninck, who in an interview with the historian Marcel Trudel stated that agnostic parents who sincerely believed that religious teaching in confessional schools was harmful to their children had not only a right but a duty to secure non-confessional schools at public expense. "Freedom of religion," de Koninck concluded, "implies the freedom to adhere to no religion. This is a right that all religions must protect if they wish to preserve their own freedom."[51]

Underlying the positive responses of a number of articulate Catholics to the MLLF's plan for non-confessional schools was the hope that the very existence of such a network would reinvigorate Quebec Catholicism. According to Jean LeMoyne, the MLLF's initiative would prove to be the "means of saving the Catholic system through a reaction of cleansing and maturation," a process in which religious education would be purged of magical, sentimental, and moralistic elements to concentrate entirely on the personal relationship of the believer with God.[52] Indeed, many both within and outside the MLLF would have agreed with the assessment of Pierre de Bellefeuille, editor of Le Magazine Maclean, when he stated that the main problem facing Quebec education was not the creation of non-sectarian schools, but the reform of the Catholic system. Seeking to allay fears that the MLLF was trying to foist atheism as a public creed on Quebec society, de Bellefeuille wrote at the end of 1962 that most Catholic children would continue to attend Catholic schools. Catholicism, he believed, would emerge as the beneficiary of the social dialectic brought to Quebec society by new ideas of secularism. The presence of groups like the MLLF would ensure that the Church would no longer be captive to either its more conservative elements or to a spiritually-deadening alliance with the state.[53]

What is striking about the public debate on education is that even conservative Catholic commentators did not deny the rights of religious minorities, even agnostic ones, to have their own schools. An important feature of the conservative argument was that the laws governing the public confessional system were flexible enough either to allow minorities to have their own schools or, where numbers did not warrant, to dispense individuals from religious instruction.[54] As early as 1961, Maurice Blain, the first president of the MLLF, warned his supporters that they should not not be assuaged by these arguments, which would make them victims of the "mortal danger" of dissidence. It was not enough, he advised them, to rest content with agitating for a parallel school system built on the idea of religious dissent. This would simply allow the Catholic majority to make rather limited concessions and retain control of all levels of the public system while relegating religious minorities to a second-rate, underfunded educational system. The establishment of "neutral schools" for the minority was a negation of the democratic right to equality in all public services, and would merely legitimate a de facto institutional segregation of minorities from the majority.[55] More importantly, it would perpetuate the notion that the distinction between Catholic majority and other religious minorities was the defining feature of Quebec society, and negate the search for secular ideals of social cohesion.

Consequently, the educational rights of dissident religious minorities were but of secondary concern to the MLLF. Its goal was less the opening of separate "neutral" schools, than the deconfessionalization of the entire public system, through the removal of the clergy from bastions of public influence and the introduction into the school system of a more secular "humanism" which valued research, creativity, and discovery. In this way, the movement postulated the creation of a new society in Quebec which was no longer organized on the basis of religion. Conscious of the need to secure support among modernist Catholic personalists, the MLLF was careful not to couch this as an assault on Catholicism, but as a critique of the clergy's presence in public institutions. This went well beyond jibes at the pedagogical incompetence of religious orders, to blaming the clergy for creating a whole climate of conservatism and authoritarianism which had stunted and perverted the psyches of individuals and that of the entire society. Because so many prominent young social scientists and historians sympathized with the MLLF, the debate on the clergy's presence in the schools served to publicize widely an alternative account of Quebec's past, one in which the presence of Catholicism and the clergy were at best marginal elements, and, at worst, reactionary, obstructive forces in the dynamic creation of a national community.

Writing in 1961, Mme Alberto Droghini of Ville St Laurent informed Maurice Blain that although she had been educated by nuns, she would refuse to send her own daughters to Catholic schools because her own education had been marred by the preoccupation with "mortal sins," which had been instilled in her by the nuns. "Because I wish to raise my children in a Christian manner," she stated, "I wish to remove them from a system which teaches them more about doctrines than right living in a suspicious and mediocre atmosphere!"[56] Two hundred years of clerical dominance of education in Quebec, stated a number of participants in the

MLLF, had stunted any creativity or spirit of discovery among generations of students. This was responsible for fostering a climate of intolerance and fanaticism among the population, and had signally failed to produce a single saint, philosopher, or moralist "of virile and pure faith."[57] As Pierre de Bellefeuille remarked in 1962, a modern educational system could no longer substitute religious devotion for professional competence. Quebec's Catholic schools could not instill modern values so long as they were dominated by sentimental piety, conformity, and a lack of creativity among its administrators and teachers, many of whom were celibate clergy.[58]

Perhaps the most devastating indictment of the presence of the clerical element in Quebec's public education system came from André Lussier, a professor of psychology at the Université de Montréal. Lussier asserted a link between non-confessional education and the healthy psychological development of children, which he believed was possible only in a plural-ist environment. This he juxtaposed against what he negatively character-ized as the educational philosophy of Catholic religious orders: a "moral-ity of panic" which insisted upon "eternal salvation ... conditional upon obedience, submission, the belief that man is nothing."[59] The prominence of the religious factor in education, these critics charged, was that it urged students to consider eternal salvation to the exclusion of all else, thus teaching them the "art of dying," rather than achieving competence in the humanistic and scientific disciplines that they would need in order to func-tion in the professions, the economy, and politics.[60] The pedagogical style evolved by the clergy over the course of two centuries had excelled in afflicting children with the "monster of terror" by inculcating an overly-scrupulous, rigid moral training which was obsessed with sexual vice.[61] Using modern child psychology to subvert the claim of nuns and teaching brothers to educational supremacy because they were celibate and thus more devoted to the task of teaching than were laity, Lussier took dead aim at the notion of chastity. The chastity taught in Quebec's monasteries and convents, he charged, was unheroic and undemanding, and was based upon "a repressed sexuality tending to regress from the genital level to the sadistic-agressive level." Although he shied away from any overt charges of homosexuality against the clergy, he did blame them for "the cancer of authoritarianism, dependence, and infantile submission" which emascu-lated men and embroiled women in the conflicting claims of maternity and virginity. Such psychosexual terrorism lay at the root of the conformity and sterile intellectualism that stultified the school system and, worse still, poisoned Quebec Catholicism through persistent injections of "Jansenism, Manicheanism and fundamentalism."[62] Lussier's point was that the well-balanced, modern teacher was "frankly and joyously heterosexual,"[63] a choice which he linked to the positive values of creativity, discovery, self-assertion, and a rational humanism. As a way of creating well-adjusted personalities, Lussier thus posited a firm separation between "secular" and "religious" subjects. While the latter could continue to be taught by the clergy, the implication clearly was that these would occupy a much reduced place in Quebec's schools. "Secular" instruction would now be the sole preserve of a new generation of lay pedagogues who would definitively banish the clerical "monsters" of conformity, incompetence, and perverted sexuality to the shadows of a best-forgotten past.[64]

These arguments were, at various conferences and public gatherings, broadened into a secularist reconstruction of Quebec's past in which the preponderant presence of the Catholic Church was written off as the "exceptional" product of unfortunate historical circumstances. Proponents of a more secular Quebec society were, however, hampered by a rather compelling historical argument that, in fact, justified the continued presence of the clergy in the public life of the nation despite the allegations of mass psychological torture: Was it not the Catholic clergy's devotion and abilities that had built and maintained the entire system of public education and social welfare since colonial times?

Speaking to a special session of the Institut Canadien des Affaires Publiques in 1961 devoted to the theme of the relations of church and state in Quebec, the Université Laval sociologist Fernand Dumont proffered a reconstruction of Quebec history that sought to account for the religious unanimity of Quebec and the dominant role played by the Catholic clergy in public life. Dumont adduced the fact of the British Conquest to explain the absence and weakness of secular French-speaking elites, and argued that this was what had allowed the Church to assume "all the essential social tasks." In a society dominated by British foreigners, political allegiance was at a premium, and the Catholic Church gained new privileges and institutional control as a reward for its loyalty, but at the cost of weakening its ties with the popular struggle for liberty pursued by secular, liberal-democratic politicians who after 1800 competed with the clergy for social and cultural authority. Central to Dumont's thesis was the belief that religious unanimity was not the thread holding Quebec's history together: indeed, it was only at the end of the nineteenth century that the Catholic clergy imposed this hegemony. The persistence of clerical power into the mid–twentieth century was again a product of Quebec's "exceptionalism," the argument being that, with French Canada having preserved many attributes of being a "folk society," the clergy were able to exercise leadership by linking Catholic belief with those magical practices and beliefs that characterized backward, rural people.[65]

In one sense, Dumont's interpretation of Quebec history was unoriginal, marrying the negative views of the British Conquest propagated by the Université de Montréal historians Guy Frégault, Michel Brunet, and

Maurice Séguin to the critical view of the Church's cozy relationship with the British colonial authorities advanced by his Université Laval colleague, Marcel Trudel.[66] What was significant about Dumont's intervention, however, was that he was a Catholic believer and budding modernist lay theologian interested in identifying a secure basis for Christian faith in the modern world.[67] In exhorting Catholics to elaborate a purified doctrine and spirituality that could speak to modern secularist ideologies, unbelief, and the existential alienation which he believed modern human beings experienced in their daily lives, Dumont advanced a clear rationale as to *why* the clergy should be excluded from social functions like education and social welfare. Their legitimate task, he argued, was confined to properly spiritual and liturgical duties;[68] for them to assume wider social authority, not only hurt the spiritual vitality of Catholic religion, but perpetuated the servitude, "alienation," and "abnormality" that had plagued Quebec society since 1760, namely, its domination by a foreign government and the consequent weakness of lay, middle-class political and social elites. As Quebec industrialized and modernized its social fabric, the values of the "folk society" – in which "religion," as coextensive with "nature," occupied a wide scope of human endeavour – were rapidly disappearing. Although in Dumont's estimation the clergy *had* performed a vital social task, their services, except in the areas encompassed by a much narrower, entirely spiritual, and private definition of "religion," were no longer required in a modern, rational society where the state was now ready to assume its "proper" function. The clergy must "disengage" from their public functions in education and social welfare and cede their social and cultural authority to lay elites.

The prominence of a group of younger, professional historians in the MLLF[69] ensured that the historical dynamic which made the Conquest the central causal factor in a power vacuum in which the Catholic Church exercised abnormal – read illegitimate – "state" responsiblities to remedy the absence of both lay elites and a government controlled by French Canadians gained a certain currency in the early years of the Quiet Revolution. In a brief to the Parent Commission, the Association des Professeurs de l'Université de Montréal rejected the conservative argument that, from the earliest times, the Church had occupied the entire field of public education. While absolving the clergy from a Machiavellian quest for power, the professors stated that, in the area of schooling, "the Church had assumed responsibilities that were too heavy," and they traced this to the absence of a "French-Canadian bourgeoisie that was powerful enough to effectively direct the national collectivity."[70] For its part, the greatest difficulty afflicting the cause of education in Quebec, stated the Fédération des Travailleurs du Quebec, was "the absence of the state and the remedial presence of the clergy,"[71] a view echoed by Bertrand Rioux, who declared that "if clericalism exists in our society, it is powerfully assisted by the lack of energy of the temporal power."[72] Following this logic, as soon as the state was able to modernize and assume its responsibilities, the inevitable corollary was the withdrawal of the Church and clergy from the public life of the national community.

That this view of history propounded by the MLLF and a number of modernist Catholics had gained hold over an influential minority by the early 1960s was evident from the responses of more conservative Catholic elements who took great pains to offer a systematic refutation. Lorenzo Paré, the editor of the Quebec City Catholic daily *L'Action*, accused historians like Trudel of peddling secularist and Marxist propaganda under the cloak of dialogue and debate. The history presented by Trudel and his colleagues, Paré observed, was simply a brand of dialectical materialism, ascribing the religious origins of an entire people to the pressures of the economic and social environment, and thus dethroning the Church from its stature of leading the "resistance of a conquered people" to "the paid servitude of Religion as an instrument of Power."[73] As the periodical review *Tradition et Progrès* argued in its brief to the Parent Commission in 1962, the whole notion of the Church having served a "remedial" function in Quebec society was bunk. The clergy possessed the same right as secular elites to perform educational tasks, as Catholic doctrine assigned an explicit teaching function to the Church, which it would have exercised no matter what social arrangements prevailed in post-Conquest Quebec.[74]

In an important pastoral address on education delivered just after the founding of the MLLF in 1961, Cardinal Léger approved the aspirations of the laity who aspired to a greater role in the educational system, even in private institutions like the classical colleges where religious orders had traditionally held pride of place. However, Léger roundly rebuked the secularizers in offering an alternative theory to explain the pre-eminence of the Church in education. Confessionality and the presence of the clergy, Léger stated, was a matter of democratic consensus and public need, not of collusive dealings with the British occupying power. Confessional public schools, in his estimation, "had arisen spontaneously out of the needs of our society. History demonstrates abundantly that the initiative of our clergy largely contributed to the flowering of the intellectual life of our people." At the centre of Léger's interpretation lay a darker view of the insufficiency of lay elites. It was not that they were oppressed by an alliance of the occupying power and the clergy; it was that they were improvident and uncaring of the people, obsessed only with achieving material prosperity, utterly repudiating the life of the mind. Thus, it fell to the Catholic clergy to create, literally from nothing, French civilization in North America.[75] Quite simply, Léger regarded the "secular" interpretation of Quebec's history as "an opportunistic anticlericalism" which lacked the courage of its more politicized European counterparts. By falsely blaming the clergy for denying laypeople a legitimate scope of activity, and by denigrating everything that had been done by the clergy, groups like the MLLF raised a red herring by which they hoped subtly to deny to the Church any right of intervention in social life. The new secularists, Léger charged, thus sought to "deliberately cut all ties with the traditions of the past. Instead of using what was good in the institutions that they found already there, they prefer to destroy everything to begin from ground zero. And this prodigious leap backward is what they call progress!"[76]

No less a figure than Paul Gérin-Lajoie, the minister of youth and the strongest voice in the Liberal cabinet lobbying for greater state authority in educational matters, sought to stem the secularist critique by reaffirming the faith of the government in the educational competence of Quebec's religious teaching orders.[77] However, it fell to the economist François-Albert Angers, the director of the École des Hautes Études Commerciales at the Université de Montréal, to offer a systematic repudiation of the secularist psychological and historical assessments of the presence of the clergy. In a series of articles published shortly after the celebrated Institut Canadien des Affaires Publiques meeting in 1961, Angers decried the hypocrisy of social scientists like Lussier and Dumont, who "began by praising the clergy, and draw us a list of the services that they had rendered in the past ... then declare that we no longer have any need of these services in the future. And thus begins the theory of disengagement. It was only to fill a vacuum, so it is said, that the Church so actively sought to fulfill a role in education. Then, they tip their caps to the 'magnificent effort'! It is immediately followed by the kick in the ass: 'Now laypeople can do the job.'"[78] In ridiculing these pretensions, he took dead aim at what he considered the core of the new secularism, namely, the view that the Catholic clergy could be eliminated from public education because there was an unbridgeable opposition between "a religious civilization and a profane one," which meant that "clergy and laity would each have their little domain in the cultural life of the nation,"[79] and that, in teaching, it was possible to disentangle what was religious and belonged to the Church, and what was secular and was the purview of the state.[80]

Angers asserted that, while clerical exclusivism was certainly unjustified, it was immature to critique the clergy for having had the intelligence and foresight to establish a network of educational institutions, or to blame them for retarding the cultural progress of the nation. This was simply falling into a sectarian, equally reprehensible lay exclusivism. Indeed, throughout history the clergy had placed themselves at the service of the people in accomplishing a task that was legitimate to the Christian ministry: the teaching of a humanism inspired by Christian faith, which lay at the basis of Christian civilization itself.[81] It would be far better for Quebec, stated Angers, if useless squabbling could be avoided, if people simply realized that clergy and laity were not separate castes, but individuals who originated in the same society and had similar aspirations.[82] More tellingly, clerical vows were not synonymous with repressed sexuality leading to pedagogical incompetence. Angers forcefully concluded by stating that, given equal talent, the Catholic clergy had an advantage over the laity because of their "total devotion to the task of education," free of family worries. "In the higher interests of the children of the nation," queried Angers, "can we really ask the Church to withdraw from the sphere of education?"[83]

The "theory of disengagement" sponsored by the MLLF and its modernist sympathizers remained a minority voice during the early years of the Quiet Revolution. However, what gave credence to the view that the clergy should withdraw from a task that was not properly theirs and so enable the secular state and lay elites to accomplish their legitimate tasks of fostering national culture was a rising tide of public awareness over the status of the French language in Quebec. Thus, the removal of the clergy became suddenly synonymous with the reorganization of the entire educational system around language differences – as a function of different French and English cultures – rather than around the older confessional religious divide between Catholics and Protestants. This link between secularism and language was astutely observed in 1963 by the Radio-Canada journalist Judith Jasmin, who emphasized in a 1963 broadcast that "promotion of the laity and salvation of the language are connected."[84] The secularist vision of history promoted by the MLLF and its sympathizers, which ended with the confining of the clergy to purely spiritual functions by the newly-empowered lay elites and a state intent on asserting its authority, thus provided the key connection between the restructuring of public education and the project of an independent Quebec.

Writing in 1962, Marcel Rioux, one of the leading spokesmen of the MLLF and a member of the recently formed Rassemblement pour l'Indépendance Nationale (RIN), drew an explicit link between a secular, public system of schools and the political project of an independent Quebec. Confessional education, he declared, was a vestige of a nineteenth-century age of "clerico-bourgeois" dominance, and was an obstacle to Quebec's ambitions to become a modern "global society," rather than a "sub-society" of Anglo-Saxon North America. Like other modern societies, Quebec was subject to the forces of individualization and secularization, and could therefore not rely in the future upon religion as a principle of social integration. Rioux forcefully argued that the school system must become a centripetal force that would provide unity for the national community, but only if language displaced religion as the basis of schooling. "It is no longer a question," Rioux stated, "of whether unbelievers should be dispensed from the clerical indoctrination of their children, or whether

Catholics can teach catechism all day long, but it is first and foremost a question of building a community where we can all live and work, one which will overcome the historical backwardness it has lived in for too many years."[85]

That same year, Paul Lacoste, a member of the law faculty at the Université de Montréal and sympathetic to the MLLF, advanced a plan for restructuring public education. Arguing from the premise that social peace was impossible if the "neutral school was to be confined to a marginal sub-sector, a kind of educational ghetto," Lacoste broached the idea that, henceforth, the cultural line of division in the Department of Public Instruction should be secular, and codified specifically by a division between French and English language committees. To avoid religious bickering, he favoured the idea of subdividing each language committee along confessional lines, with Catholic and Protestant subcommittees having full jurisdiction over religious instruction and the teaching of subjects such as history, philosophy, and literature, which touched upon religious values.[86] The Lacoste plan was eagerly endorsed by the MLLF[87] because the plan in effect substituted a positive principle of social coherence – membership in a language community – for the negative definition of "religious dissident," which in no way would change Quebec's cultural identity as a Catholic society. By making the secular principle of language the central organizing dynamic, with a secondary consideration given to religious differences, Lacoste postulated not only a radical alteration of the social imperatives of education – with language, not religion, acting as the basis of a modern, humanistic curriculum – but explicitly linked language to the continued survival and progress of the French-Canadian national collectivity.[88] To the delight of many within the MLLF, Lacoste provided a formula which dictated that, henceforth, public institutions like education would be firmly secular in their structure and composition, and which resolutely asserted the possibility of a national community in which the word "French" was no longer a synonym of "Catholic."

Implicit in the Lacoste plan of education reform was the belief that in a modern society like Quebec, religion, which was ultimately a function of private belief, was a source of divisiveness and fragmentation, rather than of social or national unity. Speaking before the Parent Commission in 1962, former teacher Georges Neray argued that "the confessional system works a profound division among tomorrow's citizens." While it might still be claimed that the Catholic element formed the majority in the francophone community, true democracy meant finding a principle of convergence, which he located in "the elements of French language and culture." Quebec should follow the example of the new state of Israel, Neray explained, by compelling all immigrants to speak a common national language.[89]

What ultimately lent credence to the arguments of the MLLF was that they identified the French language as the sole defining feature of French-Canadian social cohesion at a time when public awareness of linguistic questions had been heightened by the revelations of Frère Untel on the deficiencies of French language teaching and by the publication in 1961 of Marcel Chaput's *Pourquoi je suis séparatiste.* Chaput, a research scientist in the federal ministry of national defence, urgently proclaimed the necessity of a "new separatism, the political sovereignty of Quebec," to protect French language and culture from the inroads of bilingualism. For Chaput, linguistic colonialism was the obverse of the political colonialism that kept Quebec in a subordinate status to Canada. Thus, it was intolerable that in Quebec, English should be the language of work and public communication, while French was merely expressive of the private values of "family" and "folklore." Like Frère Untel, he pointed to the pedagogical failings of the Catholic Commmittee of Public Instruction, which had recently decided to give greater place to the study of English in the school curriculum.[90] Thus, as André Langevin concluded, the fundamental issue underlying the education debate was the immediate separation of language from religious considerations. Ethnic survival depended upon whether "French culture, of which we proclaim ourselves the heirs, will become for us a vital, rich reality, or will it continue to be a sort of indescribable magma which blends messianism with religion and anglicization with corruption."[91]

In particular, some nationalists inveighed against the confessional principle as being both the vehicle for biligualism and the assimilation of non-Catholic immigrants into the English-speaking community. As Thérèse Dumouchel noted in 1961, there were over 5,000 French-speaking Jews in the city of Montreal who had the right to be educated in French, but who could not be accommodated in the prevailing confessional structures.[92] The need to assert the priority of French as the key to achieving national independence was the bridge between the secularists of the MLLF and more conservative Catholic nationalists who wanted to preserve, through a reformed confessional education, the connection between religion, the French language, and national identity.[93] By 1963, both sides could agree that such an initiative would mean that even if the MLLF would not succeed in secularizing the schools, the confessional structure would henceforth depend upon the dynamic of the Quebec state to further French-Canadian culture. As eloquently stated by Paul Gérin-Lajoie during the debate over Bill 60, "Language is in many respects the image of the nation; the misery of the language translates all too frequently the mediocrity of thought and the poverty of culture. The situation that prevails among us ... is unworthy of a proud people and it is intolerable."[94]

"I OWE MY INTENSE PATRIOTISM TO THE NUNS WHO TAUGHT ME"[95]

One of the central imperatives of the Quiet Revolution that is unanimously cited by historians was the desire, stimulated by a rising secular nationalism, to assert and extend the authority of the Quebec state into a number of spheres hitherto dominated by religious groups or private interests. However, while moves like the nationalization of Hydro-Québec in 1962 orchestrated around the slogan "Maîtres chez nous" clearly enjoyed substantial public support, greater ambiguity attended the question of the restructuring of public education. What occurred during the public hearings of the Parent Commission and the elaboration of Bill 60 was not a straightforward, linear process in which the Church evacuated the educational field to be replaced by the state, or in which the social aims of education were rapidly transformed from religious to secular ones. Despite attempts to link the presence of the clergy in the schools to cultural backwardness, and confident assertions which anchored a modern social cohesion exclusively on the secular basis of the French language, the public debate on educational reform revealed that this ideal was hardly consensual in the French-Canadian community. What is surprising about the early 1960s is that if a consensus did exist, it continued to revolve around the necessity of articulating a harmonious synthesis between Catholicism, French culture, and national cohesion. While certainly prepared to scrape away clerical excesses from public schooling and state institutions, reformers did not envision a public realm in which Catholicism was totally eviscerated. Rather, they sought to elaborate a new, pluralistic, civic culture in which the Catholic Church was not simply relegated to the private realm, but would recommit its considerable human and cultural resources to a renewed partnership with the Quebec state and nation.

From its inception, the demand of the MLLF for non-confessional schools provoked an outpouring of public protest from Quebec Catholics who discerned that behind the assertion of democratic rights, equal treatment for minorities, and pluralistic coexistence of all creeds, there lurked a darker, and more wide-ranging design for the imposition of a single, neutral system of public schools on the children of Catholic believers. The tenor and persistence of this reponse was such that it compelled attention from Liberal politicians who were worried about the consequences of injecting religious controversy into school reform. Although rebuked as conspiratorial and reactionary fundamentalism by commentators like André Laurendeau, who was sympathetic to certain aims of the MLLF,[96] this conservative Catholic response actually established, from a very early stage, the persistence of confessionality in a modern educational system, ensuring that the plans of secularists like Lacoste and Rioux to elaborate non-religious values around which a new national consciousness would cohere could not be realized during the Quiet Revolution.

Conservative Catholics were direct and unvarnished in their reaction to the MLLF's plan for a system of non-confessional public schools. "An evil wind must be blowing over our province," wrote one anguished mother, "for anyone to want to take God away from little children."[97] "LET NO ONE BE FOOLED," trumpeted the Comité Canadien de Recherches Sociales, which linked the MLLF to a wide-ranging and insidious Marxist conspiracy. "It is the secular school that is responsible for the de-Christianization of France."[98] Aware that the democratic ideals of freedom of conscience and civil equality for minorities had considerable resonance among Quebec Catholics, conservative commentators constantly reminded their readers that the very existence of non-confessional schools was an entering wedge for anticlerical and atheist proselytizing, and thus an attack on the very principle of a public confessional system, indeed, on religion itself. Under the circumstances, Catholic conservatives maintained that the public rhetoric of the MLLF about pluralism and coexistence was simply hypocrisy, window-dressing for the eventual total secularization of Quebec's schools and society. As one Catholic weekly put the matter, an authentic Catholicism could not "even under the pretext of respect for democracy" make any accommodation that would tend to "decapitate it."[99]

What clearly worried these Catholics was that the very existence of state-subsidized non-confessional schools would, over time, ineluctably weaken the Catholic school system, and thus dissolve the partnership between church and state. The MLLF, despite its small membership, posed a serious threat, because its secularist ideals challenged the "fundamental duty" of the state, which was to allow the Church to accomplish its task of instructing and teaching.[100] Thus, the lay teachers at a Catholic school in Montreal reminded parents that "For a Catholic, confessionality is obligatory." Flowing from this axiom, "the very principle of the religiously-neutral school is inadmissible because in matters of education, religious neutrality is impossible. We believe that it is illogical to impose an education that goes against the religious convictions of the people. While we do not wish to force anyone to share our beliefs, and we respect theirs ... no one has the right to subject us to their ideas on religious matters."[101] Bitterly castigating the secularist intellectuals of the MLLF, one anonymous correspondent declared that "*we* will pay the price for *their* breadth of spirit. *Our* children, and not theirs, will be forced to attend their *godless* school. ... *The agnostics are at this moment preparing to pull the Trojan horse trick on us.*"[102]

Such views might be dismissed as the cavillings of a few arch-reactionary Catholic fundamentalists who stood in the way of progress, but a series of events that transpired between the launch of the MLLF in early April 1961 and the convocation speech of Premier Jean Lesage at the Université de

Montréal indicated that while the spirit of tolerance for religious dissidents was certainly strong among French-Canadian Catholics, so was resistance to any suggestion that confessionality or the alliance of church and state in key public insitutions might be dismantled. Commenting on the founding congress of the MLLF, Gérard Filion, the powerful editor of *Le Devoir*, aptly entitled his editorial "La rage de démolir." In it, he accused the secularists of displaying a "totalitarian spirit" which sought to demolish all school structures and impose a unitary, completely secular school system. Filion could not be accused of being a reactionary: indeed, throughout the 1950s, he had been one of Maurice Duplessis's most vocal opponents and a consistent advocate of a stronger and more activist state. However, in his estimation, the MLLF was simply sowing confusion and social conflict by positing the fallacy that, because the state was secular in nature, the logical consequence had to be the creation of a fundamentally secular system of public schools for all Quebec schoolchildren.[103] Gaston Dugas, Filion's counterpart at *La Presse*, hoped for reforms that would accommodate the legitimate demands of French-speaking non-Catholics, but he shared the ultra-conservative Catholic suspicion that the MLLF's proclamation of minority rights was but a "trampoline" permitting a jump to the next stage: total secularization of the entire school system. This, Dugas stated, was a project set afoot by "so-called avant-garde intellectuals who are flying in the face of reason by attempting to establish in Quebec a non-confessional public system that has been tried elsewhere and that has only created endless quarrelling and confusion."[104] Such sentiments were evinced by even so liberal a voice as that of Aurèle Kolnai, a former professor at the École des Sciences Sociales of Université Laval, and a colleague of Father Georges-Henri Lévesque who in the early 1950s had done much to articulate a perspective that was critical of the dominant clerical orthodoxy. In the pages of *Cité libre*, Kolnai voiced his scepticism of any "fraternal and enthusiastic" coalition between Catholic reformers and "unbelieving activists." The latter, he believed, were simply concealing their true intentions behind the shibboleth of freedom of conscience. What the secularists of the MLLF hoped for, Kolnai categorically stated, was the opportunity to "oppress the Church and persecute the faith through the instruments of government authority and social pressure organized from above."[105]

Given the apparent massive commitment among Quebec's French-speaking elites to secular values and state-centred reform in the early 1960s, the shared opposition to the ideals of the MLLF by both conservative and liberal Catholics needs to be accounted for. For reformers like Filion, fidelity to Catholic doctrine on education was at least as important as extending the authority of the state. Filion was a veteran of the vibrant Catholic social movements of the 1930s and 1940s, and his editorial credo stressed faithfulness to the social doctrines of the Church, in which modern society, far from being dominated by an all-powerful state, rested upon the bases of family and professional organizations such as trade unions, agricultural cooperatives, and business associations which harnessed private initiative to higher social purposes. In educational matters, he certainly promoted improvement, but did so while firmly adhering to the "traditional doctrine" that parents, church, and state each participated in education through a system of interlocking rights and duties. All social reform and state intervention, Filion maintained, must in the final analysis shore up the French-Canadian national family virtues of "faith, fecundity, and authority,"[106] which alone could ensure individual happiness and social peace. Indeed, these pronouncements transcended party divisions and spoke to the concerns of a group of Quebecers who stood in resolute opposition to the new secularist definition of a cohesive national collectivity organized around the state as the guardian and promoter of language, and in which Catholic faith was relegated to the private sphere and totally severed from the nation's culture. "We must," declared Maurice Allard, a professor of constitutional law at the Université de Sherbrooke, "take account of our Christian conception of life and avoid making of our history a *tabula rasa* ... especially since our heritage has bequeathed us a living faith and highly praiseworthy national virtues."[107]

The historiography of the Quiet Revolution has insisted on the fact that, throughout the late 1940s and 1950s, groups of liberal Catholics that were clustered around *Cité libre* and the Faculté des Sciences Sociales at Université Laval carried out a concerted campaign to uncouple Catholic faith and Quebec nationalism, believing that a purified and modernized Catholicism could not serve as the vehicle for reactionary and obsolete nationalist convictions.[108] For the MLLF and its sympathizers, French-Canadian society was no longer religiously-homogeneous, and therefore, to give pride of place to the modern values of freedom of conscience and pluralism, national values must flow from entirely secular sources, with the state being the preferred choice, given its role as interpreter of the interests of the nation. However, the context of the debate on public education during the early 1960s revealed, among many Quebec Catholics, the coexistence of two attitudes: a desire to make some accommodation to the educational rights of even unbelieving religious dissenters, balanced by a positive reluctance to divorce Catholicism from language and nationality. As eloquently stated by François-Albert Angers, "in a world that is largely de-Christianized, our Catholic faith, made more dynamic, is the irreplaceable key by which we can distinguish ourselves as a people and as a civilization."[109]

Such views rested upon a sophisticated theory of the relationship of religion, culture, state and nation which ultimately ran counter to both the new secularist vision of Quebec enunciated by the MLLF and the existential modernist religion promoted by social scientists like Fernand Dumont.

The symbiotic relationship between Catholicism and the French-Canadian nation was, in the post-war period, given its most systematic articulation by Esdras Minville in a work entitled *Le Citoyen canadien-français*, published in 1946. In this treatise, Minville drew careful and precise distinctions between the concepts of state and nation, based upon a vision of the dual allegiances French Canadians owed both to Canada and to their cultural homeland, Quebec. For him, the state was the political expression of human society, which frequently had to transcend a variety of heterogeneous national elements. On the other hand, the nation was a sociological entity, incarnating all elements of culture, family, religion, and language, which together contributed to form the personality of the individual.[110] Minville firmly eschewed any racialist fusion of Catholicism and French culture, arguing that there was no essential link between Catholicism and the national qualities of Frenchness. However, in the Quebec context, such an identity did exist and was a matter of historical contingency – the fact that the French-Canadian community displayed a homogeneous religious identity – and, consequently, it was possible for him to argue from Quebec's own history that "Catholic tradition, Christian humanism, must be considered as one of the guiding values of his [the French Canadian's] national heritage."[111] Given this religious homogeneity, Minville taught that public education and the social action of trade unions, cooperatives, and patriotic societies must be oriented to building a civic order that was in conformity with Catholic social doctrines. Thus, while he rejected any a priori identification of state and nation, Minville believed that if the identity of Catholic and citizen could be maintained, it would be possible, in Quebec, to fuse the political and sociological orders represented by state and nation into a single entity, the "patrie," which would increasingly pursue an autonomous course from the parallel Anglo-Saxon "nation," and be founded upon a Catholic social order and sustained by a common religious faith to which the vast majority belonged.[112]

At first glance, it might well appear that, in light of the pluralist claims and the new linguistic basis for Quebec nationalism advanced by the MLLF and its sympathizers, Minville's vision of a national cohesion anchored upon a fusion of Catholicism and French culture could be simply written off as traditionalist and hopelessly obsolete in light of the social realities of modern urban Quebec. However, to those living in the early 1960s, the grounds for divorce between faith, culture, and nationalism did not appear quite so clear-cut. Indeed, the most compelling consideration was the fact that the French-Canadian community in 1961 was much as it was when Minville wrote his treatise on civic action at the end of World War II: overwhelmingly Catholic. However, Catholic spokesmen recognized that, given the pace of social change, some reworking of the equation between faith and the promotion of French civilization was necessary. The Jesuit

Raymond Bourgault recognized that "the collusion between a unanimous faith and a unilingual national state is probably an accident of history and cannot be regarded as an eternal norm." But Bourgault cast any reform in terms of the updating or modernization of Catholic tradition, not an entire evisceration of the past.[113] Claude Ryan, the national secretary of Action Catholique Canadienne – and no supporter of easy equations of Catholicism and nationalism – disputed the logic of the secularists that the mere existence of minorities dictated the need for a complete overhaul of public institutions and a takeover by the state. Ryan maintained in a public forum held in April 1961 that the MLLF had greatly exaggerated the problem of the existence of minorities, and had signally failed to prove that there were large numbers of French-speaking unbelievers and Protestants who needed non-confessional schools.[114] Speaking in 1962, Yves Prévost, the former provincial secretary in the Union Nationale administration who can best be described as a sober and responsible conservative, called for a spirit of accommodation and dialogue between the majority and the new minorities revealed by the new pluralist climate. However, he reiterated Minville's dictum that in terms of civic identity, the French-Canadian citizen was above all "a religious being." Quebec society, Prévost told his audience of clerics and educators, was religiously-neutral from a constitutional point of view, but was "bathed in the personal religion of the immense majority of its members," who shared "a very vibrant and living Catholicism"[115] as the key element of their civic culture.

However, it should be understood that the notion of Catholicism advanced by Prévost and other conservatives differed significantly from that formulated by modernists like Fernand Dumont. Social scientists like Dumont, heavily influenced by an existential philosophy which situated faith in terms of a perpetual personal oscillation between the supposed tension in modern humans between uneasy conviction and heroic unbelief, looked with either amused contempt or frank dismay upon the "sociological religion" framed by the clerical authority, memorized prayers, liturgical kitsch, and supposed "folk" beliefs of "traditional" Catholicism. What they hoped to substitute was a new "modernist" spirituality that was entirely severed from past traditions and which would properly express the new community spirit of a modern urban culture. It would be the religious counterpart of a new republican civic culture where national values were expressed in an activist state. Catholic conservatives, however, refused to anchor religious truth in a moment of existential crisis, believing that faith was acquired in a family context which linked young people to the achievements of past generations, and especially to the signal extension of Catholicism to which French Canada as a nation had contributed. "The young French Canadian," observed La Fierté Française, "who has from an early age learned about religion from attending mass in his neighbourhood church, has slowly imbibed the pride of a parish, the history of its statues, the tradition of its pious works ... we believe that this young child will better understand the religious fact and will actively incorporate it in his daily life."[116] French Canada's fundamental national value was, in fact, its 400 years of history in which Catholic humanism had provided the nourishment for the implantation and growth of French language and culture. Because of this very close historical association, it would be no simple matter to disjoin the two elements of Catholicism and Frenchness. As the conservative weekly *Notre Temps* warned, "Remove one of the main parts of the mechanism from the French Canadian and the whole thing will fall apart! The French-speaking Canadian who ceases to be Catholic ... will soon cease to be French-speaking, as he will cease to adhere to a culture that draws heavily upon his Catholicism."[117]

So compelling and mainstream was this religiously-focused interpretation of cultural nationality in the early 1960s that voices promoting the new secular nationalism found themselves in a decided minority during the public hearings held by the Parent Commission. While the need for a reformed and restructured system of public education was unanimously admitted – with particular emphasis given to harnessing the sciences and formulating a new "humanism" which harmonized Christian doctrine and the culture of scientific discovery – powerful religious and nationalist associations made the plea that any changes should preserve the continuity with "our heritages that have marked the origin of our people and which enabled us to avoid assimilation by Anglo-Saxons."[118] The plural "heritages" referred, most specifically, to the synthesis of Catholicism and French culture in a Christian humanism that these Catholic nationalists maintained must continue to undergird the educational system. Arguing that Quebec faced a clear choice between "Christian social structures and those inspired by materialism," the Cercle d'Information Nationale pleaded vociferously for the maintenance of the confessional system, arguing that there was no need to overthrow the entire educational structure simply to placate a "noisy" group that comprised less than one per cent of the French-Canadian people.[119]

Clearly, many of these movements sympathized with the demand of the new nationalists that Quebec should be a unilingually French state, but they emphatically rejected any proposal that would see confessionality displaced in favour of the secular principle of language as an organizing dynamic. As stated by La Fierté Française, "the religious fact in French Canada exists. The French-Canadian community feels itself in possession of religious truth, which it shares with other communities ... but which is integrated into our French cultural life."[120] The idea of a national mission for French Canada, one grounded in Catholicism, remained a powerful emotional touchstone for groups preoccupied with the fate of the French language and culture in Anglo-Saxon North America. "We believe," stated the Sections Classiques de la Commission des Écoles Catholiques de Mon-·tréal, "in the 'French fact in America' and we hold the firm conviction that the French-Canadian majority is called ... to play the role of ferment by maintaining its Christian and Roman Catholic spirit ... which gives pride of place to 'the primacy of the spiritual.'"[121]

What gave this tight synthesis of Catholicism and French-Canadian cultural identity such force during the debates over public education was the fact that religion also anchored a vision of the relationship between society and state, forged in the interwar period, that had a particular resonance among Quebec's Catholic conservatives. Any project of reform, declared François-Albert Angers in 1963, must either be unanimous or represent a compromise unanimously accepted. In so weighty a matter as education, which was intimately linked to the continuity of national traditions, the government had an obligation to consult the "*pays réel*," by which he meant the opinion of the religious bodies and private interests "which incarnate the thought of the nation."[122] Angers's evocation of Charles Maurras's distinction between "*pays réel*" (the social nation) and "*pays légitime*" (the political nation) in this context is of particular significance. Like many other Quebec politicians, journalists, and educators, Angers had been raised in an environment where the principal intellectual current was a system of social values supplied by the turn-of-the-century French Right. However, where Maurras and his supporters had used the dichotomy to voice their dissent from a republican government from which they believed traditional Catholicism was excluded, these ideas were reworked in the context of Quebec to advance a particular interpretation of cultural dualism and the workings of the federal system, in which the primary allegiance must be given to the French-Canadian "nation" as it contained the primary cultural values of the human person.[123]

A second set of meanings for the terms "*pays réel*" and "*pays légitime*" gained particular credence in Quebec after World War II, when the notion served as the intellectual expression of a "liberal" society governed by Maurice Duplessis's Union Nationale. Such political notions rested upon the principle of a small state, devoted to a modernizing programme of economic progress and prosperity carried out by private business interests. Duplessis's government derived much of its social authority from its resistance to a state-centred system of modern social welfare, represented by a centralizing federal authority. In elaborating this model of a liberal society, Duplessis had decentralized political power to rural and small-town elites, and resolutely defended the management of much of public education and social welfare by private religious bodies.[124] In this case, the Maurrassian dichotomy firmly fixed the boundaries and scope of state activity. To the state it assigned responsibility for creating a legal framework and protection that would permit religious belief and endeavour to set the criteria and operate the institutional structure in which the culture of the French-Canadian "nation" would flourish and expand. When linked to Catholic doctrine which carefully assigned responsibility in education to family, state, and church, this social and cultural conservatism underpinned a concept of "organic" democracy, a notion formulated by Yves Prévost, who posited a careful distinction between the public realm, over which "the State has the right of supervision, and the private," a much broader terrain which he divided into "personal, familial, and social." Here, human freedom and intimacy were preserved through the work of various intermediate bodies, such as churches and associations, which acted to govern a "semi-public" order that served to protect the individual from encroachments from the state.[125]

In this view, if the state was called upon to play a larger role in a modern society, its activity, particularly in any realm of culture that involved the human person, should necessarily be circumscribed as long as the qualities that pertained to the "nation" continued to be assigned to the private or semi-public realms, where the Church enjoyed pre-eminence over the government. As stated by the Ligues du Sacré-Coeur in 1962, "We did not always have a State created in our image and likeness. But the Church always accompanied us, often even presiding over the destiny of our nation. She has been a part of our history; she has structured our life as a community. She has deserved well of the nation. We wish to continue to associate the Church to our future as a nation."[126] For the Commission Universitaire de la Compagnie de Jésus, all educational reform thus had to proceed from "a just conception of the role of the State in the Nation," and from an affirmation of the "continuity of the cultural tradition of French Canada."[127] The confessional character of the educational system – confirmed by the independence of the Department of Public Instruction from the inroads of "secular" influences, the latter symbolized by direct management by elected politicians – was an expression of "the thinking of the Quebec nation,"[128] whose chief cultural imperative was to assert, through the symbiotic union of Catholicism and the values of French humanism, the possibility of a Catholic social order which alone could secure Quebec's autonomy in the face of a North American civilization "of Protestant character."[129]

These cultural norms, the very definition of Frenchness, were best preserved through an educational system in which the state did not exercise a monopoly, one in which the initiative and achievements of the Church and religious orders were properly recognized and fostered. Central to this conservative argument was the belief that the fundamental social and cultural values of the "nation" did not lie in the political realm, but in a collaboration of "parents, teachers, the Church, and universities." The elected legislature, according to this view, was incompetent to "analyse and make clear that which defines the culture of a Nation."[130] While the state could certainly exercise its responsibilities to rationalize and control the educational system, it must do so in the context of scrupulous respect for private rights, and must not hamper the action of the intermediate bodies which performed an essential public service.[131] For in the final analysis, human values were forged in the crucible of the school, it being an expression of the wishes of the family and the Church rather than those of the modern state, the latter's function being not to encompass but only to represent the nation.[132]

Those who shared this outlook thus believed that the restructuring of education could not be handled in the same way as the nationalization of hydroelectricity, because the state was not the sole competent authority in the educational realm. Catholic doctrine firmly established that education was a sphere in which three entities shared jurisdiction: Church, Family, and State. Consequently, no one party could simply act without taking into account the rights of the other two, a consideration that meant that any reform must be the fruit of a friendly understanding between all three.[133] Indeed, many Catholics at this time adhered to the view, best expressed by the Dominican Father Antonio Lamarche in the pages of *Le Devoir*, that the rights of the state to serve the common good should not be exaggerated to the point of "concluding that education is simply a national function, a public service in which the State has a monopoly." In the realm of education, the family had prior rights over both church and state, because of its natural rights flowing from procreation and the fact that the family was the primary element constituting civil society. The rights of the Catholic Church to teach religion in schools extended to all of those baptized in that faith, and while the state must act to assist "unbelieving minorities," Lamarche concluded that it was "simply inconceivable that in a healthy democracy, a tiny minority should be permitted to impose its demands upon the vast majority."[134] Filion, soon to be appointed vice-chairman of Quebec's Royal Commission on Education, based his critique of those who sought the complete deconfessionalization of education on this Catholic definition of partnership between family, church, and state. He echoed Lamarche in stating that the school was an institution linked most directly to the family, rather than to the state, and must therefore incarnate the values and beliefs of Quebec's families, which were overwhelmingly Catholic. He warned his readers that if the MLLF moved from advocacy of minority rights towards "depriving parents of the democratic control of their schools and imposing a non-Christian education on people who do not want it, I fear that we will be fighting the preliminary skirmishes of a religious war of which our grandchildren will not see the end."[135]

Fears of a "religious war" over the question of secularizing Quebec's schools gained further credence soon after the founding convention of the MLLF. On 14 April 1961, Premier Lesage rose in the National Assembly to reveal that for several days he had been receiving letters from schoolchildren in St-Hyacinthe, plaintively protesting against a supposed government decision to remove crucifixes from their classrooms, and pleading that they might be allowed to keep learning their catechisms.[136] What is striking about the religio-political climate in Quebec at this time is that the premier not only angrily denounced these letters, but expended a good deal of effort to track down the culprits, who in the end, turned out to be the Soeurs de la Présentation, an order teaching in a number of schools in the St-Hyacinthe area, some of whose members had apparently advised their young charges to write letters to the premier.[137] What this apparent tempest in a teapot revealed was the extreme aversion of the political classes of Quebec at this time towards any action that might make religion a focal point of division between left and right, especially when many believed in the necessity of a delicate readjustment of the relations of church and state. Daniel Johnson, a rising star of the opposition Union Nationale, twitted Lesage about the letters, marvelling at the premier's rage. Was Lesage, queried Johnson, really worried about the relations of church and state, or was he more concerned about the effect religious controversy might have within his own cabinet, already divided between "sincere liberals" and "ambitious and pushy leftists"?[138]

That there was some truth behind Johnson's public musings was indicated by the fact that a few days later Pierre Laporte, one of Lesage's chief media allies, openly accused Johnson of importing religious strife into politics by attempting to link one party (the Union Nationale) with the preservation of the Church, and the other (the Liberals), with anticlericalism. Laporte went further. He even implied that Johnson himself had put the nuns up to the letter-writing campaign, reminding his readers of the fact that the schools in question were all located in Bagot riding, represented by Daniel Johnson himself.[139] Again showing his concern, Lesage himself prudently sent his minister of transport, Gérard Cournoyer, one of the more conservative members of the government, to speak at the annual Congress of the Knights of Columbus. There, Cournoyer reassured these staunch Catholics about the true intentions of the Liberal government regarding the place of religion in the schools. "No power in the world," Cournoyer declared, "will come to take the crucifixes out of the schools."[140]

During May and June of 1961, it was apparent that the presence of the MLLF might actually make the question of religion in the schools the focal point of political division between left and right, a fissure that could only work to the detriment of the governing Liberal party, a heterogeneous collection of factions and personalities including conservative Catholics like Cournoyer and Émilien Lafrance, the minister of family and social welfare, and elements more sympathetic to the secularist agenda, like René Lévesque, the minister of natural resources. What the Liberals hoped to do was to move cautiously to restructure public education while, through the medium of a Royal Commission, keeping the question of confessionality out of politics. However, individual members of the Church hierarchy, conservative trade unions, and a number of publicists engaged in open sniping with the MLLF, and drew a hard-line position that no dialogue or compromise was possible between Catholics and proponents of religiously-neutral schools.[141] Even liberal spirits like Frère Untel drew back from the secularist implications of the MLLF's demands. Writing to Judith Jasmin, Untel stated that if the matter was simply that of establishing neutral schools, no one would quibble, because in a pluralist society, it was important to have a spectrum of institutions to accommodate various faiths. However, he warned, "if it is a question of setting up an association that demands systematic neutrality, you will understand why I cannot go along with it." What Untel objected to was that the MLLF failed to understand that freedom of religion was double-edged: "if one cannot impose religion, in the name of freedom, one also does not have the right to prevent its teaching in the schools."[142] The danger here for the government was that extreme statements by conservatives, because they appealed to Catholic doctrine, might easily be mistaken for the official position of the Church itself, and in the public mind this would place the Church and the State at loggerheads over the question of education.

It was precisely to defuse any hint of this conflict, both within his own party and with the Church hierarchy, that Lesage used the opportunity of a speech at the convocation of the Université de Montréal to proclaim decisively where his government stood on the relationship of church and state. French Canada, the premier stated, had always been characterized by religious pluralism which dictated harmony between religious confessions. This he pledged to continue, even in the case of unbelievers, who were entitled to full civic equality before the law. However, Lesage warned the secularists of the MLLF to expect no preferential treatment, by which he clearly meant the creation of a secular school system. Religious dissent, even unbelief, was entitled to toleration, but his government would not permit the imposition of minority beliefs on the majority. It would be a mistake, he stated, for secularists to infer that because, constitutionally, church and state in Quebec were separate and there existed freedom of religion, Quebec was not an "officially Christian state." "The State," he explained, "must seek the enlightenment of the Church, not to evade its responsibilities, but to become aware of them. The Quebec state seeks this illumination from the Catholic hierarchy, which is the spiritual guide for the vast majority of the citizens. It seeks and respects at the same time the counsel and experience of other religious confessions."[143]

Of particular significance here was the fact that Lesage proclaimed Quebec not only officially "Christian," but, by coupling the Catholic Church with "enlightenment," and other religious groups with "counsel and experience," he implicitly indicated that the Quebec state was also officially Catholic. Taking dead aim at the MLLF, he accused its members of trying to destroy religious harmony by dragging arcane intellectual debates out into the open. "Never," he concluded, "will the State of Quebec be an accomplice of the propagation of atheism, that sickness of the spirit, which we must treat with as much charity as justice, but not by giving any preferential treatment which would betray the vast majority of a people which feels in quiet possession of the truth."[144]

Although the final phrase of his address left the premier open to a good deal of ridicule and public vilification from the sympathizers of the MLLF,[145] the effect of his speech was to make a number of important considerations clear. First, there would be no unilateral, state-imposed solution in the realm of educational reform and, most reassuring to Catholics, no deconfessionalization accomplished by a religiously-neutral state. By reminding his audience, which included Mgr Parent, who was the chair-designate of the Royal Commission on Education, and a number of other clerics, about the historic partnership between the Quebec government and the Catholic Church, Lesage was clearly pledging his faith that, from the standpoint of the state, this cooperation in the crucial field of education would continue through a period of reform and transition.

To properly contextualize Lesage's intervention at this stage, it is necessary to juxtapose his speech against Cardinal Léger's pastoral address on education, delivered barely three weeks later. Léger presented, from the perspective of the Church hierarchy, what in fact was the obverse of Lesage's reassurances on behalf of the state. If the premier was prepared to limit government concessions to the spirit of secularism, then the Church, according to the cardinal, was more than prepared to engage movements like the MLLF in a spirit of frank dialogue with the new democratic and pluralist spirit of Quebec society. Léger began by reiterating the doctrinal triad of family, church, and state that must continue to regulate education, in which parents had the absolute right and duty to "transmit to their children the rich heritage of Christian faith."[146] Like Filion, he believed that the school belonged far more to the parents than to the state. Secondly, Léger firmly indicated that the Church could not dispense with the confessional school, and would not settle for a structure in which it would simply purvey an optional religious instruction.

However, Léger admitted that these historic verities and doctrines must now function in a new cultural context. "Our society," declared the cardinal, "no longer has the culturally-homogeneous character that would permit a quiet possession of the truth to be shared by all." Henceforth, Quebec Catholics would be called upon to recognize that the familiar benchmarks of the old social order had ruptured under the impact of industrial civilization. For Catholicism to accommodate itself to these cultural changes, the cardinal informed his audience, the key was to incorporate the "democratic spirit" that was so much a feature of modern life. It would be a serious mistake for Catholics to engage in blanket condemnations of these new elements that now comprised Quebec society. Despite occasional "malaise and incomprehension," Léger maintained, "we must welcome with breadth of vision the developments of our society, to examine our institutions with loyalty and with a great inner freedom, and to discriminate between those elements of our cultural heritage which are permanent and those which are transitory."[147]

The combined effect of these interventions by the heads of both the civil and spiritual realms was to immediately squelch any attempt by Catholic liberals to employ the supposed opposition between Roman Catholicism and freedom of religion to move public sympathy towards the dangerously appealing Lacoste Plan advocated by the MLLF. By evoking the language of democracy and making overtures to the spirit of pluralism, Cardinal Léger, in particular, now situated the Catholic project within the liberal definition of Quebec as multi-confessional, rather than within a conservative framework of religious unanimity. Multi-confessionality, despite its pluralism, continued to relate religious faith and the public realm, a formulation which appealed far more to liberal Catholic intellectuals than the outright secularism of Marcel Rioux and Jacques Godbout. As Father Georges-Henri Lévesque declared in 1962, it was incumbent upon unbelievers, if they wanted their own freedoms honoured, to practice the democracy that they preached, and to treat with greatest respect "the beliefs of the majority of their compatriots, which were also the convictions of their ancestors."[148]

In situating Catholicism within a new pluralist orbit, what, it can be asked, was Léger really conceding? In reality, not very much. As both he and Lesage knew, although it was experiencing the pressures of modernity, French-speaking Quebec was a society where religious diversity was rather moot. In this context, multi-confessionality meant, in fact, the continuance of the traditional partnership between the state and *one* preponderant church. However, the cardinal was well aware that education was the arena in which, henceforth, the relationship between Catholicism, civic purpose, and national cohesion would stand or fall. Though articulated with intellectual clarity and precision, the Church's social teachings on labour and corporatism had, since World War II, become a hotly contested terrain between "left" and "right" Catholics, as the former, after 1956, had targeted these teachings as crucial props of the Duplessis regime. In the field of education, however, only the MLLF, which at this point could be dismissed as a few Montreal intellectuals, actually contested the Church's presence. Léger and the Catholic hierarchy gambled on the hope that, by cooperating with state initiatives in educational reform, they would see Catholic religious values remain the sheet anchor of the nation at a time of perplexing cultural change. Of equal importance, educational reform would renew the partnership of church and state in delineating a new pluralist social order founded upon a religious dynamic, one in which the imperatives of confessionality were harmoniously reconciled with the new requirements of state and society.

"NO ONE HAS THE RIGHT TO BE AN AGNOSTIC"[149]

Throughout Quebec's debate on public education in the early 1960s, the language of democracy and that defining the values of pluralism pervaded the appeals of both the secularist MLLF and the refutations of its conservative Catholic opponents. Each side, however, used these concepts in a markedly different way. For the MLLF and its sympathizers, "democracy" meant first and foremost the equality of all citizens in the context of a completely secular system of schools and other public institutions, an equality that could only be guaranteed if the state was completely separate from the church. Such transformations would enable the state to act as the supreme guarantor of the pluralism of individual belief that must characterize a modern society. Only in this way could the state then accomplish its fundamental moral purpose of incarnating the public spirit of the nation. By contrast, for most Quebec Catholics, "democracy" meant the rule of the majority. While they supported civil toleration for non-Catholic and non-Protestant minorities, most Catholics defined such rights as being exercised in the context of a social order in which the mainstream Christian denominations, and Roman Catholicism in particular, enjoyed a special relationship as collaborators of the state in the public life of the nation. "Pluralism," in this perspective, had a particular meaning, one in which "unbelief" was clearly marginal to the mainstream of society, and certainly should not enjoy equality of treatment with religious belief. According to this view, the state was not simply a "neutral" arbiter of competing private religious differences, but acted positively to enlist and integrate the religious beliefs of citizens – which were elevated as key components of "national" culture – to the wider temporal common good. This, in the final analysis, still possessed a religious, rather than a purely secular, significance.

However, in the wake of Cardinal Léger's pastoral address, Catholic spokesmen, in asserting that religion still had an intimate connection with public life, had to express the link in terms of respect for freedom of conscience. Because they recognized pluralism as characteristic of the temporal order, they were logically compelled to recognize the state as the protector and arbitrator of religious freedom or "freedom of conscience," as possessing a key role in how these virtues were to be expressed in particular social and national contexts. This assigned to the state a wider competence than what it had enjoyed in the Quebec of Maurice Duplessis, where culture and education were the sphere of religious bodies, and rigidly separated from political considerations. In the context of the early 1960s, where the vast majority of Catholics worked assiduously to preserve the equation of "public" and "confessional" in the realm of education, the meaning and application of "confessionality" was subtly altered as the relationship between family, church, and nation was recast. Under the education reforms proposed by the Parent Commission and codified in Bill 60, the Quebec state displaced both family and church as the principal agent responsible for the teaching of religion, which enabled it to play the central role in dictating what was to be henceforth the nature, content, and function of religious education. Indeed, at the behest of a large segment of Catholic opinion, what occurred was the breaching of the principle of separation which had underwritten the old division between, on the one hand, the moral and cultural realm grouping family, religion, and national values, and on the other hand that of the political order. Responsibility for the moral and cultural sphere, while still a concern of the Roman Catholic Church, increasingly came within the purview of the state.

Writing in 1961, Maurice Blain, the president of the MLLF, celebrated the arrival in Quebec of "a new pluralism, much wider and more diverse, which has exploded not only our traditional humanism and social structures, but even the monolithic nature of our Catholicism."[150] He eloquently articulated a vision of what he called "laïcité," the principle of non-confessionality applied to all public institutions and to the very relationship of the state and its citizens. Central to this new order was the absolute neutrality of the state, achieved by elevating it above all religious distinctions and factions through a declaration that its only moral obligation in the face of religious belief was to be an umpire, fairly administering the rules of the game. These rules, for Blain, took the form of absolutes: "the freedom of the act of faith, and the civil liberty of religion." These, he maintained, would enshrine the civic equality of both Catholics and unbelievers, and would in future avoid any debilitating conflicts between church and state. Central to this vision was not only the separation of church and state, but more significantly in the Quebec context, the separation of Catholicism from the French-Canadian nation, and the consecration of the state to a secular mission: that of assuring that the nation's moral anchorage no longer rested upon religious values specific to Catholicism, but upon freedom of conscience as a moral absolute.[151]

While each church would conserve the right to teach its own particular version of the faith, Blain's pronouncement signalled the necessary privatization of the spiritual realm to secure social peace and the enlistment of civic energies behind a common commitment to freedom of conscience. The collaboration of state and churches might, according to this pluralist ideal, be desirable in certain social contexts, but it was not necessary to the moral character of the state,[152] which must remain studiously aloof from all religious considerations in order to serve all citizens equally and impartially.[153] Here was an order of priority which both decisively privileged the modern democratic state over powerful religious institutions and required the secularization or deconfessionalization of all public and semi-public institutions.[154] The state, unlike the churches, offered a more comprehensive fellowship and was therefore completely autonomous from the spiritual order because it "embraced the religious community and the civic community."[155] The achievement of pluralism and democracy in this case required that even the loftiest spiritual considerations, as they impinged upon human society, be subordinate to the temporal common good, whose principle of civic cohesion was entirely rational and secular.

The MLLF and its spokesmen realized that at that particular historical conjuncture some form of confessionality was going to continue to characterize Quebec's public school system, at least for the near future. Even Maurice Blain confirmed that under his regime of secularization there would still be concord between the state and the churches; what would be abolished would be the "sociological coordination" between the two orders, which he believed had long characterized the abnormal situation of confessionality. The new equilibrium between religion and civil society, in his estimation, would be found at the level of the individual, not in social institutions or the state, which must, in the name of equal civil rights, adopt a decidedly non-religious character.[156] For that reason, during the sittings of the Parent Commission, the MLLF was intent upon securing the widest possible guarantees for freedom of conscience, either in the form of separate non-confessional schools, where possible, or at the very least an exemption from catechism and religious exercises.[157] However, the MLLF's concept of democratic pluralism clearly identified confessionality as a secondary principle – as a concession to a public whose values, at least for the moment, remained traditional – but one that would, over time, become progressively less important to Quebec society.[158] This presented a clear challenge to those Catholics who wanted to link faith with elements of modernity, and thus find a way of preserving and extending the power of religion in the public realm.

For such Catholics, in the context of educational reform, the question was how to articulate a definition of pluralism that made confessionality central to its operation, thus avoiding both the secularization of the public realm and the relegation of Catholicism to the private sphere. The answer offered by both liberal and conservative Catholics turned upon finding an interpretation of Pope John XXIII's affirmation of the "autonomy of the temporal," the spirit that so typified the hope of renewal that swept the Church during the years of Vatican II and that would speak to the cultural context which characterized Quebec in the early 1960s. Most rejected the notion propagated by the MLLF and its sympathizers that the Quebec state was theocratic or confessional in character, and needed to be "secularized" or "deconfessionalized." The Jesuit Father Richard Arès, for example, observed that in both Quebec and Canada, there was no state religion and no established church, all religious bodies legally possessing, in the eyes of the state, the status of voluntary associations. There existed no treaties or concordats with the Vatican that would confer any privileged status upon Roman Catholicism or Canon law.[159] However, the constitutional separation of church and state and the autonomy of "spiritual" and "temporal" orders did not mean, for these Catholics, opposition or conflict between these realms, or the desacralization of the temporal order.

Writing in 1963 from the more liberal end of the Catholic spectrum, Claude Ryan declared that both spiritual and temporal orders rested upon the "incontestable moral foundations" of divine sovereignty, a consideration which meant that at each stage of human society there must occur "the interweaving of concrete relationships between the two."[160] Modern society, Catholics like Arès and Ryan maintained, offered more, rather than fewer, opportunities for constructive collaboration between church and state. Commenting on the encyclical *Pacem in Terris* in 1963, Ryan advised Catholics upon a new conception of public duty that would bridge church and state: their task was no longer to "defend" the Catholic Church, but to participate in elaborating "acceptable forms of relationships between the Church and the civil societies of the modern world."[161] Such an approach was particularly suitable for the Quebec situation where, commented Richard Arès, the state simply reflected the democratic wishes of 88 per cent of the population by harmoniously collaborating with the Church. Although not confessional, the Quebec state could not simply be abstracted from all religious influences.[162]

Pluralism, democracy, and the degree of separation that would prevail between church and state could not simply be cast according to the universal absolutes propounded by the MLLF. Rather, they had to find their meaning in a society which, as Action Catholique Canadienne outlined in its brief to the Parent Commission in 1962, presented an ambiguous picture. While French Canada did not possess the "spiritual homogeneity of yesteryear," still, its people, "in a very great majority, wish to remain faithful to its religious tradition."[163] "We would not have a democracy," concluded Father Lucien Campeau, "if the large Catholic majority of our province did not exercise an overt religious influence over the spirit and the character of our political institutions."[164]

Central to the emerging Catholic concept of pluralism was the conviction that Catholicism, rather than necessarily declining as the MLLF maintained, could be rejuvenated and continue to form the preponderant element in the social and cultural identity of French Canadians. According to the tenets of majoritarian democracy, and especially in light of Quebec's Catholic preponderance, the state could not simply be a neutral arbiter between religious factions. The duty of civil tolerance to minorities must not imply, argued the Corporation des Instituteurs Catholiques, "the endorsement of neutrality as a philosophy of life or as an ideal of education."[165] Neutrality, a joint memorandum from the Corporation des Agronomes and the Union Catholique des Cultivateurs reminded the Parent Commission, "is an impossibility. The very fact of silence concerning God and our duties towards God constitutes a negation of the overriding importance of religion."[166] Thus, in the estimation of Jacques Croteau, the working out of pluralism in a social environment where the vast majority of the population adhered to one religion had to be studiously separated from the type of "dogmatically intolerant" liberalism[167] advanced by Maurice Blain. One approach, a more hard-line one that was generally adopted by conservative Catholic organizations during the debate on public education, was to urge the state to strictly limit the educational "rights" of unbelieving parents, on the grounds that agnosticism, as erroneous, could not have the same rights as Christianity. From this perspective, tolerance was simply the Christian virtue of "suffering resignation."[168] However, as Father Arès warned, the Quebec Church, because it had majority status, had to distance itself from any tone of intransigeance in proclaiming its own rights, and concentrate on a broad defence of fundamental personal freedoms in modern society, thus linking the cause of Catholicism with that of democracy.[169]

To counter the new social order postulated by the MLLF, Catholics had to somehow break the connection between freedom of conscience, which conferred equality upon all citizens; the construction of a new public sphere and definition of citizenship from which religion was entirely absent; and the consequent supremacy of a secular, religiously-neutral political authority over all religious bodies. At bottom, the dispute centred over the nature of religious truth. Was it, as the MLLF claimed, relative to the individual, and therefore a "small and inoffensive private matter"[170] or was it objective, a standard to which governments and public bodies had to adhere? The secularists' fundamental error here, stated the American Jesuit John Courtney Murray in a lengthy series of articles reprinted in

Relations, was the equation of the human conscience and God, from which was derived the equally false notion of the equal rights of belief and unbelief. This reduced religion entirely to the private sphere and made of the state an amoral entity whose sole function was to "umpire conflicts between [individual] freedoms."[171] Conscience, for Murray, was the "voice of God,"[172] and its duty lay in strict obedience to the tenets of both natural and revealed religion. From this, he drew a number of corollaries. The first was that belief and unbelief were not equal in deriving their authority from reason: the latter was an aberration, the private practice of which civil society could tolerate as a prudential consideration, but not encourage.[173] Second, because religious truth was objective, it was therefore binding upon both the individual and society, and the state was barred from according equal rights to good and evil. Although it could not invade the private realm of conscience, the duty of the political order was to recognize God as its author, to render divine worship, and to submit public life to God's law, which entailed privileging religion as an essential element of the common good. Murray argued that Catholic theology explicitly enjoined the state to prohibit those public actions or "propaganda" that would tend to weaken the community's belief in God.[174] Any concessions to the "rights" of unbelief were therefore not an indicator of a healthy democratic spirit, but were a lamentable recognition of the spread of "gangrene in the body of society."[175]

Murray's hard-edged pronouncements derived not only from the principles of Catholic theology; they came also from a more secular American cultural climate where Roman Catholics not only constituted a religious minority, but where separation between church and state had been pushed to far greater limits than in Quebec, with all confessional religious instruction banished from the realm of public education. Many Quebec Catholics would not have dissented from Murray's view that there certainly existed an objective religious truth that had implications beyond the private sphere, and that, consequently, agnosticism was irrational and aberrant, something to be tolerated rather than applauded.[176] However, there was widespread recognition that the problem facing Quebec's particular version of Catholicism was of a different order. Father Bradet, the Dominican editor of the liberal Catholic review *Maintenant,* ridiculed fears that in a society that was 88 per cent Catholic, the faith was in actual danger. It was time, Bradet urged, for Quebec's Catholics to put aside "minority complexes" and engage with the new pluralist climate by deepening faith and conviction through better education.[177] Bertrand Rioux, a philosophy professor who firmly opposed clerical excesses, perhaps best articulated the concerns of most Quebec Catholics in the early 1960s when he informed those at the colloquium on church and state of the Institut Canadien des Affaires Publiques (ICAP) that "religious forces play a very important role in the life of a nation."[178]

The connection which most Catholic spokesmen wished to preserve between the religious beliefs of the majority and national values required the presentation of Catholic doctrine in a manner inclusive of all citizens. If Catholicism was not the official religion of the Quebec state, it was the religion of the nation, however, and had imperative civic reponsibilities. Its leaders thus sought to downplay any potential of conflict between its theological tenets, public sensibilities, and the needs of an expanding modern liberal state. Their language most frequently evoked, therefore, not the confrontation between "truth" and "error," but the need to "improve" Catholic teaching, to present the faith positively and appealingly. Most importantly, they sought to demonstrate that although the "spiritual" and "temporal" were autonomous orders, they were subject to similar progressive cultural currents like democracy. Thus, practically without dissent, it was accepted by Quebec Catholics that their brand of Christianity was compatible with the highest human values and achievements, and anchored upon the canons of scientific and humanistic reason.[179]

Through this approach, and through a more "spiritual" presentation of the Catholic Church's message, many clergy hoped that the Church could aspire to a firmer commitment from its faithful, and thus retain its public authority. However, although reform-minded Catholics were prepared to concede that a climate of spiritual pluralism could certainly include atheists and agnostics, they stopped far short of the basic minimum demanded by the MLLF: the "right to error" that was a concomitant of the absolute freedom of conscience,[180] and, given this right, a secularized public sphere, or a state that did not concretely recognize the presence of religion. Pluralism, stated Jacques Croteau in 1962, did not mean a liberal conception of a social order reduced to atomized individuals presided over by an aggressively secular state. Rather, what was essential to its practice was a recognition of the fact that there was, indeed, "a truth that had to be truly adhered to," a realization that imposed a positive obligation on the secular state to promote the spiritual well-being of its citizens by assisting them in their search for truth. This was to be accomplished, not through prohibitions, denials, or the creation of categories of second-class citizens, but through the positive encouragement by the state of "the different spiritual families" of the nation.[181]

Through this language of dialogue and mutual comprehension, Catholic educational reformers hoped that the concessions to ideological pluralism could be limited. The Church could thus retain the substance of the alliance between the public school and a refurbished and revitalized confessional instruction. In this way, they believed that Quebec would be spared the brandishing of freedom of conscience as a "political dagger," and a debilitating series of abstract disputes over freedom of conscience.[182] Moreover, the emphasis upon freedom and dialogue, rather than dogma,

as essential attributes of confessionality would serve a second vital imperative: it would limit fragmentation and balkanization within a school system
that was already divided into Catholic and Protestant. As the sociologist
Guy Rocher, one of the key experts employed by the Parent Commission
wrote, while the school system should strive to accommodate religious
diversity, it would be inadvisable to enshrine any concessions to religious
dissidence within the administrative machinery of the state by opening a
third "non-confessional" school sector. The potential existence of such
schools, he argued, should be the subject of local option, which would still
recognize the freedom of conscience of parents.[183] However, it should be
emphasized that this apparent concession would leave substantially intact
the principle of confessionality, because any dissidence could still be
regarded as an exception to the rule.

By early 1962, it was apparent that the MLLF had lost the battle for a
secular public school system. As Jules LeBlanc commented in *Le Devoir*, "it
is no longer a question of opposing the two systems; but to know whether,
within the confessional system, it is possible to permit the erection of non-
confessional schools for those who demand them."[184] It was to this dominant consensus, and to the "personalist" model of pluralism,[185] that the
Parent Commission spoke when it tried to balance the competing claims
of freedom of conscience, allegiance to confessionality, and the need to
separate religion and state while keeping a necessary coordination
between the two. The state, the commissioners argued, must preserve a
strict religious neutrality, and in particular, exercise its ultimate responsibility to assure equal access for all citizens to public schooling. This did not
imply, however, that they accepted the American constitutional model of
rigidly separating public institutions and confessionality. Indeed, this form
of secularity as advocated by groups such as the MLLF was firmly reproved
as the source of unending "social discontent." "The equal rights of all citizens to education," their report proclaimed, "by no means implies the
impairment of the advantages presently granted to Roman Catholics and
to Protestants."[186] Rather than acting as a secularizing force that opposed
and limited the initiative of churches and religious bodies, the state
should, the Parent Commission believed, function as a facilitator and promoter of religion. "Whenever it is possible to do so without compromising
the general welfare or lowering educational standards," declared the
Report of the Royal Commission in its 1965 statement on confessionality, "it is
quite in order for the state to try to accede to requests relating specifically
to religious training in the schools and to their confessionality."[187] This
assertion of a more exalted status for Roman Catholics and Protestants was
intended as a firm signal that the reform and modernization of Quebec's
institutions did not mean a submergence of its traditions into the Anglo-
Saxon mainstream of North America. Indeed, in more subdued and

implicit language, the Parent Commission simply articulated what Premier Lesage had stated more openly in 1961: that Catholicism would retain, as the religion of the majority of the nation, an official status in the public school.

Writing in 1961, two of the most outspoken critics of theocracy, Fathers Gérard Dion and Louis O'Neill, contended that while the Catholic Church had no actual temporal jurisdiction and thus could not impose its own institutions upon the state, it still had a mission to ensure that the Christian principles of justice and charity inspired all national and political values.[188] At the 1961 ICAP colloquium, O'Neill went much further in stating that because the Catholic Church was "omnipresent" and played a "preponderant" role in the social life of Quebec, "it would be unrealistic to demand that politicians either feign to ignore it or treat it as simply one religious group among others."[189] The message was clear, and was publicly reiterated as the consensus of the Parent Commission in the spring of 1963: egalitarian definitions of democracy must be studiously tempered in a society in which the vast majority shared a common religious faith. "Parents," the *Report of the Royal Commission of Inquiry on Education* concluded, "can insist upon the right to give their children an education consonant with their religious beliefs, and the churches can demand the right to safeguard the religious instruction of their members. But both must also recognize the same rights for others. ... The responsibility of the democratic State consists in allowing diversity while avoiding chaos, in respecting all rights while preventing abuses, in guaranteeing freedom within the boundaries of the common good."[190] Despite the evocation of the universal concepts of freedom, democracy, and diversity, there were two overriding considerations which, in the context of the early 1960s, distinguished Quebec from a number of other Western democracies. One was respect for the "right" of churches to count on the support of the state in attending to the religious instruction of their members in the context of the school,[191] a "right" that in the early 1960s stood prior to the claims of those who desired a completely secular system of public institutions. The other was the avoidance of "chaos." Here, what the commission meant was not the assuaging of the demands of the MLLF, but, through the affirmation of the confessional principle, the removal of any possibility of conflict between Roman Catholicism and the state.

With the Parent Commission having asserted the necessity of the continued existence of confessionality within state schools, the central problem for religious authorities, Catholic groups, and government officials, was how to formulate its operation so as to safeguard the supremacy of the church over doctrine, the dominance of the state over temporal institutions, and the freedom of religion that individual citizens were guaranteed in modern society. Reassured by the pronouncements of political leaders like Paul Gérin-Lajoie, the minister of education–designate, who stated in 1963 that "in a truly democratic system, we can never secularize the school, so long as the majority of citizens has not willed it,"[192] liberal and conservative Catholics recognized that in Quebec the danger to Catholicism would not emanate so much from the existence of a state unfriendly to religion or a large, militant, agnostic community, but from internal rot. In Catholic circles, the early 1960s were dominated by an apprehension that the faith of many Catholics was "shaky." This situation was ascribed to the fact that the religious message of the Church had been frequently presented in an overly-negative, dogmatic manner.[193] Speaking to the Semaines Sociales in 1962, Cardinal Léger assigned the burden of blame for the existence of an agnostic minority to the religious ignorance and intolerance of Quebec Catholics who, in his estimation, limited their religious faith to "the legalistic observance of a few external practices and a few unconscious memories of a religious instruction received in childhood." If Christianity, the cardinal warned, continued to offer Quebec the repetition of "traditions and formulae" rather than the universal solidarity of "an elect people," modern youth would simply conclude, like the MLLF, that religion was simply a "segregationism" that inhibited the community from coalescing around universal social ideals.[194] Such views were not original to Léger; indeed, they had been standard criticisms of Quebec Catholicism from the perspective of the personalism that had suffused the various Catholic Action movements since the late 1930s. However, the fact that Quebec's most visible Catholic cleric was repeating them at a time when the relationship between confessionality and public education was subject to renegotiation was highly significant. Indeed, the public attention given to this personalist critique of Catholic religious education was crucial to the way in which the practical implementation of confessionality, and, thus, the whole relationship between church and state, was redefined in the early 1960s.

One of the main reasons for the embedding of a form of confessionality in public education during the Quiet Revolution was the awareness among clerics, politicians, and opinion-makers that a cultural "crisis" characterized French-Canadian society. Many of these figures had thoroughly imbibed the teachings of the Catholic Action movements which had been a particular feature of Quebec's post-Depression culture. Since the 1940s, these social movements had contributed what in fact was the critical element of the Quiet Revolution mentality: the belief that there had developed a great gulf between the religious convictions and practices of older and younger generations, and a consequent "crisis" in religious faith and practice that urgently required outside intervention. Despite the lip service that Catholic theology paid to the primordial rights of parents in education, there existed, by 1963, a substantial public consensus that the family unit could no longer fulfill its role as moral and religious educator. The result was that many Catholics were prepared to confer upon the state a palpable accentuation of initiative and responsibility, not simply over the "secular" political, economic, and organizational imperatives of education, but with actual jurisdiction over moral and religious matters.

In a 1962 memorandum strongly supporting the maintenance of confessional religious instruction, the Femmes Diplomées des Universités reiterated its opposition to the MLLF's notion that sufficient religious instruction could be assured outside of class hours by the family or by "Sunday School" style methods. "To count exclusively on the climate of the home," it stated, "would be to destroy the scientific character of religious instruction. ... It is the school that builds upon the religious formation given in the home."[195] For Catholics, formal religious instruction in school was a vital necessity because, as Gérard Beaudoin observed, "Catholicism essentially rests upon precise dogmas which must be properly taught."[196]

Such convictions were articulated all the more forcefully during the debate on public education because many Catholics in Quebec had become convinced that what had begun in Catholic Action youth circles as a personalist critique of the values of an older generation had in fact become the characteristic of the urban, industrial society that had emerged since 1940: intergenerational solidarity had irretrievably ruptured, and the family had signally failed in its role to transmit religious and moral values to the younger generation. No less a personage than Cardinal Léger raised the alarm when he spoke to the Cercle Richelieu in 1963. "An industrial society that conceives everything as a function of production and consumption," he lamented, "does not prepare adults to understand youth."[197]

Significantly, the cardinal did not use the occasion, as he would have in the past, to insist upon the authority of parents over their children and the duty of obedience. Instead, he squarely placed the burden of blame upon the older generation for teaching the young nothing but materialistic values which engulfed Quebec society in a morass of individualism. Nor were such views simply confined to clerical circles. From a more "secular" perspective, two Université Laval sociologists, Gérald Fortin and Marc-Adélard Tremblay, articulated conclusions similar to those of the Catholic Action movements in a study of popular attitudes towards education, prepared for the Caisses Populaires Desjardins. Lamenting the prevailing utilitarianism which linked schooling to the acquisition of personal wealth, Fortin and Tremblay identified as the root of the problem a "weak preoccupation of parents for the education of their children," and asserted, in particular, the need to "place a higher value on the humanistic and cultural aspect of knowledge."[198] To rise to its destiny as a modern, democratic society, Quebec urgently needed, in the estimation of the Association

Générale des Étudiants de l'Université de Montréal, a rapid transfusion of a "communitarian sense" of values through a school system in which "the present generation" made a self-sacrificing "investment" in progress.[199]

However, what became rapidly apparent during the public debate on education was that few in either the Church, state, or media actually believed that the older generation was, left to its own devices, capable of such a massive shift of priorities from acquisitive individualism to an ideal of spiritual and social solidarity. Parents born before the great upsurge in Catholic Action personalism during the mid-1930s were either simply too ignorant or too tied to routine and tradition to provide anything in the way of proper religious guidance for their adolescents. In February 1963, *Le Devoir* brought to the attention of its readers a survey conducted among 2,000 Catholics by the Office Catéchétique Provincial which, by raising serious doubts about the capacities of parents to teach religion to their children, actually strengthened the hand of the Church in demanding a full-fledged system of confessional education. "A large number of parents," the survey concluded, "although conscious of their responsibilities, have neither the education nor the means" to provide religious education. A significant two-thirds of those surveyed stated their intention to rely upon priests for religious education.[200] Writing just before Bill 60 passed into law, the Dominican Father Paul-Marcel Lemaire observed that "few adolescents have any ties of a religious nature with their parents, because they are disappointed and unsatisfied with the Christian life of their parents." Specifically, he pointed to what he considered the heart of the problem. At best, some parents might have "authentic" Christian faith, but they were mired in routine and convention, unable to "put a bit of mystical folly" into their lives. At worst, the majority were indifferent and uncaring, "languishing in the pathways of a conformist Christianity."[201] From a more conservative perspective, the journal *Notre Temps* reported that Quebec's parents were themselves ignorant of religion, which in many families simply took the form of superstition. The only remedy for this lamentable situation would come from the children themselves who, by experiencing the much-vaunted improvements in religious instruction in Quebec's Catholic schools, would, "by their example, induce their parents to live their faith."[202]

By the early 1960s, the leaders of both the Church and government concurred that only a massive intervention by institutions external to the family could resolve Quebec's religious "crisis," and, through the younger generation, graft onto society those personalist, communitarian values that would sustain the momentum of the great *déblocage* (unblocking) undertaken in the name of a *politique de grandeur* (politics of grandeur). Indeed, there was no surer indication of the fact that, in the public mind, the failings of the older generation had produced a religious crisis than the fact that the pronouncements of a number of conservative Catholic organizations evinced a fundamental confusion. On the one hand, they firmly adhered to a notion of an educational "partnership" in which the rights of the state were strictly subordinate to the initiatives of family and church. However, as the Chevaliers de Colomb declared before the Parent Commission, "the State must even protect the child against his parents, if they refuse him education, or attempt to give him an education contrary to divine law."[203] The largest of Quebec's teachers' federations, the Corporation des Instituteurs Catholiques, emphatically rejected the notion "that the child would have a real right not to know God ... and to dispense with the help of the Church ... We will never accept that the child has the right to adopt erroneous religious beliefs."[204] The concern of these groups was not simply to restrict the rights of agnostics to be dispensed from religious instruction, but to bridge a crucial gap which the failings of many Catholic parents had left in the education of Quebec's children. The state, these Catholics maintained, had a precise duty in relation to the child's right to religious truth, which in this case superseded the parents' freedom of conscience. The state, concluded Father Louis Lachance, would exceed its rights if it attempted to impose one kind of religion, but it did have a duty to promote the practice of religion, and in particular, to facilitate the instruction of the child in the truths of Christianity.[205]

Between 1960 and 1964, the Catholic personalist critique of Quebec's spiritual values converged with the aspirations of Quiet Revolution reformers to inaugurate a more efficient and active state structure. The casualty in the process was the authority of parents over the religious values of their children. Arthur Tremblay, deputy-minister of Youth, chief technical advisor to the Parent Commission, and, after 1964, deputy-minister of education, told the Semaines Sociales in 1962 that, henceforth, the school could not be treated as an extension of the family, an instrument of intergenerational solidarity, but must become a "factor of social innovation"[206] which itself would transform and modernize the values of the family. The parents themselves, however, were not to be equal partners in this new enterprise. Speaking at the Congrès des Commissions Scolaires de l'Archidiocèse de Québec, Cardinal Maurice Roy evoked the vision of a partnership between church and state to reconstitute the community spirit of the parish inside the large regional high schools being enthusiastically erected by Gérin-Lajoie and his bureaucrats.[207] What was missing from Roy's address was any reference to the role of parents, who were summarily relegated to the shadows by the two key public entities, the Catholic Church and the Quebec state, which would henceforth share power in determining the content, values, and organization of the school curriculum. It was to this decisive cultural transformation that the Parent Commission attested when it declared that parents themselves could no longer ensure proper education for their children. Under the new educational dispensation, the only right that they would retain was the negative one of freedom of conscience, the right to state their religious preferences, but not to participate in that education.[208]

During the Quiet Revolution, church and state in Quebec divided up the field of public education in the name of saving the spiritual values of the rising generation. However, the partnership proposed by the Parent Commission and enacted by Bill 60 did not replicate the situation that had prevailed during the previous phase of early twentieth-century liberalism, and which still held sway under the administration of Maurice Duplessis. Under this dispensation, many sectors of education had escaped direct state management, being administered and organized by quasi-independent confessional committees, private religious orders, or diocesan authorities. Under this brand of liberalism, the separation of church and state meant that cultural and moral imperatives were left explicitly as the purview of the church, with the state's role restricted to providing funding.[209] By 1960, however, an influential segment of Quebec Catholic opinion had become convinced that such arrangements were deeply offensive to newer international Catholic Church sensibilities which stressed the "autonomy of the temporal" and a more precisely-defined spiritual realm.

Writing in 1961, Fathers Gérard Dion and Louis O'Neill firmly located the source of legitimate civil authority in the state. By virtue of this, the state, they argued, was the supreme guardian of the common good, and "possessed a right of supervision over all temporal institutions," a superior right which extended even to institutions like schools in which the Church exercised certain functions of management.[210] Although an overwhelming consensus united Catholics over the right of the Church to teach religious matters, liberal commentators like Father Gérard Dion reminded their audience of the necessity to draw precise distinctions in defining the respective rights of church and state, especially if confessionality was going to function smoothly in the context of a public system of schools. In an article written in the fall of 1963 at the height of the public debate over Bill 60, Dion explained that the Catholic Church's absolute right to teach religion must operate in tandem with the prior right of the state over what pertained to the common good. Thus, the Church's oversight over the "spirit of instruction" did not extend to controlling, directing, or determining the content of that instruction, which would involve an unacceptable subordination of the state to the church, and ultimately, a theocracy. Ultimately, while he saw modern education as entailing a relationship between the state and other social groups, the partnership was not an equal one. Ultimately, in a public school system, the state must have the final authority over *all* aspects of teaching.[211] Dion's colleague Father Louis O'Neill, who after 1976 was to serve as a cabinet minister in the government of René Lévesque, advanced a similar argument. The Church was constitutionally and doctrinally correct in demanding guarantees for confessional education, but once these provisions had been secured, "it is the State that must finally approve school regulations, even in religious matters, insofar as this schooling is a part of official teaching and forms an aspect of the temporal common good."[212] Significantly, however, O'Neill firmly defended compulsory religious instruction at the elementary, secondary, and collegiate levels of the educational system.[213]

The institutional compromise between Catholic confessionality and the purposes of a modernizing state was made possible by a shared sense of meanings between reformist and conservative Catholics as to what constituted the nature of the "temporal." Unlike many English-Canadian Protestants, who in the wake of World War II imposed a rigid separation between sacred and secular, and emptied the latter of any spiritual purpose or significance, Quebec Catholics during the early 1960s remained convinced that the "temporal" order played a key role in human salvation. Where much of the post-war Protestant mainstream had come to believe that religion was a private matter separate from the public realm of the state, and that Christian action in society would be undertaken as a function of individual conscience,[214] Quebec Catholics in the early 1960s drew upon two mutually-reinforcing currents of thought in attempting to articulate a set of connections between religion and the public realm. In this sense, although the Second Vatican Council, which met from 1962 to 1965, the years in which Quebec's debate over education was at its height, proclaimed the "autonomy" of the temporal sphere, it did not endorse the idea that in welcoming a modern socio-political order characterized by pluralism, Catholicism must withdraw and become a purely private set of convictions.[215] Rather, because the temporal sphere constituted a key element in human salvation, it must be exposed to the continuing influence *both* of the actions of Christian individuals *and* of the collective purpose supplied by Christian institutions. And this newer strand of international Catholic thinking reinforced one of the bedrock convictions that animated religious and political elites in Quebec: the need to reinvigorate the close fit between Catholicism and the consciousness of the Quebec nation. Both reformist and conservative Catholics would have thus agreed with the Jesuit Father Raymond Bourgault when he argued that the "secularity" of the state simply meant its autonomy from the church, not the evisceration of its moral or religious qualities. Thus, he frankly welcomed the new climate in Quebec in which the state asserted its initiative and rights in the field of education, as this would eliminate any confusion between "Cross and Sword." This would allow Christians to more fully practice the gospel precept of "rendering unto Caesar the things that are

Caesar's" and, in a parallel manner, "rendering to God what belongs to God." The application of the principle of the "secularity" of temporal institutions, Bourgault reckoned, was essential to achieving the full catholicity and comprehensiveness of Christ's Church.[216]

Thus, the dynamism and power of the state evoked by the language and institutional achievements of Quiet Revolutionaries like Paul Gérin-Lajoie can be understood less as the displacement of Catholicism in the name of non- or anti-religious values than as the desire by public officials to harness Roman Catholicism in order to reaffirm a sense of cohesion and national purpose in a society undergoing rapid institutional modernization and cultural change. Born in 1920, Gérin-Lajoie belonged to the Quebec generation that, during the 1930s and 1940s, was the first group of Catholic laity to fully participate in the social movements which sought to implement the ideal of a re-Christianization of all modern social institutions that was announced by Pope Pius XI.[217] This generation, as we have seen, although frequently critical of the abuses of authority by the Church hierarchy, took as its great aim the task of assuring the close identity of Roman Catholicism in public life, not through the presence of the clergy, but through the activities of a religiously-awakened laity, conscious of its rights and responsibilities. Speaking to the Semaine d'Éducation in 1961, Gérin-Lajoie affirmed, on behalf of the state, that the "principal mission of the school is the teaching of truth." While conceding to parents the "*physical liberty*" to refuse their children knowledge of divine truth, the minister stated that it did not follow that "parents have the right ... to place obstacles in the path of their children's religious upbringing."[218] For these public figures, then, the state, as the "servant and protector of Quebec,"[219] itself had a vital and dynamic role in the economy of salvation, a place attested to by no less a figure than Gérin-Lajoie's colleague Georges-Émile Lapalme, the minister of culture, who testified before the Parent Commission that state initiative in school reform was a necessary instrument of "cultural progress and eternal salvation."[220]

The inauguration of a fully-fledged ministry of education was the centrepiece of the "national revolution"[221] trumpeted by Gérin-Lajoie. However, a closer look at the minister's pronouncements, and the actual institutional machinery set in place by Bill 60, raises the question of whether this aspect of the Quiet Revolution in fact constituted a desire to displace religion from public institutions. In the first place, Gérin-Lajoie publicly sought to allay fears that the state would become too powerful and all-encompassing, countering instead with a rationale of "State-as-servant" drawn from the papal encyclicals of John XXIII and from the French democratic socialist Pierre Mendès-France, with both having assigned to the state the decisive duty of promoting the public good.[222] Nor was this a mere exercise of rhetoric. Bill 60 itself explicitly recognized not only concepts of "organic," corporative social thought that were characteristic of Catholicism,[223] but actually incorporated confessionality into the state apparatus by making religious belief a fundamental criterion of appointment to public office.

Central to Gérin-Lajoie's design for his new ministry was the institution of a "Conseil Supérieur" of 24 members, a consultative organ through which the minister hoped to secure a "real representation" of a permanent, organized public opinion. Democracy, in his estimation, was not simply the "hard and implacable" application of majority wishes, but an effective coordination between the state bureaucracy and intermediate bodies that would give to Quebec a more genuine democracy.[224] Significantly, two-thirds of the places in the Conseil Supérieur were to be reserved for Roman Catholics and four seats for Protestants, thus serving notice that the principal "organic" interest that the state would recognize was a religious one. Indeed, through the institution of the Conseil Supérieur, the government sought to give an official, institutional character to currents of Catholic social thought which had gained wide currency among the Catholic social movements, and business and labour circles during the post-war era. If anything, the public hearings of the Parent Commission were characterized by a curious paradox: nearly all organizations clamoured for an educational reform, rationalization, and coordination that implied a considerable extension of state initiative, but they at the same time voiced fears of excessive bureaucratization and regimentation, and a loss of personal freedom.

The educational debate in Quebec was heavily influenced by the publication of the papal encyclical *Mater et Magistra*, which defined "socialization" as the tendency of modern society towards closer, cooperative relationships. These, however, could not be achieved through a state monopoly, but through an equilibrium of direction and coordination by the state, and the multiplication of intermediate bodies and associations that exercised real power in modern society, by enlisting and directing the energies of individual citizens to participate in the achievement of a more just temporal order.[225] These Catholic views drew their inspiration from the heavy influence of pre-war corporatism in Quebec, but during the 1950s, the tenor of corporatist thought began to shift and place greater stress upon the "democratic" and "pluralistic," rather than the "hierarchical" or authoritarian, elements within the ideology. As the Société Saint-Jean-Baptiste de Montreal stated in 1963, "the intervention of the State must take account of the role of intermediate groups and respect democratic traditions."[226] The solution advocated by a number of groups, which included the Quebec Chamber of Commerce and the two powerful union centrals, was premised upon institutionalizing, within the new ministry of education, an equilibrium between direct state control and a real delegation of powers to intermediate bodies, whose representatives would constitute a permanent body with decision-making powers.[227] What was indicative of the heavy influence of Catholic ideology on public debate during the early stages of the Quiet Revolution was the fact that much of the public opposition to Bill 60 centred, not on the guarantees of confessionality itself, but on the mode of nomination of representatives to the Conseil Supérieur and on the apparent lack of real power in what the cabinet was willing to delegate to this body.[228]

The actual implementation of confessionality was left to two subcommittees of fifteen members each – one Protestant, the other Roman Catholic. Each committee was headed by an associate–deputy minister of that faith and had the authority to make regulations, subject to the approval of the cabinet, over religious and moral instruction in public elementary and secondary schools. In the case of the Catholic subcommittee, an equal number of representatives would be nominated by the Assembly of Bishops and by organizations of parents and teachers.[229] Through this reform, Gérin-Lajoie hoped to place the Quebec state at the centre of a new republican vision of civic purpose, and thus focus the rising energies and ambitions of a citizenry conscious of its rights and responsibilities. However, it was a notion of republicanism that eschewed the secularist imperatives of its American and French analogues, in which state and church were rigidly separate. Quebec's mission, Gérin-Lajoie told the readers of *Le Devoir*, was the traditional one of progressing in the face of the power of Anglo-Saxon peoples of North America. This progress, however, would be achieved in the modern context not by adopting their ways, but by carving out "a place, a role, and a witness" to be accomplished by "an effort of rigour and of quality in which the entire nation will participate."[230] The "witness," he referred to was, of course, nothing other than the dedication of the state to the cause of furthering the Christian religion.

Roman Catholicism's place in this new republican order was guaranteed by the explicitly confessional character of the ministry of education's machinery. With Bill 60, Quebec had made a decisive choice, rejecting both secularization and religious fragmentation in the name of a single system which recognized both confessionality for the majority, and freedom of choice, so far as it was practicable at the local level, for minorities which chose to exercise their rights. This, it should be pointed out, embroiled the state in helping the Church provide subsidized, compulsory religious instruction at both primary and secondary levels, and make chaplaincies and pastoral services available at senior collegiate institutions.[231] However, the fact that, insofar as it provided religious instruction, the Church was now formally an element of state administrative machinery meant that it was subject to considerations of the temporal common good, and thus could not operate in an exclusivist or triumphalist manner, as it could under Duplessis when education and culture were regarded as separate from the imperatives of the political order. As the Parent Commission emphatically stated, the common good in a modern society was to be assured, not by the state directly teaching religious doctrine, but by respecting individual liberties and the "autonomy of the person."²³² Under conditions of pluralism, Gérin-Lajoie observed, the confessional nature of education could not be assured, in the final analysis, by state laws or regulations, which must, in the name of freedom of conscience, be as minimal as possible. Catholics themselves must make the effort to reinvigorate confessionality and make themselves into worthy partners of a dynamic state by applying the new culture of competence, rigour, and quality to the proclamation of the "*gospel*" message.²³³

The new definition of confessionality in the context of a reformed public school became clear during the hearings of the Parent Commission. In 1962, a group of parents from Quebec City, headed by Mme Malcolm Vachon, Mme Jean-Charles Falardeau, who was the wife of the Université Laval sociologist, and Mme Marcel Richard drew to the attention of the commission a highly negative assessment of the current state of Catholic religious teaching in Quebec's elementary schools. Contrasting the "attitude of indifference" towards and profound ignorance of the Catholic faith that was displayed by children to the "overabundance" of religious instruction offered to French Canadians, these concerned parents located the heart of the problem in the failure of catechism texts to meaningfully connect the Christian message with the actual life of the child. Current concepts of religious instruction, they maintained, were actually contributing to the waning of Catholicism in society by presenting the faith as a series of dogmatic precepts to be memorized by rote. This type of religious teaching thus imposed upon the young child "a wounding and irritating feeling of perpetual prohibitions, which prevent his personality from flowering through use of intelligence and imprison his desire for freedom. [It] falsifies the notion of religion, by presenting it solely under the rubric of duty and obligation."²³⁴

The remedy offered for this lamentable state of religious training was familiar to those raised in the post-war Catholic Action circles: less reliance upon the pronouncements of clerical authority figures, greater familiarity throughout the entire course of religious instruction with the wellsprings of faith, that is, the Bible, the teachings of the Church Fathers, and the history of the Church. Above all, children had to be aware from an early age of a concept of Christianity that was highly influenced by the existential quality of Catholic personalism: this was the notion that "religion is not narrow moralism; it is faith in a mystery." In this way, a new generation of Catholics would reject older, more selfish notions of individual salvation that were based upon a legalistic, conditioned adherence to moral codes, and they would recover the communitarian aspects of Christ's message. This heightened emphasis upon social solidarity would, in turn, affirm the bond between Christianity and the civic sense in the modern age.[235]

Another consideration injected a new and paradoxical element into the attempt to construct a new synthesis between the public educational system and the principle of confessionality. "We wish," stated the group of Quebec City parents, "that our children should be educated to understand those who do not share our beliefs."[236] What was at stake here went far beyond merely a desire to improve the intellectual quality of catechism or religious teaching in the modern school.[237] On the one hand, all of these prescriptions for reform were articulated within the context of a commitment to the continued alliance of the confessional principle and the public school. However, the fact that words like "respect," "usefulness to others," and the emphasis on questioning and dialogue suffused the presentation of these parents[238] indicated an awareness that, increasingly, because the confessional system was "public," Catholic schools would contain a variety of religious options and practices, ranging from fervent piety, to occasional participation, to outright unbelief. All of these would somehow have to be accommodated if some connection between Catholicism and the cultural values of the nation was to be maintained. In the interests of identifying the public school as inclusive, the main concern of the Parent Commission was to find a balance between its desire to retain confessional education as "obligatory" for Catholics who, it should be pointed out, constituted the vast majority, and the need to avoid violating the religious freedoms of those who dissented. Thus, in their 1965 disquisition on confessionality, the commissioners articulated as a fundamental principle of the primary school the "absolute" right of non-Catholic or non-Protestant children to be excused from religious instruction or exercises upon the request of the parents.[239] However, the commission went even further in attempting to make confessionality non-threatening or inoffensive to religious minorities. "In practice," their report intoned, "the number of daily prayers must be restricted to certain times during the day, or else ... a brief period of reflection and silence must be suggested at the beginning of each class, during which pupils could pray as they see fit."[240]

Thus, what emerged from the debate on education was a newer sensibility regarding the proper balance of "sacred" and "profane" elements in the curriculum of public confessional schools. Even the conservative Catholic family movement Les Foyers Notre-Dame warned against "mixing religion with all sauces; we should not slide it into the teaching of all other subjects in a way contrary to the wishes of parents and students."[241] Indeed, during the early 1960s, a variety of Catholic groups that were interested in educational reform specifically questioned the uses to which religion had been put under the old confessional dispensation. For example, Action Catholique Canadienne contended that, henceforth, religion should not be used by teachers for purposes of school discipline, as this simply perpetuated the sense that religion was a set of negative moral precepts.[242] Religious instruction, declared François Loriot of the ultra-nationalist Alliance Laurentienne, a group which favoured the continued close relationship of Roman Catholicism and Quebec nationalism, should be carefully distinguished from religious practices and liturgical exercises. While he believed that religious instruction should certainly remain compulsory in public confessional schools, adolescent students should have the freedom to choose whether or not to attend mass and the sacraments.[243] Animating all these organizations was the common conviction that Catholic religion remained a central element in forming the human personality, but that this must be done without heavy-handed "conditioning" or indoctrination, as the Femmes Diplomées des Universités reminded the Royal Commission. What was to be scrupulously avoided in a reformed public system was any religious instruction tainted with anthropomorphism, fables, and magical or supernatural usages, or the insinuation of religious messages into mathematical, scientific, or, indeed, other humanistic subjects of study.[244]

Despite the overriding consensus on the desirability of a public, confessional system, a curious reordering of priorities occurred during the early 1960s among some influential Catholics. As the influential Association de l'Éducation du Québec (AÉQ) judiciously stated in 1962, the school must be animated by a Christian humanism. Significantly, however, this body cautioned that religious apologetics must be banished from the public school. What this group meant was that disciplines like science, philosophy, history, language, and literature should no longer be taught in a way intended to serve the ends of Catholic dogma. Christianity, the AÉQ maintained, would find its support and justification in the ideal of freedom and in a celebration of "natural values," such as intelligence. Implicit in their proposals for education reform was the sense that the school could meet both its public and religious functions, not by explicitly teaching the Catholic faith, but by meeting the "requirements of a human society in evolution towards a new stage of adult life." This "dynamic," "open" confessionality[245] drew heavily upon a personalist ethos which interpreted faith in a context of freedom of choice, rather than adherence to authority and tradition. Thus, it legitimated the downplaying of an overt religious presence in the schools, historically represented by priests and members of religious orders. As Father Georges-Henri Lévesque declared at the height of the debate over Bill 60, because faith was personal, it had a mysterious, intangible quality that lay beyond the external influence of the clergy in the lives of believers.[246] This was resoundingly approved by the Parent

Commission itself, which explicitly declared that "religious influences are much more effective if exerted by a pastoral ministry, by appropriate instruction in the religious sciences and by the presence of a Christian community than by repeated exhortations which in the end involve the danger of repelling adolescents and young people."[247]

By the time the Royal Commission published its recommendations regarding the scope and nature of religious instruction in a reformed system in 1965, it was apparent that the overriding concern was less for improving the quality of catechism and religious teaching itself, than for ensuring that religion be scrupulously separated from other elements of the curriculum, and that the amount of school time devoted to teaching Catholic religion be drastically reduced. The situation to be avoided at all costs, wrote Marcelle and Bernard Vanasse, was the "'profanation' of the profane" by the excessive infusion of Catholic teaching into other school subjects.[248] Indeed, although the confessional principle remained the essential groundwork of the educational system, the convergence between personalism and the need to preserve the identity between Catholicism and nationality, both of which involved according considerable latitude if not equality to unbelievers and the lukewarm, made of religion the exceptional, non-essential element in the curriculum. Its secondary and separate status was confirmed by the commissioners' recommendation that it not be a subject of examination or regular grading. "Outsiders" like teachers and clergy were barred from judging the "reality of the relationship between the child and God." Because inner adherence was fundamental to the personalist view of religion, the Parent Report likewise took a dim view of "compulsory and regular participation in ceremonies of worship and endless religious exercises."[249] Religious teaching thus preserved a presence as the outward badge of the alliance between confessionality and public purpose in Quiet Revolution Quebec. However, it was a confessionality whose limits and operations, if not actual doctrines, were closely regulated and applied by the state, with the latter's primary mission being ultimately a religious one: to protect the convictions and sensibilities of its citizens by acting *directly* as the religious instructor.

Between 1960 and 1964, the Quebec state moved to assert a more forceful presence in the sphere of public education. It did so, not by removing religious imperatives from social and cultural life, but by creating institutional machinery and reforms that would ensure a closer coordination between the Catholic religion of the majority and the public purpose of the nation, in future to be defined principally by the political authorities. The guiding imperative of both church and state was the need to reaffirm and reinvigorate Roman Catholicism as the repository of the fundamental national values of social solidarity and community spirit, particularly in a period of cultural tension, when the ability of the family to transmit these cohesive values appeared to be in rapid decline. In the name of what they deemed the "rights" and more authentically Christian values of the younger generation, leaders of church and state undertook a far-reaching renegotiation, not only of their own relationship, but of the very character, assumptions, and place of religious instruction in Quebec's schools. The crucial test, however, was whether a refurbished confessionality could even claim to speak to the values of a generation already questioning the very need of eternal salvation, obsessing over the relativity of existence, and doubting the validity of the very question of "whether God exists or not, whether Jesus lived or not, or if Teilhard de Chardin's *Point Oméga* is more or less religious than the nirvana of one of Jack Kerouac's dharma bums."[250]

7

"An Old, Ill-fitting Garment"[1]

Fernand Dumont, Quebec's Second Revolution, and the Drama of De-Christianization, 1964–1971

A significant part of the religious impulse is today invested in the political realm, understood in its widest possible sense: political action has replaced Catholic Action.[2]

In 1971, a high-profile commission appointed by the Quebec Catholic hierarchy reported its findings. Ostensibly created to undertake an inquiry into the collapse of Catholic Action in the mid-1960s, and to chart a new direction in the relationship between clergy and laity, the Commission d'Étude sur les Laïcs et l'Église (more usually known as the Commission Dumont) was chaired by the Université Laval sociologist Fernand Dumont and included a number of prominent Catholic activists.[3] Through a series of public consultations and a final report, the Commission Dumont posed a number of anguished questions concerning the steep decline in religious practice which had occurred over the course of a single decade among Quebec Catholics, a transformation that signalled not only a profound crisis within the Catholic Church itself, but the de-Christianization of a society indelibly stamped, until very recently, by Catholic beliefs, values, and institutions. Between 1961 and 1971, the rate of religious practice in the highly urbanized diocese of Montreal fell from 61 per cent to 30 per cent, and even allowing for higher allegiance to Catholicism in rural areas and smaller towns in Quebec as a whole the 1971 figure stood at between 37 and 45 per cent.[4] "Religious practice," concluded the Commission Dumont, "is abandoned without drama, as one would throw off an old, ill-fitting garment. ... more often, people leave the Church without making a sound, sneaking out by the back door." However, what most troubled the Commission Dumont, whose members emphatically identified with Catholic Action's commitment to foster the intersection between Catholic values and modern institutions, was that religion seemed to arouse no wider debate or division over Quebec's future social or political values: the abandonment of Catholic practice was an act accomplished in the realm of private values, and evinced a worrisome tendency to separate religion from society. "Could this," wondered the commission, "be a measure of the incapacity of the Church in Quebec to arouse conflicts involving the collectivity? Could it be that these debates have no resonance in the fundamental values of our people?"[5] Such questions indicated an apprehension that a great reversal had affected Quebec Catholics in the space of a few years, a reversal that, for a society that had conceived of itself as religiously homogeneous and that viewed religious values as being essential for the articulation of both personal identity and public solidarity, constituted a dramatic de-Christianization.

Such questions placed the Commission Dumont at the conjunction of two critical events that marked the years between 1964 and 1971, and which were to forever mark the history of Quebec during the next quarter-century. The first was the extremely rapid dissolution of the central dynamic of the cultural Quiet Revolution: the attempt to articulate an intimate intersection between Catholicism and modern identities that had engaged the reformist elements of Catholic Action since the early 1930s. This effort to enhance the presence of a purified, modern, personalist Catholicism in both the personal and familial identities and in the public culture of Quebec was translated into political terms during the early 1960s when it forcefully etched the key institutional achievements of the Quiet Revolution – the social welfare reforms of the Lesage government and the massive educational reforms advocated by the Parent Commission. Far from blaming a "traditional," unchanging Catholicism for failing to adapt to the realities of a highly urban, industrial society, those Catholic activists who were most involved in the governmental reforms of the 1960s simply did not accept the "fatal" equation between an urban form of society and the loss of religious conviction.[6] Indeed, it might well be said that the central emphasis of the Lesage government was to elaborate a new democratic culture by bringing Catholicism more firmly within the machinery of the modern state, so that a tight synthesis might be coordinated between "the data of social progress and the foundations of Christian humanism."[7] Reformist Catholics like the new minister of education, Paul Gérin-Lajoie, aimed to accomplish a "grand quiet revolution" in both church and state by bringing to an end "the opposition of clergy and laity, the spiritual and the temporal, religion and politics," distinctions which he dismissed as "purely idealistic" as the two orders "naturally interpenetrated one another."[8] In this scenario, democracy was defined as both the enhancement of the power of the state, which would acquire the capacity to direct the destiny of the entire society, and the cultivation and preservation of relatively autonomous intermediate public bodies or communities – many of which had explicit links to Catholicism – that fostered a healthy civic identity by mediating the relationship between the state and the individual.

By the late 1960s, however, many within Quebec's elite were confronted with the realization that the Quiet Revolution's attempt to fuse Catholicism and public authority had seriously faltered in the face of a second cultural revolution that between 1964 and 1973 did not spare any highly industrialized Western society. This revolution so privileged the right of the individual to self-expression and self-fulfillment[9] that it rejected the legitimacy of there being a civic order outside the political realm mediated by the corporate claims of familial and religious identities. In contrast to the aspirations of the cultural Quiet Revolution, this second cultural revolution, although never overtly atheistic or anti-religious, was so wedded to an untrammelled individualism that its central implication, as far as Quebec was concerned, was the forceful rejection of a public role for Catholicism. During the late 1960s, Quebec's social and political elites discerned this heightened individualism in an apparently anarchic sexual revolution and manifestations of a "counter-culture," in a wave of youth contestation that complicated the laborious task of restructuring educational institutions, in an increasingly bellicose climate of labour relations, and most troublingly, in a wave of urban terrorism aimed at a revolutionary achievement of Quebec independence that directly challenged the legitimacy of the state. Elites from all shades of the political spectrum believed that these events had created a crisis of authority that urgently required the elaboration of new mechanisms and structures of political cohesion that would resituate public authority on firmer foundations.

During these years, many prominent Quebecers became convinced that it was necessary to bring an end to the Quiet Revolution's attempt to construct an intermediate civic order and instead to articulate a new type of democratic citizenship premised upon a direct relationship between the individual and the state. At a meeting of politicians, social scientists, and journalists held in 1970, participants concurred that "the succession of crises that Quebec has encountered over the last six or seven years constitutes a new stage in the tormented historical era that we are currently living."[10] Such crises, they believed, were characterized by violent reactions against established institutions and "current practices and traditions," and evinced not a commitment to a new type of democratic freedom, but a "social pathology" whose main characteristic was an "incapacity among individuals and groups to foster mutual communication and understanding that would allow the orderly resolution of these conflicts."[11]

For an articulate Catholic avant-garde, and in particular, for Fernand Dumont, one of the leaders of a prominent intellectual wing within the new Parti Québécois, the democratic citizenship required by this second cultural revolution necessarily entailed the elaboration of a new public creed of nationalism characterized by an indissoluble bond between the independence of Quebec from Canada and a social democracy in which social solidarity would be achieved through a direct, unmediated access of the individual to the state. Although they sought such a direct relationship, however, the central argument in this chapter is not that Dumont and his allies were solely responsible for the de-Christianization of Quebec. Rather, the socio-political context of the Dumont Commission – regarded as one of the key benchmarks that set the course for contemporary Quebec Catholicism[12] – illustrated that in the climate of international "cultural revolution" that affected Quebec and other Western societies in the 1960s, attempts to effect a fusion between post–Vatican II Catholicism and "secular" political values represented by democratic socialism and modern nationalism were to prove intensely conflictual, and ultimately illusory as the basis for political and social cohesion in a post-industrial society.

What Dumont and a coterie of like-minded Catholics hoped to achieve was, in the first instance, to radically purge Catholic values of any remaining "sociological," traditionalist tincture. They would then critique and try to re-launch the Quiet Revolution in a socialist direction by directing their fire against the type of liberal reformism that had emerged in the early 1960s, in which Quebec elites sought to forge an accommodation of public values between Catholicism and an interventionist liberal state by anchoring democracy on an order of intermediate bodies. What Dumont and his left Catholic allies desired was a full acceptance of the logic of social pluralism, which required a rapid abandonment of the Church's institutional privileges in education and social services. Catholicism, however, would not be absent from Quebec. Rather, through a more community-oriented, fully democratized parish life, it would play an important political role by fostering within the individual the values of communitarian solidarity that would create a shared cultural bond between Catholic believers and other committed social democrats. This would, in the estimation of this Catholic elite, allow Quebec to become truly independent by conferring upon it the cultural resources to resist the hedonism and privatization associated with Quebec's proximity to North American capitalism. However, between 1967 and 1970, this direct attempt by elite lay Catholics and a number of allies within the upper clergy to resolve the crisis of authority by subordinating Catholicism to a political creed failed to forge a new consensus in Quebec around the ideal of a social-democratic nation, and instead aroused the widespread alienation of numerous Catholic faithful. The effort to secure a place for a politicized, communitarian Catholicism within the second cultural revolution not only failed to arrest, but arguably was a contributing factor in accelerating, the de-Christianization of the entire society.

Indeed, the 1960s cultural revolution, on its own, is not sufficient to explain the dramatic drop in religious attendance and public identification with Catholicism in Quebec. As Callum Brown, a leading revisionist historian of secularization has suggested, the United States was arguably more affected by the cultural consequences of the 1960s than was any other Western society. However, it did not experience as dramatic a drop in both personal and public religious commitments.[13] What distinguished Quebec from anglophone North America during the 1960s was what Fernand Dumont came to represent: a full-scale cultural assault led by vocal Catholic elites and powerful elements of the upper clergy, whose project of modernization was to rapidly reform and purify what they considered "traditional" Catholicism, which they criticized for its routine practices and lack of communitarian social content. In the case of Quebec, the consequence was that influential lay and clerical elements within Catholicism promoted what can only be described as a cultural schism. The act of labelling large numbers of ordinary Catholics as non-Christian effectively countenanced, in the name of a purer, more socially-oriented religion, the permanent alienation of large segments of francophone Quebecers from Church institutions. De-Christianization must thus be understood, not so much as the decline of private belief, but as the rapid loss of a Catholic public identity.

"THE FATHERS OF THE CHURCH BAPTIZED CONVERTS, BUT WE WILL HAVE TO CONVERT THE BAPTIZED"[14]

In March 1965, Cardinal Maurice Roy, the primate of the Quebec Church, began his address to a joint sitting of the legislature with the confident affirmation "*civis sum*: I am a citizen of Quebec." He thus asserted Catholicism's participation in the adventure of defining a new ideal of citizenship. Like the overwhelming majority of the legislators, Roy emphatically rejected a notion propagated by extremists within the Mouvement Laïque de Langue Française and a coterie of academic Marxists, namely, that the priest was a "suspicious-looking stranger," and the necessary corollary that church and state must operate in "watertight compartments." Evoking the new partnership that he and Premier Lesage had hammered out over Bill 60 in the late summer of 1963, in which confessionality was harnessed to the purposes of public education, the cardinal proclaimed that Catholicism was not something to be enjoyed privately by a favoured few. Rather, because Christianity was the principle of civic culture in modern society, the institutional presence of the Church at the heart of the civic order was thus absolutely essential, for it bore within it "a life that human society needs, a spiritual life that the State cannot give itself, but must treat as the wealth of the nation and do its utmost to assist its flowering." The transmission of this spiritual life from the Church to the faithful of Quebec, the fundamental element in building a new social harmony, would, Roy indicated, not simply take place in the weekly Sunday liturgy and sacraments administered through the parish church; rather, "it is in the public arena, and especially in the school," that Catholicism would cement its connection with the people of Quebec. [15]

At one level, Cardinal Roy's address marked the clearest expression of the Quiet Revolution's definition of democratic citizenship: that Catholicism was essential to the liveliness of an intermediate public realm comprising a range of institutions that mediated between the individual and the political order of the state, acting like a conductive material that would supply a constant flow of spiritual energy transmitted back and forth between private concerns and public imperatives. However, Roy's address was equally significant because he said so little about the precise institutional forms through which Catholicism would infuse public culture. Although he was most insistent upon the presence of Catholicism in Quebec's schools through the overt and continued recognition of confessionality as a central attribute of public education, he was far less concerned to declaim upon the managerial role that the clergy would play in the new educational structure. Rather, he seemed to detach Catholicism from institutional frameworks by dwelling upon the priority of an effective and improved pastoral message through a massive program of evangelizing and catechizing children and modern youth, which in his estimation was the only way to permanently cement Catholic priorities and Quebec's destiny as a modern state.

The priority that the Quebec hierarchy now placed upon the pastoral and educative, rather than managerial, aspects of Catholicism was not simply a matter of political tactics. Nor was it a plea to use the school, as the extension of the family and parish, to shore up "traditional" values in an age of social and ideological stress, although many Catholics would have maintained that the system of education should perform these social functions. Rather, Roy's intervention signalled the existence of a growing religious fissure within Quebec society that was ultimately to compromise the synthesis of Catholicism and civic values upon which the cultural dynamism of the Quiet Revolution rested. The evocation of the terms astoral and atechesis by prominent members of the Church hierarchy and the concomitant downplaying of the Church visible institutional role during the mid-1960s was hardly neutral, for it testified to a growing sense of instability caused by the attempts of a number of influential Catholics to overtly politicize religion. This effort was most clearly expressed in the work of Fernand Dumont, a sociologist and lay theologian whose activities aimed at subordinating Catholicism to nationalism with the explicit aim of promoting a new form of social cohesion based upon a synthesis between nationalism and social democracy. In so doing, Dumont and his allies not only aggravated the religious division in Quebec that a number of post-war Catholic Action elites had promoted as essential to their society journey to modernity, but in no small measure these democratic nationalists contributed to rupturing what religious consensus the Quiet Revolution had attempted to achieve.

Like many of his contemporaries, Fernand Dumont participated in Catholic Action circles during his college and university years in the late 1940s, but unlike the professional and lower-middle class elements that usually led the student movements, Dumont own social origins were explicitly working-class. While his religious reading resembled that of a number of his counterparts in that it reflected the influence of French personalists like Mounier, his earliest intellectual encounter was with the philosophy of Maurice Blondel, a Catholic modernist whose philosophy of immanence explicitly enjoined action, rather than the creation of coherent systems of reason. The initial attraction of Blondel thinking was that it contained an implicit critique of popular Catholic religious practices, whose ensual, naturalistic elements always compromised efforts to make spirituality more solid. More than ever, Dumont believed, Christians needed a philosophy such as Blondel's because they had to engage Marxists and existentialists by demonstrating that religion and human values could be integrated.[16]

As a devotee of action, Dumont was not entirely comfortable with the anti-political stance officially espoused by Catholic Action leaders like Claude Ryan, who saw the task of modern youth as the creation of organizations to promote cultural democracy and not engagement in nationalist politics. Dumont was far more positive about the potential of political action, and evinced a particular fascination with the experience of early twentieth-century French Catholic modernists who had sought to bring Catholicism within the ambit of the nation by fusing religion with republican democracy.[17] Writing on the occasion of the nationalist celebration of the hero of New France, Dollard des Ormeaux, Dumont drew a studious distinction between those "carping nationalists afflicted with excessive patriotism and oratorical diarrhea," and his own generation. However, he did not reject the choice of nationalist politics; rather, he urged modern youth to exemplify the existential values of "lucidity and choice," not just in their personal or religious lives, but in their engagement in the cause of nationalism. "We must," he declared, "be constantly aware of these when we evoke the memory of Dollard des Ormeaux. Since 1660, the facts have not changed much; the Iroquois are present, but wearing other garb. ... Defeatism is within our walls and, in the face of American materialism and a civilization of self-fulfillment, we sense an immense sigh of resignation in our people. We must either choose this defeatism or survival."[18]

Of equal significance, because he was nearly a decade younger than activists like Gérard Pelletier, Dumont had not experienced the Catholic Action emphasis of the 1930s, which had aspired to re-Christianize civilization through a blend of personal commitment and institutional initiatives. Rather, when he attended university in the late 1940s, he experienced a very particular and radical type of personalism which, in the case of Emmanuel Mounier, explicitly rejected the entire effort to anchor Christianity in institutional forms – and thus the entire notion of a "Christian civilization" – because this simply reproduced the psychological and social alienations of bourgeois individualism, and by drawing an artificial distinction between contemplation and action, exacerbated class polarizations in modern industrial society.[19] Dumont minutely dissected this mentality in a 1952 study session of the Jeunesse Étudiante Catholique, and particularly critiqued the religious attitudes of middle-class professional elites who, in his estimation, took refuge in a vague "humanism" that he regarded as ultimately illusory because it separated religion from life. Modern man, he believed, had come to see the world in purely functional terms, as a heterogeneous assemblage of social groups whose ideologies and activities were merely juxtaposed and did not communicate or interpenetrate one another. In order to transcend these alienations, Dumont explicitly warned Christians against forms of religious expression that exalted a contemplative retreat into the individual self; rather, his starting point for a new spirituality was not religious practice itself, but the Marxist belief that social solidarity was created through work. However, he did not posit an ineluctable dialectic of class conflict, believing that both the working class and middle classes, Christians and unbelievers, could be brought to accept a communitarian vision that affirmed through labour "the authenticity of participation in the human community."[20] For Quebec's university elites, this effort to achieve class solidarity meant an engagement with the social sciences as a way of transcending the compartmentalization of knowledge fostered by the old Catholic humanistic curriculum, and a realization of "the sovereign importance of the study of popular cultures in the past."[21]

However, it was Dumont's personal involvement with a number of Catholic missionary initiatives during the years he spent pursuing graduate work in sociology in Paris that enabled him to fuse political conviction, a radical form of Catholic personalism, and social science technique together into a potent myth of religious crisis and ineluctable de-Christianization. Upon his arrival in France in 1953, Dumont joined the Action Catholique Ouvrière, while his wife was enlisted as a lay catechist in a working-class parish. Through these contacts, Dumont encountered an applied social activism and spirituality that sought a conjunction between Christianity and Marxism through the commitment exemplifed by worker-priests and a group of Catholic clergy and laity centred around the journal *Économie et humanisme.* From *Économie et humanisme*, the young sociologist drew the liberationist imperatives of community and solidarity: this was the vision of a direct democracy in which all distinctions between the people were abolished through the creation of organic "communities of destiny," and in which no barriers of class or competence existed between the people and the political state. As Dumont wrote in 1967, while the poor certainly wanted a more prosperous society, their central desideratum was "a fraternal society, where there would be a sharing, not only of the fruits of economic growth, but of an ideal." In such a social democracy, a Christianity shared by all classes was the essential foundation of social solidarity, because religion allowed the poor a voice, a means of communicating with other social groups so that all could contribute to the transformation of society.[22] Such a utopia would achieve the suppression of class differences, and would be especially dedicated to the promotion of socially marginal individuals and groups, such as the working class, as the central progressive dynamic of human history.[23]

During the post-war period, this "Catholic left" promotion of the social and spiritual significance of the working class converged readily with a second current of religious endeavour that joined social science insights to the articulation of new forms of pastoral techniques in order to arrest what it considered the de-Christianization and religious denudation of French urban workers. What was compelling about the central text of this movement – *La France, pays de mission?* written in 1943 by Fathers Godin and Daniel – was its bleak vision of the paganization of the working class and of the ineffectiveness of traditional Catholic practices and organizations in competing with secular ideologies such as Marxism. These clergymen were especially critical of what they denounced as "bourgeois" Catholicism, the attempt to Christianize individual workers by separating them from their natural neighbourhood and workplace solidarities by forcing them to conform to middle-class moral and religious standards. This had the effect of alienating them from their communities by placing them within an unreal environment of parishes whose practices were completely divorced from real life. The result was that entire swaths of France, in their estimation, had become completely devoid of religion, to the extent that in some working-class suburbs only 10 per cent of people could be deemed to be practicing their faith.[24] Catholicism, they concluded, simply had no presence across large swaths of urban France because the parish community, the basic local unit of the Church, was not anchored in daily lived reality, a situation in which working-class "paganism" was a recipe for the resurgence of permanent class conflict.[25] Of more significance for Catholics like

Fernand Dumont who were attracted to political action, Godin and Daniel implicitly conferred religious sanction upon social democratic experimentation, arguing that new forms of pastoral renewal and religious action were inseparable from projects that sought to renovate social and political structures: only in tandem could "the effort to re-Christianize the masses" create a new, classless, republican community in which a purified new spirituality, encompassing all facets of work and life, would provide a new basis of social solidarity.[26]

Dumont's personal religious engagement and professional commitment to sociology came together through his involvement with the French Centre de Pastorale Rurale in the early 1950s, where he was exposed both to clergy who were sympathetic to the communitarian emphasis of *Économie et humanisme,* and to the work of Gabriel LeBras, a participant in the centre whose precise cartography of religious practice had powerfully influenced the bleak vision of working-class paganization. Through the power of statistics, LeBras posited a direct and ineluctable connection between urbanization, industrialization, and de-Christianization, and seemed to offer irrefutable proof of a French national community that was divided into "compartments of religious practice and indifference."[27] At one level, LeBras's measurement of religious practices was particularly troubling for Christian activists, because although it presented a society characterized by high levels of religious participation in the solemn rituals of baptism, marriage, and death, regular religious observance was in dramatic decline. French society, LeBras concluded, was rapidly becoming "global" rather than local in its beliefs and practices: because large cities exhibited the highest levels of religious indifference, and because cultural tendencies moved from urban areas to the countryside, the movement was inevitably towards Christianity as a minority religion.[28] However, far from lamenting this de-Christianization, LeBras argued that it enabled Catholicism to establish a crucial distinction between vital, committed religious adherence – which he identified with heroic, missionary activist minorities – and religious practice, by which he meant the conventional religion of the parish, which he maintained was mired in formalism, a residue of folkloric "magical" elements incompatible with the rational outlook of the "global" society and distant from what he estimated was "true Christianity."[29] When applied by social thinkers like Dumont in the Quebec context, LeBras's absolute division between the activist religion of elites and the formalistic, quasi-pagan religion of ordinary people served as both a social description of the process of de-Christianization, and a catalyst that ultimately provoked the very de-Christianization that Catholic modernists hoped to counteract.

That Dumont viewed this religious divide as central to his personal, political, and professional identity was apparent when he located its existence within the contrasting personal religious practices of his parents. While he described his mother as being conventionally pious, a woman whose religiosity was encompassed by the devotional exercises prescribed by "parrotting" the catechism of the Church, he maintained that his father's more withdrawn piety was more authentic, because by forcing the believer to confront the absence of God, it ultimately opened the solitary person to a greater solidarity with God that went "beyond practices and formulae."[30] Indeed, while his father's piety appeared to be more solitary, and carried on at the margins of prescribed institutional devotional culture, Dumont considered it to be more communitarian because it reflected the deeper human realities of workplace camaraderie, and more particularly, implicitly bore the national consciousness of a French-speaking proletariat condemned to poverty and unremitting toil by Anglo-Canadian owners and bosses.[31]

Upon his return from France to a position in the sociology department at Université Laval, Dumont was given an immediate opportunity to apply LeBras's synthesis of pastoral technique and social analysis to his own society. This occurred in 1956, when the enterprising bishop of St-Jérôme diocese, Monseigneur Frenette, sought to domesticate the notions advanced in *La France, pays de mission?* by applying the new French spirituality through *grandes missions* (large-scale diocesan missions) or a *pastorale d'ensemble* (collective pastoral) to the task of "re-Christianization." Here was an interesting choice of terminology, as Catholic clergy and lay activists had previously assumed that their religious efforts were directed at a population that was fully Christian in belief and practice, and that periodic missions were simply directed at revivifying tepid faith, or directing the opprobrium of the community at derelictions from Catholic morality. However, the new French spirituality no longer considered that faith was a cultural given or that youth were naturally Christian. The fundamental concern that was expressed in the language of the modern personalism so fashionable in the post-war French Catholic left and in Catholic Action circles was to provoke a "crisis of conscience" at the level of the community, to ensure "THE PRIMACY OF CHRISTIAN EXISTENCE over any and all institutions" and that the "theological dimension of the faith was understood and embodied in the daily life of those baptized."[32]

Following the lead of his French episcopal counterparts, Frenette enlisted the collaboration of sympathetic sociologists like Fernand Dumont and Yves Martin of Université Laval to undertake a thorough preliminary study of the "social milieus" of the diocese in order to enable the bishop and clergy to identify and choose committed religious leaders among the laity,[33] specifically, men and women who would share the new spirituality of "crisis" and work to purify Catholicism by awakening a new understanding of the implications of dogma. Through this, the clergy, advised by social science experts, sought to accomplish a thoroughly modernist project, that of remaking a transcendent spiritual community – one defined by religious elites from the top down – by coordinating and synthesizing catechesis, liturgy, preaching, lay apostolate, and charitable works over an entire diocese.[34] The infusion of personalist Catholicism would break apart the old, enclosed, "natural" solidarities of the parish community that they dismissed as outmoded at best, or at worst, as conduits for de-Christianization. The weakness of old-style Catholicism, wrote Mgr Paul-Émile Charbonneau, bishop of Hull in 1966, was its supposition that religious practice was naturally acquired. It therefore lacked "an anxiety for evangelization," and aimed exclusively at consolidating Christian institutions as a "supplement to the soul." Not surprisingly, Charbonneau concluded, many Quebec Catholics had become aware, since 1945, that there was "a profound divide between religious practice and real life," the consequence of an inward-looking, somewhat selfish spirituality which exalted the parish as a "little, self-sufficient Christian family."[35] The new, activist, communitarian spirituality was the necessary religious corollary of a society that had henceforth resolved to shed all its quaint, local, "folk" trappings, in the name of conforming to the inevitable sociological laws that would transform it into a "global" society of urban, rational values.

At the heart of the religious reform they sought to accomplish was a very specific notion of faith, the idea, as Fernand Dumont stated in 1964, that "in a certain and essential sense, the Christian religion is in a state of permanent crisis."[36] For these Catholic intellectuals who had thoroughly imbibed the message of French personalist spirituality and the call of *La France, pays de mission?* and who had sought to emulate the passionate humanistic style of existentialists like Jean-Paul Sartre,[37] "crisis" was not a negative or troubling condition for the Christian faith. Rather, it was described as "a real confrontation between the Gospel and human life, a difficult struggle to be waged in order to pass from an infantile to an adult stage of faith."[38] Crisis was something to be frankly welcomed and provoked, a necessary "test" between belief and doubt in which each individual human would have to make an all-or-nothing choice between an affirmation of being and the "feeling of nothingness." This, they maintained, would reconstruct Catholic faith less around the notion of allegiance to a clerical hierarchy or received traditions and practices, than on a basis of "personal conviction, born of a closer study of one's religion." Apostles of this modernist Catholicism adopted a Marxian dialectical concept which stressed what they believed was an inevitable conflict within Catholicism between spontaneous community experiences, which remained close to the transcendent Message, and the abstract legalism of official structures. The only way in which modern Catholics could resolve the alienation resulting from the contradiction between their faith and the modern world was to shed, as rapidly as possible, any lingering loyalty to old pious traditions and their dependence on clerical authority, and to practice a purified spirituality of direct personal access to the Gospels.[39] The goal, they maintained, was a faith more adapted to an urban society and one in the process of rapid change, one in which Catholicism, far from safeguarding traditional values, would be the source of new models of identity and social cohesion.[40]

Two convictions were central to the dialectic posited by these modernist Catholics: first, the belief that two forms of religious experience were locked in conflict; and second, as derived from the objective social science data supplied by investigators like LeBras, the belief that there had never been any authentic Christianity practiced by ordinary Quebec people. As stated by Father Jacques Grand'Maison in 1964, "in daily life, the mass of Christians are still in fact at the level of pre-evangelization. Faith never intervenes practically in human relations. Many have retained the religious habits of their forefathers without holding onto their faith."[41] The religion historically supplied by Catholicism in Quebec, stated Fernand Dumont in the language of modern sociology, sought to forge the cohesion of a "Christian people" through representations of the sacred that had been "spontaneously secreted by social settings close to nature and rural traditions."[42] This form of religious expression, in Dumont's estimation, was inappropriate to modern Quebec because it ultimately rested upon a refusal of reality, an unwillingness to directly confront the social consequences of industrialism. In attempting to foster the image of religious homogeneity, the Church had in fact privileged a moral code constructed around conformity, culpability, and fear. Worse still, the old religious tradition had envisioned too close a correspondence between the folk beliefs of the natural human order and the religious community, and, consequently, Catholicism in Quebec was anchored upon "a dog's breakfast of pseudo-beliefs that are in reality superstitions barely disguised by a thin coat of Christian veneer."[43] The form of religion deemed desirable flowed instead directly from the "juxtaposition of religion and real conscience,"[44] and permitted humans to finally resolve the alienations of modern existence by encountering a more troubling, questioning God. This God, declared Dumont, "is no longer a familiar God that we have tamed once and for all by ritual, ceremonies, 'retreats,' a type of God that is ready to use. The God of the man of our time is a God that we unexpectedly bump up against, a God that we find when we have experienced constant alienation ... a God that we find through painful searching only when we have questioned the entire basis of our society or our family. ... A God whose existence is always placed in question by our own conditions of existence."[45] Catholic modernists like Dumont were thus intent upon drawing a fundamental distinction between what they meant by "authentic" or "adult" faith, and the religion currently practiced in Quebec, whose continued adherence to which would only perpetuate a conformist evasion into individual, petit-bourgeois self-satisfaction, and ultimately aggravate both individual and social pathologies.[46]

In the early 1960s, this new spirituality entered the mainstream cultural world of the university-educated social scientists and the upper clergy through the monthly journal *Maintenant*, established in Montreal by the Dominican Order at the beginning of 1962. Although not a mass-circulation magazine, it claimed 12,000 subscribers and a readership of 50,000,[47] easily surpassing its older and better-known counterpart, *Cité libre*. Through articles on spirituality, religion, birth control, education, and political questions, and through periodic symposia on issues ranging from the nature of religious sentiment among contemporary youth, to the deficiencies of traditional parish organizations and confraternities, and to religious conformity in Quebec, *Maintenant* adopted a self-conscious "left Catholic" identity. As two of its editors stated in 1965, the magazine rested upon two fundamental convictions: "first, that the Gospel is a little-understood *revolutionary* document; and second, that the Vatican Council was convened to give the green light to this profound *revolution* of Christian consciences." The clientele was frankly ecumenical: comprising anxious and doubting Christians, and sincere non-Christians or unbelievers who desired the advancement of the dignity and personal values of all humanity.[48]

However, beneath this democratic language lurked the elitist cultural refrain of those who had imbibed the radical post-war French personalism: the utter and complete contrast between the "true" Catholicism forged in a conversation with modern existential humanism and the realism of the new social sciences, and the "false" Christianity of Quebec's supposedly-disappearing rural past. Guy Rocher, who was another Université Laval sociologist, was a key member of the Parent Commission, and later was deputy-minister of culture under Camille Laurin after the Parti Québécois achieved power in 1976, stated that the worst failing of Quebec's traditional religion was that it was simply an empty shell of observances and social conformities, utterly lacking in mysticism or a principle of fraternal cohesion, a sort of "Confucian Catholicism" devoid of any spiritual life.[49] The promoters of this synthesis of existentialism and Catholicism were forthright about proclaiming their conviction that, by these criteria, Quebec was not, in spite of the nearly universal character of its Catholic identity, a truly Christian society. For this reason, they looked upon the process of secularization with rather sanguine equanimity, convinced that secular modernity would only weaken the traditional folk religion – which was the antithesis of true Christianity – and would permit the unfolding of an authentic spirituality.[50]

This Catholic existentialism was both the product of and directed towards a social and intellectual avant-garde, which its advocates exalted as a kind of "vanguard prophetic movement."[51] It is difficult to escape the conclusion that the proponents of this new Catholicism, by emphasizing the participation of Christians in economic, political, and social struggles for human liberation, and by systematically severing their supporters from any historical or family connection with older forms of piety, deliberately designed their movement to make it easier for a left-leaning cultural and political coterie to retain its Catholic identity. The modern Christian believer, stated Guy Rocher, had a great deal to learn from the "weight of sorrow and the fervent hope in history and human destiny" exhibited by atheists and Marxists.[52] The Catholic modernists clustered around *Maintenant* made no secret of the fact that their desire was for a Catholicism reconstructed, not as a continuous development from Quebec's religious past to the present day, but in accordance with questions and expectations formulated by Marxists, doubters, and unbelievers. Something of this mood was captured by the student leader Pierre Marois, at that time president of the Association Générale des Étudiants de l'Université de Montréal, and later a member of René Lévesque's government. "More than ever," proclaimed Marois in 1964, "Quebec has need of great men, of profoundly spiritual 'madmen'; I do not say Catholics, atheists, communists: these words are too charged with emotion ... I remain convinced that the spiritual crisis of our time can only favour the bursting forth, the unfolding of such men."[53] In 1965, the new editorial team of *Maintenant* openly declared that it would rather publish an article "by an agnostic trade-unionist than one written in the cloying and sermonizing style of a zealous propagandist of pious works."[54]

Much of this Catholic modernist solicitousness towards unbelief can be attributed to the fact that both Catholic modernists and agnostics drew upon an international existentialist language of alienation and personal engagement in human struggle. However, in the case of Quebec, "left Catholics" also had another imperative, the maintenance of a post-war climate in which religion had united a wide spectrum of "progressive" opinion among students, university faculty, journalists, and trade union leaders. In a celebrated article written in 1960, Gérard Pelletier bemoaned the loss of religious "unanimity" in Quebec. What he meant by this, however, was not the sundering of liberals and traditionalists along religious lines, nor even the existence of greater religious "pluralism" in Quebec society. Rather, he expressed his anguish at the spread of agnosticism among thoughtful people disgusted by "a religion of sleep walkers ... utterly lacking in vitality." What this reformer particularly feared was a situation in which "the militants ... the most conscious, talented, and most active of each social category," would simply abandon any identification with the Church.[55] This in turn would, in the long run, severely diminish the public influence and authority of Catholicism, which "left Catholics" like Pelletier without exception desired to shore up and extend.

In this respect, the "crisis" model of faith proposed by the Catholic modernists of the 1960s, which rested upon the premise of inevitable conflict, induced them to agonize less over the defections of traditionalist Catholics, than over the perceived de-Christianization of the educated middle classes of Quebec society. According to Father H.M. Robillard, the unbelievers and atheists most opposed to the Church were not "gross and unrefined souls," but rather "the delicate souls, the souls of artists ... those that are profoundly religious."[56] Far better, in the estimation of these "left Catholics," was the loss of traditional Catholics, whose faith was at best "infantile," if it existed at all, than a compromise between traditionalists and modernists which would offer at best a "ghetto Christianity" of blind adherence to ritual. This would only succeed in marginalizing the Church in the long term from the new currents of public life, which required a conscious engagement with social reality.[57] Indeed, as Father Bradet, the director of *Maintenant,* declared in a 1963 editorial statement, it would be most unwise to even attempt to work out a synthesis between the traditionalist and progressive elements in Quebec Catholicism. Tolerance was only possible, he stated, at the level of human persons, not at the level of ideas. He reminded those who already possessed the "truth," meaning, of course, the new existentialist Catholicism, that any concessions in the direction of their old-guard opponents would only ensure that Quebec's salutary religious "crisis" would unfold in an atmosphere of "sadness, which would make it harder to endure and less rapid."[58] The "left Catholics" clustered around *Maintenant* easily lumped all Catholics who did not share their existentialist vision of faith under the rubric "fundamentalist," and accused them of propping up a joyless, inward-looking "religion of mortal sin."[59]

What was significant about this imported French pastoral sociology, with its arrogant dismissal of the on-Christian character of Quebec working-class and small-town religious faith in the late 1950s, was that it did not function in a watertight religious compartment. First and foremost, many of those lay activists and clergy associated with the new evangelistic emphasis sought to work a spiritual reformation of Quebec as the foundation of a cultural and political revolution. In the hands of Fernand Dumont and a number of younger social scientists, it not only was accorded a status as the central cultural litmus test for Quebec entry into modernity, but, more importantly, it became inextricably fused with a vision of socio-political nationalism that during the early 1960s irrevocably shattered the old equilibrium between Catholicism and nationalism that had existed in the mainstream of Quebec intelligentsia.

Despite some disagreements over whether Quebec national character was determined by "rural" or "urban" characteristics, "traditional nationalists" and their critics[60] accepted the personalist notion that a hierarchy existed between nationalism and religion, and that the former was always subordinated to the latter.[61] Whatever their perspective on political action, Catholic personalists until the late 1950s accepted the main premises of Catholic sociology, a pluralist notion that the "nation" was primarily an intermediate cultural terrain that encompassed local familial, occupational, and religious identities.[62] The corollary to this was the idea that the "nation" stood outside the political state, and advocates of this position could thus maintain that a number of "nationalisms" could coexist within one political regime. Thus, nationalism was not necessarily coextensive with politics or the state, a definition which allowed most of the Catholic intelligentsia to participate in a Quebec nationality that functioned within a decentralized federal system of limited sovereignties. Because national consciousness flowed from the particularities of the biological and familial social order, it was subordinate to Catholicism – which represented the universalizing qualities of humanism and the rationality of the spirit – in the hierarchy of human values. Thus, while the Catholic Action youth movements certainly applauded the positive virtues of patriotism – loyalty to family, local cultures, and traditions – expressed by nationalism, they always worried about the potential for xenophobic excess that would detract from the wider humanism and religion, and especially sought to counteract the seductions of political action that would draw young people away from the priorities of apostolic endeavour.[63] Indeed, it was the Catholic religion – an international institution not distinctive to Quebec – and not the "particular" values inherent in the French language, that encompassed and expressed qualities that connected individual and society in Quebec to universal realities.

In an article written for *Cité libre* in 1958, just after his participation in the St-Jérôme *grande mission*, Dumont boldly reversed this order of priorities in a savage attack on both old and new Catholic nationalists and their liberal Catholic critics, such as Pelletier and Trudeau.[64] What stimulated his intervention were the implications of the historical writing of a group of historians associated with the department of history at the Université de Montréal, whose pessimistic interpretation portrayed Quebec as a decapitated or truncated nation, incapable of normal development towards political sovereignty because its commercial elite had been destroyed during the British Conquest of 1760. Quebec's collective destiny, its entire system of psychological and social identities, had, in their estimation, been consistently frustrated because the nation's leadership was in the hands of a conservative clergy and a collaborationist petit-bourgeois element that was incapable of providing the necessary impetus towards full independence, a situation which placed Quebec in a permanent status of inferiority.[65] A number of social scientists discerned two exits from their society's historical dilemma. Dumont's Université Laval colleague, the political scientist Léon Dion, drew from this pessimistic nationalism the conclusion that Quebec should frankly accept the political and cultural possibilities offered by the cultural dualism of the Canadian federation. "The old ideal that each people should have exclusive possession of cultural resources," he stated, was frankly outmoded. Surely, according to Dion, "each people would be richer through a sharing of resources and the internationalization of certain political functions." In the end, however, his liberal federalism rested upon the old premises of Catholic sociology, which accorded the "nation" a strictly limited role in that "it could not encompass the entire reality and the being of individuals, social groups, or institutions."[66]

Fernand Dumont's central contribution to the debate lay, in fact, in a complete rethinking of the premises out of which both the Montreal school and Dion worked. It was not nationalism itself, but a particular type of nationalism identified with the petit-bourgeois intelligentsia, that was responsible for Quebec's collective sense of frustration. In his diagnosis, the problem that afflicted both pessimistic nationalists and the new liberal federalists lay in their acceptance of the subordination of nationalism to Catholicism. Because the Catholic elites were all universally educated in the traditional humanistic curriculum of the classical colleges, it was this clericalized education, and not so much the events of the distant past, that had systematically occluded the achievement of both personal and collective self-awareness in Quebec. Rather than encouraging adolescents to look forward to the future, such a view erected the past into a dogmatic system that blocked access to universal values because this Catholic humanism was "too abstract" and "illusory." Quebec's social and cultural leaders thus offered a ridiculous spectacle: either they claimed that rigid adherence to the past opened people to a broad humanism, or "those who have broken the nationalist shell seek to proceed directly to the human without the mediation of culture, and thus they run up against the solidarity of conscience and culture and ... thus become men from nowhere."[67] Ultimately, the impasse of bourgeois nationalism was that it had divorced itself from cultural reality. What in fact hampered both groups was their conviction that nationalism expressed only those psychosocial verities that were local and particular. In Dumont's estimation, this definition was appropriate to the world of "little local traditional cultures such as existed in the nineteenth century," and relied upon the knowledge and values provided by oral traditions and the immediate neighbourhood. Worse still, the identification of nationalism with the natural and the instinctive realm, and religion with reason and humanism, made the achievement of a broader sense of community impossible, because such identifications were quintessential expressions of the cultural aspirations of the professional middle classes, whose existence was increasingly vapid and unreal next to the working-class majority created by modern industrial growth.[68]

Dumont's exit from the impasse flowed from his adherence to what he believed was Quebec's trajectory from a "folk" to a "global" society. Building upon the "objective" social data of Gabriel LeBras, Dumont was able to pronounce the demise of local, natural, and instinctive identities in Quebec, as Quebec had ineluctably become a "global society" whose values penetrated and transformed all the local cultures, welding them into a whole. The individual no longer encountered reality through the mediation of family and parish, but was now directly exposed to the influence of large-scale social, economic, and political organizations, and to the messages and techniques propagated by mass media. Quebec's destiny, he emphatically averred, was no longer in the hands of precious petit-bourgeois social elites, because the new industrial order and the cultural life of large cities had not only created a significant working class, but had opened both city workers and rural dwellers "to a social horizon that takes in French-Canadian society in all its dimensions."[69]

In Dumont's hands, however, the notion of "global society" was not simply a heuristic device for the formulation of social science hypotheses: it was effectively equated with the nation itself. "Fatherlands," he declared, "are obsolete; there now exists only the nation."[70] Effectively, nationalism could no longer be the expression of any one class, but had to articulate "a *destiny* and a *choice*" that reflected the aspirations of all classes to achieve a higher realization of community.[71] Thus, for humans confronted with the implications of the "global society," the old Catholic definition of patriotism as a function of the local and the particular could no longer be sustained, and had to be abandoned. Where prior to the mid-1950s Quebec's intellectual and social leadership had concurred that Catholicism was the vehicle through which people gained access to universal values, Dumont argued that nationalism must now replace religion. Nationalism alone could perform this universalizing function because, unlike Catholicism, it was a constant struggle to "realize a deeper sense of community" among all classes.[72] Dumont further universalized nationalism by assimilating its Quebec manifestation to a homegrown social democracy, an international movement that sought to perfect democracy by satisfying the aspirations of the working-class proletariat for fraternity, social and political promotion, and inclusion in the civic polity. Because Quebec nationalism, like that of other independent nations, seamlessly incarnated what appeared to be the progressive values of human community, because, more specifically, it sought to transcend class differences and create a more just human community, Dumont asserted that

Quebec's aspirations to a separate nationhood must be satisfied. Thus, because modern society itself was now total, the nation was a total entity that required expression in a sovereign political state.[73]

However, if the nation now constituted the supreme collective expression of human personal, social, and political aspirations, what relationship would Quebec Catholicism continue to have to this modern, "global" society? As a fervent Catholic activist, Dumont could not countenance a complete evisceration of Catholicism from the nation, but neither could he accept the old identification of Catholicism with universal values, as this was but the expression of a bankrupt, class-exclusive humanism. Dumont's search for a new relationship between church and nation involved a reading of the past that differed both from that of the pessimistic nationalist historians and that of the liberal federalists. Where both these groups identified clerical supremacy as a consequence of the British Conquest, with the consequent stunting of other lay elites, Dumont contended that the vision of a unanimous society clustered around its clergy was a relatively recent construct, dating from only the 1850s, and was not the product of a conspiracy between the clergy and British overlords. Rather, it was a choice made by lay elites, who opted for nationalism instead of democracy, and turned the Church into the "armature of nationality."[74]

Significantly, Dumont did not read this situation as a simple ultramontane subservience of the Quebec nation to the Catholic Church; rather, the situation was more ambiguous because it also made the Church the servant of the nation,[75] a position which opened the possibility of lay elements one day recouping their social and political powers. Given this historically close relationship, the question then became, Could the values that Catholicism supplied be coordinated with a nation whose values were democratic? Dumont emphatically answered yes, provided that Catholicism could give up its old sociological idea of intermediate, quasi-independent orders that stood between the state and the individual, and merely served to block and disaggregate the collective social will of the nation. In his estimation, Catholicism provided values that were absolutely vital to nurturing this national collective sense. Dumont argued that, because religion was "essentially the creator of community,"[76] it supplied an essential element of social cohesion by enabling people to "found their choices in fidelities." Despite his fervent commitment to a cult of nationalism as progress, as a committed Catholic activist he could scarcely ignore the close historical association between Catholicism and most of Quebec's social institutions. "Fidelity," for a global society, implied using religion as a principle of stability and cohesion, as a medium which would allow the citizens of the new Quebec to commune with their past as the way of informing choices in the present and future.[77] While Catholicism could not fulfill its older role of supplying the basic structure of the national community – a task that would now be performed by the political state – Dumont emphatically maintained that the Church supplied a "perpetual appeal to a sense of common life," specifically, a suspicion of large, impersonal bureaucratic powers, and a concern for justice and equality, values from the past that could be re-expressed in modern ideologies like social democracy.[78] By incarnating these values in its own appropriate community, the Catholic parish, rather than seeking to manage social welfare and educational institutions, would play a central task in bringing Quebec to accept the social democratic creed. In this way, the values of a shared religious fellowship would ultimately enable Quebec to link both political and cultural independence in the act of resisting the pressures towards conformity to a mass civilization whose values tended towards a vapid, individual self-satisfaction.

"IN QUEBEC, DUPLESSISM IS NOT DEAD"[79]

As outlined by Fernand Dumont and the "left" Catholics clustered around the journal *Maintenant,* the synthesis of a Catholicism shorn of its "folkloric" elements and a nationalist social democracy constituted a full-scale assault on one of the central achievements of the Quiet Revolution, the attempt to reconcile Catholic social thought – with its ascending hierarchy of collective familial, occupational, and social identities – with the primacy of the state in order to assure the direction and coordination of a modern economy. What the educational and social welfare reforms undertaken by the Lesage administration indicated was the desire to erect a liberal notion of public authority that combined greater state initiative and coordination with the existence and vitality of a sphere of intermediate, sub-political authorities that assured the health of the civic order, a type of "neo-corporatism" that privileged a political and social stability based upon a working partnership of institutionalized consultation between the state and social "powers" like the Catholic Church,[80] who would retain a large degree of independent initiative within their spheres of competence. In this respect, it can be argued that the Quebec government was not engaged in an aggressive secularization that aimed at displacing the Church from the social sphere, but was in fact acting within the Catholic framework of "socialization" as outlined in the Vatican II encyclical *Mater et magistra.*

In an address to the Confédération des Syndicats Nationaux (the former Catholic confessional trade unions) in 1961, Claude Ryan interpreted the encyclical as an updating and revision of Catholic social doctrines. Unlike the papal pronouncements of 1891 and 1931, which had specifically cited corporatism as the ideological system most compatible with Catholic doctrine, *Mater et magistra* did not mention the term "corporatism." Indeed, Ryan argued that the pope was perfectly reconciled to an enhanced role for the political state in social and economic life as a way of responding to the increased "socialization" of human experience, in which the collectivity impinged far more upon the individual. However, as Ryan observed, the pope was adamant that the individual should not simply be confronted with an all-encompassing state. Thus, the encyclical preserved the older corporatist principle of the subsidiary function of the state, in which intermediate bodies retained their independence and functions, and more importantly, it retained the differentiation between the economic and social on the one hand, and the political on the other.[81]

In this way, "corporatism" was transformed into a model of "organic democracy," a form of organization in which the tendency of the state to assume more responsibilities and to absorb the individual was balanced by an order of intermediate bodies whose actions contributed to the evolution of the civic sphere. According to Father Richard Arès, it was the imperative duty of the modern state to actively promote "the presence and action of those groups, associations, organizations and institutions that flow from private initiative and which are to a considerable extent the intermediaries between the individual and the public powers."[82] Catholic spokesmen like Father Gérard Dion were most intent on demonstrating the superiority of this synthesis of corporatism and democracy over individualist notions of liberalism, in which organized private interests had no way of expressing themselves except through the mechanism of political parties, where they assumed the insidious, quasi-clandestine role of lobbies and pressure groups. Under the rubric of "organic democracy," such organized economic, professional, and institutional groups had a precise legal definition and powers as para-public bodies which enjoyed an independence from the actual machinery of the state. However, their social action did not operate in a watertight compartment, because these groups enjoyed a close association with the political order. Their role was to organize opinion through properly-constituted mechanisms of consultation which were defined and concerted by the state, where their influence on government measures was permanent, recognized, and open.[83] As liberal spokesmen like Claude Ryan recognized, such intermediate bodies and a structured system of consultation were absolutely necessary in a modern democracy, where elected legislatures had been progressively weakened by the assumption of ever-greater social and economic powers by the executive branches. And, more specifically, in the Quebec context, "organic democracy" meant that in the key sectors of education, social security, hospital care, and education the state that desired to "truly respect the personality of its citizens ... would seek to promote the existence, for each of the major spiritual families, of institutions that answer the legitimate aspirations of their members."[84]

Here, Ryan expressed what was the central imperative of the Quiet Revolution as it was manifested in the politics of the 1960s, the elaboration of a system of public authority in which Catholic values continued to be expressed in specific institutional frameworks, and the Church continued to be a power in society. Quebec would not only retain its character as a Christian society, but, under a regime of "organic democracy," Catholicism would attain a far more effective cultural and social purchase – and an even more pervasive cultural authority – through partnerships between church and state that would effectively integrate and express religion in efficient modern institutions like the public confessional school and the mixed publicly regulated and funded but privately managed social welfare system of the Boucher Report. Although subject to standards set by the state, understood as being the guardian of the interests of civil society, Catholicism would retain its freedom of action and internal self-government. Thus, it would serve as an effective basis of social cohesion because of its closer integration with the political realm through ongoing mechanisms of consultation and coordination.

However, in this key aspect – the effort to elaborate a relationship of Catholicism to the state around the idea of institutional partnerships – the Quiet Revolution did not enjoy a consensual status among influential Catholics. Indeed, those like Fernand Dumont and the *Maintenant* group, who sought to reinterpret Catholicism as the expression of a nationalist social democracy, rejected the institutional dynamic of the Quiet Revolution, that is, the attempt to accommodate Catholic sociology to a modern polity. From the perspective of the "global society," the whole concept of "intermediate bodies" – and Christian institutions other than the Church hierarchy and the parish community – was retrograde, utterly incompatible both with their modernist notion of spirituality and with their idea of a socio-political national will organized by and around the state.

As a former national secretary of Catholic Action, Claude Ryan had as his bedrock commitment the necessity for modern society to articulate an "intermediate," sub-political culture of educative and civic institutions as a means of linking human persons to the state without the annihilation of individuality in collective structures. His political convictions, both as editor of *Le Devoir* and later as leader of the Quebec Liberal party, were anchored upon finding an equilibrium between personal and collective freedom, a balance which depended upon a studious adherence to the proper boundaries between private effort, cooperative initiative, and government. Ryan was thus a caustic critic of statist models of social democracy because he considered them both economically inefficient and overly-restrictive of personal liberty. Indeed, for Quebec to follow the socialist model would entail "an excessive insistence upon machinery of collective protectionism and ultimately, of authoritarian methods, and an exaggerated dependence on state institutions and a tendency ... to structure all facets of human life according to a pattern whose imprint stressed the collective and the orthodox."[85]

Catholics like Fernand Dumont, however, saw in Ryan's attempt to refurbish the synthesis between Catholic sociology and liberalism the negation of their own attempt to build a new collective solidarity out of political nationalism, Catholicism, and social democracy. Dumont warned that the greatest threat facing his society in the mid-1960s was the resurgence of conservative social values, which he believed would fragment and diffuse the effort to elaborate a state-centred nationalism that joined all classes together in a single collective purpose. He discerned the main obstacle to national cohesion as the resurgence of an indigenous petite-bourgeoisie, and he particularly denounced the marriage of neo-corporatism and Catholic sociology – that is, the concept of an "organic democracy" of intermediate bodies – as the principal manifestation of this conservatism.[86]

What Dumont especially feared was that through this combination of Catholicism and liberalism, religion, rather than grounding the nation in a communitarian spiritual solidarity, thus anchoring democratic socialism in a political theology, would legitimate its very antithesis, a vague individualistic pluralism that obliterated any distinction between Quebec and North America. "While we can congratulate ourselves," he observed, "for escaping the ideological intolerance of the past, are we to be satisfied with an ideological hodge-podge in which freedom will be as empty as it is absolute? In the end, this would so privilege an individualistic notion of freedom that it would leave us no principle of social cohesion but the empty dreams of consumerist abundance."[87] In order to transcend both the "proletarian condition" in which the Quebec nation had been placed, and to avoid the ideological shoals of a liberal pluralism of individual self-fulfillment, Dumont urged a breach with the tenets of Catholic sociology. This necessitated a twofold realization: first, the abandonment of any notion that society was somehow independent from the political state, and second, a merciless exposure of the unrepresentative nature of the "intermediate bodies," and especially their inability to encompass a national, collective ideal, a task that could only be effectively organized by the state itself.[88] However, this did not mean a disjuncture between Catholicism and the public realm, only the insistence that "religious faith would no longer be the shabby prop for an underdeveloped society,"[89] and a definition of ways in which Catholic spirituality could nourish the unanimous cohesion and fellowship that was essential to socialism. One of Dumont's colleagues, the social scientist Guy Rocher, was equally forceful about the need for a conjunction of mutual spiritual values between Catholicism and socialism. "I am persuaded," he concluded, "that francophone Quebecers have behind them a long religious and spiritual tradition from which they will not be suddenly detached, and that they do not have to deny in order to build a society that is socialist in both spirit and structure."[90] In this way, Catholics like Rocher and Dumont could maintain that although the principle of social cohesion would be emphatically political in nature, the synonymity of values between religion and socialism ensured that Catholicism would be an indispensable adjunct to the achievement of political independence through the building of a just society whose principle of social cohesion flowed in an unmediated way from the state to the individual.

In this respect, the priority that Dumont and Rocher assigned to the state, and their subordination of Catholicism to the political order in the task of building a human community, brought the Catholic "left" close to the more aggressive secularism of the Mouvement Laïque de Langue Française (MLLF). Speaking in 1966, Marcel Rioux had declared that the fundamental civic identities in a modern community were not a function of membership in religious communities, but were directly derived from the "global society" whose sole legitimate organ was the state. "Before being Catholics, Protestants, or Jews," Rioux maintained, "the individuals who comprise a contemporary state are first and foremost citizens, and the good qualities of citizenship, not religious allegiance, have first claim upon their obligations."[91] From this standpoint, the primary purpose of the state was to assure a collective will to live, and to resist those forces, in particular pluralist liberal notions of "organic democracy," that sought to fragment this national will. In such a society, it was incumbent upon Catholics to "put their religion in parentheses," and to cease clamouring for institutional recognition and "privileges" that would only stunt the maturation of the state-centred collectivity.[92] Similarly, the young historian René Durocher, already formulating what was to be the central tenet of the "normal society" master-narrative – the irrelevance of religion to those socio-political forces that built a modern nation – contended that religion should be completely eviscerated from Quebec society as a category of public identity. "Religion," he concluded, "pertains to individuals, families, groups and churches, but has nothing to do with the State."[93] The statism of Rioux and Durocher rested upon the claim that in a modern society where all facets of human existence tended to become ineluctably public in character, religion – and in particular Catholicism – was destined to lose those institutions that connected it to the public realm, and consequently fade into the background as an expression of a less dynamic "private" culture whose tendencies to exalt personal satisfaction constituted a socially fragmenting impulse that must always be carefully circumscribed by the state.

The Catholic nationalist social democrats were forced to confront the secularist critique of an ongoing connection between religion and public culture head-on at a December 1966 "teach-in" held in Montreal. There, Dr Jacques Mackay argued that Catholicism could never produce more than a "bastardized" accommodation with the scientific, libertarian, and rational values of modern humanism, because the need of the faithful to adhere to dogma produced "a complete passivity in the face of the constituted authorities and an adherence to an immobile conservatism." To those on the Catholic "left" who believed that religion could be the foundation of social and political dynamism, Mackay retorted that, while progressive elements in the Church had been forced to "cohabit" with people who did not share their philosophy in order to effect necessary social change, their power relative to the weight of conservatism was quite limited. At best, the existence of a "left" current in the Church was evidence of a psycho-pathology among Catholics, a dichotomy between "their real life and that of their beliefs" that could ultimately not be reconciled.[94]

Two Catholic participants in the symposium, Father Norbert Lacoste and Dr Camille Laurin, countered Mackay's aggressive secularism with the argument that Catholicism had to distance itself from the "core of fundamentalists who remain in the Church." Laurin, in particular, was adamant that "through their dynamism and energy, the forward-looking elements in the Quebec Church will sooner or later triumph over the obscurantists."[95] It should be recognized that the social-democratic Catholic left fully accepted the central premise of the MLLF: that Quebec society was now "global" rather than particularist, and that the state was the sole legitimate articulator of personal and social identities. However, it could not accept the corollary to this secularist vision of modernity, the notion that in such a society religion must be divorced from the public sphere and function purely within the ambit of private identities. Change, dynamism, and revolution, those watchwords of Quebec during the 1960s, were not words that were divorced from the Christian experience. As Guy Rocher observed in 1970, "the ideology of transformation and revolutionary ideologies [is] profoundly rooted in an old Judeo-Christian tradition which ... views the world through a historical consciousness where, in a way that is sometimes coherent and sometimes violent, the action of humans and the intervention of God are mingled together."[96] And from this standpoint, the aim of the MLLF to separate Catholicism arbitrarily from the contemporary world, to compel it to adopt an attitude of retreat and opposition, would be to "impoverish" Quebec society, depriving it of an important wellspring of socio-political radicalism.[97] The most serious danger that faced Quebec society, in the estimation of social scientists like Fernand Dumont and Guy Rocher, was not the connection between Catholicism and the state, but the marginalization of religion from the great issues of social change and nationalism.

In the years after 1966, the attempt to ground a thoroughgoing critique of North American liberalism in a fusion of Catholicism, nationalism, and social democracy entailed a growing identification with René Lévesque and the emergent Parti Québécois. However, what attracted "left" Catholics like Dumont to this fledgling political movement was less the idea of Quebec independence that it espoused, than the direct relationship Lévesque postulated between political sovereignty and social democratic conviction. As the Liberal minister of family and social services after 1965, Lévesque had come to the attention of Catholic progressives through his assertion that social welfare needed to be coherent, democratic, and universal, and that it must rest on the principle that "the citizen had a fundamental right to security, and that this must not be confused with assistance to the needy or indigent," a principle which logically compelled him to question the efficacy of the role of religious institutions of public charity that stood between the citizen and the state. [98] Indeed, in 1966 and 1967, as Lévesque moved towards the idea of sovereignty-association as the vision of Quebec's future, his views converged with those of Catholic social democrats, especially around the notion of resistance to liberal theories of "organic democracy."

Politics, stated the editors of *Maintenant* in 1967, "is all-encompassing and covers everything. ... The State structures everything and becomes the keystone which holds the national edifice in place. In this context, we cannot be content with the parcelling of power; this is to resign ourselves to paralysis."[99] During the discussions undertaken to establish the Mouvement Souveraineté-Association in the fall of 1967, the new political movement most emphatically rejected any ties with neo-corporatist theories of liberalism, arguing instead for the need for a state-centred "policy of development that would do more than just plug the holes left by capitalism." The theory of "intermediate bodies" was simply a cloak for the defence of special interests, as opposed to those of the national collectivity, and the concomitant of national independence was the replacement of obsolete liberalism by a new dynamic in which the state would enlist the direct democratic participation of citizens through regular consultation.[100] And of considerable symbolic significance, Lévesque chose to launch his political movement in the auditorium of the Dominican Monastère de Saint-Albert-le-Grand, which also functioned as the editorial headquarters of the Catholic "left" organ, *Maintenant*.[101]

More significantly, leading elements within the new Parti Québécois welcomed Catholicism as an indispensable auxiliary in the task of eliciting a cohesive set of values in the new nation, especially given the expectation that state and society must form a seamless whole. René Lévesque, for example, recognized that Quebec could not return to "the age of automatic unanimity," but was acutely aware of the need for a principle of order that legitimated the new social democratic ideology of the state as directing, coordinating, and humanizing both individual and collective life.[102] While the visible institutions of the Catholic Church could not, in a pluralist social environment, provide this bedrock of authority, influential péquistes were adamant that Catholicism should not be dismissed as a synonym of repression. According to Camille Laurin, one of the most prominent individuals who made the transition from Catholic activism to sovereignist militancy, Catholicism had been forced to assume an unnatural authoritarianism as a consequence of the British Conquest, a situation that had artificially severed it from its own rich heritage of humanism. The project of political independence, the undoing of the psychological legacy of national oppression, would free Catholicism to participate in defining a new balance of freedom and authority. In a North American world characterized by atomization and individualistic excess, Catholic values, in Laurin's estimation, testified to "the unity of the Quebec soul."[103] The synthesis of state-centred nationalism and Catholicism in a new system of collective identities, Laurin concluded, would do for Quebec what Constantine's conversion had done for the Roman Empire: "It would bring a hardened people out of the catacombs, to joyously assume their unity and unanimity."[104]

A social democratic nation whose ideology of "development" was founded upon the direct and equal access of the citizen to the state – here was the way of resolving the conundrum identified by Fernand Dumont, that of discerning an equilibrium between public and private. To participate in this democratic culture, however, Catholics would have to work to make the Church a viable community that would truly bring its members together; in other words, the preservation of religion as a principle of social authority and cohesion in Quebec depended on removing all barriers between the Church's teachings and the faithful understood as a collectivity.[105] Thus, the preservation of a seamless relationship between Catholic values and a public culture in which the political state held the paramount position necessitated a thoroughgoing and rapid purge of all "traditional" elements in Catholicism that were considered obstacles to this new sense of communion. Only a purified Catholic faith could fulfill its appointed role as the central element in a new vision of spiritual and social cohesion that would underpin and legitimize Quebec's achievement of modernity. For these Catholic modernists, the main impediments to the realization of this new democracy lay within Catholicism itself: this was a complex of attitudes, assumptions, practices, and institutions that these modernists lumped together under the rubric chrétienté, or "Christendom," an expression both of Quebec's "folkloric" religious past and the close institutional partnership between a clericalist Church and the political state.[106] Here was the absolute antithesis of the society they wished to build, in which christianisme, or the true "Christian" faith, freed of these corrupt, socially divisive, and ultimately de-Christianizing social privileges, would participate in society on a footing of equality with other creeds and ideologies, but would hold a heightened, and ultimately more secure, public role as the conduit between an intense personal faith and public engagement.

Writing in 1962, Father Bradet bluntly informed the readers of *Maintenant* that Quebec Catholics must "pass from a stage of institutional Christianity" to discover "a purified Christianity." In a modern age in which secular values and institutions were assuming an increasingly autonomous existence, the Church must "rely less and less on protective structures and institutions that are empty of spiritual sustenance, and develop personal convictions."[107] In this respect, Bradet echoed the French Dominican Father P.-A. Liégé, who in a guest article written for the magazine in February 1962, had urged Catholics to abandon the notion of a unified "Christian civilization." Liégé took particular aim at the tendency of a previous generation of Catholic social reformers to idealize the Middle Ages in an attempt to create a Christian society characterized by religious unanimity, and a close conjunction between the Church and the political order. That there had once been "a fairly harmonious dialogue between Christianity and the fact of civilization," Liégé reminded his readers, should not be elevated to the status of universal principle. In the future, he maintained, Christianity would find itself in the presence of multiple and fragmented forms of civilization, a pluralistic climate in which the Church would have to engage in dialogue with a multiplicity of partners. Thus, there would never again be a "Christian civilization" in the global sense, and the Church must at all costs avoid "contracting alliances, which would risk becoming a concubinage, with any privileged elements of civilization that might declare themselves Christian."[108]

From the general Catholic modernist assumption that the incarnation of Catholicism in visible institutions was secondary to personal conviction, and that in defining its mission the Church must prioritize "evangelism" even over the building of human society,[109] it was a relatively short step to the denunciation of *any* measure that might perpetuate separate confessional educational, charitable, or medical institutions. The concern of these "left Catholics" was not so much that such interventions would involve the Church in spiritually debilitating collaborations with political authority. Rather, these interventions were thought to simply epitomize an outmoded spirit that was characteristic of a "folkloric" age dominated by a sentimental female spirituality or, following the analysis of their mentor, Emmanuel Mounier, by an individualistic, "bourgeois" piety which they held in supreme contempt.[110] These were simply barriers to the formulation of a new Catholic spirituality of collective purpose. In the words of Fernand Dumont, it was high time that Quebec Catholics threw away the "crutch" of Christian schools, trade unions, cooperatives, social clubs, and "official Christian ideologies." These, in his estimation, were insuperable barriers to Christians and unbelievers working together to erect a democratic society and nation.[111] More significantly, the whole project of creating Christian institutions was simply counterproductive: as Jacques Leclerc stated in 1964, even the much-heralded educational compromise worked out between the bishops and the liberal state was destined to failure. Such efforts could not broaden the appeal or authority of Catholicism in modern society, but merely reconstitute "Christendom" on an ever-narrower basis, ultimately severing Catholicism from all progressive developments in modern culture. Adoption of this strategy, he believed, would simply indicate that Quebec Catholics had fallen into a state of immobilism.[112]

The urgency with which a number of vocal "left Catholics" urged an immediate and complete liquidation of "Christian institutions" appeared, by the end of the 1960s, to legitimize an impatience among many elements in the Church with any kind of institutional structure. For example, Father Vincent Harvey's controversially titled *Maintenant* editorial, "*La mort des Églises*" ("The Death of the Churches"),[113] could be read as an open assault on any kind of religious structure, although it was far more moderate in simply inviting Catholics working in secular institutions to demonstrate openness and dialogue. The message was that what was needed was a thorough renovation of the Church from within, not simply a liquidation of "Christian institutions. This task could be accomplished not by the clergy or by reforming the parish, but by the action of small, informal faith-communities,[114] whose main imperative centred upon the cultivation of an intense, largely inward-looking spiritual life through personal and private fellowship. Here, in the revolt of many "left Catholics" against the heritage of "Christendom," lay the ultimate negation of an idea of Catholicism as a dynamic force in the public culture of a modern society.

Indeed, for conservative voices within the Church, the anti-institutional imperative of modernist Catholicism rested upon the flawed premise that the spirit of Christianity could perform its task in human society through the sum total of individual human vocations acting without well-defined institutional conduits. The Jesuit Father Richard Arès, one of the most thoughtful conservative commentators during the 1960s, stated that the very acceptance of Vatican II's proclamation that the Church constituted "an immense people" implied the necessity of both "milieus where the Christian vocation can flourish and institutions that root religion in the people."[115] "Left Catholics," Arès believed, had erred in substituting an aristocratic principle of spiritual election, which relegated the church to the status of a small sect of initiates. In an open attack on Fernand Dumont, Arès quoted the works of the French cardinal Jean Daniélou, declaring that the Church must defend "the right of prayer" for the mass of the people.[116] While intellectuals like Dumont might not need the "crutches" of Christian institutions to lead saintly lives, "the weak, the humble, the poor in faith" needed an institutional framework of explicitly Catholic schools and social agencies in order to sustain their "interior attitude," because their lived existence was less a matter of understanding doctrinal substance than a more natural, rythmic adherence to universal religious imperatives shared by both pagans and Christians. Ordinary people, conservatives believed, could only feel betrayed by the spectacle of spiritual elitists among clergy and laity whose desire to engage in a dialogue with Marxists and unbelievers led them to advocate demolishing Christian institutions.[117]

The "left Catholic" conviction that religion must continue to serve a crucial public function in the modern world flowed from the way in which they defined the passage of a "traditional" society to modernity, and from the very way in which, following existentialism, they juxtaposed faith and unbelief. According to Fernand Dumont, one of the most thoughtful Quebec advocates of Catholic modernism during the late 1960s, the defining element of a "modern" society was the development of a "sphere of private life" that was characterized by free, authentic personal contacts between individuals and a "deepening of personal conscience, of the feeling that values are an act of free choice that we do not find in ancient societies." However, in Dumont's estimation, modern Quebec faced a dichotomy: this sense of personality and freedom could not, without great difficulty, be translated into the public realm of work, community, and collective values, because "the civilization of technique" insisted upon precise and absolute divisions in which the personal and the collective stood opposed. Thus, urban civilization, although it favoured the development of personal life, gave rise to a situation in which collective existence had become "rationalized," "very formalistic," and "frequently anonymous." This, concluded Dumont, ensured that the dominant characteristic of modern society was "the tendency to materialism" in the realm of values,[118] a world in which the "sacred" was exclusively the purview of the private and the personal. "The old myths," lamented Dumont, "have disappeared from collective life and are spoken of no more; but they have taken refuge more deeply in the unconscious from which they periodically well up to remind people of the old sacral meanings of life."[119]

It was thus a central imperative for modern Quebec, in its effort to find a sense of collective purpose, to connect the personal values of freedom and authenticity to a sense of public engagement, and in this respect, for many of this generation of Quiet Revolutionaries, a Catholicism shorn of its "folkloric" aspects and appealing to a well-educated society of professionals and technocrats was still the ideal conduit. Indeed, even so forceful a critic of "traditional" religion as the sociologist Colette Moreux emphatically stated in 1969 that religion was still "the foundation of the collective being and Catholicism in particular is still the essence of the French-Canadian *people*."[120] The underscoring of the collective "people" in this context is very revealing. It was redolent of the hope of so many "left Catholics" that, in an age of religious reform and political and social democracy, Quebec Catholicism would lead North America in pointing to the intersection of new forms of social solidarity and spiritual communion. For this reason, their condemnation of "old-style" Catholicism, with its clustering of Christian institutions and devotional culture was that its idea of community was essentially petit-bourgeois and that it was causing de-Christianization by alienating the working-class masses from the Church. As stated by Father Jacques Grand'Maison, one of the most vocal theological apologists for "left" Catholicism, "those faithful most active in our parishes belong mainly to the lower middle class. We find very few poor people, very few professionals, few young people, and more men than women. The people who are at the cutting edge of secular society are practically absent."[121] This created a climate in which religion was essentially bound up with ranking the moral failings of individuals, did not engage the participation of the faithful in a true fraternity, and thus forced ordinary Catholics back upon a notion of individual, rather than collective, salvation, which would ultimately render religion a completely marginal phenomenon. In the words of Jeanne Lapointe, such a religion could not serve in the modern age. "Our sense of the nation and undoubtedly also our sense of the Church," she concluded, "will become more and more vacuous unless it is rooted in the social."[122]

Reformers like Dumont ultimately considered the culture of Christian institutions as the ultimate in vacuity because it focused exclusively on religious experience as private. Such an individualistic religion, these "left Catholics" feared, would lead to a completely atomized civilization, the ultimate nightmare of existentialist alienation in which people would become complete solitaries. The key lay in "the invention of mechanisms of meeting and social intercourse"[123] appropriate to a modern society. In this respect, the personalist type of Christianity promoted by the Catholic modernists dictated an expansion, rather than a shrinking, of Catholicism. Because they envisioned the relationship between faith and unbelief as a kind of continuum, always characterized by unresolved doubt, they in fact viewed unbelievers as profoundly religious people who were different in no essential respect from Christians. According to Father Paul Doucet, all modern people, whether believers or unbelievers, were united by the reality of a world in which the solitary individual was powerless: in such a universe, the example of the individually heroic agnostic existentialist could offer no sustenance. People needed solidarity and collective effort, and it was in this "consciousness of a community of destiny and struggle" that modern people would find "the privileged route for the recognition of the true God."[124] The challenge for Catholics was to overcome the anomie of modern urban life by embodying a new communal spirituality, one that would express a "primordial sense of community" upon which social movements and ideologies could draw.[125]

The goal of these "left Catholics" was nothing less than the articulation of a new, inclusive humanism, one in which religion courageously abandoned its privileges in social, political, and cultural structures, one that would express a new vision that placed a priority upon the collective advancement of Quebec.[126] The emergence of such a secular culture, Louis Racine informed the readers of *Maintenant*, was not an anti-religious phenomenon, nor did it mean the retreat of the Church into a ghetto of Christian institutions or private piety; rather, it permitted the Church a wider influence in the process of defining common values that united both believers and unbelievers in a new brotherhood that transcended membership in any particular religious community.[127] In order for Quebec Catholics to play a part in the advent of this new humanism, "left Catholic" spokesmen like Dumont urged the revival of "the collective dimensions of the Church, hidden under the mask of the institutions of Christendom," as the essential precondition for the construction of a society ruled by the egalitarian, republican, and social democratic principles of "reciprocity of services, civil peace, fraternity and love ... the fulfillment of the self in the service of others."[128] It was precisely because of the need to ensure a connection between private faith and public social and political engagement – to remind the world that Quebec was a place in which, as Father Jean-Paul Lauzon put the matter, "new values and a renewed way of living traditional values" could be reconciled under the spiritual and cultural "*primacy*" of the Christian tradition[129] – that many "left Catholics" refused to accept that "Christianity was merely a personal, private matter."[130] "Although Christian experience is a personal act," wrote Dumont, "it is always mediated by adherence to a Mystery and to community standards."[131]

LA COMMISSION DUMONT:
"ISRAEL WANTS A KING"[132]

Writing in 1971, the members of the Commission Dumont ominously noted the reversal of the relationship between Catholicism and public values that an entire generation had sought to establish. The process of secularization, which Catholic Action had sought to impregnate with religious values, had abruptly shifted in the mid-1960s, not only exposing Catholicism to "the backwash of profane ideologies in the religious universe,"[133] but working a rapid and thoroughgoing de-Christianization in

Quebec society. It was only in the years after 1964 that Catholic social and political elites had begun to doubt the power of religion to infuse secular society with fundamental values. The key to the older, more benign view of secularization was the notion, propagated among both clergy and laity who shared a commitment to personalism, that a viable democratic order was only guaranteed by the presence of active, civically-conscious spiritual elites. Secularism, or *laïcisme*, explained the Jesuit Father Raymond Bourgault in 1963, was not in essence anti-religious or anti-clerical, but constituted a revolt against the irrational. Ingeniously, Bourgault traced the etymology of *laïcisme* to the Greek *laos*, "an elite corps of men who believe that the human community must endure and progress, and that this sacred duty is enjoined by an Authority which embraces in its love not only the living but also the dead." These religiously-inspired guardians would remove all barriers to reason, and ensure the advent of true democracy through the diffusion of culture to the masses.[134] Thus, in a society where even in the mid-1960s there existed no competing sources of religious identity, both conservatives and modernists urged co-operation with secularization and deconfessionalization[135] because neither group could envision a situation in which the public realm of politics, media, or trade unionism would not bear the impress of Catholic values, which would express the fundamental consensus that defined the nation. Indeed, for Claude Corrivault, the existence of a fundamental moral consensus built upon explicitly religious values was essential for modern Quebec in order to counteract the pressures for a materialistic egalitarianism or soulless technocracy.[136] Claude Ryan perhaps best expressed the mainstream view when he declared that, despite the displacement of clergy from directorial and managerial roles in public institutions, "the power of the religious idea itself remains considerable." For this reason, he foresaw that although the social authority of the clergy was certainly weaker, Catholicism, through the commitment and activism of lay elites, would continue to hold considerable sway over public opinion in Quebec.[137]

Writing in 1971, the sociologist Guy Rocher observed that "unbelief" had now become the cultural mainstream in Quebec society. He was, however, quick to point out that this phenomenon could not be construed as a simple absence of religion; rather, "it bears an extraordinary witness of a hope beyond all hope: it is animated by such a serious disposition, a willingness to search for truth and authenticity in the face of humans and their destiny, that it forces religous faith to justify itself."[138] Rocher recapitulated an older Catholic personalist consensus that linked the qualities of "authenticity" and "truth" to the achievements of his own age cohort, whose youthful experiences in the late 1930s and early 1940s had so marked Quebec politics, religion, and society. In particular, Rocher's article expressed the faith that a unifying moral consensus binding

Catholics and thoughtful unbelievers, youth and elders, could still be articulated. During the late 1960s, however, the elitist democratic quest that had given birth to the Quiet Revolution found itself under increasing challenge from manifestations of a cultural revolution then breaking upon both Quebec and other Western societies, a movement in which men like Guy Rocher and Fernand Dumont found themselves cast in the unlikely role of cultural conservatives.

In 1963, Yves Prévost, a perceptive conservative and former minister under Maurice Duplessis, reached conclusions that were somewhat different from those of Rocher. In a speech launching the new conservative newspaper *L'Action*, he described what he feared was a wave of "de-Christianization" breaking over the society. Quoting from the work of the French personalist philosopher Jean Lacroix, Prévost declared that atheism was no longer confined to aristocratic or intellectual circles, but "had become democratic and political." By atheism, he did not mean the ideas espoused by elite groups such as the MLLF, but, rather, transformations he sensed occurring in the area of mass popular values, evident in "a lowering of family morals, of professional ethics and the values of leisure."[139] In particular, conservatives like Prévost most feared the relativism of diverse moral standards which Vatican II appeared to condone in the name of "pluralism."

Such views, however, were not simply the lamentations of conservative old-guard Catholics. Jean Francoeur, national director of the Jeunesse Étudiante Catholique and later a journalist at *Le Devoir*, advanced similar conclusions in a memorandum assessing the values of the new, well-educated, professional, suburban middle classes in Quebec. Old-style authoritarian education, claimed Francoeur, had given individuals an internal moral compass or "automatic pilot" whose point of reference was a hierarchy of values, uniformly accepted, that enabled them to respond to certain situations. This no longer held for the world of suburbia, where egalitarian "horizontal relationships" that deprived the individual of internal moral standards prevailed. Although the new middle classes displayed their own species of conformity, this was inherently unstable because there was no external moral sanction, and individuals were governed only by fleeting caprices and appetites.[140]

By the late 1960s, a growing number of Quebec Catholics no longer associated secularization with the adjustment of relations between church and state or the anticlerical ideas espoused by a radical avant-garde such as the MLLF. Rather, many began to define secularization as the encounter of Christian values with a rising tide of mass democratic cultural values that offered a panoply of competing ethical standards and modes of conduct. In a piece entitled "Le laïc dans le Québec d'aujourd'hui" ("The Layperson in Quebec Today"), included in a collection of essays published just after he accepted the leadership of the Quebec Liberal party in 1978, Claude Ryan captured the magnitude of the cultural and religious change when he stated that the real dynamic of secularization was not the replacement of the church by the state, but the replacement of the church by "the sovereign individual conscience."[141] International cultural movements, through the increasingly pervasive agency of television, transmitted these ideas in a way that subverted and relativized the authority of elites, less through direct confrontation, than through broadening public awareness of social and cultural diversity. As the Jesuit Father Julien Harvey astutely noted in 1970, mass media never overtly presented an anti-religious message. However, "its action involved the inevitable relativization of the scale of values, by the simple presentation of multiple ways of living according to different cultures and milieus."[142]

This perceived moral relativism was the target of a number of conservative voices who excoriated the lack of civic discipline and the self-indulgent, anarchic conduct of middle-class students, teachers, and trade-union leaders, and who openly sympathized with those who were fearful and perplexed by change. The Association des Parents Catholiques de Montréal deplored the tendency to "direct against the Church the same ideas, methods, and publicity that has been used at other levels of our society to discredit what is tradition, established order, and discipline." In particular, this lack of respect for authority, which even extended to elements within the clergy, tended to relativize the word of God, erase the distinction between the Church and the world, and treat religious practices and sacraments as entirely secondary – which was an obvious swipe at Catholic personalists whose creed was founded upon a demarcation between faith and religion.[143] Religious conservatives like Jean Genest, editor of *Action Nationale*, viewed the new accent on personal freedom, not as cause for celebration, but as a disaster that was "paganizing" rather than secularizing Quebec society.[144] "This rage of contestation, of criticism, of vilification," wrote one anonymous Catholic, "can be described as 'a prodigious humiliation of Christianity.'"[145] Father Bernard Lambert, theological advisor to Cardinal Maurice Roy, and certainly no extremist conservative, deplored the daily practice in the Quebec media of "every ecclesiastical mistake being seized upon and made into a public spectacle and those among the clergy who have doubts and problems feel compelled to lay them before the public in order to secure recognition as prophets."[146]

Worse, modern society compelled the participation of individual Catholics in a pervasive climate of moral and religious relativism at the level of daily existence, thus sapping any distinctive religious contribution that Catholicism might bring to modern culture. It was this, far more than any compromises that the hierarchy had made with the state, that weakened the influence of Catholicism over the public values of the society. At its apogee, the mass democratic culture of the 1960s appeared to mockingly parody the Catholic personalist concept of authority in which values flowed from adventurous, "authentic" youth to the conformist elder generation. Guy Rocher evoked the spectacle of parents who learned television-gazing and drug-taking from their children, and then moved on to mimic the "religious doubt and unbelief" of the younger generation.[147] More troubling still for both Catholic modernists and the Church hierarchy, a religious culture of private security and self-fulfillment appeared to characterize the religious attitudes even of the older generation. One rural woman informed the Commission Dumont that, although she was a practicing Catholic, religion was essentially irrelevant to the way in which she lived her daily life. Many adults, though raised by devout Catholic families and in Catholic educational institutions, expressed indifference rather than anger, defining religion either as something entirely personal, with no wider social or communitarian ramifications, or as compartmentalized from daily existence as "something that one does on Sunday."[148] Indeed, Catholic personalists who were frustrated by the absence of collective spirituality and the popular preference for a privatized religion warned that the Church in Quebec was, under the impact of the new modernity, fast becoming a "lonely crowd."[149]

Catholicism offered little resistance to the corrosive power of mass democracy in Quebec during the late 1960s. Indeed, in one of the great ironies of the post-1964 period, Quebec bishops decided to abandon Catholic Action, one of the key organizational forms in which several generations of young Quebec Catholics had been initiated into public life. What prompted this decision to drop official Church sponsorship of these youth movements was the fear that intellectual and institutional links were developing between the leaders of Catholic Action and more radical, quasi-Marxist student and labour movements. What most troubled the bishops and conservative lay activists like Claude Ryan was the growing pressure on the Catholic youth groups to overtly link religious commitment to political action, essentially an engagement to link the promotion of socialist causes to the advancement of the struggle for national independence.[150] Quebec's bishops firmly rejected "the illusion of any 'domestication' of Marxism or of any softening of this system relative to the Christian religion."[151] Significantly, Ryan, a staunch federalist who defended the episcopal view of confessionality in the debate over Bill 60, during his tenure as national secretary of Catholic Action always cultivated a public posture of prudence as regards political action. Eschewing any overture to the Marxist left, Ryan emphatically stated that "whatever may be the differences of Church organizations with the civil power, they must always demonstrate an unflinching loyalty to the constituted authorities when exercised in their proper sphere."[152] Thus, for more conservative Catholic leaders like Ryan, the youth organizations were primarily apostolic in character, and whatever the personal engagement of Catholic individuals, the movements themselves, as intimately linked with the Church hierarchy, must at all costs avoid following the practices of pressure groups or of organizations directed to material or temporal ends.[153] Thus, the national directors of Catholic Action decided in 1964 to close the newspapers of the Jeunesse Étudiante Catholique (JEC) because conservative laity and clerics alleged that they harboured known Marxists and agnostics.[154]

Left Catholics like Father Jacques Grand'Maison, director of Catholic Action for the Diocese of St-Jérôme, also questioned whether the Catholic Action movement had a future in light of the social and political evolution of Quebec. However, their motivation differed from that of Ryan and the conservative bishops, as they certainly favoured a Catholic overture to the Marxist left. For Grand'Maison and his allies at *Maintenant*, Catholic Action had rendered valuable services to Quebec society, but it was the product of an age in which there had been close solidarities between parish and school. The reforms of the 1960s had finally exploded these illusions, and, in consequence, Catholic Action found itself in the invidious position of fostering a compartmentalization between a secularized daily life and religious practices. Worse still, Catholic Action was caught between two worlds, that of the lay activists who had fully imbibed the culture of social and political democracy, and that of the organizations' subservience to the dictates of the bishops. The erection by Catholics of parallel structures to those of civil society was, in the final analysis, simply the recipe for a "ghetto," an institutional isolation that prevented Catholics from exerting a dynamic influence over the wider culture of Quebec.[155]

Indeed, many within the youth organizations themselves questioned whether the methods of the JEC, which had evolved within completely confessional structures, could be effectively transposed to "the monster school concentrations" that existed in the new comprehensive and pluralistic secondary schools. Internal studies suggested that the modern student was completely indifferent to movements like the JEC which appeared to be too closely tied to the institutional Church and the creature of religious educators.[156] In early 1966, even Claude Ryan candidly admitted that "the issues which gave rise to Catholic Action are now obsolete."[157] The Church hierarchy, confronted by the growing left-wing orientation of the youth movements, was unwilling to rethink the place of Catholic Action in the new educational environment,[158] preferring to rely upon what it believed was the more conservative and non-political new religious pedagogy, carried out by clergy and adult lay experts. The bishops seized upon the excuse of a budget shortfall in the national Catholic Action movements in 1966 to bring the more politicized national directorates of the youth movements to heel, and impose a more effective control by the diocesan authorities. This triggered a crisis within the movements and the effective end of any overall sense of purpose that Catholic Action might have possessed.[159]

At one level, both the bishops and leading Catholic laity accepted the termination of Catholic Action with considerable equanimity, believing that the new educational partnership between church and state would ensure a more efficient initiation of children and adolescents into the essential doctrines of the faith. As well, the new social teachings of the Second Vatican Council expressed a considerable confidence that Catholicism could still play a leading public role in Quebec society by acting in a climate of cultural pluralism, and could act more effectively without being expressed in overt institutional forms like Catholic Action. However, these elites arrived at their conclusions without an awareness of one of the more profound cultural legacies of Vatican II, one that legitimized within Catholicism a new climate of subjectivity based upon the right of the individual conscience to interpret Church teachings.[160] It was in this way that ordinary Catholics began to incorporate into their lives, with some approval from leading elements in the Church, aspects of the "cultural revolution" of the 1960s. Thus, during the late 1960s, leading clerics like Father Bernard Lambert began to refer with perplexity to the rise of the phenomenon of the "third man" in modern society: Father Lambert described these Catholics as those "who make their own choice among the teachings of the Church. Neither totally outside the Church, nor totally within it, this is a person who holds in one and the same breath to free will and to the authority of the magisterium." The consequence of these developments, Lambert warned, was "the establishment of an implicit and anonymous Christianity" that would be a largely invisible and purely private religion.[161] Indeed, left Catholics like Father Jacques Grand'-Maison pointed to the lack of a strident ideological atheism in Quebec as the source of Catholicism's loss of purpose. This allowed the "co-existence between a powerful impetus of secularization and a relative permeability of the culture to religious values." However, this lack of tension rendered "specifically religious behaviour rather marginal with reference to those of other institutions."[162] There now existed an irresolvable contradiction between a "Church that perpetuates an order of traditional values, closed and immutable" and "profane society, which expresses a pluralism of values that are relative rather than absolute."[163] Under the impact of democratic moral and cultural relativism, the religious beliefs of individuals and their public activities would henceforth exist in watertight compartments.[164]

The left Catholics of the *Maintenant* circle and the Church hierarchy found themselves in agreement over the need to halt this rapidly diffusing miasma of mass democratic individualism that was rendering both the official voice of the Church and the communitarian, socially-oriented spirituality of the personalists simply irrelevant. To this end, the Catholic hierarchy in April 1968 launched the Commission d'Étude sur les Laïcs et l'Église, ostensibly to study the failure of Catholic Action, but whose real aim was to end both the internal turmoil and raise the battered public profile of Catholicism by delineating some precise social project that would enlist the energies of the faithful. After nearly two years of research and background studies, the commission held public hearings between January and September 1970, receiving over 800 briefs and involving over 15,000 people in its work.[165] Despite its mandate to search for new ways of expressing the public presence of the Church, the commission remained thoroughly dominated by a particular vision of the past and by an inflexible cult of personalist elitism that precluded any real attempt to mediate between modernist and traditionalist directions. What is less well-known is that through the person of the commission's chair, Fernand Dumont, and the comments of a section of the upper clergy, the whole exercise appeared designed to align Catholicism with a particular nationalist political agenda. This in turn offered no assurances to those troubled about the relativization of the Christian message, and seemed to seriously compromise the independence and universality of the Church. The members of the commission comprised the familiar faces of former Catholic Action militants, now occupying positions of authority in universities, trade unions, and the new educational bureaucracy.

The public hearings of the Commission Dumont opened in an atmosphere of escalating social and political violence. The noisy protests that accompanied the abortive language legislation of the weak Union Nationale government, the student occupation of universties and CEGEPs in the fall of 1969, and the renewal of the terrorist bombings by the Front de Libération du Québec convinced many academics and political figures that there was a widespread rejection of all cohesive values, and that Quebec was on the high road to anarchy. As the political scientist Léon Dion exhorted his readers, only the "convergence of all parts of the social body in the planning and carrying out of common tasks" could avert the rule of fanaticism and unreason.[166] The underlying concern, however, was that an escalating cycle of violence would lead to the repression of basic civil liberties by conservative elements, or worse, that the impetus to further reform would be halted as individuals abandoned political activism to take refuge in the private and the personal.[167] Like its political counterpart, the Commission d'Enquête sur la Santé et le Bien-Être Social, established by the former Liberal government in 1966, the Commission Dumont took as its mandate the elaboration of a collective project, the elucidation of some consensual values that would rescue Quebec from the cycle of "contestation"[168] and the abyss of violence.

The Commission Dumont was forced, from the outset, to steer a course between two tendencies that had taken firm root in Quebec Catholicism in the years following Vatican II and which threatened to undo the connection between religion and a continued direction of political and social reform. The first, described by Father Bernard Lambert in 1968, was a preoccupation with internal matters of liturgy and catechism, which turned the Church away from attention to "the Christian orientation of secular society." This, Lambert maintained, had accelerated a disaffection of committed Catholics from the wider parish community, with many of them seeking spiritual solace and friendship in smaller, private faith-communities, only tenuously linked to official Catholicism, a kind of "underground Church."[169] At a 1969 panel about debate and contestation in the Church, a number of participants affirmed that the "institutional Church was a dictatorship and must be destroyed,"[170] an indication that a growing number of believers found that even the parish community, the basic element of the Church, was an unsatisfactory forum for the expression of their spiritual commitment.[171] So long as it remained attached to a hierarchy and a structure of laws and regulations, stated a self-proclaimed group of Christians, "religion appears like a sad reality, utterly moribund and lifeless. It arouses no interest among modern humans."[172] This direction, argued Fernand Dumont, entailed a separation of Christian faith and the institutional Church that Catholic personalists had never intended, and would, if given further encouragement, simply disconnect Catholics from the wider society by exalting private friendship over civic culture.[173] In a lecture given at the Institut Pastoral des Dominicains in 1970, Lambert returned to the theme of the "base communities," the existence of which had been defended by his colleague, Father Jean-Paul Audet, as a way of overcoming the breakdown in relations between the clergy and laity. Lambert concluded that this was a dangerous direction to pursue, because these faith communities would simply eviscerate any imperative of public action and influence from modern Catholicism and would turn the Church into an irrelevant religious sect. "Do we want," demanded Lambert, "a Church of small spontaneous groups, a Church of confrontationists, an 'underground' Church or the Church of a diaspora, a collection of atomized individual particles?"[174]

The second current was the reaction of conservative Catholics whose concept of religion was not the communitarian ethic of the personalists, but an older spirituality centred around the traditional liturgy and sacraments. Many of these people were severely shaken, not only by the innovations of Vatican II, but by certain local practices of Quebec Catholicism, which in some parishes had gone to great lengths to interest young people in Catholicism by incorporating some aspects of 1960s youth culture into the ritual. One devout Catholic, Mme Richer of Granby, denounced this as "irreverence towards the Church. Lack of respect for the Blessed Sacrament. These women and girls in mini-skirts who serve mass, read the Epistle and take up the collection. Soon they will even be giving Holy Communion. Scandal. Scandal."[175] For these conservative voices, for whom ritual and liturgy comprised *the* very essence of Catholicism, these changes – designed to satisfy modern youth and encompassing everything from new Church architecture to folk and "go-go" dancing, and slide shows during sermons – simply represented a decline in the vigour and quality of the Church's message.[176] Because many felt abandoned and their spirituality assailed by the clergy and left Catholic elites, they tended to dismiss the soul-searching of the Commission Dumont as "the proliferation of mini-sociologists."[177] In the words of Joseph O. Jean, the public hearings held by the commission might have been something "more or less enthralling for those who see in it nothing more than the elaboration of a new sociological system." For believers, however, "who constitute the core of the People of God, these things offend their deeply-held sentiments and their fidelity to the Church."[178] Significantly, here the new Vatican II collectivist language of "People of God" was being turned in a more conservative direction by Catholic faithful who were anxious and perplexed about the impact of religious change.

Both these tendencies within contemporary Quebec Catholicism found themselves firmly reproved by the Commission Dumont. To the advocates of the private religion represented by the "base communities," the commission's final report, *L'Église du Quebec: un héritage, un projet* counterposed the image of Christ who, after all, had brought universal salvation in his character as a "public person." While admitting that the small fellowship communities might have some scriptural justification in the New Testament, commission members like Father Jacques Grand'Maison brought the critical light of modern sociology to bear, stating that an organizational model based on the extended family was incorporated by the old primitive Church, but that in an age of urbanization the whole idea of "base communities" was simply obsolete. To adopt this practice, cautioned the commission, would be to sanction "a leisure-time religion reserved for domestic spaces, far from the public sphere and the events that arouse and motivate our collectivity ... a stranger to the multi-faceted expressions of popular life ... its collective effervescence."[179] Traditionalist sentiment in the Church fared scarcely better, despite some half-hearted attempts by commission members to placate it. Writing in 1971, Fernand Dumont had publicly professed his anxiety at seeing a society mesmerized by the spectacular revolt of youth to the point of forgetting "the more interiorized revolt of adults and the elderly."[180] However, the anguish of the traditionalists found no supporters within the commission itself, as all its members had been shaped within the climate of the personalist revolt against these older models of Catholic spirituality and authority. From this standpoint, the commission's report could not offer a compromise between tradition and modernity, but instead cast Catholic conservatism as atavistic, as hankering after a long-vanished, stable order based upon images of "Christendom" that had once nourished the old ultramontane clerico-nationalism.[181]

The attempt by the Commission Dumont to summarily purge Quebec Catholicism of any association with its ultramontane past affords what is perhaps the best clue to the real agenda of the Catholic modernists at the end of the 1960s. To counter the momentum towards a religion of quiescence and private security that seemingly offered a respite from clashing political and social ideologies, Dumont and his associates promulgated a refurbished personalism, linked explicitly to democratic socialism and the quest for an independent Quebec, which, they believed, would challenge Quebecers to a new, and far more dynamic intersection of religion and public life, to a political theology that Catholic modernists hoped would be the spiritual legacy of the Quiet Revolution. "We will not recreate ... social cohesion in Quebec by a return to the past or by a new religion," Dumont proclaimed. He accepted that the diversity of lifestyles and social and ideological options that now existed within Quebec required "a consensus that will be defined at the level of politics."[182] However, this was emphatically not an argument for the irrelevance of the Christian presence in a completely secular society. "It is at the heart of profane engagements," maintained Dumont, "that the Christians of Quebec must work. ... This engagement is that of the State and society of Quebec."[183]

At the core of the Commission Dumont's outline for a new form of Catholic public action lay the highly politicized left Catholic vision of the *Maintenant* circle. Fernand Dumont himself had, since the early 1960s, been one of the most prominent academic sympathizers of the idea of an independent Quebec, and had applauded the birth of movements such as the Rassemblement pour l'Indépendance Nationale and the Mouvement Souveraineté-Association as a necessary "revolution of the spirit."[184] In his own estimation, personalism offered a corrective to the "bourgeois," individualistic piety promoted by Catholic ultramontanism, and sought to effect a creative fusion between suppressed, collectivist elements of Catholic spirituality and the imperatives of a democratic, socialist republic.[185] Left Catholics like Dumont regarded the political and social changes of the 1960s not as an end but as a beginning: the Quiet Revolution, he wrote at the end of 1970, "was first and foremost a cultural revolution. The great economic and political transformations remain to be achieved."[186] For these Catholics, the direction to be avoided at all costs was the articulation of a "liberal pluralist" order, as this would simply perpetuate a decadent "bourgeois" civilization. For this reason, in a society which they believed was still characterized by a high degree of religious unanimity, it was essential to the adumbration of a new national dignity that the "fundamental solidarities" of Catholicism find their counterpart and ideological expression in democratic socialism.[187] The washing away of its "bourgeois," clericalist excrescences and the recovery of the collectivist quality of Christian truth, was, for modern Catholic Quebec, the realization of its old messianic dream of being the homeland of a separate people in North America.

Between 1967 and 1970, it appeared to Dumont and his associates that they could effect such a synthesis, and at a stroke overcome the cultural legacy of 130 years of an unholy alliance of clericalism, bourgeois individualism, and Anglo-Saxon colonialism. The survival of ultramontane Catholicism until the advent of the Quiet Revolution had, through the leadership of the clergy, accomplished the cultural survival of the nation, but at a terrible price – the constriction and stunting of political nationality. Commenting on the cultural legacy of his own generation, which had drawn its intellectual sustenance from the experience of the 1930s, Fernand Dumont declared that their task had been a primarily negative one, that of "making our society appear like a vast historical shipwreck."[188] The emerging fusion of personalist Catholicism and a socialist neo-nationalism, he explained, would bind together the great wound inflicted by personalism, the loss of solidarity between past and present. The traditional traits that Catholicism had taught Quebecers, "suspicion towards great anonymous powers, a concern for justice and equality ... constitute a great crucible in which old attitudes will be transformed into new ones, the latter often borrowing the vitality of the older values."[189] The *Maintenant* circle, which spoke for a large and articulate constituency of modernist Catholics, discerned the signs of change in a rising tide of pro-independence sentiment, which they interpreted not as the mere creation of another political party, but as the expression, welling up from below, of a new, cohesive, and healthy spiritual identity, one that would heal the divisions of class and age and the psychological scars of an authoritarian colonialism.[190]

The promptings of Fernand Dumont and his associates notwithstanding, the close ties between the left Catholics of *Maintenant* and the movement to express the fundamental unity of a new Quebec nation by assembling nationalists of various stripes around the charismatic leadership of René Lévsque indicated, not a new relationship between Catholicism and nationalism, but the desire to explore a road not taken in the aftermath of the Rebellions of 1837. Like François Hertel's young hero Pierre Martel and the youthful activists of the 1930s, many progressive Catholics who sought to forge links with social democracy believed that it was possible to excise the more recent, ultramontane past and, in effect, return the society history to a new starting point where a new synthesis of nationalism and religion might be articulated. Background studies undertaken under the auspices of the Commission Dumont suggested that the religious unanimity fostered by the alliance of political conservatism and ultramontanism was, in fact, historically contingent and not ingrained in the mentality of the people. The ills that had, until very recently, afflicted Quebec had resulted from a wrong choice made by the Church hierarchy to refuse a conjunction with liberal nationalism that might have accelerated the drive to political independence, rather than an unworkable, colonialist Confederation.[191]

The alliance that Dumont and his associates desired to forge between "left Catholicism" and the "neo-nationalism" of René Lévesque was, under modern guise, a neo-Gallican revision of Quebec's history, a rehabilitation of the minority *rouge* project of the 1840s and 1850s, in which a "nationalist" clergy should have acted as true defenders of the nation by joining with liberal politicians who promoted the project of greater independence for Quebec.[192] In light of the liberal Catholic challenge to extreme assertions of papal authority apparently legitimized by Vatican II, the building of a relationship between the new Catholicism and radical nationalism in the interests of forging "an original society, different from the American model, secular, and socialist"[193] seemed at the end of the 1960s to be on the verge of realization in the massive, and emotional public support garnered by Lévesque and his movement.

The attempt to effect a convergence between a new public identity for the Catholic Church and the gathering of all French-speaking Quebecers around a republican political movement exerted a decisive influence over the prescriptions offered by the Commission Dumont. Because of the presence of staunch federalist voices like Claude Ryan and the desire to keep the official hierarchy free from political controversy, the criteria laid down in the final report dictated that the Church must not be dragged into identification with ideological political factions. As well, the official hierarchy should assiduously refrain from sponsoring mass crusades and associations to promote the aims of the Church.[194] However, the commissioners emphatically urged the Church to take its place in the building of a collectivity, and thus to be, in effect, the religious expression of the Quebec nation. Weaving together Vatican II's collectivist ideal of the Church as the "people of God" – expressed in the contemporary liturgical reforms, and the religious nationalism of ancient Israel – the commissioners deduced that the Church must consciously *act* as the fraternal expression of the communitarian values that underpinned Quebec's national identity as a historically distinct people. Although precise socio-political doctrines could not be deduced from the Gospel, Catholicism's purpose was not that of other-worldly, spiritual consolation: its role was emphatically political, critical, and prophetic.[195]

In a very real sense, the Commission Dumont was a key symbol of the end of the Quiet Revolution. In its rejection of the methods of institutional involvement and the spirituality of pre-1960s Catholic Quebec, it firmly eschewed any compromise with old-guard Catholicism, and it thus marked the advent of a personalist definition of religion within the Church itself. Its call for a public engagement of the Church that would be in close relationship with the new nationalism opened the door to a religious messianism that would, in effect, abolish the cultural legacy of the years between 1760 and 1960 by offering Quebec a creative synergy of Catholicism and democratic nationalist aspiration. Without violent revolution, Quebecers would experience national liberation simply by following the logic of the community solidarities implicit in Catholicism but obscured by reactionary clergy and a collaborationist petty bourgeoisie. Dumont and his fellow commissioners thus charted a direction that sought to move their society beyond the achievements of the personalists of the era that lay between 1931 and 1964, who had launched the Quiet Revolution as a cultural and spiritual rupture between traditional values and those of modernity.

But even as the Commission Dumont began its public hearings, a concatenation of religious, political, and cultural forces effectively blocked the conjunction of Catholicism and the new political nationalism. In December 1969, in a gesture reminiscent of the palmy days of ultramontanism, Pope Paul VI had assured the visiting Pierre Elliott Trudeau, the new prime minister of Canada and an implacable foe of Quebec independence, that from the perspective of the official Church, Canada constituted "one nation."[196] Despite the apparent groundswell of popular support for René Lévesque's crusade to unify Quebec behind the idea of independence, Quebec's electors, including a majority of francophones, opted, in April 1970, for a new Liberal team led by the technocrats Robert Bourassa and Claude Castonguay, whose promises of job creation and social justice through public investment in a welfare state dovetailed with what left Catholics had feared all along, the attraction to Catholic Quebecers of a North American culture of privacy, self-fulfillment, and security. Later that year, the events of the FLQ crisis and the heavy-handed federal military intervention severely shook the confidence of the Parti Québécois in a crusading, quasi-revolutionary militant activism. By 1973, Lévesque and his associates had largely cast aside any messianic overtones, adopting the methods of traditional political parties in calling for good government and independence only after one (or several) referenda. For those Catholics who had imbibed the Commission Dumont's call for a new prophetic spirit, the combination of these "signs of the times" indicated that the Quiet Revolution, which had both altered the content of Catholic values and their relationship to Quebec, could not be transmuted into a social or national revolution.

Conclusion

What Then Was
the Quiet Revolution?

Understood within the framework of cultural, rather than political, history, the Quiet Revolution is inseparable from the encounter of a particular type of Catholicism with Quebec society. It was the product of a very specific response to the social challenges of the Great Depression, and was an experiment brought to a rather sudden end in the mid-1960s by the irruption of a set of cultural values and notions of political society that ultimately could not be reconciled with Catholicism. This book began with the premise that it is necessary to move historical analysis away from the conventional trajectory, with its emphasis on viewing the Quiet Revolution as an act that reformed politics and state structures, or originated in post-war changes that occurred in nationalist political rhetoric. Such approaches see modern Quebec history as being ruled by a secularizing process in which the Catholic Church as an institution was simply displaced by the state, and they view this process as having been largely consensual and as having aroused very little conflict or tension.[1] However, when Quebec history during the four decades after 1930 is viewed through the lens of culture, the central role of Catholicism emerges, for much of the social and cultural ferment, and the very rhetoric that historians have identified with the Quiet Revolution, was a function of conflicts between rival social groups over divergent meanings of Catholicism.

The Quiet Revolution began with the importation of a variety of Catholic Action movements into Quebec in the 1930s. Although conservative in intent because they were sponsored and encouraged by the Church hierarchy in order to foster greater social cohesion and a large-scale project of re-Christianization, these movements flourished because of the relative absence of powerful ideological challenges to Catholicism. Thus, Catholic Action quickly became the focal point for the religious ambitions of a group of self-conscious laity, both working-class and middle-class, who employed a language that stressed the spiritual superiority of

youth and the sense of an unbridgeable gap between generations to critique both their elders and the clergy as spiritually somnolent, and hopelessly chained to routine, rather than expressing a commitment to the task
of heroically building new community ideals. In the process of articulating
this youthful, new Catholicism, its lay promoters originated the central cultural concept undergirding the Quiet Revolution: that a fundamental
rupture divided the present from the past, a gulf that necessitated an
entirely new framework of personal, familial, and social identities.
However, it should be stressed that while Catholic Action expressed anticlerical tendencies, this anticlericalism was not antireligious,[2] because it
measured the social leadership of the clergy by a religious standard, albeit
one framed around a more egalitarian interpretation of Catholicism that
continually validated the initiative of the laity. Between 1935 and the mid-
1950s, these Catholic movements, controlled by the laity and particularly
concentrated in the spheres of youth sociability, marriage preparation,
and family life, articulated an inclusive type of social activism that was especially tailored to the needs of working-class people and women. Although
these movements certainly contained some conservative elements, particularly among the clergy, they projected themselves to their urban Catholic
audience as something entirely new, as sponsoring ideologies and forms of
social relationships that were discontinuous with – and thus superior to –
the arrangements of the pre-Depression past.

In this way, much of what historians would characterize as the primary
categories of cultural modernity – namely, the affectional nuclear family,
the family's function as primarily directed to fulfilling the emotional
needs of its individual members, the greater assertion of human control
over reproductive choice, and a more horizontal, less hierarchical view of
family relationships – were in Quebec first enunciated and found their
institutional promotion, and thus wider cultural authority, within a type of
activist, more left-leaning Catholicism. To be sure, there were constant
underlying tensions within these movements between the clergy and laity:
for example, more conservative clergy advocated a structured marriage
preparation as an antidote to divorce and family instability, while many
working-class women who attended these lectures were more interested in
acquiring sexual knowledge. Likewise, palpable differences existed over
birth control, with Catholic women in particular asserting far greater latitude in interpreting what many would construe as rather restrictive
Church teachings. However, the strength of this type of social Catholicism
lay in its focus on issues of family and marriage; these were issues which
enlisted a good deal of popular interest and participation because they
were bound up with the daily lives of their members. Despite an under-
current of anticlericalism, the emphasis on family during the 1940s
and 1950s afforded a terrain of collaboration between clergy and laity,

one which downplayed the fine points of theological discussion as a test of Catholic orthodoxy.

However, the thrust of Catholic Action was blunted by a fundamental ambiguity. While at one level, the Catholic Action movements aspired to carve out a central place and to posit a dominant voice for ordinary people within Catholicism, during the early 1950s, this socially-activist lay Catholicism was forced into the background by an ambitious liberal political agenda epitomized by a small, but vocal group of intellectuals, activists, and social scientists clustered around the journal *Cité libre*. This group, which included Pierre Trudeau and Gérard Pelletier – names irrevocably associated with the politics of the Quiet Revolution – largely turned its back on the social achievements of Catholic Action, which had emphatically fostered the engagement of Catholicism with the reform of family relationships and with feminist values. In the name of rendering Catholicism and modern values synonymous, this group of intellectuals instead turned the language of Catholic Action into an aggressive, male-centred spiritual elitism that was profoundly contemptuous of popular religious practice in Quebec. In their estimation, working-class religion was vacuous and conformist, relied too heavily upon ritual, was too tailored to female forms of piety to appeal to an educated male leadership that was aware of public issues, and was too deferential to clerical leadership. They interpreted these defects as advanced symptoms of Quebec Catholicism's social and cultural sclerosis, and they feared that it would ultimately lead to de-Christianization. Although these intellectuals appeared "liberal" in their opposition to conservative nationalism, they were in fact profound cultural conservatives, arguing that this type of popular Catholicism constituted a threat to a middle-class culture based upon rationality, professionalism, and education. More tellingly, however, their religious critique became a form of political identity, as they turned their equation of religious vacuity and clerical dominance to an assault on the government of Maurice Duplessis. For them, Duplessis became the symbol of the corrupt alliance of old-style popular piety and a top-heavy institutional Church.

This group of intellectuals possesses a double significance for the relationship of Quebec Catholicism to the Quiet Revolution. In the first instance, they successfully displaced the more inclusivist social imperatives of Catholic Action with an exclusivist, theologically centred spiritual authoritarianism. At the level of the Catholic Action movements themselves, this highly intellectualist emphasis was evident by the mid-1950s in the thinking of leaders like Claude Ryan, who imbibed much of the *citélibriste* critique of contemporary Catholicism. The working-class family movements, previously noted for their activist and educative involvement, now largely abandoned their educative, and inclusivist stance in favour of emphasizing a rather inward-looking spirituality.[3] Secondly, the intellectuals' emphasis

upon the centrality of intellectual matters identified the Church completely
with a traditionalist clergy and with largely immobile, visible institutions in
the areas of education and social welfare, fields that an unholy alliance of
clerical ambition and colonialist connivance had arrogated from lay effort.
This unwarranted clerical usurpation, they believed, was the very antithesis
of the modern social order, which they held must be premised upon the
social, cultural, and political leadership of middle-class, professional elites.
Further, they interpreted Catholicism entirely through its interactions with
obsolete forms of conservative, ruralist nationalism and with the machina-
tions of the political state. More importantly, however, their spirituality dis-
closed, in embryonic form, the central tenets of the dominant historical
paradigm that was to emerge after the 1960s: the vision of Quebec as a
"normal" society in which Catholicism was no more and no less than the
ideologies and social projects of the clergy, which ideologies and social projects were either marginal to, or a reactionary brake upon, the economic
structures that were the purview of rational, liberal lay elites. In this sense,
they constructed what has become a historical truism, the notion that the
Quiet Revolution that unfolded after the death of Maurice Duplessis was
consensual because it involved nothing more than a long-delayed secularization, the recapturing of the top levels of political and social power by a
lay leadership that had been unjustly kept waiting in the wings since 1840.

What gave a particular cast to the contestation that occurred in Quebec
society in the 1960s was that the principal achievements of the political
quiet revolution – the creation of a new education system and the reform
of the social welfare system – were an effort to enshrine this intellectual-
ized Catholicism at the expense of other forms of interaction between the
Church and society. In this respect, the events that occurred between 1960
and 1964 did not constitute a simple, painless secularization in which state
structures caught up to social realities, a process reflected in the simple
substitution of lay professional technocrats for clerical elites. Rather, the
attempt to infuse the new theological priorities of Catholic Action into the
political order was a direction that enlisted the enthusiasm of liberalizing
elites clustered around Paul Gérin-Lajoie and a number of key figures in
the upper clergy. For them, social reform meant enlisting the intellectual
prestige of Catholicism in the task of legitimizing public authority in
Quebec, which would allow the state to liberalize without capitulating to
cultural tendencies that advocated a greater degree of individualism. This
alliance aroused enormous resistance and resentment from ordinary
Catholics, many of whom felt simply abandoned by the Church's connivance with this intellectualist exclusivism. De-Christianization was,
during the 1960s, not the ejection of clerics from education and social services, nor simply a function of declining church attendance, but a far more
aggressive denigration by Catholic intellectuals of working-class religious

practices – and implicitly, of the authority and expertise of adults in their families – which practices were regarded as incompatible with modern society.

In the process of investing this new intellectualist emphasis with cultural authority, Catholicism completely eviscerated its social activist wing, and thus severed the links that it had established in the 1930s with students, women, and working-class people. It was the ending of a relationship that was emphatically punctuated by the assertion of a secular, political feminism in the mid-1960s. This growing disjuncture between the Church and popular values, and the climate of contestation within the Church itself, was compounded by a more radical assertion of the *citélibriste* intellectualist argument by the sociologist-cum-theologian Fernand Dumont and a self-styled Catholic "left," which constituted a kind of conscience for the mainstream of the nascent sovereigntist movement. Despite a kind of social-democratic solicitude for the common people, Dumont was, in religious matters, an even more virulent cultural elitist than the *citélibristes*, and his negative views of Quebec popular Catholicism bore the added sanction of social-scientific law. Intellectuals of his stripe sought to elaborate a new set of connections between Catholicism and Quebec society, but did so by an even more all-encompassing identification of the Church and political order. By seamlessly equating individual values with a new nationalism incarnated in an independent Quebec political state, Dumont and his colleagues preached an anti-historical return to an old form of Gallicanism in which Catholicism was simply an auxiliary to the primacy of the state, an order in which the task of religion was to produce individuals devoted to the communitarian imperatives of nationalist citizenship.

One of the most problematic features of Quebec's "revisionist" master-narrative is the place it accords to religion. This stems from the fact that, although revisionists rejected the older historiographic canons that Catholicism made Quebec society monolithic and unique, or kept it hermetically sealed from innovation,[4] they not only failed to displace, but largely adopted the cultural conservatism of the new Catholic intelligentsia of the 1950s. In particular, "revisionists" incorporated the earlier anti-feminist, elitist dismissal of popular religion, the identification of the Church with the political alliances of the clergy and conservative politicians, and the equation of the institutional Church with a conservative nationalism. Historians working within the "revisionist" trajectory adhered to a vision that pronounced Quebec a "normal" society and they for the most part viewed the Quiet Revolution as a largely painless, and emphatically positive process of modernization that brought the structures, values, and institutions of the state into line with the imperatives of "modernity" – a rationality which they defined in predominantly economic terms. Although these historians who wrote from the 1970s onwards were committed to the primacy of economic forces in historical causation, these operated, in their historical scheme, with reference to a particular vision of Catholicism – a Catholicism that was largely unchanged from the 1950s – that stood at the centrepiece of their account of a "normal" society. It was a notion that Catholicism was somehow divorced from or at odds with the "real" experience of ordinary people, and could be completely defined by the pronouncements and actions of the clergy and the hierarchical institution. For the "revisionists," religion was a negative, residual category that encapsulated a "tradition" destined to disappear under a rising tide of modernity.[5]

By paying attention to the production and content of public ideologies,[6] particularly those centering on youth, family, and gender identity, and by carefully analysing the language of rupture and discontinuity that lay beneath the Quiet Revolution, this book avoids the pitfall of asserting as an a priori that Catholicism was "traditional." Powerful elements of conservatism certainly existed within the Church, but if the historical specificity of post-1930 Quebec is to have any meaning, what distinguished that society from others in North America and Europe was that for three critical decades many aspects of its encounter with modernity, both ideological and institutional, were mediated through varieties of Catholicism. This very diversity of currents within Catholicism explodes the central myth of the Quiet Revolution: the idea that, first, Catholicism was purely the expression of elites, either clerical or political, second, was thoroughly invested with nationalist agendas, and, third, in its manifestation as popular religion existed only as a folkloric backdrop adding some local colour to the more "rational" concerns of francophone elites. These emphases certainly characterized the ideologies and actions of some Catholics, but post-revisionist historiography will have to begin from the premise that Catholicism's relationship to Quebec was primarily social and cultural, and only secondarily political. This is a consideration that would substantially reorient social history in Quebec by shifting the emphasis away from demography, economic history, and labour history and instead giving far more scope to questions of family, gender, and institutions. By emphasizing the study of lay religious initiatives, this book suggests that social and cultural power was not monolithic or concentrated in the hands of the clergy, but highly dispersed and subject to constant calibration and renegotiation.

Further, it would testify to the maturity of Quebec history as a discipline if Catholicism itself could be disaggregated from the polemics of the Quiet Revolution – with the latter's enormous burden of moral opprobrium – and instead viewed, as a number of scholars are beginning to do, more dispassionately as a highly mutable system of social regulation and cultural authority that has been capable of functioning within a variety of political and social arrangements, and in a constantly-evolving set of relationships with other social institutions and sources of power.[7] This method would also have the advantage of suggesting an exit from the impasse in the debate between revisionists and post-revisionists. It would enable historians to navigate the always problematic relationship between the need for sensitivity to cultural differences and the need to locate particular societies within the framework of wider processes of transformation. To study Quebec Catholicism according to these criteria asserts the historical specificity of Quebec without falling back into a national (some would say nationalist) history that relies excessively on a conflictual political event history, or on a political-ideas approach that privileges the reflections of nationalist intellectuals,[8] and without resolving Quebec's history into a rather bland chronicle of impersonal economic forces, thus rendering its experience indistinguishable from that of other societies, and of little interest or concern to international practitioners of the discipline of history.

Notes

ABBREVIATIONS

ACC	Action Catholique Canadienne
ANQM	Archives Nationales du Québec, Montréal
ANQQ	Archives Nationales du Québec, Québec
AUM	Archives de l'Université de Montréal
AUQÀM	Archives de l'Université du Québec à Montréal
AN	*Action Nationale*
AQ	*Aujourd'hui Québec*
C&F	*Collège et Famille*
CAC	*Cahiers d'Action Catholique*
CC	*Communauté Chrétienne*
Chat	*Châtelaine*
CL	*Cité Libre*
CRLG	Centre de Recherche Lionel-Groulx
FO	*Le Front Ouvrier*
ICEA	Institut Canadien d'Éducation des Adultes
JC	*Jeunesse Canadienne*
JEC	*JEC: journal jéciste*
JIC	Jeunesse Indépendante Catholique
JO	*Jeunesse Ouvrière*
JOC	Jeunesse Ouvrière Catholique
LD	*Le Devoir*
LF	*La Famille: Revue d'Action catholique*
LOC	Ligue Ouvrière Catholique
LP	*La Presse*
LR	*La Relève*
LT	*Le Travail*
Maint	*Maintenant*

MCMUL   McMaster University Library
MLLF   Mouvement laïque de langue française
MM   *Le Magazine Maclean*
MTC   Mouvement des Travailleurs Chrétiens
NAC   National Archives of Canada
NT   *Notre Temps*
ON   *Ordre Nouveau*
PP   *Parti Pris*
Pros   *Prospectives*
Rel   *Relations*
RD   *Revue Dominicaine*
RS   *Recherches Sociographiques*
SPM   Service de Préparation au Mariage
SS   *Le Service Social*
VE   *Vie étudiante*

INTRODUCTION

1 Archives Nationales du Québec, Québec (ANQQ), Fonds Action Sociale Catholique, P428, S2, 1970.

2 Paul-André Linteau, René Durocher, Jean-Claude Robert, and François Ricard, *Histoire du Québec contemporain: Le Québec depuis 1930* (Montreal: Boréal, 1989), 421–2.

3 This interpretation of the Quiet Revolution, articulated in a number of influential synthesizing treatments of Quebec's social and economic history, has become the conventional wisdom among historians. See, for example, Linteau et al., *Histoire du Québec contemporain*, 808–9; John A. Dickinson and Brian Young, *A Short History of Quebec*, 2d ed. (Toronto: Copp Clark, 1993), 294, 306–7.

4 For Gignac's career, see Pierre Godin, *René Lévesque: héros malgré lui*, vol. 2, *1960–1976* (Montreal: Boréal, 1997), 50–3.

5 For a critique of this tendency in post-1970 Quebec historical writing, see Ronald Rudin, "Revisionism and the Search for a Normal Society: A Critique of Recent Quebec Historical Writing," *Canadian Historical Review* 73, no. 1 (March 1992): 30–61.

6 This view was popularized in the 1950s by social critics who sought to liberate Quebec from what they considered reactionary attitudes in both church and state. See, for example, Pierre Elliott Trudeau, *The Asbestos Strike* (Toronto: James Lewis and Samuel, 1974; 1st ed. 1956). Two important monographs also subscribe to this liberal interpretation of the Quiet Revolution. See Michael Behiels, *Prelude to Quebec's Quiet Revolution: Liberalism versus Neo-Nationalism, 1945–1960* (Montreal and Kingston: McGill-Queen's University Press, 1985); and Léon Dion, *Québec 1945–2000*, vol. 2, *Les intellectuels et le*

temps de Duplessis (Québec: Les Presses de l'Université Laval, 1993). While resisting the older demonization of Maurice Duplessis, Dion continues to adhere to the notion that the modern outlook of the Quiet Revolution originated among a small circle of liberal intellectuals.

7 This interpretation relies upon three decades of historical scholarship, the main outlines of which are effectively synthesized in Paul-André Linteau, Rene Durocher, and Jean-Claude Robert, *Histoire du Quebec, 1867–1929* (Montreal: Boréal 1982); Linteau et al., *Histoire du Québec contemporain;* Dickinson and Young, *A Short History of Quebec.* A whole school of Quebec historians now asserts that, prior to 1930, powerful currents of liberalism were present in Quebec society and politics. See Antonin Dupont, *Les relations entre l'Église et l'État sous Louis-Alexandre Taschereau* (Montreal: Guérin, 1972); Bernard L. Vigod, *Quebec before Duplessis: The Political Career of Louis-Alexandre Taschereau* (Montreal and Kingston: McGill-Queen's University Press, 1986); Fernande Roy, *Progrès, harmonie, liberté: le libéralisme des milieux d'affaires francophones à Montréal au tournant du siècle* (Montréal: Boréal, 1988); Patricia Dirks, *The Failure of l'Action liberale nationale* (Montreal and Kingston: McGill-Queen's University Press, 1991); Yvan Lamonde, *Combats libéraux au tournant du XXe siècle* (Montreal: Fides, 1995). For an analysis of this current of historical writing, and for a critical assessment of its presentation of Catholicism, see Rudin, "Revisionism and the Search for a Normal Society."

8 For a critical analysis of the secularization theory, see Roy Wallis and Steve Bruce, "Secularization: The Orthodox Model," in Steve Bruce, ed., *Religion and Modernization: Sociologists and Historians Debate the Secularization Thesis* (Oxford: Clarendon Press, 1992), 11.

9 Linteau et al., *Histoire du Québec contemporain,* 806–7.

10 For an important suggestive treatment that firmly anchors Catholicism within the structure and values of the nineteenth-century "liberal" state in Quebec, see Jean-Marie Fecteau, "La construction d'un espace social: les rapports de l'Église et l'État et la question de l'assistance publique au Québec dans la seconde moitié du XIXe siècle," in Yvan Lamonde and Gilles Gallichan, eds, *L'histoire de la culture et de l'imprimé: Hommages à Claude Galarneau* (Sainte-Foy: Les Presses de l'Université Laval, 1996), 61–89.

11 For the central tenets of this new line of interpretation that amount to a wholesale critique of the secularization thesis, see for Britain, Callum G. Brown, "A Revisionist Approach to Religious Change," in Bruce, *Religion and Modernization,* 31–58. More recently, Brown has pursued the criticism of the secularization thesis, arguing that it stems from the appropriation by sociologists and historians of categories and insights first generated by late eighteenth-century clergymen who feared that the churches were losing influence among the urban working classes. See Callum G. Brown, *The Death of Christian Britain: Understanding Secularisation, 1800–2000* (London and New York: Routledge, 2001). For Protestant Canada, the work of Nancy Christie and Michael

Gauvreau, 'A Full-Orbed Christianity': The Protestant Churches and Social Welfare,
1900–1940 (Montreal and Kingston: McGill-Queen's University Press, 1996),
has revised both the chronology and nature of the classic secularization thesis
first put forward by Ramsay Cook, The Regenerators: Social Criticism in Late Victo-
rian English Canada (Toronto: University of Toronto Press, 1986), which
focuses too exclusively on theological change and decline, rather than on
social and institutional factors. More recently, we have attempted to advance
a historical framework, based on the notions of social regulation and cultural
authority, to explain the cross-class vitality of both religious institutions and
practices in both Protestantism and Catholicism: see Nancy Christie and
Michael Gauvreau, "Modalities of Social Authority: Suggesting an Interface
for Religious and Social History," in Nancy Christie and Michael Gauvreau,
eds, Intersections of Religious and Social History, special theme issue, Histoire
sociale/Social History, spring 2003. For Quebec, preliminary findings on nine-
teenth- and early twentieth-century urban Montreal published by Lucia Ferretti, Entre voisins: La société paroissiale en milieu urbain: Saint-Pierre-Apôtre de
Montréal, 1848–1930 (Montreal: Boréal, 1992) suggest that Catholicism was
able to initiate considerable institutional vitality and was successful at enlisting religious participation among all classes in its urban parishes.

12 Gilles Bourque, Jules Duchastel, and Jacques Beauchemin, La société libérale
duplessiste (Montreal: Boréal, 1994), 26–9, 42–54.

13 On this opposition between the two interpretive frameworks, see the critical
assessments of the Bourque thesis by both Jacques Rouillard and Michael
Behiels: Jacques Rouillard, "Le Québec vire à droite," in Alain Gagnon and
Michel Sarra-Bournet, eds, Duplessis: Entre la Grande Noirceur et la société libérale
(Montreal: Éditions Québec-Amérique, 1997), 183–206; Michael Behiels,
"Duplessis, le duplessisme et la prétendue reconstitution du passé," in
Gagnon and Sarra-Bournet, Duplessis, 317–26.

14 Bourque et al., La société libérale duplessiste, 251–309. It is of particular significance that even modern treatments of Quebec Catholicism during the Quiet
Revolution accept the framework of "orthodox liberalism": a clericalist, politi-
cally-subservient Church that followed the prescriptions of the upper clergy; a
society that, until 1945, was monolithically defined by its adherence to
Catholicism. For an expression of these views, see Gregory Baum, The Church
in Quebec (Ottawa: Novalis, 1991), 15–49; and more recently, Gregory Baum,
"Catholicism and Secularization in Quebec," in David Lyon and Marguerite
Van Die, eds, Rethinking Modernity: Canada between Europe and America
(Toronto: University of Toronto Press, 2000), 149–65; David Seljak, "The
Catholic Church and Public Politics in Quebec," in Lyon and Van Die,
Rethinking Modernity, 131–47.

15 Jean Hamelin and Nicole Gagnon, Histoire du catholicisme québécois: Le XXe siècle,
vol. 2, De 1940 à nos jours (Montreal: Boréal Express, 1984). A similar tendency to conflate Catholicism and clergy also characterizes the more recent

synthesizing treatment by Lucia Ferretti, *Brève histoire de l'Église catholique au Québec* (Montreal: Boréal, 2000).

16 For the main analytical framework and chronological periodization of nineteenth-century Quebec religious history offered by this historigraphy, see Louis Rousseau, "Crises, choc et revitalisation culturelle dans le Québec du XIXe siècle," in Michel Lagrée, ed., *Chocs et Ruptures en histoire religieuse (fin XVIIIe-XIXe siècles* (Rennes: Presses Universitaires de Rennes, 1998), 5–69; René Hardy, *Contrôle social et mutation de la culture religieuse au Québec, 1830–1930* (Montreal: Boréal, 1999); Christine Hudon, *Prêtres et fidèles dans le diocèse de Saint-Hyacinthe, 1820–1875* (Québec: Septentrion, 1996). For an especially stimulating treatment of pre-ultramontane Quebec Catholicism that is based around the different notions of ritual practice that prevailed, see Ollivier Hubert, *Sur la terre comme au ciel: La gestion des rites par l'Église catholique du Québec (fin XVIIe-mi XIXe siècle)* (Sainte-Foy: Les Presses de l'Université Laval, 2000).

17 Rudin, "Revisionism and the Search for a Normal Society," 61. See, for example, Gilles Paquet, *Oublier la Révolution tranquille: Vers une nouvelle socialité* (Montreal: Liber, 1999).

18 This is the central thesis of the recent critique of post-Quiet Revolution Quebec intellectuals authored by the sociologist Joseph-Yvon Thériault, *Critique de l'américanité: mémoire et démocratie au Québec* (Montreal: Éditions Québec-Amérique, 2002), 177–220.

19 The Catholic Action movements have recently begun to attract the attention of a number of historians of twentieth-century Quebec. For specific working-class movements, see especially Jean-Pierre Collin, *La Ligue ouvrière catholique canadienne, 1938–1954* (Montreal: Boréal, 1995); Lucie Piché, "La Jeunesse ouvrière catholique feminine: un lieu de formation sociale et d'action communautaire, 1931–1966," *Revue d'histoire de l'Amerique française* 52, no. 4 (spring 1999): 481–506. The most complete analytical treatment, centred upon Catholic Action's promotion of "youth" as a category of public identity, has been provided in the recent study by Louise Bienvenue, *Quand la jeunesse entre en scène: L'Action catholique avant la Révolution tranquille* (Montreal: Boréal, 2003). An assessment of popular Catholic Action endeavours in the field of family, marriage, and women's identities is offered in Michael Gauvreau, "The Rise of Personalist Feminism: Catholicism and the Marriage Preparation Movement in Quebec," in Nancy Christie, ed., *Households of Faith: Family, Gender and Community in Canada, 1760–1969* (Montreal and Kingston: McGill-Queen's University Press, 2002), 319–47. See also the older history of the Catholic Action organizations by Gabriel Clément, *Histoire de l'Action catholique au Canada français* (Montreal: Fides, 1972).

20 Dion, *Québec 1945–2000*, vol. 2, 357.

21 Jocelyn Létourneau, "La Révolution tranquille, catégorie identitaire du Québec contemporain," in Gagnon and Sarra-Bournet, *Duplessis*, 95–118.

22 For this definition of cultural "modernity" as a phenomenon distinct from a
    process of economic "modernization," see T.J. Jackson Lears, *No Place of Grace:
    Antimodernism and the Transformation of American Culture, 1880–1920* (New
    York: Pantheon Books, 1983), xiii; Modris Eksteins, *Rites of Spring: The Great
    War and the Birth of the Modern Age* (Toronto: Lester and Orpen Dennys,
    1989). For a recent exploration of the varieties of cultural modernity in
    Quebec which focuses on literary and artistic movements rather than reli-
    gion, see Yvan Lamonde and Esther Trépanier, eds, *L'avènement de la modernité
    culturelle au Québec* (Montreal: Institut Québecois de Recherche sur la culture,
    1986).

23 Recent Quebec scholarship has begun to look again at Roman Catholicism as
    a "dynamic," rather than a purely "reactionary," institution and set of values
    in this transition. See Raymond Lemieux, "Le dynamisme religieux des cul-
    tures francophones: ouverture ou repli?" and Gilles Routhier, "Quelle sécula-
    risation?: L'Église du Québec et la modernité," in Brigitte Caulier, ed., *Reli-
    gion, sécularisation, modernité: Les expériences francophones en Amérique du Nord*
    (Sainte-Foy: Les Presses de l'Universite Laval, 1996); Michael Gauvreau,
    "From Rechristianization to Contestation: Catholic Values and Quebec
    Society, 1931–1970," *Church History: Studies in Christianity and Culture* 69,
    no. 4 (Dec. 2000): 803–33.

24 Thus, it was possible for the sociologist Gregory Baum to write an entire book
    on Catholic attitudes to the Quiet Revolution by citing only the public pro-
    nouncements of bishops and senior clergy. See his *The Church in Quebec*,
    15–49. Terence Fay's recent synthesis, significantly entitled *A History of Cana-
    dian Catholics: Gallicanism, Romanism, and Canadianism* (Montreal and
    Kingston: McGill-Queen's University Press, 2002), identifies "Catholics" very
    closely with "clergy."

25 For one obvious, and increasingly criticized example of this genre that is very
    close to home, see Michael Gauvreau, *The Evangelical Century: College and Creed
    in English Canada from the Great Revival to the Great Depression* (Montreal and
    Kingston: McGill-Queen's University Press, 1991).

26 Examples of this new genre are too numerous to cite, but for a historiograph-
    ical and theoretical analysis of this direction in religious history, see Christie
    and Gauvreau, "Modalities of Social Authority."

27 To cite only the example of Catholic teaching on family limitation, sexuality
    within marriage, and birth control, the official clerical doctrines, as articu-
    lated in various papal encyclicals, insists upon the eternal nature of doctrine.
    One recent historical study of French Catholicism, which has recently come
    to my attention, argues that between 1880 and 1968 there were considerable
    changes both in the *content* of such doctrines and the way in which Catholic
    faithful received and understood them, but that doctrine was actually defined
    as a type of social and cultural negotiation that took account of lay Catholic
    experiences and social movements: see the stimulating treatment by Martine

Sèvegrand, *Les enfants du Bon Dieu: les catholiques français et la procréation au XXe siècle* (Paris: Albin Michel, 1995).

28 For this stimulating new approach to the French Revolutionary era, see Colin Jones and Dror Wahrman, eds, introduction to *The Age of Cultural Revolutions: Britain and France, 1750–1820* (Berkeley: University of California Press, 2002), 10, 13. For the concept of a "quiet revolution" applied to early nineteenth-century Britain, see Brian Lewis, *The Middlemost and the Milltowns: Bourgeois Culture and Politics in Early Industrial England* (Stanford: Stanford University Press, 2001), 2–3.

29 It must be acknowledged that the sociologist Fernand Dumont termed the 1930s the "first quiet revolution." See Dumont, "Les années 30: la première révolution tranquille," in Fernand Dumont, Jean Hamelin, Jean-Paul Montminy, eds, *Idéologies au Canada Français, 1930–1939* (Québec: Les Presses de l'Université Laval, 1978), 1–20. The present study diverges from Dumont's characterization of the decade as a heightening of "traditional" ideologies and responses. Indeed, Dumont falls back upon the "orthodox liberal" chronology of identifying the post-1945 years as the "second," or "real," Quiet Revolution. Another recent account by sociologists E.-Martin Meunier and Jean-Philippe Warren reads Catholicism into the Quiet Revolution, arguing that "we have previously viewed Catholicism as preventing the Quiet Revolution, as something that we had to break away from to escape from the *grande noirceur* and join the advanced societies of the modern world. However, in Quebec, was not Catholicism's role equally that of a revolutionary force?" See their *Sortir de la 'Grande noirceur': L'horizon personnaliste de la Révolution tranquille* (Sillery: Septentrion, 2002), 31. The difficulty with their account is that, because it is not based on extensive primary historical research, it accepts at face value the liberal rhetoric of the 1950s that Quebec was a "clericalized" society and, further, it accepts the Quiet Revolution as a political event beginning in 1960. As such, it constitutes a refurbishing of "orthodox liberalism" by attempting to keep the political categories and teleologies by adding a culturalist tinge. Louise Bienvenue's otherwise excellent analytical treatment of Catholic Action groups between 1931 and 1950 likewise qualifies these as occurring "before" the Quiet Revolution, and, more significantly, relies upon the political teleology of anti-nationalist liberal federalists and neo-nationalist sovereigntists first advanced by Michael Behiels: see Bienvenue's *Quand la jeunesse entre en scène*, 241.

CHAPTER ONE

1 ANQM, Fonds Jeunesse Étudiante Catholique, P65, s6, ss6, sss2, D5/2, Action Catholique Universitaire, Session 1952, Claude Bruneau, "Profession et culture," Stage de l'A.C.U. Lac Ouareau, 1952.

2 Gérard Pelletier, "Soldats de campagne ou zouaves paroissiaux," CAC 74 (Oct. 1946): 60.

3 Sian Reynolds, *France between the Wars* (London and New York: Routledge and Kegan Paul, 1996), 51. The cultural notion of a generational divide had developed among young European intellectuals during the first decade of the early twentieth century and had become a "tradition" by the 1920s. See Robert Wohl, *The Generation of 1914* (Cambridge, Mass.: Harvard University Press, 1979), 205, 229.

4 On this gendered aspect, see Michael Gauvreau, "The Emergence of Personalist Feminism, Catholicism and the Marriage Preparation Movement in Quebec, 1940–1966," in Nancy Christie, ed., *Households of Faith: Family, Gender and Community in Canada, 1760–1969* (Montreal and Kingston: McGill-Queen's University Press, 2002), 319–47; Lucie Piché, "La Jeunesse Ouvrière Catholique Féminine: Un lieu de formation sociale et d'action communautaire, 1931–1966," *Revue d'histoire de l'Amérique française* 52, no. 4 (spring 1999): 481–506.

5 AUM, Fonds Action Catholique Canadienne, P16/B4,4.1, "Rapport Général du Comité National d'Action Catholique pour l'année 1945–46," Sept. 1946; ANQ-M, Fonds JEC, P65, art. 5, Father Hozaël Aganier, "Réflexions sur l'Église et l'Action Catholique," CAC, Mar. 1954. Just after the World War II, the *Jeunesse Ouvrière Catholique* recorded 3,715 female members and 1,286 men; the Ligue Ouvrière Catholique, 3,158 women and 1,257 men, and the middle-class Jeunesse Indépendante Catholique enrolled 1,311 women and 500 men. The more numerous Jeunesse Étudiante Catholique, well-established in Church-run schools and colleges, listed 20,000 members. It should be remembered that this membership snapshot caught the Catholic Action movements at a low point: wartime manpower requirements would have seriously decimated the associations in a number of areas.

6 For an analysis of the division in the United Church which developed in the 1930s between the promoters of social reform and evangelical revivalism, see Nancy Christie and Michael Gauvreau, *'A Full-Orbed Christianity': The Protestant Churches and Social Welfare in Canada, 1900–1940* (Montreal and Kingston: McGill-Queen's University Press, 1996), 224–43.

7 Carmel Brouillard, o.f.m., "Jeunesse et vie religieuse," AN 8 (1936): 80.

8 A wide variety of movements described under the rubric of "Catholic Action" had existed in Quebec since the early twentieth century. These included temperance leagues, such as the Cercles Lacordaire, male and female confraternities, such as the Ligues du Sacré-Coeur and the Dames de Sainte-Anne, and associations created to promote public decency and morality. "Specialized" Catholic Action proposed a far more "collectivist" model of religious activity and sought to create specific associations based upon group identity or economic activity. For the older traditions of "Catholic Action," see Jean Hamelin and Nicole Gagnon, *Histoire du Catholicisme québécois, le XXe siècle*, vol. 1, *1900–1940* (Montreal: Boréal, 1984).

9 For Cardijn's ideas, and the Belgian influence on Catholic Action in Quebec,

see Gabriel Clément, *Histoire de l'Action catholique au Canada français* (Montreal: Fides, 1972), 11.

10 For the episcopal decisions and the founding of these respective organizations, see the account by Louise Bienvenue, *Quand la jeunesse entre en scène: L'Action catholique avant la Révolution tranquille* (Montreal: Boréal, 2003), 50–66.

11 Clément, *Histoire de l'Action catholique*, 12–13.

12 On the apolitical character of the *Jeunesse Ouvrière Chrétienne* in France during the 1930s, see Susan B. Whitney, "The Politics of Youth: Communists and Catholics in interwar France," Ph.D. thesis, State University of New Jersey at Rutgers, 1994, 365–430.

13 See Antonin Dupont, *Les relations entre l'Église et l'État sous Louis-Alexandre Taschereau* (Montreal: Guérin, 1972); Bernard L. Vigod, *Quebec before Duplessis: The Political Career of Louis-Alexandre Taschereau* (Montreal and Kingston: McGill-Queen's University Press, 1986). It should be noted that the state preferred a model of "voluntarism" that provided some level of subsidies for Church-sponsored social institutions but left their direct management in the hands of religious authorities.

14 For a comparative perspective on large cities like London, Berlin, and New York, see Hugh Macleod, *Piety and Poverty: Working-Class Religion in Berlin, London, and New York, 1870–1914* (New York and London: Holmes & Meier, 1996). In his conclusion, Macleod remarked that during the late nineteenth century, Catholicism was far more adept than its Protestant counterparts in adapting to an urban society and idiom (209). His insights have borne out for Quebec, seen particularly in the work of Lucia Ferretti on working-class Montreal parishes, which discerned a pattern not only of high working-class church attendance, but of participation and activism in associations and voluntary groups attached to the Church. See Ferretti's *Entre voisins: La société paroissiale en milieu urbain: Saint-Pierre-Apôtre de Montréal, 1848–1930* (Montreal: Boréal, 1992).

15 Well into the 1950s, church attendance among Catholics in urban Quebec remained relatively high. As late as 1961, it stood at 61 per cent in Montreal, although concerned clergy and lay activists were quick to point out that it was probably closer to 50 per cent in some working-class parishes.

16 For the activities and role of the ACJC, see Abbé Lionel Groulx, *Une croisade d'adolescents* (Montreal: Librairie Granger Frères, 1938; 1st ed. 1912), and the analysis in Michael Behiels, "L'Association catholique de la jeunesse canadienne-française and the Quest for a Moral Regeneration, 1903–1914," *Journal of Canadian Studies* 13, no. 2 (summer 1978): 27–41. For the fusion of Catholicism and nationalism that characterized the Jeune-Canada, a movement of young Montreal intellectuals, see CRLG, Fonds Jeune-Canada, P21/A1, André Laurendeau, "Droits et Devoirs de la Nation par rapport à l'Individu," 26 May 1934.

17 CRLG, Fonds Georges-Henri Lévesque, P8/B1, Georges-Henri Lévesque, o.p., *La Mission des intellectuels Canadiens-français (Qu'ils soient un …)*, lecture delivered 5 April 1935 at the Palestre Nationale at the awarding of the *Prix d'action intellectuelle* (Montreal: Imprimerie Populaire, 1935), 2. For the statement subordinating "national" to "Catholic" action, see ibid., P8/A,8, Lévesque, "Action Catholique et Action Nationale," 24 June 1936.

18 For the accounts by the protagonists, see Georges-Henri Lévesque, *Souvenances; entretiens avec Simon Jutras*, vol. 1 (Montreal: La Presse, 1983); Lionel Groulx, *Mes mémoires*, vol. 3 (Montreal: Fides, 1970–74). For historical treatments, see Robert Parisé, *Georges-Henri Lévesque: Père de la renaissance québécoise* (Montreal: Alain Stanké, 1976); Bienvenue, *Quand la jeunesse entre en scène*, 42–5. This typology, which privileges attitudes towards political nationalism, has been given sustained and sophisticated historical treatment in Michael Behiels, *Prelude to Quebec's Quiet Revolution: Liberalism versus Neo-Nationalism, 1945–1960* (Montreal and Kingston: McGill-Queen's University Press, 1985).

19 Even Georges-Henri Lévesque did not despair that "a Christian renaissance" and "a national renaissance" could ultimately be combined by individuals working within Catholic organizations. See "Action Catholique et Action Nationale."

20 Louise Bienvenue has noted the numerical weakness and marginal nature of both Communist and extreme nationalist youth organizations in 1930s Quebec. See *Quand la jeunesse entre en scène*, 116–24.

21 Henri Roy, o.m.i., *Un problème et une solution* (Montreal: Éditions Jocistes, 1934), 23–4.

22 "Lettre-Préface de S.E. Mgr. Georges Gauthier, Archévêque-Coadjuteur de Montréal," in Roy, *Un problème et une solution*, 5.

23 For the long persistence of the public ideology of the interdependent family in Canada, see Nancy Christie, introductionto Christie, ed., *Households of Faith*. In *Engendering the State: Family, Work, and Welfare in Canada* (Toronto: University of Toronto Press, 2000), Christie argues that in the 1930s, the notion of the family as an interdependent unit was increasingly challenged by working-class children and their parents (153–9). For the interdependent family in Montreal during the industrial era, see Bettina Bradbury, *Working Families: Age, Gender and Daily Survival in Industrializing Montreal* (Toronto: McClelland and Stewart, 1993).

24 My analysis on this point is indebted to the work of Ollivier Hubert, who argues that the ultramontane clergy always acted to reinforce parental power in dealing with adolescent wilfulness or restlessness in matters of marriage, courtship and family formation. See "Ritual Performance and Parish Sociability: French-Canadian Catholic Families at Mass from the 17th to the 19th Centuries," in Christie, ed., *Households of Faith*.

25 M.-C. Forest, o.p., "Notre avenir religieux" (suite), RD, Nov. 1936, 203.

26 R.P. Victor-M. Villeneuve, o.m.i., head chaplain of the JOC and the LOC, "Le

dixième anniversaire de la J.O.C. Canadienne," in *Rapport des Journées d'Étude Sacerdotales de la Jeunesse Ouvrière Catholique à l'occasion du dixième anniversaire de la J.O.C. canadienne (1932–1942)* (Montreal: Éditions Ouvrières, Éditions Fides, 1942), 40.

27 For this view, see Hubert, "Ritual Performance and Parish Sociability." Hubert argues that full membership and participation in the parish community required an adult status that was demonstrated by marriage. Recent work on nineteenth-century rural parish notables in Quebec has demonstrated that only male heads of family of good religious and moral conduct and having a superior level of landed wealth or material prosperity could aspire to serve on the parish vestry. See Christian Dessureault and Christine Hudon, "Conflits sociaux et élites locales au Bas-Canada: le clergé, les notables, la paysannerie et le contrôle de la fabrique," *Canadian Historical Review* 80, no. 3 (Sept. 1999): 413–39. Lucia Ferretti's research on working-class Montreal in the early twentieth century reveals a similar pattern in which leading roles in voluntary associations were monopolized by those individuals and families who were better-established in the parish, and that by contrast, recreational clubs directed at adolescent males were rather poorly attended. See her *Entre voisins,* 116, 182.

28 AUM, Fonds ACC, P16/K1.12, Monseigneur Joseph Charbonneau, "L'Action Catholique: Lettre Pastorale," published in CAC, July 1941.

29 Simonne Monet-Chartrand, *Ma vie comme rivière,* vol. 1, *Récit autobiographique, 1919–1942* (Montreal: Les Éditions du Remue-ménage, 1981), 228.

30 AUM, Fonds ACC, P16/A1,2, "Pour comprendre l'Action Catholique: Notes sur les fondements doctrinaux et la méthode de l'Action catholique," Jeunesse Catholique des Classes Moyennes, Sept. 1950; ANQ-M, Fonds JEC, P65, art. 2, Maurice Lafond, c.s.c., and R.F. Gaston-Adrien, e.c., "Cours d'Action Catholique."

31 For this argument, see John R. Gillis, *Youth and History: Tradition and Change in European Age Relations, 1770–present* (New York: Academic Press, 1981), 133. The contortions engaged in by French Catholic Action movements to mask the extent of control and direction by the youth chaplains have been described in Whitney, "The Politics of Youth," 172–5.

32 Gillis, *Youth and History,* 142.

33 ANQM, Fonds JEC, P65, art. 5, "Urgence de l'A.C. pour les Étudiantes et le Jécisme Féminin," ca late 1930s.

34 Monet-Chartrand, *Ma vie comme rivière,* vol. 1, 221. It could also be claimed that the movement provided similar opportunities for working-class youth, who in the traditional lines of authority in Catholic parishes could have exercised little initiative in associational life. See Piché, "La Jeunesse Ouvrière Catholique Féminine."

35 Guay, in *Jeunesse. Les Semaines Sociales du Canada, 1945* (Montreal: École Sociale Populaire, 1945), 141.

36 Ibid., 142.

37 Gérard Pelletier, "La responsabilité laïque mythe ou realité," CAC 44 (Apr. 1944): 350; J.-H. Langoumois, "Propositions sur la spiritualité étudiante," CAC 5 (Feb. 1941): 151.

38 For an excellent short analytical account of the personalist "ethos," see Meunier and Warren, *Sortir de la 'Grande noirceur,'* 52–3, 69.

39 For a discussion and definition of these key concepts of personalism as articulated in France, see John Hellman, *Emmanuel Mounier and the New Catholic Left, 1930–1950.* (Toronto: University of Toronto Press, 1981).

40 In France, the concept of a "spiritual revolution" as a response to the disorder of the 1930s was a conviction that spanned the intellectual spectrum between the non-Marxist left and quasi-fascist elements of the right. The best guide to the various "nonconformist" tendencies remains Jean-Louis Loubet del Bayle, *Les Non-conformistes des années 30: Une tentative de renouvellement de la pensée politique française* (Paris: Éditions du Seuil, 1969). For a treatment that emphasizes the notion of "community," see the suggestive treatment by Daniel Lindenberg, *Les années souterraines (1937–1947)* (Paris: Éditions La Découverte,1990), 53. For the emergence of "personalism," see Hellman, *Emmanuel Mounier,* 5–6.

41 Gilmard, "Individualisme ou Solidarité," JEC 2, no. 10 (Oct. 1936). Personalism was part of a wider European climate in which, during the 1930s, there was a flowering of attempts to emulate mythical or primitive notions of community. See John Hellman, *The Knight-Monks of Vichy France: Uriage 1940–1945* (Montreal and Kingston: McGill-Queen's University Press, 1993), 5–6; Lindenberg, *Les années souterraines,* 82–3, 166.

42 On the complex relationship between the Vichy state, personalism, and Emmanuel Mounier, see Hellman, *The Knight-Monks of Vichy,* and most recently, Michel Bergès, *Vichy Contre Mounier: Les non-conformistes face aux années 40* (Paris: Economica, 1997).

43 For an analysis of this rather ambiguous transition within Catholic Action, see Bienvenue, *Quand la jeunesse entre en scène,* 167.

44 André-J. Bélanger, *L'apolitisme des idéologies québécoises. Le grand tournant de 1934–1936* (Québec: Les Presses de l'Université Laval, 1974).

45 J. Proulx, Juniorat Montfortain Papineauville, "Génération neuve," JEC 2, no. 5 (May 1936).

46 The contrast is particularly telling when the responses to the Depression of English Canada's Protestant churches are examined. No new structures or approaches premised on an idea of "youth" were proffered by mainstream Protestantism, and the churches remained wedded to an "individualistic" style of religion premised upon promoting personal conversion, rather than changes to the structures of society. See Christie and Gauvreau, *'A Full-Orbed Christianity,'* 224–43.

47 La Rédaction, "Révolution," JEC 1, no. 10 (Oct. 1935).

48 J. Proulx, Juniorat Montfortain Papineauville, "Génération neuve", JEC 2, no. 5 (May 1936).

49 Jean-Marie Parent, "Daniel-Rops", JEC 2, no. 7 (July 1936).

50 For the reception of Maritain in Quebec, see AUM, Fonds ACC, P16/K1.47, Jacques Maritain, "Les conférences de M. Maritain," LD, 1934; La Direction, "Positions," LR 2 (May 1934): 3–5; La Direction, "Les problèmes spirituels et temporels," LR 5 (July 1934), 122; Jean-Robert Bonnier, "Désespérance des jeunes," AN 6 (1935): 127. For the monopoly enjoyed by scholastic philosophy in Quebec's *collèges classiques* and universities, see Yvan Lamonde, *La philosophie et son enseignement au Québec, 1665–1920* (Montreal: Hurtubise, 1980). For the influence of the personalism of *Ordre Nouveau*, see Robert Charbonneau, "Réponse à Jean-Louis Gagnon," LR 2, 163–5; Charbonneau, "Jeunesse et Revolution," LR 2, 5; Parent, "Daniel-Rops," and Guy Frégault, "Révolution et liberté," AN 11 (1937): 232–9. For Mounier's presence on the Quebec cultural scene, see Emmanuel Mounier, "Le Mouvement 'Esprit,'" LR 2, no. 7: 227–33.

51 Brouillard, "Jeunesse et vie religieuse," 81.

52 "Appel à la violence," JEC 1, no. 1 (Jan.–Feb. 1935). See also "La droiture de conscience," JO 2, no. 4 (Jan. 1934).

53 Maurice Lafond, c.s.c., "À la source d'un renouveau chretien," CAC 18 (Nov. 1942): 314; "Un genre de vie," JEC 1, no. 1 (Jan.–Feb. 1935).

54 Maurice Tremblay, "Pourquoi la J.E.C." [*La Vie Écoliere*], Séminaire de Rimouski, JEC 2, no. 4 (Apr. 1936); Jean-René, "Notre Jeunesse – Carnet de Route" [*J.E.C. Française*], JEC 3, no. 7 (July 1937); F. Sénécal, "Un Défi," JEC 2, no. 10 (Oct. 1936); "Au Séminaire Sainte-Croix," JEC 2, no. 2 (Feb. 1936); "CONSCRIPTION," JEC 3, no. 3 (Mar. 1936); Maurice Lafond, c.s.c., "Lénine... un vrai jéciste," JEC 3, no. 3 (Mar. 1936); "À TOUTE VAPEUR," JEC 1, no. 6 (June 1935); "Appel à la violence," JEC 1, no. 1 (Jan.–Feb. 1935); "Être moderne," JEC 1, no. 1 (Jan.–Feb. 1935); Paul Doncoeur, s.j., "La jeunesse chrétienne dans la crise moderne," LR, 2 (Apr. 1934), 10; AUM, Fonds ACC, P16/G2, 1.38, Spiritualité, Alex Pelletier and Gérard Pelletier, "Caractères de la spiritualité étudiante," CAC, special issue on "Spiritualité étudiante," Dec. 1944; ibid., Jeanne Benoît, general propagandist for the JECF, "La J.E.C., mouvement d'action," CAC, special issue on "Spiritualité étudiante," Dec. 1944; ANQ-M, Fonds JEC, P65, s6, ss6, sss1, D1, "Notes sur l'Action Catholique a l'Université," 4 June 1942.

55 Adrien Malo, o.f.m., "L'Action Catholique: Christianiser," CAC 7 (Apr. 1941): 199; "Message de Rome!" JEC 1, no. 3 (Mar. 1935).

56 Monet-Chartrand, *Ma vie comme rivière*, vol. 1, 227.

57 "Message de Rome!" JEC 1, no. 3 (Mar. 1935).

58 AUM, Fonds ACC, P16/G2, 1.20, Jeunesse Étudiante Catholique, Guy Cormier, "J.E.C. en fonction du milieu," 1943.

59   Bonnier, "Desespérance des jeunes," 121.

60   Guy Frégault, "Où est la révolution?" AN 9 (1937): 81.

61   Dorothée, "Non mais cette Devise," JEC 1, no. 12 (Dec. 1935); "... *jeunesse neuve*," JEC 1, no. 5 (May 1935); Madeleine Dufour, "Le salut de la J.E.C.F. ," JEC 1, no. 8 (Aug. 1935); "J.O.C. ," JO 3, nos 3–4 (Dec.–Jan. 1935); AUM, Fonds ACC, P16/G5,4.1, "Premier Congrès Général – juillet 1935."

62   "Faut-il rompre avec le passé?" JEC 1, no. 3 (Mar. 1935).

63   This process occurred in the articulation of a modern historical conscious-ness by certain key Quebec historians in the early 1940s who turned away from a political history of constitutional precedent to an identification with a "heroic" French colonial past when Quebec society appeared to have control of its own destiny. See Jean Lamarre, *Le Devenir de la Nation Québécoise, selon Maurice Séguin, Guy Frégault et Michel Brunet, 1944–1969* (Sillery: Septentrion, 1993). In this context, it is not coincidental that the three historians exam-ined by Lamarre were all strongly influenced by their participation in Catholic youth movements in the 1930s, Séguin as a Scout leader, Frégault in the Jeunesse Étudiante Catholique, and Brunet as a member of the Associa-tion Catholique de la Jeunesse Canadienne. See ibid, 91–2.

64   Guy Frégault, "Séparatisme? État français? ... à l'Abbé Lionel Groulx," *Jeunesse*, Sept. 1937.

65   Emile Deguire, c.s.c., "Notre dévotion envers le Christ total," CAC 42 (Feb. 1944): 243; Maurice Lafond, c.s.c., "La Paroisse," CAC 123 (Nov. 1950): 114; Gilmard, "Face au Sacrifice de la Messe: une solide étude sur le caractère social de la messe et la participation du chrétien," JEC 9, nos 4–5 (Apr.–May 1943); Réginald Boisvert, "Monsieur Atlee a bien parlé" (editorial), VE 12, no. 3 (Mar. 1946). The doctrine of the Mystical Body of Christ was officially proclaimed by Pope Pius XII in 1943. Based upon the works of the German theologian Karl Adam, these ideas had been widely discussed in France and infused French Catholic personalism during the 1930s. See Lindenberg, *Les années souterraines*, 208; Hellman, *Emmanuel Mounier*, 7.

66   Lafond, "À la source," 312.

67   Both Pelletier and Trudeau warmly mention Hertel as one of the central influences in their college life. See Gérard Pelletier, *Les années d'impatience, 1950–1960* (Montreal: Alain Stanké, 1983), 36–8; Pierre Elliott Trudeau, *Memoirs* (Toronto: McClelland and Stewart, 1993), 22. Hertel's influence on René Lévesque was more indirect, as Lévesque attended the Séminaire de Gaspé. But Hertel's works were certainly made available by Father Charles Dubé, Hertel's cousin and one of Lévesque's instructors. It is apparent from the latest biography of Lévesque that his early commitment to Quebec's inde-pendence was strongly fostered by a reading of Hertel's *Leur inquiétude* in 1936. See Pierre Godin, *René Lévesque: un enfant du siècle (1922–1960)* (Montreal: Boréal, 1994), 54.

68 François Hertel, *Leur inquiétude* (Montreal: Éditions 'Jeunesse' A.C.J.C., 1936), 89.

69 Ibid., 14.

70 Ibid., 128.

71 Ibid., 70; Robert Élie, "De l'esprit bourgeois," LR 2, no. 4: 114.

72 Suzanne Manny, "Le beau risque: le livre," JEC 6, no. 3 (Mar. 1940); Gérard Pelletier, "Le beau risque: l'auteur," JEC 6, no. 3 (Mar. 1940).

73 François Hertel, "D'une sainteté contemporaine: Lettre aux redacteurs à demi-ouverte au profit des lecteurs," JEC 7, no. 1 (Jan. 1941).

74 François Hertel, *Le Beau risque* (Montreal: Fides, 1940), 26.

75 Hertel, "D'une sainteté contemporaine."

76 Hertel, *Le beau risque*, 82–3, 114–5.

77 Roy, *Un problème et une solution*, 47; AUM, Fonds ACC, P16/G2, 1.20, "Caractères fondamentaux de la J.E.C. Canadienne," CAC, Montreal, 1943, "Numéro special: La J.E.C., mouvement apostolique," Émile Deguire, c.s.c., "Présentation."

78 "Ce que veut la J.O.C. ," JO, June–July 1939; Charbonneau, "L'Action Catholique: Lettre Pastorale."

79 M.D. Chenu, o.p., "Paroisse et Oeuvres," RD (May 1934): 350–1.

80 Ibid., 351–2.

81 AUM, Fonds ACC, P16/G, 1.38, Spiritualité, Alex and Gérard Pelletier, "Caractères de la Spiritualité Étudiante." Before her marriage to Gérard Pelletier, Alexandrine Leduc was president of the women's section of the Jeunesse Étudiante Catholique. Pelletier was president of the men's section and editor, in the 1940s, of JEC, the monthly newspaper published by the Catholic student movement.

82 Dominique, "Le billet de Dominique: Bravo Jeunesse! – Au lendemain des Journées Thomistes d'Ottawa," JEC 2, no. 6 (June 1936).

83 André Picard, c.s.c., deputy chaplain-general, JEC and JECF, "J.E.C. mouvement de masse," CAC 63 (Nov. 1945): 117; AUM, Fonds ACC, P16/G2, Histoire de la J.E.C. – Documents, "Élite et Masse," ca 1940–41.

84 Benoît, "La J.E.C."; Malo, "L'Action Catholique: Christianiser"; Pierre Juneau, "La Semaine d'étude generale," CAC 23–24 (Aug. 1942): 543–7; Guy Rocher et Jean-Paul Lefebvre, "Vie d'Équipe," CAC 56: (Apr. 1945), 357–62; Maurice Lafond, c.s.c., "À base de christianisme social," CAC Dec. 1943; AUM, Fonds ACC, P16/G3, 3.2, Jeunesse Indépendante Catholique, Roland Duhamel, p.s.s., "Christianisme de choc"; ibid., Raymond Dunn, s.j., "Corps mystique et sens social"; ibid., P16/G2, 1.20, Guy Cormier, general propagandist, "J.E.C. en fonction du milieu," 1943; ibid., Jeanne Benoît and Jean Dostaler, "Mémoire à la Commission Canadienne de la Jeunesse sur l'éducation," n.d.; JEC, "Fraternité," JEC, 8, no. 4 (Apr. 1942); Germain-M. Lalande, c.s.c., *Conversion au réel: un essai sur l'Action Catholique: expériences étudiantes* (Montreal: Fides, 1948), 180, 185, 222.

CHAPTER TWO

1 Pierre Elliott Trudeau, "In Memoriam: Albert Béguin et Jacques Perreault," CL 17 (June 1957): 2.

2 Jean-Marc Léger, "Le Canada français à la recherche de son avenir," *Esprit* 1952 (special issue on French Canada), 279.

3 R.P. Robert Fortin, s.s.s., professor of theology in the Sherbrooke Grand Séminaire, "Notre Jeunesse," in *La Jeunesse. Les Semaines Sociales du Canada, 1945* (Montreal: École Sociale Populaire, 1945), 50.

4 The French sociology that Catholic Action relied upon was anti-Marxist in the sense that the milieu did not have an exact correspondence with economic class. Writing in 1946, Father Michel Doran stated that concepts of class were derived from social function, while the milieu involved "a similarity of mentalities." The milieu, according to this commentator, was "a homogeneous group with a common culture, identical aspirations, one that possesses a common ideology. ... Like the individual, the milieu possesses a conscience." See Michel Doran, o.p., chaplain-general of the LIC and JIC, "L'Action catholique specialisée," *RD* (Sept. 1946): 68.

5 Claude Ryan, cited in *La Jeunesse*, 50. For Ryan's early education, training, and call to the national Catholic Action secretariat, see the biography by Aurélien Leclerc, *Claude Ryan: l'homme du devoir* (Montreal: Les Éditions Quinze, 1978).

6 Georges-Henri Lévesque, *Souvenances*, vol. 2, *Entretiens avec Simon Jutras* (Montreal: La Presse, 1983), 155. The Quebec committee of the Canadian Youth Commission included Father Georges-Henri Lévesque of the École des Sciences Sociales of Université Laval, the sociologist Jean-Charles Falardeau, Eugene Bussières, and Maurice Lamontagne, all of whom were associated with the Laval tradition of social service. The Montreal community was represented by Esdras Minville, director of the École des Hautes Études Commerciales; Jacques Perreault; Mme Claudine Vallerand of the École des Parents; Father Gonzalve Poulin; Maximilien Caron; Adrien Pouliot; Roger Duhamel; Senator Léon-Mercier Gouin; and Gérard Lemieux, editor of *Jeunesse Ouvrière* and later head of the Institut Familial at the Université de Montréal. For the changing imperatives of the Canadian Youth Commission, see Michael Gauvreau, "The Protracted Birth of the Canadian 'Teenager': Work, Citizenship, and the Canadian Youth Commission, 1943–1955," in Nancy Christie and Michael Gauvreau, eds, *Cultures of Citizenship in Postwar Canada, 1940–1955* (Montreal and Kingston: McGill-Queen's University Press, 2003), 201–38.

7 Claude Ryan, "La Fédération Provinciale des Mouvements de Jeunesse," JC, Jan. 1948.

8 For the articulation and prevalence of these "economic" notions of citizenship during the waning years of the Depression, see Christie, *Engendering the State*, 196–248.

9 "Les jeunes ouvriers devant l'après-guerre," JO (Apr. 1942).

10 AUM, Fonds ACC, P16/04.57, Commission Canadienne de la Jeunesse, "Jeunesse et Après-guerre" (pamphlet, n.d.); ibid., P16//04.59, Commission Canadienne de la Jeunesse, "Committee on Religion," conference held at Université de Montréal, 27–28 January, 1945.

11 Marcel Côté, as quoted in Gérard Lemieux, *Jeunesse du Québec: Bilan d'une génération* (Montreal: Jeunesse Indépendante Catholique, 1946).

12 AUM, Fonds ACC, P16/J16, 1, "Ministère de la Jeunesse – Mémoire," Feb. 1946.

13 Ryan, "La Fédération Provinciale." Louise Bienvenue, *Quand la jeunesse entre en scène* (Montreal: Boréal, 2003), 134, likewise insists on the episcopal hierarchy's fear of lay insubordination and its concern to regulate and control the Catholic Action movements.

14 Ryan, "La Fédération Provinciale." For Ryan's assimilation of Anglo-Saxon traditions of liberalism, see Leclerc, *Claude Ryan*, 104. Ryan's own Catholicism was strongly marked by the influence of Cardinal Newman, in contrast to the French personalist variety experienced by many of his contemporaries.

15 Gérard Pelletier, "Ce fameux 'après-guerre,'" JEC 11, no. 3 (Mar. 1945).

16 AUM, Fonds ACC, P16/G3, 5.1, Jeunesse Indépendante Catholique, École civique d'été, 1950, Pierre Juneau, "Les Mouvements de jeunesse: Formateurs ou rongeurs d'homme"; Guy Cormier, "Le mal de notre jeunesse," JC (Apr. 1947).

17 For an account of these international student encounters and their new, universal definition of youth, see Bienvenue, *Quand la jeunesse entre en scène*, 191–205.

18 Pelletier, "La responsabilité laïque: mythe ou réalité," CAC 44 (Apr. 1944): 350; Gérard Pelletier and P.P. Asselin, chaplain-general of the LOC, "Pour une littérature d'Action catholique," CAC 62 (Oct. 1945): 68. While editor of JEC, Pelletier refused to offer unconditional loyalty to the war effort, arguing that in religious terms the elaboration of a Christianity infused with personalism was "independent of the war itself and of all imperialisms": Gérard Pelletier, "L'appel des armes" (editorial), JEC 8, nos 5–6 (May–June 1942). On a less elevated note, as editor of JEC Pelletier warmly praised Marshal Pétain's "National Revolution." See André Laurendeau, "Jouer à la balle au chasseur," JEC 6, no. 8 (Aug. 1940); "Regards sur le Monde – France," JEC 7, no. 4 (Apr. 1941); "Extrait d'une lettre de France," JEC 7, no. 10 (Oct. 1941); "Message de Pétain aux Élèves de France," JEC 8, no. 1 (Jan. 1942); "La guerre et nous," JEC 8, nos 5–6 (May–June 1942). For the dominance of pro-Pétain sympathies within the Jeunesse Étudiante Catholique, see the memoirs of Guy Rocher, *Entre les rêves et l'histoire* (Montreal: VLB Éditeur, 1989), 165.

19 Gérard Pelletier, "Soldats de campagne ou zouaves paroissiaux," CAC 74 (Oct. 1946): 55.

20 Gérard Pelletier, "La responsabilité laïque," 341; AUM, Fonds ACC, P16/G4, 10.3, Présence, Louis Beaupré to Claude Ryan, 29 March 1947.

21 AUM, Fonds ACC, P16/K1.53, Gérard Pelletier, Gérard Pelletier, "Visage de notre société, Perspectives 1946."

22 Gérard Pelletier, "D'un prolétariat spirituel," Esprit 1952 (special issue on French Canada), 190, 193.

23 Ibid., 199.

24 Jean-Charles Falardeau, "Comment préparer l'apres-guerre," RD (June 1941): 309–12; Guy Cormier, "Un grand bouquin," JEC 9, no. 9 (Sept. 1943); Henri-Irénée Marrou, "Préface française," Esprit 1952 (special issue on French Canada), 174.

25 ANQM, Fonds JOC, P104, art. 181, "Rapport Camille Laurin, 1950."

26 AUM, Fonds ACC, P16/G3, 5.1, Libres pour Vivre Pleinement – Rapport de l'École Civique d'été, Lac Stukeley, juin 1950, Claude Ryan, "Gravité du problème de la liberté"; Gérard Desagne, ptre, Séminaire de Chicoutimi, "Les Services dans l'Église," CAC (1943).

27 Guy Rocher, "Images étudiantes d'outre-Atlantique," VE 12, no. 10 (Oct. 1946); Réginald Boisvert, "Affaire de Famille?" JEC 11, no. 7 (July–Aug. 1945); Pierre Juneau, "Images Étudiantes d'outre-Atlantique," VE 12, no. 4 (Apr. 1946). For an account of these contacts in the 1950s and the suspicions they aroused among university authorities at the Université de Montréal, see Nicole Neatby, Carabins ou activistes? (Montreal and Kingston: McGill-Queen's University Press, 1998).

28 Jacques Dubuc, "Le monde et la foi" [Quartier latin], JEC 11, no. 2 (Feb. 1945); Robert Élie, "Gide et l'expérience communiste," LR 3, no. 8: 209–15.

29 Guy Rocher, "Lettre ouverte au Directeur," VE 12, no. 5 (May 1946); Rocher, "Présence chrétienne," VE 13, no. 5 (May 1947); Fernand Jolicoeur, "Une internationale de la jeunesse," RD 52 (Apr. 1946): 240–5; Roger Varin, "L'Armée Rouge," JC (Jan. 1948).

30 Claude Ryan, "Anti-Communisme ... ou Quoi?," JC (June 1947).

31 For a critical analysis of the official culture of anti-Communism in post-war Canada, see Reg Whitaker and Gary Marcuse, Cold War Canada: The Making of a National Insecurity State, 1945–1957 (Toronto: University of Toronto Press, 1994).

32 Juneau, "Images etudiantes d'outre-Atlantique."

33 Gérard Pelletier, "L'Europe Oublie Abraham," JC (Mar. 1947).

34 Ibid.,; Pelletier, "Un boulet dans chaque main?" JEC 11, no. 2 (Feb. 1945); Fortin, "Notre jeunesse," 56–7.

35 ANQ-M, Fonds JEC, P65, Action Catholique Universitaire, Marc Lalonde, "Risque chrétien et profession," 1950; Pierre Vadeboncoeur, "L'irréalisme de notre culture," CL 1, no. 4, (Dec. 1951).

36 To date, there have been few sustained attempts to precisely analyse Mounier's influence on Quebec. However, see the recent work by Simon

Lapointe, "L'influence de la gauche catholique française sur l'idéologie de la CTCC-CSN de 1948 à 1964," *Revue d'histoire de l'Amérique française* 49, no. 3 (winter 1996): 331–56, which traces the influence of Mounier's personalism on key leaders of Quebec's Catholic labour movement.

37 AUM, Fonds ACC, P16/12.56, "Correspondance R," Claude Ryan, "projet de lettre rédigé le 4 mars 1953 mais jamais envoyé, à M. Léopold Richer." A few years later, another Catholic Action document identified a "personalist" network controlling the intellectual agenda of the national broadcasting system. See ibid., P16/J6, 1, Commission Nationale pour Cinéma-Radio-TV, "Le problème de la télévision au Canada," 26 April 1956.

38 For an excellent analysis of the Paris intellectual scene that draws together the experiences of both Communist and non-Communist intellectuals, see Tony Judt, *Past Imperfect: French Intellectuals 1944–1956* (Berkeley: University of California Press, 1992), 1, 18, 21, 30, 49. The impact of Marxism on the direction of French intellectual life, and in particular, on varieties of existentialism has been described in Mark Poster, *Existential Marxism in Postwar France: From Sartre to Althusser* (Princeton: Princeton University Press, 1975). For the "Left Christian" version, see Hellman, *Emmanuel Mounier,* 227–8. For the impact of this French anti-Americanism among Catholic circles in Quebec, see AUM, Fonds ACC, P16/G3, 5.1, "Camp civique ... 1949," speech of M. Beauchet, national vice-president of the French Jeunesse Independante Catholique.

39 Lindenberg, *Les années souterraines (1937–1947)* (Paris: Éditions de la Découverte, 1990), 189.

40 Fernand Dumont, *Récit d'une émigration: Mémoires* (Montreal: Boréal, 1997); Rocher, *Entre les rêves et l'histoire,* 28.

41 Fernand Dumont, "Un maître inconnu," VE 16, no. 5 (June 1950).

42 Emmanuel Mounier, *Personalism,* trans. Philip Mairet (London: Routledge and Kegan Paul, 1952; original French ed. 1950), 9, 12–13, 17–19, 21, 80–1. For Mounier's attempt to equate personalism with Marxism, and for his evocation of the humanist traditions of French socialism, see Hellman, *Emmanuel Mounier,* 207, 211–12.

43 Mounier, *Personalism,* 102.

44 Jean LeMoyne, "Jeunesse de l'homme," CL 1, no. 2 (Feb. 1951): 10–14.

45 Gilles Marcotte, "Un chrétien nomme Mounier," CL 16 (Feb. 1957); Madeleine Poisson, "Vision d'espérance," JC (Apr. 1947); Albert Breton, "Accélérer la montée humaine," VE 19, no. 4 (Apr. 1953); Gilles Marcotte, "L'homme de la communion," VE 19, no. 4 (Apr. 1953); Gérard Pelletier, "Trois paroles d'Emmanuel Mounier," CL 1, no. 3 (Mar. 1951): 45–6.

46 Pelletier, *Les années d'impatience,* 40–1.

47 Trudeau, *Memoirs,* 40.

48 AUM, Fonds ACC, P16/G3, 5.1, Jeunesse Indépendante Catholique, Camp Civique d'Été, 1949, Pierre Elliott Trudeau, "Où va le Monde!" This address

seems to have been based on the insights that Trudeau gained from his travels in Asia, where he was researching the Harvard thesis that he briefly alludes to in *Memoirs*.

49 Ibid., "Où va le Monde!"

50 Trudeau, *Memoirs*, 40, 47. Trudeau's biographers have tended, in part to explain his attractiveness to Anglo-Canadian audiences, to overplay the "English" influences on his intellectual makeup. See, for example, Stephen Clarkson and Christina McCall, *Trudeau and Our Times*, vol. 1, *The Magnificent Obsession* (Toronto: McClelland and Stewart, 1990), 46–51, for a lengthy discussion of the rather tangential intellectual influences of Harvard and the London School of Economics.

51 Maurice Blain, "Sur la liberté de l'esprit," *Esprit* 1952 (special issue on French Canada): 203; ANQM, Fonds JEC, P65, S6, SS6, SSS2, D1/4, "Document de travail," Oct. 1950; ibid., P65, S6, SS6, SSS2, D5/2, Action Catholique Universitaire, Stage au Lac Ouareau, 1952, Marc Lalonde, "Risque chrétien et profession."

52 ANQM, Fonds JEC, P65, S6, SS6, SSS6, D5/2, Action Catholique Universitaire, Stage du Lac Ouareau, 1952, Abbé Norbert Lacoste, "Progrès et profession."

53 Jean-Charles Falardeau, "Reflet de l'homme," VE 27, no. 10 (Feb. 1961).

54 ANQM, Fonds JEC, P65, S6, SS6, SSS6, D5/2, Action Catholique Universitaire, Stage du Lac Ouareau, 1952, Fernand Dumont, "Spiritualité et profession"; Jean-Paul Geoffroy, "Le capitalisme ... au rancart!," JC (Oct. 1947); Guy Frégault, "Le travail et l'homme," LR 4, no. 2: 74–7; Robert Élie, "Discussion sur l'idée du travail," LR 4, no. 5: 142–7; Réginald Boisvert, "Comment on clame les vérités d'ouvriers," JEC 11, no. 4 (Apr. 1945); Égide Dandenault, "Le travail," JEC 17, no. 6 (June 1951).

55 Pierre-Elliott Trudeau, "L'asceticisme en canot," JEC 10, no. 6 (June 1944).

56 Pelletier, "Soldats de campagne ou zouaves paroissiaux," 57, 60.

57 Mounier, *Personalism*, 43.

58 Réginald Boisvert, "Foi chrétienne et mission temporelle," CL 13 (Nov. 1955): 6.

59 Pierre Vadeboncoeur, "Hommage: Henri Bourassa," CL 2, no. 3 (Dec. 1952): 71–2.

60 For the emergence of this exclusively male definition of citizenship in Canada during the 1930s, see Christie, *Engendering the State*, 245–8. Mounier's personalism contained a strong admixture of Nietzschean admiration for masculine, self-reliant, vigorous "supermen." See Hellman, *Emmanuel Mounier*, 199, 220.

61 Henri-Irénée Marrou, "Préface française," *Esprit* 1952 (special issue on French Canada), 170.

62 This line of interpretation originates with the personal mythology and political self-promotion of the principals themselves *after* they acceded to key positions in the federal Liberal party. See Pierre Elliott Trudeau, *Approaches to*

Politics (Toronto: McClelland and Stewart, 1970), especially the introduction by Ramsay Cook. A generally similar, but more sophisticated and refined line of argument is offered by Michael Behiels, *Prelude to Quebec's Quiet Revolution: Liberals vs. Neo-Nationalists, 1945–1960* (Montreal and Kingston: McGill-Queen's University Press, 1985). Behiels posits a dialectic, originating in the early 1950s, between, on the one hand, staunchly federalist *citélibristes* who were wedded to a "liberal" agenda of civil liberties and labour activism, and, on the other hand, a "neo-nationalist" current, centred around *Le Devoir*, which advanced more state-centred ideas of economic nationalism that were linked to the achievement of greater independence for Quebec.

63 Behiels, *Prelude to Quebec's Quiet Revolution*, 70–8.

64 Léon Dion, *Quebec, 1945–2000*, vol. 2, *Les intellectuels et le temps de Duplessis* (Sainte-Foy: Les Presses de l'Université Laval, 1993), 357–9. Dion also argues in regard to the intellectuals of the 1950s that "they wasted their energy in issuing peremptory condemnations of the dogmatism and conformity of the Church and popular religion. However, there was no expression of a powerful breath of spirituality among them, and the sense of mystery, tragedy, and the sacred was generally absent." While during the 1950s Dion was a young professor of political science at Laval and a sometime contributor to *Cité libre*, by the 1990s he was chiding the journal for not having done enough to regenerate the Catholic Church in Quebec. Such opinions are more revealing of Dion's own nostalgia and yearning for the simpler life before the far-reaching social changes of the 1960s. His assessment of the 1950s intellectuals must be read against his own desire for the "strong man," paternal leadership of a Duplessis-type figure, for the village school-house, and for the fellowship that he believed characterized the old-style village parish.

65 On this point, see Shirley E. Woods, *Her Excellency Jeanne Sauvé* (Toronto: Macmillan, 1986), 43. Based upon the reminiscences of Jeanne Sauvé, who was president of the women's section of the Jeunesse Étudiante Catholique in the mid-1940s as Jeanne Benoît, it is apparent that the decision to marry meant that one would have to relinquish one's official functions and membership in the youth movements.

66 Internal documents from the late 1940s and early 1950s testify to a "tension between lay responsibility and ecclesiastical control." See AUM, Fonds ACC, P16/B4, 1.1, Coordination de l'A.C.C. entre 1945 et 1952, Jan. 1950–Feb. 1953, "IV. Analyse de la conjoncture présente"; ibid., P16/B5, 5.3, Fernand Cadieux, "Notes Introductoires à la question d'un centre d'entraînement."

67 AUM, Fonds ACC, P16/G4, 10.3, Groupe Présence, Jacques Dubuc, "Lettre Circulaire," 19 Mar. 1948.

68 AUM, Fonds ACC, P16/G4, 10.3, Groupe Présence, 21 déc. 1945–sept. 1950, "Autres dépliants," n.d.; ibid., "Groupes d'Action Civique – Programme d'Activités 1947–48." "Présence" included as its members Claude Ryan, Fernand Cadieux, Guy Cormier, Jacques Dubuc, Camille Laurin, Gérard

Lemieux, Claude Mailhiot, Jean Marchand, Jacques Dubuc, Gérard Pelletier, Roger Varin, and Guy Beaugrand-Champagne. Several of these names were later key contributors to *Cité libre.*

69 Dubuc, "Lettre Circulaire."

70 Claude Ryan, "Circulaire," *Jeunesse Canadienne* (Montreal), 1946. The editorial board of this magazine included Roger Varin, Guy Beaugrand-Champagne, Jeanne Benoît, Réginald Boisvert, Guy Cormier, Jacques Dubuc, Jean-Paul Geoffroy, Françoise Lavigne, Gérard Lemieux, Charles Lussier, Claude Ryan, Guy Rocher, Suzanne Casgrain, Yolande Cloutier, Georges Bilodeau, Renée Blanchard, Gustave Boulanger, and Colette Fortier. Foreign flavour was added by a team of "correspondents," which at times included Pierre Juneau (Paris), Camille Laurin (Geneva), and Maurice Sauvé and Pierre Elliott Trudeau (London).

71 AUM, Fonds ACC, P16/G3, 5.1, Écoles Civiques d'Été, Ryan, "Circulaire," 24 July 1947.

72 Pelletier, *Les années d'impatience*, 141–3. Pelletier listed the following names as having been involved with founding *Cité libre*: Guy Cormier, Réginald Boisvert, Pauline Lamy, Jean-Paul Geoffroy, Renée Desmarais, Pierre Juneau, Fernande Saint-Martin, Alec Leduc (Alec Pelletier). Significantly, most of these had also been involved with the journalistic enterprise of *Jeunesse Canadienne*. Interestingly, Claude Ryan refused to give the official blessing of Catholic Action to the magazine, on the grounds that he estimated it an "overdose of writing." Indeed, while Ryan agreed generally with the progressive aims of the *Cité libre* circle, what he objected to was the "excessive bitterness" among "certain advanced elements of the younger generation." In particular, Ryan deplored their tendency to "express themselves on too many fronts and to fall into ... imprecision and mere literature ... many ... took as their starting-point the ill-digested memories of their youthful and adolescent years." See Ryan, "L'Église Catholique au Canada français," *Chronique sociale de France* 65 (1957): 454.

73 Gérard Pelletier, "Premières questions: Histoire de collégiens qui ont aujourd'hui trente ans," CL 1, no. 1 (June 1950): 5–9.

74 La Rédaction, "Règle du jeu," CL 1, no. 1 (June 1950): 1.

75 Ibid., 1–2.

76 Gérard Pelletier, "'Cité libre' confesse ses intentions," CL 1, no. 2 (Feb. 1951): 3; Vincent Harvey, o.p., "Une expérience religieuse," RD (July–Aug. 1953): 24.

77 Pelletier, "Premières questions," 8–9.

78 La rédaction, "Règle du jeu," 1.

79 Fernand Cadieux, "Orientation spirituelle," CAC 148 (Dec. 1952): 101–2. Cadieux was the national president of the Jeunesse Etudiante Catholique and had close links to the *Cité libre* circle. Similar criticisms of Quebec Catholic Action had been advanced by Pelletier as early as 1946, as he contrasted his

encounter with the "harsh duties" that Christians had to perform in post-war Europe to the sentimental, unreal climate that existed in Catholic Action circles in Quebec. See Pelletier, "Soldats de campagne ou zouaves paroissiaux."

80 Pelletier, "Premières questions," 8–9: "We were tormented, unstable, hampered on all sides, but we were also impatient, full of fire, and violent. We thirsted to go beyond ourselves."

81 Ibid., 8; Pelletier, "Faites vos jeux: Le Diagnostic du R.P. Anjou, s.j.," CL 1, no. 3 (Mar. 1951): 42–5.

82 Pelletier, "'Cité libre,'" 4; ibid., "Y a-t-il un malaise chez les catholiques français?" CL 2, nos 1–2 (June–July 1952): 48–51.

83 Pelletier, "'Cité libre,'" 7.

84 For this estimate of Cité libre's influence, see Behiels, Prelude to Quebec's Quiet Revolution, 70–8; surveys by Linteau, Durocher, and Robert, Histoire du Québec contemporain: de 1930 à nos jours; and John Dickinson and Brian Young, A Short History of Quebec, 2d ed. (Toronto: Copp Clark Pitman, 1993), 284–9.

85 Mounier's "dialogue" with Marxism meant that he reached this position as early as the mid-1930s, a key element of his thought that always distinguished him from the Catholic "Right." See Loubet del Bayle, Les non-conformistes des années 30, 121–57, 269–326.

86 Cadieux, "Orientation spirituelle," 102–3; AUM, Fonds ACC, P16/B6, 3.18, Claude Ryan, "Le vrai visage de l'espérance," Apr. 1955.

87 AUM, Fonds ACC, P16/E2,6, 5.1, "Congrès International, Rome 1956"; ANQM, Fonds JEC, P65, S6, SS6, SSS3, D6, Action Catholique Universitaire, Correspondance Générale 1935–1955, Guy Rocher à Fernand Cadieux, 13 December 1949; Gérard Pelletier, "Crise d'autorité ou crise de liberté?" CL 2, nos 1–2 (June–July 1952): 3.

88 Charles Lussier, "Réhabilitation de l'autorité," CL 1, no. 3 (May 1951): 23.

89 Mounier, Personalism, 121–2.

90 Ibid, 124; Emmanuel Mounier, "Feu la chrétienté," in Carnets de route, 1 (Paris: Editions du Seuil, 1950).

91 Mounier, Personalism, 122.

92 Fortin, "Notre jeunesse," 58–9, quoted an anonymous Canadian student leader as rejecting "a moderate social Christianity" like that proffered by the French Mouvement Républicain Populaire, characterizing it as "'a lacklustre compromise formula.'" For the impact of Mounier's "Feu la chrétienté," see ANQM, Fonds JEC, P65, S6, SS6, SSS3, D6, Action Catholique Universitaire, "Correspondance Générale, 1935–1955," Fernand Cadieux à Claude Saint-Laurent, 20 Sept. 1950.

93 For Mounier's "Christian agnosticism" during the 1940s, see Hellman, Emmanuel Mounier, 198.

94 Fernand Dumont, "Tâches de l'étudiant," VE 16, no. 3 (Mar. 1950). See also Dumont, "Un prophète: Bernanos," VE 15, no. 10 (Dec. 1949): "in our rationalized universe, pervaded by technique, one way alone is open to us: that of

mysticism." Here, Dumont was commenting on the work of the Christian existentialist novelist Georges Bernanos.

95 Blain, "Sur la liberté de l'esprit," 213; Pelletier, "D'un prolétarisme spirituel," *Esprit* 1952 (special issue on French Canada): 200.

96 Pierre Vadeboncoeur, "Le sort fait à la révolution," CL 1, no. 3 (May 1951): 17–20.

97 Pelletier, "'Cité libre,'" 4.

98 Pelletier, "Crise d'autorité," 2; Pierre Elliott Trudeau and Roger Rolland, "Matériaux à servir à une enquête sur le cléricalisme," CL 3, no. 7 (May 1953): 29.

99 Pelletier, "Crise d'autorité," 6–7.

100 For an analysis of the 1952 episcopal decision, see Bienvenue, *Quand la jeunesse entre en scène*, 249–50.

101 See, for example, Robert Rumilly, *L'infiltration gauchiste au Canada français* (Montreal, 1956).

102 Pelletier, "Crise d'autorité," 7.

103 Trudeau and Rolland, "Matériaux," 30.

104 Ibid., 37.

105 Blain, "Sur la liberté de l'esprit," 201; Pierre Vadeboncoeur, "Pour une dynamique de notre culture," CL 2, nos. 1–2 (June-July 1952): 19; Robert Élie, "Reflexions sur le dialogue," CL 1, no. 3 (May 1951): 31–7; ibid., "Au-delà du refus," RD (July-Aug. 1949): 5–18; Benoît Pruche, o.p., "La recherche religieuse dans la classe indépendante de la France d'aujourd'hui," RD (June 1951): 342–52; Jean-Noel Tremblay, "La vie quotidienne," RD (July–Aug. 1951): 11–19.

106 Catholic Action's role in mediating aspects of existential philosophy during the immediate post-war years was evident. See, for example, Camille Laurin, "Sur Bergson," JEC 9, nos. 4–5 (Apr.–May 1943); Réginald Boisvert, "Un film: Crime et Châtiment," JEC 11, no. 3 (Mar. 1945); Pierre Juneau, "Présence chrétienne," VE 12, no. 11 (Nov. 1946); Maurice Blain, "Où va notre littérature?" JEC 12, no. 11 (Nov. 1946); Guy Rocher, "Fedor Dostoievsky," VE 14, no. 12 (Dec. 1948); Fernand Dumont, "Blondel présent," VE 15, no. 7 (Sept. 1949); AUM, Fonds ACC, P16/G4, 10.3, Groupe Présence, Pierre Trottier, "Esprit, Pensée, Action"; Charles Michaud, "De l'Eden au Jourdain," in Centre Catholique des Intellectuels Canadiens, *Le rôle des laïcs dans l'Église. Carrefour 1951* (Montreal: Fides, 1952), 40–1.

107 Pelletier, "D'un prolétariat spirituel," 199.

108 Ibid., 200.

109 Jean-Guy Blain, "Inquiétude et Tradition," *Esprit*, 1952 (special issue on French Canada), 243–4.

110 Blain, "Sur la liberté de l'esprit," 203.

111 Pelletier, "Crise d'autorité," 2; Boisvert, "Foi chrétienne et mission temporelle," 6.

112 Trudeau and Rolland, "Matériaux," 42.

113 Jean-Charles Falardeau, "The Changing Social Structures," in Jean-Charles Falardeau, ed., *Essais sur le Québec contemporain* (Québec: Les Presses de l'Université Laval, 1953), 120.

114 For an exploration, in a radically different context, of attempts to foster a notion of "eternal youth," see Laura Malvano, "The Myth of Youth in Images: Italian Fascism," in Giovanni Levi and Jean-Claude Schmitt, eds, *Stormy Evolution to Modern Times*, vol. 2, *A History of Young People in the West* (Cambridge, Mass.: Belknap Press, 1997), 233.

115 Hertel, *Leur Inquiétude*, 121–2; Henri Charlier, "Remarques sur le Canada," JEC 5, nos 3–4 (Mar.–Apr. 1939); Antonin Lamarche, o.p., "Que vaut la foi de notre peuple?" RD (Nov. 1934): 241–55; M.-A. Lamarche, o.p., "Notre américanisation," RD (Jan. 1936): 1–5; M.-C. Forest, "Notre avenir religieux," RD (Oct. 1936): 150–7; "Petit examen de conscience sur les paroles du P. Doncoeur, 1934," JEC 6, no. 10 (Oct. 1940).

116 Hertel, *Leur Inquiétude*, 125.

117 Vianney Décarie, "Tous sont appelés," JEC 5, no. 6 (Jun. 1939).

118 François Hertel, "De notre chrétienté et de ses assomptions possibles," RD (July 1941): 27–8.

119 Gérard Pelletier, "Ce faux moine," JEC 9, no. 3 (Mar. 1943); "Tous dans le jeu!: Manifeste étudiant sur la messe," JEC 9, nos 4–5 (Apr.–May 1943); Paul Dumas, "Nous n'avons pas merité d'etre épargnés," RD (July 1941): 18–26; Germain-M. Lalande, c.s.c., *Conversion au réel: un essai sur l'Action catholique: experiences étudiantes* (Montreal, Fides, 1948), 228–9. For the attempt of the specialized Catholic Action movements to promote a more vigorous model of "masculinity," see Whitney, "The Politics of Youth," 157–8.

120 Falardeau, "Comment préparer l'après-guerre," 312.

121 R.P. André Guay, o.m.i., "Le problème de la déchristianisation des masses," *Rapport des Journées d'Étude Sacerdotales* (Montreal: Fides, 1942), 70.

122 Horace Miner, *Saint Denis: A French-Canadian Parish* (Chicago: University of Chicago Press, 1939), 95, 97, 104.

123 Pelletier, "Ce faux moine."

124 Gérard Pelletier, "Une vérité: trois attitudes," JEC 9, no. 2 (Feb. 1943).

125 AUM, Fonds ACC, P16/B6, 3.18, Claude Ryan, "La Rencontre de Deux Mondes," lecture delivered by Claude Ryan, 20 Feb. 1955, for the Corporation des Escholiers Griffonneurs.

126 Ibid. See also, Claude Ryan, "Les étudiants s'interrogent: Quel serait pour le chrétien le vrai visage de l'espoir?" VE 21, no. 8 (May 1955); "Un document ... sur l'Église canadienne en devenir," VE 20, no. 12 (Oct. 1954).

127 Ryan, "La Rencontre de Deux Mondes."

128 AUM, Fonds ACC, P16/E3,6, 4.3, Congrès International – Rome 1961,"La Femme Canadienne-Française, Instrument d'Unité."

129 AUM, Fonds ACC, P16/B6, 3.18, Claude Ryan, "Rencontre de Deux Mondes," ca 1955.

130 Historians of cultural life in Quebec currently lack a body of research or analysis dealing with involvement in the religious practices of parish communities during the post-war period.

131 Jean Francoeur, "Témoins d'une crise?" VE 22, no. 5 (Mar. 1956); Maurice Blain, "Lettre à des chrétiens divisés," CL 9 (Mar. 1954): 20.

132 Francoeur, " Témoins d'une crise?"; ibid., "Éditorial," VE 24, no. 15 (May 1958); ANQM, Fonds JEC, P65, art. 3, Maurice Lafond, c.s.c., "Cours sur l'Action Catholique," 1951; AUM, Fonds ACC, P16/J6, 1, Commission Nationale Cinéma-Radio-TV, "Le problème de la Télévision," 20 Apr. 1956; ibid., P16/J6, 3.18, Claude Ryan, "Un divorcé à la tête de l'Angleterre," Apr. 1955; ibid., "La Rencontre de Deux Mondes."

133 AUM, Fonds ACC, P16/K1.53, Gérard Pelletier, Gerard Pelletier, "Visage de notre société."

134 Jean-Charles Falardeau, "Avant-propos," in Jean-Charles Falardeau, ed., *Essais sur le Québec contemporain* (Québec: Les Presses de l'Université Laval, 1953), 20. See also Vadeboncoeur, "L'irréalisme de notre culture," 213; AUM, Fonds ACC, P16/E3, 6, 4.3, "La Femme Canadienne-Française, Instrument d'Unité."

135 Jean-Charles Falardeau, "Les recherches religieuses," in Fernand Dumont and Yves Martin, eds, *Situation de la recherche sur le Canada français* (Québec: Les Presses de l'Université Laval, 1962), 208–9; Falardeau, "Perspectives," in *Essais sur le Québec contemporain,* 257. Falardeau's comments were significant because he always eschewed any association with Catholic youth organizations. Born in 1914, he was slightly older than the group that had pioneered Catholic Action in the 1930s, but he acknowledged the same intellectual influences of Jacques Maritain, Mounier's *Esprit,* and existentialists such as Sartre. More importantly, he was driven by the vision of a distinctive youth identity that he encountered through his contacts with international student groups during the 1930s. See Jean-Charles Falardeau, *Roots and Values in Canadian Lives,* Alan B. Plaunt Memorial Lectures, Carleton University, Ottawa, 24, 26 Mar. 1960 (Toronto: University of Toronto Press, 1961), 21–3.

136 Blain, "Sur la liberté de l'esprit," 208.

137 ANQM, Fonds JOC, P104, art. 181, Rapport Camille Laurin.

138 François Hertel, "Les évolutions de la mentalité au Canada français," CL 10, no. 7, (Oct. 1954): 40–51.

139 For a stimulating discussion of these issues among American social commentators in the late 1940s and early 1950s, see Richard H. Pells, *The Liberal Mind in a Conservative Age: American Intellectuals in the 1940s and 1950s* (New York: Harper & Row, 1985), 180–261.

140 AUM, Fonds ACC, P16/I2.43, Mgr. Ménager, "L'Action Catholique en

France," n.d.; ibid., P16/J6, 1, "Commission Nationale Cinéma-Radio-*TV*," Apr. 1956; ibid., P16/D1, 4.10, "La Culture," programme d'action 1959–60, Fr. Albini Girouard, "La Vie de l'Esprit Chez le Jeune Travailleur," Journées d'étude, 28 fév.–1 mars 1959; Fernand Cadieux, "Influence du cinéma américain au Canada Français," CAC 129 (May 1951): 335–6; Fernand Dumont, étudiant au Séminaire du Québec, "Quelle liberté?" VE 15, no. 4 (Apr. 1949); ANQM, Fonds JEC, P65, art. 5, "Rôle de la JEC Canadienne," ca 1954.

141 Claude Ryan, "La Religion des Canadiens-français," CAC 172 (Feb. 1955): 244. See also AUM, Fonds ACC, P16/B6, 3.18, Claude Ryan, "Les laïcs et la vie liturgique au Canada," n.d.

142 Ryan, "Les laïcs et la vie liturgique au Canada"; AUM, Fonds ACC, P16/B6, 3.18, Claude Ryan, "Le vrai visage de l'espérance," Apr. 1955: "a tearful and subjective halfway religion, of Jansenist or Romantic origin"; ANQM, Fonds JEC, P65, s6, ss6, sss2, D5/2, Action Catholique Universitaire, Fernand Dumont, "Spiritualité et profession," Sept. 1952.

143 T.R.P. Louis-M. Régis, o.p., "La Religion et la philosophie au Canada français," in Mason Wade, *The Canadian Duality/La dualité canadienne* (Toronto: University of Toronto Press/Québec: Les Presses de l'Université Laval, 1960), 63. See also Philippe Garigue, "Saint Joseph's Oratory," in *Études sur le Canada français* (Montreal: Faculté des Sciences Sociales, Économiques et Politiques, Universite de Montréal, 1958), 75–87.

144 Louis O'Neill, "Vie de l'Eglise au Canada Français," in Centre Catholique des Intellectuels français, *Le Canada français aujourd'hui et demain*, Recherches et débats, no. 34 (Paris: Arthème Fayard, 1961), 93–5.

145 Ibid., 96.

146 Ryan, "Le vrai visage de l'espérance." See also ANQM, Fonds JOC, P104, art. 4, Comité consultatif des mouvements specialisés, "Situation de la Jeunesse Ouvrière Canadienne, Rapport de la J.O.C. preparé pour la Réunion du Bureau International de la J.O.C., tenue à Rome, les 6–10 nov. 1954"; ibid., art. 181, Commission 2: Pour une Action Catholique vraiment Canadienne, 1950, "Que Penser de la Prédominance Actuelle du Secteur *Féminin* et du Secteur *Masculin* dans le développement de l'A.C.C.?"; AUM, Fonds ACC, P16/E3, 6.4, "Personnalité de la Femme Rurale," ca 1961; ibid., P16/H3, 34.38, Journées d'Étude pour les Mouvements d'A.C. Générale, 1960, Guy Bélanger, ptre, "L'apostolat laïc dans L'Église," 24 June 1960; ibid., P16/I3.109, "Oratoire St. Joseph," Claude Ryan à R.P. Roland Gauthier, c.s.c, supérieur, Oratoire St. Joseph, 7 July 1960; Benoît Lacroix, o.p., "'Je me souviens', donc je prévois: Méditation pour le 24 juin," RD 60 (June 1954), 259–63; Pelletier, "Visage de notre société."

147 Pierre Elliott Trudeau, "La province de Québec au moment de la grève," in Pierre Elliott Trudeau, ed., *La grève de l'amiante: Une étape de la révolution industrielle au Québec* (Montreal: Les éditions Cité Libre, 1956), 61. For

other reflections of this view, see Hubert Guindon, "The Social Evolution of Quebec Reconsidered," *Canadian Journal of Economics and Political Science* 27 (Nov. 1960), reprinted in Marcel Rioux and Yves Martin, eds, *French-Canadian Society*, vol. 1 (Toronto: McClelland and Stewart, 1964), 153–5; ANQM, Fonds JOC, P104, art. 181, "Rapport Camille Laurin."

148 Guindon, "The Social Evolution of Quebec Reconsidered," 161.

149 Pelletier, "D'un prolétariat spirituel," 190–200. Pelletier's notion of "spiritual proletariat" was hardly original, and supplies further evidence of his ongoing debt to Catholic Action. The concept seems to have been directly derived from a series of lectures given in Montreal in 1948 by Joseph Folliet, the director of the *Semaines Sociales de France*. See AUM, Fonds ACC, P16/K1.23, Joseph Folliet, "Essai d'explication de sociologie de notre temps." In 1951, Fernand Cadieux, president of the Jeunesse Etudiante Catholique, used the phrase "intellectual proletarianization" to describe the impact of American cinema on Quebec youth. See Cadieux, "Influence du cinema américain," 336.

150 Pelletier, "D'un prolétarisme," 195–6. See also Blain, "Sur la liberté de l'esprit," 24; Jean-Charles Falardeau, "Parish Research in Other Countries: Canada," in C.J. Nuesse and Thomas J. Harte, eds, *The Sociology of the Parish: An Introductory Symposium* (Milwaukee: Bruce Publishing Company, 1951), 329–32; Jean-Charles Falardeau, "The Seventeenth-Century Parish in French Canada," in *Paroisses de France et de Nouvelle-France au XVIIe siècle,* Cahiers de l'École des sciences sociales, politiques, et économiques de Laval, vol. 2, no. 7, n.d., reprinted in Marcel Rioux and Yves Martin, eds, *French-Canadian Society*, vol. 1 (Toronto: McClelland and Stewart, 1964), 31–2.

151 Guindon, "The Social Evolution of Quebec Reconsidered," 157. Guindon acknowledged a particular debt to information and insights supplied by Fernand Cadieux, a leading figure in the Jeunesse Étudiante Catholique during the 1950s. For the dominant view among French-Canadian social scientists during the 1950s, the notion that the province's expansion was now a function of impersonal, large-scale, monopolistic industries, see Albert Faucher and Maurice Lamontagne, "History of Industrial Development," in Marcel Rioux and Yves Martin, eds, *French-Canadian Society*, vol. 1 (Toronto: McClelland and Stewart, 1964), 35; Everett-C. Hughes, "Regards sur le Quebec," in Falardeau, ed., *Essais sur le Québec contemporain*, 229.

152 Pelletier, "D'un prolétarisme"; Blain, "Sur la liberté de l'esprit," 206, in which he argued that the Quebec bourgeoisie was the "spiritual progeny" of the clergy, and that the Church itself had become a "Third Estate."

153 Pelletier, "D'un prolétariat," 195. It is interesting to note in this context that Pelletier's highly negative opinion of Protestant sects like the Jehovah's Witnesses resembled that of his arch-enemy, Premier Maurice Duplessis. Pelletier and Duplessis, however, differed sharply over the means to combat

them, the premier favouring legislative restriction of their activities, Pelletier, taking measures to restore the spiritual appeal of Catholicism.

154 For the popularization of this view, see H. Godin and Y. Daniel, *La France, Pays de Mission?* (Paris: Les Éditions de l'Abeille, 1943). For the influence of this work on an individual whose concerns are central to this study, see Fernand Dumont, *Récit d'une émigration*, 96–7.

155 Blain, "Sur la liberté de l'esprit," 206.

156 The most complete historical analysis of the perspective of Catholic elites on the labour question has been offered by Behiels, *Prelude to Quebec's Quiet Revolution*, 121–48, and more recently, in a work which explores the influence of personalism, Lapointe, "L'influence de la gauche catholique française."

157 See, for example, *L'Avenir de notre bourgeoisie*, lectures delivered at the First congress of the Jeunesse Indépendante Catholique, Montreal, 25–27 Feb. 1939 (Montreal: Editions J.I.C., 1939); CRLG, Fonds Jeune-Canada, P21/B,4, Jean-Louis Dorais, "La Crise Morale de Notre Bourgeoisie," n.d.

158 For the alteration in post-war definitions of youth within the Catholic Action movements, see Bienvenue, *Quand la jeunesse entre en scène*, 233–4.

159 The equation of university student and "intellectual worker" as a result of contact with European student movements has been explored by Karine Hébert, "Between the Future and the Present: Montreal University Student Youth and the Postwar Years, 1945–1960," in Christie and Gauvreau, eds, *Cultures of Citizenship in Postwar Canada*, 163–200.

160 Claude Ryan, *Les classes moyennes au Canada français* (Montreal: Éditions de l'Action Nationale, 1951), 14.

161 Ibid., 27, 40, 43.

162 AUM, Fonds ACC, P16/04.153, Institut Canadien des Affaires Publiques, *Le peuple souverain*. Rapport de la première conférence annuelle de l'Institut Canadien des Affaires Publiques, Ste-Marguerite, 29 Sept.–2 Oct. 1954, Pierre Elliott Trudeau, "Obstacles à la Démocratie."

163 Pierre Elliott Trudeau, "Des avocats et les autres dans leurs rapports avec la justice," *Notre Temps*, 27 Dec. 1947.

164 Pierre Elliott Trudeau, "Citadelles d'orthodoxie," *Notre Temps*, 15 Nov. 1947.

165 Trudeau, "Obstacles à la Démocratie."

166 Simonne Monet-Chartrand, *Ma vie comme rivière*, vol. 1, 162; Charles Péguy, "Sur le travail," JEC 7, no. 10 (Oct. 1941); Roger Duhamel, "Préoccupations spirituelles de notre temps," RD Jan. 1945, 81–7; ANQM, Fonds JEC, P65, art. 3, Maurice Lafond, c.s.c., "Cours sur l'Action Catholique, la J.E.C.," 1951; "L'Homme Décadent," VE 19, no. 1 (Jan. 1953); André Duranleau, "La taille de l'homme moderne," VE 20, no. 2 (Feb. 1954); Fernand Cadieux, "Le programme de l'année," CAC 145 (Sept. 1952): 8.

167 Wohl, *The Generation of 1914*, 212. Such themes were particularly evident in the French-Catholic literary revival that occurred between 1880 and 1914,

and which profoundly influenced the French-Canadian proponents of Catholic Action. See Richard Griffiths, *The Reactionary Revolution: The Catholic Revival in French Literature, 1870–1914* (London: Constable, 1966); Paul M. Cohen, *Piety and Politics: Catholic Revival and the Generation of 1905–1914 in France* (New York: Garland Publishing, 1987).

168 Falardeau, "The Changing Social Structure," 119; Falardeau, *Roots and Values in Canadian Lives*, 12–14; AUM, Fonds ACC, P16/J15, 7, "Enquête sur les Classes Moyennes," 1954; ibid., P16/K1.53, Gérard Pelletier, "Les implications chrétiennes de la télévision," 20 Feb. 1956; ibid., P16/J6, 1, "Le problème de la télévision nationale au Canada," 26 Apr. 1956; Roger Varin, "Étapes chrétiennes," JC (Feb. 1948).

169 Marcel Côté, "Jeunesse Chrétienne, Jeunesse Moderne," JC (Apr. 1947); AUM, Fonds ACC, P16/G3, 5.1, "Deuxième école civique," 1949; ibid., P16/C2, 3.2, "Rapport de la Rencontre des Dirigeantes Nationales, les 28 et 29 août, 1947"; Albert Breton, étudiant en science économique, "Vers un humanisme 'TECHNICIEN,'" VE 20, no. 8 (May 1954).

170 For an illuminating comparative discussion, see Luisa Passerini, "Youth as a Metaphor for Social Change in Fascist Italy and America in the 1950s," in Levi and Schmitt, *A History of Young People in the West*, 318–22. The negative image of the post-war adolescent has been explored in the American context by James Gilbert, *A Cycle of Outrage: America's Reaction to the Juvenile Delinquent in the 1950s* (New York: Oxford University Press, 1986). Recent scholarship in both English Canada and Quebec has generally echoed the American historical emphasis on the "cohesiveness" of the post-war generation of adolescents. See Doug Owram, *Born at the Right Time: A History of the Baby Boom Generation* (Toronto: University of Toronto Press, 1996); François Ricard, *La Génération lyrique: Essai sur la vie et l'oeuvre des premiers-nés du baby-boom* (Montreal: Boréal, 1992).

171 Gilbert, *A Cycle of Outrage*, 91–126.

172 AUM, Fonds Paul-Larocque, P52/K19.7, Mlle Jeanne Lapointe, "Humanisme et Humanités," 15 May 1958. Jeanne Lapointe was during the 1960s a member of Quebec's Royal Commission on Education, better known as the Parent Commission, and was later a member of the federal government's Royal Commission on the Status of Women.

173 See, for example, AUM, Fonds Paul-Larocque, P52/K19.11, Pierre Angers, s.j., Collège Jean-de-Brébeuf, 15 May 1958; ibid., P52/K19.9, "Mémoire présenté ... par M. le chanoine Pichette, aumônier de la C.T.C.C.," May 1958; ibid., P52/K19.17, Abbé Gérard Dion, "Mémoire présenté ...," 20 Jan. 1958; ibid., P52/K19.17, Frère Clément Lockquell, e.c., "Notre milieu culturel," 2 May 1958.

174 Lapointe, "Humanisme et humanités."

175 AUM, Fonds ACC, P16/B6, 3.1, Hozaël Aganier, "Mémoire préparé à l'intention de la Commission des Programmes de la Faculté des Arts de l'Univer-

sité Laval," 18 Apr. 1958; Andrée Lajoie, "Où va la jeunesse française?" VE
   23, no. 14 (Apr. 1957).
176 AUQÀM, Fonds Pierre-Dansereau, 22P4/153, I.C.A.P. Montreal, 1956:
   "Thème: Éducation – Septembre 1956, "Le Dilemme de l'Éducation Contemporaine," outline of the lecture by Henri-Irénée Marrou.
177 For the curriculum and the values that sustained these colleges, see Claude
   Galarneau, *Les collèges classiques au Canada français* (Montreal: Fides, 1978).
178 Jean LeMoyne, "Témoignage d'un laïque sur l'enseignement religieux,"
   CAC 14 (Nov. 1941): 137–44. It is interesting to observe that so staunch a
   defender of the *collèges* as the conservative economist Esdras Minville was
   likewise very harsh in his criticisms of the teaching of religion in the colleges. See Esdras Minville, *Invitation à l'étude* (Montreal: Fides, 1945), 51–2;
   AUM, Fonds ACC, P16/G5, 8.1, Jeunesse Ouvrière Catholique, "Le problème
   des jeunes qui ne fréquentent plus l'école," 6 Dec. 1942.
179 Guy Bélanger, ptre, "Des étudiants d'Écoles Supérieures devant la Messe,"
   CAC 175 (May 1955): 355. See also, "L'opinion des éducateurs," CAC 175
   (May 1955): 346–50; "Problèmes de vie sentimentale des étudiants canadiens," CAC 154 (June–Aug. 1953): 293–316; Frère Albéric, s.g., "Problème
   religieux chez nos jeunes," CAC 139 (Mar. 1952): 214–16; AUM, Fonds ACC,
   P16/D1, 4.10, Gérard Lemieux, "Les valeurs de l'esprit chez les Gens de
   Classes Moyennes."
180 ANQM, Fonds JOC, P104, art. 181, "Rapport Camille Laurin."
181 Cadieux, "Le programme," 6.
182 Blain, "Sur la liberté de l'esprit," 206. For further explorations of this perceived crisis of humanism, see François Hertel, "De notre chrétienté," RD
   (July 1941); Jean LeMoyne, "L'atmosphère religieux au Canada français:
   Esquisse et notes" (1951), in Jean LeMoyne, *Convergences* (Montreal: Hurtubise HMH, 1977), 49–51; Maurice Blain, "L'écrivain devant la crise de conscience religieuse," CL 18 (Nov. 1957): 19–25; Hyacinthe-Marie Robillard,
   o.p., "Sommes-nous jansénistes?" RD (July–Aug. 1957): 4–16; Pierre
   Vadeboncoeur, Maurice Blain, and Jean-Guy Blain, "Pour une dynamique
   de notre culture," CL 2, nos 1–2 (June–July 1952): 11–30; Maurice Blain,
   "L'écrivain devant la crise de conscience religieuse," CL 18 (Nov. 1957):
   23–4; AUM, Fonds ACC, P16, K1.16, Vianney Décarie, "L'université, centre de
   culture et de recherche," 24 Nov. 1960; ibid., P16/13.43, Centre Catholique
   des Intellectuels Canadiens, Carrefour 1956, "La crise de conscience
   religieuse des Intellectuels canadiens-francais"; Gilles Marcotte, "*La nuit
   privée d'étoiles*: un temoignage significatif du catholicisme américain," VE 18,
   no. 6 (June 1952); Gilles Marcotte, "C'est vous et moi en face de la vie," VE
   18, no. 5 (May 1952); Clément Lockquell, "Notre littérature s'interroge –
   mais non pas suffisamment," VE 21, no. 9 (May 1955).
183 Blain, "Sur la liberté de l'esprit," 208.
184 Marcel Rioux, "Remarques sur l'éducation secondaire et la culture

canadienne-française," CL 3, no. 8 (Nov. 1953): 34–42; François Hertel, "L'évolution de la mentalité au Canada français," CL 10, no. 7 (Oct. 1954); Marcel Rioux, "Idéologie et crise de conscience au Canada français," CL 14, no. 9 (Dec. 1955): 1–29.

CHAPTER THREE

1 AUM, Fonds ACC, P16/04.88, "École des Parents – Journées d'Etude, 16–17 fév. 1957," "Vie Spirituelle du Foyer."

2 NAC, MG 28 I117, Canadian Conference on the Family, vol. 11, file 4, Paul-Émile Roy, c.s.c., "La Famille à l'Heure du Québec," *L'Oratoire*, Apr. 1964.

3 This argument of conservatism, immobility, and quiescence between 1945 and 1960 in the sphere of the family has been advanced in the American context by Elaine Tyler May, *Homeward Bound: American Families in the Cold War Era* (New York: Basic Books, 1988); and for Canada, by Doug Owram, *Born at the Right Time: A History of the Baby Boom Generation* (Toronto: University of Toronto Press, 1996), 10–30; and Owram, "Canadian Domesticity in the Postwar Era," in Peter Neary and J.L. Granatstein, eds., *The Veterans Charter and Post-World War II Canada* (Montreal and Kingston: McGill-Queen's University Press, 1998), 205–23. That such a climate was particularly repressive towards youth, women, and sexual "deviants" has been the theme of a number of recent studies. See, for example, Mona Gleason, *Normalizing the Ideal: Psychology, Schooling, and the Family in Postwar Canada* (Toronto: University of Toronto Press, 1999); Mary Louise Adams, *The Trouble with Normal: Postwar Youth and the Making of Heterosexuality* (Toronto: University of Toronto Press, 1997), 53–106; Mariana Valverde, "Building Anti-Delinquent Communities: Morality, Gender, and Generation in the City," in Joy Parr, ed., *A Diversity of Women: Ontario, 1945–1980* (Toronto: University of Toronto Press, 1995), 19–45.

4 For a close analysis of these new definitions, see Nancy Christie, *Engendering the State: Family, Work and Welfare in Canada* (Toronto: University of Toronto Press, 2000), 196–248.

5 ANQM, P116, Fonds Service de Préparation au Mariage [SPM], art. 36, "La crise de l'amour dans le monde moderne," resumé de la conférence de M. Gustave Thibon, 1 Nov. 1956.

6 For recent studies of the German and Italian youth movements in this period, see Alexander von Plato, "The Hitler Youth Generation and its Role in Two Post-War German States," in Mark Roseman, ed., *Generations in Conflict: Youth Revolt and Generational Formation in Germany, 1770–1968* (Cambridge: Cambridge University Press, 1995), 210–26; Dagmar Reese, "The BDM Generation: A Female Generation in Transition from Dictatorship to Democracy," in Roseman, *Generations in Conflict*, 227–46; Peter Stachura, *The German Youth Movement, 1900–1945* (London: Macmillan, 1981); Luisa Passerini, "Youth as

a Metaphor for Social Change in Fascist Italy and America in the 1950s," in Giovanni Levi and Jean-Claude Schmitt, eds., *A History of Young People in the West*, vol. 2, *Stormy Evolution to Modern Times* (Cambridge, Mass.: Belknap Press, 1997), 281–3.

7 For an exploration of the wider cultural consequences of this crisis from the perspective of largely Anglo-Canadian youth initiatives, see Gauvreau, "The Protracted Birth of the Canadian 'Teenager,'" in Nancy Christie and Michael Gauvreau, eds, *Cultures of Citizenship in Postwar Canada, 1940–1955* (Montreal and Kingston: McGill-Queen's University Press, 2003), 201–38.

8 Servite, "Un grand problème d'ordre social," JO 7, no. 1 (Sept. 1938): 7. See also ANQM, Fonds JOC, P104, art. 104, "Union de la Jeunesse Catholique Canadienne – Rapports de Réunions," Rapport préliminaire du Premier Congrès National, Ottawa, 8–10 Oct. 1938; ibid.; art. 104, "Belle Victoire de la J.O.C.," 23 Apr. 1937.

9 Léon Lebel, s.j., "Les prérogatives fondamentales de la famille," in *Pour une société chrétienne*, 16e Semaine Sociale, Sherbrooke, 1938 (Montreal: École Sociale Populaire, 1938), 109. For Lebel's role as an early promoter of family allowances, see Christie, *Engendering the State*, 179–81. For the erosion of the idea of the economically interdependent family among social scientists and policy-makers during the Depression, see Christie, *Engendering the State*, 247. For its earlier manifestations in the context of working-class Montreal, see Bettina Bradbury, *Working Families: Gender, Work and Daily Survival in Industrializing Montreal* (Toronto: McClelland and Stewart, 1994) and Denyse Baillargeon, *Ménagères au temps de la crise* (Montreal: Éditions du Remue-ménage, 1991), 28, 71. Baillargeon notes that this pattern persisted well into the 1930s in Montreal.

10 Guillaume Lavallée, o.f.m., "La Préparation au Mariage: La Vocation au Mariage," LF 1, no. 4 (Dec. 1937): 52–3. *La Famille* was founded under the aegis of the Franciscan Order in 1937 and was published until 1954 as a journal specifically devoted to parent education and family issues. Its collaborators included Franciscan clergy, medical specialists, early childhood experts, and specialists in applied hygiene.

11 Henri Roy, o.m.i., *Un problème et une solution* (Montreal: Éditions Jécistes, 1934), 23; Gilbert Laverdure, o.f.m., "Au secours du foyer," LF 1, no. 2 (Oct. 1937): 19.

12 Fernand Jolicoeur, chef du secretariat de l'Action Sociale du diocese de Joliette, *La Jeunesse Ouvrière* (Montreal: J.O.C., 1946), 31; Roy, *Un problème et une solution*, 21.

13 Jolicoeur, *La Jeunesse Ouvrière*, 21. Jolicoeur was later appointed the director of education for the *Confédération des travailleurs catholiques canadiens* (CTCC), the Catholic trade union central. See also Bernardin Verville, o.f.m., "Notre famille canadienne," LF 3, no. 6 (Feb. 1940): 146.

14 Verville, "Notre famille canadienne," LF 3, no. 6 (Feb. 1940): 146; Gérard Pelletier, "La famille est-elle menacée," JEC 7, no. 5 (May 1941).

15 R.P. André Guay, o.m.i., "Le problème de la déchristianisation des masses," in *Rapport des Journées d'Etude Sacerdotales de la Jeunesse Ouvrière Catholique à l'occasion du dixième anniversaire de la J.O.C canadienne (1932–1942)* (Montreal: Éditions Ouvrières, Éditions Fides, 1942), 71.

16 Pope Pius XI, *Encyclical: On Christian Marriage – Casti Connubii* (New York: Paulist Press, 1941; first issued 1930) [henceforth cited as *Casti Connubii*], 52–3. On the discourse surrounding the sexual instruction of Catholic youth in Quebec, see Gaston Desjardins, *L'Amour en patience: la sexualité adolescente au Québec, 1940–1960* (Sainte-Foy: Presses de l'Université du Québec, 1995), 78, 118. Desjardins observes that a number of Catholic circles in the 1930s recognized the need for sex education for youth, but that Catholic commentators resolutely sought to avoid a collective sexual instruction given in educational institutions.

17 Colette, "Éducation de la pureté" [*Revue de presse famialale*], LF 2, no. 3 (Nov. 1938): 56; Bernard Verville, o.f.m., "Préparation au mariage à l'école primaire, secondaire, universitaire," LF 3, no. 3 (Nov. 1939) 57.

18 Verville, "Notre famille," 147.

19 A general outline history of these Catholic family movements has been provided by Marie-Paule Malouin, *Le Mouvement familial au Québec: les débuts: 1937–1965* (Montreal: Boréal, 1998). For specific case studies, see Jean-Pierre Collin, *La Ligue ouvrière catholique canadienne, 1938–1954* (Montreal: Boréal, 1995). The Service de Preparation au Mariage, initially an offshoot of the Jeunesse Ouvrière Catholique, has been analysed by Michael Gauvreau, "The Emergence of Personalist Feminism: Catholicism and the Marriage Preparation Movement in Quebec, 1940–1966," in Nancy Christie, ed., *Households of Faith: Family, Gender and Community in Canada* (Montreal and Kingston: McGill-Queen's University Press, 2002), 319–47. For the École des Parents, see the important study by Denyse Baillargeon, "'We Admire Modern Parents': L'École des Parents du Quebec and the Post-war Quebec Family, 1940–1959," in Christie and Gauvreau, *Cultures of Citizenship in Postwar Canada*, 239–74. Both Baillargeon and Gauvreau suggest that these organizations tried to tailor their message to audiences and participants having a mix of working-class and middle-class backgrounds.

20 "Vibrant témoignage rendu à la cause jociste, par Son Excellence Mgr. Georges Gauthier," JO 8, no. 11 (Aug.–Sept. 1939): 4. Contemporary accounts of this famous mass marriage spectacle are available in ANQM, Fonds Mouvement des Travailleurs Chrétiens [MTC], *P*257, art. 12, "Scrap-Book, Les cents-mariés, 1939," "La digne apothéose du travail chrétien," LP, 24 July 1939; ibid., "La reconstruction sociale par la Jeunesse Ouvrière Catholique," LD, 24 July 1939; ibid., art. 13, "20e anniversaire 1959"; ibid., Bill Bantey, "Mass Marriage Couples Renew Vows," *Montreal Gazette*, 31 Aug. 1939.

21 The mass marriage ceremony was preceded by 115 days of intensive study and 600 meetings for adults that widely disseminated the teachings of the

papal encyclical *Casti Connubii,* not only among those celebrating their marriage in the stadium, but to hundreds of other interested adults. See R.P. Victor-M. Villeneuve, o.m.i., "Le dixième anniversaire de la J.O.C. Canadienne," in *Rapport des Journées d'Étude Sacerdotales,* 29–30.

22 In the aftermath of World War I, and continuing until the mid-1930s, Quebec Catholicism continued to articulate a certain nostalgia for older types of multi-generational kinship, patriarchal families. See the papers presented in *La Famille: 4e Session des Semaines Sociales du Canada, 1923* (Montreal: École Sociale Populaire, 1923) and Andrée Lévesque, *Making and Breaking the Rules: Quebec Women, 1919–1939* (Toronto: McClelland and Stewart, 1991), 19–21. On the cohabitation of generations among both elite and working-class Quebec Catholic families, see Denise Lemieux and Lucie Mercier, *Les femmes au tournant du siècle, 1880–1940* (Montreal: Institut Québécois de Recherche sur la Culture, 1989), 168–71; Baillargeon, *Ménagères au temps de la crise,* 94–6. For the widespread existence in Canada of family types that diverged from the classic model of the "nuclear family," see Nancy Christie and Michael Gauvreau, eds., *Mapping the Margins: Families and Social Discipline in Canada, 1700–1980* (Montreal and Kingston: McGill-Queen's University Press, 2004); and in the same collection, the article by Denyse Baillargeon, "Les orphelins au Québec: en marge de quelle famille?," which outlines the clerical attempt to substitute Church-controlled institutions for parents.

23 *Casti Connubii,* 24. By "companionate" marriage, the encyclical specifically meant those marriage unions which were not considered indissoluble, and not the efforts to assign a higher priority to the emotional satisfaction of husbands and wives within existing marriages.

24 *Casti Connubii,* 5; Fr Ferdinand, "Le Mariage: 1. Doctrine catholique sur le mariage," LF1, no. 5 (Jan. 1938): 75; R.P. Joseph-Papin Archambault, s.j., "Dédication d'ouverture," *Le Chrétien dans la famille et dans la nation.* 17e Semaine Sociale, Nicolet, 1940 (Montreal: École Sociale Populaire, 1940), 19–20.

25 Adélard Provencher, "Le chrétien dans la famille," in *Le Chrétien dans la famille et dans la nation,* 48.

26 *Casti Connubii,* 9.

27 Guillaume Lavallée, o.f.m., "La préparation au mariage," LF 1, no. 2 (Oct. 1937): 21; "Avant de vous marier," JO 2, no. 3 (Dec. 1933): 4, 6.

28 M.-A. Lamarche, o.p., "Sanctification mutuelle des époux," RD (Jan. 1940); 4.

29 *Casti Connubii,* 11–12.

30 Mgr L.-A. Pâquet, "La doctrine de l'Église," ON.

31 Jeba-Tirai, "Ce qu'il faut penser du mariage," JO 7, nos 5–6 (Jan.–Feb. 1939): 6. See also J.C., "Le Mariage, *foyer* de la vie!," JO 4, no. 9 (May 1936): 5; Maurice-H. Beaulieu, s.j., "Le vrai sens du mariage," *Rel* (Feb. 1941): 94–6.

32 AUM, Fonds ACC, P16/R.61, "Prêtre et Famille," *Le Prêtre et la famille: Revue de pastorale familiale,* Nov.-Dec. 1947.

33 Jeba-Tirai, "Ce qu'il faut penser du mariage," JO 7, no. 7 (Mar. 1939): 2.

34 "Mon Épouse," JO 3, no. 2 (Sept. 1935): 7.

35 Quebec Catholics were not alone in proclaiming the sacredness of human sexuality. For the existence of a similar, although later post-war current within the United Church of Canada, see the analysis by Nancy Christie, "Sacred Sex: The United Church and the Privatization of the Family in Post-War Canada," in Christie, *Households of Faith*, 348–76.

36 "Le courrier de José," FO, 30 Nov. 1946. See also Jacques B., "Vers l'avenir ... Face à l'éternel féminin," FO, 9 Dec. 1944; Lionel Pelland, "Mariage et bombe ... atomique," *Rel* (May 1948): 135–7; Mme Claudine Vallerand, "Madame Vallerand de l'École des Parents nous invite à soigner notre ÉDUCATION SENTIMENTALE," VE 18, no. 4 (Apr. 1952).

37 For the structure of the courses in the period prior to 1955, see ANQM, Fonds JOC, P104, art. 4, "17e session intensive, 1952," Jacques Champagne, "Le Service de Préparation au Mariage, 1952." The courses were as follows: (1) Making Sense of the Period of Engagement; (2) Complementary Psychologies of Man and Woman ; (3) Love and Happiness; (4) Mutual Adjustment of Personalities; (5) Managing the Household's Finances; (6) Marriage and the Civil Law; (7) Marriage and Ecclesiastical Law; (8) The Marriage Ceremony; (9) The Mystique and the Sacrament of Marriage; (10 and 11) Anatomy, Hygiene, and Health – Sexual Relations in Marriage; (12) The Early Days of Marriage; (13) Conjugal Morality; (14) Expecting a Child. See also ANQM, Fonds SPM, P116 art. 2, Germain Lemieux, "Allocution, 1950"; ibid., art. 1, "Journée d'étude, 23 sept. 1952."

38 ANQM, Fonds SPM, P116 art. 1, "Semaine des fiancés, 1955," Marie Bourbonnais, "Les fiancés d'aujourd'hui sont les parents de demain," LP, 8 Jan. 1955; ibid., art. 19, "Aumôniers," ca 1968–69; ibid., art. 36, "Spicilèges," n.d.; AUM, Fonds ACC, P16/D5, 3.1, "Réunions 15 déc. 1955–16 mars 1964."

39 ANQM, Fonds SPM, P116, art. 1, "Session d'étude, 1954," Résumé de l'allocution de M. l'abbé Gérard Lalonde"; ibid., art. 2, "Allocution du président du S.P.M. à la clôture de la semaine des fiancés," 15 Jan. 1950.

40 ANQM, Fonds SPM, P116, art. 36, "Spicilèges," "Mémoire sur le Service de Préparation au Mariage de la J.O.C. Canadienne," Jan. 1958.

41 ANQM, Fonds SPM, P116, art. 6, "Appréciation des cours," Marcel Lefebvre, rue Marquette, Montréal, au rédacteur, *Le Petit Journal*, 19 June 1952; AUM, Fonds ACC, P16/D5.1, Fonction des foyers responsables – exposé presenté par M. Paul Meloche, lors de la réunion du 13 décembre 1963." See also ANQM, Fonds SPM, P116, art. 24, "Résumé de l'allocution de M. L'abbé Gérard Lalonde, aumônier diocésain du S.P.M., à la recollection des couples-conférenciers," 6 May 1955.

42 ANQM, Fonds SPM, P116, art. 2, "Semaine des fiancés, 1949," "Un professeur et un élève," LD, 8 Jan. 1949; "Un appui: la vie familiale," LT, 20 May 1953, 7; L'équipe, "Le forum a 3 Voix," VE 15, no. 7 (Sept. 1949).

43　ANQM, Fonds SPM, P116, art. 1, "Historique du SPM."

44　Thomas-A. Audet, o.p., "Sainteté des epoux," RD 51 (July-Aug. 1945): 4.

45　ANQM, Fonds SPM, P116 art. 2, "Semaine des fiancés, 1949," Gérard Pelletier, "Réflexions sur un mot malheureux," LD, 8 Jan. 1949. For similar views, see ibid., art. 1, "Semaine des fiancés, 1955," Bourbonnais, "Les fiancés d'aujour-d'hui sont les parents de demain"; ibid., art. 1, Chanoine Clavel, "La semaine de la famille et la préparation au mariage," Le Canada, Apr. 1950; ibid., art. 24, "Conférences données au Service, 1947–1954," "Substance de la con-férence de M. Marcel Clément," Nov. 1954. Clément's intervention is most significant. A conservative French social Catholic, he was a virulent opponent of Pelletier on labour-management issues, but largely agreed with his ideas of family and the necessity for marriage preparation. For Clement's right-wing political involvements and opposition to the citélibristes, see Léon Dion, Québec 1945–2000, vol.2, Les intellectuels et le temps de Duplessis (Quebec: Les Presses de l'Université Laval, 1993), 233.

46　AUM, Fonds ACC, P16/I.85, Fédération des Étudiants des Universités Catholiques du Canada, Charles Terreault, "Conception Étudiante du Mariage," Symposium à Duchesnay, les 22, 23 et 24 octobre 1953, Rencontres: Bulletin National de la Fédération des Étudiants des Universités Catholiques du Canada, affiliée à Pax Romana.

47　Ibid. See also Provencher, "Le chrétien dans la famille," 61.

48　Jean LeMoyne, "Du sens et de la fin du mariage," LR 4, no. 8 (1938): 237–43; and LeMoyne, "Du sens et de la fin du mariage," LR 4, no. 9 (1938): 276–82. LeMoyne's articles were based on the work of the German theologian Herbert Doms, whose teachings were later condemned by Rome.

49　Robert-E. Llewellyn, "Problèmes," LF 10, no. 2 (Feb. 1946); Simone and Roland Germain, "Le mariage, route de sainteté," LF 14, no. 8 (Oct. 1950): 478–9.

50　AUM, Fonds ACC, P16/R.61, Le Prêtre et la famille; ibid., P16/D1, 4.9, "Le corps humain 1958–59," Claude Mailhiot, "L'homme est un tout."

51　Marie-Joseph d'Anjou, s.j., "Respect au mariage chretien," Rel (Jan. 1952): 8, 10.

52　Provencher, "Le chrétien dans la famille," 58; Simone and Roland Germain, "Un livre unique sur le mariage," LF 14, no. 2 (Feb. 1950): 92–6, 114, which explained the views of Chanoine Jacques Leclerc on the centrality of sexual partnership and compatibility in a successful marriage; Le Prêtre et la famille. For the influence of French and Belgian models in post-war Quebec family organizations, see Baillargeon, "'We Admire Modern Parents.'"

53　AUM, P16/G3.5.1, Jeunesse Independante Catholique, École Civique d'été, 1950, Guy Cormier, "Qu'est-ce qu'être libre?" 19 June 1950; ibid., Claude Mailhiot, "L'équilibre sexuel et les conditions psychologiques d'exercice de la liberté," 23 June 1950.

54　"L'amour humain chez les jeunes," CAC 113 (Jan. 1942): 148; AUM, P16/G2,

1.38, "Spiritualité étudiante – numero spécial," *Cahiers d'action catholique*, Dec. 1944.

55 Simonne Monet-Chartrand, *Ma vie comme rivière*, vol. 2, *Récit autobiographique: 1942–1959* (Montreal: Éditions du Remue-ménage, 1981), 87.

56 Gérard Pelletier, "Le laïque marié, image de l'union du Christ et de son Église," *Le rôle des laïcs dans l'Église*, Carrefour 1951, organisé par le Centre Catholique des intellectuels canadiens, Université de Montréal (Montreal: Fides, 1952), 111. For the "sacerdotal" concept of marriage, see AUM, Fonds ACC, P16/G2, 1.38, Spiritualité, Alex and Gérard Pelletier, "Caractères de la spiritualité étudiante," special issue on "Spiritualité étudiante," CAC (Dec. 1944).; Llewellyn, "Problèmes."

57 Paul Vanier, s.j., "Virginité et mariage," *Rel* (May 1951): 119–22.

58 Philippe Ariès, "Familles du demi-siècle," in R. Prigent, ed., *Renouveau des idées sur la famille* (Paris: Presses Universitaires de France, 1954), 167–170.

59 Marguerite Cardinal, "Pourquoi l'amour?," C&F 4, no. 3 (Nov. 1948).

60 Gérald Fortin, "L'Amour et le mariage," LF 16, no. 8 (Oct. 1952): 7, 11.

61 For Kinsey's views on human sexuality, see Jonathan Gathorne-Hardy, *Sex the Measure of all Things: A Life of Alfred C. Kinsey* (London: Chatto & Windus, 1998), 343–5. For discussions of Kinsey within Catholic Action circles, see AUM, P16/G4, 10.3, "Groupe 'Présence'," 21 déc. 1945–sept. 1950, Claude Ryan, president, à R.P. Henri Samson, s.j., 16 April 1948. Here, Ryan invited the priest to address this men's group of labour leaders and Catholic social activists on the subject of the Kinsey Report. For a more explicit Catholic critique, see ANQM, Fonds SPM, P116 art. 24, "Conférences 1960–1966," Bernard Mailhiot, o.p., "De l'esprit de géometrie en psychologie," n.d.

62 Gérard Lemieux, "Paternité par Joseph Kuckhoff," VE 16, no. 2 (Feb. 1950); Luce Beauchemin, "Le mariage est-il une vocation?," LF 3, no. 4 (Dec. 1939): 81–3.

63 Desjardins, *L'Amour en patience*, 96.

64 Fortin, "L'Amour," 12–13.

65 Fernand Dumont, "Les causes de la désintegration familiale: les facteurs socio-culturels," in *Les causes de la désintegration familiale* (Montreal: Caritas-Canada, 1956), 35.

66 Recent studies of the emergence of the social sciences in Quebec during the 1930s and 1940s have insisted upon the close relationship between social Catholicism and the development and diffusion of these disciplines. See Jean-Philippe Warren, *L'engagement sociologique: La tradition sociologique du Québec francophone (1886–1955)* (Montreal: Boréal, 2003); Denyse Baillargeon, "'We Admire Modern Parents.'"

67 For the concept of post-war domesticity as "privatization," see May, *Homeward Bound*; "Home and Family at Mid-Century" in Owram, *Born at the Right Time*. In a different twist on this argument, Nancy Christie has shown that the casting of the family as "private" by Protestant churches in English Canada

was in fact an emphatically political statement, and flowed from a post-war climate of suspicion regarding the sudden expansion of the welfare state during the Second World War. See Christie, "'Look out for Leviathan': The Search for a Modernist Conservative Consensus," in Christie and Gauvreau, *Cultures of Citizenship in Postwar Canada*, 63–94.

68 Gonzalve Poulin, o.f.m., "La famille ouvrière canadienne-française," LF 16, no. 7 (Aug.-Sept. 1952): 8.

69 Ibid., 12.

70 Ibid., "Le foyer chrétien," in *Le Foyer: Base de la société*, 27e Semaine Sociale, Nicolet, 1950 (Montreal: Institut Social Populaire, 1950), 43.

71 ANQM, Fonds JOC, P104, art. 104, "Rapport Camille Laurin"; Pierre Laplante (directeur des sections d'études du Conseil central des oeuvres de Quebec), "En attendant les 'unions de familles,'" *Rel* (Sept. 1951): 246–8.

72 AUM, Fonds ACC, P16/04.88, École des Parents – Journées d'Étude, 16–17 fév. 1957, Dr Claude Mailhiot, "L'Évolution des Écoles de Parents." Mailhiot's reference to the "large, extended kin family" drew directly upon the early work of Philippe Ariès, which was available to Catholic circles in "Le XIXe siècle et la révolution des moeurs familiales," in Prigent, *Renouveau des idées*, 111–18. See also "Après la guerre," JO (Feb.. 1943); Guy Rocher, "La Famille dans la Ville Moderne," SS 4, no. 1 (spring 1954): 81; Marc A. Lessard, "Individualisme dans la famille," LF 18, no. 10 (Oct. 1954): 483–5.

73 Rocher, "La Famille dans la Ville Moderne," 80–4; Simone Paré, "Participation d'une population de banlieue à ses groupes de famille, de parenté, d'amitié et de voisinage," SS 9, no. 1 (Jan. 1960): 25–56; Philippe Garigue, *Vie familiale des canadiens-français* (Montreal: Les Presses de l'Université de Montréal, 1962), 31.

74 Gérard Pelletier, *Histoire des enfants tristes*, un reportage sur l'enfance sans soutien dans la Province de Québec (Montreal: L'Action Nationale, 1947), 86, 33. On the contrasting values of institutional care and that given within the family, see AUM, Fonds ACC, P16/R.64, Kaspar Fraser, "Appendice II – La Famille Canadienne en 1950," and R.S. Ste.-Mechtilde, S.M., Assistante Sociale, Service Social de l'Hôpital de la Miséricorde, Montréal, both in *Vers l'édification de la famille de demain*, rapport des premières journées d'etude de la Commission française du Conseil canadien de bien-être social, Hôpital de la Miséricorde, Montréal, 9 et 10 mars, 1951. For the institutional Church's concept of the Church as a "family" superior to the biological family, see Baillargeon, "Les orphelins"; and for the wider post-war debate on the orphanage versus the foster family, see Marie-Paule Malouin, *L'Univers des enfants en difficulté au Québec entre 1940 et 1960* (Montreal: Bellarmin, 1996).

75 Dominique Marshall, *Aux origines sociales de l'état-providence* (Montreal: Les Presses de l'Université de Montréal, 1998), explores the extent to which, in the period after 1940, Quebec rural and working-class families continued to adhere to the older model of the economically-interdependent family,

contesting attempts by reform Catholics, and provincial and federal governments to promote the idea of the nuclear family with a single breadwinner.

76 For the involvement of Guy Rocher and Fernand Dumont in the Jeunesse
Étudiante Catholique in the 1940s and its influence on their social thinking,
see Guy Rocher, *Entre les rêves et l'histoire* (Montreal: VLB, 1989),12–25, 28–9;
Fernand Dumont, *Récit d'une émigration* (Montreal: Boréal, 1997), 69–71.

77 On the sociological outlook and methods of the post-1930s Chicago School,
see Martin Bulmer, *The Chicago School of Sociology: Institutionalization, Diversity,
and the Rise of Sociological Research* (Chicago: University of Chicago Press,
1984); Robert C. Bannister, *Sociology and Scientism: The American Quest for Objec-
tivity, 1880–1940* (Chapel Hill: University of North Carolina Press, 1987). For
the influence of Everett C. Hughes on the practice of social science at McGill
University during the 1930s, see Marlene Shore, *The Science of Social Redemption: McGill, the Chicago School and the Origins of Social Research in Canada*
(Toronto: University of Toronto Press, 1987), 255–60, 269–71. The influence
of the tenets of University of Chicago sociology and anthropology on the
direction of post-war social thinking in Quebec has been perceptively treated
recently in Warren, *L'Engagement sociologique.*

78 Everett C. Hughes, *French Canada in Transition* (Chicago: University of
Chicago Press, 1943), 5.

79 Significantly, the post-war sociologists who most vociferously assigned the
concept of "folk society" to Quebec were Rocher and Dumont, who had had
a prominent involvement with Catholic Action, and Marcel Rioux, who proclaimed his "agnosticism" but acknowledged a significant influence of radical
French personalists like Emmanuel Mounier. For Rioux, see *Un peuple dans le
siècle* (Montreal: Boréal, 1993). All three sociologists helped shape a vision of
Quebec as a "global society" to counter the passivity, traditionalism, and
immobility that they believed was inherent in the concept of "folk society."
See Gilles Bourque, Jules Duchastel, and Andre Kuzminski, "Les grandeurs et
les misères de la societé globale au Québec," *Cahiers de recherche sociologique* 28
(1997). By contrast, Philippe Garigue, their colleague at the Université de
Montréal, had no significant involvement in Catholic Action, and thus did
not accept the notion of modernity as "rupture" that was inherent in the
concept of "folk society." See Garigue, "The French Canadian Family," in
Mason Wade, ed., *La dualité canadienne* (Toronto: University of Toronto Press,
1955), 187–8.

80 Horace Miner, *St. Denis: A French-Canadian Parish* (Chicago: University of
Chicago Press, 1939), xiii–xiv, 63–6.

81 Father Gonzalve Poulin, "À propos des allocations familiales," JO (Apr. 1939).

82 ANQM, Fonds Fédération Nationale de Saint-Jean-Baptiste, P120/54–3, Marcel
Labrie, sec.-gen., Ligue Ouvrière Catholique, à Mme. Thibaudeau, présidente, FNSJB, 26 Jan. 1943; François-Albert Angers, "Pour servir la personne
humaine," in Angers, *Pour orienter nos libertés* (Montréal: Fides, 1969) [*L'Action*

nationale, Oct. 1944], 103–4; AUM, Fonds ACC, P16/K1.11, Émile Bouvier, s.j., "Votre tâche, jeunesse," LD, 18 Nov. 1942. For the impact of federal welfare-state family policies, which had the effect of casting the family as a nuclear unit of consumption headed by a sole male breadwinner and of dispensing with extended kin and the wage contributions of women and adolescents, see Christie's chapters on the Depression and family allowances in *Engendering the State*.

83 Verville, "Notre famille." See also Edouard Déry, "Sauvegarde pour demain," LF 17, no. 10 (Dec. 1953): 625–32.

84 Gérard Dion, "La famille a droit à la securité économique," in *Mission et Droits de la Famille*, Semaine Sociale 1959 (Montreal: Secrétariat des Semaines Sociales, 1959), 138.

85 C.J. Magnan, "De la préparation à la vie familiale," *L'Éducation Sociale*. 13e Semaine Sociale du Canada, Montréal, 1935 (Montreal: École Sociale Populaire, 1935), 266–8, 279. For the impact of this "active" pedagogy in post-war Quebec, see Baillargeon, "'We Admire Modern Parents.'"

86 Magnan, "De la préparation," 276.

87 Yves et Mado Clermont, "La famille a le droit et le devoir d'être unie," in *Mission et Droits de la Famille*, 61.

88 Jolicoeur, *La Jeunesse Ouvrière*, 21–3; Françoise Marchand, "Les familles et leurs problèmes," *Rel* (Jan. 1952): 20–1.

89 "Ce que veut la J.O.C.," JO (June-July 1939); O.G. "L'amour chrétien, gage de paix," ON 5 and 20 Sept. 1939.

90 AUM, Fonds ACC, P16/04.52, Commission Canadienne de la Jeunesse, "Mémoire sur la Famille," ca 1945.

91 ANQM, Fonds MTC, P257, art. 13, "Crédit à l'habitation," "Conférence au poste CKCV," ca 1947–48.

92 ANQM, Fonds JOC, P104, art. 171, "Rapport national, 1954."

93 Renée Geoffroy, "Dans une société qui ne va pas, l'amour est le premier atteint," LT 11 June 1954, 6.

94 See for example, ANQM, Fonds SPM, "Semaine des fiancés, 1949," "Quelques conseils pratiques"; "Le courrier de José," FO, 21 Sept. 1946; ibid., 18 Oct. 1947; ibid., 17 Jan. 1948; "C'est ma belle-mère qui mène dans mon ménage!" FO, 11 July 1953.

95 It should be noted in this context that, as late as 1961, over 67 per cent of Montreal residents rented, rather than owned, their dwellings, and that much of even the new construction consisted of multi-family dwellings. See Paul-Andre Linteau, René Durocher, Jean-Claude Robert, *Histoire du Québec contemporain*, vol. 2, *De 1930 à nos jours* (Montreal: Boréal, 1993), 279–80. On the Catholic Action crusade for working-class housing, see Jean-Pierre Collin, "La Ligue Ouvrière Catholique et l'organisation communautaire dans le Québec urbain des années 1940," *Revue d'histoire de l'Amérique française* 47, no. 3 (Autumn 1993): 163–91.

96 R.P. Gonzalve Poulin, o.f.m., "Enjeux et fonction de la famille canadienne-française," in *Les causes de la désintegration familiale* (Montreal: Caritas-Canada, 1956), 12.

97 For Parsons's influence, especially on the sociologists trained at Université Laval, see Dumont, "Les causes," 31; and Rocher, *Entre les rêves et l'histoire*, 32–3. During the 1970s, Rocher authored a treatise on Parsons' thought. See Guy Rocher, *Talcott Parsons and American Sociology*, trans. Barbara and Stephen Mennell (London: Thomas Nelson & Sons, 1974; French ed., 1972).

98 Talcott Parsons, *The Social System* (New York: The Free Press of Glencoe, 1951), 208; W.F. Ogburn and M.F. Nimkoff, *Technology and the Changing Family* (Cambridge, Mass.: Houghton Mifflin Co., 1955), 15. For the influential role of the Chicago sociologists and Parsons's appropriation of Freudian psychology in post-war definitions of the family, see the critical account by Christopher Lasch, *Haven in a Heartless World: The Family Besieged* (New York: Basic Books, 1977), 29–33, 35–7, 39, 112–13. For a discussion that examines the wider impact of these strands of sociology on shaping post-war views of the Canadian family, see Michael Gauvreau, "The Family as Pathology: Psychology, Social Science and History Construct the Nuclear Family, 1945–1980," in Christie and Gauvreau, *Mapping the Margins*.

99 Emmanuel Mounier, *A Personalist Manifesto* (New York: Longmans, Green, 1938), 138–9. See also Mounier, "Le Mouvement 'Esprit,'" LR 2, no. 8 (1935): 231. Mounier's personalist vision of the family was elaborated in a French context where, during the 1930s and early 1940s, a number of social movements and regimes sought an extreme reassertion of male authority within the family. See, for example, Miranda Pollard, *Reign of Virtue: Mobilizing Gender in Vichy France* (Chicago: University of Chicago Press, 1998); and Cheryl A. Koos, "Fascism, Fatherhood, and the Family in Interwar France: The Case of Antoine Redier and the Legion," *Journal of Family History* 24, no. 3 (July 1999): 317–29.

100 Jean Lacroix, *Force et faiblesses de la famille* (Paris: Éditions du Seuil, 1948), 78.

101 Mounier, *A Personalist Manifesto*, 142; Mounier, *Personalism* (London: Routledge, 1950), 107; Gonzalve Poulin, o.f.m., "Rôle de la famille dans la personnalité de l'enfant," LF 10, no. 5 (May 1946).

102 De Lestapis, "La mission de la famille urbaine," Rel (August 1956): 227.

103 Mounier, *Personalism*, 108; Lacroix, *Force et faiblesses de la famille*, 112–13.

104 Claude Ryan, *Les classes moyennes au Canada français* (Montreal: Éditions de l'Action nationale, 1951), 24.

105 Mme R. Philie, "L'atmosphère du foyer," LF 4, no. 3 (Nov. 1940): 76–8; André Laurendeau, "École et foyer (Une enquête)," in *Le Foyer: Base de la Société*, 171; R.P. Richard Arès, s.j., "Pour une plus grande reconnaissance des droits de la famille," in *Mission et droits de la famille*, 21; Stanislas de

Lestapis, s.j., "Le bouleversement de la famille traditionnelle," *Rel* (July 1956): 183–6, first of three interviews at Radio-Canada.

106 Lacroix, *Force et faiblesses de la famille,* 54.

107 "La Famille" [extract from *L'Humanisme et l'humain,* by Francois Charmot, s.j.], CAC 1 (Oct. 1940): 43–6; AUM, Fonds ACC, P16/G3, 5.1, École civique d'été, 1947, M. de Laplante, "Vocation sociale," 24 June: "the realm of the private social"; ibid., P16/I.56, Commission Sacerdotale d'Études Sociales, "Dimanche de la Justice Sociale," 21 May 1950; Chanoine Raoul Drouin, "La vaste communauté des familles chrétiennes," LF 17, no. 6 (June–July 1953): 365–7, 394 (reprinted from *L'École canadienne,* Oct. 1952); "Famille," FO, 23 June 1945; Gerard Lemieux, Mme Andrée Daveluy, Guy Chabot, JC (Jan. 1949): 16; ANQM, Fonds SPM, P116, art. 2, "Programme souvenir," n.d.; ibid., art. 36, Conférences données au service, 1954 à 1958, "Fiancés d'aujourd'hui ... époux de demain," Conférence de Mgr. Léger, 11 jan. 1954 au Plateau.

108 Stanislas de Lestapis, "Pour une association des familles et une mystique chrétienne," *Rel* (Mar. 1957): 61; "Une entrevue avec Gustave Thibon, philosophe de l'amour," VE 23, no. 4 (Nov. 1956).

109 Gonzalve Poulin, o.f.m., "Que sera notre famille après la guerre?," LF 3, no. 6 (June-July 1940): 265.

110 Provencher, "Le chrétien dans la famille," 56–7.

111 Lucien Grothe (École des parents), "Sang-froid," LT (Oct. 1948): 8; Mme. Claudine Vallerand, "École et foyer," RD (Oct. 1939): 132–46; Jeanne Metivier-Desbiens, "L'atmosphère familiale moderne," LF 4, no. 10 (June 1941): 300–2; AUM, Fonds ACC, P16/D1, 4.9a, "Le corps humain, 1958–59," Claude Mailhiot, "L'Homme est un Tout."

112 NAC, Fonds Paul-Gouin, MG27 III D1, vol. 14, Colonisation – L'aide à la colonisation, 1944–1947, C.-E. Couture, "La Jeunesse Rurale et son milieu"; ANQM, Fonds MTC, P257, art. 3, "Semaine de la Famille Ouvrière, 1953," "Causerie," Poste CKCV, 20 Oct. 1953; Mgr Albert Tessier, "Le foyer, centre d'attraction," in *Le Foyer: Base de la société,* 256–8; ANQM, Fonds JOC, P104, art. 176, "Mémoire à la Commission Royale d'Enquête sur les Problèmes Constitutionnels," 18 Mar. 1954, jointly presented by Le Conseil de la Coopération du Québec, La Fédération des Coopératives d'Habitation, and the CTCC.

113 Gonzalve Poulin, o.f.m., "Le sens de l'amour," in Poulin, *Problèmes de la famille canadienne-française* (Quebec: Les Presses de l'Université Laval, 1952), 14. See also Stanislas de Lestapis, "La mission de la famille urbaine," 226–8.

114 Lacroix, *Force et faiblesses de la famille,* 55.

115 For this notion, see the work of the French philosopher Jean Lacroix *Force et faiblesses de la famille,* 94–5. This text had enormous influence among both Quebec conservatives like Father Gonzalve Poulin and social democrats like Fernand Dumont.

116 Poulin, *Problèmes de la famille canadienne-française*, 15–16.

117 Ibid., 42, 50.

118 ANQM, Fonds JOC, P104, art. 4, "17e Session Intensive," Champagne, "S.P.M., 1952"; Marcel Côté, ("La préparation au mariage," in *Le Foyer: Base de la Société*, 59–60.

119 Louise-M. Lamonde, "Préparation au mariage," *Rel* (June 1953): 162; Magnan, "De la préparation," 286; ANQM, Fonds JEC, art. 42, "Vie sentimentale des jeunes."

120 Côté, "La préparation au mariage," 68. See Lamonde, "Préparation au mariage," 162–3; Joseph D'Anjou, s.j., "Parents, c'est vous que ça regarde," *Rel* (Mar. 1959): 68–9.

121 Mgr A. Camirand, "L'éducation sexuelle," LF 2, no. 7 (Mar. 1939): 145–6; "L'amour humain chez les jeunes," CAC 113 (Jan. 1950): 147.

122 ANQM, Fonds JEC, art. 171, "Rencontre nationale des responsables et aumôniers du S.P.M.," 3–4 décembre 1955. See also ibid., art. 4, "Suggestions de programme d'action, 1961," "Amour entre garçons et filles"; ibid., art. 175, "Enquête auprès de 329 fiancés qui ont suivi le S.P.M. sur la préparation économique des jeunes au mariage," 1954.

123 AUM, Fonds ACC, P16/D5, 1.14, "Compilation du sondage auprès des fiancés sur l'amour," 1962. This study was based on the responses of 133 couples in five Quebec dioceses and eight cities. See also ANQM, Fonds SPM, P116, art. 1, "Situation des fiancés, 1955–56," which pointed to the very late sexual awareness of Quebec youth. Fully 60 per cent of the young people questioned stated that they had acquired their sexual knowledge after age fourteen.

124 AUM, Fonds ACC, P16/D5, 1.14, "Compilation du sondage," 1962; ibid., P16/H18.84, "Conclusion du Comité Éxecutif du S.P.M., jan.–mai 1956."

125 See ANQM, Fonds SPM, P116, art. 24, "Substance de la conférence de M. Marcel Clément," ca 1954; ibid., art. 2, Semaine des fiancés, 1950, Chanoine Clavel, "Les ennemis de la famille et la préparation au mariage"; AUM, Fonds ACC, P16/G3, 9.2, R.P. Jules Godin, s.j., "Le Service de Préparation à la Vie," ca 1951; ibid., P16/G5, 8.1, "Le problème des jeunes qui ne fréquentent plus l'école," 6 Dec. 1942; "Famille-École," CAC 134 (Oct. 1951): 75–6; "Le courrier de José," FO, 4 Dec. 1946.

126 Abbé Groulx, "Les traditions familiales de notre peuple," JEC 7, no. 5 (May 1941).

127 Dumont, "Les causes," 31. See also Gérald Fortin, "Socio-Cultural Changes in an Agricultural Parish," in Marcel Rioux and Yves Martin, eds., *French-Canadian Society*, vol. 1 (Toronto: McClelland and Stewart, 1964), 94–104; Guy Rocher, "Le Père," *Food for Thought* 14, no. 6 (Nov. 1954); Rocher, "La famille dans la ville moderne."

128 Dumont, "Les causes," 34. See Lacroix, *Force et Faiblesses de la Famille*.

129 De Lestapis, "La mission de la famille urbaine," 227–8; Hervé Carrier, s.j.,

"Situation et avenir de la famille," *Rel* (Sept. 1957): 233–5; Poulin, "Enjeux et fonctions de la famille canadienne-française," 15.

130 Dumont, "Les causes," 30, 34.

131 Ibid., 35.

132 ANQM, Fonds JOC, P104, art. 181, Camille Laurin, "Rapport Camille Laurin"; "La Famille, équilibre de notre societe," LF 16, no. 7 (Aug.–Sept. 1952): 43: "a new type of family is in the process of being constituted."

133 "La Famille, équilibre de notre sociéte," 32.

134 For this historical trajectory, which relies heavily on a Foucauldian analysis of discourse and power, see Mona Gleason, "Psychology and the Construction of the 'Normal' Family in Postwar Canada, 1945–1960," *Canadian Historical Review* 78, no. 3 (Sept. 1997): 442–77; Gleason, *Normalizing the Ideal: Psychology, Schooling and the Family in Postwar Canada* (Toronto: University of Toronto Press, 1999). For the definition of heterosexuality as "compulsory," and therefore as marginalizing homosexuality, see Mary Louise Adams, *The Trouble with Normal: Postwar Youth and the Making of Heterosexuality* (Toronto: University of Toronto Press, 1997). For a recent study of single mothers in post-war Ontario, see Margaret Jane Hillyard Little, *'No Car, No Radio, No Liquor Permit': The Moral Regulation of Single Mothers in Ontario, 1920–1997* (Toronto: University of Toronto Press, 1998), 107–38. A number of articles have explored aspects of the post-war moral regulation of delinquent youth. See Mariana Valverde, "Building Anti-Delinquent Communities: Morality, Gender, and *Generation* in the City," in Joy Parr, ed., *A Diversity of Women: Ontario, 1945–1980* (Toronto: University of Toronto Press, 1995), 19–45; Franca Iacovetta, "Parents, Daughters, and Family Court Intrusions into Working-Class Life," in Franca Iacovetta and Wendy Mitchinson, eds., *On the Case: Explorations in Social History* (Toronto: University of Toronto Press, 1998), 312–37.

135 For a critique of postmodern historical analyses of the family in another cultural context, see James Walter, "Designing Families and Solid Citizens: The Dialectic of Modernity and the Matrimonial Causes Bill, 1959," *Australian Historical Studies* 116 (Apr. 2001): 55–6. Walter characterizes this type of postmodernism as a type of "covert whig history," and correctly argues that elite social scientists, government officials, and church leaders who sought to design policies for the post-war family were neither unified nor hegemonic. For a critique of "master-narratives" which stress the hegemonic aspects of post-war Canadian social history, see Christie and Gauvreau, "Introduction," *Cultures of Citizenship in Postwar Canada*.

136 Claudine-S. Vallerand, "Ce que donne L'École des Parents," *Rel* (May 1941): 156. See also "L'Enfant éducateur de ses parents," LF 18, no. 10 (Oct. 1954): 514–6 (first published in *Mon Village*, Paris). For the formation and early activities of the *École des Parents*, see Malouin, *Le Mouvement familial au Québec*, 31–6; and Baillargeon, "'We Admire Modern Parents.'"

137 Magnan, "De la préparation," 272;

138 Ibid., "Sens social dans la famille," LF 3, no. 6 (Feb. 1940): 153.

139 Marguerite St. Germain-Lefebvre, "L'Autorité, premier devoir des parents," LF 5, no. 3 (Nov. 1941): 76–7. See also Louis Clairval, "Enfants acceptés et enfants rejetés! ...," LF 10, no. 1 (Jan. 1946): 26–7.

140 AUM, Fonds ACC, P16/04.57, "Commission Canadienne de la Jeunesse," *Jeunesse et Après-guerre* (pamphlet, n.d).

141 Louis Clairval, "Autorité et liberté," LF 14, no. 1 (Jan. 1950): 23; Lacroix, *Force et faiblesses de la famille*, 72, 78, 86, 110. See also Dumont, "Les causes," 110; Provencher, "Le chrétien dans la famille," 72; AUM, Fonds ACC, P16/13.85, Terreault, "Conception Étudiante du Mariage."

142 Stephane Valiquette, s.j., "École des Parents: Papa Hitler," C&F 9, no. 1 (Feb. 1952): 7–9; Valiquette, "Papa gâteau," C&F 9, no. 2 (Apr. 1952): 54–8; Marie-Joseph d'Anjou, s.j., "L'autorité dans l'éducation familiale," C&F 10, no. 3 (June 1953): 110–16; L. Valois, ptre, "Le sacrifice, loi essentielle de la vie familiale chrétienne," LT (Oct. 1943): 8; Garigue, "The French Canadian Family," 97.

143 AUM, P16/14.57, *Jeunesse et Après-guerre.*

144 This insight, the implications of which have been explored in Baillargeon's superb treatment of the *École des Parents*, is critical for precisely describing and situating the ideology of the "democratic family" within post-war Quebec society.

145 Claudine-S. Vallerand, "Pour une 'pédagogie à la page,'" C&F 1, no. 3 (May 1944): 81–6; Jean Laramée, s.j., "Pour une pédagogie éternelle," C&F 1, no. 3 (May 1944): 87–92.

146 AUM, Fonds ACC, P16/D1, 4.10, "La Culture, Programme d'Action, 1959–60," Gérard Lemieux, "Les Valeurs de l'Esprit Chez les Gens de Classes Moyennes." See also Clermont, "La famille a le droit et le devoir d'être unie," 55.

147 Jeanne Benoît, "Entr'aide possible?" JEC 10, no. 4 (Apr. 1944). Benoit's views were similar to those articulated by the Canadian Youth Commission. See AUM, Fonds ACC, P16/04.52, "Commission Canadienne de la Jeunesse," *Accent on Action: A Report of the National Conference of Agencies Serving Youth.* Chateau Laurier Hotel, Ottawa, 30 Nov. and 1 Dec. 1946, Dr Sidney E. Smith, "An Interpretation of the Canadian Youth Commission."

148 AUQÀM, Fonds Institut Canadien d'Éducation des Adultes (ICEA), 56P, 11k/3, "Documents de travail, 1947," David Bosset, "La Famille Urbaine et la Formation du Sens Moral."

149 "L'amour humain chez les jeunes," CAC 113 (Jan. 1950): 147. See also "Vos adolescents et Votre milieu familial, Votre autorité," LF 18, no. 2 (Feb. 1954): 107–23; Soeur Marie-Alice, s.f.a., "Une bonne famille canadienne-française," LF 16, no. 6 (June–July 1952): 11–18; Ryan, *Les classes moyennes*, 27.

150 "Le courrier de José," FO, 28 Dec. 1946; Jacques Baillargeon, "Peuvent-ils
     être nos amis," JEC 9, no. 7 (July 1943); Daniel A. Lord, "Un problème qui
     n'en est pas un: les mariages mixtes," *Rel* (Oct. 1943): 123–4; Gaston Leury,
     "Comprenons nos jeunes gens," FO, 4 Oct. 1947.

151 Here, I dissent from much of the current historical literature that uses Fou-
     cault's attention to language to posit a monolithic, monocausal "construc-
     tion" of family structure and relations through the imposition of language.
     A more open-ended and pluralist application of Foucault's method would
     suggest that, while family practices may have remained patriarchal, the lan-
     guage of the "democratic family" amounted to a significant shift in the way
     in which the discourse of social agencies, media, churches, and govern-
     ments conceptualized the nature of marriage, family authority, and patterns
     of child-rearing, and thus amounted to a significant change in *public* atti-
     tudes rather than individual practices.

152 ANQM, Fonds SPM, P116, art. 2, Gérard Lemieux, "Allocution du président,
     1950." See also ibid., art. 2, "La semaine des fiancés, 1948"; Claudine
     Vallerand, "Madame Vallerand."

153 Gérard Lemieux, *Jeunesse du Québec: Bilan d'une génération* (Montreal:
     Jeunesse Indépendante Catholique, ca 1946), 26.

154 For a more complete discussion of the intersection of youth ideologies with
     post-war ideas of social citizenship, see Gauvreau, "The Protracted Birth of
     the Canadian 'Teenager.'"

155 "Devant l'enfant moderne," LF 18, no. 1 (Jan. 1954): 40 (first published in
     Nouvelle Revue Pédagogique, Belgium); Claude Ryan, "Jeunesse d'aujour-
     d'hui," JC (Nov. 1946).

156 For the father as economic provider, see Cynthia Comacchio, "'A Postscript
     for Father': Defining a New Fatherhood in Interwar Canada," *Canadian His-
     torical Review* 78, no. 3 (Sept. 1997): 385–408. For the consumerist and
     escapist self-perceptions of post-war Canadian males, see Robert Rutherdale,
     "Fatherhood, Masculinity, and the Good Life during Canada's Baby Boom,
     1945–1965," *Journal of Family History* 24, no. 3 (July 1999): 351–73. For
     pre–World War II concepts of male domesticity in which the father's role as
     moral educator of his children was strongly emphasized by both Protestant
     and Catholic religious traditions, see Nancy Christie, "Introduction: Family,
     Community, and the Rise of Liberal Society," in Christie, *Households of Faith*.

157 Jean-Marc Chicoine, "Paternité, vocation des temps actuels," CAC 161 (Mar.
     1954): 237–8.

158 For the genesis and definition of these policies during the latter stages of
     the Depression and during World War II, see Christie, *Engendering the State*.

159 André LaRivière, psychologue et psychanalyste, "Ce que doit être le rôle du
     père dans l'éducation," LF 15, no. 4 (Apr. 1951): 247.

160 Pelletier, "Le laique marié," 115, 120–1. See also AUM, Fonds ACC, P16/G3,
     5.1, "Écoles civiques d'été," Raymond Beriault, "L'amour," 20 June 1947.

161 Théo Chentrier, "Fête des pères: Présence paternelle," c&f 8, no. 3 (June 1951): 102.

162 Henri Messier, "Donnez à vos enfants la chance de se corriger," *FO*, 10 Mar. 1948. See also LaRivière, "Ce que doit être le rôle du père dans l'éducation," 247; "Miriam," "L'École des maris," c&f 1, no. 2 (Mar. 1944): 19; auqàm, Fonds icea, 56p 11k/3, "Documents de travail à l'intention des membres de la délégation canadienne au 2e Congrès Mondial de l'Apostolat des laïcs, 5–13 Oct. 1947," "Les problèmes de la famille rurale."

163 "Miriam," "L'École des maris." See also "Moins de femmes en pantalon et plus d'hommes en tabliers," fo, 23 Aug. 1947; Pierre Dufoyer, "Le procès des maris," lf 16, no. 10 (Dec. 1952): 9–12; Old Fashion, "L'action syndicale 'presque toujours' en opposition avec la vie familiale, lt, 1 May 1953, 6; Léopold Godbout, "Les causes de la désintegration familiale: les facteurs d'ordre morale," in *La prévention de la désintegration familiale*, 42.

164 Father Léandre Poirier, o.f.m., ed., "Repos-Jeu-Loisir," lf 14, no. 6 (June-July 1950): 306.

165 aum, Fonds acc, p16/d5, 1.10, "Travaillera-t-elle?," n.d.; anqm, Fonds spm, p116, art. 1, "Session d'étude 1957," Solange Pitre à Madeleine Meloche, secrétaire spm; Roger Mathieu, "Allocations familiales," jo (Apr. 1943); "Après la guerre," jo (Feb. 1943); aum, Fonds acc, p16/k1.22, "Gérard Filion," "Positions – Sur les problèmes sociaux," ld, Apr. 1947; ibid., p16/04.63, "Confédération des Syndicats Nationaux," *Bulletin des dirigeants de la C.T.C.C.* 1, no. 4 (Nov. 1954); R.P. Léon Lebel, s.j., aumônier général de l'Union Catholique des Cultivateurs, "Les prérogatives fondamentales de la famille," in *Pour une société chrétienne*, 102–3.

166 Marcel-Marie, o.f.m., "À Qui Appartient l'éducation?" lf 3, no. 11 (July-Aug. 1940): 305; Jeanne and Gerard Corbeil, "Pour hommes seulement," lf10, no. 7 (Aug.-Sept. 1946); Monique-B. Dufresne, "Profession et foyer: deux forces à conjuguer," lf 12, no. 10 (Dec. 1949): 579–82; Jeanne d'Arc and Bernard Trottier, "L'union au foyer," lf 12, no. 2 (Feb. 1948); Provencher, "Le chretien dans la famille," 60–1; Clermont, "La famille a le droit et le devoir d'être unie," 56–8; Suzanne, "Une perle de mari," jo 12, no. 2 (Oct. 1943): 10; Jean-Paul Geoffroy, "Qui doit tenir le budget familial? Lui ou elle?" lt, 17 Apr. 1953; Rocher, "Le père"; Rocher, "La famille urbaine," 83.

167 Jeanne and Guy Boulizon, "Rôle respectif du père et de la mère dans l'éducation des enfants," lf 8, no. 10 (Dec. 1944): 428.

168 Chentrier, "Fête des pères," 105; Boulizon, "Rôle respectif," 428.

169 LaRivière, "Ce que doit être," 248.

170 Chicoine, "Paternité," 239; Jeanne and Gerard Corbeil, "L'Homme d'aujourd'hui," lf 11, no. 7 (Aug.–Sept. 1947); Dumont, "Les causes," 33–4.

171 Rocher, "La famille dans la ville moderne," 82; aum, Fonds acc, p16/r62,

Spiritualité familiale, "Spiritualité familiale: problèmes pratiques et experiences," n.d.; Ryan, *Les classes moyennes.*

172 Lacroix, *Force et faiblesses de la famille,* 131–3.

173 Renée Geoffroy, "À qui appartiennent nos maris? À leurs femmes ou au
syndicalisme?" LT, 27 Feb. 1953, 6. See also Corbeil, "Pour hommes seulement." It is significant to note that in this connection, although Catholic
personalists placed a high value upon sexual communion within marriage,
they diverged from their Protestant counterparts in Anglo-Canada, who
posited female sexual satisfaction as the only criterion that would keep
women attached to the domestic sphere. For this strand of thinking in the
United Church of Canada, see Christie, "Sacred Sex."

174 Lacroix, *Force et faiblesses de la famille,* 114, 134.

175 Esdras Minville, *Le citoyen canadien-français,* vol. 2 (Montreal: Fides, 1946),
160; ibid. *Le citoyen canadien-français,* vol. 1 (Montreal: Fides, 1946), 141–2.
Minville was quoting the French social thinker and jurist Father J.-T. Delos,
who fled France during the Nazi occupation and taught at Universite Laval.
For Minville's career, see Pierre Trepanier, "Esdras Minville (1896–1975) et
le traditionalisme canadien-français," *Les Cahiers des Dix 51* (1995): 255–94.
For further Catholic commentary on the links between family and nation,
see Claudine Vallerand, "Ce que donne l'École des Parents," 156; Romain
Légaré, o.f.m., "Le nombre: puissance fondamentale d'une nation," LF 1,
no. 8 (Apr. 1938): 131; Roger Mathieu, "Du pain S.V.P. Monsieur," JO (Mar.
1943); Côté, "La préparation au mariage," 58; "Notre grande richesse, ce
sont nos familles chrétiennes," *Rel* (Jan. 1951): 14–15.

176 Dumont, "Les causes," 35. See also Fernand Jolicoeur, "Les qualités de la
classe ouvrière," LT (June 1949): 2; Gilmard, "Autorité et liberté," JEC 6, no.
4 (Apr. 1940); "JEC et le sens familial," JEC 6, no. 9 (Sept. 1940).

177 Poulin, "La Famille," 43. See also AUM, Fonds ACC, P16, 13.85, "Le mariage
étudiant," 1953; Philippe Garigue, "St. Joseph Oratory," in Garigue, *Études
sur le Canada français* (Montreal: Faculté des sciences sociales, économiques,
et politiques, 1958), 86; T.R.P. Louis-M. Régis, o.p., "La Religion et la
philosophie au Canada français" (1955), in Wade, *La dualité canadienne,* 60:
"to be papists means, for us, first and foremost that we have a father, a
daddy."

178 Poulin, "La Famille," 44.

179 Valiquette, "Papa gâteau," 58.

180 "Pour réformer la famille!" JO (Feb. 1938). See also C.H. Denzo, "Restaura-
tion sociale et familale," JO (Nov. 1942); R.P. Joseph-Papin Archambault, s.j.,
"Déclaration d'ouverture," in *Le Chrétien dans la famille,* 19; Léon Lebel, s.j.,
"Pour une politique familiale. 1. – Le principe," ON, 5 Jan. 1937; François
Hertel, "Législation familiale et esprit de famille," ON, 5 and 20 Sept. 1939.

181 Hellman, *Emmanuel Mounier and the New Catholic Left* (Toronto: University of
Toronto Press, 1981), 191–2. Hellman also notes (201), and at greater

length in *The Knight-Monks of Vichy France*, that Mounier and Jean Lacroix, author of *Force et faiblesses de la famille*, had initially given their allegiance to Vichy's National Revolution. For Mounier's rejection of capitalist notions of corporatism in the 1930s, see Jean-Louis Loubet del Bayle, *Les Non-conformistes des années 30* (Paris: Éditions du Seuil, 1969), 393–4.

182 For the strong hold of corporatism on social and economic thinking in twentieth-century Quebec, see Pierre Trépanier, "Quel corporatisme? (1820–1965)," *Les cahiers des Dix* 50 (1994): 186–7; Clinton Archibald, *Un Québec corporatiste?: corporatisme et néo-corporatisme: du passage d'une idéologie corporatiste sociale à une idéologie corporatiste politique, le Québec de 1930 à nos jours* (Hull: Éditions Asticou, 1983). The central contribution of both these works is to separate corporatism from an exclusive identification with right-wing, quasi-fascist ideological tendencies. However, neither of these works explore the link between ideologies of family and forms of social corporatism, a connection that was of enormous significance in Catholic thinking.

183 AUM, Fonds ACC, P16/G2. 7.1, "Semaines Étudiantes," Gérard Pelletier et Alex Leduc, "Pour Servir: Campagne Familiale, avril-mai 1941."

184 Esdras Minville, "Quelques aspects du problème social dans la province de Québec," in *Pour une société chrétienne*, 176.

185 Gonzalve Poulin, o.f.m., "Esquisse d'une politique familiale pour le Québec," *Rel* (Jan. 1944): 6–8; Stanislas de Lestapis, s.j., "Le Mouvement familial en France," *Rel* (Feb. 1947): 38; Gonzalve Poulin, "L'État et la politique familiale," LF 3, no. 1 (Sept. 1939): 6–7; André Laurendeau, "École et foyer," in *Le Foyer, Base de la Société*, 172–3; Laurendeau, "Aspect national de la Famille," LF 17, no. 2 (Feb. 1953): 84–92; "Importance de la famille ouvrière," LT, 18 avril 1952; Hélène Lamontagne, "Après une reconstruction," JO 10, no. 6 (Feb. 1942); Gilmard, "La Famille qui bâtit la chrétienté, les pays, les nations," JEC 7, no. 5 (May 1941); AUM, P16/K1.11, R.P. Émile Bouvier, s.j., "Votre tâche, jeunesse"; ibid., P16/04.63, *Bulletin des dirigeants de la C.T.C.C.*; Lebel, "Les prérogatives fondamentales de la famille."

186 In *Les Non-conformistes*, Loubet del Bayle argues that Jean Lacroix, whose treatise on the family was read widely in post-war Quebec, defined democracy simply as the equality of all human persons before the law, and expressed very little liking for either parliamentary institutions or universal suffrage (376).

187 Poulin, *Problèmes de la famille*, 43; Lacroix, *Force et faiblesses de la famille*, 155.

188 Poulin, "Esquisse," 6; Gilmard, "La Famille"; Poulin, "L'État et la politique familiale"; Gaston Leury, "La Famille d'abord!" FO, 31 jan. 1948; AUM, Fonds ACC, P16/R.64, "L'Apport des services publics," communication présentée par M. Edgar Guay, professeur à l'École de Service Social, Université Laval, in *Vers l'édification de la famille de demain* (Montreal: n.p., 1951); Bernardin Verville, o.f.m., "Réagissons," LF 8, no. 12 (Feb. 1945): 576.

CHAPTER FOUR

1 Gonzalve Poulin, o.f.m., *Problèmes de la famille canadienne-française* (Quebec: Les Presses de l'Université Laval, 1952), 51, quoting the French journalist Jacques Madaule.

2 Jules LeBlanc, "Le Cardinal Léger: il faut repenser nos moyens d'action auprès des adolescents," LD, 13 Sept. 1963.

3 Philippe Garigue, "L'Église et la politique familiale,"lecture delivered to the Bishops of the Canadian Catholic Conference, at Ottawa, 7 Apr. 1970, in Philippe Garigue, *Famille et humanisme* (Montreal: Leméac, 1973), 205–6.

4 Ibid., 205–6, 211–13.

5 Roch Duval, ptre, Université Laval, "La fréquentation des adolescents," CAC (Jan.–Feb. 1954): 148.

6 Doug Owram, *Born at the Right Time: A History of the Baby Boom Generation* (Toronto: University of Toronto Press, 1996), outlines these developments (136–58). However, his analysis fails to provide chronological specifics as to when these developments occurred, beyond stating that "Teenagers were an American invention, but television, magazines, and the general pervasiveness of American culture quickly carried it north of the border," and that "sometime in the 1950s, the cult of the teenager was born" (145).

7 For examples of this approach in the Canadian context, see Valverde, "Building Anti-Delinquent Communities: Morality, Gender, and Generation in the City," in Joy Parr, ed., *A Diversity of Women: Ontario, 1945–1980* (Toronto: University of Toronto Press, 1995); Mary Louise Adams, *The Trouble with Normal: Postwar Youth and the Making of Heterosexuality* (Toronto: University of Toronto Press, 1997), 53–82; and Franca Iacovetta, "Gossip, Contest, and Power in the Making of Suburban Bad Girls: Toronto, 1945–1960," *Canadian Historical Review* 80, no. 4 (Dec. 1999): 585–623. Owram, *Born at the Right Time*, also notes that in the early 1950s, "obsession with the juvenile delinquent was at an all-time high" (144). Broadly speaking, such interpretations build on the classic American work on the subject, James Gilbert's *A Cycle of Outrage: America's Reaction to the Juvenile Delinquent in the 1950s* (New York: Oxford University Press, 1986). Gilbert's treatment, however, is highly contextualized and nuanced, and he does not begin from the starting point that the discourse on youth was monolithic. British "subcultural" studies of working-class youth phenomena, such as the Teddy Boys, Mods, Rockers, and punks, focus on the ways in which distinctive clothing and musical styles constitute a "resistance" to hegemonic forms of culture. See for this trajectory, Dick Hebdige, *Subculture: The Meaning of Style* (New York: Methuen & Co., 1979); Stuart Hall and Tony Jefferson, eds, *Resistance Through Rituals: Youth Subcultures in Postwar Britain* (London: Hutchinson & Co., 1976); Angela McRobbie, *Feminism and Youth Culture* (Boston: Unwin Hyman, 1991). It is ironic in this context that while both Valverde and Iacovetta assume – by solely studying youth culture

through the "gaze" of legal and social welfare experts – that working-class
youth universally "resisted" the imposition of norms by outside adult authority, they make little attempt to identify the musical or fashion elements
among young people themselves that would constitute such a "subculture,"
preferring to highlight sexual transgressions.

8 For a Canadian example of this traditional chronology, see *Born at the Right
Time*, in which Owram posits a sharp break between the 1950s and the 1960s.
More recently, a number of revisionist works have sought to re-periodize this
cultural transition, locating important elements of the more radical climate
of the 1960s in aspects of earlier post-war cultural practices. See, generally,
Arthur Marwick, *The Sixties: Cultural Revolution in Britain, France, Italy, and the
United States, ca. 1958–ca. 1974* (Oxford: Oxford University Press, 1998); and
for a recent American revisionist treatment, Dominick Cavallo, *A Fiction of the
Past: The Sixties in American History* (New York: St. Martin's Press, 1999).

9 Canadian Youth Commission, *Youth, Marriage, and the Family* (Toronto:
Ryerson Press, 1948), 21.

10 Ibid.

11 Ibid. For a more complete analysis of the assumptions and definitions that
governed notions of "youth" in the wartime and post-war Canadian Youth
Commission, see Gauvreau, "The Protracted Birth of the Canadian
'Teenager,'" in Nancy Christie and Michael Gauvreau, *Cultures of Citizenship
in Post-war Canada, 1940–1955* (Montreal and Kingston: McGill-Queen's
University Press, 2003).

12 For American definitions, see Grace Palladino, *Teenagers: An American History*
(New York: Basic Books, 1996), 5. Palladino notes that by the mid-1930s,
American teenagers were already considered an age group, and not simply a
wealthy social class. For the proportions of American youth enrolled in high
school in 1940, see John Modell, *Into One's Own: From Youth to Adulthood in the
United States, 1920–1975* (Berkeley: University of California Press, 1989), 36.

13 See Wolfgang M. Illing and Zoltan E. Zsigmond, *Enrolment in Schools and Universities 1951–2 to 1975–6* (Ottawa: Economic Council of Canada Staff Study
No. 20, 1967), Appendix table B-2.

14 For Quebec, see the images analysed by Gaston Desjardins, *L'Amour en
patience: la sexualité adolescente au Québec, 1940–1960* (Sainte-Foy: Presses de
l'Université du Québec, 1995); and for English Canada, Adams, *The Trouble
with Normal*, 83–106.

15 For a critical analysis of this rather heavy-handed use of the category "Americanization" by scholars, see Heide Fehrenbach and Uta G. Poiger, eds, introduction to *Transactions, Transgressions, Transformations: American Culture in
Western Europe and Japan* (New York: Berghahn Books, 2000), xiii–xiv. In *Born
at the Right Time*, Owram describes Canadian teens' emulation of American
patterns of teenager consumption and purchasing power (147–8). However,
it is significant that his evidence is drawn almost entirely from the late 1950s,

a period in which Canada, like Britain, France, and Germany, entered, for the first time, a period of widely-diffused consumer affluence. For a fuller discussion of the consequences of the later timing of Canada's entry into the social framework of mass consumption, see Christie and Gauvreau, "Introduction: Recasting Canada's Postwar Decade," in Christie and Gauvreau, *Cultures of Citizenship in Postwar Canada.*

16 John R. Seeley, R. Alexander Sim, Elizabeth W. Loosley, *Crestwood Heights* (Toronto: University of Toronto Press, 1956), 112–13. This volume, which explored a wealthy older suburb of Toronto, was one of two influential studies of Anglo-Canadian suburbias. The other was Frederick Elkin and William Westley, "The Myth of Adolescent Culture," *American Sociological Review* 20 (1955): 682 – which examined the Westmount area of Montreal. Interestingly, French-Canadian sociologists of the period produced no comparable studies of middle-class urban neighbourhoods, preferring to concentrate on the "folk society" theme or the socio-cultural transition from agriculture to urban areas.

17 "Problèmes de Vie Sentimentale des Étudiants Canadiens," CAC 154 (June–July–Aug. 1953): 283. See also Frère Alberic, s.g., "Problème religieux chez nos jeunes," CAC 139 (Mar. 1952): 214–16; Marie-Paule Demers, "Les adolescentes, des incomprises?" *CAC* 140 (Apr. 1952): 244–9; AUQÀM, Fonds ICEA, 56P, 11k/3, Documents de Travail, 1947, "Les problèmes de la famille rurale dans un diocèse du Québec, vus par Mme. Lucien Dugas"; ANQM, Fonds JEC, P65, art. 3, Maurice Lafond, c.s.c., "Cours sur l'Action Catholique, la J.E.C.," 1951.

18 AUM, Fonds ACC, P16/G5, 8.12, Maurice Crête, "Les jeunes ne sont pas prêts à se marier," LD, 24 Sept. 1955.

19 Léopold Godbout, curé de Notre-Dame-d'Assomption, Sherbrooke, "Les causes de la désintégration familiale," in *Les causes de la désintégration familiale* (Montreal: Caritas-Canada, 1956) 47; ANQM, Fonds JOC, P104, art. 171, "Rencontre nationale des responsables et aumôniers du S.P.M.," 3–4 Dec. 1955; "Individus, foyers, professions et sociétés sont malades," FO, 8 aout 1953.

20 ANQM, Fonds JEC, P65/s6, ss2, sss1, D4/2, "Le probleme de la J.E.C. des jeunes," ca 1955, préparé par André Juneau. See also ibid., P65/s6, ss2, sss1, D1, "Historique de la J.E.C. des Jeunes, 1950–1958."

21 AUM, P16/D1, 4.10, La Culture, programme d'action, 1959–60, Fr. Albini Girouard, "La Vie de l'Esprit Chez les Jeunes Travailleurs," 28 Feb.–1 Mar. 1959. See also ibid., P16/G5, 4.16, Session Intensive, 1958, "Rapport de la 23ième Session Intensive, JOCF et conjointe," 21–24 June 1958.

22 ANQM, Fonds JEC, P65/s6, ss2, sss1, D3/2, Problématique et lignes de solution face au secteur jeunes, "Rencontre des Permanentes, 23 au 27 fev. 1954"; Andrée Lajoie, "Où va la jeunesse française?" VE 23, no. 14 (Apr. 1957).

23 Ariès, "Familles du demi-siècle," in R. Prigent, ed., *Renouveau d'idées sur la famille* (Paris: Presses Universitaires de France, 1954), 164–5.

24 "Problèmes de Vie Sentimentale," 295–8, 303, 311. See also "La psychologie de l'adolescent," VE 16, no. 2 (Feb. 1950).

25 Sidlauskas, "L'Adolescente et son premier amour," in "Les Voies du Coeur en Éducation," CAC 159–160, (Jan.–Feb. 1954): 137. For the "dating culture" as it developed in American high schools in the 1920s, and in particular the ways in which it was perceived as offering more freedom for young women than previous patterns of supervision of courtship by parents, see Beth L. Bailey, *Front Porch to Back Seat: Courtship in Twentieth-Century America* (Baltimore and London: Johns Hopkins University Press, 1989), 77–80; Modell, *Into One's Own*, 83–8.

26 Roch Duval, ptre, Université Laval, "La fréquentation des adolescents," CAC 159–60, (Jan.–Feb. 1954): 139, 148, 156–7.

27 La Rédaction, "Présentation," "Les Voies du Coeur en Éducation," CAC 159–160 (Jan.–Feb. 1954): 129; Soeur Marie-de-Sainte-Jeanne-Louise, c.s.c., and Soeur Gabriel-Lalement, s.g.c., "L'Adolescence, cet âge riche," CAC 156 (Oct. 1953): 31.

28 Norbert Fournier, c.s.v., "Les éducateurs et le problème des fréquentations," C&F 16, no. 3 (June 1959): 107–9.

29 Ibid., 110.

30 Modell, *Into One's Own*, observes that "going steady" was the linchpin of the whole post-war system of adolescent heterosexual relationships. Further, he argues that while the dating culture itself was widely accepted by most parents, the concept of "going steady" was much more contested, because it seemed to incorporate a progression in sexual relations (233–8).

31 Jean-Paul Labelle, s.j., "Les 'petites' fréquentations," C&F 14, no. 1 (Feb. 1957): 12–14. See also ANQM, Fonds JEC, P65 art. 42, "Vie sentimentale des jeunes," 1961; Fournier, "Les éducateurs et le problème des fréquentations," 107–9. English Canadian opinion from the late 1950s also tended to express considerable doubt regarding the wisdom of "going steady," and out of similar concerns for the effect that such relationships would have upon young men. For an analysis, see Gauvreau, "The Protracted Birth of the Canadian 'Teenager.'"

32 Indeed, the age brackets that were used by various groups – ranging from Catholic Action militants to late-Depression federal youth initiatives to the writings of the educators, Church leaders, and policy-makers of the Canadian Youth Commission – tended to target as "youth" anyone aged fifteen to twenty-four, thus conflating teenagers with young adults. See Gauvreau, "The Protracted Birth of the Canadian 'Teenager.'"

33 For the emergence of these views, and the impact of psychologists and sociologists such as Erik Erikson and S.N. Eisenstadt, see Gilbert, *A Cycle of Outrage*, 199; John Davis, *Youth and the Condition of Britain: Images of Adolescent Conflict* (London & Atlantic Highlands, N.J.: The Athlone Press, 1990), 132–3. For

the prevalence of these views among Catholic reformers in Quebec by the middle of the 1950s, see Desjardins, *L'Amour en patience*, 45–6.

34 Marie-Paule Demers, "Les adolescentes, des incomprises," CAC (Apr. 1952): 247–8.

35 "Problèmes de vie sentimentale," 294, 303; "Famille contemporaine et problèmes étudiants," CAC 164–6 (June–July–Aug. 1954): 341; Jean LeMoyne, "La femme et la civilisation canadienne-française," CL 17 (Jan. 1957): 30–6; ANQM, Fonds JEC, P65, S6, SS1, D3/1, art. 286, "E.P.S. – Programme – Préparation – Relations Gars et Filles – Problématique," ca 1954; AUM, Fonds ACC, P16/D1, 4.14B, "Commission du programme d'action – Vie sentimentale des jeunes," 23 octobre 1961, "Compte-rendu de la réunion du 23 octobre 1961"; ibid., P16/D5, 1.14, "Compilation du sondage auprès des fiancés sur l'Amour," 1962; Andrée Lajoie, "Les teddy-boys anglais ont de l'agressivité à revendre," VE 25, no. 10 (Feb. 1959).

36 AUM, Fonds ACC, P16/G2, 7.4, "Programme d'action 1953–54, Vie sentimentale," préparé par Albert Breton et Maurice Pinard. Both Pinard and Breton were later to have prominent careers as sociologists during the 1960s and 1970s.

37 This is the argument advanced in Adams, *The Trouble with Normal*, 83–106.

38 Duval, "La fréquentation," 158.

39 AUM, Fonds ACC, P16/R68, Fréquentations entre adolescents, "Précisions sur un essai psychologique relatif aux fréquentations entre adolescents," par l'abbé Roch Duval, professeur à l'Université Laval.

40 A number of recent historical works have explored the emergence of these more benign attitudes towards youthful dress, music, and sexuality. See, for example, Uta G. Poiger, *Jazz, Rock, and Rebels: Cold War Politics and American Culture in a Divided Germany* (Berkeley: University of California Press, 2000); Susan Weiner, *Enfants Terribles: Youth & Femininity in the Mass Media in France, 1945–1968* (Baltimore and London: Johns Hopkins University Press, 2001), 140; Esther Faye, "Growing Up 'Australian' in the 1950s: The Dream of Social Science," *Australian Historical Studies* 111 (1998): 357.

41 For the argument that the dating culture and "going steady" represented a simple, nostalgic search for security through the emotions and consumption, see Elaine Tyler May, *Homeward Bound: American Families in the Cold War Era* (New York: Basic Books, 1988), 101; this argument is echoed in the Canadian context by Owram, *Born at the Right Time*. Another facet of this argument maintains that the the positive revaluation of teen heterosexuality by psychologists, medical experts, and educators constituted evidence of post-war conservatism. See Adams, *The Trouble With Normal*; Mona Gleason, *Normalizing the Ideal: Psychology, Schooling, and the Family in Postwar Canada* (Toronto: University of Toronto Press, 1999). In a more revisionist assessment drawn from comparisons between the United States and a number of European societies,

Arthur Marwick has identified the distinguishing marks of the 1960s "cultural revolution" as a challenge to established authorities and hierarchies in human relations, a climate of "permissiveness," and an outburst of new individualism and youth subcultures having an increasing influence on the rest of society. Significantly, Marwick locates a number of these cultural tendencies in social changes occurring in the later 1950s. See Marwick, *The Sixties*, 18–19.

42 Guy Rocher, "Ambiguités et fonctions de l'initiative privée dans le bien-être social," ss 9, no. 2 (July–Aug. 1960): 69.

43 Philippe Garigue, "La famille canadienne-française dans la société contemporaine," text of a speech delivered to the Congress of Caritas-Canada, 24 May 1957, in Garigue, *Famille et humanisme*, 51.

44 Ibid., 59. For statements of the opposing viewpoint, which emphasized the discontinuities attendant on modernization, see Georges-Henri Lévesque, o.p., "Les nouvelles tâches du Service social en face des problèmes que l'industrialisation pose à l'institution et à la vie familiales," RD (Nov. 1956): 223–38; Fortin, "Socio-Cultural Changes in an Agricultural Parish," in Marcel Rioux and Yves Martin, eds, *French-Canadian Society*, vol. 1 (Toronto: McClelland and Stewart, 1964), 94, 104.

45 Philippe Garigue, *La vie familiale des Canadiens-français* (Montreal: Les Presses de l'Université de Montréal, 1962), 25, 31, 34–5, 93. For a similar perspective advanced by a social investigator from the rival École de Service Social at Universite Laval, see Simone Paré, "Participation d'une population de banlieue à ses groupes de famille, de parenté, d'amitié et de voisinage," ss 9, no. 1 (Jan. 1960): 36–7. Paré did observe, however, some generational particularities, noting that young people tended to have more interaction with friends in their peer group than with members of their extended families.

46 Garigue, *Vie familiale*, 26–7.

47 For this definition, see Clinton Archibald, *Un Québec corporatiste?: corporatisme et néo-corporatisme: du passage d'une idéologie corporatiste sociale à une idéologie corporatiste politique, le Québec de 1930 à nos jours* (Hull: Éditions Asticou, 1983), 45.

48 "Encore un appel pour une association familiale," *Rel* (Apr. 1955): 99.

49 For this new trajectory which saw even a socially-conservative regime like that of Maurice Duplessis forced to begin articulating a new relationship between public authorities and private welfare initiatives, see Yves Vaillancourt, *L'évolution des politiques sociales au Québec, 1940–1960* (Montreal: Les Presses de l'Université de Montréal, 1988).

50 Stanislas de Lestapis, s.j., "Pour une association des familles et une mystique chrétienne," *Rel* (Mar. 1957): 59. See also AUM, Fonds ACC, P16/05.81, "Fédération des Unions de Familles," *Les Unions de familles: ce qu'elles sont, ce qu'elles font*, ca 1962. For the role of the École des parents, see Marie-Paule

Malouin, *Le Mouvement familial au Quebec: les débuts: 1937–1965* (Montreal: Boréal, 1998), 95–8.

51 R.P. Richard Arès, s.j., "Pour une plus grande reconnaissance des droits de la famille," *Mission et Droits de la Famille*, Semaine Sociale, 1959 (Montreal: Secrétariat des Semaines Sociales), 16. See also ANQM, Fonds SPM, P116, art. 16, "Dignité infrangible de la famille chrétienne," 1958.

52 Arès, "Pour une plus grande reconnaissance," 20–2.

53 Ibid., 26.

54 Dion, "La famille a droit à la sécurité économique, fondée principalement sur le travail de ses membres, principalement du père de famille" in *Mission et Droits de la Famille*, 116.

55 Arès, "Pour une plus grande reconnaissance," 23.

56 Ibid., 22–6.

57 Claude Morin, "La famille a droit à la justice distributive et à la securité sociale," in *Mission et Droits de la Famille*, 167.

58 Claude Morin, "Le respect des charges de famille dans la taxation et la sécurite sociale au Canada," SS 9, no. 2 (July–Aug. 1960): 112.

59 Ibid., 170.

60 Morin, "Le respect des charges de famille," 112. See also Morin, "La famille a droit," 169–70.

61 AUM, Fonds ACC, P16/R.64, "Discours de Me Jean Lesage au déjeuner de clôture," *Vers l'édification de la famille de demain*, 1951.

62 Gouvernement du Quebec, *Rapport du Comité d'études sur l'assistance publique* (June 1963), 3. Boucher was president of the Société Nationale de Fiducie; Marcel Bélanger, a chartered accountant, was a professor in the Université Laval faculty of business; and Claude Morin, also a Laval professor, was already acting as an informal advisor to government. See also "Discours de Me Jean Lesage au déjeuner de clôture," for his conviction that the expansion of social security must not result in the disappearance of private agencies.

63 Ibid., 27.

64 Ibid., 97, 108.

65 Ibid., 64.

66 Ibid., 98.

67 Ibid., 126–7, 157, 159–61.

68 Ibid., 164.

69 AUM, Fonds ACC, Ministère de la Famille et du Bien-être Social, "Exposé de M. Émilien Lafrance, sur le Bill 25, créant un Ministère de la Famille." Lafrance also stated at the outset that the creation of the ministry had been asked for by the École sociale populaire, the Jesuit *Relations*, and the nationalist Société de Saint-Jean-Baptiste.

70 Ibid.

71 The argument here diverges from that advanced in *Aux origines sociales de l'État-providence* (Montreal: Les Presses de l'Université de Montréal, 1998), where Dominique Marshall argues that the Quebec climate of the early 1960s favoured centralization, technocratic management, and expansion of social services (255–91). In the estimation of Claude Morin, technocratic expertise largely identified with the maintenance of a strong private social welfare sector, and not with state control.

72 For the prevalence of neo-corporatist thinking in the Lesage government, see Archibald, *Un Québec corporatiste?* 181, 206. For the older current of liberalism represented by Maurice Duplessis, in which there was a rigid separation between the state machinery and bodies such as trade unions, business associations, the Church, and welfare agencies, see Bourque, Duchastel, Beauchemin, *La société libérale duplessiste* (Montreal: Boréal, 1994).

73 "Yves Thériault au Club Richelieu," LD, 29 Jan. 1965.

74 For links between the "counter-culture," the new insistence upon individual freedom, and 1960s youth, see Cavallo, *A Fiction of the Past*; Sabine Von Dirke, *'All Power to the Imagination!': The West German Counterculture from the Student Movement to the Greens* (Lincoln and London: University of Nebraska Press, 1997); Owram, *Born at the Right Time*, 159–84; and for Quebec, François Ricard, *La Génération lyrique: Essai sur la vie et l'oeuvre des premiers-nés du baby-boom* (Montreal: Boréal Compact, 1994). More recently, revisionist treatments of the 1960s have begun to question the extent to which the new interpretations of freedom can be exclusively associated with youth. Marwick argues in *The Sixties*, for example, that much of the new insistence on personal freedom that underlay the "counter-culture" was in fact shared by members of the older generation (694). For a revisionist Canadian treatment of the origins of the "sexual revolution" in the more "traditional" climate of the United Church, see Christie, "Sacred Sex," in Nancy Christie, ed., *Households of Faith: Family, Gender, and Community in Canada, 1760–1969* (Montreal and Kingston: McGill-Queen's University Press, 2002).

75 ANQM, Fonds Judith Jasmin, P143, Reel 853, "Pour un nationalisme positif." See also AUM, Fonds Paul-Larocque, P52/A38, Jean Saint-Louis, ptre, Aurèle David, "Mémoire: École et Loisir," ca 1962.

76 Marwick, *The Sixties*, 34.

77 Le Directeur, "Qu'est la jeunesse étudiante de 1964?" C&F 21, nos 2–3 (Apr.–June 1964): 54–5. See also Gilles Casson, "Le pluralisme en éducation religieuse et la perspective pastorale," *Pros* 3, no. 1 (Feb. 1967): 28–32.

78 AUM, P16/D1, 4.16, "Monde des Jeunes et Monde des Adultes," thème pour le programme d'action, 1963–64, 18 Aug. 1962.

79 Abbé Gerard Marier, séminaire de Nicolet, "Les jeunes sont-ils à l'avant-garde du progrès de notre société," *Pros* 3, no. 1 (Feb. 1967): 8–9; Florian Lariviere, "L'autorité et le changement social dans la relation jeunes-adultes," *Pros* 3, no. 4 (Sept. 1967): 260–6; Yves Thériault, "Un croulant fait le procès des

jeunes," VE 30, no. 11 (Mar. 1964); Jules-Bernard Gingras, "Conflit des générations," AN 56, no. 2 (Oct. 1966): 135–42.

80 AUM, Fonds ACC, P16/05.37, Congrès des Mouvements de Jeunesse du Québec, "Charte du Congrès des Mouvements de Jeunesse du Québec," Sept. 1965, "Déclaration des Droits et Devoirs du Jeune Québécois."

81 Committee on Youth, *It's Your Turn*. A Report to the Secretary of State by the Committee on Youth. (Ottawa: Information Canada, 1971), 3.

82 Réal Pelletier, "Le sociologue Rioux explore de nouvelles avenues marxistes: Demain, la société verra-t-elle plus de grèves de 'jeunes' que de grèves de 'prolétaires' ...?" LD, 12 Mar. 1965; Claude Beauregard, "Jeunes et adultes: affrontements occasionnels ou lutte à finir?" *Pros* 1, no. 3 (June 1965): 3–4. Beauregard's article was likewise based on an interview with Marcel Rioux. See also Joffre Dumazédier, "L'action étudiante révolutionnaire," LD, 5 Sept. 1968; Jean-Marc Léger, "Une voix pour les étudiants, une présence pour les étudiants," LD, 19 May 1965; "Des étudiants decrètent un état d'urgence au secondaire," VE 30, no. 9 (Feb. 1964).

83 Léon Dion, "L'anarchie est-elle inévitable?" CC (Jan.–Feb. 1970): 56. Similar views were articulated a number of years earlier by Georges-Henri Lévesque, "L'orientation culturelle des jeunes," RD (Jan. 1961): 19–24, talk given at the Maison Montmorency, to the wives of delegates of the A.P.I., 17 November," .

84 Anselme d'Haese, "L'adolescence, produit moderne," C&F 23, no. 3 (June 1966): 132. See also AUM, Fonds ACC, P16/D1, 4.19, "Les jeunes dans la société: mouvements de jeunes 1964–65," Jean-Claude Leclerc, "L'intégration des étudiants dans la société"; ibid., P16/D1, 4.16, "Programme d'Action, 1963–64," "Monde des Jeunes et Monde des Adultes."

85 AUM, Fonds ACC, P16/13.13, "Association d'Éducation du Quebec," "Semaine de l'Éducation, 1961," Corporation des Instituteurs Catholiques, "Le conflit des générations," Mar. 1961. See also Jacques Pelletier, "La politique: s'en occuper dès maintenant," VE 28, no. 7 (Dec. 1961); Jacques Laliberté, "'La pire race des crasseux ...'" VE 28, no. 8 (Jan. 1962).

86 Gilles Desmarais, "The Younger Generation," in Jean Morrison, ed., *The Canadian Conference on the Family*, Proceedings of sessions held at Rideau Hall and at Carleton University, Ottawa, June 7–10, 1964 (Ottawa: Vanier Institute of the Family, 1965), 109.

87 Jean Brassard, "Le conflit des générations," C&F 24, no. 2 (Apr. 1967): 46; Gingras, "Conflit des génerations." See also Garigue, "Une politique familiale pour le Quebec," in *Famille et humanisme*, 269.

88 S. Saint-Andre-de-Jésus, c.n.d., and S. Sainte-Lucie-de-Jésus, c.n.d., "Monde cassé," C&F 21, nos 2–3 (Apr.–June 1964): 69. One such survey, undertaken by the sociologists Marcel Rioux and Robert Sévigny, argued that, whatever continuity of values there might be, 86 per cent of eighteen- to twenty-one-year-olds believed that on the whole, they differed from their parents' generation. See Marcel Rioux and Robert Sévigny, *Les nouveaux citoyens: enquête*

sociologique sur les jeunes du Quebec (Montreal: Radio-Canada, 1965), 35. For an analysis of the role of opinion surveys in constructing "youth" as a social and cultural category, see Weiner, *Enfants Terribles*, 170–96.

89 Léon Girard, "The Younger Generation," in Morrison, *Canadian Conference on the Family*, 109.

90 René and Claudine Vallerand, "Isocrate, les vingt, les quarante ans et la libération," LD, 27 July 1963.

91 Ibid, "Isocrate," 27 July 1963.

92 Ibid., "Isocrate, les vingt ... – II," LD, 29 July 1963.; See also Brassard, "Le conflit des générations"; Beauregard, "Jeunes et adultes."

93 Gérard Pelletier, "Le Québec et les québécoises," *Chat* 5, no. 11 (Nov. 1965): 81.

94 Committee on Youth, *It's Your Turn*, 77.

95 LeBlanc, "Le Cardinal Léger."

96 For the most sustained contemporary interpretation of Quebec's sexual revolution as being ineluctably identified with the energies of young people, and underpinning a wider spectrum of desired political and educational changes, see the sociological essay by Jacques Lazure, *La jeunesse du Québec en révolution: essai d'interprétation* (Montreal: Les Presses de l'Université du Québec, 1970). Lazure, a former Oblate priest and a professor of sociology, had been active earlier in the decade as a prominent Catholic commentator on the changes taking place in the nature of Quebec's youth movements. See AUM, Fonds ACC, Jeunesse Ouvrière Catholique, P16/G5, 4.22, "Conférence: le rôle représentatif de la J.O.C.," par R.P. Jacques Lazure, o.m.i., professeur en sociologie, Université d'Ottawa; Jacques Lazure, o.m.i., "L'Action catholique dans l'arène," *Maint* (July-Aug. 1965): 248–9. Standard Canadian historical treatments such as Owram, *Born at the Right Time*, 248–79, see the "sexual revolution" as a function of the 1960s, linked largely with the ready availability of the birth control pill, and dismiss the 1940s and 1950s as a time of "contradictory" moral messages. For two works that accent the changes in sexual attitudes that occurred among the "older generation" prior to the 1960s, see Marwick, *The Sixties*; Christie, "Sacred Sex."

97 Here, I follow the direction of the chronology we have already outlined in the introduction to *Cultures of Citizenship in Postwar Canada*, and in Gauvreau, "The Protracted Birth of the Canadian 'Teenager.'" Unlike the United States, where mass consumer prosperity characterized the entire post-war period, Canada did not experience this type of prosperity until the years following 1955.

98 For explorations of these concerns in West Germany and France in the late 1950s, see Poiger, *Jazz, Rock, Rebels*, and Weiner, *Enfants Terribles*, 66, 103, 152–3.

99 AUM, Fonds ACC, P16/P6.24, Université Laval, Commission du Programme de la Faculté des Arts, 1958, Mgr. Guillaume Miville-Dechêne, P.D., curé de St.-Francois-d'Assise de Québec, "Formation religieuse de la jeune fille," 8 May 1958.

100 AUM, Fonds ACC, P16/B6, 3.1, Hozaël Aganier, Hozaël Aganier, "Mémoire preparé à l'intention de la Commission des programmes de la Faculté des Arts de l'Université Laval," Apr. 1958.

101 "Famille contemporaine et problèmes etudiants," 311.

102 In examining the Catholic Action membership figures for the 1950s, Jean Hamelin and Nicole Gagnon have determined, by averaging all the movements, that 75 per cent of the effectives were women. See Jean Hamelin and Nicole Gagnon, *Histoire du catholicisme québécois, le XXe siècle*, vol. 2 (Montreal: Boréal, Express, 1984), 127.

103 Miville-Dechêne, "Formation Religieuse de la Jeune Fille"; AUM, Fonds ACC, P16/D1, 4.15, Vie affective, programme d'action 1962–63, André Thibault, "Rapport d'une enquête exploratoire sur les relations entre jeunes gens et jeunes filles."

104 Despite its revision of a number of other facets of 1960s culture, Marwick's *The Sixties* follows this conventional pattern in describing a shift in public attitudes regarding the liberation of women, identifying it with a "later" period of the decade, the years after 1969 (679–724). According to Owram, *Born at the Right Time*, "'women's liberation' came late to the 1960s, and most of the impact of the changing attitudes towards women belongs to the 1970s or after" (273).

105 "Famille contemporaine et problèmes etudiants," 341–2.

106 Garigue, *Vie familiale*, 78–9, 91. See also Centre Catholique des Intellectuels Français, *Le Canada français aujourd'hui et demain*, Recherches et débats, no. 34 (Paris: Arthème Fayard, 1961), 95.

107 Papal prohibitions on coeducation at the level of secondary schooling had been stated as recently as 1929 in Pius XI's encyclical *Divini illius magistri*.

108 Jean Genest, "La coéducation et le rapport Parent," C&F 22, no. 2 (Apr. 1965): 74.

109 For this critique, see André Lussier, "La sexualité prend le large," *Maint* (July–Aug. 1966): 221. See also "Vie affective."

110 AUM, Fonds ACC, P16/G5, 4.20, Session Intensive, juin 1962, "Programme social, 62–63, La verité sur l'amour."

111 "Vie affective."

112 AUM, Fonds Paul-Larocque, P16/A10, "Mémoire de J.E. Havel."

113 Québec, Gouvernement du Québec, *Report of the Royal Commission of Inquiry on Education*, vol. 2. *Pedagogical Structures of the Educational System*, 1965, 137–8; Jean Gaudreau, "L'école mixte: peut-on faire confiance à la nature?" *Maint* (Sept. 1966): 274–5; Solange Chalvin, "L'école mixte ou le coenseignement," LD, 16 May 1965.

114 ANQM, Fonds SPM, P116 art. 24, Dr Camille Laurin, "Les Services que le S.P.M. rend à la société," Conférence, Banquet annuel, 4 June 1966.

115 Ibid.

116 Camille Laurin, "La liberté sexuelle," in Camille Laurin, *Ma traversée du Québec* (Montreal: Les Éditions du Jour, 1970), 65.

117 Laurin, "Les Services."

118 Alice Parizeau, "La Famille Québécoise est-elle depassée par les problèmes de l'enfant moderne?" *Chat* 7, no. 1 (Jan. 1966): 21.

119 Ibid., 21.

120 Significantly, Laurin's propaganda work on behalf of the Parti Québécois, a book of essays entitled *Ma traversée du Québec*, contained an important essay on the nature of authority in a newly democratic society.

121 David Seljak, "Resisting the 'No Man's Land' of Private Religion: The Catholic Church and Public Politics in Quebec," in David Lyon and Marguerite Van Die, eds, *Rethinking Church, State, and Modernity: Canada Between Europe and America* (Toronto: University of Toronto Press, 2000), observes that "Catholics supporting an independent Quebec were in a strict minority." Since 1976, opinion polls have consistently indicated that "churchgoing Catholics have been the least likely among all francophone Quebeckers to support independence, sovereignty association, or the PQ as a political party" (147n16).

122 René Raymond, "La famille américaine," SS 12, no. 1 (Jan.–Sept. 1963): 148–54.

123 "Ce que pensent ... ceux qui pensent: Philippe Garigue: La famille, chez les Canadiens francais, se désintègre," AQ 1, no. 6 (Sept. 1965): 49. See also André Daigneault, "Dégradation ou renaissance?" AQ 2, no. 3 (May 1966): 17.

124 ANQM, Fonds JEC, P65/S6, SS2, SSS1, D2/1, "Champ d'Action de la J.E.C. Chez les Jeunes," ca 1963.

125 Georges P. Vanier, Governor-General of Canada, "The Crisis in the Family: Inaugural Address delivered Sunday afternoon, June 7, 1964 at Rideau Hall," in Morrison, *Canadian Conference on the Family*, 4–5.

126 AUM, Fonds ACC, P16/05.158, "Institut Vanier de la Famille," n.d. See also ibid., *P16/H3*, 18.86, Service de Préparation au Mariage, "Enquête sociologique sur les mariages des adolescents." For a longer discussion of this tendency among psychologists, educators, and sociologists in the 1960s, see Michael Gauvreau, "The Family as Pathology: Psychology, Social Science and History Construct the Nuclear Family, 1945–1980," in Nancy Christie and Michael Gauvreau, eds, *Mapping the Margins: Families and Social Discipline in Canada, 1700–1970* (Montreal and Kingston: McGill-Queen's University Press, 2004).

127 Committee on Youth, *It's Your Turn*, 66.

128 AUM, Fonds Commission d'étude sur les laïcs et l'Église, (henceforth cited as Commission Dumont), P21/G9.14, "Mémoire d'un groupe d'étudiants du secondaire V."

129 MCMUL, Royal Commission on the Status of Women, Briefs. Mémoire #120,

"Conseil étudiant des Filles, Collège Ste-Anne-de-la-Pocatière," Mar. 1968. For the negative valuation of marriage among American youth in the late 1960s and early 1970s, see Modell, *Into One's Own*, 266.

130 Royal Commission on the Status of Women, Briefs. "Mémoire #120" For similar views among Quebec young people aged eighteen to twenty-four, see Rioux and Sévigny, *Les nouveaux citoyens*, 32–3.

131 Fernande Saint-Martin, "Le mariage civil et le bonheur des époux," *Chat* 7, no. 3 (Mar. 1966): 1. See also Saint-Martin, "Qu'est-ce qu'un peuple heureux?" *Chat* 2, no. 7 (July 1961): 1.

132 Parizeau, "La Famille Québécoise," 20.

133 ANQM, Fonds SPM, P116, art. 19, Raymonde Charron, "Le Service de Préparation au Mariage: Une institution nationale," ca 1962; ibid., Renaude Lapointe, "Les cours de préparation au mariage déglamorisent-ils l'amour," LP, 19 Jan. 1963.

134 Ibid., Renaude Lapointe, "Les Cours de Préparation au Mariage" reported in 1963 that the Montreal SPM engaged the energies of 700 to 800 volunteers, and reached about 8,000 fiancés per year, about 45 per cent of Catholic couples marrying in the diocese. Raymonde Charron reported in "Le Service de Préparation au Mariage" that, of this percentage, it was reckoned that the movement reached 53 per cent of upper middle-class couples, 47 per cent of middle class couples, and 38.6 per cent of the working-classes. The clientele tended to be relatively well-educated, 60 per cent of participants having at least Grade 10 education, with 19 per cent of women and 28 per cent of men having more than thirteen years of schooling.

135 AUM, Fonds ACC, P16/H18.83, Service de Préparation au Mariage, Madeleine Trottier and André Normandeau, "Le Mariage des Adolescents à Montréal: Étude Sociologique sur leurs chances d'Ajustement Marital," Mar. 1965.

136 Hyacinthe-Marie Robillard, o.p., "Sommes-nous jansénistes?" RD (July–Aug. 1957): 6–10.

137 Joseph d'Anjou, s.j., "Nos adolescentes ouvrières," *Rel* (July 1959): 177–80; AUM, Fonds ACC, P16/D1, 4.14B, Commission du programme d'action, "Vie sentimentale des jeunes," 23 Oct. 1961.

138 AUM, Fonds ACC, P16/D1, 4.15B, Enquête, vie sentimentale, Résultats d'un sondage fait à Chicoutimi en décembre 1961, "L'Amour avant et après le mariage." See also ibid., P16/H18.83, "Les Cours du Service de Préparation au Mariage sont-ils adaptés aux Fiancés," n.d.

139 AUM, Fonds ACC, P16/D5,3.1, Commission de la Préparation au Mariage, "compte-rendu de la 5e réunion," 19 Mar. 1964. See also ibid., P16/D1, 4.15B, "Sondage, Chicoutimi," 1961.

140 Philippe Garigue, "Permanence and Change in Ideas Regarding the Family," principal address delivered 7 June, 1964, Carleton University, in

Morrison, *Canadian Conference on the Family*, 39. For Garigue's views on the
continued reality of male authority in the modern nuclear family, see *Vie
familiale*, 31, 34–5, 93.

141 Michelle Lasnier, "Trop parfaites, nos mémères sont-elles Esclaves ou
Tyrans?" *Chat* 3, no. 1 (Jan. 1962): 26–7, 54–5. See also books by Dr Lionel
Gendron, *Qu'est-ce qu'une femme?* , vol. 2, *Inquiétudes de la femme moderne*
(Montreal: Les Éditions de l'Homme, 1961); Jean LeMoyne, *Convergences:
essais* (Montreal: Éditions HMH, 1961); Théo Chentrier, *Psychologie de la vie
quotidienne; ou, L'art de vivre avec soi-même et avec les autres* (Montreal: Éditions
du Jour, 1961).

142 AUM, Fonds ACC, P16/D1, 4.15, Vie Affective, André Thibault, "La Vie Sentimentale des Jeunes dans une Grande Ville: Images et Approches," 1962–63.
See also Solange Chalvin, "La Sexualité expliquée aux enfants," LD, 9 Apr.
1965.

143 Lasnier, "Trop parfaites," 54.

144 Ibid., 54–5.

145 Garigue, "Permanence and Change," 26. See also NAC, Canadian Conference on the Family, "Round Table 12a, Roles and Relationships"; ibid., vol.
9, file 2, "The Fragmented Family."

146 Garigue, "Permanence and Change," 47; Jean Genest, "Jeunes gens et
jeunes filles," C&F 21, no. 1 (Feb. 1964): 27.

147 Rocher, "La famille dans la ville moderne," SS 4, no. 1 (spring 1954): 83;
Fortin, "Socio-Cultural Changes in an Agricultural Parish," 94; AUM,
P16/D5, 1.10, "S.P.M. de Montreal," n.d. For comparable worries among
Anglo-Canadian post-war social observers, see Gauvreau, "The Family as
Pathology."

148 Fernande Saint-Martin, "Un mythe à détruire: aucun matriarcat au
Québec," *Chat* 5, no. 12 (Dec. 1964): 1.

149 Solange Chalvin, "Création a Montréal d'un Institut de sexologie et
d'études familiaux," LD, 2 Apr. 1966.

150 Fernande Saint-Martin, "La paternité est-elle un mythe?" *Chat* 3, no. 2 (Feb.
1962): 1; Françoise Cholette-Perusse, "Le père – au foyer!" *Maint* (Mar.
1967): 99–100; Lasnier, "Trop parfaites," 55; Solange Chalvin, "Le couple
moderne en proie au mythe de l'érotisme, vu par Violette Morin," LD, 8 July
1967; ibid, "Le mythe de la Femme tue les femmes, déclare Andrée Michel,
sociologue français," LD, 12 Oct. 1964.

151 It should be noted in this context that Catholic Action's marriage preparation movement was not aimed at adolescents in secondary education institutions, but at engaged couples who had already signified their intent to
marry. It was also a purely voluntary format, and thus could not be considered to breach the 1929 papal prohibition against mass sex education.

152 Fernande Saint-Martin, "Nos moeurs familiales," *Chat* 2, no. 5 (May 1961): 1.

153 Lussier, "La sexualité prend le large," 222. See also, Guy Brouillette,

"L'Amour, mythe d'un autre âge?" *Maint* (July–Aug. 1966): 223–6; "La 'révolution sexuelle' chez les étudiants américains," LD, 15 Aug. 1968.

154 Chalvin, "Création à Montreal d'un Institut de sexologie," observed that this was not a drastic innovation, pointing to the fact that even the Catholic universities of Lille and Louvain had already established such institutes. Chalvin noted, however, the prominent participation of clergy alongside doctors and social workers.

155 Jean Genest, "L'éducation de la sexualité," C&F 24, no. 4 (Oct. 1967): 182. See also Genest, "Quelle éducation sexuelle," C&F 24, no. 5 (Dec. 1967): 223–30.

156 Gaston Lapointe, "À propos d'éducation sexuelle," LD, 17 Jan. 1969.

157 AUM, Fonds Commission Dumont, Diocese de Chicoutimi, P21/G19.14, "Office du Secondaire." See also ibid., Diocèse de Quebec, P21/G1.36, Constance Fortier, Gisèle Royal, Claire Marchand, Ernestine Lepage, "Rapport présenté ... par le membres de l'Équipe de réflexion chrétienne du Centre Pilote Laval," 18 June 1970.

158 AUM, Fonds Commission Dumont, P21/G5.8, Diocèse de Nicolet, "Rapport d'un Comité d'Études."

159 MCMUL, Royal Commission on the Status of Women, Briefs, Mémoire #17, "Groupe de Femmes de Roberval," 1968. See also ANQQ, P428, Fonds Action Sociale Catholique, *Action Catholique* (Journal), "La parole est aux lecteurs," Lucien Caron, Ste.-Foy, "Réflexions sur 'Un Sens au Voyage'," Catéchèse pour Secondaire II – 9e année"; ibid., Denis Duval, ptre, "Le catéchisme oui, la catéchèse non"; ibid., Abbé Anselme Longpré, *L'Action*, 1968; AUM, Fonds Commission Dumont, Diocèse de Quebec, P21/G1.37, "Mémoire de la Jeunesse Étudiante Catholique, Diocèse de Québec, mai 1970."

160 ANQQ, P428S2, *Action Catholique* (journal), J. Alphonse Beaulieu, ptre, Mont-Joli, lettre, *L'Action*, n.d., ca 1971.

161 Hélène Pelletier-Baillargeon, "Le droit des parents," *Maint* (Sept. 1966).

162 For the images evoked by the transistor radio in the early 1960s in France, see Weiner, *Enfants Terribles*, 144. *Maintenant* was launched by the Dominican Order in 1962, as part of a commitment to challenging the old order. By 1965, the journal claimed 11,000 subscribers and a readership of 50,000. For further information on this periodical, see David Seljak, "Catholicism's 'Quiet Revolution': *Maintenant* and the New Public Catholicism in Quebec after 1960," in Marguerite Van Die, eds, *Religion and Public Life in Canada: Historical and Comparative Perspectives* (Toronto: University of Toronto Press, 2000), 257–74.

163 "Les étudiantes de 16 a 20 ans devant la Messe," CAC 175 (May 1955): 341–2. See also "La Messe et les Étudiants," CAC 175 (May 1955): 330–2; Guy Bélanger, ptre, "Des étudiants d'Écoles Supérieures devant la Messe," CAC 175 (May 1955): 351–5.

164 See AUM, Fonds ACC, P16/E3,6, 4.3, Comité des Jeunesses Féminines Catholiques du Canada, Congrès International – Rome 1961, "La femme canadienne-française, instrument d'unité." See also AUM, Fonds Paul-Larocque, P52/F1, Louis O'Neill, "La formation religieuse des étudiants au niveau collégial et universitaire": "spiritual schizophrenia"; ibid., P52/K19.9, "Mémoire présenté à la Commission du programme de la Faculté des Arts de Laval par M. le chanoine Pichette, aumônier de la C.T.C.C.," 1 May 1958, "Communication de quelques aumôniers de mouvements sociaux"; AUM, Fonds ACC, Comité Des Jeunesses Féminines Catholiques du Canada, P16/E2, 5.7, "La Jeune Fille, Membre Vivante de la Communauté," enquête préparatoire au Seminaire International de Buenos Aires, 24 au 31 juillet, 1962; ibid, P16/D1,4.19, "Les jeunes dans la société: mouvements de jeunes, 1964–65," Jean-Claude Leclerc, "L'intégration des étudiants dans la société."

165 AUM, Fonds ACC, P16/D1, 4.10, Fr. Albini Girouard, "La Vie de l'Esprit Chez le Jeune Travailleur," Journées d'étude pour les dirigeants nationaux des mouvements specialisés, 28 fév.–1er mars 1959.

166 Hozaël Aganier, "Mémoire préparé à l'intention de la Commission des programmes de la Faculté des Arts de l'Université Laval."

167 Marcel Marcotte, s.j., "L'évolution religieuse des adolescents," C&F 14, no. 6 (Oct. 1957): 153.

168 Paul Francoeur, "De la foi a l'incroyance," VE 28, no. 12 (Mar. 1962); Jean-Charles Falardeau, *Roots and Values in Canadian Lives*, 18; Paul Francoeur, "Nous étouffons sous le poids des choses inexprimées," VE 28, no. 6 (Dec. 1961).

169 AUM, Fonds ACC, P16/D1.4.16, André Thibault, "Rapport d'une Enquête Exploratoire," Programme d'action, 1963–64.

170 Emmanuel Rioux, "L'engagement chrétien des jeunes d'aujourd'hui," C&F 18, no. 5 (Dec. 1961): 224.

171 Marcel Marcotte, s.j., "La formation religieuse des adolescents," C&F 14, no. 5 (Dec. 1957): 193. See also Guy Bélanger, ptre, "Une marche vers l'Aventure: la Bible chez nos élèves," VE 28, no. 6 (Dec. 1961); Luce Francoeur, "Enseigner la religion – courrier de l'étudiante," VE 27, no. 8 (Jan. 1961).

172 For an analysis of Quebec Catholic religious culture that presents the parish community and the family as mutually reinforcing social structures, see Ollivier Hubert, "Ritual Performance and Parish Sociability," in Christie, *Households of Faith*.

173 Gilles Cusson, s.j., "Éducation religieuse de l'adolescent," *C&F* 16, no. 2 (Apr. 1959): 51–6; Gilles-M. Bélanger, o.p., "Redécouverte de la catéchèse," CC 1, no. 5 (Sept.–Oct. 1962): 283–5; Paul Doucet, o.p., "Feu de paille ou revolution?" *Maint* (July–Aug. 1966): 217–20; Paul-Marcel Lemaire, "La confession: un problème aigu de notre pastorale," CC 19 (Jan.–Feb. 1965): 5–15; Henri Dallaire, o.p., "Les jeunes: faillite ou carrefour?" *Maint* (Sept. 1964): 274.

174 Pierre Saby, c.s.v. and Roland Robert, c.s.v., "La situation religieuse de nos étudiants," c&f 21, nos 2–3 (Apr.–June 1964): 137–141.

175 Guy Paiement, "Ou en est la liturgie dans les collèges," c&f 19, no. 5 (Dec. 1962): 190–1.

176 Pierre J.-G. Vennat, "Un certain silence rompu," cl 41 (Nov. 1961): 25. See also Gérard Pelletier, "Un certain silence," cl 40 (Oct. 1961): 3–4; aum, Fonds acc, Comité des Jeunesses Féminines Catholiques du Canada, "La Jeune Fille": "personal effort."

177 "Nos colloques et leurs resultats," *Maint* (May 1964): 159. This particular article reported on a colloquium on the subject of young people and religious faith held 20 January 1964. It included an appreciation by eight university students, some of whom were to have distinguished careers in the Quebec university system: George Marchand (physics), Louis Gueret (Medicine), Francois Caron (history), Marcel Bellavance (history), Lise Pageot (pedagogy), Vincent Ross (sociology), Denise Lemieux (sociology), Gilles Pineault (physics). For the concept of the "lyrical generation" and an assessment of its religious values, see Ricard, *La génération lyrique*, 75–8.

178 Pierre Audet and Régine Binette, "La religion qu'est-ce que c'est pour Nous? Qu'est-ce que nous attendons d'un professeur de religion?" ve 31, no. 2 (Oct. 1964).

179 Henri-M. Bradet, o.p., "Une foi pour un temps de combat," cc 2, no. 11 (Sept.–Oct. 1963): 384.

180 aum, Fonds acc, Thibault, Rapport d'une enquête exploratoire, "Relations entre jeunes et adultes." See also Jean-Paul Labelle, "Y-a-t-il conflit entre les générations?" c&f 19, no. 4 (Oct. 1962): 166–72.

181 Paul-Marcel Lemaire, o.p., "Crise religieuse et jeunesse," *Maint* (Dec. 1963): 374; Magdelaine Verdon, "Haro sur les 'croulants'!" *Maint* (June 1963): 199–200.

182 "Vont-ils perdre la foi," Pierre Marois"... à Montreal," *Maint* (May 1964): 154. See also ibid., Claude Beauchamp, "...à Laval," *Maint* (May 1964): 153; Fr. Alphonse Caron, "...Collégiens?" *Maint* (May 1964): 157; Jocelyne Pelchat, Achille Tassé, "Nouveaux carabins," *Maint* (Nov. 1963): 343–4; André Major, "Jeunesse québécoise et morale de l'échec," *Maint* (Dec. 1962): 404–5.

183 Louis Racine, o.p., "La nouvelle catéchèse aura-t-elle son 5 juin?" *Maint* (Sept. 1966): 269.

184 aum, Fonds acc, p16/d6, 8.4, "La pastorale en éducation."

185 "Selon le Centre de Catéchèse de Montréal: les 'infiltrations' religieuses dans les matières profanes sont nefastes à la foi," ld, 27 Nov. 1965.

186 Jean-Paul Labelle, s.j., "Le nouveau catéchisme," *Rel* (Sept. 1964). Marcel Marcotte, s.j., "Le Rapport Parent et la formation religieuse – iv," *Rel* (June 1965): 175.

187 "La pastorale en éducation." For a brief overview of the chronology and

official intent of the new catechism texts, see Hamelin and Gagnon, *Histoire du catholicisme québécois, le XXe siecle*, vol. 2, 302–5.

188 L.-M. Regis, o.p., "Dialogue avec la vérité," *Maint* (Jan. 1962): 5–7.

189 Marthe Henripin, "Qui sont-ils?" CC (July–Aug. 1966): 274.

190 Jacques Castonguay, "École secondaire, foi religieuse," *Maint* (Mar. 1966): 99; "La pastorale en éducation"; Aurore Bonneau, "La situation présente de l'enseignement religieux," CC 15 (May-June 1964): 174.

191 Paul-Marcel Lemaire, o.p., "La liberté religieuse à l'école," *Maint* (Jan. 1966): 28.

192 ANQM, Fonds MLLF, P295, 9/1/29, Correspondance generale, Mme. G. Sylvestre, Montréal, à Jacques Mackay, ca 1964.

193 Ginette Deschênes, "Une religion de crucifix," *Maint* (June 1965): 200.

194 Pierre Fortin, "L'Étudiant et la religion," *Maint* (Feb. 1966): 67; Clément Moisan, "Foi des adultes, foi des enfants," *Maint* (Mar. 1965): 108. See also Henripin, "Qui sont-ils?" 266–73; Lemaire, "La confession: un probleme aigu de notre pastorale," 5–15.

195 "Vont-ils perdre la foi?" Mère Ste.-Thérèse-de-Lisieux, " ...Collégiennes?" *Maint* (May 1964): 155; "Vont-ils perdre la foi?" Françoise Stanton, ... Nos Enfants," 158; Jean Proulx, "La foi au défi?" *Maint* (July–Aug. 1966): 236–7.

196 Guy Rocher, "L'incroyance comme phénomène sociologique," CC 60 (Nov.–Dec. 1971): 359.

197 Fernand Dumont, *Pour la conversion de la pensée chrétienne: essai* (Montreal: Éditions HMH, 1964), 31.

198 "La pastorale en éducation"; Yvon Poitras, F.I.C., "L'éducateur chrétien d'aujourd'hui," *Rel* (July 1965): 208.

199 AUM, Fonds Commission Dumont, P21/C1.16, Pierre Ménard, "La Catéchèse des Adultes, Groupes adultes et foi," Apr. 1970. See also ibid., P21/G4.9, Diocèse de Montréal, "Réflexions et recommandations ... par un groupe d'adultes catholiques pratiquants," Montreàl, 16 Feb. 1970; ibid., Diocèse de Saint-Hyacinthe, P21/G2.7, M. Guy Pépin, enseignant, "Mémoire"; ibid., Diocèse de Quebec, P21/G1.23, "Direction diocésaine de la pastorale scolaire, écoles secondaires publiques, 1969–1970," 27 Feb. 1970; ibid., Entrevues, P21/D.23, H-87; Paul Doucet, o.p., Louis Racine, o.p., "Les parapluies de la confessionnalité," *Maint* (June 1966): 182.

200 AUM, Fonds Commission Dumont, Diocèse de Saint-Jérôme, P21/G9.7: "Mémoire des Mouvements Familiaux," 4 Apr. 1970.

201 AUM, Fonds Commission Dumont, "Entrevues," P21/D.1, A-212.

202 Madame Paul David, "L'éducation de la foi en milieu familial," *Rel* (May 1966): 144.

203 "Note à la Commission Dumont," Association des parents de Sainte-Anne-de-la-Pocatière, AN 60, no. 3 (Nov. 1970): 230. See also Gustave Thibon, "Les jeunes et la violence," AQ 3, no. 3 (May 1967): 43–8.

204 Commission d'étude sur les laïcs et l'Église, *L'Église du Québec: un héritage, un projet* (Montreal: Fides, 1971), 176, 187.

205 Morrison, *Canadian Conference on the Family*, 94; André Charbonneau, "La famille entre hier et aujourd'hui," *Maint* (Dec. 1967): 396–8.

206 Morrison, *Canadian Conference on the Family*, 142.

207 Ibid., 68–9.

208 Fortin, "Socio-Cultural Changes," 104; Marc-Adélard Tremblay and Gérald Fortin, *Les comportements économiques de la famille salariée au Québec* (Québec: Les Presses de l'Université Laval, 1964), 11–13.

209 AUM, Fonds ACC, P16/G2, 7.1, "Semaines étudiantes," "Campagne pour les loisirs, Secteur secondaire, 1962," based upon an article by J. Stoetzl, "Sociologie de la récréation," *Esprit* (1959).

210 AUM, Fonds ACC, P16/05.29, Confédération des Loisirs du Québec, "Semaine d'éducation sur les loisirs: La famille face aux loisirs," 1965.

211 Ibid., "Campagne pour les loisirs"; "Semaine d'éducation sur les loisirs: La famille face aux loisirs."

212 AUQÀM, Fonds Centre de Planning Familial, 113P/210A/001, Philippe Garigue, "Au Canada et au Québec, la famille se désintegre," discours au Club Richelieu, Québec, 28 Dec. 1967. See also Garigue, "Un politique familiale pour le Quebec," in *Famille et humanisme*, 269.

213 AUQÀM, Fonds du Centre de Planning Familial, 113P/210A/001, "À Québec: Contre l'Opération-pilule," "Allocations," *La Patrie*, 11 Feb. 1968.

214 AUM, Fonds ACC, P16/N5, 1.7, "Conseil Supérieur de la Famille," "Mémoire du S.P.M. National au Conseil," n.d.; AUM, Fonds Commission Dumont, P21/C1.3, Jocelyne Bernier, "Les Foyers Notre-Dame Canadien," équipe de recherche sous la responsabilité de Normand Wener, Sept. 1969; "Le sociologue Garigue souhaite l'avènement d'une législation sociale familiale au Québec," LD, 17 July 1965.

215 Garigue, "Permanence and Change" in Morrison, *Canadian Conference on the Family*, 41–6; Garigue, "L'Église et la politique familiale," 210; Germaine Bernier, "'La famille nouvelle' aura-t-elle tous les atouts?" LD, 26 July 1965.

216 Garigue, "Une politique familiale pour le Quebec," 273.

217 For Lévesque's key role in the 1963–64 old-age pension negotiations with Ottawa, see P.E. Bryden, *Planners and Politicians: Liberal Politics and Social Policy, 1957–1968* (Montreal and Kingston: McGill-Queen's University Press, 1997), 114–17.

218 Jean Francoeur, "C'est la fin du 'laisser-faire' dans le domaine du bienêtre," LD 18 Mar. 1965; "Lafrance annonce une réorganisation profonde du ministère de la famille et du bien-être," LD, 12 Mar. 1965.

219 Claude Déry, "Session Pré-Électorale," *Maint* (fall 1965): 295–6.

220 Dery, "Session Pré-Électorale."

221 ANQM, Fonds René Lévesque, P18/D265, Mouvement Souveraineté-Association, "Notre Vie Sociale."

222 Although the work of Clinton Archibald on social and neo-corporatism in Quebec does not analyse social security, it does make the observation that the Bourassa Liberals, in contrast to both the Lesage government and the post-1976 regime of the Parti quebecois, were uninterested in neo-corporatist state structures, preferring to evoke a more "egalitarian" model of government. See Archibald, *Un Québec corporatiste?* 210.

223 Québec, Gouvernement du Québec, *Rapport de la Commission d'Enquête sur la santé et le bien-être social, 4e partie, Vol. VI, tome 1*, (1972), 79, 91.

224 Québec, Gouvernement du Québec, , *Commission d'enquête sur la santé et le bien-être social, tome 1* (Québec: Gouvernement du Québec, 1971), 18, 27, 164; ANQM, Fonds René Lévesque, P18/23/D245, Claude Castonguay, ministre des affaires sociales, "Les droits sociaux dans le monde moderne," LD, 10 Mar. 1971.

225 Garigue, introduction to *Famille et humanisme*, 16.

CHAPTER FIVE

1 Hélène Pelletier-Baillargeon, "Un Concile pour le deuxième sexe?" *Maint* (May 1966): 149.

2 ANQM, Fonds SPM, Camille Laurin, "Les services que le SPM rend à la société," 1966.

3 The outlines of this argument have been advanced in a number of synthesizing and more specific treatments of Quebec women's experience and organization between 1900 and 1960. See, for example, The Clio Collective (Micheline Dumont et al.), *Quebec Women: A History,* trans. Roger Gannon and Rosalind Gill (Toronto: The Women's Press, 1987), which employs the phrases "contradictions," "impass," and "collective silence" (185–324). True feminism, for these authors, begins only in the later 1960s, especially after the founding of the Fédération des Femmes du Québec, an organization that eschewed any ties to the Catholic Church. A similar assessment is evident in Alison Prentice et al., *Canadian Women: A History* (Toronto: Harcourt Brace & Co., 1996), 414–15, 324–7, 206–7. Much of the impetus behind this interpretation flows from earlier analyses of the first francophone Catholic middle-class women's organization, the Fédération Nationale de Saint-Jean-Baptiste, founded in 1907, whose feminism was deemed "paradoxical" because it was apparently forced by Church authorities to retreat from its initial advocacy of political and social equality. See Marie Lavigne, Yolande Pinard, and Jennifer Stoddard, "La Fédération nationale Saint-Jean-Baptiste et les revendications féministes au début du 20e siècle," in Marie Lavigne and Yolande Pinard, eds, *Travailleuses et féministes: Les femmes dans la société québécoise* (Montreal: Boréal Express, 1983), 199–216. For the only sustained attempt to offer a balanced and nuanced discussion of the Catholic discourse on woman's nature and role, particularly as it affected concepts of women's

education between 1900 and 1960, see the article by Lucia Ferretti, "La philosophie de l'enseignement," in Micheline Dumont and Nadia Fahmy-Eid, eds, *Les couventines: L'Éducation des filles au Québec dand les congrégations religieuses enseignantes, 1840–1960* (Montreal: Boréal, 1986), 143–85. However, Ferretti concludes that during the 1920s and 1930s Catholic educators evinced a strong desire to "*counter* the feminist movement, either by discrediting it, or by 'incorporating' it in turning it away from its true objectives." (157).

4 Karine Hébert, "Une organisation maternaliste au Québec: la Fédération Nationale Saint-Jean-Baptiste et la bataille pour le vote des femmes," *Revue d'histoire de l'Amérique française* 52, no. 3 (winter 1999) offers a new assessment of the FNSJB as "maternalist" rather than "feminist," thus avoiding the conventional story of paradox and recuperation by conservative elements (315–44). Hébert argues that the FNSJB played a significant role until the 1930s, but she fails to link its decline to the rise of Catholic youth organizations with a different message during that decade.

5 This polarity has also been recently challenged by Piché, "La Jeunesse Ouvrière Catholique Feminine: un lieu de formation sociale et d'action communautaire, 1931–1966," *Revue d'histoire de l'Amérique française* 52, no.4 (spring 1999): 481–506. Piché, however, confines her analysis to the potential offered by young women's activism within the Catholic Action movements.

6 I employ the designation "personalist feminism," not only to distinguish it from earlier twentieth-century manifestations of maternalism, but because of its egalitarian content. Karine Hébert defines the FNSJB as "maternalist" rather than "feminist" because its outlook lacked an egalitarian argument.

7 François Hertel, *Leur inquiétude* (Montreal: Éditions 'Jeunesse' A.C.J.C., 1936), 66.

8 Pope Pius XI, *Encyclical: On Christian Marriage -Casti connubii* (New York: Paulist Press, 1941), 12.

9 Gina Lombroso, *The Soul of Woman: Reflections on Life* (New York: E.P. Dutton, 1923), 5, 112.

10 Ibid., 47, 111–12, 140, 146, 226.

11 Ibid., 13. For a useful and subtle discussion of the similarities and oppositions in the French context between social Catholics and the ultra-conservatives of Vichy that is entailed in the concept of a distinct "feminine nature," see Francine Muel-Dreyfus, *Vichy et l'éternel féminin* (Paris: Éditions du Seuil, 1996), 15, 75, 165, 169–75. For fascist and Nazi uses of the concept of biological maternity to restrict women's rights and social roles, see Claudia Koonz, *Mothers in the Fatherland: Women, the Family and Nazi Politics* (New York: St. Martin's Press, 1987).

12 Emmanuel Mounier, "Woman also a Person," in Mounier, *A Personalist Manifesto* (New York: Longmans, Green, 1938), 128–9, 131–2. Alexandrine Leduc,

who headed the Jeunesse Étudiante Catholique in the early 1940s, later married Gérard Pelletier. In an interview done with *Châtelaine* in 1962, she recalled, with a none-too-veiled barb at her husband, that she had read *Esprit* in the 1930s, long before it became the daily fare of a certain elite. See Michelle Lasnier, "Reportage exclusif: le couple Alec et Gérard Pelletier," *Chat* 3, no. 11 (Nov. 1962): 50.

13 Emmanuel Mounier, "The Person of the Married Woman," in *A Personalist Manifesto*, 109, 142–48.

14 Mariana Jodoin, "La meilleure ouvrière de progrès humain: La femme, mère et éducatrice," ON, 20 Sept. 1940. See also M. l'abbé P. Perrier, "La Femme au Foyer," LF 4, no. 1 (Sept. 1940): 8–10; Jacqueline Rathé, "Lettre de guerre," JEC 7, no. 10 (Oct. 1941).

15 Fr. Ferdinand, o.f.m., "Le Mariage. II. Vices contraires au mariage," LF 2, no. 2 (Oct. 1938): 28–9. See also, Gilles Dupré, "Moderne ou Éternelle," LF 3, no. 4 (Dec. 1939): 90–1; Gaby Gérard, "Future reine du foyer," JO 2, no. 7 (Apr. 1934): 5, 8; "Propos de mariage: la vie normale de la femme," JO 3, no. 4 (Feb. 1935): 5, 11; "Le vrai féminisme: être femme et etre mère," JO 5, no. 9 (June 1937): 5.

16 Hermin Filiatrault, "Pédagogie familiale – 'La Collaboratrice,'" *Jeunesse* 3, no. 7 (Mar. 1938); Rathé, "Lettre de guerre"; Perrier, "La Femme au Foyer."

17 NAC, Fonds Thérèse-Casgrain, MG 32 C25, Marie-Jeanne Patry, "Le suffrage féminin, une arme défensive," *La Patrie*, 26 Apr. 1941.

18 Esdras Minville, *Le citoyen canadien-français*, vol. 2 (Montreal: Fides, 1946), 313–16.

19 Simonne Monet-Chartrand, *Ma vie comme rivière*, vol. 1, *1919–1942* (Montreal: Les Éditions du Remue-ménage, 1981).

20 Robert Charbonneau, "Troisième annee," LR 2, no. 7 (1935): 197.

21 Piché, "La Jeunesse ouvrière catholique féminine," 505–6; Sian Reynolds, *France between the Wars* (London and New York: Routledge and Kegan Paul, 1996), 51, 57.

22 Jeannette Bertrand, présidente-génerale, JECF, "Pourquoi nous en sommes," JEC 2, no. 8 (Aug. 1936).

23 Lucette St. Cyr, "À mes Soeurs les Étudiantes," JEC 2, no. 5 (May 1936).

24 Jeannette Bertrand, Collège Ste-Croix, JEC 2, no. 5 (May 1936).

25 Claire Gélinas, étudiante en médecine, "Gina Lombroso," JEC 3, no. 9 (Sept. 1937).

26 "Vers les cîmes – Helene Boucher," *Jeunesse* 5, no. 4 (Dec. 1937); Irène Cloutier, "Comme épouse et comme mère," *Jeunesse* 5, no. 5 (Jan.-Feb. 1938); Françoise Clément, College Bruyère, Ottawa, "Madame la baronne de Hueck nous a parlé," JEC 2, no. 4 (Apr. 1936); Jeanne Benoît, "Ne conviendrait pas?" JEC 9, no. 10 (Oct. 1943); Robert-E. Llewellyn, professeur à Stanislas, "Sport vs. Feminité," JEC 9, no. 11 (Nov. 1943).

27 "Reconquête du monde par toi! jéciste, femme de demain," JEC 1, no. 11

(Nov. 1935); Dorothée, "Non mais cette Devise!!" JEC 1, no. 12 (Dec. 1935); Jeannine Morissette, Collège Ste-Croix, St. Laurent, "Aux armes," JEC 2, no. 2 (Feb. 1936).

28 "Allô ...! Allô ... Radio Monique," JEC 3, no. 3 (Mar. 1937). See also Jeannine Morissette, "J.E.C. École de vie sociale," JEC 2, no. 11 (Nov. 1936); "Reconquête du monde part toi!"

29 Jeannine Morissette, présidente-generale JECF, "Le Féminisme que nous voulons," JEC 4, no. 4 (Apr. 1938).

30 Ibid.

31 Madeleine Labrecque, "Semaines Sault-au-Recollet," JEC 5, no. 8 (Aug. 1939).

32 "Allô ...! Allô ... Radio Monique."

33 Y.D., "La Femme Nouvelle," JEC 4, no. 10 (Oct. 1938).

34 "Maternité sublimisée; Maternité divinisée, Maternité au foyer," JEC 2, no. 5 (May 1936). See also Jeannette Bertrand, présidente de la JEC, "Héroisme d'amour, à l'occasion de la fête des mamans," JEC 3, no. 4 (Apr. 1937).

35 Herve Blais, o.f.m., *L'Éducateur: Revue des parents et des maîtres* 1, no. 4 (May 1942): 53.

36 ANQM, Fonds SPM, P116, art. 1, Semaine des fiancés, 1955, Marie Bourbonnais, "Les fiancés d'aujourd'hui sont les parents de demain," LP, 8 Jan. 1955.

37 ANQM, Fonds JOC, P104, art. 4, Jacques Champagne, "S.P.M., 1952." See also AUM, Fonds ACC, P16/K1.24, Jean-Paul Gagnon, "Cours donné par M. Jean-Paul Gagnon à Montréal et Québec, juillet 1952," "Comment contribuer au bien commun par mon travail."

38 Simone Comeau, "Comme on se trompe!," FO, 7 Apr. 1945. See also "Madame, c'est vous," FO, 7 Apr. 1945.

39 Jacques B., "Vers l'avenir ... Face à l'éternel féminin," FO, 9 Dec. 1944.

40 AUM, Fonds ACC, P16/13.85, Fédération des Étudiants des Universités Catholiques, *Rencontres*, 1953, Remy Gagné, "Le mariage étudiant." See also "Miriam," "L'École des maris," C&F 1, no. 2 (Mar. 1944): 18–19; Jean Laramée, s.j., "En marge de 'l'École des maris,'" C&F 1, no. 2 (Mar. 1944): 21–4.

41 AUM, Fonds ACC, P16/H3, 18.86, Madeleine Trottier, André Normandeau, "Le mariage d'adolescents à Montréal: Étude sociologique sur leurs chances d'ajustement marital," Mar. 1965; AUM, Fonds ACC, P16/A1, 19, "Secteur féminin, mars 1957"; ANQM, Fonds MTC, P257, art. 3, Semaine de la famille ouvrière, 1955; Ibid., Semaine de la famille ouvrière 1957, "Causerie prononcée par Mme. Albina Arcand, CKCV, 11 oct. à 4.50 heures."

42 ANQM, Fonds JOC, P104, art. 4, Champagne, "S.P.M., 1952."

43 ANQM, Fonds SPM, P116, art. 6, Appréciation des cours, Marie-Ange à "Ma chère Reine," 28 Nov. 1947; ibid., Madeleine à "Chère Marie-Paule," 26 Nov. 1947.

44 Ibid., C. Frappier, Montréal, à directeur SPM, 31 Aug. 1961; ibid., art. 22, "Sondage auprès des fiancés," 1963–64.

45 For the presence of this current in discussions of marital sexuality within the United Church of Canada, see Nancy Christie, "Sacred Sex," in Nancy Christie, ed., *Households of Faith: Family, Gender and Community in Canada, 1760–1969* (Montreal and Kingston: McGill-Queen's University Press, 2002), 359–60.

46 For a recent treatment of pre-1940s Quebec Catholic sexual values and practices, although in a rural context, see Gérard Bouchard, "La sexualité comme pratique et rapport social chez les couples paysans du Saguenay (1860–1930)," *Revue d'histoire de l'Amérique française* 54, no. 2 (autumn 2000): 189–98. For the official discourse delimiting the narrow scope for female sexual expression, see Andrée Lévesque, *Making and Breaking the Rules: Women in Quebec, 1919–1939* (Toronto: McClelland and Stewart, 1991), 53–73.

47 ANQM, Fonds P116, Fonds SPM, art. 6, Appréciation des cours, Jeannette Gingras, Montréal-Nord, à Père J. de B. Laramée, 24 June 1946. In her study of working-class women in Montreal during the Depression, Denyse Baillargeon has observed that for the pre-war generation, the qualities of a good husband were defined in negative terms, and many of the women of this generation referred to the lack of communication or discussion with their husbands. See Baillargeon, *Ménagères au temps de la crise* (Montreal: Les Éditions du Remue-ménage, 1991), 82–4.

48 ANQM, P116, Fonds SPM, art. 6, Appréciation des cours, Pauline Fontaine à Mlle G. Bates, 29 mai 1947; Thérèse Brault à SPM, 10 May 1947; ibid., Lucille Ducharme à Julienne Croteau, 20 Mar. 1947.

49 Monet-Chartrand, *Ma vie comme rivière*, vol. 1, 98–9.

50 Une mère, "A propos d'éducation familale au couvent et à l'école," LF 1, no. 9 (May 1938): 150–1. See also the reminiscences in Monet-Chartrand, *Ma vie comme rivière*, vol. 1, 124–5, 127.

51 ANQM, Fonds SPM, P116, art. 1, Session d'étude 1955, "Commission des couples."

52 Ibid., art. 6, Appréciation des cours, anonymous letter to editor, *Front Ouvrier*, n.d.

53 Ibid., art. 24, Conférences 1960–1966, Bernard Mailhiot, o.p., "De l'esprit de géometrie en psychologie," n.d.

54 Father Léopold Godbout, "Les causes de la désintégration familiale: les facteurs d'ordre morale," in *Les causes de la désintégration familiale* (Montreal: Caritas-Canada, 1956), 44–5; Jean-de-Brébeuf Laramée, o.f.m., "Maternité menacée," LF 13, no. 5 (May 1949): 247–9; R.P. Joseph d'Anjou, s.j., "La famille a le droit et le devoir d'être féconde," *Mission et Droits de la Famille. Semaine Sociale 1959.* (Montreal: Secrétariat des Semaines Sociales, 1959), 72.

55 In examining the Catholic Action movements as a whole during the 1950s, Jean Hamelin has determined that, on average, the female component stood at approximately 75 per cent. See Jean Hamelin and Nicole Gagnon, *Histoire du catholicisme québécois*, vol. 2 (Montreal: Boréal Express, 1984), 127.

56 Marie-Joseph d'Anjou, s.j., "Amour procréateur et éducateur," C&F 10, no. 2 (Apr. 1953): 71.

57 Miriam, "L'École des maris," 19; "Qu'est-ce qu'aimer?" FO, 4 Aug. 1945.

58 Marie-Joseph d'Anjou." See also d'Anjou, "La famille a le droit et le devoir d'être féconde," 85, 91–2.

59 For a discussion of this post-war tendency in American sexology, see Jenny Neuhaus, "The Importance of Being Orgasmic: Sexuality, Gender and Marital Sex Manuals in the United States, 1920–1963," *Journal of the History of Sexuality* 9, no. 4 (Oct. 2000): 447–73. Neuhaus observes that in the 1930s there was a greater primacy placed on the female orgasm and the responsibility of husbands to satisfy wives' needs. By the 1950s, however, women's sexuality was viewed as dysfunctional, but correspondingly, sexual satisfaction came to centre upon the husband's achievement of orgasm. For a Quebec example of this tendency, significantly written by a medical professional and not by a Catholic clergyman or lay activist, see Dr Lionel Gendron, *Qu'est-ce qu'une femme?* vol. 2 (Montreal: Les Éditions de l'Homme, 1961), 101. For an analysis of French sexology of the 1920s and 1930s, which likewise affirmed that married women should "enjoy a sexual identity," see Mary Louise Roberts, *Civilization without Sexes: Reconstructing Gender in Postwar France, 1917–1927* (Chicago and London: University of Chicago Press, 1994), 197–205.

60 ANQM, Fonds SPM, P116, art. 24, Conférences données au Service, 1960–1966, "Compte-rendu de la rencontre des conférenciers du S.P.M. avec le Révérend Père Jules Paquin, s.j., 16 mars 1960."

61 Ibid.

62 ANQM, Fonds SPM, P116, art. 2, "Semaine des fiancés, 1951."

63 Clio Collective, *Quebec Women: A History*, 304–6; Angus McLaren and Arlene Tigar McLaren, *The Bedroom and the State: The Changing Practices and Politics of Contraception and Abortion in Canada, 1880–1930* (Toronto: McClelland and Stewart, 1986), 124–32; Bouchard, "La sexualité comme pratique et rapport social."

64 For the overall pattern of declining fertility, see Danielle Gauvreau et Peter Gossage, "'Empêcher la famille': Fecondité et contraception au Québec, 1920–1960," *Canadian Historical Review* 78, no. 3 (Sept. 1997): 478–510; and for a cultural treatment of the effect of the baby-boom that offers a more nuanced context for Quebec than do the standard Anglo-American treatments, see François Ricard, *La génération lyrique: Essai sur la vie et l'oeuvre des premiers-nés du baby boom* (Montreal: Boréal Compact, 1994), 38–9, 44.

65 For these policies and their impact on women in post-war France and Germany, see Elizabeth J. Heinemann, *What Difference Does a Husband Make?: Women and Marital Status in Postwar Germany* (Berkeley: University of California Press, 1999); Robert Moeller, "Reconstructing the Family in Reconstruction Germany: Women and Social Policy in the Republic, 1949–1955," in Robert Moeller, ed., *West Germany Under Construction: Politics, Society and*

Culture in the Adenauer Era (Ann Arbor: University of Michigan Press, 1997); and for France, Claire Duchen, *Women's Rights and Women's Lives in France, 1944–1968* (London and New York: Routledge, 1994), 126. The federal family allowance policy, the only post-war social legislation that appeared to have natalist implications, was in fact intended to encourage consumption, and was deliberately designed to reduce benefits to large families. See Nancy Christie, "Family Allowances and the Politics of Abundance," in *Engendering the State: Family, Work, and Welfare in Canada* (Toronto: University of Toronto Press, 2000). A provincial policy of family allowances had to wait until the late 1960s, when the connection between Catholicism and the state had become much more tenuous.

66 *Casti connubii*, 8–9, 25.

67 Ibid., 27.

68 For accounts of these efforts, see McLaren and McLaren, *The Bedroom and the State*, 22, 175; Lévesque, *Making and Breaking the Rules*, 28.

69 M.-C. Forest, o.p., "La théorie Ogino-Knaus – Un remède contre le néo-malthusianisme," RD (Jan. 1934): 69.

70 ANQM, Fonds SPM, P116, art. 2, Semaine des fiancés, 1948, "Sermon prononce par le R.P. Lorenzo Gauthier, c.s.v., à la semaine de clôture de la Semaine des Fiancés du S.P.M., le 18 jan. 1948"; AUM, Fonds ACC, P16/04. 52, Commission Canadienne sur la Jeunesse, "Mémoire sur la Famille."

71 Hervé Blais, o.f.m., *L'Éducateur: Revue des parents et des maîtres* 1, no. 4 (May 1942): 53.

72 Hervé Blais, o.f.m., "Crescite et multiplicamisis," *Nos enfants* 1, no. 5 (June–July 1942): 68.

73 AUM, Fonds ACC, P16/K1.14, Dr. Brock Chisholm, Camille L'Heureux, "Une expérience douteuse," *Le Droit*, 23 Apr. 1952.

74 Fr. Ferdinand, o.f.m., "Le Mariage. II. Vices contraires au mariage," LF 1, no. 11 (July 1938): 190–1; Gilles Dupré, "Dénatalite et esprit chrétien," LF 2, no. 2 (Oct. 1938): 25, 27; Gonzalve Poulin, "Le dur pain quotidien," LF 3, no. 6 (Feb. 1940): 154–7; Albert Tessier, ptre, "'Onze enfants, mais c'est immoral!" *Rel* (Nov. 1943): 296–7.

75 Mme Berthe Lepage, Saint-Jérôme, "Réponse," FO, 18 July 1953; Fernand Rainville, 3625, rue Hochelaga, Montréal, lettre, FO, 18 July 1953; "Jeune mari," "Pouvons-nous fixer le nombre des enfants?" FO, 18 July 1953; Mme Roger Belisle, Shawinigan-Sud, "Réponse," FO, 18 July 1953; Tessier, "'Onze enfants.'"

76 Jeanne Grisé-Allard, "L'égoisme chez l'enfant: faiblesse ou défaut?" LF 10, no. 4 (Apr. 1946): 134; "Enfant unique," LF 1, no. 12 (Aug. 1938): 210.

77 Mounier, *A Personalist Manifesto*, 108–9.

78 AUM, Fonds ACC, P16/D5, 1.10, "Psychologie de l'homme et de la femme," n.d.; ANQM, Fonds SPM, P116, art. 24, "Différents articles sur la préparation

au mariage ... 1942 à 1960," lettre de Jean Lemieux, "On accepte les enfants que le bon Dieu envoie," LD, 9 Sept. 1959.

79 AUM, Fonds ACC, P16/D5, 1.14, "Compilation du sondage," 1962; ANQM, Fonds SPM, P116, art. 6, Appréciation des cours, Madeleine à "Chère Marie-Paule," 26 Nov. 1947.

80 AUM, Fonds ACC, P16/H18.83, "Commission médecins-infirmières," 2 Oct. 1955.

81 This, of course, did not exhaust the variety of birth control practices such as prolonged breast-feeding and *coitus interruptus* that had been practiced throughout the nineteenth and early twentieth centuries. For the existence of practices such as prolonged breast-feeding, abstinence, and *coitus interruptus*, see Bouchard, "La sexualité comme pratique et rapport social"; Danielle Gauvreau and Peter Gossage, "Avoir moins d'enfants au tournant du XXe siècle: une realité même au Quebec," *Revue d'histoire de l'Amérique française* 54, no. 1 (summer 2000): 39–65; Danielle Gauvreau and Peter Gossage, "'Empêcher la famille,'" 478–510.

82 ANQM, Fonds SPM, "Compte-rendu de la rencontre des conférenciers du S.P.M. avec le Révérend Père Jules Paquin, s.j."

83 Rodophe and Germaine Laplante, "Les parents devant l'éducation," *Rel* (Jan. 1943): 2.

84 For the popularity and wide diffusion of the "planning" metaphor during the later stages of the war and early post-war period in Canada, see for debates on social policy, Christie, *Engendering the State*, especially the final chapter, "Family Allowances and the Politics of Abundance," and for a suggestive look at how the language of planning infused concepts of high and popular culture during this period, see Leonard Kuffert, "'Stabbing our Spirits Broad Awake': Reconstructing Canadian Culture, 1940–1948," in Nancy Christie and Michael Gauvreau, eds, *Cultures of Citizenship in Post-war Canada, 1940–1955* (Montreal and Kingston: McGill-Queen's University Press, 2003), 27–62.

85 Adélard Provencher, "Le chrétien dans la famille," in *Le Chrétien dans la famille et dans la nation: Les Semaines Sociales du Canada, 18e session* (Montreal: École Sociale Populaire, 1941), 66–8.

86 Jeanne d'Arc and Bernard Trottier, "Spiritualité à deux," LF 12, no. 9 (Nov. 1948); Jeba-Tirai, "Ce qu'il faut."

87 AUM, Fonds ACC, P16/R.62, "Spiritualité familiale, problèmes pratiques et expériences," n.d.; Gaston Pouliot, "Intervious avec le directeur de *La Famille*," LF 7, nos 2–3 (Feb.–Mar. 1941).

88 Dr Albert Guilbeault, ed., "Introduction," *Nos Enfants* 1, no. 1 (Dec. 1940): 5–6; See also R.P. Joseph d'Anjou, s.j., "La famille a le droit et le devoir d'être féconde," 75.

89 AUM, Fonds ACC, P16/D5.1, "Nouveaux résumes," ca 1963–64, "Famille nouvelle."

90 Jacques Henripin, "Aspects démographiques," in Wade, ed., *La dualité canadienne/Canadian Duality* (Québec: Les Presses de l'Université Laval; Toronto: University of Toronto Press, 1960), 179–80.

91 AUM, Fonds ACC, P16/D5, 1.10, S.P.M. de Montréal, n.d., "Pour un amour enrichissant (morale conjugale)."

92 Ibid.

93 AUM, Fonds ACC, P16/04.88, École des Parents – Journées d'Étude, 16–17 fév. 1957, "Vie Spirituelle du Foyer." See also "Le problème du nombre des enfants," *FO*, 25 July 1953; Fernand Rainville, lettre, 18 July 1953.

94 Ariès, "Familles du demi-siècle," in R. Prigent, ed., *Renouveau des idées sur la famille* (Paris: Les Presses Universitaires de France, 1954), 166.

95 Gauvreau and Gossage, "'Empêcher la famille,'" 488. These figures have been confirmed by Jacques Henripin et al., *Les enfants qu'on n'en a plus au Québec* (Montreal: Les Presses de l'Université de Montréal, 1981), 162. Neither of these works examines the wider cultural influence of Catholic Action, although Gauvreau and Gossage note that 80 per cent of Catholic women relied exclusively on the Ogino-Knaus method and abstinence to regulate births (491). Contemporary social surveys also revealed the heavy prevalence of the rhythm method. See Philippe Garigue, *La vie familiale des canadiens-français* (Montreal: Les Presses de l'Université de Montréal, 1962), 89. As early as 1957, the demographer Jacques Henripin observed that "Parents control their fertility more effectively *after* they have had a few children." See "From Acceptance of Nature to Control: The Demography of the French Canadians since the Seventeenth Century," in Marcel Rioux and Yves Martin, eds, *French-Canadian Society*, vol. 1 (Toronto: McClelland and Stewart, 1964), 213.

96 Recent revisionist historiography has emphasized in English-speaking cultural contexts the liberalization of sexual morality and practices prior to the youth revolts of the 1960s. See, for example, Arthur Marwick, *The Sixties* (Oxford: Oxford University Press, 1998), 111; Christie, "Sacred Sex."

97 Garigue, "La famille canadienne-française dans la société contemporaine," 62."

98 Jacques Henripin, "From Acceptance of Nature to Control," in Rioux and Martin, *French-Canadian Society*, vol. 1, 216.

99 Garigue, "La famille canadienne-française," 59.

100 Claudine Vallerand à Simonne Monet Chartrand, 28 May 1947, quoted in Chartrand, *Ma vie comme rivière*, vol. 2, 326.

101 For the historiography that sees the post-war period as constraining women's public roles and heightening domesticity, see, for the American context, Elaine Tyler May, *Homeward Bound: American Families in the Cold War Era* (New York: Basic Books, 1988). Canadian works which follow in this current include Ruth Roach Pierson, *'They're Still Women After All": The Second World War and Canadian Womanhood* (Toronto: McClelland and

Stewart, 1986); Owram, "Canadian Domesticity in the Postwar Era"; and for the existence of a conservative discourse reasserting traditional gender hierarchies as "normal," Mona Gleason, *Normalizing the Ideal: Psychology, Schooling and the Family in Postwar Canada* (Toronto: University of Toronto Press, 1999).

102 For an exploration of this contradiction in the American context, see Joanne Meyerowitz, "Beyond the Feminine Mystique: A Reassessment of Postwar Mass Culture, 1946–1958," *Journal of American History* 79, no. 4 (Mar. 1993): 1455–1482. For a suggestive study that explores the ways in which the suburban domestic ideal offered far greater scope for married women than has hitherto been acknowledged, see Veronica Strong-Boag, "'Their Side of the Story': Women's Voices from Ontario Suburbs, 1945–1960," in Joy Parr, ed., *A Diversity of Women: Ontario 1945–1980* (Toronto: University of Toronto Press, 1995), 46–74.

103 Guy Rocher, "A. – Les modèles et le statut de la femme canadienne-française," in Paul-Henry Chombart de Lauwe, *Images de la femme dans la société* (Paris: Les Editions Ouvrières, 1964), 197. In 1951, the female percentage of the Quebec labour force stood at 23.2 per cent, above the national average, but only 3.37 per cent of Quebec's married women worked, a figure well below the national average of 30 per cent. See André Roy, "Les femmes à l'usine," LT, 8 May 1953, 3.

104 AUM, Fonds ACC, P16/G5, 4.1, Jeunesse Ouvrière Catholique, Premier Congrès Général, juillet 1935, "La Jeunesse, C'est l'Avenir." Examples of this public discourse abounded between the late 1930s and the early 1950s. See, for example, ibid., P16/04.52, Commission Canadienne de la Jeunesse, "Comité de la Famille"; ibid., P16/13, 85, Fédération des Étudiants des Universités Catholiques du Canada, *Rencontres*, 1953, Hélène Laberge, "Le mariage et la profession"; R.P.M.-Ceslas Forest, o.p., "La mère au foyer: une exigence de bon sens et de la sociologie chrétienne," ON, 20 Dec. 1939; Monique Deschamps, "Nos Droits," JO 9, nos 3–4 (Dec. 1939–Jan. 1940): 13; Simonne Comeau, "La mobilisation de la main-d'oeuvre féminine," JO 9, no. 12 (Aug. 1940): 4; Laurette Larivière, "La J.O.C.F. prépare la jeune fille à son rôle futur," JO 10, no. 2 (Oct. 1940): 4;"Beau travail et les projets d'un congrès feminin," LD, 28 Apr. 1941; "Un beau travail de la J.O.C.," JO 10. nos 5–6 (Jan.–Feb. 1941); "Les excès de travail féminin pendant la guerre," JO 11, no. 3 (Nov. 1942); "En marge du travail féminin," JO 11, no. 3 (Nov. 1942); ANQM, Fonds FNSJB, P120/54–3, Mme Henri Vautelet, *Mémoire sur l'orientation du travail féminin d'après-guerre*. Préparé pour le Conseil d'Orientation Économique (ca 1943); Madeleine Maillé, "En marge de l'après-guerre: La jeune ouvrière doit rester femme," JO 12, no. 9 (May 1944): 4; Gérard Pelletier, "Pour une guerre vraiment sainte," JEC 8, no. 11 (Nov. 1942); ANQM, Fonds JOC, P104, art. 155, Communiqués aux journaux, Sept. 1943, "La jeune ouvrière et son avenir." For the ideology of the Con-

féderation des Travailleurs Catholiques, see Louis-Marie Tremblay, *Les idéologies de la C.S.N. et de la F.T.Q., 1940–1970* (Montreal: Les Presses de l'Université de Montréal, 1972), 261. The CTCC's Declaration of Principles explicitly declared in favour of "the right of the father of the family to provide for the subsistence of his dependents, the right of the mother to accomplish in the household her task of guardian, housekeeper, and educator." For the wartime and post-war social policies that enshrined these imperatives, see the analysis in Christie, "Family Allowances and the Politics of Abundance."

105 Raymond Tanghé, ed., *Opinions: Tribune d'information sur les problèmes de l'après-guerre* (originally broadcast on Radio-Canada) (Montreal: Fides 1943), 30.

106 Marguerite Perroy, "La mère dans un monde à rebâtir," *Rel* (Jan. 1948): 10.

107 Gonzalve Poulin, o.f.m., "Orientations nouvelles de la femme canadienne," *Culture* 5 (1944): 403, 407, 410, 412, 414. See also R.P. Antonin Lamarche, o.p., "La Semaine de la Famille," RD (Mar. 1945): 176–8; Ernest Pallascio-Morin, "La femme sauvegarde de la morale," RD (Mar. 1946): 168–75; Godbout, "Les causes de la désintegration familiale," 42.

108 Perroy, "La mère dans un monde à rebâtir," 10.

109 "Le courrier de José," FO, 25 Oct. 1947.

110 Rita Racette, "La femme éternelle," VE 15, no. 4 (Apr. 1949); Laurette Larivière, "Service social ou instinct maternel," FO, 23 Nov. 1946; Constance Tousignant, "Mission de femme," VE 16, no. 4 (Apr. 1950).

111 AUM, Fonds ACC, P16/J2,3, Campagne de Moralité – Étude Sociale 1945–46, "Le rôle social de la femme." See also P.M., "La vocation de mère," FO, 4 Jan. 1947; Alice Franchère, "'Gardons' le foyer," FO, 6 Dec. 1947; Gaston Leury, "… et notre métier de femme!" FO, 29 Nov. 1947.

112 Madeleine Vaillancourt, "Femme forte, femme moderne," VE 17, no. 1 (Feb. 1951). For the argument that "sublimation" of the maternal ideal was a form of post-war conservatism that devalorized women's roles, see Ferretti, "La philosophie de l'enseignement," 158.

113 Gertrud Von Le Fort, *The Eternal Woman*, trans. Placid Jordan, Order of St. Basil (Milwaukee: Bruce Publishing Co., 1962; German ed. first published 1934), 6–8, 39. For a contrasting view, see Simone de Beauvoir, *Le Deuxième Sexe: I, Les faits et les mythes* (Paris: Gallimard, 1949), 14–15.

114 Von Le Fort, *The Eternal Woman*, xiv.

115 Ibid., 21, 24.

116 Ibid., 83.

117 Ibid., 36, 53.

118 Ibid., 36, 48–9.

119 Ibid., 82.

120 Ibid., 31–2, 36.

121 Ibid., 26.

122 Rita Racette, "Mots d'appel pour une liberté authentique," VE 17, no. 5

(May 1951). For the reception of Von Le Fort's book in the late 1940s, see Guy Cormier, "'La Femme Éternelle,'" JC (Apr. 1947); Racette, "La femme éternelle"; Roland Germain, "La femme éternelle," LF 12, no. 6 (June–July 1949): 348–50. It should be noted that the latter article stressed the "norm" of physical maternity, while the appreciations of Racette and Cormier were more intent on elucidating the personalist language of "free gift of self" and the cooperative aspects of male and female natures and roles.

123 Françoise-M. Lavigne, "Grandeur et servitude de la mère," C&F 12, no. 1 (Feb. 1955): 12, Radio-Canada broadcast, 18 Oct. 1954. Similar views were held in Catholic Action working-class circles. See "Le courrier de José," FO, 12 July 1947; "Le courrier de José," FO, 25 Oct. 1947.

124 A similar emphasis on the spousal relationship, rather than on the strictly maternal identity, was also made by Father Léopold Godbout, "Les causes de la désintegration familiale," 41: "To be good parents, you must first be good spouses. The spouses are the twin pillars of the family. The fate of the family is played out between the spouses, and today, the crisis of the family can be found in the relationship between the spouses." See also Jeanne d'Arc and Bernard Trottier, "Un pas en avant," LF 12, no. 1 (Jan. 1948): 5–6.

125 Lavigne, "Grandeur et servitude," 12.

126 Fernande Juneau, "Femmes Modernes," VE 16, no. 2 (Feb. 1950). See also Janet Kalven, "La mission de femme dans le monde moderne," LF 17, no. 1 (Jan. 1953): 6–19; Monique Leboeuf, étudiante en Sciences Sociales, Montréal, "Si tu veux être moderne," VE 14, no. 1 (Jan. 1948); Jeanne Benoît, "Orientation vers ta personne," VE 12, no. 3 (Mar. 1946); ibid., "Les nouveaux Brigitte," VE 12, no. 5 (May 1946).

127 Simonne Monet-Chartrand, "Noviciat au mariage," extraits d'un cours donné à la Maison des oeuvres de Longueuil, 10 mai 1945, cited in Chartrand, *Ma vie comme rivière*, vol 2, *1942–1959* (Montreal: Les Éditions du Remue-ménage, 1981), 252–3.

128 Ibid., 252, 254.

129 ANQM, Fonds JOC, P104, "Rapport des Journées d'Étude Nationale," Rapport de Camille Laurin, "Évolution du Canada depuis le début du siècle en regard de l'Idéal Chrétien," 1950.

130 *Casti connubii*, 34–5.

131 AUM, Fonds ACC, P16/04.52, "Mémoire presenté par la Jeunesse Indépendante Catholique Féminine," ca 1946.

132 See for an analysis of the Dorion Commission, Jennifer Stoddart, "Quand les gens de robe se penchent sur les droits des femmes: le cas de la commission Dorion, 1929–1931," in Marie Lavigne and Yolande Pinard, *Travailleuses et féministes: Les femmes dans la société québécoise* (Montreal: Boréal Express, 1983), 307–35.

133 Rosabèle Saint-Amant, "La femme conseillère," LF 1, no. 2 (Oct. 1937): 24.

134 Maximilien Caron, "La femme mariée dans le droit du Quebec," LF 8, no. 8 (Oct. 1944): 378. See also ibid, "Conditions juridiques de l'épouse," LF 8, no. 10 (Dec. 1944): 501–2; and for similar objections, AUM, Fonds ACC, P16/05.84, "Ligue des Droits de la Femme," Chambre des Notaires de la Province de Quebec, "Mémoire soumis à Me Léon Méthot, C.R., commissaire spécial sur les demandes de modification au Code Civil relativement à la femme mariée."

135 AUM, Fonds ACC, P16/05.84, "Ligue des Droits de la Femme," Thérèse F. Casgrain, "Les droits civils de la femme," in *Le code civil et la femme mariée dans la Province de Québec: Article publié par la Ligue des Droits de la Femme, extrait du Devoir, des 28 et 29 janvier, 1946.*

136 ANQM, Fonds JEC, P65, S6, SS6, SSS2, D1/4, "Document de travail, 1950."

137 AUM, Fonds ACC, P16/D5, 10.1, "Commission sur le Statut Juridique de la Femme Mariée dans le Québec," Apr. 1947; ibid., P16/J22.2, "Cours donné par Mme. Thais Lacoste-Frémont au Cercle de l'Amicale J.M. de Sillery, Québec," 23 Oct. 1947; ibid., P16/05.52, "Commission Canadienne sur la Jeunesse," Jacques Perreault, "Congrès Provincial – Comité de la Famille," ca 1946.

138 Antonio Perreault, "Condition juridique de la femme mariée," Rel (Mar. 1952): 58–66.

139 "Faut-il faire un contrat de mariage?" FO, 20 Jan. 1945. The sixth session in the fourteen-week marriage preparation course was "Lois civiles du mariage," in which the couple was advised to make a marriage contract to protect the legal rights of wives within the marriage. See ANQM, Fonds JOC, P104, art. 4, 17e session intensive, 1952, Jacques Champagne, "Le Service de Préparation au Mariage"; ANQM, Fonds SPM, P116, art. 2, "Service de préparation au mariage: quelques conseils pratiques."

140 For the Instituts Familiaux, see Nicole Thivierge, "L'enseignement ménager, 1880–1970," in Nadia Fahmy-Eid and Micheline Dumont, eds, *Maîtresses de maison, maîtresses d'école: Femmes, famille et éducation dans l'histoire du Québec* (Montreal: Boréal Express, 1983), 126–30.

141 For the establishment of the classical curriculum for women, see Michèle Jean, "L'enseignement supérieur des filles et son ambiguïté: Le collège Marie-Anne, 1932–1958," in Fahmy-Eid and Dumont, *Maîtresses de maison*, 144–58.

142 Albert Léonard, s.j., "Femme forte," C&F 7, no. 4 (Oct. 1950): 180–3. See also Colette Fortier-Lépine, "Inspiratrice, dors-tu?" LF 15, no. 2 (Feb. 1951): 110–12.

143 Louise Mireault, "Plaidoyer pour la jeunesse," RD (Sept. 1945): 96. See also AUM, Fonds ACC, P16/G4, 1.5, Jeunesse Indépendante Catholique Feminine, Divers, 1946–1958, "Culture et Personnalité Feminine," n.d.; Françoise April, Institut Familial de Ste.-Martine, "Avons-nous un avenir?" VE 19, no. 8 (May 1953).

144 AUM, Fonds ACC, P16/P5.12, Instituts Familiaux Canadiens, *Les Instituts Familiaux du Québec*. See also Mgr Albert Tessier, visiteur-général des Écoles d'Enseignement Ménager, "Le foyer, centre d'attraction," in *Le Foyer: Base de la Société: compte-rendu des cours et conférences, 27e Semaine Sociale du Canada* (Montreal: Institut social populaire, 1952), 254–6.

145 AUM, Fonds Paul-Larocque, P52/K19.22, Paul-H. Carignan, "Humanité féminine," 21 Mar. 1958.

146 Paul-H. Carignan, ptre, "Vocation à la maternité," CAC 113 (Jan. 1950): 152. In March 1942, the Vichy government, which like other authoritarian regimes subscribed to an extreme notion of male/female physiological and psychological dichotomy and division of the social world, had made household education mandatory for all girls. See Muel-Dreyfus, *Vichy et l'éternel féminin*, 138, 271; Miranda Pollard, *Reign of Virtue: Mobilizing Gender in Vichy France* (Chicago: University of Chicago Press, 1998). The ambiguities of the discourse of the Instituts Familiaux, which advocated a liberalized discipline within a more ironclad definition of female roles, has also been noted by Thivierge, "L'enseignement ménager," 130–2.

147 Albert Tessier, ptre, "Les Écoles Ménagères au service du foyer," *Rel* (Sept. 1942): 235–7.

148 Lombroso, *The Soul of Woman*, 145–6.

149 Willie Jacob, "Deviendront-elles des hommes?" VE 19, no. 8 (May 1953). See also Pauline Demers, Couvent Notre-Dame-du-Rosaire, Ottawa, lettre, VE 10, no. 5 (May 1944); Pauline Gagné, "À la rescousse de la femme maternelle," C&F 8, no. 3 (June 1951): 137–40; Abbé Paul-H. Carignan, visiteur-propagandiste de l'Enseignement ménager, "Pour préparer des foyers heureux," LF 12, no. 7 (Aug.–Sept. 1949): 398–401.

150 André Raynauld, Belles-lettres, "Tribune libre: les études supérieures," JEC 11, no. 6 (June 1945).

151 Monique Dufresne, "Femme savante, femme épatante," LF15, no. 4 (Apr. 1951): 211–2. See also J.and G. Corbeil, "Pour hommes seulement"; AUM, Fonds Paul-Larocque, P52/K19, "Memoire présenté à la Commission du Programme de la Faculté des Arts de Laval par les Collèges Féminins," 16 Oct. 1958.

152 Lucia Ferretti, "La philosophie de l'enseignement," has observed that the partisans of household education were able to impose their views as the reference point for all other discourses on female education.

153 Françoise Lavigne, "La femme est-elle une personne?" JC (Nov. 1948): 28–9.

154 Renée Geoffroy, "Un climat d'amour," LT, 21 May 1954, 6; J. and B. Trottier, 'Un pas en avant," 5–6; J. Templier, "Gestes de femme," LF 17, no. 5 (May 1953): 320–3; Jeanne, "Les mamans doivent-elles se faire mourir au ménage?" LT, 1 May 1953, 6; "L'activité syndicale: un enrichissement pour le foyer," LT, 5 June 1953; Renée Geoffroy, "Un syndicat de mamans? – Pourquoi pas?" LT, 20 Nov. 1953, 6; Jeanne Sauvé, "L'épouse et la mère en

regard du syndicalisme," LT, 9 Apr. 1951, 6; Jeanne, "Quand la maman est fatiguée," LT, 30 Jan. 1953, 6; Renée Geoffroy, "Des maisons humaines: première condition de travail de nos mamans," LT, 17 Apr. 1953, 6.

155 Micheline Robitaille, Pensionnat St. Lambert, "Pourquoi une femme instruite serait-elle moins attrayante?" VE 19, no. 10 (June 1953).

156 Monique Dufresne, "La femme et la vie intellectuelle," LF 14, no. 9 (Nov. 1950): 513–18; Dufresne, "Femme savante, femme épatante," LF 15, no. 4 (Apr. 1951): 313–4; Madeleine Mathieu, Couvent Notre-Dame-du-Rosaire, Ottawa, lettre, JEC 10, no. 5 (May 1944); Thérèse Roy, Collège Marguerite-Bourgeois, "Les Études supérieures: le plus grand bienfait," JEC 11, no. 4 (Apr. 1945); Pierre Godin, (e.e. Philo, UdeM), "Les études secondaires: la bataille bat son plein!" JEC 11, no. 9 (Sept. 1945); Vous et Moi, "Autour de l'humanisme féminin," C&F 7, no. 5 (Dec. 1950): 223–32.

157 Soeur Sainte-Madeleine-des-Anges, "Histoire d'une évolution – II," C&F 5, no. 2 (Mar. 1948): 83–7.

158 "Mémoire présenté à la Commission du Programme de la Faculté des Arts de Laval par les Collèges féminins." See also Marie-Joseph d'Anjou, s.j., "Préambule à une éducation féminine," C&F 11, no. 5 (Dec. 1954): 201–14.

159 Thivierge, "L'enseignement ménager," 136–7 observes that, while the provincial government of Maurice Duplessis funded the Instituts Familiaux, no public funds were made available for women's classical colleges.

160 Dufresne, "Femme savante, femme épatante," 313. For arguments linking a culture of individual achievement and educational reform, particularly of the *collèges classiques* in 1950s Quebec, see Michael Behiels, *Prelude to Quebec's Quiet Revolution: Liberalism versus Neo-Nationalism, 1945–1960* (Montreal and Kingston: McGill-Queen's University Press, 1985), 149–84.

161 Monique Béchard, D.Ps., "Véritables jeunes filles???" C&F 8, no. 1 (Feb. 1953): 44.

162 Ibid., "'Le complexe …' d'où vient tout le mal," C&F 8, no. 5 (Dec. 1951): 222–3.

163 Monique Béchard, "Vocation universelle," C&F 10, no. 2 (Apr. 1953): 65–9; Béchard, "Encore l'éternel féminin!," C&F 8, no. 3 (June 1951): 131.

164 Béchard, "Véritables jeunes filles???" 41–8. Françoise Maillet-Lavigne denounced Lombroso in the following terms: "her thought is inspired by paganism, and even reflects the mentality of a prostitute, and displays the extremely crass ignorance of fascism." She added that Lombroso's works should have been long ago placed on the Index. See "La femme est avant tout une personne humaine," C&F 8, no. 4 (Oct. 1951): 177.

165 Béchard, "Véritables jeunes filles???" 85.

166 Ibid., "Encore l'éternel féminin!" 135–6; ibid., "'Le complexe'" 215, 220; AUM, Fonds ACC, P16/G4, 7.1, Semaines nationales, Germaine Bernier, "À propos d'une revue sur l'amour," LD, 15 May 1954. For an assessment of

Friedan that accents her participation in a cultural current that asserted the importance of identity in an age of mass conformity, see Daniel Horowitz, *Betty Friedan and the Making of the Feminine Mystique* (Amherst: University of Massachusetts Press, 1998), 172, 197. It should be emphasized in this context that feminists like Béchard would have dissented from Friedan's overweening prioritization of paid work – what they would have dismissed as "economic feminism" – as the touchstone of women's equality.

167 Monique Béchard, "Est-elle aussi un être humain?" c&f 8, no. 4 (Oct. 1951): 167–74; Maillet-Lavigne, "La femme est avant tout une personne humaine," 179.

168 Monique Béchard-Deslandes, "Activités, tâches et professions féminines," c&f 10, no. 5 (Dec. 1953): 200; Béchard, "Femme idéale?" 82.

169 Monique Béchard, "Vocation universelle," c&f 10, no. 2 (Apr. 1953), 65; ibid., "Femme idéale?" 85, 89, 179–80; Françoise-M. Lavigne, "Grandeur et servitude," 11.

170 AUM, Fonds ACC, P16/C2, 3.2, "Rapport de la Rencontre des Dirigeantes Nationales, le 28 et 29 août 1947."

171 AUM, Fonds ACC, P16/A1, 19, "Secteur féminin en AC," Mar. 1957; ibid., P16/D6, 5.2, Rapport de la Rencontre des Dirigeantes Nationales, les 28 et 29 août 1947, Suzanne d'Arsigny and Rita Bibault, "Notre rôle dans la centrale," 29 Aug. 1947.

172 AUM, Fonds ACC, P16/B6, 3.15, Denise Messier, Denise Messier, "Morale familiale – De l'indépendance de la femme dans la hiérarchie du foyer," 6 Feb. 1956, Philosophie IIIe année, Université de Montréal.

173 Ibid.

174 Ibid.

175 Ibid.

176 See Karen Offen, "Body Politics: Women, Work and the Politics of Motherhood in France, 1920–1950," in Gisela Bock and Pat Thane, eds, *Women and the Rise of the European Welfare States, 1880s-1950s* (London and New York: Routledge, 1991), 144.

177 Marion Provencher, séminaire de Nicolet, "Le docteur angélique affirme la supériorité de l'homme," VE 19, no. 10 (June 1953).

178 Michel Dansereau, "À propos du 'Deuxième Sexe' de Simone de Beauvoir," CL 17 (June 1957): 57.

179 AUM, Fonds ACC, P16/E2.2.1, "Correspondance, 23 mai 1945–12 mars 1964," "Quelques notes prises, à l'occasion du Congrès."

180 ANQM, Fonds JEC, P65, SS6, SSS2, D5/2, Rita Racette, "La Femme et la Profession," Session de l'Action catholique universitaire, Lac Ouareau, Sept. 1952.

181 Adèle Lauzon, "Égalité et civilisation," RD (Jan. 1950): 31–5," See also Vallerand, "Madame Vallerand"; "Forum," JC (Feb. 1948): 8–9; Jeanne

Benoît, "La femme dans nos temps," JC (Feb. 1948): 25–6; Rita Leclerc, "'L'âme féminine, par Paul Thouvignon," JC (Apr. 1947): 25–6; Béchard, "Femme idéale?" 90.

182 AUM, Fonds ACC, P16/D5, 1.10, "Travaillera-t-elle?" n.d.; ibid., P16/D1, 4.10, "La Culture, programme d'action, 1959–60," Madeleine Ryan, "Vie de l'esprit chez les jeunes de classes moyennes"; Francine Laurendeau and Louise Holtved, collège Basile-Moreau, Ville St. Laurent, lettre, VE 19, no. 11 (Sept. 1953); Michèle Leclerc, "Le Courrier de l'Étudiante: Intelligence, culture sont toujours des atouts précieux," VE 22, no. 7 (Apr. 1956).

183 "Être femme de son temps," VE 17, no. 5 (May 1951).

184 Racette, "La Femme et la Profession."

185 AUM, P16/E2, 1.2, Comité des Jeunesses Féminines Catholiques du Canada, "Journée mondiale de prières, 30 novembre 1960 – 1er juillet 1961."

186 ANQM, Fonds JEC, P65, S6, SS6, SSS2, D1/5, Programmes, Action Catholique Universitaire, *S'Inscrire dans l'Histoire.* Élements pour une présence chrétienne à la société politique, Sept. 1955.

187 AUM, Fonds ACC, P16/D6, 5.2, Questionnaire, Anna-Maria Pigeon, secrétaire, à Union Feminine Civique et Sociale, Paris, 18 Jan. 1953. See also ibid., P16/D6, 5.1, Développement de la Personnalité de la Femme, "Personnalité de la Femme Ouvrière." AUQÀM, Fonds ICEA, 56P 11b/9, "Symposium 1958: Rencontre consultative auprès des organismes féminins," 20 Mar. 1958.

188 ANQM, Fonds SPM, P116, art. 36, La crise de l'homme dans le monde moderne, résumé de la conférence de M. Gustave Thibon, 1 Nov. 1956; ibid., Spicilèges, Chanoine Clavel, "À la conquête des Foyers de Demain," conférence, 9 May 1950; AUM, Fonds ACC, P16/D6, 5.2, Marcel Clément, "Chômage et travail féminin," *L'Action Catholique,* 21 Mar. 1953.

189 Jacqueline Billette, "Carrières féminines," JC (Sept.–Oct. 1948). See also Renée Blanchard, "Carrières feminines," JC (Mar. 1948); Mlle L. Gaudreau, "Émancipation de la femme et syndicalisme," LT, 18 Jan. 1952, 6.

190 AUM, Fonds ACC, P16/K1.24, Jean-Paul Gagnon, "Cours donné par M. Jean-Paul Gagnon à Montréal et Québec – juillet 1952," "Le rôle du travail féminin dans le monde moderne." For a similar view, see also André Roy, "Pourquoi travaillent-elles?" LT, 13 May 1953, 8.

191 AUM, Fonds ACC, P16/G4, 7.1, Semaines nationales, Germaine Bernier, "À propos d'une revue sur l'amour," LD, 15 May 1954. See also AUM, Fonds ACC, P16/E3, 4.3, "La Femme Canadienne-française: Instrument d'unité," 1961.

192 AUM, Fonds ACC, P16/K1.24, Jean-Paul Gagnon, "Cours donné par M. Jean-Paul Gagnon à Montréal et Québec – juillet 1952," "Le rôle du travail féminin dans le monde moderne."

193 Ibid., "Comment contribuer au bien commun par mon travail."

194 Adèle Lauzon, "La femme au travail: Chercher une réponse," LT, 6 Nov. 1953, 4.

195 Gagnon, "Le rôle du travail féminin dans la société moderne."

196 Carignan, "Humanité féminine."

197 ANQM, Fonds MLLF, box 3, Fernande Saint-Martin, *La femme et la société cléricale*. (Collection MLF, no. 14, Ottawa: MLLF, 1967).

198 Racette, "La Femme et la Profession."

199 "La Femme Canadienne-française: Instrument d'unité." See also AUM, Fonds ACC, P16/G5, 8.7, Jeunesse Ouvrière Catholique, "Situation religieuse des jeunes travailleuses," May 1957; Racette, "La Femme et la Profession." Perhaps the most eloquent expression of the dichotomy between male and female religious psychologies was provided by Fernand Dumont, who recalled that his mother was "naturally religious" and that her piety was exhibited in the form of external devotions accompanied by a strict moralism. His father, who was not devout in the conventional sense, apparently taught him an intensely "personal religion" that Dumont sought to equate with the modernizing currents within the Church that he enthusiastically identified with. See Fernand Dumont, *Récit d'une émigration* (Montreal: Boréal, 1997), 36–7.

200 AUM, Fonds ACC, P16/D6, 5.2, Claude Ryan, "Dangereuse prédominance de l'élément féminin dans l'A.C."

201 AUM, Fonds ACC, P16/C2, 3.8, "Notes sur l'État actuel des Mouvements specialisés d'Action Catholique au Canada," June 1950; ibid, P16/12.23, Claude Ryan à Mlle Madeleine Guay, 17 June 1953: "inevitably, in the long run, the secularization of those sectors of life which more commonly pertain to men"; ibid., P16/D6, 5.2, Ryan, "Dangereuse prédominance de l'élément féminin dans l'A.C."; ANQM, Fonds JOC, P104, art. 181, Commission 2, Pour une Action Catholique vraiment Canadienne, 1950, "Que Penser de la Prédominance Actuelle du Secteur *Féminin* et du Secteur *Masculin* dans le développement de l'A.C.C.?"

202 For the cultural fears regarding a developing matriarchy, see Barbara Ehrenreich, *For Her Own Good: 150 Years of the Experts' Advice to Women* (New York: Anchor Books, 1989). For the fears of Canadian Protestant religious leaders, see Christie, "'Sacred Sex,'" in Christie, *Households of Faith*, 361. In the Quebec context, the theme of female dominance and consequent male emasculation was a theme sounded by a variety of Catholic activists and social scientists during the 1950s, most eloquently by Jean LeMoyne, "La femme et la civilisation canadienne-française," CL 17 (June 1957): 14–36. See also Guy Rocher, "La famille dans la ville moderne," SS 4, no. 1 (spring 1954): 83; Gérald Fortin, "Socio-cultural Changes in an Agricultural Parish," in Rioux and Martin, eds, *French-Canadian Society*, vol. 1 (Toronto: McCelland and Stewart, 1964), 94. For further analysis of this theme, see Michael Gauvreau, "The Family as Pathology: Psychology, Social Science and History Construct the Nuclear Family, 1945–1980," in Nancy Christie and Michael Gauvreau, eds, *Mapping the Margins: Families and Social Discipline in*

Canada, 1700–1970 (Montreal and Kingston: McGill-Queen's University Press, 2004).

203 For a similar argument, which views the secularization of Britain as characteristic of the 1960s, and also centres it on the problem of the intersection of Christianity and women's identities, see Callum G. Brown, *The Death of Christian Britain: Understanding Secularization, 1800–2000* (London and New York: Routledge, 2001), 176–9.

204 AUM, Fonds ACC, P16/D6, 5.6, "La Femme au travail dans le monde," ca 1957; ANQM, Fonds JOC, P104, art. 288, "Programme social, 1955–56, JOCF." In this respect, married women in Quebec participated in a common North American pattern in the 1950s, although they seemed to enter the dynamic only after the mid-1950s. For example, Jessica Weiss has noted in the American context that in 1950, 52 per cent of married women worked, and that during that decade there was a tremendous expansion among the work of married and older women due to the abolition of marriage bars in most states, the availability of part-time work, and the expansion of the tertiary sector. See Jessica Weiss, *To Have and to Hold: Marriage, the Baby Boom, and Social Change* (Chicago: University of Chicago Press, 2000), 49–52; and for Ontario, Joan Sangster, "Doing Two Jobs: the Wage-Earning Mother, 1945–70," in Parr, *A Diversity of Women*, 98–134.

205 Jeanne Duval, "La femme au travail," *Maint* (June 1963): 202–4. See also AUM, Fonds ACC, P16/N4.21, Ministère du Travail, *A travail égal, salaire égal: progrès du concept au Canada* (Ottawa: Ministère du Travail du Canada, 1959).

206 In this respect, Quebec Catholic attitudes were far less conservative on the issue of married women working than were the prevalent attitudes in the United Church at the end of the 1950s. See on this debate in Canadian Protestantism, Christie, "'Sacred Sex,'" 361–2.

207 Renée Geoffroy, "La mère de famille peut-elle allier une carrière a sa vie domestique?" LT, 7 Sept. 1956, 6.

208 "La Femme Canadienne-française: Instrument d'unité."

209 Renée Geoffroy, "Cette femme forte: la mère de famille à l'usine," *Chat* 5, no. 9 (Sept. 1964): 25; Fernande Saint-Martin, "Pourquoi travaillent-elles?" *Chat* 2, no. 2 (Feb. 1962): 1; AUM, Fonds ACC, P16/E2, 5.6, Étude sur le travail féminin, "Le travail féminin au Canada français," 1960, which cited the need for the development of the human person "in and through work"; ibid., P16/J4.3, Le milieu des classes moyennes et professionnelles, document de travail, 6 Dec. 1957, "Opinions sur les Filles et les Femmes"; ibid., P16/E3.4.2, Congrès International, Rome 1957, Marthe Beaudry, "A travail égal, salaire égal – Qu'est-ce que cela signifie chez-nous?" undated news clipping; ibid., P16/E2, 5.7, La Jeune Fille, Membre Vivante de la Communauté,Enquête préparatoire au Séminaire Internattional de Buenos Aires, 24 au 31 juillet, 1962, "Participation de la jeune fille à la vie de travail"; AUM, Fonds Paul-Larocque, P52/A10, "Mémoire … par J.E. Havel."

210 AUM, Fonds ACC, P16/D5, 1.10, SPM de Montréal, "Travaillera-t-elle?" n.d. This realization owed a good deal to the efforts of personalist feminists in the Catholic labour movement who since the mid-1950s had brought to light the situation of married women who had been forced to perform a "double duty" as both workers and wives and mothers. See "La C.T.C.C. et le travail féminin," LT, 11 June 1954, 6; Renée Geoffroy, "La femme à l'usine," LT, 4 Feb. 1955, 6; Renée Geoffroy, "La mère de famille peut-elle allier une carrière à sa vie domestique?" LT, 7 Sept. 1956, 6.

211 "La Femme Canadienne-française: Instrument d'unité." See also Marie Raymond, "La femme et la civilisation," CL 17 (June 1957): 3–13. For the timing of the arrival of post-war consumerism in the cultural realm in the latter half of the 1950s, see Christie and Gauvreau, "Introduction: Recasting Canada's Postwar Decade" in Christie and Gauvreau, eds, *Cultures of Citizenship in Postwar Canada*. The impact of this consumerism on public ideologies of female identity is only beginning to be explored by historians. For a particularly illuminating study in the West German context, see Erica Carter, *How German Is She? Postwar West German Reconstruction and the Consuming Woman* (Ann Arbor: University of Michigan Press, 1997), 62–5.

212 ANQM, Fonds SPM, P116, art. 2, "Semaine des fiancés, 1951."

213 AUM, Fonds ACC, P16/D5, 1.10, SPM de Montréal, Session d'étude, 1957, Solange Pitre à Madeleine Trottier, secrétaire SPM.

214 "Mère de famille et citoyenne – Courrier de l'étudiante," VE 27, no. 2 (Oct. 1960); MCMUL, Royal Commission on the Status of Women, Briefs, "Mémoire #120: Conseil Étudiant des Filles, Collège Sainte-Anne-de-la-Pocatière," Mar. 1968; Rocher, "Les modèles et le statut de la femme canadienne-française," in Marie-José Chombart de Lauwe, *La femme dans la société: son image dans différents milieux sociaux* (Paris: Centre national de la recherche scientifique, 1963), 204.

215 AUM, Fonds ACC, P16/N5, 1.7, Conseil supérieur de la Famille, "Mémoire du SPM," n.d.

216 AUM, P16/D5, 1.10, "SPM de Montréal," n.d." See also ibid., P16/H3, 18.84, "Le S.P.M. de Montréal et le travail de la femme mariée," ca 1963–64; Mme Michèle Stanton-Jean, ancienne collaboratrice au quotidien *Le Soleil* de Québec, "Le travail de la mère hors du foyer," *Mission et droits de la famille*, 142–53; Michèle Rivet, "Les jeunes filles – Des inférieures au plan social," VE 28, no. 16 (May 1962).

217 Jacques Laliberté, "La femme de demain élèvera de futurs astronautes – une entrevue avec Mme. Alex Pelletier," VE 28, no. 15 (May 1962). This Friedanesque type of critique of family life became widespread in Quebec during the mid-1960s. See for example, "La dépression nerveuse guette les femmes 'cloîtrées' au foyer," LD, 4 Apr. 1966; Germaine Bernier, "Betty Friedan," LD, 8 Apr. 1965; Michelle Lasnier, "La femme de trente ans," *Chat* 3, no. 5 (May 1962): 37, 113–16, 118–19; Fernande Saint-Martin, "Femmes,

unissez-vous," *Chat* 3, no. 9 (Sept. 1962): 1; Michelle Lasnier, "Pourquoi se séparent-ils?" *Chat* 4, no. 9 (Sept. 1963): 34–5, 84–90; Cathy Breslin, "La femme domestiquée," *Chat* 6, no. 2 (Feb. 1965): 22–3, 48–9; Margaret Mead, "Toutes les femmes ne sont pas aptes au mariage," *Chat* 6, no. 6 (June 1965): 24, 50–2.

218　Garigue, *Vie familiale des canadiens-français*, 34–5.

219　AUM, Fonds Paul-Larocque, P52/A69, "Mémoire de l'Association des Instituts Familiaux"; "La Femme Canadienne-française: Instrument d'unité."

220　Camille Laurin, "Le statut de la femme," in Laurin, *Ma traversée du Québec*, 58–9. See also MCMUL, Royal Commission on the Status of Women, Briefs, "Mémoire #349, Association des Femmes Diplômées des Universités (Montréal)," Apr. 1968.

221　For this assessment, see Marwick, *The Sixties*, 9–11.

222　Government of Canada, *Royal Commission on the Status of Women* (Ottawa: Queen's Printer, 1970), 4–6.

223　Solange Chalvin, "Le couple moderne en proie au mythe de l'érotisme, vu par Violette Morin," LD, 24 Nov. 1967. See also Margaret Mead, "L'homme nord-américain est-il encore un homme?" *Chat* 4, no. 7 (July 1963): 17, 40, 42; NAC, Fonds Thérèse-Casgrain, vol. 6, "Fédération des Femmes du Québec," "Office de la Femme," "Mémoire présentée a l'Hon. Robert Bourassa," Nov. 1971. The rapidity of the transformation in Quebec can be gauged by a 1968 *Châtelaine* survey that indicated that of 3,000 women surveyed, only 12 per cent agreed with the traditional structure of family with a single male breadwinner; 73 per cent of women stated that they wanted to combine marriage with a career; and 87 per cent said they would advise their daughters to continue their careers after marriage. See Fernande Saint-Martin, "La majorité des québécoises voudraient unir mariage et carrière," *Chat* 9, no. 6 (June 1968): 1; Mme L. Caron, Montréal, "Le débat se poursuit," lettre, *Chat* 5, no. 10 (Oct. 1964): 84; AUQÀM, Fonds Centre de planning familial, 113P/207/001, Les implications de la planification des naissances, Mémoire présenté à la Commission Royale d'Enquête sur la situation de la femme au Canada."

224　AUM, Fonds ACC, P16/E3, 3.5, "Réunions 1966, 1967, 1968," "Procès-verbal de la réunion tenue mercredi 13 septembre 1967"; ibid., P16/B6, 7.15, Volume sur la vie politique, Lucie Ryan, "La Femme et la Politique," ca 1967. See also AUM, Fonds Paul-Larocque, P52/A137, André Dagenais, "Témoignage pour le Concile et Mémoire sur l'éducation," 4 July 1962; ANQM, Fonds JEC, P65, art. 1, Abbé Louis-R. Dumas, "Principes d'une spiritualité du laïcat étudiant," 1962.

225　NAC, Canadian Conference on the Family, MG28 I117, vol. 6, file 4, Raymond Doyle à Marguerite Mathieu, 20 May 1964.

226　AUM, Fonds ACC, P16/E3, 4.2, Congrès international, Rome 1957, "Circulaire," 15 May 1959.

227 Dr Mirra Komarovsky, "Women in the Modern World," in Canadian Broadcasting Corporation, Department of Public Affairs, *The Real World of Women* (Toronto: Canadian Association for Adult Education, 1962), 3–4, 6–7, 11.

228 Camille Laurin, "Woman in the Modern World," in *The Real World of Women*, 61.

229 Ibid., 60–2.

230 Ibid., 65–7. For the new prominence of Simone de Beauvoir's existentialist feminism in Quebec middle-class circles in the 1960s, see Fernande Saint-Martin's interview with the French philosopher, "Le bonheur ou le malheur d'être femme," *Chat* 5, no. 4 (Apr. 1964): 1; Michelle Lasnier, "'Le Deuxième Sexe' c'est notre bible," *Chat* 5, no. 4 (Apr. 1964): 19, 62–6.

231 Jeanne Sauvé, "Comments on Interviews – II," in *The Real World of Women*, 55.

232 Ibid., 56–7.

233 Ibid., 54, 57.

234 Thérèse Forget-Casgrain, "Bill 16: Des Miettes," *Maint* (Apr. 1964): 127; NAC, Fonds Thérèse-Casgrain, MG32 C25, vol. 8, file "Régimes matrimoniaux," "Toujours trop peu," ca 1964; ibid., Thérèse Casgrain, "Le Statut de la femme au Québec"; ibid., vol. 8, "Correspondance, 1960–1966," H.M. Charette, avocat, à Thérèse Casgrain, 11 Mar. 1964; ibid., vol. 5, "Le mariage et le divorce," Mémoire de la Chambre des Notaires du Québec, Mar. 1968; Fernande Saint-Martin, "Le Code et le mépris de la femme," *Chat* 4, no. 9 (Sept. 1963): 1; Fernande Saint-Martin, "Un appel a tous les hommes," *Chat* 5, no. 3 (Mar. 1964); Marcel Thivierge, "La capacité juridique de la femme mariée est soumise aux députés," LD, 28 Jan. 1964.

235 Bernard Mailhiot, o.p., "Des mythes et mystères de la femme," *Maint* (Mar. 1964): 89. See also Hélène Pelletier-Baillargeon, "Fete des mères," *Maint* (May 1964): 151–2; Colette Carisse, "Nouveau dialogue conjugal," *Maint* (July–Aug. 1965): 250–1; Hélène Pelletier-Baillargeon, "Un Concile pour le deuxième sexe?" *Maint* (May 1966): 145–9; ANQM, Fonds JEC, P65, art.1, Jean LeMoyne, "La qualité de la vie religieuse dans l'Église," ca 1962.

236 Saint-Martin, *La femme et la société cléricale.*

237 AUM, Fonds Commission Dumont, P21/G1.28, Diocèse de Québec, Mme Germaine Laplante, Ste.-Foy, "Les laïcs dans l'Église," May 1970.

238 Saint-Martin, *La femme et la société cléricale.*

239 Ibid.

240 Pelletier-Baillargeon, "Un Concile pour le 'deuxième sexe,'" 147.

241 AUM, Fonds Commission Dumont, P21/G1.28, Laplante, "Les laïcs dans l'Église"; MCMUL, Royal Commission on the Status of Women, Briefs, "Mémoire #102, Cercles de Fermières de la Province de Québec, jan. 1968"; ibid., "Mémoire #127, Dames Hélène-de-Champlain, 11 mars 1968."

242 "Programme et objectifs de la FFQ pour l'année 66–67," LD, 23 Apr. 1966.

See also Solange Chalvin, "Jeanne Sauvé réclame une enquête nationale sur le statut des femmes au Canada," LD, 11 Mar. 1966.

243 NAC, Fonds Thérèse-Casgrain, vol. 8, "Régimes Matrimoniaux," "Mémoire soumis au Comité des régimes matrimoniaux de l'Office de Revision du Code Civil," Fédération des Femmes du Québec, Dec. 1966; ibid., vol. 5, "Commission Royale sur le statut de la femme au Canada, 1968," "L'Éducation des femmes au Québec: situation et perspectives," Mémoire présenté a la Commission ... par la Fédération des Femmes du Québec, Mar. 1968.

244 Claude Déry, "Session Pré-Électorale," *Maint* (autumn 1965): 296.

245 MCMUL, Royal Commission on the Status of Women, Briefs, "Mémoire #17, Groupe de Femmes de Roberval, L'Ère de la femme," 16 Jan. 1968; ibid., "Mémoire #49, Association féminine d'éducation et d'action sociale, village de Richelieu," 24 Jan. 1968; AUM, Fonds ACC, Conseil Supérieur de la Famille, "Mémoire du S.P.M."; Alice Parizeau, "La femme: pupille ou paria?" *Maint* (May 1965): 158–60; ANQM, Fonds René-Lévesque, P18/23/D207, "Bulletin de liaison, C.C.C.E.," "La Femme et la Politique," n.d.

246 Carole, cited in Marie-Josée Beaudoin, *Pouvez-vous 'empêcher la famille'?* (Montreal: Les Éditions de l'Homme, 1964), 60.

247 "La Femme Canadienne-française: Instrument d'unité."

248 Dr Lionel Gendron, *Qu'est-ce qu'une femme?* vol. 2, 33–4; Laurin, "Woman in the Modern World," in *The Real World of Women*, 61. Writing in 1968, June Callwood characterized 25 to 50 per cent of North American women as "frigid," arguing that most unstable marriages and family tensions could be blamed on the lack of female sexual gratification. See Callwood, "La Femme nord-américaine découvre une nouvelle sexualité dans le mariage," *Chat* 9, no. 6 (June 1968), 64.

249 Marwick, *The Sixties*, 18.

250 "La Femme Canadienne-française: Instrument d'unité"; AUQÀM, Fonds Centre de planning familial, 113P/210A/001, Revues et coupures de presse, Solange Chalvin, "Un teach-in prend l'allure d'un cours magistral sur la sexualité," LD, 12 Mar. 1970, citing the address of Jean-Marc Samson, theologian; AUM, Fonds Commission Dumont, P21/G2.13, Diocèse de Saint-Hyacinthe, Jean H. Massey, avocat, "Plaidoyer pour l'homme," Granby, 2 Mar. 1970; André Major, "Jeunesse québecoise et morale de l'échec," *Maint* (Dec. 1962): 405. For a recent study of the growing tension between Catholic moral teaching and the need for sexual fulfilment within marriage, a tension that affected many ordinary Catholics, see Diane Gervais, "Morale catholique et détresse conjugale au Québec: la réponse du service de régulation des naissances Seréna, 1955–1970," *Revue d'histoire de l'Amérique française* 55, no. 2 (autumn 2001): 185–215.

251 "Amour difficile," lettre, *Chat* 4, no. 11 (Nov. 1963): 88.

252 ANQM, Fonds SPM, P116, art. 24, Camille Laurin, "Les services que le S.P.M.

rend à la société." See also AUM, Fonds Commission Dumont, P21/D2, Entrevues, "Entrevue 2, 02-B-22."

253 Gérard Pelletier, "Le Québec et les québécoises," *Chat* 5, no. 9 (Sept. 1965): 8. See also Denis Duval, aumônier, l'Académie de Québec, "Quand le sexe va, tout va," *Maint* (Jan. 1965): 24–5; M.D., lettre, *L'Action*, 12 Sept. 1968.

254 Pelletier, "Le Québec et les québécoises," 73.

255 Marie-Josée Beaudoin, *Pouvez-vous*, 72; AUM, Fonds ACC, P16/D1, 4.15b, "Sondage à Chicoutimi."

256 AUM, Fonds ACC, P16/G2. 2.1,3, "Problèmes a la centrale de la J.E.C., 1961–62," "Jean Francoeur." See also AUQÀM, Fonds Centre de planning familial, 113P/103A/001, Procès-verbaux, 27 Sept. 1965, observation by the Services Familiaux du Quartier St.-Henri; Jacques Baillargeon and Hélène Pelletier-Baillargeon, "Éducation populaire et régulation des naissances," *Maint* (June 1963): 195.

257 Baillargeon and Pelletier-Baillargeon, "Éducation populaire," 196; Marcel-Marie Desmarais, "Une Encyclique de Jean XXIII sur le mariage?" *Maint* (May 1963): 154–7; Michel Trottier, "Contrôle des naissances et contrôle de la sexualité," SS 12, nos 1–2 (Jan.–Feb. 1963): 56–70; André Lussier, "Mariage et psychanalyse," *Maint* (Mar. 1964): 86–7; Joseph-M. Parent, o.p., "Limitation ou régulation des naissances," *Maint* (Apr. 1962): 141–2.

258 ANQM, Fonds JOC, P104, art. 4, "S.P.M. de la J.O.C.: Rapport du Congrès national, 1961," M. et Mme Jacques Baillargeon, "Le problème de la régulation des naissances."

259 Beaudoin, *Pouvez-vous*, 18–19. See also Colette Carisse, *Planification des naissances en milieu canadien-français* (Montreal: Les Presses de l'Université de Montréal, 1964), 171; André Laurendeau, "Le 'Birth Control' hier et aujourd'hui," MM (Aug. 1966): 44; Colette Carisse, "Le nombre des enfants," *Chat* 5, no. 6 (June 1964): 63–4; "Vous avez le dernier mot – Contrôle des naissances," *Chat* 4, no. 8 (Aug. 1963): 52.

260 AUM, Fonds ACC, P16/05.29, "Confédération des Loisirs du Québec, 1965"; ibid., P16/D1, 4.15b, Sondage à Chicoutimi, 1961; ANQM, Fonds JEC, P65, art. 42, "Vie Sentimentale des Jeunes, jan. 1961"; Carisse, *Planification des naissances*, 99–100; Alice Parizeau, "Contrôle des naissances," *Chat* 4, no. 6 (June 1963): 25.

261 "Sondage – La régulation des naissances – comment se comportent les Québecoises?" MM (June 1966): 11–13; Colette Carisse, "Le nombre des enfants," *Chat* 5, no. 6 (June 1964): 27, 63–5; Fernande Saint-Martin, "Des femmes qui crient au secours," *Chat* 4, no. 6 (June 1963): 1; Beaudoin, *Pouvez-vous*, 57: opinion of "Anne" a university student, who noted that she had consulted a priest, who referred her to a doctor who then prescribed the Pill; Ian Sclanders, "Une seule solution: 'Empêcher la famille?" MM (May 1964): 32, 45–50.

262 ANQM, Fonds SPM, P116, art. 24, Paquin, "Compte-rendu, 1960."

263 AUM, Fonds ACC, P16/D5, 1.12, SPM de Montréal, "Amour conjugal," n.d.; ibid., P16/D5, 1.10, SPM de Montréal, "Pour un amour enrichissant," n.d.

264 Dr Jacques Baillargeon and Hélène Pelletier-Baillargeon, "Régulation des naissances," *Maint* (Jan. 1966): 10. See also Solange Chalvin, "Le premier but du 'planning familial': faire échec a l'avortement," LD, 19 Oct. 1964; "L'Église de Toronto et les contraceptifs oraux," LD, 23 Oct. 1964; Solange Chalvin, "C'est à chaque couple qu'incombe le devoir moral et social de planifier les naissances," LD, 23 Oct. 1964; "Un religieux se demande si le problème de la limitation des naissances devrait être résolu en conscience par chacun," LD, 19 Feb. 1965.

265 AUQÀM, Fonds Centre de planning familial, 113P/101B/001, Serge Mongeau, "Historique du Centre de planning familial du Québec"; ibid., 113P/103A/001, Procès-verbaux, 27 Sept. 1965, Vincent Harvey. For Harvey and *Maintenant*, see Vincent Harvey, o.p., "L'amour conjugal chrétien," *Maint* (Feb. 1963): 48–9; Harvey, "Morale conjugale: Régulation des naissances," *Maint* (Sept. 1964): 258, in which he condemned "irresponsible *natalism*" and dwelt upon the serious limitations of the rhythm method; Jacques Baillargeon & Hélène Pelletier-Baillargeon, "Le médecin et la régulation des naissances," *Maint* (Jan. 1965).

266 "Les médecins et la contraception," *Maint* (May 1966): 157–9.

267 AUQÀM, Fonds Centre de planning familial, "Compte-rendu de la réunion tenue ... 1er fév. 1967, par le Comité Aviseur"; ibid., "Compte-rendu, 2 mai 1967 ... par le Comité Aviseur."

268 Baillargeon and Baillargeon, "Régulation des naissances," 15; AUQÀM, Fonds Centre de planning familial, Robert Riendeau, ptre, "Résumé des discussions d'un comité chargé ... d'examiner le projet ... du point de vue des implications morales et religieuses," 3/1/67.

269 Marthe Handfield, "Mimétisme et aggiornamento," AN 54, no. 8 (Apr. 1965): 809–14.

270 AUM, Fonds Commission Dumont, P21/D1, Entrevues, 01-E-667; Commission d'étude sur l'Église et les laïcs, *L'Église du Québec: un héritage, un projet*, 33; AUQÀM, Fonds Centre de Planning familial, "Communiqué spécial du Centre de planification familiale," Aug. 1968.

271 Hélène Pilotte, "La sexologie: une science en conflit avec la tradition," *Chat* 9, no. 10 (Oct. 1968): 28–9; Claude Ryan, "L'encyclique sur la régulation des naissances," LD, 30 July 1968; Solange Chalvin, "Un grand choc pour les catholiques," LD, 31 July 1968; Solange Chalvin, "L'encyclique ne changerait rien ... au comportement professionnel des médecins, travailleurs sociaux, conseillers familiaux," LD, 1 Aug. 1968; Fernande Saint-Martin, "On ne peut vouer la femme à la seule maternité physique," *Chat* 9, no. 10 (Oct. 1968): 1.

CHAPTER SIX

1　Jacques Godbout, "Chronique de l'éducation – l'égoisme sénile ou les amendements de N.N.S.S.," PP 2, no. 2 (Nov. 1963): 59.

2　ANQ-M, P 295, Fonds MLLF, 9/1/26, Correspondance générale, cl-Ge, René Guilbeault à Pierre Lebeuf, coupure de presse, 13 July 1962.

3　Maurice Blain, "La guerre de Troie n'a pas lieu," CL 36 (Apr. 1961): 10, 13.

4　Gilles Dussault, "La Commission d'Enquête sur l'Enseignement: les 42 premiers mémoires," Rel (Mar. 1962): 70. As Charles Taylor, a member of the secularist Mouvement Laïque de Langue Française, recognized in 1963, two cultural currents were converging in modern Quebec: "the evolution of the modern State in the direction of religious neutrality; the other the evolution of the Catholic Church ... towards a spiritualization that will free it from that will to power that has weighed for centuries upon its history." See Taylor, "L'État et la laïcité," CL 54 (Feb. 1963): 3. Such a view was not markedly different from that of the more conservative commentator, the Jesuit Father Richard Arès. See Richard Arès, s.j., "L'éducation, problème social," in L'éducation, problème social. Semaines sociales du Canada, 38e session, Montréal 1962 (Montreal: Les Éditions Bellarmin, 1962), which stressed the need for accord and collaboration between Church and State in order to preserve the "soul" of the educational system while adapting it to the conditions of an urban, industrial, scientific civilization (10).

5　Réginald Boisvert, "La guerre de Troie est-elle souhaitable?" CL 35 (Mar. 1961): 19.

6　For analysis of the social and political constituencies behind the 1943 school reforms, see Dominique Marshall, Aux origines sociales de l'État-providence (Montreal: Les Presses de l'Université de Montréal, 1998), 26–38.

7　For a recent analysis of Vatican II that focuses largely on matters internal to the Catholic Church, see Terrence Fay, A History of Canadian Catholics: Gallicanism, Romanism, and Canadianism (Montreal and Kingston: McGill-Queen's University Press, 2002), 295–6; and for its impact on the life of the Quebec Church, see Gilles Routhier, ed., L'Église canadienne et Vatican II (Saint-Laurent, Quebec: Fides, 1997).

8　NAC, Fonds Paul Gérin-Lajoie MG31 E106, vol. 64.1, "Allocution de l'Hon. Paul Gérin-Lajoie, ministre de la Jeunesse, au Comité Catholique du Conseil d'Instruction Publique," 28 Sept. 1961.

9　Richard Arès, s.j., "Au congrès laïque," Montréal-Matin, 8 May 1961.

10　See Louis-Philippe Audet, Histoire de l'enseignement au Québec, 1840–1971, vol. 2 (Montreal: Holt, Rinehart et Winston, 1971).

11　On the education debate of the 1950s, see Michael Behiels, Prelude to Quebec's Quiet Revolution: Liberalism versus Neo-Nationalism, 1945–1960 (Montreal and Kingston: McGill-Queen's University Press, 1985), 159–61. Behiels notes that most of Duplessis's critics, particularly André Laurendeau, Gérard Filion, and

Arthur Tremblay, the latter two who were to play key roles as architects of the 1960s education reforms, were wary of advocating complete state control of the education system.

12 Paul Gérin-Lajoie, *Pourquoi le Bill 60* (Montreal: Les Éditions du Jour, 1963), 56.

13 Two of these proposed institutions were to be located in Montreal: Loyola, an English-language facility, and Sainte-Marie, a French-language institution.

14 On Lesage's attitude, see Dale C. Thomson, *Jean Lesage and the Quiet Revolution* (Toronto: Macmillan, 1984).

15 For the composition of the commission, see *Report of the Royal Commission of Inquiry on Education in the Province of Quebec* (Quebec: Province of Quebec, 1963). The English-language commissioners were David Munroe (Protestant) and John McIlhone (Catholic). Only Jeanne Lapointe, Guy Rocher, and Arthur Tremblay, the deputy-minister of Youth who was Associate Commissioner without voting rights, would qualify as representatives of the new "secular" professional elite, and even their credentials as believing Catholics were never in doubt. On Filion's attitude throughout the 1950s, see Behiels, *Prelude to Quebec's Quiet Revolution*, 157.

16 Frère Pierre-Jérôme [Jean-Paul Desbiens, préf. d'André Laurendeau] *Les Insolences du Frère Untel* (Montreal: Les Éditions du Jour, 1961), 24–5, 49.

17 Ibid., 26.

18 Ibid., 81.

19 Ibid., 71–2, 81. For similar views regarding the corruption of the French language under the system of clerical teaching, see AUM, Fonds ACC, P16/05.80, Fédération des Sociétés St.-Jean-Baptiste du Québec, Raymond Barbeau, "La langue franglaise, un patois de trahison," *Alerte. Revue mensuelle* (June-July 1959): 165–6.

20 AUM, Fonds Paul-Larocque, P52/A260, "Mémoire ... présenté par les requérants du bill de l'Université Sainte-Marie," 10 July 1962.

21 Association des professeurs de l'Université de Montréal, *L'Université dit NON aux Jésuites* (Montreal: Les Éditions de l'Homme, 1961, 3d ed.; 1st ed. 1960), 17, 83–4.

22 Ibid., 17, 26.

23 In addition to the serialized letters in *Le Devoir*, Frère Untel's book sold over 100,000 copies, while even the more specialized *L'Université dit NON aux Jésuites* had sold 18,000 by 1961.

24 The founding executive and council were as follows: Maurice Blain, a lawyer and contributor to *Cité libre*, as president, and Judith Jasmin and Pierre Lebeuf, both Radio-Canada broadcasters, as vice-president and secretary. On the council were Jean-Marie Bédard, the film-maker Jacques Godbout, Jacques Guay, and the literary critic Jean LeMoyne.

25 See Robert Élie, introduction to *L'École laïque* (Montreal: Les Éditions du Jour, 1961).

26 Jacques Mackay, "Positions du Mouvement laïque de langue française," in *L'École laïque,* 22. See also ANQM, Fonds MLLF, 9/1/9, "Congrès – Réunions – Assemblées," "Déclaration relative à un projet d'Association Laïque de Langue Française," 3 au 4 février, 1961; Fonds MLLF, 9/1/1, "Constitution."

27 Mackay, "Positions du Mouvement laïque," 21, 26.

28 André Langevin, "Le peuple et les intellectuels s'interrogent dans le même sens," *Le Nouveau Journal,* 10 June 1961.

29 Georges-Henri Lévesque, o.p., "Le Nouveau laïcat," *Maint* (Oct. 1963): 294; Gérard Pelletier, "Feu l'unanimité," CL 30 (Oct. 1960): 8; Jean Genest, "Le mouvement laïc de langue française au Quebec," AN 52 (Feb. 1963): 543.

30 "Fondation du Mouvement laïc de langue française," LD, 10 Apr. 1961. For the views of the "jeune gauche," see André Major, "Jeunesse québécoise et la morale de l'échec," *Maint* (Dec. 1962): 404–5; Jacques Guay, "Voilà ce que je pense," CL 41 (Nov. 1961): 27; Jacques Godbout, "'Un Certain Silence' Rompu," CL 42 (Dec. 1961): 28; Yves Dionne, "Le laïcisme au Canada-français," PP (Jan. 1964): 4–22.

31 For Rioux's interpretation, see Denis Duval, ptre, "Le Mouvement laïque – incompris," *Maint* (July–Aug. 1962): 245.

32 AUM, Fonds Paul-Larocque, P52/A186, "Mémoire du MLF"; ANQM, Fonds MLLF, 9/1/2, "Procès-verbaux, 1961," which declared that religious teaching would be permitted, but on condition that it did not seek to "become the norm of Rational life"; editorial, "Ni cléricalisme, ni trahison des anticlercs," PP 2, no. 8 (Apr. 1965): 2–6.

33 Mackay, "Positions du Mouvement laïque," 22.

34 ANQM, Fonds MLLF, 9/1/26, "Correspondance Générale," Secrétaire MLLF à M. Jean-Pierre Guillemette, Trois-Rivières, 4 Feb. 1966.

35 Ibid., 9/1/2, "Procès-verbaux, 1961," Jean Lebas, secrétaire, section de la Ville de Québec, 23 May 1961.

36 Marcel Trudel, "'Il faut libérer l'Église de la servitude de l'État," LD, 19 Nov. 1962.

37 Richard Arès, s.j., "Le fait religieux au Quebec," *Rel* (Feb. 1962): 38; Pelletier, "Feu l'unanimité."

38 ANQM, Fonds MLLF, 9/1/26, Correspondance Générale, Thérèse Dumouchel, faculté de philosophie, Université de Montréal, à Maurice Blain, 28 Apr. 1961; ibid., 9/1/28, Correspondance Générale, H. Lefranc, Candiac, à MLLF, 13 Nov. 1964.

39 Gérard Filion, "Une solution raisonnable," LD, 5 Apr. 1961.

40 Gérard Pelletier, "Chez Qui Sommes Nous," in *L'École laïque,* 86–89: "I have drawn from Christian sources the sense of justice that inspires this commitment on my part"; ANQM, Fonds MLLF, 9/1/12, "Commission sociologique et politique, 1961," Maurice Hébert, St. Eustache Lac à Maurice Blain, 10 Oct. 1961.

41 Arès, "Au congrès laïque," *Montréal-Matin,* 8 May 1961.

42 "Après le discours de M. Lesage, le Mouvement laïc proteste," LD, 3 June 1961.

43 "Le Mouvement laïque n'a jamais réclamé autre chose que l'école neutre pour ceux qui la désirent," LD, 25 May 1961.

44 Élie, introduction to *L'École laïque*, 12–13.

45 AUM, Fonds Paul-Larocque, P52/A186, "Mémoire du Mouvement laïque de langue française," May 1962.

46 Maurice Blain, "La guerre de Troie," 13.

47 ANQM, Fonds MLLF, 9/1/25, "Correspondance Générale," Gilbert Beloeil, Rimouski, à Pierre Lebeuf, 27 Apr. 1961; ibid., 9/1/26, "Correspondance Générale," Raymond Laplante, Montréal, à Pierre Lebeuf, 5 Feb. 1962.

48 Ibid., 9/1/25, "Correspondance Générale," Très R.P. Ulric Arcand, M.A. à président MLLF, 25 Mar. 1963; 9/1/29, André-M. Billette, o.p., Couvent des Dominicains, Montréal, à Pierre Lebeuf, 14 July 1962; Abbé Robert Rivest à Pierre Lebeuf, 24 July 1962. Rivest, the first Catholic clergyman to adhere openly to the MLLF, believed in the separation of church and state pushed to its extreme, but declared that his notion of secularism was that of "President Kennedy, which is that of the group of Harvard sociologists."

49 "Un message courageux," LP, 20 June 1961.

50 "L'abbé Louis O'Neill: l'école non-confessionnelle: une aspiration légitime des non-catholiques," LD, 13 June 1961.

51 ANQM, Fonds MLLF, "Interview accordé par M. de Koninck à M. Marcel Trudel, le 29 mars 1962"; "Comme chrétien et comme citoyen, M. Gérard Pelletier dit: Oui, nous avons BESOIN d'écoles neutres dans la province de Québec," LD, 31 May 1961; Élie, introduction to *L'École laïque*, 10, where he stated that his membership in the MLLF was more a function of his Catholicism than of his belief in democracy.

52 Jean LeMoyne, "Foi et laïcité," in *L'École laïque*, 77; Élie, introduction to *L'École laïque*, 13; Miriam Chapin, "Quebec's Revolt against the Catholic Schools," *Harper's Magazine* (July 1961).

53 Pierre de Bellefeuille, "Editorial," MM (Dec. 1962): 4.

54 AUM, Fonds Paul-Larocque, P52/A55, "Mémoire des Chevaliers de Colomb," which noted that as a result of the 1957 Court of Appeals decision in the case of *Chabot* vs. *Les Commissaires d'École de La Morandière*, Jehovah's Witnesses had the right to attend Catholic schools while being exempted from religious instruction and exercises. See also ibid., P52/F22, Guy Rocher, "Essai d'introduction préliminaire à une tentative pour une première approche en vue d'un début de solution approximative à ce qui peut sembler être la méthode pour éviter de moins en moins le problème de la confessionnalité," n.d.; "L'école confessionnelle au Québec: situation juridique," *Rel* (Feb. 1962): 44–6; ANQM, Fonds MLLF, 3, "Mémoires," Yves Prévost à Pierre Lebeuf, 23 July 1962.

55 Blain, "La guerre de Troie," 13; ANQ-M, P295 Fonds MLLF, 9/1/26, "Corre-

spondance générale," Thérèse Dumouchel à Maurice Blain, 28 Apr. 1961, in which she qualified the MLLF as "this anti-segregationist movement." At a November 1961 meeting of the MLLF's Commission Sociologique et Politique, many in attendance were unfavourable to the idea of a separate non-sectarian school sector, arguing that it would be difficult to administer in areas outside Montreal and Quebec City. See ibid., 9/1/12, "Congrès d'étude ... Commission sociologique et politique – 4 novembre 1961," par Pierre de Bellefeuille.

56 ANQM, Fonds MLLF, 9/1/26, "Correspondance Générale," Mme Alberto Droghini à Maurice Blain, 17 Apr. 1961.

57 "La campagne pour l'École laïque se développe au Canada," LP, 1 Aug. 1961; ANQM, Fonds MLLF, 9/1/25, "Correspondance Générale," Roland Berger, Longueuil, à Pierre Lebeuf, 9 Dec. 1961; Mackay, "Positions du Mouvement laïque," 32–3.

58 Pierre de Bellefeuille, "Chasser les bondieuseries de l'ecole pour ne pas en chasser Dieu," MM (Aug. 1962): 4; Vincent Prince, "Au lieu de se lamenter ..." LP, 21 Sept. 1961; AUM, Fonds Paul-Larocque, P52/A10, "Mémoire par J.E. Havel, dr. es. lettres, dipl. en sciences politiques, lic. en droit, pr. en sc. politique à l'Université de Montréal."

59 André Lussier, "Notre école confessionnelle et l'enfant," in J. Mackay, ed., *Justice et Paix scolaires* (Montreal: Les Éditions du Jour, 1961), 82.

60 "L'opinion d'André Langevin: À la manière de François-Albert Angers," *Le Nouveau Journal,* 5 Dec. 1961; Wilfrid Martin, "Gros plan d'un adversaire de la laïcisation," LD, 14 Dec. 1961.

61 André Lussier, "Les dessous de la censure," CL 28 (June-July 1960): 15–17.

62 Ibid., 93, 97–8.

63 Ibid., 99.

64 Martin, "Gros plan d'un adversaire de la laïcisation"; AUM Fonds Paul-Larocque, P52/D3, Coupures de journaux, André Langevin, "Réforme qui ne peut attendre," *Le Nouveau Journal,* n.d.; André Major, *Liberté étudiante: Nous accusons nos éducateurs* (Montreal: n.p., 1961).

65 Fernand Dumont, "Réflexions sur l'histoire religieuse du Canada français," in Marcel Rioux, ed., *L'Église et le Québec* (Montreal: Éditions du Jour, 1961), 49, 55, 60–3.

66 On the formulation and professional context of these interpretations of Quebec's past, see Ronald Rudin, *Making History in Twentieth-Century Quebec* (Toronto: University of Toronto Press, 1997), 109–10, 140–1.

67 For this aspect of Dumont's career, see Fernand Dumont, *Récit d'une émigration* (Montreal: Boréal, 1997), 101–25.

68 Dumont, "Réflexions sur l'histoire religieuse du Canada français," 65.

69 In addition to Marcel Trudel, who was president of the Quebec City section of the movement, other active figures included Laurier LaPierre, Jean Hamelin, Fernand Ouellet, and Louise Dechêne. See ANQM, Fonds MLLF, 9/1/26, Correspondance Générale, Louise Dechêne à Pierre Lebeuf, 2 Apr.

1962; ibid., 9/1/12, "Commission sociologique et politique," 1961; ibid., P295/3, Laurier LaPierre, "Discours," Loyola College, ca 1963. Fernand Ouellet became president of the Quebec City branch in 1964, and he was a frequent participant in MLLF colloquia on themes such as "Nationalisme et laïcité." See ibid., 9/1/5, "Procès-verbaux, 1964."

70 AUM, Fonds Paul-Larocque, P52/A25, "Mémoire de l'Association des Professeurs de l'Université de Montréal," 21 June 1962.

71 Ibid., P52/A229, "Mémoire de la Fédération des Travailleurs du Québec," 21 June 1962.

72 Bertrand Rioux, "Réflexions sur notre chrétienté," CL 31 (May 1960): 16; AUM, Fonds Paul-Larocque, P62/A85, "Mémoire présenté par Georges Neray," 4 July 1962; R. Boisvert, "La guerre de Troie est-elle souhaitable?" CL 37 (May 1961); Maurice Beaulieu, André Normandeau, "Le rôle de la religion à travers l'histoire du Canada français," CL 71 (Nov. 1964): 15–24.

73 Lorenzo Paré, "Le Dialogue des laïcistes," L'Action (formerly L'Action catholique), 1 Mar. 1963.

74 AUM, Fonds Paul-Larocque, P52/A19, "Mémoire de la revue Tradition et Progrès."

75 Réflexions pastorales sur notre système d'enseigment par S. Em. le cardinal Paul-Émile Léger," LP, 19 June 1961; "Deuxième partie," LP, 20 June 1961.

76 ANQM, Fonds JEC, P65, art. 1, Cardinal P.-E. Léger, "Dangers du Laïcisme au Canada Français," Oct. 1960. Allocution prononcée à un Dîner-Causerie du Club du Premier Vendredi du Mois à l'Oratoire Saint-Joseph le 7 octobre 1960.

77 "Monsieur Gérin-Lajoie: Le respect de la liberté de chacun est le fondement même des écoles confessionnelles," LD, 23 Oct. 1961. The minister's view resembled that of Cardinal Léger as he believed that the clergy came to prominence in the educational system, not because they desired a monopoly, but because the laity refused to accept fiscal responsibility for schooling, and to pay teachers proper salaries.

78 François-Albert Angers, "La singulière théorie du désengagement," LD, 20 Sept. 1961.

79 François-Albert Angers, "La singulière théorie du désengagement – II," LD, 21 Sept. 1961.

80 Julia Richer, "Dialogue à une seule voix," NT, 23 Dec. 1961, in which she accused the MLLF of wanting to "kick out the clergy, relegating them to the sacristy or forcibly extirpating them."

81 Angers, LD, 20 Sept. 1961. See also Pierre Angers, s.j., "Clercs et laïcs dans l'enseignement," Rel (Nov. 1961), who put the matter as follows: "All instruction, even that in profane subjects, is a task of the Church. The Church holds the right to open schools; she has exercised that right in all periods of history, and for all levels and all forms of instruction. ... This instruction is a

task of the Church. When a priest fulfills a task of the Church, he is not fulfilling a remedial role; he is exercising a ministry" (299).

82 Angers, LD, 20 Sept. 1961; Genest, "Le Mouvement laïc," 556.

83 François-Albert Angers, LD, 21 Sept. 1961. See also for a defence of clerical
celibates as educators, Gérard St. Pierre, ptre., "La Soeur enseignante," NT,
11 Nov. 1961; Gérard St. Pierre, "L'éducateur religieux," NT, 25 Nov. 1961.

84 ANQM, Fonds Judith-Jasmin P143, bobine 853, "Émissions à Radio-Canada,
1963," "Reportage imaginaire sur le Canada Français."

85 Marcel Rioux, "La décléricalisaton de l'éducation et la communauté
nationale du Quebec," in Mackay, *Justice et Paix scolaire,* 145–52. See also
Massue Belleau, "Le Canadien français est un apatride," *Maint* (May 1963):
167; Pierre Saucier, "L'unilinguisme et le Rapport Parent," *Maint* (July-Aug.
1963): 230–1; ANQM, Fonds MLLF, P295, 9/1/17, "Congrès – Réunions –
Assemblées," "Nationalisme et Laïcité: Parallèle, Antithèse, ou Convergence,"
3 May 1963.

86 Paul Lacoste, "Réforme et confessionnalité," CL 47 (May 1962): 17–18.

87 "Le M.L.F. fait sienne la 'solution Lacoste,'" LD, 19 Feb. 1962; ANQM, Fonds
MLLF, 9/1/26, "Correspondance Générale," Amédée Green à MLF, ca 1962;
Jacques Tremblay, "L'Instruction Publique: une dictature sans dictateur," MM
(Feb. 1962): 42.

88 AUM, Fonds Paul-Larocque, P52/A46, Gérard Dagenais, "Mémoire"; ANQM,
Fonds MLLF, 9/1/6, "Procès-verbaux, 1965," "Procès-verbal de la réunion
regulière du Conseil national du M.L.F., le 14 décembre 1965 ..."

89 "Mémoire présenté par Georges Neray." Interestingly, Frère Untel also
pointed to the example of Israel as a democratic, unilingual state that
Quebec should follow. See ANQM Fonds Judith-Jasmin, P143, bobine 853,
Fr. Pierre-Jérôme à Judith Jasmin, 13 Dec. 1960.

90 Marcel Chaput, *Pourquoi je suis séparatiste* (Montreal: Les Éditions du Jour,
1961), 23, 37, 39.

91 AUM, Fonds Paul-Larocque, P52/D3, "Coupures de journaux," André
Langevin, "Réforme qui ne peut attendre," *Le Nouveau Journal,* n.d.

92 ANQM, Fonds MLLF, 9/1/26, Dumouchel à Maurice Blain, 28 Apr. 1961;
André Laurendeau, "Blocs-Notes: L'école non-confessionnelle et les parents
non-chrétiens," LD, 24 July 1961; "Le Mouvement laïque n'a jamais reclamé
autre chose que l'école neutre pour ceux qui la désirent," LD, 25 May 1961;
Jacques Ferron, "Roger Brien et nos laïcisants," *LD,* 14 Feb. 1962; AUM, Fonds
Paul-Larocque, "Memoire par J.E. Havel"; ibid., P52/A203, "Erreurs tragiques
touchant l'enseignement pémature de l'anglais au cours primaire," mémoire
présenté par Gertie Kathleen Hart, diplomée de la Sorbonne, Paris, auteur, et
ex-professeur à l'Université Laval, traductrice et publiciste.

93 See, for example, AUM, Fonds Paul-Larocque, P52/A45, François Loriot,
"Mémoire de l'Alliance Laurentienne," 10 Nov. 1961; ibid., P52/A105,
"Mémoire présenté ... par la Société Pierre Boucher les Trois-Rivières," Mar.

1962. The latter group, comprising Denis Vaugeois, Jacques Lacoursière, Pierre Gravel, and Claude Brouillette, declared that the school system must be "Catholic and French," but that Quebec must be a society in which only the French language was official, and minorities, though treated with justice and consideration, must be regarded as minorities.

94 J.-M. Léger, "Je me refuserai de diriger un ministère fantoche," LD, 13 Aug. 1963. See also ANQM, Fonds Paul-Gerin Lajoie, P88/vol. 40, "Bill 60 – Textes des Principaux Mémoires," "Étudiants"; ibid., "Fédération Libérale du Québec," which also favoured abandoning the division of schooling based on religion, and the substitution of language as the principle of organization.

95 S.G. "Chère correspondante," NT, 20 May 1961.

96 André Laurendeau, "Un secteur 'neutre,'" LD, 29 May 1961; "À propos de 'projets diaboliques,'" Blocs-Notes, LD, 22 Apr. 1961. For Laurendeau's own personal agnosticism, which seems to have developed during the 1950s, see Denis Monière, *André Laurendeau et le destin d'un peuple* (Montreal: Québec-Amérique, 1983).

97 "Une mère" à Chère Simone, "Au courrier de l'amitié: Faut-il croire à la menace des écoles neutres?" NT, 20 May 1961.

98 Le Comité canadien de recherches sociales, "Dénonciation du mouvement laïciste," lettre, LD, 28 Apr. 1961. The French example was a compelling tool in the conservative arsenal. There, as Chanoine Charles Ledit pointed out, the public school system was secular, with optional religious instruction provided on an extra-curricular basis by chaplains. While 80 per cent of students made their first communions, by late adolescence, Catholic faith had been so thoroughly eroded by teachers who were unsympathetic to religion that only 10 per cent of the urban population practised its faith, a figure that declined to between 2 and 3 per cent among the working classes. See Chanoine Charles-J. Ledit, "Liberté ... Liberte chérie," LD, Oct. 1961.

99 Jules-Paul Pinsonneault, "Les tenants de l'école neutre s'en vont en guerre," *Salaberry: Hebdomadaire Social Catholique*, 6 Apr. 1961.

100 "Réprobation du mouvement de laïcisation scolaire," LP, 1 May 1961.

101 "L'opinion du lecteur: Réagir...ou périr!" NT, 3 May 1961; S.G. "Chère correspondante," NT, 20 May 1961; "Éducation et verité," *Rel* (May 1961).

102 ANQM, Fonds MLLF, 9/1/26, Correspondance Générale, René Guilbeault, "L'École Neutre, Cheval de Troie," coupure de presse, s.d., inclus dans lettre à Pierre Lebeuf, 13 July 1962; ibid., 9/1/25, Correspondance Générale, Mgr O. Bonin, curé, St. Jacques, à MLLF, 7 Mar. 1964.

103 Gérard Filion, "La rage de démolir," LD, 11 Apr. 1961; ibid., "Une solution raisonnable." For Filion's championing of a larger and more active state in the 1950s, see Behiels, *Prelude to Quebec's Quiet Revolution*, 108–10.

104 Gaston Dugas, "Le Mouvement laïc de langue française: Une erreur de tactique qui pourra retarder la solution du problème," LP, 15 Apr. 1961; "Mémoire des Chevaliers de Colomb"; ANQM, P88, Fonds Paul-Gérin Lajoie,

art. 35, "Bill 60 – Amendements," Marguerite Tessier, Secrétaire-Souveraine Dames Hélène de Champlain à Paul Gérin-Lajoie, 18 Aug. 1963.

105 Aurèle Kolnai, "Société 'unanime' ou société 'neutre,'" CL 36 (Apr. 1961): 7. For Kolnai's career in the social science faculty at Université Laval, see Léon Dion, *Le Québec 1945–2000*, vol. 2, *Les intellectuels et le temps de Duplessis* (Quebec: Les Presses de l'Université Laval, 1993).

106 AUM, Fonds ACC, P16/K1.22, "Gérard Filion," "Positions," LD, Apr. 1947.

107 ANQM, Fonds Paul Gérin-Lajoie, art. 35, "Bill 60–Amendements," Me Maurice Allard, avocat et professeur en Droit constitutionnel, Université de Sherbrooke, à Paul Gérin-Lajoie, 28 Aug. 1963.

108 Behiels, *Prelude to Quebec's Quiet Revolution*, 61–96.

109 François-Albert Angers, "Faut-il imiter les autres à propos du bill 60?" LD, 18 Sept. 1963.

110 Esdras Minville, *Le Citoyen canadien-français*, vol. 1 (Montreal: Fides, 1946), 16–19. For a recent analysis of Minville's thought and career as director of the École des Hautes Études Commerciales, see Pierre Trepanier, "Esdras Minville (1896–1975) et le traditionalisme canadien-français," *Les Cahiers des dix* 52 (1995): 255–294.

111 Minville, *Le Citoyen*, 66.

112 Ibid., 67, 73, 84–5.

113 Raymond Bourgault, s.j., "Le laïcisme," *Rel* (Mar. 1963): 60. From a more liberal Catholic perspective, see "La langue, sauvegarde de la foi?" *Maint* (Mar. 1962), which reported a speech by the Jesuit, Father Belcourt, at a colloquium of the AEFO held in North Bay, Ont.: "'the French language, in and of itself, is no more Catholic than any other. It is a natural means that Providence has offered us to assist us in conserving our religion. The affirmation that language is the guardian of faith is far less true today in Canada'" (98). It should be noted in this context that Belcourt was unwilling to completely sever faith and language. Adopting the cautious view of Minville, he nonetheless indicated that in the future some recasting of the relationship would no doubt occur.

114 Gilles Constantineau, "Colloque chez les Pères dominicains: L'enseignement devant le fait religieux," LP, 21 Apr. 1961. In this respect, the views of Ryan closely resembled those of the conservative nationalists clustered around the review *Tradition et Progrès*. They similarly argued that it was unreasonable to demand the "breakup of our whole system of confessional schooling in order to substitute neutral schools" simply to accede to demands advanced by less than one-half of one per cent of the francophone population. See "Mémoire de la revue *Tradition et Progrès*."

115 Yves Prévost, c.r., "Le citoyen et l'éducation," in *L'Éducation, problème social*, 125–6. Prévost was a member of the federalist wing of the *Union Nationale*, defeated in the 1962 election. See Pierre Godin, *Daniel Johnson*, vol. 1 (Montreal: Les Éditions de l'Homme, 1980).

116 AUM, Fonds Paul-Larocque, P52/A54, "Mémoire de la Fierté Française," 7 Dec. 1962.

117 S.G., "Au courrier de l'amitié," NT, n.d.; "La valeur culturelle," NT, 9 Dec. 1961; François-Albert Angers, "École Confessionnelle et École Laïque," conférence prononcée au Congrès des Amicales de Frères du Sacré-Coeur, in F.-A. Angers, *Pour Orienter nos Libertés* (Montreal: Fides, 1969).

118 AUM, Fonds Paul-Larocque, P52/A35, "Mémoire du Cercle Mgr. Rouleau"; "Mémoire de la revue *Tradition et Progrès.*"

119 Ibid., P52/A33, "Mémoire du Cercle d'Information Nationale," Oct. 1961.

120 Ibid., La Fierté Française, "Mémoire," 7 Dec. 1962; ibid., P52/A121, "Résumé du mémoire présenté ... par les Foyers Notre-Dame Canadien," 12 Apr. 1962; "Mémoire de l'Alliance Laurentienne."

121 AUM, Fonds Paul-Larocque, P52/A218, "Mémoire des Sections Classiques de la Commission des Écoles Catholiques de Montréal," June 1962; ibid., P52/A163, "Mémoire de la Fédération Nationale des Ligues du Sacré-Coeur," 21 June 1962.

122 François-Albert Angers, "Contre le 'passage à vapeur' du bill 60," LD, 6 July 1963.

123 On the influence of a right-wing French version of modernity on the interwar generation of Quebec intellectuals, see the stimulating account by Catherine Pomeyrols, *Les intellectuels québécois: formation et engagements, 1919–1939* (Paris and Montreal: L'Harmattan, 1996), 59, 294.

124 For a study of the social composition, language, and practices of Duplessis and the Union Nationale between 1944 and 1960, see Bourque, Duchastel, Beauchemin, *La société libérale duplessiste* (Montreal: Les Presses de l'Université de Montréal, 1994). The concept of the Duplessis government and society as "liberal" has been subject to much recent criticism and debate. See the collection of essays edited by Alain-G. Gagnon et Michel Sarra-Bournet, eds, *Duplessis: entre la Grande Noirceur et la société libérale* (Montreal: Éditions Québec-Amérique, 1997).

125 ANQ-M, Fonds Paul Gérin-Lajoie, art. 35, Yves Prévost, c.r., "De Quelques Principes en Éducation: Corps intermédiaires et groupes d'intérêts," Fédération des Commissions scolaires catholiques du Québec, 16ième congrès annuel, Hôtel Reine Elizabeth, 14 Nov. 1963.

126 "Mémoire de la Fédération Nationale des Ligues du Sacré-Coeur."

127 La Commission universitaire de la Compagnie de Jésus, "Le Rapport de la Commission Parent," *Rel* (July 1963): 196–7.

128 F.-A.A., "Confusion autour de la motion Prévost," AN 52 (Sept. 1962): 85.

129 Ibid.; Angers, "Faut-il imiter les autres à propos du bill 60?"

130 Commission Universitaire de la Compagnie de Jésus, "Le Rapport de la Commission Parent," 198. See also ANQM P88, Fonds Paul Gérin-Lajoie, art. 35, Bill 60 – Amendements – Correspondance, Marguerite Tessier à Gérin-Lajoie, 28 Aug. 1963; ibid., art. 40, Textes des Principaux Mémoires,

"Mémoire de la Fédération des Collèges Classiques, La Corporation des Instituteurs Catholiques, la Fédération des Commissions Scolaires du Québec"; "Le ministère de l'Éducation," *Rel* (Aug. 1963): 218–19; François-Albert Angers, "Ce ministère de l'Éducation!" AN 53, no. 1 (Sept. 1963): 4–25; Jean Genest, "Le rapport Parent," AN 53, no. 1 (Sept. 1963): 135–40; Richard Arès, s.j., "Jusqu'où l'État," *Rel* (May 1962): 127–9; AUM, Fonds Paul-Larocque, P52/A222, "Mémoire de la Fédération des Collèges Classiques."

131 AUM, Fonds Paul-Larocque, P52/A111, "Mémoire du Collège des Ursulines de Rimouski," Apr. 1962; ibid., "Notre Réforme Scolaire: Mémoire de la Fédération des Collèges Classiques," 1 June 1962.

132 Albert Lévesque, "L'étatisation est-elle l'unique formule de réforme? – I," LD, 12 Sept. 1963; "F.-A. Angers: sans mandat explicite des parents et de l'Église, l'État n'a pas le droit de créer un ministère de l'éducation," LD, 17 Sept. 1963. For an expression of the belief that the national community and the school were an extension of the family, rather than the state, see Albert Lévesque, *Les mensonges du bill 60* (Verchères: n.p., 1963).

133 ANQM, Fonds Paul Gérin-Lajoie, art. 35, Correspondance à Classer, R. de Pinte, secrétaire, L'Exécutif Provincial du Tiers-Ordre de St. François, à Jean Lesage, 14 Oct. 1963; ibid., Me Allard à Gérin-Lajoie, 21 Aug. 1963; AUM, Fonds Paul-Larocque, P52/A237, "Mémoire de la Corporation des Instituteurs Catholiques," June 1962.

134 R.P. Antonio Lamarche, o.p., "La hiérarchie des droits en éducation," LD, 31 July 1961; AUM, Fonds Paul-Larocque, P52/A233, "Mémoire de la Fédération des Commissions Scolaires du Québec," June 1962; "Deux évêques demandent des amendements au bill 60," LD, 21 Aug. 1963; François-Albert Angers, "Les droits des parents en éducation," LD, 31 Aug. 1963; Albert Lévesque, "L'étatisation est-elle l'unique formule de démocratisation? – II," LD, 13 Sept. 1963; ANQM, Fonds Paul Gérin-Lajoie, art. 40, Bill 60, M. et Mme. Wilbrod Gingras, Laverlochère, comté Témiscouata, à Gérin-Lajoie, 3 Feb. 1964.

135 Filion, "Une solution raisonnable"; ibid., "La rage de démolir."

136 "Protestation de M. Lesage: Des 'empoisonneurs' font écrire des lettres par des ENFANTS," LD, 14 Apr. 1961. The text of one of the letters was as follows: "I have heard it said that the authorities were intending to remove the Catholic religion from the schools. I beg you to keep our catechism. For us Catholic girls, it is our favourite subject. Keep it in the school, please."

137 "Aucune déclaration des religieuses," LD, 17 Apr. 1961; "Regrets de l'Évêque et du maire de Saint-Hyacinthe," LD, 15 Apr. 1961.

138 "Plutôt que les lettres d'enfants – C'est la division du parti qui inquiète M. Lesage – M. Daniel Johnson," LD, 17 Apr. 1961.

139 Pierre Laporte, "D'où vient cette hystérie," LD, 18 Apr. 1961; "M. Jean Lesage répond aux enfants qui lui ont demandé de conserver la religion," LD, 21 Apr. 1961.

140 "Aucune puissance au monde ne viendra décrocher les crucifix dans les écoles," LP, 22 Apr. 1961.

141 "En matière d'éducation scolaire," LD, 16 June 1961; "Mgr. G.-L. Pelletier et l'école neutre," LD, 17 June 1961; J.M. [Julien Morrissette], "Les conditions d'un dialogue," NT, 17 June 1961; "Déclaration de l'évêque de Sherbrooke – Le système scolaire du Québec maintient les droits de l'Église, de la famille et de l'État," LD, 14 Apr. 1961; "L'école non-confessionnelle violemment prise à partie," LP, 19 May 1961.

142 ANQM, Fonds Judith-Jasmin, Frère Pierre-Jérôme à Judith Jasmin, 11 Mar. 1961; Boisvert, "La guerre de Troie est-elle souhaitable?" 17–19.

143 "Principaux Extraits du discours de M. Lesage, à la collation des grades de l'U. de Montréal," LD, 1 June 1961.

144 Ibid.

145 Dominique Clift, "Charge of Atheism Rebounds on Lesage," *Globe and Mail*, 3 June 1961; "Autres répercussions: M. Lesage et l'école neutre," LD, 2 June 1961; "Après le discours de M. Lesage: Le Mouvement laïc proteste," LD, 3 June 1961; André Laurendeau, "M. Lesage et l'école neutre," LD, 3 June 1961. Laurendeau accused Lesage of totalitarianism for the latter's invocation of the right of the majority not to be disturbed by atheist propaganda.

146 "Cardinal," LP, 19 June 1961; "Réflexions pastorales ... Deuxième partie," LD, 20 June 1961.

147 Ibid.

148 Lévesque, "Le nouveau laïcat," 294. For other Catholic liberal opinion hostile to the MLLF's vision of "fundamental secularism," see, "L'abbé O'Neill: les corps intermédiaires risquent d'être ecartés du Conseil Supérieur," LD, 8 May 1963; Denis Duval, ptre, "Le Mouvement laïque ... incompris?" *Maint* (July–Aug. 1962): 243–46; Un prêtre, "Évolution ou révolution," *CL* 44 (Feb. 1962): 4–10; Guy Poisson, p.s.s., "Confessionnalité ou liberté," *Maint* (Jan. 1963): 19–20; Jacques Cousineau, s.j., "La guerre scolaire aura-t-elle lieu?" *Rel* (Dec. 1961): 327–9; ANQM, Fonds MLLF, 9/1/29, "Correspondance Générale," Abbé Robert Rivest à Pierre Lebeuf, 24 July 1962; ibid., 9/1/25, Raymond Beaugrand-Champagne à MLLF, 16 Mar. 1963; "M. Paul Desrochers propose: Des écoles neutres au non-catholiques par un comité protestant modifié – Mais l'école neutre pour la majorité, jamais!" LD, 8 July 1961; "Me Daniel Johnson: Les agnostiques ont droit à leurs écoles, mais ..." LD, 26 July 1961; Robert Giroux, "Le Mouvement Laïque de Langue Française reçoit un Dur Coup," *L'Action*, 11 Mar. 1963. The latter article described a public forum on "Laïcisme et laïcité" held at Motel des Laurentides, Beauport, attended by 200 people. Abbé Gérard Dion, one of the leading lights of Catholic liberalism, denounced secularism as a form of neutrality "which takes a deliberately misleading position with respect to religion."

149 R.P. Maurice Lamarche, s.j., "L'école neutre," LD, 12 Dec. 1961.

150 Blain, "La guerre de Troie," 12.
151 Maurice Blain, "Situation de la laïcité," in *L'École laïque*, 51–3.
152 "Mémoire du Mouvement laïque de langue française."
153 ANQM, Fonds MLLF, P295/3, Laurier Lapierre, "Discours," ca 1963; AUM, Fonds Paul-Larocque, "Mémoire de Gérard Dagenais."
154 ANQM, P295, Fonds MLLF, "Procès-verbaux, 1961."
155 Blain, "Situation de la laïcité," 50–1; Blain, "La synthèse laïcité et démocratie, ou une recherche d'unité dans le pluralisme," in Mackay, *Justice et paix scolaires*, 159–69. Blain stated that the secular character of the state must be fundamental: "the operation of the State must be placed above the churches. ... The State affirms that the unity of the nation rests upon another foundation than that of unity of faith" (160).
156 Blain, "La synthèse," 165–6; Blain, "Situation de la laïcité," 51.
157 "Mémoire du Mouvement laïque de langue française."
158 "Mémoire de la Fédération des Travailleurs du Québec," which argued that we must think of the future, in which unbelief and non-practice of religion would become the social norm. Thus, "The confessional school will be guaranteed more effectively for the future because it will not arouse opposition." See also ibid., P52/A231, "Mémoire de l'Association Générale des Etudiants de l'Université de Montréal."
159 Richard Arès, s.j., "Situation de l'Église au Québec – II," *Rel* (Aug. 1963): 223.
160 Claude Ryan, "Église et questions temporelles," LD, 4 Sept. 1963; Bertrand Rioux, "Réflexions sur notre chrétienté," CL 31 (May 1960): 14.
161 Claude Ryan, "Jalons pour une présence chrétienne dans le monde actuel," *Rel* (June 1963): 175.
162 Richard Arès, s.j., "Le statut religieux de l'État québécois – III," *Rel* (Oct. 1963): 285–7.
163 AUM, Fonds Paul-Larocque, P52/A228, "Mémoire de l'Action Catholique Canadienne," June 1962.
164 Lucien Campeau, s.j., "Démocratie et neutralité scolaire," *Rel* (June 1961): 154.
165 "Mémoire de la Corporation des Instituteurs Catholiques"; "Mémoire de la Fédération des Commissions Scolaires du Québec"; "Interview accordé par M. de Koninck à M. Marcel Trudel, le 29 mars 1962"; Kolnai, "Société 'unanime' ou societe 'neutre,'" 8.
166 AUM, Fonds Paul-Larocque, P52/A108, "Mémoire de la Corporation des Agronomes et de l'Union Catholique des Cultivateurs," Apr. 1962. For similar statements, see "Déclaration de la Société Saint-Jean Baptiste de Montréal sur le Mouvement Laïque," *Le Bulletin* (May 1961); "Solutions proposées par M. Yves Prévost," NT, 3 Feb. 1962. Prévost introduced into Quebec's Legislative Assembly a series of resolutions which, while affirming the rights of religious dissident taxpayers to establish schools, firmly stated

that any recognition of public schools as non-confessional was "inadmissible" because it conflicted with "the fundamentally different conception of education held and required by the quasi-totality of the Quebec nation."

167 Jacques Croteau, "Les exigences laïques du pluralisme," *Maint* (Sept. 1962): 288–9.

168 "Mémoire de la Corporation des Instituteurs Catholiques"; "Mémoire des Chevaliers de Colomb"; Mgr Robert Lacroix, "L'École neutre," lettre, LD, 16 June 1961; Gilles-M. Lemire, o.p., "En marge de 'catholiques et agnostiques,'" LD, 2 Aug. 1961. The Corporation des Instituteurs Catholiques further stated: "No democracy can claim to assure every and each one of its citizens, at every moment of his existence, a mechanically identical treatment."

169 Richard Arès, s.j., "L'Église et l'état," *Rel* (Oct. 1962): 264–6; Marcel Faribault, Philippe Garigue, Jacques Girard, "Dialogue: L'université catholique?" *Maint* (Apr. 1962): 124–8.

170 John Courtney Murray, s.j., "La liberté religieuse et la doctrine libérale," *Rel* (Dec. 1962): 333.

171 John Courtney Murray, s.j., "La liberté et la loi," *Rel* (July 1962): 182. The Quebec Jesuits paid close attention to developments in American constitutional law during the 1960s, particularly as they affected interpretations of the freedom of religion and school prayer. See "Dieu et l'école américaine," *Rel* (Aug. 1962): 205–06.

172 John Courtney Murray, s.j., "La Conscience – la Liberté de religion – IV," *Rel* (Aug. 1962): 208.

173 Murray, "Le Droit à l'Incroyance," *Rel* (Apr. 1962): 91–2.

174 Murray, "Les Devoirs de la Conscience – La liberté de religion – V," *Rel* (Sept. 1962): 236; "La Conscience – La liberté de religion – IV," 208–10.

175 Murray, "Les devoirs," 238; "Terrain de rencontre – La liberté de religion – VIII," *Rel* (Jan. 1963): 4.

176 In its public submission to the Parent Commission, the Ligues du Sacré-Coeur went so far as to maintain that the "neutral schools" desired by agnostics to protect their rights would simply introduce a rival religion to Christianity: "worldliness." See "Mémoire de la Fédération Nationale des Ligues du Sacré-Coeur." See also J. D'Anjou, "Autour du 'droit' à l'incroyance," *Rel* (June 1961); Joseph-M. Parent, "Catholiques et Agnostiques," lettre, LD, 5 June 1961.

177 Jules LeBlanc, "Le père Bradet et 'Maintenant' à la défense du bill 60: Le plus grand danger pour l'Église, ce'st un système scolaire inefficace," LD, 19 Sept. 1963. Bradet's call was echoed other voices, including that of Claude Ryan, who argued that the "new pluralism," far from merging all religions into a meaningless syncretism, "is an invitation for each Church to give its members a more serious education in order to make them effective in bearing witness to their faith among men of other faiths that they are called upon to live in proximity with everyday." See Ryan, "Jalons pour une

présence chrétienne," 175; Gilles Dussault, "La Commission d'Enquête sur l'enseignement," *Rel* (Mar. 1962): 70.

178 Bertrand Rioux, "Comment Doivent Évoluer les rapports de l'Église et de l'État dans le Québec," in *L'Église et le Québec*, 106. This was precisely the same view that was articulated by the more conservative François-Albert Angers in his critical assessment of the ICAP colloquium. See Angers, "La singulière théorie du désengagement"; "Mémoire de la Fédération Nationale des Ligues du Sacré-Coeur": "Our entire humanism is linked to our religious conceptions ... it is the characteristic element and that which unites our people."

179 This was the vision evoked in the opening section of the Parent Report, published in 1963. See *Report of the Royal Commission of Inquiry on Education in the Province of Quebec, 1963, Part 1*: "Ideas in Evolution," 63, 69.

180 Bertrand Rioux, "Réflexions sur notre chrétienté," 15, stated that while the Church could certainly promote civil tolerance for agnostics, it could not practice a dogmatic tolerance.

181 Croteau, "Les exigences laïques du pluralisme," 288–91.

182 Gérard Filion, "Retour au bons sens," LD, 10 June 1961.

183 AUM, Fonds Paul-Larocque, P52/F22, Guy Rocher, "Essai d'introduction ..."; ibid., "Mémoire des Professeurs de l'Université de Montréal."

184 Jules LeBlanc, "Apres Cinq Mois et Demi d'Audiences Publiques – II. Les droits scolaires des 'neutres' généralement reconnus," LD, 12 May 1962; "La Non-Confessionnalité: Reconnaître Juridiquement le Principe," LD, 19 Feb. 1962.

185 Croteau, "Les exigences laïques du pluralisme" qualified his ideal as "personalist" to contrast with the "ideological pluralism" of Maurice Blain.

186 *Report of the Royal Commission of Inquiry on Education in the Province of Quebec, Part 4* (1965), 60, 115.

187 Ibid., 30–1.

188 Abbés Gérard Dion and Louis O'Neill, *Le Chrétien en démocratie* (Montreal: Les Éditions de l'Homme, 1961), 27.

189 Louis O'Neill, ptre, "Église et état: Réflexions théologiques sur le probleme," in M. Rioux, ed., *L'Église et le Québec* (Montreal: Éditions du Jour, 1961), 72; Claude Ryan, "L'ancien et le nouveau," LD, 12 Aug. 1963.

190 *Report of the Royal Commission of Inquiry on Education in the Province of Quebec, 1963, Part 1*: "Ideas in Evolution," 72.

191 Ibid., 109.

192 Gérin-Lajoie, *Pourquoi le Bill 60*, 11.

193 Joseph-M. Parent, o.p., "Catholiques et Agnostiques," LD, 5 June 1961.

194 Cardinal Paul-Émile Léger, "Le magistère de l'Église devant le monde moderne," in *L'Éducation, problème social*, 155–9.

195 AUM, Fonds Paul-Larocque, P52/A128, "Mémoire des Femmes Diplomées des Universités."

196 Gérard Beaudoin, notaire, "La religion à l'école, " lettre, LD, 15 Apr. 1961.

197 Jules LeBlanc, "Le cardinal Léger: il faut repenser nos moyens d'action auprès des adolescents," LD, 13 Sept. 1963.

198 AUM, Fonds Paul-Larocque, P52/A216, "La Conception Populaire de l'Instruction, étude preparée par Gérald Fortin et Marc-Adélard Tremblay, Université Laval ..."

199 Ibid., P52/A231, "Mémoire de l'Association Générale des Étudiants de l'Université de Montréal," June 1962.

200 "La formation religieuse des enfants," LD, 9 Feb. 1963; "Initiation religieuse au foyer," *Rel* (Mar. 1963): 77.

201 Paul-Marcel Lemaire, o.p., "Crise religieuse et jeunesse," *Maint* (Dec. 1963): 374.

202 S.G., "L'offensive des écoles neutres."

203 "Mémoire des Chevaliers de Colomb."

204 "Mémoire de la Corporation des Instituteurs Catholiques." A similar view that children had a right to religious education was stated by the Corporation des Agronomes and the Union Catholique des Cultivateurs. See ibid., P52/A108; R.P. Maurice Lamarche, s.j., "L'École neutre," LD, 12 Dec. 1961.

205 Louis Lachance, o.p., "Le partage des droits et responsabilités en éducation," in *L'Éducation, problème social*, 173; R.P. Maurice Lamarche, s.j., "L'École neutre" (suite), LD, n.d.

206 Arthur Tremblay, "Notre système d'enseignement face à l'évolution de notre société," in *L'éducation, problème social*, 19, 21.

207 "Les programmes scolaires: Nous voulons TOUT changer à condition que ce soit UTILE – Mgr Maurice Roy," LP, 19 June 1961.

208 *Report of the Royal Commission of Inquiry on Education, Part 4*, 108–9; ibid., *Part 1*, 72.

209 Bourque, Duchastel, Beauchemin, *La société libérale duplessiste.*

210 Gérard Dion et Louis O'Neill, *Le Chrétien en démocratie* (Montreal: Les Éditions de l'Homme, 1961), 31.

211 "En refusant un vrai ministère ..." LD, 19 Sept. 1963.

212 "O'Neill: plus que les formules politico-cléricales," LD, 9 Aug. 1963. See also, Jules LeBlanc, "Le père Bradet"; "Mémoire de la Fédération des Travailleurs du Québec": "We recognize all the rights of the parents and of the Church which the State must always scrupulously respect. But neither the parents nor the clergy can assume responsibility for the entirety of the system. ... We hear a great deal about the collaboration of the public and private sectors. All this is excellent, so long as we fully recognize the primacy of the public sector."

213 AUM, Fonds Paul-Larocque, P52/F1, Abbé Louis O'Neill, "La formation religieuse des étudiants au niveau collégial et universitaire," n.d.

214 On the existence of this mentality in the United Church of Canada, see Christie, "'Look out for Leviathan'" in Nancy Christie and Michael Gauvreau, *Cultures of Citizenship in Post-war Canada, 1940–1955* (Montreal and Kingston: McGill-Queen's University Press, 2003).

215 For the continued commitment in Quebec to the notion of Catholicism as a "public" religion, see David Seljak, "Resisting the 'No Man's Land' of Private Religion: The Catholic Church and Public Politics in Quebec," in David Lyon and Marguerite Van Die, eds, *Rethinking Church, State, and Modernity: Canada Between Europe and America* (Toronto: University of Toronto Press, 2000), 131–48.

216 Raymond Bourgault, s.j., "La Laïcité," *Rel* (Feb. 1963): 32: "It is perhaps not possible to keep rendering to Caesar except where an institution independent of Caesar teaches its faithful, who are also citizens, that we must at the same time render to God that which is God's."

217 For Gérin-Lajoie's participation in Catholic youth movements such as the Pax Romana, see Paul Gérin-Lajoie, *Combats d'un révolutionnaire tranquille: propos et confidences* (Montreal: Centre éducatif et culturel, 1989), 14, 18–19.

218 "Éducation et vérité," *Rel* (May 1961).

219 ANQM, Fonds Paul Gérin-Lajoie, art. 40, "Notes pour le discours de M. Paul Gérin-Lajoie en Chambre lors de la troisième lecture du Bill 60," le 5 février 1964.

220 AUM, Fonds Paul-Larocque, P52/A73, "Resumé des Conclusions de l'Office de la langue française, mémoire presenté jan. 1962 par Hon. Georges-Émile Lapalme, Ministre des Affaires Culturelles."

221 Léger, "Je me refuserai."

222 Gérin-Lajoie, *Pourquoi le Bill 60*, 46.

223 Clinton Archibald, *Un Québec corporatiste?* (Hull: Éditions Asticou, 1984).

224 Gérin-Lajoie, *Pourquoi le Bill 60*, 9, 85; Marcel Thivierge, "Lesage dépose le projet de loi instituant un ministère de l'éducation," LD, 27 June 1963.

225 Abbé Gérard Dion, "Socialisation: Colloque," *Maint* (Nov. 1963): 331–2; Dion, "Église et socialisme," *Maint* (Dec. 1963): 370–1.

226 ANQM, Fonds Paul Gérin-Lajoie, art. 40, "Bill 60: Mémoires," Société Saint-Jean Baptiste de Montréal.

227 For the proposal of a "Conseil Supérieur," see AUM, Fonds Paul-Larocque, P52/A160, "Mémoire de la Confédération des Syndicats Nationaux," May 1962; ibid., Fierté Française, "Mémoire"; "Mémoire de la Fédération Nationale des Ligues du Sacré-Coeur"; AUM, Fonds Paul-Larocque, P52/A174, "Mémoire des Instituteurs et Institutrices Catholiques," May 1962; "Mémoire de l'Action Catholique Canadienne"; "Mémoire de la Fédération des Travailleurs du Quebec." Even Paul Lacoste, though sympathetic to many of the aims of the MLLF, rejected excessive state authority, arguing in 1961 for "une certaine délégation du pouvoir législatif à un Conseil." See "La réforme du Conseil de l'Instruction Publique," CL 41 (Nov. 1961): 7.

228 For this debate, see ANQM, Fonds Paul Gérin-Lajoie, art. 35, Bill 60 – Amendements, Marguerite Tessier à Gérin-Lajoie, 28 Aug. 1963; ibid., art. 35, Me Allard à Gérin-Lajoie, 28 Aug. 1963; ibid., art. 40, "Bill 60 – Mémoires," Madeleine Joubert, secrétaire-générale de l'Institution

Canadien d'Éducation des Adultes à Gérin-Lajoie, 30 Aug. 1963; Jacques Cousineau, s.j., "Bill 60 et démocratie," *Rel* (Sept. 1963): 268–70; "Le père Cousineau: c'est un recul de la démocratie organique," LD, 12 Oct. 1963; Francois-Albert Angers, lettre, LD, 12 Oct. 1963; "La prétendue 'dépolitisa- tion' du systeme scolaire de la province n'est qu'un mythe," LD, 16 May 1963; "L'abbé O'Neill: les corps intermédiaires risquent d'être écartes du Conseil supérieur de l'éducation," LD, 8 May 1963.

229   Thivierge, "Lesage dépose."

230   Léger, "Je me refuserai."

231   *Report of the Royal Commission of Inquiry on Education in the Province of Quebec, Part 4,* 78–84, 36.

232   *Report of the Royal Commission of Inquiry on Education, Part 1,* 72.

233   Gérin-Lajoie, *Pourquoi le Bill 60,* 100. Here, the minister cited the injunc- tion of the French Catholic philosopher Jacques Maritain, a particularly important intellectual mentor in the post-Depression Catholic Action movements.

234   AUM, Fonds Paul-Larocque, P52/A120, "Rapport sur l'Enseignement du Catéchisme au Cours Primaire ... par Un groupe de parents de la ville de Québec," 1962. For similar criticisms, see ibid., P52/A204, "Mémoire des Parents Catholiques de la Ville Mont-Royal," 29 June 1962; "Mémoire de l'Action Catholique Canadienne." Many of these views had first been sug- gested by Marthe Henripin, "L'essentiel, est-ce le ciel?" CL 37 (May 1961): 23–7. Marthe Henripin was the wife of the celebrated demographer, Jacques Henripin.

235   "Rapport sur l'Enseignement du Catéchisme au Cours Primaire"; "Mémoire de l'Action Catholique Canadienne"; AUM, Fonds Paul-Larocque, P52/A121, "Mémoire des Foyers Notre-Dame," 12 Apr. 1962; "Mémoire des Femmes Diplomées des Universités"; "Mémoire de la revue *Tradition et Progrès*"; Felicien Rousseau, ptre, "Droits et responsabilités de l'Église en éducation," in *L'éducation, problème social,* 228; Jean Lacroix, "Crise de civilisation, crise de l'école: le point de vue chrétien," in *L'éducation, problème social,* 106, 118–20; Cardinal Léger, "Réflexions pastorales sur l'enseignement, deuxième partie," LP, 20 June 1961.

236   "Rapport sur l'Enseignement du Catéchisme au Cours Primaire."

237   This was one significant aspect of the debate on confessionality. The Quebec City parents called for an acceleration of the preparation of cate- chists at institutes specifically devoted to this purpose, while the French philosopher Jean Lacroix, who spoke to the Semaines Sociales in 1962, stated that in a post-industrial society, religious education could not be left in the hands of priests who were at the intellectual level of "unskilled workers." See Lacroix, "Crise de civilisation": "manual workers" in a "world where the service sector will dominate" (118).

238　Even so conservative a figure as Yves Prévost stated in 1962 that the "school of the nation," if it was to demand the support of minorities, must provide a religious instruction that accentuated dialogue with other religious traditions, and broke decisively with routine. See Prévost, "Le citoyen et l'éducation," 136.

239　*Report of the Royal Commission of Inquiry on Education in the Province of Quebec, Part 4,* 81.

240　Ibid., 82.

241　"Mémoire des Foyers Notre-Dame." In this respect, they resembled the MLLF, which criticized the "massive dose" of religious teaching which was "completely maladapted to actual needs." See "Mémoire du Mouvement laïque de langue française"; ANQM, Fonds Paul Gérin-Lajoie, art. 40, "Bill 60," Pierre Marois, A.G.E.U.M à Jean Lesage, 27 Jan. 1964. Even Action Catholique Canadienne overtly cautioned that the "Christian spirit" must not deform or misuse the "profane subjects in the name of a so-called religious apostolate."

242　"Mémoire de l'Action Catholique Canadienne."

243　"Mémoire de l'Alliance Laurentienne."

244　"Mémoire des Femmes Diplomées des Universités," in which they stated that religion was not "a system of acquired reflexes," but "a sense, an education of human freedom"; La Fierté Française, "Mémoire"; Chapin, "Quebec's Revolt Against the Catholic Schools"; de Bellefeuille, "Chasser les bondieuseries"; ANQM, Fonds MLLF, 9/1/12, "Commission Sociologique et politique, 1961"; ibid., 9/1/29, Correspondance générale, Abbé Robert Rivest à Pierre Lebeuf, 24 July 1962; Guy Viau, "Un Élève sous-doué," *Maint* (Jan. 1962): 15–16; Lucille de St. André, "Religious Education in Quebec Berated," *Montreal Star,* n.d.; "Au courrier de l'amitié: 'Une de vos fidèles lectrices,'" NT, n.d.

245　AUM, Fonds Paul-Larocque, P52/A, "Mémoire de l'Association de l'Éducation du Quebec," 10 July 1962.

246　Levesque, "Le Nouveau laïcat," 293–4.

247　*Report of the Royal Commission on Education Part 4,* 37–8.

248　Marcelle et Bernard Vanasse, "La parole entendue au 20e banc," *Maint* (Jan. 1963): 8; AUM, Fonds Paul-Larocque, P52/A262, "Mémoire de la Fédération des Sociétés Saint-Jean-Baptiste de Québec," 11 July 1962, which argued against the clericalization of profane structures and the denaturing of civic professional, and political institutions into "*mere ancillaries of Catholic action institutions by the administrative subservience of the temporal to the spiritual.*"

249　*Report of the Royal Commission on Education in the Province of Quebec, Part 3, Programmes of Study* (1965), 216–17.

250　Editorial, "Ni cléricalisme, ni trahison des anticlercs," PP 2, no. 8 (Apr. 1965): 5.

CHAPTER SEVEN

1 Commission d'Étude sur les laics et l'Église (Commission Dumont), *L'Église du Québec, un héritage, un projet* (Montreal: Fides, 1971), 20.

2 Guy Rocher, "L'incroyance comme phénomène sociologique," CC 60 (Nov.–Dec 1971): 366.

3 The members of the Commission Dumont included Fernand Dumont, director of the Institut supérieur des Sciences humaines de l'Université Laval as chair; Hélène Chénier (vice-chair) secretary-general of the Alliance des Professeurs de Montréal; Claude Ryan (vice-chair) editor of *Le Devoir* and former national secretary of Catholic Action; Msgr Paul-Émile Charbonneau, bishop of Hull; Janine Dallaire, student, Université de Montréal; Anne-Marie Frenette, ex-director of Jeunesse Ouvrière Catholique; Father Jacques Grand'Maison, professor in the faculty of theology, Université de Montréal; Jean-Paul Hétu, director of the Service de l'Éducation, Confédération des Syndicats Nationaux; Father Jean-Marie Lafontaine, vicar-general of the Archdiocese of Montreal; Jean-Marie Poitras, president of l'Alliance Laurentienne insurance company; Rolande Vigneault, ex-director of the Jeunesse Catholique Rurale; Jacques Champagne (commission secretary), ex-director of Catholic Action.

4 For the attendance figures, see Paul-André Linteau, René Durocher, et al., *Histoire du Québec contemporain: le Québec depuis 1930* (Montreal: Boréal, 1989), 653.

5 Commission Dumont, *L'Église du Québec, un héritage, un projet*, 20

6 ANQM, Fonds SPM, P116 art. 24, Gérard Filion, "Une prise de conscience réaliste et saine," LD, editorial, 24 May 1961.

7 NAC, Fonds Paul Gérin-Lajoie, MG 31E106, vol. 64.10, Discours 1964, "Allocution ... prononcée par le sous-ministre M. Arthur Tremblay, lors de la première réunion du Conseil supérieur de l'éducation tenue à la Salle des réunions de la Commission des écoles catholiques de Montréal," 31 Aug. 1964.

8 NAC, Fonds Paul Gérin-Lajoie, vol. 64.12, "Discours 1965," "Allocution à l'occasion du 25e anniversaire du sacerdoce de Mgr. H. Aganier, vicaire-général du diocèse de Valleyfield, 26 juin, 1965, au Séminaire de Valleyfield."

9 Arthur Marwick, *The Sixties: Cultural Revolution in Britain, France, Italy, and the United States, ca. 1958–ca. 1974* (Oxford: Oxford University Press, 1998), advances the notion of the centrality of individualism to the cultural revolution of this decade.

10 ANQM, Fonds Judith-Jasmin, bobine 853, "Réunion 1970," circulaire 30 novembre 1970.

11 Fonds Judith-Jasmin, bobine 853, "La Contestation et la santé mentale," May 1969. This panel included Claude Castonguay, minister of Health and Social Services in the Liberal cabinet of Robert Bourassa; the journalists Judith Jasmin, Raymond Laliberté, and Claude Ryan, later leader of the Liberal

party; the Dominican priest Father Vincent Harvey, editor of *Maintenant*; and social scientists Fernand Dumont, Charles Taylor, and Guy Rocher.

12 For a recent appreciation of the Dumont Commission as an attempt to "democratize" Catholicism in Quebec, see Gregory Baum, "Catholicism and Secularization in Quebec," in David Lyon and Marguerite Van Die, eds, *Rethinking Church, State, and Modernity: Canada between Europe and America* (Toronto: University of Toronto Press, 2000), 149–65.

13 Callum G. Brown, "A Revisionist Approach to Religious Change," in Steve Bruce, ed., *Religion and Modernization: Sociologists and Historians Debate the Secularization Thesis* (Oxford: Clarendon Press, 1992), 54.

14 Jacques Grand'Maison, ptre, "L'Église du Québec en état de concile – III: Les provocations missionnaires du mouvement de sécularisation," LD, 1 Oct. 1965.

15 "L'Église et l'État au Québec," *Rel* (Apr. 1965): 124.

16 Fernand Dumont, "Blondel présent," VE 15, no. 7 (Sept. 1949); ibid., *Récit d'une émigration* (Montreal: Boréal, 1997), 66–7.

17 ANQM, Fonds JEC, P65, S6, SS6, SSS6, D5/2, Action Catholique Universitaire, Stage du Lac Ouareau, 1952, Fernand Dumont, "Spiritualité et profession"; Claude Ryan, "Ferons-nous de la politique?" AN 35, no. 5 (May 1950): 451–77.

18 Fernand Dumont, "Trêve de discours," VE 15, no. 5 (May 1949).

19 ANQM, Fonds JEC, P65, S6, SS6, SSS2, D6, "Questionnaire d'auto-critique, mai 1953."

20 Dumont, "Spiritualité et profession."

21 Fernand Dumont, "La crise de l'histoire," VE 16, no. 1 (Jan. 1950).

22 Fernand Dumont, "La lutte contre la pauvreté," exposé présenté au symposium sur "les inégalités socio-économiques et la pauvreté au Québec," organisé par le Conseil du bien-être du Québec, Lévis 1967," in Fernand Dumont, *La Vigile du Québec, Octobre 1970: L'impasse?* (Montreal: Hurtubise HMH, 1971), 130, 127.

23 For an analysis of the social-democratic ideology of the *Économie et humanisme* group, see Denis Pelletier, *Économie et humanisme: de l'utopie communautaire au combat pour le tiers-monde, 1941–1966* (Paris: Cerf, 1996), 108–9, 111, 114–9, 151, 235–8; and for the French worker-priests, see Oscar L. Arnal, *Priests in Working-Class Blue: The History of the Worker-Priests (1943–1954)* (New York: Paulist Press, 1986), 19–21. For Dumont's own involvement with French Catholic Action and the influence of these models on his thinking, see his *Récit d'une émigration*, 96–7.

24 H. Godin and Y. Daniel, *La France, pays de mission?* (Paris: Les Éditions de l'Abeille, 1943), 46, 36–7, 11.

25 Ibid., 15, 18, 33–7.

26 Ibid., 160–1.

27 Gabriel LeBras, *Études de sociologie religieuse*, vol. 1, *Sociologie de la pratique*

religieuse dans les campagnes françaises (Paris: Les Presses Universitaires de
France, 1955), 366, 380. Dumont, *Récit d'une émigration*, recalled that he was
strongly influenced in the 1950s both by Godin and Daniel's pastoral work,
and by LeBras, whom he met both at academic colloquia and at sessions of
the Centre de pastorale rurale at Saint-Brieuc (95–6).

28 Gabriel LeBras, *Études de sociologie religieuse*, vol. 2, *De la morphologie à la typologie* (Paris: Les Presses Universitaires de France, 1956), 400, 559–60, 481.

29 Ibid., 586, 641.

30 Dumont, *Récit d'une émigration*, 27, 36–7, 47–8.

31 Ibid., 28.

32 Mgr Paul-Émile Charbonneau, "Le renouveau pastoral," *Rel* (Feb. 1966): 44.
For the St Jerome mission, and the 1960 and 1962 missions in the Montreal
and Chicoutimi dioceses, see Jean Hamelin and Nicole Gagnon, *Histoire du
catholicisme québécois*, vol. 2 (Montreal: Boréal, 1984), 215.

33 For Dumont's method and these activities, which included the participation
of students such as Robert Sévigny, Vincent Lemieux, and Gerard Lapointe in
the St Jerome mission, see *Recit d'une émigration*, 96–7, 116–17. The term
milieu, as interpreted by the French sociologists upon whom their Quebec
counterparts relied, was summarized by Fathers Godin and Daniel in *La
France, pays de mission?*, as a setting defined according either to physical, economic, or cultural criteria, either by geographic unity, organization and type
of work, and conception of life and institutions and customs (23).

34 Hamelin and Gagnon, *Histoire du catholicisme québécois*, vol. 2, 214.

35 Charbonneau, "Le renouveau pastoral," 42. See also Robert Llewellyn,
"L'abbé Llewellyn à Paris," *Maint* (Oct. 1963): 300; Yvon Hamel, "Un hardi
effort d'adaptation suscite des expériences inédites," *VE* 17, no. 5 (May 1951).

36 Fernand Dumont, *Pour la conversion de la pensée chrétienne: essai* (Montreal:
Éditions HMH, 1964), 11.

37 For the self-conscious identification of *Maintenant*'s editorial board with
French existentialism, see L'équipe de direction, "Lettre à Sartre," *Maint*
(Apr. 1967): 114. In a recently-published cultural history of the 1960s,
Arthur Marwick has observed that the existentialism of Sartre appealed to
many young intellectuals of the 1960s because of "its insistence on political
commitment and ... its demand that people should reject 'bad faith', that is,
living lives according to the false conventions of society." See Marwick, *The
Sixties*, 32.

38 Paul-Marcel Lemaire, o.p., "Crise religieuse et jeunesse," *Maint*, (Dec. 1963):
374; Michèle Jean, "Changement de menu," *Maint* (Mar. 1964): 79; H.-M.
Bradet, o.p., "Sommes-nous dans une crise religieuse?" *Maint* (Mar. 1963):
73–6.

39 Bradet, "Sommes-nous dans une crise religieuse?," 73; Dumont, *Pour la conversion de la pensée chrétienne*, 14; Dumont, *Récit d'une émigration*, 47–8.

40 Marthe Henripin, "Qui sont-ils," *CC* 28 (July–Aug. 1966): 274.

41 Grand'Maison, "L'Église du Québec en état de concile – III: Les provocations missionnaires du mouvement de sécularisation." See also Colette Moreux, "Le Dieu de la québécoise," *Maint* (Feb. 1967): 67; AUM, Fonds Paul-Larocque, O'Neill, "La formation religieuse au niveau collégial et universitaire," n.d.: "mere attachment to religious ritual is not an indicator of progress in the Catholic faith"; P.-A. Liégé o.p., "L'Église et les civilisations," *Maint* (Feb. 1962): 51.

42 Dumont, *Pour la conversion de la pensée chrétienne*, 15.

43 Dumont, "L'authenticité de l'expérience chrétienne dans la société d'aujourd'hui," cc 29 (Sept.–Oct. 1966): 382.

44 Dumont, "Sur notre situation religieuse," *Rel* (Feb. 1966): 37; Dumont, "Réflexions sur l'histoire religieuse au Canada français," in Rioux, ed., *L'Église et le Québec* (Montreal: Les Éditions du Jour, 1961), 60–1. See also the views advanced by Maurice Bouchard, an economist at the Université de Montréal, in "Conformisme religieux," *Maint* (Nov. 1964): 330.

45 Dumont, "L'authenticité de l'expérience chrétienne," 395. Significantly, this was delivered at a summer session of the Fédération des Collèges Classiques for "those in charge of pastoral activities in the colleges."

46 O'Neill, "La formation religieuse"; André Lussier, "Les dessous de la censure," cl 28 (July–Aug. 1960); Jean Francoeur, "Réflexions sur le problème de la liberté religieuse au Québec," *Pros* 2, no. 11 (Feb. 1966): 21–8; Armand Croteau, ptre, "Travailler le moins possible?" *Maint* (Nov. 1963): 333; AUM, Fonds ACC, P16/12.43, Mgr. Ménager, bishop of Antioche-la-Mineure, ca 1957.

47 David Seljak, "Catholicism's 'Quiet Revolution': *Maintenant* and the New Public Catholicism in Quebec after 1960," in Marguerite Van Die, ed., *Religion and Public Life in Canada: Historical and Comparative Perspectives* (Toronto: University of Toronto Press, 2001), 261.

48 Hélène Pelletier-Baillargeon and Pierre Saucier, "Le couple clercs-laïcs," *Maint* (autumn 1965): 276.

49 Guy Rocher, "Préface," in Colette Moreux, *Fin d'une religion?: monographie d'une paroisse canadienne-française* (Montreal: Les Presses de l'Université de Montréal, 1969), xi. Readers of *Maintenant* were treated to a sneak preview of these findings in 1967. See Colette Moreux, "Le Dieu de la québécoise," 67–8. Like Fernand Dumont, Guy Rocher was a veteran of the Catholic Action movements, active in the Jeunesse Étudiante Catholique between 1943 and 1947, and an ardent disciple of Emmanuel Mounier. For details of his career, see Guy Rocher, *Entre les rêves et l'histoire* (Montreal: VLB Éditeur, 1981).

50 AUM, Fonds Commission Dumont, P21/B1, Julien Harvey, s.j., "Laïc chrétien et sécularisation," Mar. 1970; O'Neill, "La formation religieuse."

51 "L'Église et les défis de la laïcité," *Rel* (Jan. 1967): 20. This article reported the series of lectures given by Father Christian Duquoc at the Université de Montréal.

52 Rocher, "L'incroyance comme phénomène sociologique," 372; AUM, Fonds Paul-Larocque, P52/K19.7, Jeanne Lapointe, "Humanisme et humanité"; "L'Église et les défis de la laicité," 20.

53 Pierre Marois, "... à Montréal," *Maint* (May 1964): 155.

54 Vincent Harvey, o.p., Pierre Saucier, Hélène Pelletier-Baillargeon, and Paul Doucet, o.p., "Après l'Entracte," *Maint* (autumn 1965).

55 Gérard Pelletier, "Feu l'unanimité," CL 30 (Oct. 1960): 10.

56 H.-M. Robillard, "La Religion du péché mortel," *Maint* (May 1965): 175.

57 O'Neill, "La formation religieuse."

58 Bradet, "Sommes-nous dans une crise religieuse?" 75.

59 Robillard, "La Religion du Péché Mortel," 173–5; Doris Lussier, "L'intégrisme contre la foi," *Maint* (Mar. 1964): 82–3; ANQM, Fonds JEC, P65, art. 1, Jean LeMoyne, "La Qualité de la Vie Religieuse dans l'Église," ca 1962.

60 See Michael Behiels, *Prelude to Quebec's Quiet Revolution: Liberalism versus Neo-Nationalism, 1945–1960* (Montreal and Kingston: McGill-Queen's University Press, 1985), for the differences between the "traditional" nationalism of the 1930s and the views of two influential post-war nationalists, Gérard Filion and André Laurendeau (48). Although *citélibristes* like Gérard Pelletier and Pierre Trudeau were powerful critics of the tendency of French-Canadian nationalism to identify with social conservatism, they accepted a similar hierarchy of values between the universal and the particular, so much so that they directed much of their criticism towards reforming Catholicism. In political terms, during the 1950s they concurred with conservatives such as Esdras Minville, François-Albert Angers, and Maurice Duplessis in promoting a decentralized federal structure, although they abhorred what they perceived as the latter's abuse of human rights.

61 Even so uncompromising a critic of the institutional Church as Emmanuel Mounier held to this conventional hierarchy, in which the nation was indispensable as a mediating element of human culture and society, but was not coextensive with the state or political society. See Mounier, *Personalism*, 109–12. From a more "traditional" perspective, Esdras Minville argued that patriotism was first and foremost an instinct, and that "the relationship of the national to the religious is of the same order as that of the temporal to the eternal." See Esdras Minville, *Invitation à l'étude* (Montreal: Fides, 1945), 31, 47–8.

62 For a discussion of the pluralist implications of Catholic social thinking in Quebec, especially after 1931, see Michael Gauvreau, "From Rechristianization to Contestation: Catholic Values and Quebec Society, 1931–1970," *Church History: Studies in Christianity and Culture* 69, no. 4 (Dec. 2000): 803–33.

63 AUM, Fonds ACC, P16/D1, 4.5, "Notes pour servir à l'étude du civisme," 1957–58; ibid., P16/G3, 5.1, "Libres pour vivre pleinement," Dr Camille Laurin, "L'Unité Nationale," École civique, 1950; ibid., P16/B4, 4.1, Anna-

Maria Pigeon, "Circulaire," 18 Mar. 1952; ANQM, Fonds JEC, P65/s6, ss6, sss2, D5/2, Abbé Norbert Lacoste, "Progrès et profession," 1952.

64 Fernand Dumont, "De quelques obstacles à la prise de conscience chez les Canadiens français," CL 19 (Jan. 1958).

65 For an analysis of the professional techniques employed by the "Montreal school" of Guy Frégault, Michel Brunet, and Maurice Séguin, see Ronald Rudin, *Making History in Twentieth-Century Quebec* (Toronto: University of Toronto Press, 1997). The intellectual content and nationalist engagements of these historians have been more effectively treated in Jean Lamarre, *Le devenir de la nation québécoise: selon Maurice Séguin, Guy Frégault et Michel Brunet, 1944–1959* (Sillery: Septentrion, 1993).

66 Léon Dion, "Le nationalisme pessimiste: Ses sources, sa signification, sa validité," CL 18 (Nov. 1957): 17–18.

67 Dumont, "De quelques obstacles," 24–5.

68 Ibid., 26–7.

69 Ibid., 27; AUM, Fonds ACC, P16/04.92, Etats Généraux, Fernand Dumont, "Essai de schéma, domaine social," 10 Jan. 1964; Jacques Grand'Maison, "L'Église, le monde, et le Québec," *Maint* (Dec. 1964): 391.

70 Dumont, "De quelques obstacles," 27.

71 Ibid., 28.

72 Ibid., 27–8.

73 "Fernand Dumont au congrès biennial de l'Association internationale des sociologues: une néo-nationalisme axé sur l'État et l'industrialisation," LD, 5 Oct. 1964; Réal Pelletier, "Fernand Dumont Enumère 3 tâches immédiates du socialisme au Québec," LD, 13 Feb. 1967; Fernand Dumont, "Un socialisme pour le Québec," in Dumont, *La Vigile du Québec*, 149.

74 Fernand Dumont, "Sur notre situation religieuse," *Rel* (Feb. 1966): 36.

75 Dumont, "Réflexions sur l'histoire religieuse du Canada français," 52–6.

76 Jean Francoeur, "Une douloureuse récupération des valeurs humaines," LD, 18 oct. 1965.

77 Dumont, "De quelques obstacles," 28.

78 Fernand Dumont, "Depuis la guerre: la recherche d'une nouvelle conscience," in Dumont, *La Vigile du Québec*, 33–4; Dumont, "Un socialisme pour le Québec," 152–3.

79 ANQM, Fonds MLLF, P295, 9/1/28, Correspondance générale, Martial Légaré, Bed 21, Département 3400, Notre-Dame-de-la-Merci, Montréal, à Pierre Maheu, 16 Apr. 1966.

80 For the development of a more politicized "neo-corporatism" in Quebec after 1960, see Clinton Archibald, *Un Québec corporatiste?: corporatisme et néo-corporatisme: du passage d'une idéologie corporatiste sociale à une idéologie corporatiste politique, le Québec de 1930 à nos jours* (Hull: Éditions Asticou, 1983), 160.

81 AUM, Fonds ACC, P16/B6, 3.18, "Claude Ryan," "L'Encyclique Mater et Magistra de sa Sainteté Jean XXIII," résumé d'un cours donné au collège du travail

de la Confédération des Syndicats Nationaux le 15 novembre 1961; ibid., P16/D1, 4.20, "Les attitudes du chrétien à l'intérieur des politiques," Fr Gérard Bouchard, "Les attitudes du chrétien à l'intérieur des politiques sociales – III. Jalons pour une réflexion chrétienne," 1966; AUM, Fonds Commission Dumont, P21/A7, Germain Lesage, o.m.i., "La pensée pastorale des évêques Canadiens-Français, 1830–1962."

82 Richard Arès, s.j., "L'État et les corps intermédiaires," in Les Semaines Sociales du Canada, *L'État et les corps intermédiaires, 39e session, Québec, 1964* (Montreal: Les Éditions Bellarmin, 1964), 6.

83 Gérard Dion, "Corps intermédiaires: groupes de pression ou organismes administratifs?" in Les Semaines Sociales du Canada, *L'État et les corps intermédiaires,* 14–20; Jean Rivero, "La démocratie organique," in ibid., 35–7.

84 Claude Ryan, "L'avenir des 'institutions chrétiennes," LD, 6 Apr. 1966; Claude Ryan, "Les conditions d'une collaboration entre l'État et les corps intermédiaires," in Les Semaines Sociales du Canada, *L'État et les corps intermédiaires,* 24–6.

85 Claude Ryan, "Pourquoi j'entre en politique, et au Parti libéral," 10 Jan. 1978, in Claude Ryan, with Robert Guy Scully, *Une société stable: le Québec après le PQ* (Saint-Lambert: Héritage, 1978), 52, 55. See also Ryan, "1967: le choix de René Lévesque," in Claude Ryan, *Une société stable,* 75. For Ryan's personal efforts to promote the civic culture of "intermediate bodies," see Claude Ryan, *L'éducation des adultes: réalité moderne* (Montreal: Institut Canadien d'Éducation des Adultes, 1958).

86 Dumont, "Un socialisme pour le Québec," 147; Guy Rocher, "Le conservatisme québécois," in Guy Rocher, *Le Québec en mutation* (Montreal: Hurtubise HMH, 1973), 37, 47.

87 Dumont, "Un socialisme pour le Québec," 152

88 Dumont, "L'idéal coopératif," allocution au Congrès des mouvements coopératifs, 1959, in Dumont, *La Vigile du Québec,* 123–4; Dumont, "Un socialisme pour le Québec," 149.

89 Dumont, "Un socialisme pour le Québec," 153.

90 Rocher, "Un incertain avenir," in Rocher, *Le Québec en mutation,* 59.

91 Marcel Rioux, *La nation et l'école* (Ottawa: Collection MLLF, 1966).

92 Ibid.

93 ANQM, Fonds MLLF, P295/3, Coupures de presse, René Durocher, "L'école neutre," LD, 8 June 1967.

94 ANQM, Fonds MLLF, P295/3, Jacques Mackay, *Le catholicisme: un carcan* (Montreal: Collection MLLF, 1966). See also "Le catholicisme est-il devenu un obstacle au progrès du Québec?" LP, 3 Dec. 1966.

95 "Le catholicisme est-il devenu un obstacle au progrès du Québec?"

96 Guy Rocher, "L'idéologie du changement comme facteur de mutation sociale," CC 49 (Jan.–Feb. 1970): 20.

97 Guy Rocher, "Déclin ou renouveau religieux?," in Rocher, *Le Québec en mutation,* 205.

98 Jean-Marc Léger, "La sécurité sociale: une révolution à faire," LD, 18 Oct.
1965; Solange Chalvin, "René Lévesque, ministre de la famille et du bien-
être, fait le point de la nouvelle politique de sécurité sociale au Québec,"
LD, 20 Nov. 1965. For other critiques from the Catholic "left" of the
Church's direct role in managing health and welfare institutions, see Pierre-
J.-G. Vennat, "Socialisation de la charité," *Maint* (Jan. 1965): 35; Pierre Pelletier, o.p., "Catholicisme, obstacle au progrès," *Maint* (Jan. 1967): 20.

99 La Rédaction, "To Be or Not to Be," *Maint* (Sept. 1967): 235. See also
André Charbonneau, "Avec René Lévesque: à bas la démagogie des 'élites,'"
Maint (Feb. 1967): 47–50; Fernand Dumont, "La critique, DÉJÀ?" *Maint*
(Mar. 1970): 69–70.

100 ANQM, Fonds René-Lévesque, P18/D265, "Mémoire soumis à la Commission
politique du M.S.A." ca 1967; ibid., "Notre vie sociale"; ibid., J.C. Guy Joron,
"Mémoire soumis à la Commission politique du M.S.A.," 11 Feb. 1968.

101 For this information, see Pierre Godin, *René Lévesque: héros malgré lui,*
1960–1976 (Montreal: Boréal, 1997), 353. Lévesque was a close friend of
the Dominican Father Bradet, a former editor of *Maintenant* who invited
him to use the premises. For the links between the Parti Québécois and the
Catholic "left," see Jacques-Yvan Morin, "Du nationalisme duplessiste au
nationalisme progressiste," *Maint* (Nov. 1970): 289: "The péquiste spirit …
revolves around the themes, questionings, and conclusions of MAINTENANT."

102 René Lévesque, *An Option for Quebec* (Toronto: McClelland and Stewart,
1968; French ed. first published 1968), 15–16, 23.

103 Camille Laurin, *Témoignage de Camille Laurin: Pourquoi je suis Souverainiste*
(Montreal: Les Éditions du Parti Québécois, 1972), 19, 22.

104 Dr Camille Laurin, "Le centenaire de la Confédération," in Laurin, *Ma traversée du Québec* (Montreal: Éditions du Jour, 1970), 97; Laurin, "Autorité et
personnalité au Canada français," in Laurin, *Ma traversée du Québec*, 24–6,
33–4.

105 Fernand Dumont, "L'impasse d'une doctrine sociale," *Maint* (Aug.–Sept.
1969): 202.

106 I have somewhat unsatisfactorily translated *chrétienté* as "Christendom," to
describe a set of values, practices, and social and political institutions that
reflected the dominance of Christianity within a particular culture or
society.

107 H.-M. Bradet, o.p., "Sommes-nous engagés?" *Maint* (May 1962): 159.

108 Liégé, "L'Église et les civilisations," 49–51.

109 AUM, Fonds Commission Dumont, P21/G1.1, Diocèse de Quebec, "Mémoire
de M. l'abbé J.G. Pagé Québec."

110 Jean Proulx, "L'Église renaît au 'Pays d'en-haut," *Maint* (Apr. 1967): 117. In
his memoirs, Fernand Dumont significantly linked the "old" piety of
rosaries, devotions, and public prayer to his mother, while he claims that he
learned an "existential" spirituality of solitude and personal conviction from
his father. See Dumont, *Récit d'une émigration*, 36–7.

111 Dumont, "Sur notre situation religieuse," 38; Dumont, "I. Chrétienté impuissante, défis d'aujourd'hui," *Maint* (Feb. 1966): 52–5; AUM, Fonds ACC, P16/04.63, Confédération des Syndicats Nationaux, Gérard Dion, Louis O'Neill, *Autour d'une querelle de principes. En marge du mémoire de cinq anciens aumôniers sur la confessionnalité de la C.T.C.C.* (Quebec, 1960).

112 Jacques Leclerc, "Feu la chrétienté?" *Maint* (Dec. 1964): 378; Jacques Girard, "L'intégrisme des laics," *Maint* (Mar. 1963): 89–90; Vincent Harvey, o.p., "La mort des Églises," *Maint* (15 May–15 June 1968): 131–2.

113 Harvey, "La mort des Églises."

114 AUM, Fonds Commission Dumont, P21/G2.9, Diocèse de St. Hyacinthe, Réal Proulx, ptre, "Mémoire presenté ... Tracy, le 24 janvier 1970."

115 Richard Arès, s.j., *Faut-il garder au Québec l'école confessionnelle?* (Montreal: Bellarmin, 1971), 38.

116 Ibid., "'L'oraison, problème politique' et l'Église du Québec," *Rel* (Dec. 1965): 347–8.

117 "L'avenir des institutions chrétiennes," *Rel* (Apr. 1966): 97. See also La Direction, "Où Sommes-nous?" *Aujourd'hui-Québec* 3, no. 7 (Sept. 1967): 2–4, 58; Jean Francoeur, "Le p. Daniélou crie casse-cou à un christianisme d'élite, LD, 9 Oct. 1965.

118 Fernand Dumont, "I. Chrétienté impuissante," 53; Dumont, "L'idéal coopératif," in Dumont, *La Vigile du Québec*, 107–8.

119 Dumont, "L'authenticité de l'expérience chrétienne," 381. A similar analysis was offered by Jean-Charles Falardeau, "Les paroisses dans nos villes: aujourd'hui et demain," CC 24 (Nov.–Dec. 1965): 482–8.

120 Moreux, *Fin d'une religion?* 336.

121 Grand'Maison, "L'Église du Québec en état de concile – III: Les provocations missionnaires du mouvement de sécularisation," See also Gérard Pelletier, "Associations pieuses et besoins paroissiaux," *Maint* (Mar. 1963): 78–9; Chanoine Armand Racicot, "La fosse aux lions: Mouvements paroissiaux, Église en marche," *Maint* (Mar. 1963): 77; H.-M. Bradet, o.p., "Feu les retraites paroissiales," *Maint* (Feb. 1964): 40–1.

122 Jeanne Lapointe, "Que deviendront les institutions privées?" *Maint* (Sept. 1966): 272; Racicot, "La fosse aux lions," 77; Hélène Pelletier-Baillargeon, "Qui est le Nouveau Directeur?" *Maint* (autumn 1965): 264; Moreux, "Le Dieu de la québécoise," 67.

123 ANQM, Fonds René Lévesque, P18/D355, Affaire Cross-Laporte, Courrier Favorable, Jacques Beauséjour, St. Césaire, René Lévesque, 4 Nov. 1970; Dumont, "L'authenticité de l'expérience chrétienne," 382.

124 Paul Doucet, o.p., "Les Horizons sans Dieu," *Maint* (Feb. 1966): 41.

125 Falardeau, "Les paroisses dans nos villes," 488; AUM, Fonds ACC, P16/G2, 2.1, Jeunesse Étudiante Catholique, Jean Francoeur, "Rapport," 1962.

126 Philippe Garigue, "Une nouvelle vision du monde est née dans la société

québécoise," LD, 27 July 1965; "M. Philippe Garigue au colloque de l'ACELF sur le sens national: Le nouveau nationalisme,-purement québécois, se présente comme pragmatiste et réformateur," LD, 20 May 1965.

127 Louis Racine, "Québec nouveau, Église nouvelle," *Maint* (Sept. 1967): 282–5.

128 Fernand Dumont, "Morale et moralisme," CC 13 (Jan.–Feb. 1964): 14; Dumont, "Sur notre situation religieuse," 38; Harvey, "La mort des Églises," 133; Dumont, "II. Pour sortir du ghetto: une anthropologie nouvelle," *Maint* (Feb. 1966): 55–60.

129 AUM, Fonds Commission Dumont, P21/G4.30, Diocèse de Montréal, Jean-Paul Lauzon, ptre, "Mémoire ... du service de la pastorale du CEGEP de Vieux-Montréal," 1970; Fernand Dumont, "Chrétien et socialiste," *Maint* (autumn 1965): 289.

130 AUM, Fonds Commission Dumont, P21/G9.29, Diocèse de St. Jérôme, "Mémoire de M. Gerard Lemay," 21 Apr. 1970.

131 Dumont, *Pour la conversion de la pensée chrétienne*, 147.

132 Jacques Grand'Maison, in Jean-Pierre Proulx, "L'Église du Québec mettra-t-elle le cap sur le projet de la société québécoise?" LD, 24 Jan. 1970.

133 Commission Dumont, *L'Église du Québec, un héritage, un projet*, 51.

134 Raymond Bourgault, s.j., "Le Laicisme," *Rel* (Mar. 1963): 59–61.

135 Louis Racine, o.p., "L'École unique," *Maint* (Nov. 1967): 338; AUM, Fonds Commission Dumont, P21/A7, Germain Lesage, o.m.i., "La pensée pastorale des évêques Canadiens-Français, 1830–1962," 2e partie, Université Saint-Paul, Ottawa, 1970.

136 Claude Corrivault, "Commentaire," RS (1966): 1–2, 110–12.

137 Claude Ryan, "Pouvoir religieux et sécularisation," RS (1966): 1–2, 101–9. See also Jean Genest, "Le pluralisme," AN 60, no. 2 (Oct. 1970): 102–3.

138 Rocher, "L'incroyance comme phénomene sociologique."

139 AUM, Fonds ACC, P16/K1.57, "Me Yves Prévost," Yves Prévost, "C'est l'heure de L'ACTION ... pourquoi?" Lancement des Compagnons de l'Action, Château Frontenac, 6 May 1963.

140 AUM, Fonds ACC, P16/G2, 2.1, "Jean Francoeur."

141 Claude Ryan, *Une société stable*, 347–8.

142 AUM, Fonds Commission Dumont, P21/B1, Julien Harvey, s.j., "Laic chrétien et sécularisation," Mar. 1970. See also ibid., Diocèse de St. Hyacinthe, P21/G2.16, Gilles Baribeau, responsable de Section pour les Foyers Notre-Dame, "Opinion d'un laic engagé dans un Mouvement d'Église," Granby, 18 Feb. 1970. The interlocking notions of international cultural exchange, the unprecedented influence of television, and the idea that Western democracies are collections of multicultural societies, all of which subverted the authority of established elites, are central to what Arthur Marwick defines as the criteria of the cultural revolution of the 1960s. See Marwick, *The Sixties*, 17–20.

143 AUM, Fonds Commission Dumont, P21/G4.32, "Memoire de l'Association des Parents Catholiques de Montréal," 18 Apr. 1970. See also François-Albert Angers, "Où va l'Église?" AN 58, no. 4 (Dec. 1968): 358–60; Lucien Saulnier, "Le drame de notre révolution tranquille," AN 56, no. 8 (Apr. 1967): 858–65. Saulnier was the powerful chairman of the executive council of the City of Montreal, the deputy to Mayor Jean Drapeau.

144 Jean Genest, "Jusqu'à la lie?" AN 60, no. 3 (Nov. 1970): 181–2.

145 ANQQ, Fonds Action Sociale Catholique, P428S2 (Action Catholique, Journal), "Un lecteur inquiet mais confiant," L'Action, 13 July 1968.

146 Bernard Lambert, o.p., "Allons-nous vers une crise dans l'Église du Québec?" LD, 18 May 1968.

147 Rocher, "L'incroyance comme phénomène sociologique," 359.

148 AUM, Fonds Commission Dumont, "Entrevues," P21/D.1, F-1059, B-191, B-271; ibid., P21/D.2, B-230; ibid., P21/D.13, C-82; ibid., P21/D.9, A-198: "even if there was no religion, it would change nothing at the centre of our lives"; ibid., P21/D.6, K-216.

149 Rocher, "Préface," in Moreux, Fin d'une religion? xii.

150 For these internal pressures, see ANQM, Fonds JEC, P65, s6, ss3, sss3, D7/1, "Secteur secondaire: Document de travail," ca Feb. 1964; AUM, Fonds ACC, P16/G2,8.2, "Problématique sur la vie politique, oct. 1965–mai 1966," "Les jeunes et la politique," exposé de M. Jacques Laliberté à l'intérieur du Conseil, Oct. 1965; ibid., P16/D4.12, "Projet de volume sur la vie politique," 1966; ibid., P16/G5,4.22, Statut de la jeunesse travailleuse canadienne (1964); ibid., "Conférence: le rôle représentatif de la J.O.C.," par R.P. Jacques Lazure, o.m.i., professeur en sociologie, Université d'Ottawa; Jacques Lazure, o.m.i., "L'Action catholique dans l'arène," Maint (Sept. 1964): 277–8; Louis Fournier, "Étudiants et ouvriers," Maint (July–Aug. 1965): 248–9; "Les étudiants et les autres: rendez-vous à l'an prochain," MM (May 1964): 23. Arthur Marwick observes that, in the wider cultural context of the industrialized West, Marxist and quasi-Marxist notions enjoyed considerable vogue during the 1960s in disciplines ranging from literature to anthropology and sociology. The Quebec student environment, which became politicized during the 1960s over the issue of nationalism, was very receptive to these currents. See Marwick, The Sixties.

151 AUM, Fonds ACC, P16/A1.1, Documents épiscopaux, 1957–1963, "Exigences particulières de la situation en Italie."

152 ANQM, Fonds JEC, P65 art. 2, Claude Ryan, "L'Action Catholique a-t-elle un avenir?" Apr. 1962.

153 AUM, Fonds ACC, P16/G2, 2.2, Correspondance 1960–1966, Claude Ryan Jean Francoeur, centrale nationale de la J.E.C., 20 Apr. 1960.

154 For the controversy over the presence of André Major later a member of the radical Parti Pris – and the closure of the newspapers, see AUM, Fonds ACC, P16/G2, 1.40, "La J.E.C. et la démission des journalistes des Journaux:

État de la Question"; ibid., "Rapport de la Commission d'Enquête sur les journaux de la J.E.C.," 14 Apr. 1965; ibid., "La J.E.C. et le sens de la Possession," *Le Quartier latin*, 3 Nov. 1964; ibid., Michel Cantin, "Monsieur Major et Cie, ou la construction d'un enfer," *L'Action*, 16 Nov. 1964.

155 André Charbonneau and Héléne Pelletier-Baillargeon, "Du servant de messe à l'électeur," *Maint* (15 Mar.–15 Apr. 1968): 67–70; Jacques Grand'-Maison, "L'Église, le monde et le Québec," *Maint* (Dec. 1964): 388–91.

156 ANQ-M, Fonds JEC, P65, S6, SS2, SSS1, D5/5, Situation et orientation en 1963, "Deuxième stage du secteur 'Jeunes,' juin 1963"; AUM, Fonds ACC, P16/D6,8.4, "La pastorale en éducation."

157 Claude Ryan, "Les laics et l'évolution de l'Église au Québec: Réflexions partir de l'expérience de l'Action Catholique," *Rel* (Feb. 1966): 57.

158 AUM, Fonds Commission Dumont, Diocèse de St. Jérôme, P21/G9.33, "Mémoire de M. l'abbé Charles Valois," 4 Apr. 1970. Valois observed that the bishops emphatically did not want the JEC to become a "movement of Christian thought."

159 Gabriel Clément, *Histoire de l'Action catholique au Canada français* (Montreal: Fides, 1972), 315.

160 For this aspect of Vatican II, which had an enormous impact on ordinary Catholics, see Terence J. Fay, *A History of Canadian Catholics: Gallicanism, Romanism, and Canadianism* (Montreal and Kingston: McGill-Queen's University Press, 2002), 296.

161 Lambert, "Allons-nous vers une crise?" See also "Sommes-nous encore chrétiens?" *Rel* (Oct. 1968): 269.

162 Jacques Grand'Maison, "L'Église, le Monde et le Québec," *Maint* (Dec. 1964): 388. See also Harvey, "La mort des Églises," 131; Gérard Marier, ptre, "Les jeunes Québécois et l'athéisme – II," *Rel* (Mar. 1967): 73.

163 AUM, Fonds Commission Dumont, Diocèse de St. Jérôme, P21/G9.6, "Mémoire de M. Paul-Henri Bordeleau," 4 Apr. 1970.

164 AUM, Fonds Commission Dumont, Diocèse de Montréal, D21/G4.36, "Mémoire – Mouvement des Femmes Chrétiennes de Montréal," 1970; ibid., Diocèse de Québec, P21/G1.2, "Mémoire de la Jeunesse Indépendante Catholique," Jan. 1970; ibid., Diocèse de Montréal, P21/G4.30, "Mémoire ... du CEGEP de Vieux-Montréal"; ibid., Diocèse de Montréal, P21/G4.66, "Recherche sur l'ouvrier au Québec"; ibid., "Mémoire de M. Paul-Henri Bordeleau."

165 Commission Dumont, *L'Église du Québec, un héritage, un projet*, 9.

166 Léon Dion, "L'anarchie est-elle inévitable?," CC 49 (Jan.–Feb. 1970): 52–3.

167 This was the theme of a gathering held in November 1970, presided over by Claude Castonguay, the minister of Health and Social Affairs in the Liberal cabinet of Robert Bourassa. The high-powered panel included Fernand Dumont, Pierre Harvey, Vincent Harvey, Guy Rocher, Claude Ryan, Charles Taylor, Raymond Laliberte, Jean Gérin-Lajoie, and Judith Jasmin. See ANQM,

Fonds Judith-Jasmin, P143, bobine 853, "Réunion 1970," "circulaire, 30 novembre 1970."

168 Province de Québec, *Commission d'enquête sur la santé et le bien-être social*, vol. 1, 41.

169 Lambert, "Allons-nous vers une crise?"

170 ANQQ, Fonds Action Sociale Catholique, P428 S1, "Contenu et Présentation, 1961–1969," "L'Église devrait être détruite pour que vive le prêtre, affirme-t-on," *L'Action*, 8 May 1969.

171 AUM, Fonds Commission Dumont, P21/G4.9, Diocèse de Montréal, "Réflexions et recommandations ... par un groupe d'adultes catholiques pratiquants," Montréal, 16 Feb. 1970; ibid., P21/G5.1, Diocèse de Nicolet, "Sondage réalisé par le M.F.C. dans la paroisse de St.-Germain de Grantham, co. Drummond, Diocèse de Nicolet, 28 f . 1970"; ibid., P21/G1.12, Diocèse de Québec, "Quelques notes sur la paroisse ... par M. l'abbé François Routhier au nom du Conseil Presbytéral du Diocèse de Québec," 17 Jan. 1970; ibid., P21/G1.22, "Mémoire présenté à la Commission ... par le groupe 'Apr S.O.F.' de Sainte-Foy," 11 Mar. 1970; André Beauchamp, ptre, "Le renouveau dans la paroisse," *Rel* (Feb. 1966): 45; AUM, Fonds ACC, P16/K1.48, Chanoine Maurice Matte, "Pour une paroisse missionnaire, par l'apostolat laïque," n.d.; Dumont, *Pour la conversion de la pensée chrétienne*, 23.

172 AUM, Fonds Commission Dumont, P21/G1.12, Diocèse de Québec, "Mémoire présenté à la Commission d'Etude," 17 Jan. 1970; ibid., P21/G1.2, Diocèse de Québec, "Mémoire de la Jeunesse Indépendante Catholique, Diocèse de Québec," Jan. 1970.

173 Fernand Dumont, "Le silence de l'Église du Québec," *Rel* (Dec. 1969): 348–50.

174 Bernard Lambert, o.p., "L'enjeu historique d'une société écclesiale nouvelle au Québec," LD, 24 Jan. 1970. See also Proulx, "L'Église du Québec."

175 AUM, Fonds Commission Dumont, Diocèse de St. Hyacinthe, P21/G2.20, Mme Richer, Granby, lettre à Me Jean Massey, 18 Feb. 1970.

176 AUM, Fonds Commission Dumont, Diocèse de St. Hyacinthe, P21/G2.19, Soeur Thérèse de Jean Crucifié, lettre à Me Jean Massey, n.d.; ibid., Diocèse de St. Hyacinthe, P21/G2.17, Dame Jeanne Morin, 347 rue St.-Viateur, Granby, "Lettre addressée à la Commission ..."; ibid., Diocèse de Montréal, P21/G4.46, "Mémoire de la Paroisse St. René Goupil," 4251 rue Frégault, 4 May 1970; ibid., Diocèse de Québec, P21/G1.28, Mme Germaine Laplante, Ste-Foy, "Les Laics dans l'Église," 6 May 1970; ibid., "Entrevues," P21/D.1, A-133; Claude Panaccio, "Le Christianisme 'dans le vent,'" *Maint.* 39; "Note à la Commission Dumont," AN 60, no. 3 (Nov. 1970): 226–7; ANQQ, Fonds Action Sociale Catholique, P428s2, Action Catholique (Journal), "La parole est aux lecteurs," letter of Ida Fréchette, 23 Sept. 1968; ibid., letter of

Lucienne Turgeon, Québec, n.d.; ibid., letter of Claude Morin, "Folklore local," 10 f . 1970; ibid., letter of André Roy, ptre aum., Vallée-Jonction, Beauce, s.d.; ibid., letter of Pauline Tremblay Carrier, Levis, s.d. See also François-Albert Angers, "L'heure de la foi," AN 57, no. 1 (Sept. 1967): 29.

177 ANQQ, Fonds Action Sociale Catholique, P428S2, "La parole est aux lecteurs," 1968, A. Larouche, Le Mouvement social chrétien, "Quand le Chat sort du Sac!"

178 Ibid., Joseph O. Jean, "Information impartiale?," ca 1970. See also ibid., J. Alphonse Beaulieu, ptre, Trois-Pistoles, "La Commission Dumont en voit de toutes les couleurs!" n.d.; ibid., G.P., "La Commission Dumont Montreal," n.d.

179 Commission Dumont, L'Église du Québec, un héritage, un projet, 47–8; Jacques Grand'Maison, "Une glise nouvelle en gestation," Maint (Dec. 1969): 311.

180 Fernand Dumont, "Ce qui a fait défaut et manque encore au Québec: un modèle de développement qui lui appartienne en propre," in Claude Ryan, ed., Le Québec qui se fait (Montreal: Hurtubise HMH, 1971), 171.

181 Commission Dumont, L'Église du Québec, un héritage, un projet, 43–4.

182 Dumont, "Ce qui a fait défaut et manque encore au Québec," 173.

183 Proulx, "L'Église du Québec."

184 Dumont, Récit d'une émigration, 134–5.

185 Dumont, Pour la conversion de la pensée chrétienne, 36–7; Fernand Dumont, "Mounier toujours présent," Maint (June 1970): 203; ANQM, Fonds JEC, P65, S6, SS6, SSS2, D5/2, Dumont, "Spiritualité et profession." For the injection of the categories of the French "left" and "right" into the Quebec political scene in the 1960s, see Roger Duhamel, "La vérité a-t-elle choisi son camp?" Maint (May 1962): 165.

186 Fernand Dumont, "Notre culture entre le passé et l'avenir," Maint (Nov. 1970): 92.

187 Dumont, "Chrétien et socialiste," 287–8.

188 Fernand Dumont, "Le temps des aînés," paper presented to a colloquium on Saint-Denys Garneau at the University of Montreal, in Dumont, La vigile du Québec, 25.

189 Fernand Dumont, "Depuis la guerre," 33–4.

190 See La Rédaction, "To Be or Not to Be," 235–7; Dr Camille Laurin, "Autorité et personnalité au Canada français," in Laurin, Ma traversée du Québec, 24–6, 33; Dumont, Récit d'une émigration, 148.

191 See, for example, Pierre Hurtubise, o.m.i., "Rôle et statut du laic dans l'Église au Canada français," 1970.

192 It is not entirely coincidental that the years around the sittings of the Commission Dumont saw a spate of work on the Rouges and an attempt to recover "radical" and "liberal" ideologies in Quebec's past. See, for example, Jean-Paul Bernard, Les rouges: libéralisme, nationalisme et anticléri-

calismeau milieu du XIXe siècle (Montreal: Les Presses de l'Université du Québec, 1971); Fernand Dumont, ed., *Idéologies au Canada français* (Quebec: Les Presses de l'Université Laval, 1971).

193 Jacques Grand'Maison, "Jonas et le nationalisme de Baptiste," *Maint* (Feb. 1969): 46.

194 Commission Dumont, *L'Église du Québec, un héritage, un projet,* 136–7, 224.

195 Ibid., 129–30, 96–7. See also ANQM, Fonds René Lévesque, P18/D288, "Coupures de Presse – Église 1971–1974," Gilles Provost, "Le Rapport de la commission Dumont: pour une action sociale des chrétiens," LD, 17 Dec. 1971.

196 "Paul VI évoque la coexistence au Canada de deux communautés linguistiques et culturelles," LD, 17 Jan. 1969; and for criticism of the pontiff by Quebec Catholics, see Claude Ryan, "Faut-il confondre oecuménisme et rapports diplomatiques?" LD, 17 Jan. 1969; Louis Rousseau, "Fraternité chrétienne et unité politique," LD, 21 Jan. 1969.

CONCLUSION

1 Some scholars of Quiet Revolution Catholicism, relying mainly on evidence from the views of the upper clergy, are adamant that the process of political modernization aroused little in the way of cultural schism. See Gregory Baum, *The Church in Quebec* (Ottawa: Novalis, 1991), 15–49; David Seljak, "Why the Quiet Revolution was 'Quiet': The Catholic Church's Reaction to the Secularization of Nationalism in Quebec After 1960," Canadian Catholic Historical Association, *Historical Studies* 62 (1995): 109–24. It should be clear that this book runs counter to this line of interpretation, arguing that the cultural schism in the key identities of gender, marriage, family, youth, and notions of religion occurred in Quebec before 1960.

2 The religious role of anticlericalism as a factor in the relationship between clergy and people is only beginning to be analysed in the Quebec context. See, however, the perceptive treatment by Christine Hudon, "Beaucoup de bruits pour rien? Rumeurs, plaintes et scandales autour du clergé dans les paroisses gaspésiennes, 1766–1900," *Revue d'histoire de l'Amérique française* 55, no. 2 (autumn 2001): 217–40.

3 This shift in emphasis has been observed, but not accounted for, in the treatments of Catholic social movements by Marie-Paule Malouin, *Le Mouvement familial au Québec: les débuts, 1937–1965* (Montreal: Boréal, 1998), 93–4, and Jean-Pierre Collin, *La ligue ouvrière catholique, 1938–1954* (Montreal: Boréal, 1995).

4 Paul-André Linteau, René Durocher, et al., *Histoire du Québec contemporain: Le Québec depuis 1930* (Montreal: Boréal, 1989), 810.

5 For the values of the Quiet Revolution as the touchstone of both "revisionists" and "post-revisionists," see Ronald Rudin, "Revisionism and the Search for a

Normal Society: A Critique of Recent Quebec Historical Writing," *Canadian Historical Review* 73, no. 1 (March 1992): 30–61.

6 As it has evolved during the 1990s, this has become the methodological terrain of cultural history. See for a discussion, Roger Chartier, "Writing the Practices," *French Historical Studies* 21, no. 2 (spring 1998): 255–64, and Jonathan Dewald, "Roger Chartier and the Fate of Cultural History," *French Historical Studies* 21, no. 2 (spring 1998): 221–40.

7 On the use of these concepts for the broader intersection of religious and social history in Canada, see Nancy Christie and Michael Gauvreau, "The Modalities of Social Authority: Suggesting an Interface for Religious and Social History," *Histoire Sociale/Social History* 35, no. 71 (spring 2003): 1–30. Special issue, *Intersections of Religious and Social History*. For important Quebec examples of this new tendency, see especially Christine Hudon, *Prêtres et fidèles dans le Diocèse de Saint-Hyacinthe, 1820–1875* (Quebec: Septentrion, 1996); Ollivier Hubert, *Sur la terre comme au ciel: La gestion des rites par l'Église catholique du Québec (fin XVIIe – mi XIXe siècle)* (Sainte-Foy: Les Presses de l'Université Laval, 2000).

8 This is the post-revisionist approach outlined in Joseph-Yvon Thériault, *Critique de l'américanité: mémoire et démocratie au Québec* (Montreal: Éditions Québec-Amérique, 2002).

Index